OXFORD READINGS IN CLASSICAL STUDIES

The series provides students and scholars with a representative selection of the best and most influential articles on a particular author, work, or subject. No single school or style of approach is privileged: the aim is to offer a broad overview of scholarship, to cover a wide variety of topics, and to illustrate a diversity of critical methods. The collections are particularly valuable for their inclusion of many important essays which are normally difficult to obtain and for the first-ever translations of some of the pieces. Many articles are thoroughly revised and updated by their authors or are provided with addenda taking account of recent work. Each volume includes an authoritative and wide-ranging introduction by the editor surveying the scholarly tradition and considering alternative approaches. This pulls the individual articles together, setting all the pieces included in their historical and cultural contexts and exploring significant connections between them from the perspective of contemporary scholarship. All foreign languages (including Greek and Latin) are translated to make the texts easily accessible to those without detailed linguistic knowledge.

Aeschylus
Edited by Michael Lloyd

Ovid
Edited by Peter E. Knox

The Attic Orators
Edited by Edwin Carawan

Lucretius
Edited by Monica R. Gale

Catullus
Edited by Julia Haig Gaisser

Seneca
Edited by John G. Fitch

Vergil's *Eclogues*
Edited by Katharina Volk

Vergil's *Georgics*
Edited by Katharina Volk

Homer's *Odyssey*
Edited by Lillian E. Doherty

Livy
Edited by Jane D. Chaplin and Christina S. Kraus

Persius and Juvenal
Edited by Maria Plaza

Tacitus

Edited by

RHIANNON ASH

OXFORD
UNIVERSITY PRESS

OXFORD
UNIVERSITY PRESS

Great Clarendon Street, Oxford, OX2 6DP,
United Kingdom

Oxford University Press is a department of the University of Oxford.
It furthers the University's objective of excellence in research, scholarship,
and education by publishing worldwide. Oxford is a registered trade mark of
Oxford University press in the UK and in certain other countries

British Library Cataloguing in Publication Data
Data available

Library of Congress Cataloging in Publication Data
Data available

ISBN 978-0-19-928508-2 (hbk)
978-0-19-928509-9 (pbk)

Printed in Great Britain by
MPG Books Group, Bodmin and King's Lynn

Preface

As any editor working in this series will testify, the process of selecting the articles to appear in an Oxford Readings volume is never easy,
but in the case of Tacitus, such a giant of the ancient world, the task is
particularly difficult. Scholarly interest in Tacitus' works takes so
many forms, ranging from the historians, who turn to his narratives
for a wide variety of information about the imperial period, to the
historiographers, who offer close readings of his expressive language
and artistic methods of narrative composition which channel the
historical material. The broad range of genres across which Tacitus
operates means that his writings are central to anyone interested in
Roman identity and imperialism, intellectual history, the process of
commemoration, rhetoric, exemplarity, intertextuality, practical
ethics, military history, antiquarian matters, and reception. No single
volume could ever hope to represent every aspect of Tacitean scholarship, and in compiling this selection, the editor has been faced with
some very difficult choices, resulting in a cutting-room floor littered
with an embarrassing array of wonderful items.

In essence, this book is aimed primarily at university teachers and
their students. It sets out to offer a representative sample of some of
the most important articles on Tacitus, as well as further guidance
about the scholarly context which generated them. The articles are
preceded by an introduction which offers an overview of the older
scholarship on Tacitus; a summary of current issues being addressed
in Tacitean scholarship, with some bibliographical guidance for those
who wish to pursue particular areas in further detail; and a synopsis of
the articles in the volume, including suggestions about how these
pieces are representative (or not) of the field. Living authors of
individual articles have either left their work in the original form,
updated their pieces with relevant bibliography, or added a postscript
to indicate where they view their articles as standing in relation to the
'state of play' of scholarship today. I am immensely grateful to all
these authors for their efficiency in submitting revised versions of
their pieces. For articles appearing posthumously, some supplementary bibliography has been added, either in postscripts or in the notes,
but any additions to the notes have been included in square brackets,

and translations of the Latin and Greek have been added to the main text, except in the article of Goodyear, whose primary focus is philological. Francesca Albini and David Ash translated two of the pieces in this volume, and their help has been invaluable. Chris Pelling was also kind enough to read and comment on a draft of my introductory chapter, for which I am very grateful. I would also like to thank warmly Merton College, Oxford, for granting me a term of sabbatical leave, which enabled me to complete this project. Hilary O'Shea has been remarkably patient during its long gestation.

Finally, I want to say something about the evolution of this volume. The original editor was to have been the inimitable Michael Comber, whose sharp eye and immense knowledge of Tacitus (and so much else) would have produced an invaluable addition to the series. When it became clear, however, that his deteriorating health was not going to allow him to serve as editor, I became involved. At different points, Michael and I had animated discussions about which articles and authors we should try to include and inevitably we produced multiple lists of essential items, with individual pieces jockeying for position. The current volume reflects at least some of Michael's thinking on the selection of articles, although no doubt the final cut would have been rather different in his capable hands. It seems entirely appropriate, then, to dedicate this volume to the memory of Michael, still sadly missed.

RA

Oxford
December 2010

Contents

Acknowledgements

Only the Introduction by Rhiannon Ash appears here for the first time. Permission to reprint original or revised versions of the following items is gratefully acknowledged:

Katherine Clarke, 'An Island Nation: Re-reading Tacitus' *Agricola*', *Journal of Roman Studies* 91 (2001), 93–112.

W. Liebeschuetz, 'The Theme of Liberty in the *Agricola* of Tacitus', *Classical Quarterly* 16 (1966), 126–39.

Ellen O'Gorman, 'No Place Like Rome: Identity and Difference in the *Germania* of Tacitus', *Ramus* 22 (1993), 135–54.

Shadi Bartsch, 'Praise and Doublespeak: Tacitus' *Dialogus*', pp. 101–25 in Shadi Bartsch, *Actors in the Audience: Theatricality and Doublespeak from Nero to Hadrian* (Cambridge, Mass., 1994).

Sander Goldberg, 'Appreciating Aper: The Defence of Modernity in Tacitus' *Dialogus de Oratoribus*', *Classical Quarterly* 49 (1999), 224–37.

Ettore Paratore, *Tacito* (2nd edn, Rome, 1962), pp. 182–90 (given the new title 'The *Agricola*: Stepping-Stone to History').

N. P. Miller and P. V. Jones, 'Critical Appreciations III: Tacitus, *Histories* 3.38–9', *Greece and Rome* 25 (1978), 70–80.

David Levene, 'Pity, Fear, and the Historical Audience: Tacitus on the Fall of Vitellius', pp. 128–49 in S. Braund and C. Gill (eds), *The Passions in Roman Thought and Literature* (Cambridge, 1997).

Ronald Martin, 'Tacitus and the Death of Augustus', *Classical Quarterly* 5 (1955), 123–8.

Sir Ronald Syme, 'Obituaries in Tacitus', *American Journal of Philology* 79 (1958), 18–31.

Judith Ginsburg, 'The Beginning of the Year in Tacitus', pp. 10–30 in Judith Ginsburg, *Tradition and Theme in the Annals of Tacitus* (New York, 1981).

Christopher Pelling, 'Tacitus and Germanicus', pp. 59–85 in A. J. Woodman and T. J. Luce (eds), *Tacitus and the Tacitean Tradition* (Princeton, NJ, 1993).

A. J. Woodman, 'Nero's Alien Capital: Tacitus as Paradoxographer', pp. 173–88 in J. Powell and A. J. Woodman (eds), *Author and Audience in Latin Literature* (Cambridge, 1992).

T. J. Luce, 'Tacitus' Conception of Historical Change: The Problem of Discovering the Historian's Opinions', pp. 143–57 in I. S. Moxon,

J. D. Smart, and A. J. Woodman (eds), *Past Perspectives: Studies in Greek and Roman Historical Writing* (Cambridge, 1986).

F. R. D. Goodyear, 'Development of Language and Style in the *Annals* of Tacitus', *Journal of Roman Studies* 58 (1968), 22–31.

René Bloch, 'Tacitus' Excursus on the Jews through the Ages: An Overview of its Reception History', pp. 187–216 in R. S. Bloch, *Antike Vorstellungen vom Judentum* (Stuttgart, 2002).

Arnaldo Momigliano, 'Tacitus and the Tacitist Tradition', in A. Momigliano, *The Classical Foundations of Modern Historiography* (Berkeley, Calif., and Oxford, 1990), 109–31.

Lionel Trilling, 'Tacitus Now', pp. 198–204 in Lionel Trilling, *The Liberal Imagnation: Essays on Literature and Society* (New York, 1976).

Abbreviations

The titles of Tacitus' works are abbreviated as follows:

A., Ann.	*Annales*
Agr.	*Agricola* (*De vita e moribus Iulii Agricolae*)
D.	*Dialogus de Oratoribus*
G., Ger., Germ.	*Germania* (*De origine et situ Germanorum*)
H.	*Historiae*

Introduction

Rhiannon Ash

Tacitus is without doubt a challenging author, with constant capacity to surprise and delight. His uniquely expressive Latin prose, built creatively on the foundations of his predecessors, especially (but not only) Cato the Elder and Sallust, has embedded within it a sharply moralizing voice, often wry and wise, always demanding a reaction. That voice was both shaped by and pointedly situated at a distance from, the murky world of the principate on which our author comments so acerbically.[1] Tacitus is in many ways a product of his times, but not passively so. Even the generic trajectory and publication dates of his five works (*Agricola, Germania, Dialogus, Histories, Annals*) have fundamentally shaped ancient and modern assessments of Domitian's regime (and the principate as an institution more generally). While many authors in the Classical world boldly embarked on their literary careers from an early age, Tacitus was different. Only when he was about 41 years old in AD 98 did he publish his literary debut, the *Agricola*. This purports to be a biography of his father-in-law, but it is constructed around an outspoken, highly politicized prologue and epilogue, casting Domitian as a menacing and malicious tyrant: for Tacitus, this is the *princeps* who oversaw book-burning in the Forum (*Agricola* 2) and unleashed butchery on members of the Roman senate (*Agricola* 45). By deferring publication of the *Agricola* until after Domitian's assassination, Tacitus at one stroke eloquently endorsed the powerful ideological message of his

---

[1] On Tacitus' artificially constructed status as 'outsider' within his writings (despite his impressive path through the *cursus honorum* in reality), see Sailor (2008).

first work and set in motion a kind of literary *damnatio memoriae* of the tyrannical emperor which has proved highly enduring.[2] Where Tacitus led, others soon followed, particularly Pliny the Younger, whose *Panegyricus* is centred on a series of sharp polarizations involving negative images of Domitian (AD 81–96) set against positive representations of Trajan (AD 98–117). The intervening emperor, the elderly Nerva (AD 96–8), conveniently gets lost in the emotive contrasts at play within the speech. Tacitus has left us a rich legacy of works in different genres, all of which are explored in the articles and essays contained in this volume.

STANDING ON THE SHOULDERS OF GIANTS: TACITUS AND THE SCHOLARS OF THE PAST

Modern editions of Tacitus' works can be seen as the culmination of intellectual engagement and hard graft over the centuries by a succession of scholars who operated across Europe and beyond. It is impossible to tell the full story here, with all of its highs and lows, but it is still salutary to underscore how much we owe to our predecessors.

Although the works of Tacitus were circulating during the fifteenth century, it was Philippus Beroaldus the Younger's publication of his *editio princeps* of *Annals* 1–6 in 1515 which brought Tacitus to a wider audience, (crucially) reuniting the various parts of his scattered historical corpus. The first printed edition (c.1468 or 1470) of *Histories* 1–5 and *Annals* 11–16 had been produced by the 'Spira' press in Venice, but this had not included *Annals* 1–6.[3] After Beroaldus, further editors took up the baton, but two editions stand out, one by the Alsatian humanist Beatus Rhenanus (1485–1547), published in 1533, with a revised second edition appearing in 1544, and the other by the Flemish philologist and humanist Justus Lipsius (1547–1606), who first published an edition of Tacitus in 1574 (seven revised versions followed). Lipsius also built on his engagement with the

---

[2] Flower (2006) discusses sanctions against memory in Roman culture (though she has sensible reservations about the term *damnatio memoriae* itself, which is not found in ancient texts).

[3] See Mendell (1957: 349–78) for a comprehensive survey of the history of the printed texts of Tacitus.

text by publishing the first full-scale commentary on Tacitus in 1581, thereby initiating a mode of scholarly engagement with Tacitus which is still flourishing today.[4] That year also saw the publication of another important commentary on Tacitus in Paris by Carolus Paschalius, who examined Tacitus' text for useful *exempla*, as opposed to Lipsius' project, which focused instead on offering clarification of the historical material in the text.[5] The final (posthumous) edition (1607) of Lipsius' text of Tacitus was published in part as a response to Curtius Pichena's ongoing engagement with textual problems in Tacitus, published in two collections of notes in 1600 and 1604. Although Lipsius clearly feels a sense of scholarly rivalry with Pichena, in his address to the reader in the 1607 edition he presents his own editorial work as a means for his readers above all to *enjoy* Tacitus.[6] Pichena, meanwhile, had been working on his own edition of Tacitus, which also appeared in 1607, and which was based on the two Medicean manuscripts of Tacitus (not consulted by Lipsius).[7] These early editors and commentators blazed a trail and put Tacitus prominently on the map.[8] As Martin observes, the period 1600–1649 saw more editions of the works of Tacitus appearing than any other Greek or Roman historian.[9]

Not all of the early responses to Tacitus' texts were so strictly philological. He also inspired creative engagement. For instance, the Warden of Merton College, Oxford, Sir Henry Savile (1549–1622), who had served as Queen Elizabeth's tutor in Greek, took the

---

[4] Another figure operating in the tradition of Lipsius was Nicolas-Abraham Amelot de la Houssaye (1634–1706), a prolific commentator on and translator of Tacitus. See further Soll (2000).

[5] Goodyear (1972: 5–10) surveys the major figures of Tacitean scholarship in the sixteenth century. On Lipsius and the text of Tacitus, see further Brink (1952). Mellor (1995) offers a useful overview of Tacitus from the Renaissance to the twentieth century.

[6] Morford (1993: 130).

[7] See ibid. 129–30 on the relationship between Lipsius and Pichena. *Annals* 1–6 survive in the Mediceus (M), now in the Biblioteca Laurenziana in Florence, copied in c.AD 850 in Germany. *Annals* 11–16 and *Histories* 1–5 survive in Laurentianus 68.2, the 'second Mediceus', written in Beneventan script at Monte Cassino in the eleventh century. The manuscript history of the minor works is particularly murky. See further Tarrant and Winterbottom in Reynolds (1983: 406–11).

[8] Mellor (1993: 137–62) usefully traces the impact of Tacitus. Ash (2006b: 96–147) discusses as case studies the afterlife of Julius Civilis in the Netherlands and Arminius in Germany.

[9] Martin (1981: 239).

opportunity, while preparing an English translation of Tacitus, to construct a 'bridge' over the missing portions of the *Annals* and the *Histories* by writing his own *The ende of Nero and the beginning of Galba* (1591) to fill in the unfortunate gap.[10] What is striking about this enterprise is that in formulating this narrative, Savile appears to have had a contemporary political agenda, namely supporting the Earl of Essex's political strategy of the early 1590s: distinctive elements such as Savile's encomium of Julius Vindex as exemplifying successful, principled intervention of military commanders have been thought to cast a positive light on Essex.[11] In other spheres, drama also saw creative engagement with Tacitus' texts, perhaps not surprisingly when one considers his talents as a creator of vivid visual scenes (the return of Agrippina with the ashes of Germanicus at the start of *Annals* 3 is one memorable instance). So, Ben Jonson (1572–1637) was inspired to write his *Sejanus* (1603), and Jean Racine (1639–99) composed his *Britannicus* (1669). The reception of Tacitus' works by society at large is a huge topic in its own right, but it must have been exciting for the early pioneers of Tacitus' corpus to see their scholarly work bearing creative fruit in so many different spheres.

It was probably not until the nineteenth century that the recognizably modern age of Tacitean scholarship began. This was an era which saw the professionalization of history as a discipline in the universities, the establishment of learned journals for the publication of scholarly research and book reviews, and the institution of series such as the Teubner library of Greek and Latin Classics and the Oxford Classical Texts.[12] Christopher Stray formulates such developments in terms of 'a movement from an earlier world of gentlemanly amateur scholars to that of professional researchers ... in university environments'.[13] A rich legacy of material from this period of Tacitean studies is still in use. The Oxford don Henry Furneaux (1829–1900) produced his extensive two-volume commentary on

---

[10] One can compare here Syme (1991: 647–62), a parodic 'fragment' of Tacitus *Histories*, apparently narrating events of AD 79 soon after the death of Vespasian, including Titus' dismissal of Berenice, and written in a style evocative of the *Annals*.

[11] See Womersley (1991: esp. 341–2).

[12] See Whitaker (2007) on the evolution of Teubners and *OCTs*. Stray (1998: 117–40) is particularly helpful in tracing this evolution of academic scholarship in a British context.

[13] Ibid. 117.

the *Annals*,[14] in which he made use of nascent tools such as the *Lexicon Taciteum* (Leipzig 1877–1903) of Adolf Gerber and Adolf Greef. That work was started in 1877, and took more than 25 years to complete, although it was published at regular intervals in fascicles before the whole lexicon was finished.[15] After Gerber died in 1888, Greef (1845–1910) was left the lonely task of completing the lexicon by himself, finally publishing the whole volume in 1903.

One conspicuous and widespread scholarly pursuit of the nineteenth century is 'Quellenforschung', the attempt to read ancient historical accounts in a bid to peel back the layers and identify the hidden sources used by the historian to construct his narrative. In its least satisfying form, this activity potentially 'demotes' historians so that they are seen merely as uncritical transcribers, slavishly following one source at a time, rather than engaging in more complex modes of composition and using multiple sources simultaneously; but more constructively, thoughtful analysis of sources and parallel accounts can shed light on an author's creativity and distinctive narrative features. In Tacitean studies, important early practitioners of Quellenforschung in the nineteenth century include Mommsen and Fabia, even if it was perhaps not quite such a dominant strand of scholarship as it was in those working on Livy in the same period.[16] What characterized Tacitean scholarship of the late nineteenth and early twentieth centuries in general was a dichotomy between academics analysing his works from the perspective of Quellenforschung (and in some cases raising doubts about his reliability as a historian) and those examining Tacitus as an accomplished stylist and tracing the evolution of his Latin (with more positive representations of him as a remarkable literary artist).[17]

---

[14] Furneaux's secluded life as a don contrasts sharply with that of his adventurous ancestor, the English navigator Tobias Furneaux, the first man to circumnavigate the world in both directions and discoverer of the Furneaux islands near Tasmania.

[15] Furneaux in his 2nd edn of 1896 says that he was able to consult Gerber and Greef as far as *reliquus*. He had also used the *Lexicon Taciteum* of Bötticher (1830).

[16] Mommsen (1870) and Fabia (1893). Questa (1960: 17–34) offers a useful survey of scholarly work on Tacitus' sources from the nineteenth century onwards, while Haupt (1885: 132–63) provides a contemporary overview. Nissen (1863) is the dominant figure at this time for Livy. See further Chaplin and Kraus (2009: 2–3). Today, there is still creative interest in Tacitus' sources amongst modern scholars, such as Devillers (2003).

[17] Martin (1981: 241).

Against this backdrop, scholars produced further useful tools, such as the *Onomasticon Taciteum* (Paris and Lyons 1900) of Philippe Fabia (1860–1939).[18] This work lists alphabetically the proper names which features in Tacitus' works and cites the Latin at each point where a name appears. In the modern era when we have easy access to fast and efficient searchable electronic databases such as Musaios and the Phi discs, it is easy to overlook the practical value of such pioneering resources, often produced laboriously over a number of years. So, in the Latin preface to the *Onomasticon Taciteum*, Fabia tells readers that he spent almost three years compiling the work. Interestingly, his assertion of scholarly *labor* ('hard work') which he deemed *non ita per se iucundus*, 'not so much pleasant in itself', but an endeavour which was *operae pretium*, 'worth the effort', pointedly calls to mind some of the *topoi* associated with the genre of ancient historiography itself (cf. Tacitus *Annals* 4.32.2, *nobis in arto et inglorius labor*, 'my work is confined and inglorious'; Livy Preface 1.1.1, *operae pretium*, 'worth the effort').

As the work of Fabia demonstrates, in the early twentieth century, there was particular admiration for Tacitus in France. Notable publications on Tacitus include the study by Gaston Boissier (1823–1908),[19] who considers Tacitus' conception of history, his political opinions, and attitudes towards the Caesars. One of the striking features of Boissier's work is how in his preface he celebrates Tacitus in a contemporary context, and casts him as an author who defies the trend whereby Classical writers are fading from view: 'Not only is he still read, though the ancient authors scarcely have readers any longer . . . ' In the body of the study, he offers some spirited comments: 'What I know and what I can affirm is this: that on the day when ancient history has disappeared from our schools, there will be something lacking in them.'[20] Boissier writes with great passion and ranges widely, including in his analysis the revival of interest in Tacitus during the French Revolution. Another scholar with broad interests in Tacitus working in France at this time was Joseph Vianey (1864–1939) of the University of Montpellier. His study considers

---

[18] Later in his career, Fabia published on the famous Lyons tablet containing Claudius' speech about the possible admission of Gauls to the senate (on which see Griffin 1982). Fabia's long and fruitful association with the University of Lyons is celebrated today in a street named after him (rue Philippe Fabia).

[19] Boissier (1903).

[20] Ibid. 107.

from a literary point of view the implications of Racine's famous assertion that Tacitus was 'the greatest painter of antiquity', and sets out to illustrate Tacitus' considerable talents as a descriptive writer.[21] In much the same spirit, Edmond Courbaud (1868–1927) produced a study devoted to the artistic elements of the *Histories*, including the scenes of battle, an emotive topic to consider in a work published at the end of the First World War.[22]

The nineteenth century also saw the airing of some bold theories about Tacitus. John Wilson Ross (1818–87), for example, published anonymously in 1878 a study arguing that the *Annals* were not in fact written by Tacitus, but were a brilliant forgery concocted by the Italian humanist Poggio Bracciolini, who was aided in his scheme by a helpful monk from the abbey of Fulda who transcribed the forgery. By a series of close comparative readings of the *Histories* (considered genuine) and the *Annals* (an 'immortal and wonderful forgery'),[23] Ross argues that Bracciolini produced an audacious forgery in order to make himself rich and promote his own career. The theory did not win supporters, but Ross certainly constructs an exciting and dramatic narrative.[24]

At the same time as Ross was arguing that Tacitus' *Annals* was an elaborate forgery, other scholars, particularly those in Germany, were hard at work producing careful, rigorous studies of Tacitus' language and style. A central figure in this area was Eduard Wölfflin (1831–1908), who began the systematic investigation of Tacitus' language and style in a series of reports published in *Philologus*.[25] Amongst other things, Wölfflin advanced the idea that Tacitus, after writing the *Histories*, appears to have self-consciously adopted an increasingly archaic and artificial style of writing in the *Annals*. The linguistic focus of other scholars included dedicated studies of topics such as archaic language in Tacitus,[26] Tacitus' imitation of

---

[21] Vianey (1896). Racine's description appeared in the second preface (1676) to his *Britannicus* (Martin (1981: 240)).

[22] Courbaud (1918: 120): 'Il est surtout un peintre de batailles.'

[23] Ross (1878: 88). Hochart (1890) and (1894) rejects both the *Histories* and the *Annals* as forgeries. Wiener (1920) argues that the *Germania* is a forgery. For an overview of such (discredited) theories, see Mendell (1957: 219–20).

[24] Furneaux (1896: 8–12) defends the *Annals* as a genuine work. In debates about authenticity, one particularly contentious passage is *Annals* 15.44 on Nero and the Christians.

[25] Wölfflin (1867; 1868; 1869). Meyer (1933) assembles some selected papers.

[26] Degel (1907).

Virgil[27] and Lucan,[28] his use of the genitive case,[29] Tacitean alliteration,[30] and his use of the subjunctive.[31] Such projects, which proliferated in the latter half of the nineteenth century and the early part of the twentieth, often took the form of inaugural dissertations produced by young German scholars as a stepping-stone towards an academic career, but there were also wider-reaching philological studies of Tacitus' syntax and style, such as that of the formidable Anton August Draeger (1820–95), originally published in 1868 and a prelude to his ambitious *Historische Syntax der Lateinischen Sprache* (1874–8). Perhaps the most extraordinary expertise in this sphere is that of Geoffrey Fletcher (1903–95), Professor of Latin (1946–69) at King's College, Newcastle upon Tyne, who published a series of articles on Tacitus' Latin over the 1940s, which he then assembled in a single volume.[32] Fletcher also directed the graduate studies of another eminent Tacitean scholar, Ronald Martin (1916–2008), whose incisive early studies on Tacitus' language and the textual tradition were to culminate in his remarkable general study of our author, which is arguably still the best and most accessible introduction to Tacitus available today.[33]

Yet one book above all has made the most impact of Tacitus, so much so that we must divide the scholarship on Tacitus into two distinct periods, pre- and post-1958. The publication of *Tacitus* by Sir Ronald Syme (1903–89) had an immediate, longlasting and ongoing bearing on the field, not least of all because he succeeded in realigning two distinct scholarly strands, which had previously tended to consider Tacitus in a polarized fashion, either as a historical source or as a literary artist.[34] In a different context, Michael Comber, in a review of the commentary of Martin and Woodman (1989), observed: 'There was a time when the treatment of Tacitus was relatively straightforward. Stripped of bias, he could, in conjunction with other evidence,

---

[27] Schmaus (1887).   [28] Robbert (1917).   [29] Zernial (1864).
[30] Renz (1905).   [31] Carmody (1926).
[32] Fletcher (1964). Reviewing this volume, Wellesley (1965: 124) observed: 'No student of Tacitus can afford to neglect Fletcher (though some continue to do so), and certainly the textual critic cannot.' Fletcher's knowledge of Greek is also remarkable, as can be seen from his review of the revised *LSJ* Greek dictionary (*CR* 3 (1947), 82–4).
[33] Martin (1981). For his important earlier linguistic and textual studies, see Martin (1946; 1953; 1964; 1968). Martin was also an expert in the sphere of Roman comedy, particularly Terence.
[34] Dench (2009) uses the metaphor of 'scholarly bifocals', whereby historians read texts primarily for content, and philologists engaged with style and rhetoric.

provide access to the objective truth of the early imperial period. But in these sceptical, post-modern times things are far more complicated.'[35] Behind Comber's characterization of a simpler world of past scholarship on Tacitus, we can locate Syme's *Tacitus* as the transformative force. In engaging with Tacitus, Syme draws on an extraordinary range of expertise, including an unparalleled knowledge of epigraphy, prosopography, and Roman history, combined with nuanced stylistic engagement with Tacitus' Latin (and its evolution throughout his works) to create an integrated reading of the historian. Sherwin-White singles this out as a particularly positive feature of Syme's work: 'Perhaps the most impressive fact about the book is its bold march across the too often separated domains of literature, philology, and history.'[36] The 95 appendices alone contain a remarkable range of invaluable discussions, running from source-criticism to Tacitus' origin and his friends, but arguably the most substantial component is on style and words. This includes, for example, an eloquent, revealing, and resonant list of selected items of vocabulary simply entitled 'Some Words Not in Tacitus'.[37] While it is undoubtedly true that anyone setting out today to write a monograph on Tacitus would probably not be allowed the leeway granted to Syme, for example, in adopting an English style so curiously evocative of his subject's Latin, the longevity and prominence of his work on Tacitus is unlikely to be paralleled in the field.[38]

Not every scholar after Syme was prepared to embrace this reintegration of history and literature in their analysis of Tacitus. Erich Koestermann, for example, seems to be a curious throwback in the arrangement of his commentaries on the *Annals* (1963–8). So, the first two volumes of Koestermann's commentary are divided page by page into two parts running in tandem, with one section devoted to

[35] Comber (1991: 209).
[36] Sherwin-White (1959: 146). For other reviews of Syme's *Tacitus*, see Mendell (1959), Levi (1959), Balsdon (1959), Thiel (1959), and Rogers (1960). Soon after the publication of *Tacitus* (1958), Syme was awarded his knighthood in 1959.
[37] Syme (1958a: 713, appendix 43).
[38] Sherwin-White (1959: 140): 'Seldom has so long a book contained so much *breuitas.*' For obituaries of Syme, see M. Griffin in *JRS* 80 (1990), xi–xiv, G. W. Bowersock in the *Proceedings of the American Philosophical Society* 135 (1991), 117–22, and G. Alföldy in *Athenaeum* 81 (1993), 101–22. There is also a memoir by G. W. Bowersock in the *Proceedings of the British Academy* 84 (1994), 539–63. For thoughtful reflections on Syme's evolution and the role of 'rational conjecture' in his work, see Wiseman (1998: 121–52). Dench (2009) is also helpful.

content and a separate one considering style. Norma Miller, reviewing the second volume of the commentary, observes diplomatically, 'Time has not reconciled the reviewer to the dichotomy', and urges that 'Latinity, Tacitean style, text, and interpretation are inextricably fused'.[39] This polarization was a practice which Koestermann eventually dropped after his commentaries on the Tiberian hexad.

Two scholars built constructively on Syme's work and opened the door to an exciting and distinctive new sub-discipline in Tacitean studies. In 1979, T. P. Wiseman set out to address the intriguing question of why and how (now fragmentary) Roman historical narratives written in the late second century BC by authors such as Gnaeus Gellius and Valerius Antias appear to have been so much more extensive in size and scope than the more frugal narratives of their predecessors.[40] How did these writers set about constructing their monumental accounts of early Roman history, when reliable sources must have been thin on the ground? Wiseman homes in on the significance of the annalistic format, suggesting that this hitherto skeletal repository of facts compiled on a year-by-year basis was transformed by inventive historians in the late second century BC into something much more voluminous and expansive. For Wiseman, the plausible rhetorical embellishment of the past by these pioneering ancient historical writers operated on a much larger scale than modern historians were generally prepared to acknowledge. At the same time, however, ancient readers of these texts were perfectly aware that they were engaging with artfully rhetorical narratives, which had creative overlap with genres such as drama.[41]

Ten years later, through a series of careful readings, A. J. Woodman developed further the fundamental notion that creative *inuentio*, based on a plausible rhetorical expansion of the basic facts, was a crucial driving force in the formation of ancient historical narratives, both Greek and Roman.[42] Woodman's conclusions not only reinforced and developed Wiseman's earlier arguments but also encouraged further engagement with these ideas by a generation of younger scholars. Although the influence of Woodman's study certainly

---

[39] Miller (1966: 345).
[40] Wiseman (1979: 9–26).
[41] Wiseman (1998) further explores this interaction.
[42] Woodman (1988a) offers independent but interrelated studies of Thucydides, Cicero's conception of historical writing, the style of Sallust and Livy, and finally Tacitus.

extended beyond Tacitus, it did have a particularly striking and sustained impact on Tacitean scholarship, not least because of the commentary on Tacitus *Annals* 4, which Woodman and Martin published soon afterwards.[43] This stimulating volume, on which Woodman was working at the same time as his *Rhetoric in Classical Historiography*, shows how productively the thesis about *inuentio* could be explored through a close, sustained reading of an ancient text. In essence, the commentary format offers the ideal framework for demonstrating how Tacitus' literary and rhetorical aims fundamentally shaped his historical writing. Looking back on this period, Feldherr talks in terms of a 'Wiseman–Woodman revolution'.[44] Yet at the time, Wiseman and Woodman themselves appear to have been relatively cautious about likely responses to their views. So, in a review published in 1988, Woodman himself refers to the notions about the rhetorical nature of Classical historiography as 'a controversial subject on which scholars are divided'.[45] Despite such misgivings, historiography as a prominent field for study has been flourishing over recent decades, although scholars do still raise questions about its precise relationship to Greek and Roman History and whether in general we have succeeded in striking the right balance.[46] No doubt the debate will continue.

CURRENT THEMES IN TACITEAN SCHOLARSHIP

There are various distinctive areas to which Tacitean scholars have directed attention over recent years.[47] It is impossible to present an exhaustive picture here, but still worthwhile to pick out some of the main strands. In the historiographical sphere, critics have continued to engage with the visual dimension of Tacitus' narratives,

---

[43] Martin and Woodman (1989).

[44] Feldherr (2009).

[45] Woodman (1988b: 418). See too Wiseman (1988: 263).

[46] Lendon (2009) offers a spirited discussion.

[47] We have an extremely useful resource in the annotated bibliographies on Tacitean scholarship over a 50-year period (1954–2003) produced by Benario (1964–5; 1969–70; 1977–8; 1986–7; 1995–6; 2005) which appeared regularly in *CW*. Benario (1993) also ventures into creative writing via his fictional memoir of Arminius' wife, Thusnelda.

particularly in the *Histories* and the *Annals*. The work of Borszák is important here,[48] particularly his analysis of *spectaculum* as a motif of tragic historical writing, which has also been considered by Keitel.[49] A closely related topic is the notion of role-playing by characters within the narrative itself, which Woodman (1993), Bartsch (1994), Shumate (1997), and Fulkerson (2006) have explored from different angles, particularly in relation to the *Annals*. Pomeroy (2006) considers the types of public display and spectacle enacted by different protagonists within the *Histories*, demonstrating that major figures such as the emperors and their generals constantly seek to display the correct public forms, while various groups in the text offer their own evaluations (almost always different from the implied conclusions of the meta-audience, Tacitus' own readers). Finally, historiographical set-pieces such as battle-narratives have also attracted attention from a variety of perspectives.[50]

In general, since Classicists have shown themselves over recent decades as being increasingly receptive to intertextuality, the relationship between Tacitus' narratives and other texts and genres has naturally attracted sustained attention. So, Santoro l'hoir (2006) considers various aspects of the relationship of the *Annals* with the genre of tragedy (particularly Aeschylus and Seneca the Younger), while the connections between Thucydides and Tacitus are analysed by Haüssler (1996); and Kelly (2010) pursues the Herodotean elements of Tacitus' portrait of Germanicus in *Annals* 2. Intertextuality with Greek poetry has attracted attention, as in Mayer (2003), who considers the interaction between Homer and Tacitus in one suggestive case. In addition, there has been a growing interest over recent years in the interface between Tacitus and Latin poetry. Foucher (2000) explores the impact of Virgil and Lucan on Tacitus, concluding that the *Histories* is particularly rich in poetic formulae, while the edited volumes of Levene and Nelis (2002) and Woodman and Miller (2010) offer a series of useful articles on this whole issue from a broader perspective.[51] Cross-pollination between genres is also explored by

---

[48] Borszák (1970; 1973).

[49] Keitel (1992).

[50] Woodman (1979), Ash (1999b; 2002; 2007b), Morgan (1992b; 1992c; 1997; 2005b), Manolaraki (2005), Levene (2009).

[51] See too Lauletta (1998). For articles on Virgil and Tacitus, see Baxter (1971; 1972), Miller (1986), Putnam (1989), Keitel (2008), Ash (2010a). Ash (1997) considers an instance of intertextuality between Naevius, Sallust, and Tacitus.

Morello (2006), who considers the depiction by Tacitus of Tiberius as an epistolographer within the first hexad of the *Annals*.

One distinctive area which has understandably attracted scholarly attention is Tacitus' use of direct speeches, since these are a feature of every work except the *Germania*, and Tacitus himself was an accomplished orator. Speeches in ancient historiography were a particularly useful way to sharpen the moral dilemmas being faced by characters in the surrounding narrative and to add dramatic irony to an account, whether the speeches were delivered by Romans or outsiders. Interest has ranged widely, including the relationship between speeches in the text and 'real' speeches,[52] the differences between Tacitus' Latin in the speeches and the rest of the narrative,[53] the structure and function of speeches in their narrative context,[54] the impact of speeches delivered by enemies such as Calgacus and Boudica,[55] and the moralizing potential of deliberative speeches.[56] The whole question of the interaction between speech and narrative in the ancient historians formed the focus of a wide-ranging conference held at the University of Giessen in 2008, whose proceedings (edited by Dennis Pausch) were published in 2010.

Tacitus' language has attracted attention on a more detailed level too. Adams (1972) offers an invaluable analysis of how Tacitus' language evolves and develops in the later books of the *Annals*. Scholars have also been increasingly engaged with the issue of Tacitean word-play, which so often serves as a powerful and meaningful weapon in his historiographical arsenal. The study of Plass (1988) puts Tacitean wit centre-stage, while Morgan (1998) foregrounds a bitter pun put in the mouth of Sejanus' victim Sabinus at *Annals* 4.70 while he is being dragged away to his death. Woodman (1998: 218–43) discusses a particularly striking array of instances, including word-play with names (a device especially favoured by Tacitus) and translingual puns, where Tacitus plays with his audience's knowledge of Greek. As Henderson observes, 'Tacitus' dramatic writing deploys a sceptical rhetoric of *ludibrium* (mockery) to engage readers in appreciating the absurdist illogic of imperial entropy.'[57] Wit and

---

[52] Miller (1968), Griffin (1982), Brock (1995).
[53] Adams (1973).
[54] Keitel (1991; 1993).
[55] Stewart (2003) on Calgacus; Adler (2008) on Boudica.
[56] Levene (1999).
[57] Henderson (1998: 266).

word-play have certainly been a sustained focus of scholarly attention, but in a different vein, Kirchner (2001) and Stegner (2004)
pursue the important topic of Tacitus' deployment of moralizing
sententiae, the type of universalizing pronouncements of general
truths designed to add a timeless relevance to a historical narrative.
One format in particular which offers scope for sustained engagement
with all the nuances of Tacitus' Latin is the area of translation, and the
version of the *Annals* by Woodman (2004) is a notable attempt to
capture Tacitus' linguistic power in English. Tacitus' language (and
that used by his protagonists in the text) has also inspired theoretical
responses, which consider how his Latin reflects and interacts with
the power structures in Roman society more generally. Sinclair
(1995), O'Gorman (2000), and Haynes (2003) are notable examples.

There have been exciting developments too in the area of Tacitus
and epigraphy. In some cases, there has been a fresh reinterpretation
of existing evidence. So Alföldy (1995) has shed useful new light
on Tacitus' life and career by arguing that a fragmentary funerary
inscription is in fact a record of Tacitus' career.[58] Most notably,
however, there have been further discoveries of new evidence, above
all the inscription preserving the senatorial decree recording the trial
of Cn. Calpurnius Piso, charged with Germanicus' murder, which can
productively be set alongside Tacitus' account of these same events to
reveal a great deal about his narrative techniques.[59]

Analysis of evidence from Tacitus alongside other sources has also
figured as an important element in wider-reaching historical studies
dedicated to particular figures, such as Ginsburg (2006) on representations of Agrippina the Younger, and Davies (2004) on Rome's religious
history. Engagement with Tacitus' attitude to the republican past as a
focal point of memory is explored by Gowing (2005), who concentrates
particularly on the *Dialogus*. An important piece on this topic is Ginsburg (1993), who invites us to consider how and why Tacitus invokes
the past in the *Annals* as a standard against which to measure the
present. She considers in particular Tacitus' version of two senatorial
debates in which speakers allude to famous senatorial debates from the

---

[58] Birley (2000) reviews Tacitus' life in the light of Alföldy's arguments and argues
that he may well have survived well into the principate of Hadrian.

[59] See note 94 below for bibliography. Another important focal point is the bronze
tablet found at Lyons containing a version of Claudius' speech about the potential
admission of men of Gallic heritage to the senate and Tacitus' rendition of this same
speech (*Annals* 11.24–5). See Griffin (1982).

past, and argues that in so doing, the senators (ironically) reveal how far they have fallen from the standards of the past.

Finally, although the *Nachleben* of Tacitus' works has always been a focus of scholarly attention (as Benario's regular surveys of 'recent work on Tacitus' reminds us), the emergence of Reception as a distinct sub-category in the field of Classics has seen some lively activity in the sphere of Tacitus.[60] Scholars have considered topics ranging from the use of Tacitus by Ammianus Marcellinus (Riedl 2002) to Bulgakov's allusions to Tacitus' *Annals* in *The Master and Margarita* (1940) in the context of Stalin's regime (West (1996–7)). In connection with the *Germania*, studies have operated across a broad chronological sweep: Krebs (2005) considers the manipulation of this text by four humanists in the fifteenth century in the context of disputes between the papacy and the Holy Roman Empire, while the study of Lund (1995) considers the Nazi period.[61] Krebs (2011) offers a comprehensive survey. Also noteworthy here is the discussion by Schama (1995) of a commando raid, organized by Himmler and conducted by the SS, in a bid to acquire the *codex Aesinas*, containing the *Germania*.[62] This is an area of Tacitean studies which will no doubt continue to grow.

THE SELECTED ARTICLES

Three of the pieces in this volume focus on the *Agricola*. Liebeschuetz (1966; Chapter 2 below) addresses the theme of liberty in the work, a topic which continues to drive scholarship on the *Agricola* (and Tacitus' other writings) today. He acknowledges right from the start the heterogeneous qualities of this so-called biography, which is in fact a kaleidoscopic piece, showing some features reminiscent of an oration and other structural devices recalling the monographs of Sallust. Liebeschuetz dwells on the oddity of Tacitus including an

---

[60] The foundation of the *International Journal of the Classical Tradition* in 1994 marked an important development in the field of Reception in Classics. In 2009, Lorna Harwick launched the *Classical Receptions Journal* intended to cover all aspects of the reception of the texts and material culture of ancient Greece and Rome from antiquity to the present day. For an introduction to the field, see Hardwick (2003).

[61] Benario (1990) offers a useful overview, as does Rives (1999: 66–74).

[62] Schama (1995: 75–81).

ethnographical and geographical survey of Britain, which pointedly suspends the central biography, as well as a climactic battle description, which would be perfectly at home in an extended historical narrative.[63] The *Agricola* is certainly hard to pin down in generic terms (and indeed this issue is an enduring aspect of scholarship on this text).[64] Yet Liebeschuetz asserts forcefully that despite the disquieting sense of fragmentation generated by these disparate elements, Tacitus establishes a central unity of theme by exploring the consequences of loss of freedom. Liebeschuetz argues that Tacitus' distinctive and insistent emphasis on Agricola's qualities of self-effacement and subordination show him championing qualities which would not normally be seen in a positive light by his contemporaries.[65] In fact, he argues that in some sense, Tacitus is calling for an acceptance of the political world of the present day, however flawed and difficult the status quo, and that in practical terms he is setting up Agricola's conduct as an exemplar and a guiding light for his contemporaries.[66] For Liebeschuetz, this process sees Tacitus adopting contradictory attitudes to empire. On the one hand, Tacitus is showing himself to be a hard-nosed realist, advocating *modestia* and *obsequium* as survival strategies (however unattractive) which make it possible for individuals to serve the state in a beneficial way.[67] On the other hand, he embraces a nostalgic view of Roman identity, which is deeply influenced by the wider phenomenon of the

---

[63] For details of how Tacitus' dramatic description of the battle of Mons Graupius manifests many features typical of similar scenes in historical narratives, see Ash (2007b); more generally, see Levene (2009).

[64] Marincola (1999) is essential. See too Whitmarsh (2006): 'Tacitus' *Agricola* remains a bamboozling text' (305).

[65] Mayer (2001: 2) points to the possibility that the *Dialogus* and *Agricola*, with their respective focus on oratory and life as a military man, should be seen as a kind of 'diptych', revealing Tacitus' concerns about the 'emptiness that he himself found at the end of the traditional paths to glory and prestige in Rome'. Habinek (2000) explores Seneca's renegotiation of traditional paths to *uirtus* (and for this, see Rosenstein 1990).

[66] Whitton (2007) sets out to resituate Tacitus' *Agricola* and *Histories* in the original Trajanic context in which these works were written and to read them as having a positive political agenda and as being fully engaged with the contemporary political scene: thus, he argues, Tacitus' *Agricola* and *Histories* must be seen as part of a wider literary project in the post-Domitianic era which actively aimed to bolster Trajan's principate and to legitimize his position as emperor by means of a fiercely polarised periodization.

[67] See further McGing (1982) on this compromise position in relation to the 'Stoic martyrs'.

aristocracy's loss of self-respect incurred through submitting to the absolute power of the *princeps*.

The strength of Liebeschuetz's article lies in the fact that he is ready to acknowledge the many complexities and contradictions at play within the *Agricola* and to resist reductive readings of this work and its author. The issue of Tacitus' attitude to *libertas* is of course a crucial one for anyone engaging with his writings and ideology, and it continues to exercise scholars today.[68] In methodological terms, Liebeschuetz conducts his investigation in fairly traditional terms, but he certainly asks the right questions. We can briefly compare it with a recent article on the *Agricola* by Haynes (2006), who addresses the central question of liberty from another angle and considers what the figure of Agricola as constructed by Tacitus might represent for the survivors of Domitian (and also what that literary construction can tell us about Tacitus' own guilty feelings). For Haynes, the memorable description of those who outlived that emperor as *nostri superstites*, 'survivors of ourselves' (*Agricola* 3.2), suggests that tyranny (even after it has gone) generates a kind of death, even for those who did not actually lose their lives. For Haynes too, Agricola represents a kind of duality in the text that bears his name: he serves to exemplify both the best one can do under a tyrant and the worst that such a 'best' represents. Despite very different methodological standpoints, Haynes and Liebeschuetz address similar questions about how to read the figure of Agricola.

Another lively and important paper on the *Agricola* included in this volume is Clarke (2001; Chapter 1 below). She too acknowledges the tantalisingly enigmatic nature of the work and emphasizes its elusive generic status. Yet she approaches the question from a different perspective from Liebeschuetz. Drawing on her research on ancient geography and conceptions of the world, she pursues the geographical aspect of the *Agricola* as a way to gain insights into Tacitus' representation of Agricola, Domitian, and Roman political life. She firmly rejects the viewpoint of Dorey (1969a) that Britain, the location for Agricola's exploits, is really just a colourful stage, or some kind of a decorative 'backdrop' to the general's exciting personal drama. Instead, she sees the country's insularity as an integral element which must be continually reassessed and redefined by Tacitus'

---

[68] Lavan (2011) considers the other side of the coin, analysing the *Agricola* for its perspective on slavishness.

readers. As a crucial feature in responding to the text, she identifies the shifting alignment of Britain, at times portrayed as a distinct island, at times cast more as an adjunct to continental Europe (and therefore as ripe for seizure by Romans with aspirations to extend the empire).[69] According to Clarke, Tacitus manipulates Britain's liminality in various ways as an appropriate setting for imperial *res gestae*, but it becomes clear that the island undergoes a troubling redefinition through Agricola's campaigns, which results in a partial loss of insularity and an erosion of the remoteness which was crucial to its spirited independence from Rome. Agricola as the agent of this change cannot therefore be seen straightforwardly as a force for good. Yet Clarke still sees the *Agricola* as a fascinating text precisely because of its lack of resolution, whereby Britain is still left in a state of semi-detachment, despite Agricola's conquests. Other scholars too, such as Batomsky (1985), have set out to identify ambiguities in Tacitus' portrait of Agricola and to modify the impression of the work as straightforward encomium. This sort of reflective reassessment can also be seen in analyses of other leading Tacitean protagonists, such as Germanicus (Pelling 1993; Chapter 12 below) and Corbulo (Ash 2006a). It is not so much a case of such scholars knocking heroic figures from their pedestals, but rather of renegotiating our sense of the complexities involved in Tacitus' techniques of characterization and acknowledging the compromises leading figures have to make in order to function under the principate.[70]

The third piece on the *Agricola* (Chapter 6) is an extract from the monumental study of Tacitus by Paratore (1951), revised in a second edition published in 1962 and dedicated to the eminent Hellenist Gennaro Perrotta. Paratore's Italian, often effusive and richly creative in his use of metaphor, is in its own way almost as arresting as Syme's distinctive style of English.[71] Paratore is fascinated by the psychology

---

[69] The concept of insularity continues to interest Classical scholars: see Gabrielli (2007) and Constantakopoulou (2007).

[70] None of the articles selected reflects one important area of scholarly responses to the *Agricola*, namely its standing in relation to the archaeological evidence. On that important issue, see e.g. Hanson (1991a) with bibliography at 1778–84, Hanson (1991b), Dickinson and Hartley (1995), and Shotter (2004).

[71] Paratore's preface to the revised 2nd edn is expressive. He acknowledges (ix) the extraordinary work of Syme (1958a) as a watershed for Tacitean studies, even if it generated particular challenges for his own process of revising his own pre-Syme book on Tacitus and drove him to use some colourful polemic: Townend (1964), 53 points to Paratore's 'deep chagrin that his thunder has been stolen by Syme's *Tacitus*'.

of Tacitus (and of the characters in his narratives) and by his changing response to the imperial system as his literary career evolved. What this means is that he is rarely content to consider Tacitus' individual works in isolation, and develops a clear sense of the interrelationship between individual items in the Tacitean corpus.[72] For Paratore, the crucial turning-point in Tacitus' political attitudes comes, not between the minor works and the *Histories* (when, Paratore suggests, he was still relatively optimistic about Trajan), but between the *Histories* and the dark vision of *Annals* (when he had become pessimistic about the potential for any vitality surviving within the imperial system). Where both Liebeschuetz and Clarke acknowledge the importance of the generic diversity of the *Agricola*, Paratore considers through a series of close comparisons how the work represents what he sees as being the first manifestation of Tacitus' impulse to write history, particularly the kind of history which he would go on to present in the *Histories* (rather than the *Annals*). In this context, Paratore's comments on crowd scenes are especially pertinent.

Ever since the rediscovery of the *Germania* in the fifteenth century (a time which both coincided with and contributed to a rising sense of German patriotism), interpretations of this work have often been driven by its potential impact on contemporary culture (particularly in Germany). Of all Tacitus' writings, this is a text which has tended to provoke especially strong reactions over the centuries. Yet as Rives (2002) asserts, it has nevertheless been relatively neglected outside Germany over recent times.[73] One important exploration of this text is the study by O'Gorman (1993; Chapter 3 below), who is concerned to break down overly simplified polarizations of Germany and Rome in the *Germania* and to explore Tacitus' representation of Germany as a 'textual country'.[74] She rightly asserts that the monograph,

---

Tacitus was attracting the attention of other Italian scholars at this time: see Questa (1960) and Garzetti (1960). Another Italian giant in the field of Tacitean studies is Francesco Arnaldi (1897–1960). See Flores (1999).

[72] The one exception to this is the *Dialogus*, which Paratore (controversially) believed was not written by Tacitus, but by Titinius Capito.

[73] Rives (2002) offers a more nuanced reading of the *Germania* in relation to its own contemporary setting, and suggests that a work which apparently operates in the timeless present tense of ethnographical literature actually reflects quite closely the diplomatic and political context of Tacitus' own times.

[74] Krebs (2006) discusses this issue in the context of Caesar's *de Bello Gallico*.

Germania, is never an innocent text, but one where Tacitus complicates the idea of Germany as a space to be described, by intertwining it with the idea of Germany as a place to be remoulded as a Roman artefact.[75] Her analysis of the multivalent and shifting role of boundaries in this text is particularly fruitful, and indicates some common concerns with Clarke's engagement with the concept of insularity in the *Agricola*. O'Gorman advances the idea that in this context, the invasiveness of Rome is not necessarily a positive factor, and explores this further through consideration of the proprietorial act of naming by the Romans.[76]

Within the world of Tacitean scholarship, the *Dialogus* can sometimes seem to exist in something of a vacuum. Indeed, this is understandably a work often read most seriously by specialists in ancient rhetoric, who can pose rather different sorts of questions from other Tacitean scholars about this fascinating text.[77] Yet if we detach the *Dialogus* from the rest of the Tacitean corpus, we lose access to a text which in many ways is just as valuable as the other so-called minor works for plotting Tacitus' views. It has rightly been seen as closely linked with the *Agricola*,'to form a kind of diptych, which reveals their author's disillusion with the careers open to a Roman in public life'.[78] Two articles about the *Dialogus* feature in this volume and both relate in different ways to Tacitus' self-positioning in his contemporary political and intellectual world.[79]

---

[75] Murphy (2004) considers similar issues in connection with Pliny the Elder's encyclopaedia.

[76] Haynes (2004) takes up this issue more broadly within the Tacitean *corpus*.

[77] One area of specialized interest, for example, is the relationship between the *Dialogus* and Quintilian's lost *de Causis Corruptae Eloquentiae*, on which see Brink (1989). Brink (349) expresses exasperation about the marginalization of the *Dialogus*, particularly in Britain: 'In Britain it has never been very popular, whatever the reasons. But at least it used to be read. Now I find that it has disappeared from the syllabus of many British universities.' The publication of Mayer (2001), the first commentary in English on the *Dialogus* since the end of the nineteenth century, should help to reverse this trend.

[78] Mayer (2001: 2); Syme (1958a: 109 n. 5).

[79] In this connection, the dating of the *Dialogus* (often pinned to AD 102) is an important issue. The dramatic date of this dialogue (AD 75) is much less problematic than its date of publication. Bartsch (1994) 122 [Ch. 4 below] follows Murgia (1980) and favours a date of publication during Nerva's principate (AD 96–8), but Brink (1994), in a comprehensive survey of the evidence, contests this viewpoint. Mayer (2001: 22–7) offers a succinct and helpful overview, conceding that the safest assumption is that the *Dialogus* was published at some point early in the first decade of the

Goldberg (1999; Chapter 5 below), beginning from an argument that a neo-Ciceronian style does not necessarily entail Ciceronian values, addresses the issue of modernity in the *Dialogus*. He argues that, despite the apparently pessimistic focus on the decline of oratory in the body of the work, the *Dialogus* is in fact more optimistic in tone than many critics think. Goldberg stresses the openness of the *Dialogus*, in which key aspects of the question about the decline of oratory raised in the preface actually remain open to the end. Goldberg thus offers a defence of Aper, the 'champion of modernity', and urges us to reinstate him as a serious and respectable voice in the debate. We should not reduce the complexities of the *Dialogus* to a simple assertion of oratory's decline under an autocratic regime. Instead, the work should be seen as a springboard for further debate about which direction oratory should take in Tacitus' contemporary world and which aspects of the old style were worth restoring.[80]

Bartsch (1994; Chapter 4 below) sees the *Dialogus* as a less optimistic work, but one whose author pointedly embraces contradiction as a way to reveal the true *locus* for political comment in contemporary imperial Rome. She takes as her starting point the odd lack of fit created by Tacitus in choosing to open the *Dialogus* with the spotlight on the relative merits of poetry and oratory. Rather than reading this opening as simply quirky, she regards it (and the figure of the charismatic poet Maternus) as setting up a work which explores how poetry and poets can engage in political protest in a public context where free speech has been severely restricted, if not closed down altogether. In Bartsch's analysis, Aper does not seem to be a particularly admirable figure: he cautiously warns Maternus that in first writing his outspoken play *Cato* and then failing to censor it before publication, he is likely to get himself into trouble by offending the powerful.[81] Yet Maternus himself is generally acknowledged to be a curiously contradictory man: after all, in his closing speech in the dialogue (*D.* 36–41), we see him praising the present political conditions and the current emperor, Vespasian. How does this

second century AD. Where we can see at least some consensus is that the work was published after Domitian's assassination.

[80] See Ginsburg (1993) for a general consideration of the relationship between past and present in Tacitus' works. Gowing (2005: 109–17) discusses the relationship between the *Dialogus* and Cicero and the republic.

[81] Gallia (2009) has more to say on the identities of these powerful figures and argues (172–3) that they do not necessarily include the emperor himself.

relate to the initial impression we get of Maternus as outspoken and independent? Are we dealing here with an ironic panegyric, whose hyperbole actually consitutes a critique of the principate? In her analysis, Bartsch stresses the problematizing function of Maternus' final speech, which destabilizes the *Dialogus*.[82] Like Goldberg, she sees openness at the end of the *Dialogus*, but it is openness of a different variety, as Tacitus allocates praise to 'the one character from whose mouth it will have the least credibility' (113). Rather than resorting to the concept of 'irony' to salvage his character, Bartsch pinpoints as an interpretative device the notion of 'double-speak', or saying one thing and potentially meaning another, although this need not be the case.[83] In short, Bartsch's stimulating discussion vividly brings Maternus to life and allows us to pose provocative questions about what this man symbolizes. She sees him as the embodiment of a transition enacted under the principate, whereby the medium of poetry takes over from 'republican' oratory as the real vehicle for political comment.[84]

It is probably fair to say that in the past, the *Histories*, with its kaleidoscopic and complex focus on the civil wars of AD 68–9, tended to attract less attention than the *Annals*, whose dominant imperial characters tend to capture the imagination and draw in audiences. Yet this has increasingly changed, as a series of scholars have engaged with the narrative of the *Histories* and sought to make it more accessible via dedicated monographs, close readings and a series of commentaries.[85] One spirited and memorable article in this respect is

---

[82] On this speech see further Syson (2009).

[83] Mayer (2001: 43) offers rather a different explanation for Maternus' apparently contradictory position in his final speech, namely that since he is replying to what has been said before by Aper and by Messalla, his views are necessarily coloured by his adversarial position. Luce (1986), 147 [Ch. 14 below] is cautious about reformulating Tacitean irony: '. . . sarcasm and irony are not easily removed: they colour the text as a dye permeates a piece of cloth'.

[84] Luce (1986; Ch. 14 below) considers the issue of inconsistency in Tacitus from a broader perspective. Through considering the figure of Orpheus in Virgil and Ovid, Pagán (2004b) addresses the problems faced by poets engaging with the establishment in an earlier era, but raises questions important for the role of poetry as a vehicle for political comment.

[85] For monographs on the *Histories*, see Ash (1999a) and Haynes (2003). Damon (2003) and Ash (2007a) have produced commentaries on *Histories* 1 and 2 respectively; for close readings, the succession of articles by M. G. Morgan should be consulted. In particular Morgan (2006) and Wellesley (2000) set out to make the events narrated in the *Histories* accessible to the non-specialist.

Miller and Jones (1978; Chapter 7 below). In one of a series of collaborative 'critical appreciations' to appear in the journal *Greece & Rome*, Miller and Jones turn their attention to a distinct episode in the *Histories*: the dramatic narrative laying out the events leading up to the death of one Junius Blaesus, the legate of Gallia Lugdunensis who supported Vitellius and accompanied him to Rome after his victory, only to be put to death by the very emperor he had loyally helped (*H*. 3.38–9). The respective literary analyses of this episode by Miller and Jones demonstrate clearly that Tacitus' talents for shaping a searing dramatic narrative are just as prominent in the *Histories* as they are in the *Annals*. Indeed, many of the fundamental themes and creative techniques of presentation which come to fruition in the *Annals* are already clearly present in the *Histories*.

First, Miller carries out a close reading of Tacitus' Latin syntax, vocabulary, and sentence structure to demonstrate meticulously how he builds up drama and tension and draws his audience into this chilling narrative sequence. On the face of it, Blaesus is the last person who should have stirred Vitellius' suspicions, but Tacitus paints a vivid scene in which the emperor, who has fallen ill, looks out from his sickbed one night to see a tower ablaze with lights. On asking for an explanation, he is told that this is Caecina Tuscus' dinner party, at which Blaesus is the guest of honour. At this point the courtiers really start to embellish their description and to work on Vitellius' ruffled feelings. Tacitus casts these interlocutors as predatory creatures who know only too well how to exploit the emperor's weaknesses to secure Blaesus' downfall. Yet the real damage is done by Vitellius' own brother, Lucius, who has a personal grudge against Blaesus, and who bursts into the emperor's sickroom to play out a scene which will guarantee his enemy's demise.[86] Miller's perceptive engagement with the finer points of Tacitus' presentation shows how the historian uses his descriptive powers and imagination to tremendous emotional and moralizing effect: exploitative courtiers, treacherous family members, and flawed emperors who misuse their tremendous powers are all familiar figures from the claustrophobic world of the *Annals*.

Next, Jones offers his own lively analysis of the passage, which shows how the description is driven by a sharp sense of paradox

---

[86] Levene (1997) [Ch. 8 below] draws out in a nuanced way how Tacitus uses Vitellius' family to characterize the emperor.

and irony. Jones is particularly deft at capturing Tacitus' brilliant depiction of the odious brother Lucius, as he delivers his killer speech before his sick brother and exploits his family relationship with the emperor to pursue his own murderous agenda. For Jones, this passage is rendered particularly intense by the 'faceless irrationality of the unseen powers at work': Blaesus is innocent, but he is effectively dead even before he has left the party. What this collaborative analysis of Miller and Jones brings home is how many of Tacitus' primary concerns in the *Annals* about the corruption of power are anticipated in the *Histories*. No doubt we would have had a clearer sense of this if the books of the *Histories* documenting the principates of Vespasian, Titus, and Domitian had survived.

Levene (1997; Chapter 8 below) considers Tacitus' techniques of characterization in a broader way, but focusing in particular on his intriguing portrait of Vitellius. He considers how the emotions of pity and fear are brought into play by Tacitus for a historical audience, drawing a distinction between responses which are 'audience-based' (where readers are persuaded to take over the emotions of a character who is pitying another character within the text) and those which are 'analytic' (essentially concerned with explaining and evaluating from an external perspective the behaviour of those who are subject to these emotions).[87] Taking as a case study Tacitus *Histories* 3.36–86, a stretch of narrative where fear and pity feature prominently, Levene sets the whole action surrounding the fall of Vitellius against an intricate network of both fear and pity involving all the participants. While the early stages of this segment of Tacitus' narrative often prompts an 'analytic' response to the text, combining explanation and evaluation, once the account moves into the end-game of Vitellius, Tacitus increasingly uses the internal audience to trigger an 'audience-based' reaction to events. By using this narrative technique to show Vitellius as a relatively sympathetic figure, Tacitus introduces a provocative note, which works against the 'analytic' viewpoint, which has been treating him entirely critically. Levene concludes that, perhaps contrary to what we might expect, the 'audience-based' approach to the passions is far from being at odds with rational historical analysis, but can work hand-in-hand with the 'analytic'

---

[87] See Marincola (2003) on emotions in historiography more generally.

narrative mode as a powerful weapon in the arsenal of a moralizing historian.[88]

Pelling (1993; Chapter 12 below) takes up the issue of the 'problem' of Germanicus and asks how we should go about reconciling the apparently inept practitioner in Germany in *Annals* 1 with the far more competent figure we encounter in the east in *Annals* 2.[89] For Pelling, Tacitus has shaped a curiously indecisive and morally inexplicit narrative around the figure of Germanicus, but he argues that whatever the problems in appraising Germanicus, the issue of consistency is a red herring.[90] In fact, Germanicus' spontaneity and *comitas*, the very traits which lead him to give so weak a lead in the mutinies in *Annals* 1, are precisely the ones which enable him to function so constructively in the east, where showmanship and theatricality often get results. However, there is more at stake in the characterization of Germanicus than simply assessing an individual. Pelling suggests that the whole world in which Germanicus moves, and his style of leadership and politics, are carefully set up by Tacitus as a contrast to the devious and grubby world of the principate. Germanicus belongs in a simpler, older realm, redolent above all of the republic. Yet however attractive this may be, comparison with Tiberius' techniques in the realm of foreign policy is still revealing— the curmudgeonly *princeps* may be unglamorous in his working methods, but even so, he is often highly effective. In ideological terms, Pelling's arguments have interesting points of contact with the reading which Liebeschuetz (1966) applies to the *Agricola*. Perhaps the main strength of Pelling's article lies above all in his execution of a subtle literary analysis, one which serves as a timely reminder that we must consider characters in Tacitus' narratives as exemplifying similar moral complexities and problems which have prompted such nuanced debate about other genres: so, Germanicus

---

[88] Levene's careful analysis of Vitellius has many points of contact with the scrutiny of Germanicus by Pelling (1993).

[89] This perception of inconsistencies in the characterization of Germanicus between *Annals* 1 and 2 has parallels with the concerns voiced by scholars about the apparent contradictions in the portrait of Antonius Primus between *Histories* 2 and 3, sometimes put down to Tacitus' inability to handle his sources (Wellesley (1972: 15); Chilver (1979: 247)). For a different reading of these fluctuations, see Ash (1999a: 147–65).

[90] For more on the issue of consistency and inconsistency in Tacitus, see Luce (1986) [Ch. 14 below], who takes as one of his focal points for discussion 'Germanicus the bumbler versus Germanicus the hero' (149).

can and should invite the same sort of analysis as figures such as an Antigone, Aeneas, or Achilles.[91]

The extract from Ginsburg (1981; Chapter 11 below) considers rather a different aspect of Tacitus' narrative technique, but one which is just as productive in terms of adding complexity to our response to his historical account, namely his use of the annalistic method. By analysing the opening of the annual account in the twenty-one years (AD 15–29, 32–7) of *Annals* 6 for which the beginning is extant, she demonstrates how Tacitus rejects a style of annalistic historical writing often associated with Livy in favour of incorporating material relevant to the wider themes of his first hexad. Far from being an element which restricts creativity, the annalistic framework cumulatively enables Tacitus to sharpen his points. In particular, Ginsburg argues that Tacitus' overwhelming preference for the ablative absolute formula (as opposed to various other constructions used by Livy) to introduce the names of the consuls allows him a striking degree of flexibility: so, in chronological terms, the material immediately following the ablative absolute can potentially be drawn from any point in the year. Where Tacitus avoids using this ablative absolute formula, he usually does so for a reason, as in the year AD 37. Here, his emphasis on the entrance into office of the last consuls of Tiberius' principate pointedly calls attention to the emperor's failure to provide for the succession (*Ann.* 6.46.1–3). Even when Tacitus appears to open the year in a manner reminiscent of traditional annalistic techniques, he tends to introduce material which has a thematic significance.[92] So, for the year AD 24 (*Ann.* 4.4), his apparently simple focus on the annual prayers on 3 January for the emperor's safety includes the suggestive detail that the priests exacerbated Tiberius' dislike of Germanicus by including the latter's two sons in their prayers. This point puts the spotlight on the 'succession theme' and on the deteriorating relationship between Tiberius and the household of Germanicus. As Ginsburg emphasizes, Tacitus often focuses on Germanicus and the members of his (dwindling) family at the beginning of each year, drawing out the tensions

---

[91] Santoro l'hoir (2006) takes this one step further and analyses Tacitus' historical narrative in the *Annals* from the perspective of allusions to tragedy and tragic themes. Fulkerson (2006) considers the theatrical aspect of the mutiny on the Rhine.

[92] Martin (1981: 11), in connection with Tacitus' manipulation of the annalistic tradition, comments that in this respect 'much of Tacitus' originality consists of putting new wines into old bottles'. See further ibid. 13–25.

within the imperial *domus*. Ginsburg's study has made a real impact on Tacitean studies.[93] She reminds us of Tacitus' versatility in arranging his material and serves as a warning that evidence from his narrative must not be removed from its context without considerable care. The discovery of the inscription preserving the senatorial decree recording the trial of Cn. Calpurnius Piso, charged with Germanicus' murder, demonstrates how prescient Ginsburg was in her original study: although scholars disagree on points of detail, a comparison of the inscription with Tacitus' narrative of Piso's trial and its aftermath suggests that the historian has taken considerable liberties in the chronological arrangement of the material in order to enrich his narrative by means of suggestive juxtaposition.[94]

In a classic piece, Martin (1955; Chapter 9 below) considers a striking case of self-imitation in Tacitus and draws out the cluster of verbal correspondences which subtly link the description of Augustus' death and Tiberius' succession with the subsequent account of Claudius' death and Nero's succession. Essentially, Martin argues that Tacitus is using the suggestive power of words to invest the accession of Tiberius with the same air of questionable legitimacy which surrounded Nero's accession. Nor is he content just to demonstrate this parallelism without considering the important supplementary question of originality. For if Tacitus has simply taken over parallels from his source, then Martin's thesis would reveal far less about our author's historiographical concerns and techniques. Therefore, Martin conducts a meticulous comparison of Tacitus' account with the versions of Suetonius and Dio to demonstrate not only that Tacitus draws upon different sources for his material in *Annals* 1 (Augustus/Tiberius) and *Annals* 12–13 (Claudius/Nero) but also that the parallelism between the two scenes is a touch unique to him. It is possible, Martin speculates, that Tacitus may have been inspired by Livy's account (1.41) of the concealment of Tarquinius' death by his wife, Tanaquil, during the regal period.[95] What Martin demonstrates in

---

[93] See Ash and Malamud (2006: 139–41) for an overview of Ginsburg's contribution to the field.

[94] See esp. Woodman and Martin (1996: 67–75). The inscription was first published by Eck, Caballos, and Fernández (1996). Damon and Takács (1999) have edited a special volume of *AJP* dedicated to the inscription.

[95] This connection is explored further by Santoro l'hoir (2006: 47–56), who suggests that Tacitus is alluding not only to Livy but also to Attic tragedy, specifically to plays associated with Clytemnestra's murder of Agamemnon.

this stimulating and pithy article is that Tacitus is above all an author whose Latin first demands and then repays meticulous and careful reading: this type of verbal echo, which bridges so considerable a portion of continuous narrative, shows how richly layered Tacitus' narrative can be, and illustrates how thoughtfully analysing both intratextual and intertextual echoes are a fundamental way to appreciate his historical analysis.[96]

Woodman (1992; Chapter 13 below) offers a typically illuminating close-reading of a memorable section of narrative from the *Annals*, Nero's dramatic postponement of his trip to Greece and the subsequent banquet organized by the praetorian prefect Tigellinus (15.36–7). Woodman shows how particular aspects of Tacitus' account point up how the extraordinary party on Agrippa's lake is not only morally defective but also (from an idealized Roman perspective) unnatural and foreign. Even Tacitus' word order at significant moments is a calculated exercise in accentuating paradox and suspense. Such touches (cumulative and increasingly insistent) are designed, Woodman argues, to prompt Tacitus' readers to see how Nero by his transgressive conduct was transforming Rome into a foreign city in order to compensate for the aborted eastern tour. Yet this is not just Tacitus adding general rhetorical *color* to his account. The specific foreign city under which Rome is subsumed here is Alexandria: so, Nero's golden house emulates the royal palace of the Ptolemies, Tigellinus' pontoon recalls the massive royal barge of Ptolemy Philopator, and Nero's entourage is described in Horatian language in such a way as to align it with the eunuchs of the Alexandrian queen Cleopatra (gender-bending which also has resonances with Nero's climactic 'marriage' to Pythagoras at the end of 15.37). Through Tacitus temporarily assuming the role of paradoxographer, Nero is eloquently cast as a foreign aggressor, so that a

---

[96] Martin's intellectual successor in carrying out such typically fruitful close readings of Tacitus' Latin is Woodman. Their collaboration in producing two excellent commentaries, first on *Annals* 4 and then on *Annals* 3, has been an invaluable contribution to Tacitean scholarship. One engaging feature of their work is that where they disagree with one another in interpreting a particular aspect of the Latin; the divergent views are both elaborated in the commentary. Woodman (2007) argues powerfully for the need to understand Greek and Latin as a vital element in engaging with ancient texts.

figure operating beyond the normal boundaries of *historia* is presented in an aptly discordant narrative voice.[97]

Finally, we have Syme (1970; Chapter 10 below), which is itself a reprint of an article originally published in 1958 (1958b). In this lucid and far-reaching piece, Syme investigates how Tacitus' distinctive obituary notices demonstrate his autonomy and expressiveness as a historian in the *Annals*, where he formally documents the deaths of twenty men in twelve separate passages. Syme points out that one distinctive aspect of these entries is their uneven distribution within the work, so that nine out of the twelve passages (involving fifteen men) cluster in the first hexad of the *Annals* 1–6, but none features in (what survives of) the second hexad, and only three (involving five men) in *Annals* 13 and 14. Why should this be? For Syme, this clustering of death notices in the Tiberian books suggests (surprisingly perhaps) that Tacitus' aim was to show that the matter of Roman history was not quite as dynastic and monarchic as it would later became under Tiberius' successors. Celebrating the achievements of illustrious men (whether in the form of a funeral laudation or a eulogistic biography) formed part of the legacy of the Roman republic, as Tacitus himself comments at *Agricola* 1, so the top-heavy distribution of these death notices in the *Annals* is pointed. So too is the 'relative poverty of the necrological rubric in the third hexad', since what Syme calls 'the texture of history' had changed after the principate of Tiberius, with even less scope for the exercise of senatorial power and a much greater concentration of authority within the imperial palace. Syme also draws attention to how Tacitus uses the obituaries of individuals such as the aristocratic generals Cn. Cornelius Lentulus and Domitius Ahenobarbus (*Annals* 4.44), both active during Augustus' principate, to broaden the chronological scope of his narrative and to sharpen the contrast between the relatively peaceful contemporary world of Tiberius' principate and the earlier history of Augustus' principate, where warfare had been much more predominant.[98] This article is typical of Syme, as we see him applying his extraordinary prosopographical knowledge to a distinctive aspect

---

[97] For more on Tacitus and Alexandria, see Kelly (2010). Similarly, Tacitus uses Tiberius' departure for Campania and self-imposed exile on Capri to cast the emperor as alienated from and hostile towards Rome. See Woodman (1972: 155).

[98] It may be helpful to distinguish here between Tiberius' character as *princeps* (on which see Luce 1986: 152–7) and the principate over which he presided.

of Tacitus' text, thereby illuminating the historian's narrative techniques and historiographical agenda. It also offers some archetypally
vivid touches, such as when Syme pictures the young Tacitus during
the principate of Vespasian listening to the funeral laudations of
illustrious men and overhearing 'the informed commentary of old
men there present'. Syme's style of writing, densely packed, allusive,
elliptical, and full of sound effects, overlaps curiously with Tacitus'
own, but so too do his powers of imagination.[99]

Luce (1986; Chapter 14 below) is concerned with a big question,
one which is relevant to all authors from the Classical world: how one
can use the text as a way to reconstruct what a writer really thought. If
comparison of passages within a text suggests that a writer appears to
adopt inconsistent views about a particular issue, how should we
respond to this dilemma? Or should we even see it as a problem?
Luce cites Goodyear (1976) for four reasons why Tacitean opinions
can be especially elusive: first, there is the influence of rhetorical
training, which inculcated the ability to argue on all sides of a question; second, there is the desire to entertain readers, which could
involve expressing provocative views; third, we have the very real
possibility of an author's genuine *aporia* about certain issues (and
changing one's mind over time is also a relevant factor); and finally,
there is the potential impact of conflicting sources. What Luce sets
out to do is to identify the difficulty of extracting Tacitean opinions
from, for example, ideas embedded in speeches delivered by internal
protagonists, and then to acknowledge that we are dealing with an
author who is indeed inconsistent at times. Yet this is not necessarily
a problem: Luce suggests that we should see such inconsistency as a
reflection of 'the complexity of the individual moment' (151), and
argues that the impact of individual historical circumstances at a
particular time and place should caution against the practice of
extracting timeless, all purpose Tacitean opinions from the text. So,
for example, in the abstract, we might well assume that Tacitus would
regard the concept of parsimony in a positive light. Yet in the case of
the emperor Galba, his rigidity in failing to award the soldiers even a
tiny financial sweetener leads to his downfall, brought about by his
adherence to an admirable but outdated principle. For Luce, the
particularity of events and circumstances is crucial in interpreting

---

[99] See further Wiseman (1998: 135–52) on the relationship between imagination,
style, and history in Syme's scholarship.

Tacitus, and therefore, rather than being troubled by inconsistency, we should work with it in analysing his works.[100] Luce's seminal paper touches upon issues which are directly relevant to a number of articles in this volume: these include Liebeschuetz's engagement with Tacitus' sometimes inconsistent attitude towards empire, Pelling's analysis of the characterization of Germanicus, and Bartsch's scrutiny of Maternus' contradictory positions within the *Dialogus*. Luce's argument suggests that, in facing up to apparent inconsistencies rather than explaining them away, these scholars are certainly on the right track.

Next, Goodyear (1968; Chapter 15 below) considers Tacitus' Latin. He begins with the basic idea that Tacitus' language and style continually evolve over the course of his different works, persistently moving away from normal usage in search of novelty. Yet some critics have detected a shift of dynamic within the *Annals*: they suggest that although in *Annals* 1–6 Tacitus does indeed move away from normality in terms of language and style, analysis of certain features (the relative frequency of *forem* and *essem*, the use of *ni* as a replacement for *nisi*, and so on) suggests that he reverts in *Annals* 13–16 to a more conventional way of writing (at least relatively so). In a spirit of provoking further discussion, Goodyear challenges this overview, at the same time as acknowledging the difficulties in studying the development of Tacitus' language and style. As he reminds us, the loss of so much of the *Histories* and *Annals* may well give a distorted impression of how drastic any perceived stylistic change really was, and the analysis is not helped by the loss of so much of Sallust's *Histories* and Livy's *Ab Vrbe Condita*, which means that an apparently 'Tacitean' coinage may be no such thing. Goodyear does concede that there may indeed be some movement towards an easier and less affected vocabulary over the course of *Annals* 13–16, but he insists that there are also many signs of continuity with the practice of the earlier books of the *Annals*, such as Tacitus' consistently bold use of metaphorical language, and in his willingness to discard words previously used (an ongoing process throughout the *Annals*), even very colourful ones (such as *grandaeuus*). Since in a writer

---

[100] One can perhaps draw a parallel here with the sensibly cautious attitude of Goodyear (1968: 24) [see Ch. 15 below] towards studying the evolution of Tacitus' language and style between the different works: 'in detail there is no simple formula. For instance, it is mistaken to find an increasing preference for mildly poetical words.'

such as Tacitus, style is so intricately related to ideology and meaning, detailed studies such as Goodyear's are arguably as crucial to our historical interpretation of Tacitus' narratives as they are to our artistic and aesthetic response.[101]

One area of Tacitean scholarship which could easily have offered material for an independent volume of essays in its own right involves the study of the afterlife and reception of his texts. Whether we think about the role of Tacitus' rebel leader Julius Civilis from the *Histories* in helping to shape Dutch national identity or the vibrant appropriation of Arminius (Herman) from the *Annals* in German culture and beyond, the ways in which Tacitus' narratives have been used and abused over the centuries are fascinating.[102] Perhaps one of the most notorious and controversial parts of Tacitus' historical narrative is his excursus on the ethnography and history of the Jews in *Histories* 5. How Tacitus' account of the Jews was subsequently received over the centuries is the focus of Bloch (2002; Chapter 16 below). Bloch traces in chronological order the intriguing range of reactions to Tacitus' Jewish excursus, beginning with the criticism of Tertullian from a Christian perspective, where predictably a disproportionate amount of attention was paid to *Histories* 5. As a result of the spotlight directed by early Christian authors towards these chapters, the Jewish excursus became accessible in the Middle Ages to a wider audience (even though the rest of Tacitus' narrative apparently remained in the shadows for most readers between the seventh and fourteenth centuries). With the fifteenth and sixteenth centuries, Tacitus became much more visible, but he faced harsh criticism from the French humanist Guillaume Budé, even if Jean Bodin, Michel de Montaigne, and Marc-Antoine Muret rallied to his defence. What is striking about this period is that the 'battleground' was primarily Tacitus' posthumous reputation as a historian, so that material from the Jewish excursus itself was not used to provide fuel for anti-Semitic observations. Only in the seventeenth century did Jewish authors themselves (the Venetian rabbi Simone Luzzatto, the Spanish emigré to Italy Isaac Cardoso, the Dutch philosopher Baruch (Benedictus) de Spinoza) confront the polemical excursus in any detail to engage in debate and to defend Judaism. In so doing, these authors often seem

---

[101] Another scholar who has made crucial contributions to our understanding of the development of Tacitus' Latin is Adams (1972; 1973).

[102] On the 'afterlife' of Civilis and Arminius, see Ash (2006b).

to combine self-defence with respect for Tacitus' intellectual achievements in the rest of his works, expressing surprise that he could be so uncritical in this one section. During the eighteenth century we can also see writers such as Gabriel Brotier and Jean Henri Dotteville engaging in a delicate balancing act between admiration for Tacitus and adhering to their own religious beliefs (even from a non-Jewish perspective). Unfortunately, J. G. Müller, who in 1843 produced the first scholarly treatise on the Jewish excursus in the German language, felt no such qualms: his writings show signs of deeply entrenched anti-Semitism, which were to become more and more common during the nineteenth century. Bloch concludes his illuminating survey by considering one representative work from the period of National Socialism (1933–45), by the 'race researcher' E. Fischer and the New Testament scholar G. Kittel, whose collaborative study of 1943, *Das antike Weltjudentum* (World Jewry in Antiquity) draws on Tacitus to bolster National Socialist conspiracy theories concerning the Jews. Yet as Bloch argues, what is perhaps most striking about the reception of the Jewish excursus is how often writers make efforts to separate Tacitus as anti-Jewish polemicist from Tacitus the far-sighted historian.

Momigliano (1990; Chapter 17 below) focuses on the reception of Tacitus' works more generally. He analyses the 'Tacitist tradition', starting with a portrait of Tacitus himself as a rigorous and reliable historian, who crafted brilliant, innovative narratives. Tacitus' literary career culminated in two extraordinary historical works, each of which in different ways was driven by a desire to understand the most disturbing features of tyrannical regimes and to chart the consequences of the permanent suppression of liberty. Momigliano sees Tacitus fundamentally as a conservative figure, whose pessimistic outlook is shaped by the fact that he cannot realistically see any alternative to the structure of the Roman empire, whatever its problems. In essence, this is not a writer who sought to encourage revolution, but rather one who sought to open people's eyes to the effects of despotism. In the second part of the paper, Momigliano paints a vivid picture of the afterlife of Tacitus' texts and identifies a series of significant moments in their evolution running from the sixth century (the last point when we can see Tacitus being seriously read and quoted) to nineteenth-century France. For instance, after Tacitus' texts had been restricted largely to Benedictine monasteries either in Germany or associated with Germany, a crucial turning-point came early in the fifteenth century (*c.*1403) when Leonardo Bruni quotes from Tacitus in his *Laudatio Florentinae Vrbis*: thus, Italy, and more specifically Florence, saw the first appearance of Tacitus in modern political thought. Later on in the fifteenth century, in Germany too attention was being turned to the *Germania* as a text which could inculcate pride and a sense of independence. That process only gained further momentum as the publication of *Annals* 1–6 by Philippus Beroaldus in 1515 brought the German rebel Arminius back into the public eye. Momigliano then traces the significance of Tacitus' writings in the Counter-Reformation, and elaborates how scholars such as Justus Lipsius and Carolus Paschalius, both of whom published commentaries on Tacitus in 1581, added momentum to the 'Tacitist' movement. This is a typically rich, learned, and far-ranging paper, which represents the best aspects of reception studies and helpfully identifies areas where there is more work to be done.

Finally, we have a short piece by Lionel Trilling (1976; Chapter 18 below), one of the 'New York Intellectuals', who taught for many years in the English Department at Columbia University in New York.[103] Trilling's early academic publications were on Matthew Arnold (1939) and E. M. Forster (1943), but the piece on Tacitus is taken from his first collection of published essays, *The Liberal Imagination*, which originally came out in 1950. For Trilling, who consistently engaged in exploring the relationship between literature and contemporary culture and society, Tacitus may seem an incongruous subject, particularly since, as he acknowledges, American liberals were likely to be put off by the 'aristocratic colour of his libertarian ideas'. In addition to that, Trilling suggests that the nature of the American political system in the past meant that there was no shared experience which could possibly allow Americans to understand properly the repressive world depicted by Tacitus. Yet Trilling suggests that by 1950 this is no longer the case and that now Tacitus is an author who should resonate strongly with those who have

---

[103] On the 'New York Intellectuals', see Bloom (1986), Ward (1987), Wilford (1995), and Jumonville (2007).

experienced their own 'political education' in his contemporary America.[104] What ultimately captivates Trilling about Tacitus' writings, however, is 'his power of mind and his stubborn love of virtue maintained in desperate circumstances'.

[104] Trilling's only novel, *The Middle of the Journey* (1947), about a political turncoat and the response to him of a group of intellectuals spending the summer in Connecticut, is suggestive in this connection and is strangely prescient about ideological disputes which were to develop over the 1950s. Several characters in the novel have been seen as thinly veiled versions of real people, particularly the controversial figure of the former communist and classmate of Trilling, Whittaker Chambers, whose testimony (1948) against Alger Hiss proved instrumental in the subsequent trials of Hiss for perjury (1949, 1950). Trilling and his wife, Diana, were caught up in the controversy after Chambers persuaded them to let him use their mailbox as a delivery point. See further Kimmage (2009).

1

An Island Nation: Re-reading Tacitus' *Agricola**

Katherine Clarke

There's a sense of place about islands—even when they're semi-detached—that sets them apart from continents.[1]

hanc oram nouissimi maris tunc primum Romana classis cir-cumuecta insulam esse Britanniam adfirmauit ('At that time a Roman fleet circumnavigated this most remote shore for the first time and confirmed that Britain was an island', Tac., *Agr.* 10.4)

INTRODUCTION

Tacitus' *Agricola* is one of the most tantalizingly enigmatic of ancient texts.[2] Coming from the pen of one who was to become a renowned

* This article has been developed from a paper given at the Laurence Conference on Roman Britain, held in Cambridge in May 1997 and organized by Mary Beard and John Henderson. I should like to thank the organizers and the participants in the conference for their many helpful suggestions and criticisms. I should also like to thank Chris Burnand, Fergus Millar, Chris Pelling, and the anonymous *JRS* readers for their many illuminating comments. All remaining errors and infelicities are, of course, my own. I should also like to thank Rhiannon Ash most warmly for her generous help, both intellectual and practical, in updating this article. Her stimulating suggestions for revision have proved invaluable.

[1] Crane (1999: 350).

[2] See Whitmarsh (2006) for a detailed and insightful discussion of the various types of ambiguity in the *Agricola*. Whitmarsh sees the linguistic, generic, and conceptual ambiguities as inherently bound up with the complexity of Tacitus' political ideology. The enigma of this text is promised a thorough and illuminating analysis in the forthcoming commentary by C. S. Kraus and A. J. Woodman (Cambridge).

historian, it is notoriously hard to place in generic terms. It fails to conform to any commonly accepted model of political history, and yet, as I shall argue, it has much to tell us about Tacitus' views of Roman political life. We can turn to the parallel of the *Germania* for another possible way out of the dilemma, and yet the ethnographic details which the *Agricola* undoubtedly encompasses could hardly be seen as its main focus. The most natural cast to give the work draws on its ostensibly biographical aspect. Commemorating the *res gestae* ('achievements') of Tacitus' father-in-law, Agricola, is the purpose signalled to the reader from the first sentence onwards: *clarorum uirorum facta moresque posteris tradere* ('to hand on to future generations the deeds and values of distinguished men', *Agr.* 1.1). All of these interpretations have had their proponents. But I shall argue here for a different reading of the *Agricola*, one which not only highlights an aspect of the text which has tended to be sidelined, but also provides an interpretative framework within which some of the other, more extensively treated themes may be reconsidered. My reading of the *Agricola* is focused not on the state of Rome under the emperor Domitian, nor on the customs of the inhabitants of Britain, nor even on the figure of Agricola himself, but on the actual location of his *res gestae*. I shall consider how Tacitus' portrayal of Britain itself may ultimately offer us insights into Agricola, Domitian, and Roman political life.

Two possible approaches to the geographical aspect of the *Agricola* have already been explored and exploited. Dorey saw the question of location as very much subordinate, almost incidental, to Tacitus' relation of Agricola's achievements: 'the account of the achievements of Agricola's predecessors as governors of Britain and the description of the country itself and its peoples merely serve as a prologue and a backcloth to the great drama in which Agricola is to be the protagonist.'[3] This view of the location as a mere stage and of its description as a piece of literary scene-setting is one against which I shall argue strongly. I shall propound a reading of the *Agricola* in which 'the description of the country' is indeed the ideal location for the *res gestae* of Agricola, but one which permeates the work and offers

---

[3] Dorey (1969a: 4). Byre (1994) offers a study of another island which seems designed to set into relief the character of a protagonist (Odysseus). Byre notes the length of Homer's description, which goes beyond that required by the plot, and stresses the importance of the insularity of the place.

a crucial key to its wider interpretation. In contrast to Dorey's 'back-cloth', a focus on location might seem to promise a traditionally empirical approach to the *Agricola*, which entails an attempt to map Agricola's exploits and travels onto modern Britain. Archaeological research has greatly enhanced the rewards for those who pursue this approach; and if we take the text at face value and trust in its credentials as an account of Roman incursions into the British Isles and, in particular, of the campaigns of Agricola, then its value for reconstructing the history of that period is considerable.

I have chosen, however, to explore a different angle on the issue of geographical location: namely, the light shed by the *Agricola* on the Roman view of Britain as a geographical entity and as a potential subject nation. I aim to show that Tacitus manipulates traditional aspects of this geographical conception, in particular Britain's place in relation to the Continent, in ways which illuminate not only Roman Britain but also the nature of Rome itself.[4] A consideration of the *Agricola*, which takes the geographical vision of Britain as its starting-point, may unexpectedly offer new insights into set pieces such as the pre-battle speeches of Agricola and Calgacus, as well as bringing into sharper focus the question of how Romanness could be constructed and negotiated. The key to this reading lies in a feature of Britain which has remained contentious to this day, periodically threatened and fiercely defended, namely its insularity.[5]

BEYOND THE PILLARS

In order to appreciate the significance of Tacitus' portrayal of Britain as a geographical entity, it is important to consider the tradition into which he inserted his account. A first impression of the history of geographical thought and the expansion of knowledge through conquest and exploration tends to focus attention on the Mediterranean world. Who indeed would be interested in doing more than creeping

---

[4] O'Gorman (1993: 135) [Ch. 3 below] sees the *Germania* as an 'exploration of a country (Germany) in search of the ideological (Roman) self'. Many of her ideas about the *Germania* are also relevant to discussion of the *Agricola*.

[5] There are many recent and stimulating discussions of insularity as a geographical concept and reality. See e.g. Constantakopoulou (2007) and several classical contributions in Létoublon (1996).

around the shores of the Mediterranean, listing cities, villages, and peoples along the way in the manner of Ps-Scylax or Ps-Scymnus?[6] It is possible to appreciate the allure of the eastern landmass of Asia, much of which would be imagined, constructed, and reconstructed first by the companions of Alexander the Great and then by succeeding generations. But the cold, damp, miserable North-West held considerably less appeal. Tacitus himself gives some idea of the repellent nature of this part of the world in the *Germania*: *qui mutare sedes quaerebant, et immensus ultra utque sic dixerim aduersus Oceanus raris ab orbe nostro nauibus aditur. quis porro, praeter periculum horridi et ignoti maris, Asia aut Africa aut Italia relicta Germaniam peteret, informem terris, asperam caelo, tristem cultu aspectuque, nisi si patria sit?*, 'Those who wanted to change their habitat in the past travelled by sea rather than by land, and the vast Ocean that lies beyond and acts, so to speak, as a barrier, is rarely approached by ships from our world. In any case, quite apart from the danger of an inhospitable and unknown sea, who would leave behind Asia or Africa or Italy to make for Germany, ugly in its landscape, harsh in its climate, and grim to live in and to look at, unless it were his own land?' (*G.* 2.1). In what terms could such liminal areas be represented?[7]

I shall argue that it is precisely the remoteness of the North-West and particularly of Britain itself which Tacitus exploits in the *Agricola*; that Britain's isolation, and specifically its insularity, underpins Tacitus' exploration of other themes within the work. There was indeed a long-standing tradition about the nature of Britain. According to Tacitus, many authors had treated the island and its inhabitants before (*Agr.* 10.1). He mentions two of these authors by name: Livy and Fabius Rusticus, who are described as 'the most eloquent of ancient and recent authors, respectively' (*Liuius ueterum, Fabius Rusticus recentium eloquentissimi auctores, Agr.* 10.3). In spite of these earlier treatments, Tacitus still has something to contribute, because the island was only fully conquered at the time of Agricola (*tum primum perdomita est, Agr.* 10.1), thus offering new opportunities for speculation to be replaced by knowledge. Furthermore, I shall argue that the conquest of Britain, as related in Tacitus'

---

[6] For these *periplus* texts, see Müller (1855).

[7] For discussion of the text of the *Germania*, its relation to other ethnographic works, and later treatments of the land and people, see the excellent commentary by Rives (1999).

Agricola, not only enhanced empirical knowledge of the island but actually altered its location on the mental map of the Romans.[8] As Ogilvie and Richmond note in their commentary, Caesar, Strabo, Pomponius Mela, undoubtedly Posidonius, and, long before them, Pytheas of Massilia had compiled accounts of Britain.[9] But the conceptual framework for Tacitus' *Agricola* may be unexpectedly enhanced by first considering the accounts of those writers who dealt not with Britain but with the west coast of Africa. The *periplus* texts attributed to Hanno, king of Carthage, and Scylax of Caryanda may appear at first to have little to offer our understanding of the *Agricola*, but I shall argue that they give us a productive insight into the geographical conceptions which characterize the world beyond the Pillars of Hercules, a world to which Tacitus' Britain must at least partially belong.

We know of Hanno's voyage from the Greek translation of a Punic inscription, supposedly set up in Carthage to commemorate the expedition.[10] Hanno apparently set out from Carthage in *c.*480 BC to explore the west coast of Africa and to found Liby-Phoenician cities. It has been suggested that the voyage referred to in the text never actually took place, and that the text represents rather an attempt to construct non-Greek *altérité*; but for the present purpose of assessing the conceptual geography of the world outside the Mediterranean, questions of fictionality need not concern us.[11]

The text purports to recount a voyage down the coast into increasingly hostile and alien territory and its inhabitants. The world of the Outer Ocean is one in which the landscape, its inhabitants, and their languages become threateningly different from those of the Mediterranean. All of these features will be important elements in understanding the use which Tacitus makes in the *Agricola* of the earlier geographical tradition. Hanno and his men come across lands of fire and incense from which streams of fire flow into the sea, making approach impossible (§§ 15–17). Not far into the journey

---

[8] See Murphy (2004: 197), for the point that empirical knowledge was in the gift of the *principes*, who could either reveal or withhold it. They 'had the power to promote knowledge by making it institutional, or to conceal it by denying it access to the public sphere'.

[9] See Ogilvie and Richmond (1967: 165).

[10] Text, translation, and commentary are provided by Ramin (1976).

[11] For the suggestion that the voyage is an imagined rather than a real one, see Jacob (1991: 73–84). It is, of course, also possible, even likely, that not only the voyage but also its epigraphic commemoration was fictional.

they encounter elephants (§4) and wild beasts (§7). From then on the division between men and beasts becomes blurred. There are Troglodyte men who run more swiftly than horses (§7), and wild men clad in animal skins (§9). This confusion culminates in the discovery of the gorilla women, about whom I shall say more shortly. The language of the inhabitants matches the increasing oddity of the landscape. Early in their voyage the Carthaginians take on board interpreters, but on reaching the land of the Ethiopians, they discover that their language cannot be understood by even the Lixite interpreters (§11).

Furthermore, the world beyond the Pillars is a world of islands. Hesiod and the Homeric epics had established that the western Ocean contained the Isles of the Blessed.[12] Hanno's voyage confirms the insular nature of this region. He passes the island of Cerne soon after leaving the Pillars of Hercules (§8). I shall return to the significance of Cerne below. But it is also an island, and furthermore an island within a lake within another island, which provides the location for the most startling of the experiences to befall Hanno and his companions, and which marks the end of the journey. 'On the lake [sc. within the island] was another island full of wild people. By far the majority of them were women with hairy bodies. The interpreters called them gorillas. When we chased them we were unable to catch the men, for they all fled from our hands, since they climbed well and defended themselves with stones. We captured three women, however, who bit and scratched those who led them and did not want to follow. So we killed them and flayed them and took the skins to Carthage. For we sailed on no further, for our food was running out' (§17). And here the account ends. An island on an island, together with its strange inhabitants, marks the limit of exploration.

The unfamiliar nature of what lay beyond the Pillars is confirmed by the mid-fourth-century BC text attributed to Scylax of Caryanda.[13] After performing the traditional circuit of the Mediterranean basin and returning to the Pillars of Hercules with a neat sense of closure,

---

[12] See Homer, *Od.* 4.563ff. on Elysium in the Ocean (see Strabo 1.1.5 for the islands of the blessed in the context of Homeric geography); Hesiod, *Works and Days* 170–77 describes these islands in some detail. Pindar, *Ol.* 2.68ff. continues the tradition. Of course, the delightful nature of these islands is in contrast with the inhospitable places encountered and described by the explorers, but the abnormality of the island landscape and inhabitants remains a constant theme.

[13] For an extensive and detailed treatment of Scylax, see Peretti (1979). For discussion of the world beyond the Pillars more generally, see Roller (2006).

the author then breaks out beyond the confines of the Mediterranean and enters the unfamiliar territory explored by Hanno. After passing some of the landmarks noted by Hanno, he reaches the island of Cerne and runs into problems. τῆς Κέρνης δὲ νήσου τὰ ἐπέκεινα οὐκέτι ἐστὶ πλωτὰ διὰ βραχύτητα καὶ πηλὸν καὶ φῦκος ('What lies beyond Cerne cannot be reached by ship because of the shallowness of the sea and the mud and seaweed', §112). This is an island world where the sea is no longer navigable and the normal rules of physics do not apply.

Around a century after the purported voyage of Hanno down the coast of Africa, Pytheas of Massilia sailed north on emerging from the Pillars of Hercules. His reward was the reputation of being utterly untrustworthy; his name became synonymous with tall stories. Strabo picked up on Polybius' misgivings concerning the evidence produced by Pytheas on Britain and its environs. At least Euhemerus, the archetype for geographical invention, claimed to have sailed to only one country, Panchaea, fictitious though that may have been. But Pytheas claimed to have explored the whole northern region of Europe as far as the ends of the earth (μέχρι τῶν τοῦ κόσμου περάτων), an assertion which no one would believe: not even Hermes himself had made it (Strabo 2.4.2).

The claims which Pytheas apparently made concerning the area are strongly reminiscent of the world constructed by the authors of the voyages of Hanno and Scylax: a world of islands, strange landscapes, and strange peoples. According to Strabo, Pytheas claimed the existence of an island called Thule, six days' sail north of Britain and near the frozen sea (1.4.2). Pytheas managed to convince the great Hellenistic scientist Eratosthenes that the island existed, but, according to Strabo, men who had seen Britain and Ierne (Ireland) did not mention Thule, although they did speak of other small islands around Britain (1.4.3).

> Pytheas of Massilia tells us that the areas around Thule, the most northerly of the Britannic islands, are the most remote . . . but, from the other writers, I can find nothing out—neither that there exists an island called Thule at all, nor that the areas right up to the point where the summer tropic becomes the arctic circle are habitable. I believe that the limit of the inhabited world on the northern side lies much further south than this. For modern writers have nothing to say about any country beyond Ierne (Ireland), which lies close to the north of Britain and is the home of men who are utterly wild and lead a miserable

existence because of the cold; and therefore, in my opinion, the northern limit of our inhabited world is to be placed there. (2.5.8)

The sea around the Thule area, as described by Pytheas, bears
a striking resemblance to what Scylax found around Cerne. 'He [sc.
Pytheas] talked about those regions in which there was no longer
either land in its own right, or sea, or air, but a kind of substance
made up of all these elements, resembling a "sea-lung", in which the
earth, the sea, and all the elements are held in suspension; and this is a
sort of bond to hold them together, but you can neither walk nor sail
on it (μήτε πορευτὸν μήτε πλωτὸν)' (Strabo 2.4.1). Just as Scylax
described, the islands beyond the Pillars of Hercules seem again to
belong to a world in which elements behave strangely, making places
inaccessible and quite literally hard to define, as land and sea are
merged into one.

The world beyond the Pillars may seem to bear the hallmarks of a
fictional creation. As I have already noted, Strabo found Pytheas'
account incredible; Jacob has suggested that Hanno's voyage may
never have taken place, except in the imagination, and indeed the
text relating his adventures may be a later fake. The similarity in sea
quality between that around Cerne and that around Thule begins to
hint at some profound geographical problems. The use of 'stock
literary places' in geographical works has been the subject of some
recent discussion, in particular concerning the islands of Cerne and
Thule, whose precise locations prove hard to define. It has been
suggested from the fact that the name 'Cerne' was applied to several
different places—opposite the Persian Gulf according to Ephorus
(Pliny, *NH* 4.35) and beyond the Pillars of Hercules according to
Eratosthenes (Strabo 1.3.2)—that the term 'non rappresenta una
frontiera geografica, ma un confino fantastico'.[14] The island of
Thule has been found similarly elusive because 'nella letteratura
antica il nome Tule indica l'estremità settentrionale dell'ecumene'.[15]
So, Cerne as the indicator of western limits, and Thule of the north
may not be representative of 'real' islands at all, but part of a fictional

---

[14] Amiotti (1987: 45): 'It represents not a geographical boundary, but a fantastical
limit.'
[15] Cordano (1992: 107): 'in ancient literature, the name Thule indicates the northern extremity of the inhabited world'.

and schematic mapping out of the world.[16] If this is the world in which Tacitus' *Agricola* takes place, then any use of the text for the tracing of Roman campaigns in Britain may be compromised. Accurate mapping and pure fiction are not polar opposites, but the way in which real locations are perceived and 'mapped' is very much a matter of ideological and, as I would argue in the case of Tacitus' Britain, intertextual construction.[17]

Before focusing on Tacitus, I make one final allusion to the Greek geographical tradition and to its construction of the non-Mediterranean world. Homer, according to Strabo the father of geography, propagated the idea of the encircling Ocean. The encircling Ocean was important because it was suggestive of a limit, and in spite of the best efforts of the Hellenistic geographers such as Eratosthenes to argue that more lay beyond, many, including Strabo himself, clung to the Homeric world-view.[18] For those propounding a 'Roman' vision of the world there were clear advantages to be found in a geography which specified an outer boundary, which could be presented as the natural limit to imperialism.[19] Such notions may be brought into play when considering the imperialist exploits of Agricola and their presentation by Tacitus. However, it is not immediately clear how the idea of the Ocean as the outer limit of the Empire can be reconciled with the fact that the Ocean itself, as seen in the exploratory tradition, is a place of islands, and furthermore islands which may be seen as potential conquests. Where are we to locate Britain—within or without the boundary that conveniently delimits Roman imperial aspirations?[20] I shall discuss in the following sections the ambiguous location of Britain, in the ill-defined and

[16] For the close relationship between geographical literature and fiction, see Romm (1992).

[17] The idea of 'constructed landscapes' is interestingly developed in relation to the *Germania* by O'Gorman (1993: esp. 136) [Ch. 3 below]. See also similar arguments in Krebs (2006).

[18] See Strabo 1.4.6 for Eratosthenes' belief that the Western Ocean formed not a limit but a route to the world beyond and ultimately to India.

[19] That Roman commanders from Pompey onwards, and partly in emulation of Alexander the Great, made political mileage out of 'reaching the Ocean' is apparent. See e.g. Cicero, *de Imperio* 33; Sallust, *Letter of Mithridates* 17; Plutarch, *Pompey* 38.2–3; Plutarch, *Caesar* 58.6–7. For Alexander, see Pompeius Trogus, *Historiae Philippicae* 12.7.4.

[20] Braund (1996a: 12) expresses this neatly: 'Britain lay both in Ocean and beyond Ocean, so that the conquest of Britain was also the conquest of Ocean itself.'

nebulous world that characterizes the Ocean beyond the Pillars, but nonetheless the appropriate setting for Roman imperial *res gestae* ('achievements'). In particular, I shall consider Tacitus' manipulation of different geographical traditions in ways which both highlight and exploit this ambiguity.

PLACING TACITUS' *AGRICOLA* IN THE OCEAN

In many respects the world of Tacitus' *Agricola* resembles that of the Ocean beyond the Pillars, found by the Greek explorers to be full of islands and physically abnormal. Dorey says of the *Germania*, 'there is a feeling of remoteness from the subject',[21] clearly referring to Tacitus' lack of personal interest, but in a purely spatial sense both Germany and Britain, regions of the North-West, are portrayed as being remote from Rome, in a liminal position on the edge of the known world. There is no doubt that Britain is ambiguously placed. The northern shore is faced by no other land (*Agr.* 10) and is beaten by the 'great and open sea' (*uastum et apertum mare*, *Agr.* 10.2), although Britain's place here within the encircling Ocean is worth noting. The sea around Thule in the *Agricola* precisely recalls that of Pytheas' account and also Scylax' tale concerning Cerne. It is 'sluggish and heavy' (*pigrum et graue*, *Agr.* 10.5), qualities which are said to make rowing difficult. The sensible explanation has been provided by Burn: 'the meaning of this has been elucidated only by men who have been there. The Romans would have encountered the North Atlantic Drift Current running against them.'[22] Ogilvie and Richmond too offer this as an explanation for what Tacitus describes. All three scholars also mention Pytheas, but to disappointing effect. For Burn, Tacitus' description is too geographically specific to be an allusion to the world of Pytheas; for Ogilvie and Richmond, 'Pytheas was certainly alluding to the freezing sea round Iceland, but Tacitus describes a different phenomenon', thus denying the point of contact.[23] Their commentary may well be correct in asserting that

---

[21] Dorey (1969a: 17).
[22] Burn (1969: 40). See also Burn (1949: 94) for this passage as an accurate description of a 'phenomenon familiar to sailors of small craft in the Pentland Firth'.
[23] Ogilvie and Richmond (1967: 173).

Pytheas' Thule was Iceland and that of Tacitus Shetland. But this very confusion signifies that Tacitus' portrayal of these regions is coined in the currency of movable islands and jelly-like seas, the remote world beyond the Pillars, making use of standard literary topoi for geographically distant areas.[24]

The ambiguity between land and sea is yet another feature of the island world which appears in the *Agricola*. Tacitus rejects a detailed discussion of the Ocean, but he does mention the supremacy of the sea insofar as it cuts its way deep inland around Britain, blurring the natural boundaries (*Agr.* 10). Not only this, but the overthrow of the natural order is manifested in the confusion between day and night. A feature of the most remote part of Britain, and indeed a function of that remoteness, is the existence of night which is paradoxically 'bright' and 'short' (*clara* and *breuis*: *Agr.* 12.3). The implications for the question of definition and ambiguity are made explicit: 'you could hardly distinguish between evening and morning twilight' (*finem atque initium lucis exiguo discrimine internoscas, Agr.* 12.3). The sun can be seen all night, not rising and setting, but simply gliding across (*transire*). It must be, says Tacitus intriguingly, that the flat extremities of the earth, with their low shadow, do not project the darkness. Whatever the theory behind this, there is a clear connection between extremity, remoteness, and the failure of the natural world to behave according to the usual rules. Britain's failure to adhere to boundaries is further exemplified by the leadership of a woman, Boudicca, *neque enim sexum in imperiis discernunt*,'for they make no distinction between the sexes in their commands' (*Agr.* 16.1).

The view of Britain as a remote island, lying on the edge of the earth, is, however, under threat in the text. One of the quotations with which I began this chapter concerns the moment in history, namely the time of Agricola's campaign, when the island nature of Britain was firmly established, but I shall argue that this recognition also marks the first stage in Britain's removal from the island world of the Ocean. It has been argued that the passage in which this discovery is

---

[24] Further weight is given to this connection by the observation by Thompson (1948: 148–9) that there was an extensive tradition in geographical writings of discovering and describing sluggish seas in remote areas. He refers, e.g., to Himilco's exploration of the outer parts of Europe, in which were found seas that were difficult to navigate. Certain phrases in Avienus' account of Himilco's voyage are particularly revealing. See *Ora Maritima* 121: *aequoris pigri* and 128: *nauigia lenta et languida repentia*.

stated forms part of a digression, thus sidelining it from the main narrative.[25] Ogilvie and Richmond compare the digressions in the monographs of Sallust, which, they claim (p. 164), are similarly used to separate the principal stages in the narrative. However, it has more recently been suggested that the digressions in Sallust are anything but digressive.[26] I would argue that for Tacitus too the digression on the geography and ethnography of Britain is integral to the work.[27] Britain's insularity is not just a backdrop, but an element which must be continually reassessed and redefined. The other quotation which I introduced at the start provides the cue for the forthcoming discussion of Britain as an island which, though remote, may be seen as also 'semi-detached'.

BECOMING 'SEMI-DETACHED': BRITAIN AS AN ADJUNCT TO THE CONTINENT

This is the point at which to note that sailing out through the Pillars of Hercules was not the only means of reaching Britain. An alternative route, and one which would give Britain a quite different identity from that of the Oceanic world, was across land through Gaul. This was the route taken by Caesar; it was also the picture given by Strabo, who presented his description of Britain as a continuation of that of Gaul, and stressed the English Channel as a medium for communication rather than as a barrier (Strabo 4.5.1–5). Britain was the natural next step in Rome's conquest of the world, 'une suite

---

[25] Even such sensitive treatments as that of Liebeschuetz (1966) can find little to link the description of Britain with the surrounding narrative.

[26] See Wiedemann (1993). Wellesley (1969: 69) places the geographical 'digression' of the *Agricola* in the category of *origines et situs*, which Tacitus discusses at *A.* 4.32–3 as being an integral part of the historiography of imperialism. The description of Britain would thus be motivated by the fact that the island was then for the first time fully conquered. This argument is somewhat supported by Tacitus' announcement that he is moving on to discuss *Britanniae situm populosque* (*Agr.* 10.1). It is disappointing that Ogilvie and Richmond (1967) entitle their commentary on *Agr.* 10–12 'The Ethnography of Britain'. My aim is in part to reinstate the *Britanniae situs* as being of at least equal importance to the *populi*.

[27] Sailor (2008: 81–9) discusses this digression, and brings out interestingly the parallels between Agricola and Tacitus, each performing his own conquest, literal or literary, of the island. Thus the digression could be seen as further enmeshed in the surrounding narrative.

logique de celle de la Gaule', according to Dion.[28] This, I shall argue, is the other main configuration of the location of Britain which Tacitus and the characters of the *Agricola* reveal and exploit in the course of the text.

Crucial to the process of redefinition is the intellectual conquest by the Romans of their prospective new territory. This intellectual conquest must go alongside the literal one effected in the campaigns for Tacitus to be able to claim that Britain was first completely conquered (*perdomita, Agr.* 10.1) at the time of Agricola. The Romans cannot start to reassess the place of Britain in their world-view until they have become informed about the island.[29] So we hear that the Orkney islands were discovered and subdued, but had been unknown (*ignotae*) up until that time (*Agr.* 10.4); finding out about the earliest inhabitants is difficult even now (*parum compertum, Agr.* 11.1). But Agricola's mission is to reveal, uncover, bring all within the compass of Roman knowledge. In his third season of campaigning, he uncovers new peoples (*nouas gentes aperuit, Agr.* 22.1); the fifth season brings still further discoveries—the subjugation of 'peoples unknown until that time' (*ignotas ad id tempus gentes, Agr.* 24.1). But Agricola employs his knowledge discriminately: 'he knew everything, but he did not follow it all through' (*omnia scire, non omnia exsequi, Agr.* 19.2).

The final showdown at Mons Graupius provides the context not only for the military clash but also for the battle over knowledge of Britain. Calgacus, the Scottish chieftain and Agricola's worthy opponent, spurs on his men with reference to the 'remoteness and seclusion' (*longinquitas ac secretum, Agr.* 31.3) which have so far kept his land out of the Roman grasp. He characterizes the Romans as utterly unfamiliar with all that surrounds them: 'fearful through ignorance, looking around at the sky itself and the sea and the woods, all unknown entities' (*trepidos ignorantia, caelum ipsum ac mare et siluas, ignota omnia circumspectantes, Agr.* 32.2). Agricola totally reverses this picture in his speech of encouragement: 'Britain has been discovered and subdued' (*inuenta Britannia et subacta, Agr.*

---

[28] Dion (1977: 254).
[29] Burn (1969: 37) notes the disproportionate geographical interest in the work devoted to islands. 'The Romans seem to have had an appetite for British island names', adducing also Pomponius Mela's mention of 30 Orcades, Thule, and 7 Aemodae.

33.3). Although the Romans may not have a precise knowledge of the region, these are not 'new peoples and an unknown battle-line' (*nouae gentes atque ignota acies, Agr.* 34.1). From the British perspective, as portrayed by Tacitus, the less that is known about Britain by the Romans the better; for the Romans, intellectual conquest is going to be an important part of the takeover.

Tacitus' image for the Roman intellectual victory over Britain, when he states that Britain is the largest of the islands which Roman knowledge embraces (*quas Romana notitia complectitur, Agr.* 10.2), has serious implications for Britain's insular nature. Agricola's campaigns have the effect of altering Britain's status as an island, previously free from the Continent.

In his account of the history of British incursions, Tacitus recalls the Britons' view of their insularity. The Germans were disadvantaged in having only a river, rather than the Ocean, as a defence against the Romans: 'they were defended by a river, not the Ocean' (*et flumine, non Oceano defendi, Agr.* 15.3). Before Agricola's invasion, the Homeric encircling Ocean could be seen as a defence between the Continent and the British Isles. Britain lay far out in the Ocean itself. The previously remote, Oceanic nature of Britain is reinforced by Tacitus, who comments that opposite the north shore was no further land; the shore was battered by the vast, open sea (*Agr.* 10.2). Calgacus may use the Oceanic nature of Britain as a spur to his men at Mons Graupius—'no land lies beyond us' (*ultra*). But the advent of Agricola changes the conceptual geography of this part of the world, in ways which even Calgacus cannot deny.

Instead of the Ocean acting as a barrier between Britain and the Continent, it now acts as the medium by which the Romans can embrace Britain within their grasp. As Tacitus says, it was at the time of Agricola that Britain was first circumnavigated by the Roman fleet. The paradox is that although this proved that Britain was an island, and therefore remote and theoretically beyond the scope of Rome's imperial aspirations, the act of circumnavigation was a crucial stage in the removal of Britain from the Oceanic world beyond the Pillars, and its gradual attachment, both administratively and in the Roman mental map, to the world of the Continent.[30] The circumnavigation

---

[30] For earlier formulations of the idea that the Ocean might encircle and encompass Roman power, note the ambitions of Pompey (Plut., *Pomp.* 38.2–3) and Caesar (Plut., *Caes.* 58.6–7). The flexible definition of where precisely the Ocean ran, beyond

led to the embrace (*complectitur, Agr.* 10.2) of Britain by Roman knowledge, but also to a change in its insular status; a geographical realignment, so that it now fell within the compass of the Roman world, not in the world of the elusive western islands. The resultant exclusion of Britain from the world of the Outer Ocean is reinforced by the note that Agricola's men who circumnavigated Britain could not do the same for Thule. This island was sighted, but no more, allowing it to remain firmly outside the Roman world.

As the campaigns move further northwards, the island status of Britain is continually reassessed. The fourth year brings the Romans to a possible terminus, the narrow strip of land between the Forth and the Clyde. If the glory of Rome had not forbidden a halt, says Tacitus, a limit would have been found in Britain itself (*inuentus in ipsa Britannia terminus, Agr.* 23). The garrisoning of this strip of land would have resulted in the enemy being cut off, as if onto another island (*summotis uelut in aliam insulam hostibus, Agr.* 23). The island mentality is at the fore; islands mean separation, isolation, and defence. But here, the idea is to move the boundary of Britain to a point which the Romans can reach. What lies beyond would join the quite separate world of Oceanic islands, a world which is not of immediate concern to Rome—an extreme example of the way in which the Romans could redraw their mental map to match their aspirations and achievements.[31]

Britain or before one reached it from Gaul, could of course be useful in justifying either variety of Roman expansion in that elsewhere Plutarch describes Caesar's British expedition as taking him beyond the confines of the Empire, i.e beyond the Oceanic barrier and into a world that was scarcely believable. In the context of nebulous island-worlds, the phrase νῆσον ἀπιστουμένην ὑπὸ μεγέθους (Plut., *Caes.* 23) is particularly striking. Here, there is no suggestion that Caesar's conquest would threaten the insular nature of Britain; rather, its insularity is proof of Caesar's daring. As Pelling observes, Pompey's allusion to Caesar 'calling the pools of uncertain depth an Ocean' (*Oceanumque uocans incerti stagna profundi*, Lucan, *Civil War* 2.571) might suggest that Caesar himself made much of the Oceanic adventure in his dispatches concerning the British expedition.

[31] The mental division of Britain into a 'Roman' and a 'non-Roman' section is clearly seen in Appian's preface, in which he outlines Roman acquisitions, including 'the larger and better portion of it [sc. Britain], since they did not want the remainder at all' (App., *Roman History, Pref.* 5). For the unprofitability and consequent undesirability of Britain as an element in Roman rhetoric concerning the island's elusiveness from conquest, see Strabo 4.5.3. Braund (1996a: 149), however, interestingly points to the way in which Scotland, under the name of Caledonia, was used by Flavian poets to express the rulers' aspirations to conquer Britain, telling against the idea of a northern segment of the island which could be mentally detached and dismissed.

This option is rejected. Britain will be conquered wholesale. The following year's campaign opens up a new issue, the status of Ireland,[32] and raises interesting possibilities for the shifting alignment of Britain as either an island or an adjunct to the Continent. Strabo had made it clear that Ireland fell outside the intended limits of the Roman Empire, being utterly barbarian and undesirable, a place of savagery, cannibalism, and incest (4.5.4). Tacitus' *Agricola* at least harbours ambitions in that direction. As for Britain, the insular nature of Ireland is firmly established, but it is interesting that the extreme remoteness of Ireland found in Strabo's account is tempered by Tacitus. The island is smaller than Britain, but larger than those in the Mediterranean (*nostrum mare*, *Agr.* 24.2)—contexts of comparison which immediately draw Ireland and the world of the Ocean towards the Mediterranean Roman world. The notion expressed in *Agr.* 24 that conquest of Ireland would help to link together the western parts of the *imperium*—Britain, Ireland, and Spain—brings these Oceanic lands into the embrace of Rome again, redrawing the map of the Greek geographical tradition, which had placed them *outside* the world of the Mediterranean *periplus*. The new geographical grip on Ireland, which its conquest would bring, is foreshadowed by the inclusion of Ireland in the intellectual grasp of the Romans already. Tacitus says that the harbours on the island are fairly well known (*cogniti*, *Agr.* 24.2) through the reports of traders. As I discussed above with regard to Tacitus' Britain, knowing about a place is a half-way stage to conquering it with arms.

Before the arrival of Agricola, the sea, which was so much a part of the British landscape as to penetrate even far inland, proved a bonus to the British. The sixth year of the campaigns was to change all that. At this point, Agricola set in motion a marine counterpart to the landborne offensive: 'The war was pushed forward simultaneously by land and sea: infantry, cavalry, and marines would meet up in the camp and compare the conquest of land and the enemy with that of the Ocean' (*hinc terra et hostis, hinc uictus Oceanus*, *Agr.* 25.1). According to the tales of captives, the Britons were amazed, as though 'with the recesses of their own sea opened up, the last refuge for the defeated had been shut off'. The Britons consider the Ocean to be

---

[32] See further Freeman (2001: 56–62). Freeman sees Tacitus' description here as 'one of the most important and informative passages on Ireland in classical literature' (56).

their sea (*maris sui*, *Agr.* 25.2), and now it is being taken over by the Romans, who already have the Mediterranean as their own (*nostrum mare*, *Agr.* 24.2). The confidence brought by the fact that the Ocean itself, the very definer of Britain's former identity, is now in his power leads Agricola to abandon once and for all the notion of a terminus within Britain, and to seek the real terminus, the Oceanic terminus which encompasses the whole island, and ultimately the whole earth. There is no need now for subdivisions which would leave a newly created 'island' still to be conquered.

By the time of the battle of Mons Graupius, there can be no doubt in anyone's mind that the insular status of Britain has been eroded; its position among the nebulous islands that lie beyond the Pillars, the haunts of Hanno, Scylax, and Pytheas, has been taken away by Rome's conquest. The conquest is both intellectual—drawing the whole island into the realm of Roman knowledge, and forcing a redrawing of the mental map of the area—and real, in the sense that Rome has actually reached the terminus of Britain, paradoxically using as the medium of travel the Ocean itself. This part of the Outer Ocean, like the Mediterranean, had now in a sense been appropriated by the Romans as *nostrum mare*; it no longer belongs to the Britons.

The speeches before the battle of Mons Graupius provide the dramatic opportunity for this gradual process of redefinition to be brought into clearer focus.[33] Calgacus starts in encouraging fashion. Now is the dawn of freedom for the whole of Britain (*libertas toti Britanniae*, *Agr.* 30.1). You are all (*universi*, *Agr.* 30.1) gathered here, free from servitude. But it is apparent that all of these terms have now taken on a more sinister aspect. *Libertas* is a theme to which I shall return. But the united nature of Britain was a feature of its life as an island, distinct and self-contained. In the face of earlier Roman incursions, Boudicca had taken up the war for all (*universi*, *Agr.* 16.1); it was natural for Calgacus to make the same appeal. But we have seen the way in which the intervening campaigns of Agricola

---

[33] They may also, according to Martin (1981: 43), be used as a means of establishing that the *Agricola* is to be seen as a historical work. Ogilvie (1991: 1720) also sees in the pair of speeches in the *Agricola* an echo of those attributed to Hannibal and Scipio in Livy 21.40–44. For a Tacitean parallel, see *Ann.* 12.34, where Tacitus alludes to a pre-battle speech given by the British chieftain, Caratacus. Many of the themes are very similar to those raised by Calgacus—*libertas*, *uirtus*, *maiores*, the family. Just as in the case of Calgacus, Caratacus is defeated in spite of his brave words. His main speech in *oratio recta* comes after his defeat, when he has been taken to Rome.

have now made the union of Britain desirable in Roman eyes. The option of dividing Britain has been weighed up and rejected. The Romans, having encircled Britain geographically, are now happy for it to be united as a bundle which can be easily adjoined to the Empire.

No land lies beyond us, says Calgacus; not even the sea is free from the threat of Rome. But we have already seen that Ireland, lying beyond Britain, is part of the Roman plan for future conquest, and one which would take away the prospect of *libertas* from Britain. When Calgacus goes on to stress the isolation of Britain from subject peoples—'we have eyes which are undefiled by contact with domination' (*Agr.* 30.2)—he is referring to the Gauls. Britain was, for him, the safe island retreat from the Continent; for the Romans, the concern is that Britain should not be able to see liberty on the other side, out into the Ocean. But I have argued that the Roman redefinition of Britain relies on looking towards the English Channel, not the Ocean. Yet again Calgacus is made to speak in terms which curiously echo the wishes of the Romans. Rather than looking outwards, he is made to focus his sights on precisely the link that Rome wants to effect.

Up until this point, says Calgacus, Britain was defended by its very remoteness and seclusion (*recessus ipse ac sinus, Agr.* 30.3); now the terminus of Britain is revealed. The effects of Agricola's campaigns in terms of bringing Britain within the realm of Roman knowledge are accepted. As Calgacus' speech proceeds, the picture of Britain it puts forward seems to be increasingly in line with that presented in the narrative itself. Agricola himself needs only to summarize the same picture in his speech, claiming to have secured the limit of Britain (*finis Britanniae, Agr.* 33.3). Returning to the terminology of Tacitus' 'digression' in *Agr.* 10–12, it could hardly be made more explicit that the conquest is as much one over the landscape (*situs*), the insular nature of Britain and its geographical position, as over the inhabitants (*populi*) themselves.

One might see this new identity of Britain as being one of 'semi-detachment', or perhaps more accurately as one of 'semi-attachment', since the process is in the direction of assimilation rather than disjunction. As a result of Agricola's campaigns the island undergoes a redefinition which results in a loss of strict insularity, an erosion of the remoteness which was crucial to its independence from Rome and was manifested in its similarity to other landmarks of the physically strange world beyond the Pillars. Now Britain is made to adhere to the Continent, to minimize the real and conceptual gulf of the Channel, which had previously provided an important divider and kept Britain as a feature of the Oceanic world. The possibility that Britain might be subdivided and the northern half allowed to go free, redefined as an island in its own right, has been rejected. With the Roman grasp embracing not only the Channel and the whole of Britain, but even the sea beyond, the realignment is complete. However, as Crane's comment on semi-detached islands notes, even these retain a 'sense of place that sets them apart from continents'. And, as I shall argue in the next section, it is the continuing ambiguity in Britain's geographical status which provides a fitting context for Tacitus' exploration of the behaviour and values of the protagonists, both conquered and conquerors.

PROBLEMS OF IDENTIFICATION

It is one of the many complexities of the text that the same picture of Britain, as an island whose insularity is under threat and which is encircled by Roman power and knowledge, can be used as an encouragement to both sides. It is not hard to see how Agricola might use such a picture to give confidence to his troops, but the reasoning of Calgacus is more difficult to understand. For this, we need to consider what else Calgacus feeds into his picture. The definitions of Britain may to a large degree coincide, but Calgacus then turns his attention to the portrayal of the Romans, and herein reveals another significant shift from the traditional picture. I shall argue in this section that the ambiguity of Britain as a location for Roman *res gestae* is reflected in the difficulty in defining both its inhabitants and its conquerors.

It was standard practice in geographical and ethnographical works to portray peoples on the edge of the earth as pirates and brigands. Not only those far from the centre of power, but all those characterized by their 'out-of-the-way-ness' (ἐκτοπισμός) are prone to piratical behaviour. And one of Rome's greatest achievements was the suppression of such piracy. Throughout the first century BC this would be a major route to fame and power for politicians such as Lucullus and

Pompey, and we know that it was an image still being propagated by Augustus.[34]

But various leaders and authors had tried to turn this picture around. Sallust's *Letter of Mithridates* (22) designates the Romans as *latrones gentium*. Calgacus, in the words of Tacitus, follows in this tradition of criticism. The Romans are, he says, the brigands of the world (*raptores orbis, Agr.* 30.4). Not only this, but they have not been satisfied with East and West (*non Oriens, non Occidens satiauerit, Agr.* 30.4). The implication is that they also want the North, the region of Thule in the schematic layout of the earth. But we know from authors such as Vitruvius and Strabo that the Romans belonged at the centre of the earth. It was their location at this climatologically privileged point that made them naturally prone to hegemony.[35] Now their imperial ambitions had led them to the very edges of the earth, and they had started to behave according to the stereotype of the barbarians whose natural habitat was on these perimeters. This is one possible reading and I am arguing in general here for the importance of place and location; but I shall return to consider whether this picture of geographical determinism, whereby the Romans behave piratically because of their new location in barbarian lands, stands up to close scrutiny.

Furthermore, the progress of the text reveals that these 'Romans' are not necessarily Roman at all. The army is made up of Gauls, Germans, and even some Britons.[36] The Romans do not just behave like barbarians; they actually are barbarians. Just as this makes it impossible to draw a sharp distinction between the troops of Calgacus and Agricola, so too does it reveal a lack of unity within Agricola's army itself. And the same tension between unity and diversity among the Britons is also revealed in the work.[37]

---

[34] For Lucullus, see Plut., *Luc.* 23; for Pompey, see Cicero, *de imperio Gnaei Pompeii* 34–5, in which the anti-pirate command is seen as the springboard for the granting to Pompey of the command over the war against Mithridates through the *Lex Manilia*. For Augustus, see his claim at *Res Gestae* 25 (*mare pacaui a praedonibus*). This may indeed refer to the war against Sextus Pompeius in Sicily in 39-36 BC, but the point is made more general in Horace, *Odes* 4.5.19: *pacatum uolitant per mare nauitae* and in Suetonius *Life of Augustus* 98, in which the Alexandrian sailors hail Augustus: *per illum se uiuere, per illum nauigare*.

[35] See Vitruvius 6.1.10–11; Strabo 17.2.1, but esp. also 6.4.1.

[36] On the auxiliary nature of the battle, see Gilliver (1996).

[37] It is worth remembering that Agricola himself is a Gaul, a detail which further confounds any attempt at strict divisions. On the implications of this, see Richmond

Just as Agricola's army may be affected by their new location on the edges of the earth, behaving piratically as befits their 'out-of-the-way-ness' (ἐκτοπισμός), so too are the Britons affected by the presence of Agricola's men—the processes of acculturation at work. Tacitus famously catalogues in *Agr.* 21 the effects of Roman influence on the way of life of the inhabitants of Britain.

> *namque ut homines dispersi ac rudes eoque in bella faciles quieti et otio per uoluptates adsuescerent, hortari priuatim, adiuuare publice, ut templa fora domos extruerent, laudando promptos, castigando segnis: ita honoris aemulatio pro necessitate erat. iam uero principum filios liberalibus artibus erudire, et ingenia Britannorum studiis Gallorum anteferre, ut qui modo linguam Romanam abnuebant, eloquentiam concupiscerent. inde etiam habitus nostri honor et frequens toga; paulatimque discessum ad delenimenta uitiorum, porticus et balinea et conuiuiorum elegantiam. idque apud imperitos humanitas uocabatur, cum pars seruitutis esset.*

To induce a people, hitherto scattered, uncivilized and therefore prone to fight, to grow pleasurably inured to peace and ease, Agricola gave private encouragement and official assistance to the building of temples, public squares, and private houses. He praised the keen and scolded the idle, and competition to gain honour from him was as effective as compulsion. Furthermore, he trained the sons of the chiefs in the liberal arts and expressed a preference for British natural ability over the trained skill of the Gauls. The result was that in place of rejection of the Latin language there came a passion to command it. In the same way, our national dress came into favour and the toga was everywhere to be seen. And so the Britons were gradually led on to the amenities that make vice pleasant—arcades, baths, and sumptuous banquets. It was called civilization by those to whom it was all new, when really it was a feature of their enslavement.

I shall return to the implications of the last sentence, but for now simply note the change for Britain and the lifestyle of its inhabitants brought about by the advent of Agricola.

Coming back to Calgacus, it is striking that he is seen to possess and display the most Roman of virtues, *uirtus* itself. He is introduced as a man outstanding in *uirtus* and nobility (*Agr.* 29.4). He attributes

---

(1944: 44). Braund (1996a: 155) comments that Agricola's upbringing in Gaul keeps him away from the corruption of Rome itself, a point to which we shall return.

this to the Britons under his leadership: they have *uirtus ac ferocia* ('virtue and fierce courage') (*Agr.* 31.3). *Virtus* is what the Romans lack. 'Do you think that their *virtus* in war matches up to their wantonness in peace?' asks Calgacus (*Agr.* 32.1). Besides this, he attributes familial piety to the Britons: Agricola's army is without any *familia*, no wives to spur them on, no parents to chide if they run away from battle,[38] and his whole speech ends with an appeal to the ancestors and future generations (*maiores* and *posteri, Agr.* 32.4)—a standard appeal for Romans.

Even more strikingly, Calgacus' entire speech is a masterpiece of Roman oratory: full of *sententiae* (*omne ignotum pro magnifico est, Agr.* 30.3); rhetorical questions; balanced antithesis (*non Oriens, non Occidens satiauerit, Agr.* 30.4—where even the sentiment expressed entails notions of balance, spatial in this case). There is a grand rhetorical crescendo: *auferre trucidare rapere falsis nominibus imperium atque ubi solitudinem faciunt pacem appellant* ('robbery, murder and rape they falsely call empire: they create desolation and call it peace', *Agr.* 30.4). Here the rhetorical practice of *definitio*, defining one's terms, is shown off.[39]

We thus have the paradoxical scenario in which Calgacus, the barbarian chieftain, is more skilled in the art of speaking Latin than are the Romans themselves. We know that his definitions are more accurate than theirs: he knows better how to use their language. The Romans are barbarian brigands whose Latin is decidedly suspect: Calgacus and his men are the repositories of Roman *uirtus* and proper Latin usage. Has the process of acculturation resulted here in a wholesale exchange of identities? The question of language usage seems to me key. In the famous passage on Romanization at *Agr.* 21, Tacitus describes the acquisition of Roman habits and the accoutrements of civilization: *idque apud imperitos humanitas uocabatur, cum pars seruitutis esset* ('it was called civilization by those to whom it was all new, when really it was a feature of their enslavement', *Agr.* 21.2). Tacitus makes clear that the Britons have not adopted the correct

---

[38] I owe to Rhiannon Ash the interesting suggestion that this scenario represents a rerun of the Trojan war, with Agricola's men in the role of the Greeks and the Britons as Trojans.

[39] See Cicero, *de Oratore* 1.42 (189) for the definition of *definitio* as 'a short piece of description of those features which particularly characterize the thing which we wish to define'.

term for what is happening.[40] This cannot be due to their short acquaintance with the language, since Calgacus, far away in the north of Scotland, does not share this problem. Furthermore, he is actually able to correct the Latin used by the Romans themselves: his understanding of the terminology of imperialism is more accurate than theirs. It cannot be the case that one's Latin improves through contact with the invading Romans; otherwise, those in the south of Britain, rapidly becoming Romanized, would be far more advanced than Calgacus. It is, of course, in any case a conceit that Calgacus was a fluent and accomplished Latin orator.

Rather than being improved by contact with the Romans, it appears that the Britons of the south have been corrupted. Their adoption of the twisted Roman terminology justifying conquest is one example of this. They have learned to speak as the Romans do, and that means in a corrupt way. By contrast, Calgacus, hidden away in the most remote part of Scotland, on what could even be thought of as the second island, has not yet been corrupted. His Latin is pristine. As he claims for all Britons: 'we are uncorrupted and unconquered' (*integri et indomiti, Agr.* 31.4), an extravagant claim and not a true one. The unity of Britain, to which Calgacus appealed and which would have suited the Romans too, is a façade. Some have been taken over and brought into the Roman mindset, but there still remains a pocket which has not succumbed. The difficulty, then, is to consider what the state of uncorrupted Britain is, and what Calgacus stands for.

I have mentioned the many ways in which Calgacus seems to epitomize Romanness. He is almost more Roman than the Romans themselves. So we cannot say that Agricola's Roman army is corrupting a barbarian nation, but rather that there may be two types of Romanness in play. Calgacus is representative of the fact that Old Rome is to be found in the most remote parts of the Empire, or even beyond the Empire's bounds.[41] Old Roman virtues and grand Latin speeches are located at the edge of the earth, in the most peculiar

---

[40] But see Whitmarsh (2006: 319) for the view that categories of praise or blame and the search for a single meaning may be inappropriate in the context of the *Agricola*'s many ambiguities.

[41] O'Gorman (1993: 147–9) [Ch. 3 below] discusses this theme in relation to the *Germania*, raising the question of whether Germany could be seen as an equivalent to primitive Rome, or 'a re-enactment of early Roman history'. In the *Germania*, just as in the *Agricola*, this question finds no easy solution.

world of the Oceanic islands, and as far from Rome itself as one can imagine.

THE REMOTENESS OF *ROMANITAS*: BRITAIN AS THE IDEAL LOCATION FOR AGRICOLA'S *RES GESTAE*

This is one way of understanding the prominence of Calgacus, as the representative of Roman *uirtus* and Roman *eloquentia*. But the text is introduced as a commemoration of the illustrious achievements of Agricola. How can his opponent be allowed to eclipse the hero of the work to the extent that he and his land are revealed as the repository for the kinds of values we would naturally associate with the *clari uiri* of Rome?[42] I return now to the question of Britain as the ideal location for Agricola's *res gestae* ('achievements') and to some explanation of why the issue of Britain's geographical status is much more than a mere backdrop to Agricola's campaigns.

I have set out the way in which Tacitus may be playing on two geographical conceptions of Britain: placing the notion of Britain as part of the remote island world of the Outer Ocean, together with Cerne and Thule, alongside the alternative conception of Britain as an adjunct to the Continent, the logical follow-on from Gaul. Agricola, as a native of Forum Iulii (*Agr.* 4.1), and educated in Marseilles, belongs by birth to the second of these two worlds, that of Gaul, the Continent, and the Roman Empire. His military apprenticeship under Suetonius Paulinus introduced him to Britain and, as Tacitus says, he got to know his province well (*noscere prouinciam*) (*Agr.* 5.1). His final qualification as the ideal candidate for the governorship of Britain came with his magnificent term in command of Aquitania (*Agr.* 9). Public opinion demanded that he should be appointed to Britain, not because he himself suggested it, but because he was the

---

[42] See Martin (1994: 39–49). He discusses the work as one in which the figure of Agricola as hero is maintained partly through acknowledgement of the fact that times have changed since the Republic and a new type of heroism is called for. However, I disagree with his view that Calgacus' portrayal as worthy opponent is designed primarily to increase the stature of Agricola (*Agr.* 44). It seems to me rather that Calgacus actually embodies what Agricola himself might have been like if he had not been a Roman general at the time of Domitian, and subject to the concomitant constraints.

right man (*par uidebatur*, *Agr.* 9.5). Agricola, with experience of both Gaul and Britain, was the ideal person to effect the transformation of the latter into an adjunct to the Continent, to make it 'semi-detached'. But Britain was also the ideal location for Agricola by virtue of the fact that its insularity was still in question; its geographical alignment remained ambiguous. Returning to my initial quotation, I suggest that Britain was the perfect location for Tacitus' commemoration of Agricola's exploits precisely because it was still significantly set apart from the Continent, even though in the process of becoming semi-attached.

I have argued that Tacitus presents a picture of Britain as the repository of Old Roman values. In particular, Britain in its pristine state, as represented by Calgacus at Mons Graupius, is the location of true *eloquentia* and *uirtus*.[43] We know from the *Annals* and the *Dialogus de Oratoribus* something of Tacitus' views on the opportunity for *eloquentia* and *uirtus* at Rome under the Principate. Oratory was dead; *uirtus* rewarded with a rapid fall. That we may be encouraged to read these events in Roman Britain in the light of Rome itself is surely suggested by the framing of the work. Tacitus starts the *Agricola* with a lament over the hostility shown at Rome at the time of Domitian to *uirtus*: 'so hostile to virtue are the times' (*tam . . . infesta uirtutibus tempora*, *Agr.* 1.4). He moves on to mention examples of men who made a protest at the lack of senatorial freedom of speech (*eloquentia*) under Nero and Vespasian—Thrasea Paetus and Helvidius Priscus. Their eulogists, Arulenus Rusticus and Herennius Senecio, are recalled, as is the fact that not only was *eloquentia* in the Senate disallowed, but so too was *eloquentia* in the form of books recording the suppression of senatorial *eloquentia*. The books were burned in an attempt to obliterate the voice of the Roman people (*uox populi Romani*, *Agr.* 2.2) and the *libertas* of the Senate. Rome of old explored the limits of *libertas*; by the time of Domitian it was

---

[43] Again, Caratacus provides an illuminating parallel. His post-defeat speech is given in Rome, not in Britain, and it draws him closer to 'Old Rome' than even Calgacus can come, since Caratacus not only is eloquent but directly echoes the pre-death speech of Cremutius Cordus, a historian condemned for his *libertas* under Tiberius. Caratacus' claim at *A.* 12.37 that execution, the final suppression of his *libertas*, will bring him eternal memorial is strikingly reminiscent of Cordus at *A.* 4.35. This parallel is all the more resonant given the framing of the *Agricola* with reference to the loss of senatorial *libertas* at Rome.

exploring the depths of *seruitus*.[44] The *Agricola* ends, as has been noted by various scholars, with a passage strongly reminiscent of Cicero's *consolatio* in *de Oratore* 3 for the death of L. Licinius Crassus, the most renowned Roman orator until the time of Cicero himself.[45] It is not clear to what extent Agricola might be thought to display the ideals of *libertas* embodied by Crassus, and to what degree he, in Domitianic Rome, can be only a pale imitation of this Republican figure. Tacitus was, of course, not alone in observing the moral decline of Rome. For Sallust *uirtus* had been destroyed by the removal of the external enemy of Carthage in the second century BC, and it is interesting that Tacitus follows Sallust at least in the monograph form he chose to give to this work. Martin, among others, has observed the strong evocation at the start of the *Agricola* of Sallust and Cato, perhaps signifying the similarity of theme or sentiment between this work and the writings which emerged from and lamented the dying days of the Republic.[46]

But Britain, which belonged at least in part to the Oceanic world of islands and is defined in the *Agricola* by its remoteness, was a place of *eloquentia* and *libertas*.[47] It is specifically in the north of Scotland, to which the Romans considered giving special island status, where these most Roman of values are on display. Britain, as an island nation, forms the antithesis of Rome in Agricola's day, as described by Tacitus. Is Britain the paradigm for Rome of the past, and particularly of the Republic? The start of the *Dialogus*, in which oratory and eloquence are seen as features of the Republic, and destroyed by the Principate, might offer support to this reading. It seems likely from the process described in *Agricola* 21, by which contact with Romans corrupts the perceptions and modes of expression of the Britons, that Britain of the future may become like Rome of Domitian's day. But the corollary does not necessarily hold. It is not in any sense clear that Rome of the past was like Britain at the time of Agricola, except in its opportunities for *eloquentia* and *libertas*. We cannot explain the relationship between Britain and Rome and the

---

[44] The bibliography on Tacitus' views of *libertas* is vast, and a discussion of the subject lies far outside the scope of this paper. See e.g. Hammond (1963). The classic treatment is Wirszubski (1950).

[45] Martin (1994: 48); Ogilvie (1991: 1718).

[46] Martin (1994: 41); Sage (1991: 3385–3419, esp. 3388).

[47] Giua (1991: 2897) argues that the *Agricola* reveals that 'la lontananza e l'isolamento rispetto al cuore della civiltà siano considerate garanzia di autentica libertà'.

values propagated in each place simply in terms of a time-lag. The question of location must be reintroduced.

In what sense can Britain be seen as an appropriate venue for the *res gestae* of Agricola? Beyond the very obvious answer that it was in Britain that Agricola did indeed carry out his relatively successful campaigns, I suggest that Tacitus turns the location into more than just the real and suitable backdrop for those achievements; that he makes the question of geographical identity central to the commemoration of Agricola's life.

Agricola came from a family of *eloquentia* and *uirtus*. His father, Iulius Graecinus, was renowned for his *eloquentia* and *sapientia* and was punished by the emperor Gaius for these *uirtutes* (*Agr.* 4.1). His mother, Iulia Procilla, was a model of chastity (*rarae castitatis*, *Agr.* 4.2). Agricola himself was something of a philosopher; he also enjoyed marital harmony—we may note Calgacus' appeal to the familial piety of his troops. Agricola was a man of *uirtus*, so thought Domitian at any rate, for on hearing about Agricola's successes, his reaction was that 'other talents could be just about ignored, but the *uirtus* of a general was the preserve of the princeps' (*Agr.* 39.2). Agricola's danger from Domitian lies in the fact that Domitian is hostile to *uirtus*, in which Agricola excels. Agricola is finally driven headlong to destruction by his own virtues (*suis uirtutibus*, *Agr.* 41.4) and by the faults of others (*Agr.* 41.4). Thus Britain, as the location of traditional Roman virtues, provides an appropriate setting for the playing out of the *res gestae* of Agricola, a hero of the old style.[48] Here there may be some instructive parallels to draw from Pelling's work on Germanicus as a Republican-style hero.[49] It is interesting that both Agricola and Germanicus enjoy their greatest achievements right at the edges of the Roman world. The context of Germanicus' final episode in Germany before his recall is strikingly similar to that of Agricola's campaigns in Britain: a world of open sea (*aperta Oceani*), islands (*insulae*), and hidden shoals (*occulta uada*) (*A.* 2.23.3). Indeed, some of Germanicus' ship-wrecked men are carried to Britain, which they relate as a place of oddity and ambiguity, in terms both of its geography and its

---

[48] See Sage (1991: 3388–93) for the framing of the *Agricola* in a context of Republican-style *uirtus*. The opening chapters make clear that a significant contrast is to be drawn between the possibilities for outstanding deeds and their recording in the past and in the present.

[49] Pelling (1993) [Ch. 12 below].

inhabitants (*A.* 2.24.4).[50] The landscapes in which these imperial commanders operate are evocative of the heroic Republican world and the historiography which went alongside its aggressive imperialism.[51] Tacitus would, of course, famously link such geographical descriptions with the relating of Republican achievements at *A.* 4.32, and lament their passing, as Giua points out.

That observation might shed light on why even the harsh, heroic landscape of Britain and the North-West cannot provide the ideal location for the exploits of Germanicus and Agricola. Their opportunities at Rome are limited by imperial jealousy. But even here in the remoteness of Britain the atmosphere of *libertas, uirtus,* and *eloquentia* does not provide the perfect environment for Agricola's glorious *res gestae.* Instead, like Germanicus, he remains curiously unfilled.[52] Agricola's keyword is not excellence, but moderation (*moderatio*). He constantly weighs the situation up, and is not allowed to complete his campaign.

One problem in assessing the behaviour of Agricola and of his potential subjects is the ongoing ambiguity over what it means to be Roman, the difficulty over identification which I discussed in the previous section and to which I must return. For Braund, Calgacus and his views are belied by the narrative, leaving Agricola for the most part without criticism. He dissociates Agricola from Roman corruption, stressing his Gallic origins and claiming that Agricola's civilizing mission is misinterpreted and manipulated by the Britons in *Agr.* 21, who 'adopted more Romanization and a different Romanization from that which Agricola had offered'.[53] But, if Agricola is not fully Roman, then neither are the inhabitants of the land which I have characterized as one of *Romanitas, eloquentia,* and *uirtus.* Calgacus and his men are more than just worthy opponents of Agricola. They fall into a

---

[50]   On the landscape of Germanicus' campaigns, see Giua (1991: 2887–90).

[51]   However, it is worth noting the shift in the image of Ocean as no longer the proof of a great campaigning exploit (as for Caesar), but now a muted barrier, or not one at all. So, the traditional historiographical topos of the commander surpassing a mighty boundary may be toned down in accordance with the times, and the new geographical image of the encompassed Britain may be appropriate for the new muted heroism. I owe this point to Chris Pelling.

[52]   For imperial *inuidia* against Agricola, see *Agr.* 39; for that against Germanicus, *A.* 2.22.1 (*metu inuidiae*); 2.26. Shatzman (1974: 574) suggests a further parallel in that rumours surrounding both Agricola and Germanicus, unusually for Tacitus, almost always cast them in a more favourable light than reality suggests.

[53]   Braund (1996a: 63).

historiographical category of adversaries who are 'more Roman than the Romans'—so Roman that they traditionally bring out the best in their Roman counterparts. But in the Domitianic world of the *Agricola*, where achievement must be muted, the usual topoi misfire, and Agricola is not inspired by Calgacus to reach the heights of success. Furthermore, the notion that Calgacus knows Latin better than the Romans themselves is valid only if we define *Romanitas* and *eloquentia* in the outdated terms that seem to suit heroes like Germanicus and Agricola himself. There may be yet a further twist in this argument, insofar as speaking Latin well, perhaps always and certainly in Rome of this period, means being disingenuous, artful, rhetorical, even misleading, and speaking the corrupt Latin adopted by the southern Britons. If this is so, then it is no longer clear that Calgacus really is the better speaker of Latin, the better preserver of *Romanitas*.

EPISODES IN THE OCEAN: FICTION AND REALISM

The *Agricola* is full of paradox and ambiguity. It is remarkable that we might even contemplate that *Romanitas* in the age of Domitian might be found in the world of permanent day and jelly-like seas. It is significant that Agricola's campaigns in this most remote corner of the world known to the Romans should provide the context for Tacitus' exploration of 'how to be a good man under a bad emperor'.[54] If it is necessary to go so far in order to maintain one's integrity, and even then in a compromised way, then the implications for Rome itself must be bleak. It is also startling that the reader might be left with some reservations about the very subject of commemoration.

Tacitus manipulates the geographical tradition to create a shifting vision of Britain. He requires Britain to have a remote identity, both in order that he might make a point about the location of *Romanitas* and, more specifically, for Agricola's strengths to find a suitable setting. But Agricola himself threatens to undermine Britain's insularity, to remove it conceptually from the world beyond the Pillars and turn it into an adjunct to the Continent. What can there be to

---

[54] For Tacitus' belief in the opportunity for virtue and heroism even in a wicked age, see Percival (1980: 127–9). Another key example is Lepidus at *Ann.* 4.20.

commemorate in the life and career of Agricola, if he is the force behind the destruction of this pristine island world which encapsulates the values that he himself holds dear?

The precarious and ambiguous status of Britain is nowhere more clearly apparent than in the pair of episodes which frame the great showdown at Mons Graupius, in which, I have argued, the process of Britain's geographical redefinition is brought into closest focus. The first episode concerns the mysterious Usipi, who murdered their Roman commanders, hijacked three ships, and set off on a voyage around the whole of Britain.[55] Coming from Germany, they belong to the region which had once provided the context for the achievements of Germanicus, like Agricola, thwarted in his pursuit of excellence.[56] The Usipi are in many ways like Agricola's troops, made up of a cohort which had been levied in Germany and transferred to Britain. They come closest to fulfilling Calgacus' belief, as expressed in his speech before the battle of Mons Graupius, that the barbarians who made up Agricola's army would recognize their roots and switch sides. Indeed in *Agr.* 32.3, he uses the Usipi as a exhortatory *exemplum*. We hear of no such process in the aftermath of the speech; rather, Agricola's troops are the men who have been corrupting Britain as they advance. But the Usipi had found in Britain an invigoration of their 'edge of the earth' existence. Their behaviour is the least civilized to find a place in the work. Having killed the centurion and soldiers who had been set over them to teach discipline, they set sail like pirates; indeed, they were taken for pirates (*pro praedonibus habiti, Agr.* 28.3) and some ended up being sold as slaves. Their difficulty in procuring food led to acts of cannibalism (*Agr.* 28.2), by contrast with the relatively normal diet of the inhabitants of the island (*Agr.* 12.5). Their level of barbarism was so great that they appeared uncivilized even in the context of the wild North-West, with Britain providing the ultimate opportunity for behavioural *libertas*.

[55] The episode is afforded illuminating analysis by Ash (2010c), who brings out the way in which a potentially ambiguous presentation of the Usipi (through ambivalent vocabulary such as *facinus*) seems to tilt towards a sympathetic portrayal (280–88).

[56] The importance of Germany for our understanding of the *Agricola* is a recurrent theme. Not only does it provide the subject for Tacitus' other work in monograph form, but it acts as a foil in all kinds of ways. Germanicus' exploits are notoriously unfulfilled (*A.* 2.26 for the recall of Germanicus on the cusp of victory); Domitian's own expedition was incomplete (*Agr.* 39).

But the Usipi, antithetical though their behaviour may be to the civilizing force of Agricola, are also paradoxically reminiscent of some of the qualities associated with him. Their murder of the Roman soldiers might have been a dreadful crime, but it won them fame, or at least notoriety (*magnum ac memorabile facinus, Agr.* 28.1).[57] Fame and commemoration motivate the writing of the Agricola (a point to which I shall return), although Agricola himself is forced to be moderate in his seeking of such renown. In this respect the Usipi, in a perverse way, are allowed to succeed where Agricola fails, although there is of course a considerable difference between acquiring fame for great deeds and notoriety for heinous crimes.[58] Furthermore, the circumnavigation of Britain by the Usipi forms a parallel to that accomplished for the first time by the Romans with Agricola, in the passage quoted at the start. The Romans were able to establish that Britain was an island, since it had been sailed around (*circumuecta, Agr.* 10.4). As I have argued, this voyage marks an important stage in the reconceptualization of Britain; the confirmation of its insularity is the first stage in the threatening of that status. But for the Usipi, the circumnavigation of Britain (*circumuecti Britanniam, Agr.* 28.3) is part of their liberation from the constraints of civilized behaviour and from their subjection to Roman commands. Their voyage is hardly unproblematic, culminating as it does in the loss of the crucial component, the ships. It is noteworthy that this loss occurs through ignorance of the necessary skills (*amissis per inscitiam regendi nauibus, Agr.* 28.3), in stark contrast to the knowledge and preparation associated with Agricola and his army. Nevertheless, the Usipi, with their achievement of fame and their exploitation of Britain as a place of invigoration, the recapturing of a *libertas* which had now been lost in their native Germany, give us a final glimpse into the vision of Britain as a fully-fledged island, free from the corruption brought by continental attachment, and it is important that their visit

---

[57] We should perhaps in any case recall Calgacus' designation of the Romans as *raptores orbis* (*Agr.* 30.4).

[58] However, the fact that there was a fairly thin line to be drawn between great deeds and transgressive ones was neatly encapsulated in the tales surrounding Alexander the Great, whose conquests and ambitions could be seen as both mighty and hubristic, although this still does not match the transgressions of the Usipi. However, the point that greatness could be dangerous is very relevant to the question posed by the *Agricola* of how to be a good man under a bad emperor.

should involve a reaffirmation of this insularity through circumnavigation.[59]

There follow the speeches, fighting, and aftermath of the battle at Mons Graupius, on which I have commented above, and in the course of which the new vision of Britain as semi-detached, an adjunct to the Continent, is adopted. It is interesting that the final triumphal act instigated by Agricola after the battle should involve still further use of the Ocean as a means of asserting control. Agricola orders the commander of the fleet to sail around Britain (*circumuehi Britanniam, Agr.* 38.3), using the terror of Rome as his defence in the face of trouble. Unlike the voyage of the Usipi, this one is well planned, and ultimately successful. Progress is assisted by favourable winds (*secunda tempestate*) and the reputation of the Romans (*fama, Agr.* 38.4). Thus two Roman voyages around Britain frame that undertaken by the Usipi, and the Romans emerge as the masters of Britain's waters and hence of its insularity.

But there is a further Oceanic episode which provides an alternative way of configuring the text. The report of events at Mons Graupius elicited a jealous response from Domitian. We are implicitly reminded of why the Usipi were fortunate by comparison with Roman generals such as Germanicus and Agricola, insofar as their eagerness for fame and adventure could be realized, whereas Agricola must hold back. Popular reaction demanded that Domitian show restraint in his reining in of Agricola, and the province of Syria was to be offered as a sop. But, predictably, the opportunity for Agricola to excel was snatched away. A freedman was dispatched to offer the province to Agricola, but only if he was still in Britain. The story went that the messenger met Agricola's ship in the Channel (*in ipso freto Oceani, Agr.* 40.2), and returned to Domitian without even addressing Agricola himself. So, whereas the Oceanic episode concerning the Usipi and preceding Mons Graupius symbolized opportunities for exhilaration, that which follows the crucial turning point in Britain's Oceanic status reveals yet another lost opportunity for Agricola. His potential for glory is unfulfilled, but he himself had been responsible to some degree for the development of a new geographical conception

---

[59] Note the contrast drawn earlier between the Germans, for whom the only defence from Rome was a river, and the Britons, who could hide behind an Oceanic barrier. Here, the Usipi benefit from the geographical advantages afforded by Britain, and denied to their own people.

of Britain, in which the Ocean becomes a medium for suppression, rather than a symbol of *libertas*.

The fact that the whole British narrative in the Agricola (*Agr.* 10–40) falls within the framework of the Ocean, neatly mirroring its real physical location, is suggestive of the importance that might be attached to Britain's geographical status, and in particular to its insularity. Our first extensive encounter with the location in *Agr.* 10 stresses the Oceanic nature of the place and indeed hints at the possibility of more detailed study of the Ocean itself—a possibility which is rejected as exceeding the scope of the present work and, in any case, already treated by other writers.[60] However, Tacitus does acknowledge that there is nowhere more dominated by the sea than Britain (*nusquam latius dominari mare, Agr.* 10.6); in the expanse of water lies the key to Britain's identity. Our very last glimpse of Britain in the work is the near-encounter with Agricola in the Channel; again the insularity of Britain is at the fore, although by now the Ocean has been reduced to a mere strait (*fretum, Agr.* 40.2).

But there is something unsatisfactory about the Ocean and the episodes which take place within it framing the main body of the work. The Usipi, invigorated by the *libertas* of Britain, may set off on an Ocean adventure. But the whole venture has the ring of implausibility; indeed it is described as being 'like a story' (*ut miraculum, Agr.* 28.1). It was wonderful in more than one sense. Miraculous if it could be accomplished, but possibly also too astonishing to be true. Similarly, the story concerning Agricola's ship and his lost opportunity for gaining the province of Syria was suspected as a Domitianic fiction. 'It was unclear whether it was true, or whether it was fictitious and made up in accordance with the emperor's character' (*siue uerum istud, siue ex ingenio principis fictum ac compositum est, Agr.* 40.2).[61] The events of the Ocean world, especially those which take place on the sea itself, partake of a certain fictive quality. As before, it is worth noting the startling echoes of Germanicus' abortive exploits in the region. The stories brought back by his shipwrecked men of Britain

---

[60] A similar disclaimer relating to discussion of the Ocean is given by Strabo 2.3.3, referring almost without question to Posidonius. If, as Ogilvie and Richmond suggest, Tacitus knew Posidonius' works, then it is quite possible that he was entering here into well-worn topos of avoiding overlap with Posidonius' monumental work *On Ocean*.

[61] It is striking, given other similarities between Agricola and Germanicus, that, when Germanicus is recalled by Tiberius, the reason given (namely to give Drusus a share in the glory) is considered by Germanicus fictitious (*fingi: A.* 2.26.5).

were *miracula* (*A.* 2.24.4). The search for conquest in the form of knowledge cannot be said to be over for Rome, casting some doubt on its grasp on the island and leaving its ambiguous status intact.

It is this lack of resolution which gives the *Agricola* an ongoing interest. Britain is left in a state of semi-detachment. Agricola's conquest had apparently destroyed its insularity, but the fictive quality of the final episode alludes back to the Oceanic world which had characterized Britain at the start, and raises questions over the completeness of the Roman mission to embrace the island within its grasp. This might then be formulated as a Roman failure—Britain has remained an island after all, but only by the skin of its teeth.

However, the end of the British narrative does not mark the end of the work. Just as Britain wins a partial reprieve, so too does Agricola's reputation receive a final rehabilitation. I have argued above that there might not be much to commemorate in the *res gestae* of someone who destroyed the world which encapsulated the values he held dear, or perhaps in the career of a commander whose plans were continually thwarted. However, the final chapters of the work, together with the opening chapters, form a frame around the British narrative, and are similarly concerned with matters of commemoration and fame. I suggested above that Britain, by its very remoteness, could be identified as a place of invigoration, where people such as the Usipi are able to perform in a spectacular and memorable way, and where Calgacus fulfils some of the qualities which Agricola himself might have accomplished, had he not been a general under Domitianic Rome.[62] By contrast, Rome is antithetical to both the performance and the celebration of noteworthy deeds, as is very clear from the opening chapters. Indeed Agricola sinks into obscurity on his return to Rome.

An article on the shifting geographical conceptions of Britain in the *Agricola* is not the place for a detailed exploration of the non-British parts of the work. It is, however, worth noting that the closing chapters pay extensive tribute to Agricola and to his *res gestae*, and above all secure his lasting fame through Tacitus' commemoration.

---

[62] For the different view that, far from symptomatic of a decline in the opportunities for generalship, Tacitus instead depicts Agricola as superior in command to the most renowned of his predecessors in the attempt to subdue Britain, Julius Caesar, see Fear (2009). The very process of drawing Agricola into comparison with the liminal figure of Caesar is thought-provoking in terms of placing Agricola himself in relation to Republic and Principate.

This must have some bearing on our reading of the central core of the work, namely his exploits in Britain itself. I suggested that Britain, as a part of the peculiar and remote Oceanic island world, and therefore free from the corruption of Rome, was the ideal location for Agricola, even though his campaigns threatened to destroy that insular identity.[63] But the continental attachment was never quite completed, and Britain retained some elements of an almost fictive Oceanic image, as revealed by the episode which concludes Agricola's dealings with that part of the world. Agricola's rather muted fame is more appropriate to the real world of Roman politics under Domitian.[64] In answer to the puzzle of how to be a good man under a bad emperor, the opportunities offered by somewhere as distant as Britain are perhaps not sustainable for long, at least not for a Roman. In that context, Agricola's moderation is greater cause for celebration than the abandon of the Usipi or the exuberance of Calgacus. Agricola embodies a new type of *uirtus*.[65] The threats that are made to Britain's island identity in the course of the text allow for an exploration of where the true limits of *Romanitas* and *libertas* lie. But the sense of difference and remoteness which my opening quotes would attribute to insular Britain means that that location cannot match or be matched by Rome. There is, after all, 'a sense of place about islands—even when they're semi-detached'.

---

[63] Ogilvie (1991: 1117–18) argues that Tacitus deliberately belittles the achievements of Agricola's predecessors in Britain so as to increase Agricola's stature.

[64] See Classen (1988) for the realism of Tacitus' vision; also for the argument that even the definition of what constitutes *moderatio* has changed since the time of Cicero.

[65] On the new political virtue of quietism and moderation, see Liebeschuetz (1966) [Ch. 2 below]. It has, however, been argued by Luce (1991) that Tacitus is not, by praising characters in his works, necessarily setting them up as models for emulation in the manner of Livy. Tacitus is far more interested in commemoration than in paradigms.

2

The Theme of Liberty in the *Agricola* of Tacitus

W. Liebeschuetz

The *Agricola* of Tacitus[1] differs from other surviving biographies of antiquity.[2] It exhibits some features more characteristic of an oration,[3] yet the preface and composition of the biography as a whole recall Sallust's *Iugurtha* and *Catiline*.[4] Then, the central biographical section of the work is interrupted by an excursus on the geography and peoples of Britain, and an historical outline of the Roman occupation of the island. It has been argued that the style of these chapters would be more appropriate to history than to biography,[5] and this same historical style recurs in the pair of commanders' speeches which precede the account of the battle of Mons Graupius. Finally, the narrative of Agricola's life is followed by a section working out the theme that Agricola was happy in the time of his death. This and the concluding address to the mourning family clearly belong to funeral oratory.[6]

It is the object of this paper to show that all these elements, while making a contribution to the primary object of the work, laudatory

---

[1] Edition of Furneaux, revised by Anderson (1922). See also Forni (1962), Ogilvie and Richmond (1967), and Severini (2004).

[2] e.g. the biographies of Plutarch or Suetonius or the *Euagoras* of Isocrates or the *Agesilaus* of Xenophon. Cf. Leo (1901); Stuart (1928). See now Whitmarsh (2006).

[3] Thus Hübner (1866) argued that it was a published funeral oration. Gudeman (1928: 311–22) argues that it follows the rules of a *basilikos logos*.

[4] Furneaux–Anderson (1922: lxxxi–ii), with references to older literature. See now Sailor (2004: esp. 161–3).

[5] *Agr.* 10–17, with Furneaux–Anderson (1922: xxiii). On stylistic variation within the *Agricola* see now Bews (1987).

[6] *Agr.* 45. Cf. fragment of funeral speech of L. Caecilius Metellus (Pliny *HN* 7.139; cf. Cic. *de Or.* 3.3.12, *ad Fam.* 4.5.5.1; Hübner 1866).

biography, have an additional unity of theme, in that they are to a considerable extent concerned with the consequences of the loss of freedom.

According to Polybius, biography differs from history in being selective.[7] The central section of the *Agricola* conforms to this requirement. It contains no continuous account of the history of the times. Even the life story of Agricola is presented in a selective way. Thus while various facets of Agricola's personality are recognized and praised, one aspect is mentioned again and again: moderation and self-effacement in all business of private or public life.[8]

Agricola's youthful interest in philosophy left him with a sense of proportion.[9] When he served as military tribune his chief, Suetonius Paulinus, set him an example of moderation,[10] and Agricola in turn conducted himself with restraint, diligence, courage, and modesty (*Agr.* 5.4). As a tribune of the plebs, he refrained from conspicuous activity,[11] unlike his colleague, Arulenus Rusticus, who proposed to veto the trial of Thrasea Paetus (*A.* 16.26). He conducted his praetorship in a similar manner. His praetorian games preserved the mean between extravagance and stinginess (*Agr.* 6.4). Later, when he had been put in command of a mutinous legion, Agricola refused to take credit for the restoration of discipline (*Agr.* 7.6). As the governor of Britain at that time was a man of peaceful temperament, Agricola checked his own natural ardour, so as not to become too prominent. He was . . . *peritus obsequi, eruditusque utilia honestis miscere*, 'adept at obedience and trained to blend the practical with the honourable' (*Agr.* 8.1). Some time later, under a new chief, when an active military policy was adopted, Agricola showed himself ready to yield credit for success to the governor whose instrument he had been.[12] During the next stage of his career, as governor of Aquitaine, Agricola sought fame neither by making a display of his virtues nor by intrigue. He did not enter into competition with governors of neighbouring provinces, and refrained from quarrelling with the imperial procurators.[13] When

---

[7] Polybius 10.21, 8.10; Nepos *Pelop.* 1.

[8] Cf. Habinek (2000) on the same phenomenon in Seneca the Younger.

[9] *Agr.* 4.5: . . . *quod est difficillimum, ex sapientia modum.*

[10] *Agr.* 5.1: *diligenti ac moderato duci.*

[11] *Agr.* 6.3: *quiete et otio transiit.*

[12] *Agr.* 8.3. Cf. Richmond (1944: 36).

[13] *Agr.* 9.5: *ne famam quidem, cui saepe etiam boni indulgent, ostentanda uirtute aut per artem quaesiuit.*

he was consul, it was widely believed that he would be the next governor of Britain, though he had not contributed to this opinion by any words of his own (*Agr.* 9.6). In the much fuller account of his governorship of Britain, Agricola is shown as a great governor and great general, with the result that there is less scope for examples of moderation. Nevertheless, Tacitus points out the modesty of the dispatches in which Agricola announced his victories,[14] and the willingness with which he gave up his command (*Agr.* 39.4 and 40.3). Finally, the account of the last years of Agricola's life is centred on the quietness with which Agricola retired into civil life and the restraint with which he bore the fact that he was not given further posts in which to exercise his talents (*Agr.* 40.3–42.4).

The qualities of Agricola so much emphasized by Tacitus can be summed up as deliberate and consistent shunning of the limelight, with consequent avoidance of envy and enmity on the part of superiors, inferiors,[15] and most of all the emperor himself. This is made explicit in the famous passage which stands in an emphatic position, concluding and, as it were, summarizing the account of the life of Agricola[16] and followed only by the description of his death and the epilogue (*Agr.* 42.3–4):

> *moderatione tamen prudentiaque Agricolae leniebatur, quia non contumacia neque inani iactatione libertatis famam fatumque prouocabat. sciant quibus moris est illicita mirari, posse etiam sub malis principibus magnos uiros esse, obsequiumque ac modestiam, si industria ac uigor adsint, eo laudis excedere, quo plerique per abrupta, sed in nullum rei publicae usum ambitiosa morte inclaruerunt.*

Yet even Domitian was appeased by the moderation and wisdom of Agricola, who declined by a defiant and futile parade of freedom to court fame and fatality. Let those whose habit it is to admire forbidden conduct learn that great men can live under bad rulers and that obedience and self-control, when they are joined to capacity for work and energy, can reach as high a pinnacle of fame as that of those who tread precipitous paths and owe their glory, without any public service rendered, to an ostentatious death.[17]

---

[14] *Agr.* 18.7: *dissimulatione famae famam auxit.* Also, *Agr.* 39.

[15] *Agr.* 22.4: *nec Agricola umquam per alios gesta auidus intercepit*; *Agr.* 41.1: *causa periculi non . . . querela laesi cuiusquam.*

[16] Cf. Büchner (1955: 73–4).

[17] See Furneaux–Anderson (1922: 151–2 and xxx); also below, nn. 28 and 29.

The primary purpose of the passage is evidently to provide an emphatic justification of the principles of conduct which had governed the life described in the previous chapters. But this does not exhaust its function. By denigrating an alternative course of conduct as involving 'defiance', 'a parade of freedom', 'precipitous paths', and 'ostentatious death', and in criticizing men who admired such 'forbidden conduct', Tacitus suggests that his biography has a controversial as well as a laudatory aim. He indicates that the selection of a particular kind of conduct for praise implied the deliberate rejection of conduct of another kind.

When scholars[18] have sought to throw further light on the way of life rejected by Tacitus, their attention has often been drawn to the opposition group of which successive generations made gestures of senatorial independence and self-respect, and under at least three emperors paid for their courage with their lives.[19] At a time when biographies of victims of the Caesars met with wide popularity,[20] the 'martyrs' of this group received particular veneration, even among men who themselves carefully refrained from libertarian gestures.[21] They were regarded, and regarded themselves,[22] as the moral successors of the younger Cato, of Brutus and Cassius, who too received tributes from otherwise perfectly loyal career servants of the emperors.[23]

Tacitus' attitude is shown by his treatment of the group's outstanding personalities, Helvidius Priscus in the *Histories* and Thrasea Paetus in the *Annals*.[24] Both men occupy a more prominent place in the narrative than might be anticipated from their rank or the intrinsic importance of the actions related. Although Tacitus allowed his account to reveal considerable admiration[25] he nevertheless

---

[18] Paratore (1962: 99); Forni (1962: 126 n. 1, 239); Walker (1952: 229–30).

[19] Syme (1958a: 555–61); Wirszubski (1950: 138–50); MacMullen (1993: 46–81).

[20] Pliny *Ep.* 5.5.3 (Gaius Fannius), 8.12.4 (Titinius Capito).

[21] Syme (1958a: 92). Pliny had close personal links with this group, and their memory was evidently greatly revered in his circle: *Epistles* 3.16, 6.29, 7.19, 8.22, 3.11, 4.21, 9.13, 1.5, 1.15, 2.18, 4.22, 6.14.

[22] *A.* 16.22. Thrasea's biography of Cato Minor: Plutarch, *Cato Minor* 25. Juvenal 5.36–7: *quale coronati Thrasea Heluidiusque bibebant/Brutorum et Cassi natalibus.*

[23] Syme (1958a: 93) on Titinius Capito and Pliny *Ep.* 2.17.

[24] On this group see now Malitz (1985).

[25] See below, p. 81. On Tacitus' treatment, see Syme (1958a: 555–61); also Walker (1952: 229–31), who has an interesting comparison with Tacitus' view of Caratacus and Boudicca.

displays a remarkably detached and even critical attitude. A number of interpolated comments, by no means necessary to the context, suggests that these champions of liberty were motivated by a desire for fame as well as zeal for senatorial dignity.[26] He gives examples of interventions that achieved their aim (*A.* 14.49 and 15.20–22), but he also shows that success was gained at disproportionate cost. He hammers home, with comments of his own[27] and, more disconcertingly, in fully reported speeches of opponents,[28] that every intervention of these men was remembered, to be eventually used against them, and that this happened even under the 'good' Vespasian. If we compare these comments in the historical works with the critical passage in the *Agricola*, and bear in mind that three members of this group fell victims to Domitian and are commemorated in the *Agricola*,[29] the conclusion is inescapable that Tacitus had admirers of this group[30] in mind

---

[26] *A.* 14.49: . . . *Thrasea sueta firmitudine animi et ne gloria intercideret*; *A.* 16.26: *Rusticus Arulenus, flagrans iuuenis et cupidine laudis*; *H.* 4.6 of Helvidius Priscus: *erant quibus adpetentior famae uideretur*. On the speeches of Helvidius Priscus and Eprius Marcellus, see now Pigoń (1992).

[27] *A.* 14.49: Thrasea obtained commutation of a death sentence—but this was later brought up against him: *A.* 16.21; *A.* 14.12: *Thrasea Paetus . . . sibi causam periculi fecit, ceteris libertatis initium non praebuit*; *H.* 4.9: (under Vespasian) *eam sententiam modestissimus quisque silentio, deinde obliuio transmisit: fuere qui et meminissent.*

[28] *A.* 13.49: futility of Thrasea's interventions on behalf of *libertas senatoria* pointed out ironically by showing that Thrasea would not risk speaking on issues that mattered; *A.* 16.21–2: prosecutor's speech shows how Thrasea's every demonstration was remembered against him; *H.* 4.8: the evil (*A.* 16.28) Eprius Marcellus: *quo modo pessimis imperatoribus sine finem dominationem, ita quamuis egregiis modum libertatis placere*; *H.* 4.43: . . . *relinquimus tibi senatum tuum, regna praesente Caesare.* Cf. the warning given to Pliny in similar circumstances: *Ep.* 9.13.10: *notabilem te futuris principibus fecisti.*

[29] Arulenus Rusticus and Herennius Senecio: *Agr.* 2.1, 45.1; also Helvidius Priscus the Younger, *Agr.* 45.1.

[30] Is the reference wider than the conduct of the opposition group? See Wirszubski (1950: 149–50). At *Agr.* 42.4, *inani iactatione libertatis* seems to refer specifically to the group, whose practice of *libertas* was famous, e.g. *A.* 16.22, 16.24; *H.* 4.5. *contumacia* was used by his opponents to describe Thrasea's attitude (*A.* 16.22) and *per abrupta . . . ambitiosa morte inclaruerunt* (*Agr.* 42) could also describe men who were executed for more active resistance than was practised by the group, but it is parallel to the clause *quia non contumacia . . . fama fatumque prouocabat* (cf. Lepidus' verdict *A.* 4.20) and in the latter clause active resisters are evidently not meant. Also the question of resistance to tyranny has hardly (perhaps *Agr.* 40.3) been raised in the *Agricola*.

It is of course possible that there were numerous ostentatious and provocative, but not actively revolutionary, opponents of the emperors outside the group, and that these are meant. But this is unlikely. *contumacia* was too dangerous. Surely a man like

when he wrote his admonition to 'those who admire forbidden conduct'.[31]

That Tacitus chose to end his account of the active life of Agricola with a passage of criticism of the 'martyrs', and admonition of their admirers, calls for explanation. It has been suggested that Tacitus was in fact defending his father-in-law, and by implication himself, from the charge of having been an over-compliant servant of the tyrant Domitian.[32] That he was in actual danger of prosecution is unlikely.[33] After the death of Domitian there was a release of pent-up indignation, and a call for vengeance was raised by the friends and relatives of the dead tyrant's victims. This was directed against informers and achieved some results, particularly when the attack was made against non-senators.[34] Attacks on senators, even when their guilt was plain, were liable to be blocked.[35] The attack was not and could not be directed against mere office-holders under Domitian, because these men continued to hold positions of power,[36] and Nerva[37] and Trajan[38] had been among them. The circumstances which made it practically impossible to inflict any kind of retribution on even

---

Thrasea was famous precisely because he dared do what many thought. Both Thrasea (*A.* 16.25) and Helvidius (*H.* 4.6) were urged by followers to be more uncompromising. But it was they and not the followers who were to win the glory and the penalty; cf. also *A.*16.22 on admirers. To sum up: the language of the passage is sufficiently vague not to exclude wider interpretation altogether, but the indications point at the opposition group.

[31] *illicita*,'forbidden', in the sense 'not approved by the emperor', as at *A.* 6.8: *abditos principis sensus et si quid occultius parat exquirere illicitum anceps.* Furneaux–Anderson (1922: 151) cite *A.* 3.27, *honores illicitos*, but this might mean 'contrary to the constitution', which was strictly true of none of the actions reported by Tacitus or even the extreme rudeness of Helvidius at Suet. *Vesp.* 15. Dio 66.12 goes further, but see Syme (1958a: 551); Wirszubski (1950: 148–9).

[32] For discussions of this question see Furneaux–Anderson (1922: xxviii); Syme (1958a: 24–6).

[33] Furneaux–Anderson (1922: xxxi).

[34] On inquisition and informers, see now Rutledge (2001).

[35] Dio 68.1. Aquillius Regulus (cf. *H.* 4.42; Syme 1958a: 101–2) fears prosecution by Pliny (*Ep.* 1.5). For a detailed account of the attempt to avenge the younger Helvidius Priscus, see Pliny the Younger *Ep.* 9.13; 9.13.21 (leniency to senators). The praetorian guard insisted on punishment of Domitian's murderers (Dio 68.3). On the situation see Syme (1958a: 7, 77–8).

[36] See ibid. 3–6 (under Nerva), 50–54 (under Trajan), appendix 14. Also ibid. 101 and *D.* 8 for the formidable position of two notorious Neronian *delatores* under the 'good' Vespasian.

[37] Syme (1958a: 2).

[38] Ibid. 33–5.

the most notorious instruments of a dead tyrant, if they were men of standing, were to be carefully noted by Tacitus in his account of the events following the death of Nero (*H.* 4.6–8 and 42–45).

It is, of course, possible that there was widespread verbal criticism of office-holders and that Tacitus' remarks are a reply to this. That the offensive is on the side of Tacitus is, however, also possible. The passages which illustrate Agricola's self-effacement and subordination do not at all suggest that Tacitus is dealing with a well-known trait which has been misunderstood and criticized, but rather that he is deliberately putting forward for praise qualities which would hitherto have been thought unworthy of the dignity[39] of a senator. He is making the point that self-effacement and adaptability, qualities which might be associated with a knight like Atticus,[40] were characteristic of the senator Agricola, and paradoxically that these very qualities enabled him to win fame of the ancient kind as a successful leader in war.

By challenging comparison with the admired martyrs, Tacitus takes his praise of Agricola from the personal to the public sphere, and transforms the principles that had guided Agricola's life into an ideal of conduct of general validity. The opposition senators, by means of gestures which inevitably brought publicity to themselves as well as to their ideal, achieved the fame of a martyr's death but no public benefit. Agricola, by keeping his person in the background, was able to perform great public service and win fame through achievement. The comparison is an eloquent argument that careers like Agricola's deserve at least as much admiration and imitation as the lives of the others.

In a wider perspective, it might be said that Tacitus is calling for an acceptance of the present. Conduct appropriate to the present is as worthy of praise as that belonging to circumstances that are past. That this interpretation does not do violence to Tacitus' manner of thought is suggested by two famous passages from other works, in which he

---

[39] Cf. Cicero, *ad Fam.* 4.14.1: *sin autem in eo dignitas est, si quod sentias, aut re efficere possis aut denique libera oratione defendere ne uestigium ullum est reliquum nobis dignitatis.* On the republican tradition of *dignitas* and its incompatability with *otium*, see references in the index of Wirszubski (1950).

[40] Cf. Nepos, *Atticus.* Atticus' principle of keeping out of all political controversy and partisanships enabled him to survive the age of civil wars. But unlike Agricola, he kept clear of public service too.

accepts the historical determination of values in the conduct of life. In the *Annals* he has occasion to note the simpler way of life of the aristocracy of his own time compared with that of the early empire.[41] Among the causes of this development he notes that nobles no longer courted vast *clientelae*, that prominence had in the past so often meant death, that many of the new noble families originated from *municipia* in Italy or even the provinces. He comments: *nec omnia apud priores meliora, sed nostra quoque aetas multa laudis et artium imitanda posteris tulit. uerum haec nobis <in> maiores certamina ex honesto maneant,* 'Earlier times were not better than ours in every way, our own epoch too has produced many examples of praiseworthy and talented achievement for our descendants to copy. May opportunities to compete honourably with our ancestors in this respect at any rate remain open to us!'[42]

In a similar spirit he comments in the *Dialogus*: *quoniam nemo eodem tempore assequi potest magnam famam et magnam quietem, bono saeculi sui quisque citra obtrectationem alterius utatur,* 'Since it is impossible for anybody to enjoy at one and the same time great renown and great repose, let everyone make use of the blessings his own times afford without disparaging any other age...'[43]

But the judgement that the behaviour of the 'martyrs' was inappropriate to the present does not exhaust Tacitus' reaction to their example in the *Agricola*. Tacitus ends his comment on the opposition group who *in nullum rei publicae usum ambitiosa morte inclaruerunt,* 'owe their glory, without any public service rendered, to an ostentatious death' (*Agr.* 42.4). He continues: *finis uitae eius nobis luctuosus,* 'The end of his (i.e. Agricola's) life was grievous to us...' (*Agr.* 43.1). So sharp a juxtaposition of the deaths of the 'martyrs' and that of Agricola is surely intentional. Agricola is to be compared with the opposition group not only in the manner of his life but in his death. It seems as if Tacitus could not mention the deaths of members of the opposition group and thus recall what men felt most admirable about them, namely their willingness to die for their ideals, without feeling

---

[41] On Tacitus' comparison of the present with the past, see now Woodman and Martin (1996: 408–13); Ginsburg (1993).

[42] *A.* 3.55.5. Cf. Syme (1958a: 339); Virg. *G.* 2.174, Tac. *H.* 1.3.3. We can see other arguments based on historical determination of custom at *A.* 3.34, 12.6 (a dishonourable cause), *A.* 2.33.4, with Tacitus' comment: *sub nominibus honestis confessio uitiorum.*

[43] *D.* 41.5; translation of W. Petersen in the Loeb series (1914).

challenged to show that Agricola, despite his cautious demeanour, had been no less brave than they.[44] This he did to some extent by showing that Agricola too died with courage and cheerfulness, and thus won a final moral advantage over the emperor.[45] But it may be that his main answer to those who estimated the value of a man's way of life by his readiness to risk death for it was to point out that Agricola's more cautious conduct was in the long run no less dangerous than that of the opposition group. By living a life which enabled him to perform great deeds he was slowly but inevitably incurring the murderous hatred of the emperor, finally to fall victim to it. It may be that it was in the interest of this argument that Tacitus composed his manifestly distorted picture of the hatred and jealousy of the emperor, culminating in the suggestion which, though never directly asserted, is almost irresistibly insinuated: that Domitian poisoned Agricola.[46]

There are other indications of Tacitus' respect for the 'martyrs' of the opposition group (*Agr.* 2.2): *scilicet illo igne uocem populi Romani et libertatem senatus et conscientiam generis humani*[47] *aboleri arbitrabantur*, 'They imagined no doubt that in that fire disappeared the voice of the Roman people, the freedom of the senate, and the memory and judgement of mankind.' This comment on the burning of the biographies of Thrasea Paetus and Helvidius Priscus following the execution of their authors only means that Domitian and his advisers by their acts of persecution accepted the opposition group at its own valuation. But in a number of passages Tacitus seems to be doing this himself. In the *Histories* Helvidius is introduced with a highly laudatory character sketch (*H.* 4.5–6). His intention of prosecuting the man who informed against Thrasea is commended as just (*H.* 4.6.1: *ea ultio, incertum maior an iustior*). His supporters are qualified as 'the good majority' (*H.* 4.43.2: *hinc multi bonique, inde pauci et ualidi*). But the facts of power were against him.[48] In the *Annals*

---

[44] Pliny felt obliged to point out how nearly he became a victim himself (*Ep.* 3.11).

[45] *Agr.* 45.3: ... *constans et libens fatum excepisti, tamquam pro uirili portione innocentiam principi donares.* Also *Agr.* 43.4: *tam caeca et corrupta mens* (of Domitian).

[46] On Tacitus' technique see Schwinge (1963).

[47] Furneaux–Anderson (1922) on *Agr.* 2.2, *conscientiam generis humani*, quote *A.* 4.35.6: *praesenti potentia credunt extingui posse etiam sequentis aeui memoriam.*

[48] Vespasian would not allow retaliation except against scapegoats selected for their insignificance; cf. above, nn. 30 and 33.

the portrait of Thrasea, a more reasonable man, is yet more favourable. His prosecution is described as an attack on virtue itself and his death as a heroic martyrdom.[49] Even in the *Agricola* the deaths of the three members of the group are given a symbolic role, for they are made to represent the culmination of the tyranny of Domitian (*Agr.* 2.1–2, 45.1–2).

If Tacitus, perhaps in spite of himself, felt profound admiration for these men, it was no doubt partly because as a man of his time he could not fail to feel admiration for its chosen heroes, but even more because his deepest feelings rebelled at the judgement of his historical reason, and insisted that the changes resulting from the collapse of the Republic, perhaps from the moral decay that had brought about that collapse,[50] when judged by absolute standards involved a change for the worse.[51] This feeling can be sensed, as an undertone, even in the two passages which argue the historical conditioning of social values, for the first of these[52] reads a little like an attempt to persuade himself, and the second is not without irony.[53] In the *Agricola* the fact that the good of the Empire is merely relative is clearly if tactfully stated.

In the introduction to the *Agricola*[54] Tacitus proclaims his intention of recording the deeds and manner of life of a great man for posterity. This was an ancient practice and continued to some extent into Tacitus' own time. But compared with the present, the age of the Republic[55] had offered both a freer field for the performance of noble

---

[49] *A.* 16.21.1: *Nero uirtutem ipsam exscindere concupiuit interfecto Thrasea Paeto et Barea Sorano.* The trial and death are described very fully; cf. Syme (1958a: 561, n. 8).

[50] *H.* 2.38.1: *sed ubi subacto orbe et aemulis urbibus regibusue excisis securas opes concupiscere uacuum fuit.* But the idea seems less important than in Sallust.

[51] *A.* 4.32.2: *nobis in arto et inglorius labor*, with Walker (1952: 200–203).

[52] Cf. n. 42 above. The fact that Tacitus reports three debates on related topics suggests that he was not sure about the answer: cf. *A.* 2.33, 3.33–4, 3.52–5.

[53] e.g. *D.* 41: *quid enim opus est longis in senatu sententiis, cum optimi cito consentiant? quid multis apud populum contionibus, cum de re publica non imperiti et multi deliberent sed sapientissimus et unus?* Cf. Syme (1958a: 220). On *D.* 41 and Maternus' portrait of Vespasian, see Bartsch (1994: 108–10) [Ch. 4 below], who explores the contradictions between Maternus' first and second speech in his attitude to Vespasian.

[54] The following paragraphs are based on Büchner (1956), which demonstrates a close parallel in structure and argument between chs 1 and 3.

[55] When did the good age end? According to the *Agricola*, presumably later than the time of Rutilius and Scaurus. According to *A.* 3.28, in Pompeius' third consulate— or after the Twelve Tables? According to *H.* 2.38, perhaps after the destruction of

deeds and a greater incentive to men of standing to record them. Then not even autobiography on the part of great men was disbelieved or criticized as presumptuous:

> adeo uirtutes iisdem temporibus optime aestimantur, quibus facillime gignuntur. at nunc narraturo mihi uitam defuncti hominis uenia opus fuit, quam non petissem incusaturus: tam saeua et infesta uirtutibus tempora.

Noble qualities are best appreciated in those ages in which they are most easily produced. But in the present time, as I intend to relate the life of a dead man, I have to ask for indulgence which I would not have sought if I had been writing an invective. So savage and hostile to virtue are the times.[56]

This comment of Tacitus is surely not intended to refer exclusively to the grim tyranny of Domitian. In the age of Domitian, as Tacitus argues in the following chapter, it was not enough to ask for indulgence before speaking; complete silence was required—*memoriam quoque ipsam cum uoce perdidissemus, si tam in nostra potestate esset obliuisci quam tacere*, 'and if it had been in our power to forget as it was to keep silent we would have lost our memory as well as our speech' (*Agr.* 2.4). The very fact that Tacitus has the courage to write is the result of the new age of Nerva and Trajan. The age which is hostile to virtue and is unfavourably contrasted with an earlier, better age therefore of necessity includes the time when Nerva and Trajan are reigning and Tacitus is writing.[57] Certainly Nerva and Trajan receive high praise. Nerva achieved what had been thought impossible in reconciling the principate with liberty.[58] Trajan was daily increasing the happiness of the times. Tacitus' future historical work, and indeed the *Agricola*, would by portraying the slavery of the past bear witness to the blessings of the present (*Agr.*3.3). But the blessings of

---

Carthage. One suspects that as an historian, Tacitus could not assign a critical point in time.

[56] *Agr.* 1.4. Here and elsewhere, I made much use of the translation of the *Agricola* by Mattingly (1948). *uenia opus fuit* is taken by Furneaux–Anderson (1922) to refer to the time of writing, as in a letter, with reference to A. 4.5.6: *persequi incertum fuit*; A. 3.65: *exsequi haud institui.*

[57] The hostility is not only the emperor's, but society's as a whole. Individuals believe that accounts of crimes of others are intended to refer to themselves (A. 4.33). This was an age when criticism was conveyed obliquely, as by Maternus in his play (D. 3).

[58] *Agr.* 3.1; Syme (1958a: 7).

courts in order to devote himself to literature, including the writing of a provocative play about Cato.[66] The *Agricola* therefore reveals two contradictory attitudes to the Empire, both held by Tacitus. There is a realistic attitude, with emphasis on *modestia* and *obsequium* and the practical good these virtues make possible even under the worst emperors, and a romantic backward-looking view, deeply influenced by the loss of self-respect incurred by senators in submitting to overwhelming power. But perhaps there is after all no contradiction. In the course of the narrative of Agricola's life, Tacitus recommends a course of conduct which is productive of public good and appropriate to the facts of Empire. In the introduction and in the reflections on the timeliness of Agricola's death, Tacitus cautiously but unmistakably reveals his feeling that the present age and the conduct appropriate to it are only relatively good, that, even leaving aside tyrants like Domitian, the society of the Empire is less appreciative and less productive of virtue than had been that of the Republic before the civil wars.[67]

The *Agricola*, it has been truly said, does not carry its meaning on its face.[68] Ostensibly a biography of Tacitus' father-in-law, the biography is made a framework for a balanced discussion of what constitutes a claim to fame under the principate. But this theme is not obviously relevant to the considerable portions of the *Agricola* where interest is diverted from the Roman official to the land and people governed by him: Britain and the Britons. In discussing these passages we are still faced with the problem of the unity of the *Agricola*, and the place in it of the excursus on the geography and history of Britain, and the two speeches elaborating the grievances of the Britons. If we restrict ourselves to the surface meaning, it would not be difficult to show that most of the detail of these passages also has been selected to contribute to the task of laudatory biography: to magnify[69] or justify[70] or explain[71] the actions of a governor of Britain.

---

[66] *D.* 3 and 41. Cf. praise of Pomponius Secundus, *A.* 12.28.2; Syme (1958a: 338–9).

[67] Cf. *H.* 3.51.2: *tanto acrior apud maiores sicut uirtutibus gloria, ita flagitiis paenitentia fuit.*

[68] Syme (1958a: 29).

[69] e.g. *Agr.* 10, allegedly new information about the north of Britain.

[70] *Agr.* 12.6: *pretium uictoriae*, against Strabo 4.5.3. Note that giving up of Britain has been considered (Suet. *Nero* 18). Agricola's conquests were partly surrendered, *H.* 1.2.1: *perdomita Britannia et statim missa.*

[71] e.g. the character and grievances of the Britons explain Agricola's administration. So, *Agr.* 13.1: *impigre obeunt si iniuriae absint*; followed by *Agr.* 19, where Agricola eliminates *iniuriae*.

The fact that we sometimes lose sight of the hero does not alter the subsidiary[72] character of the detail. The question nevertheless remains whether here too we would be justified in looking for an underlying meaning.

In the central portion of the *Agricola*, Tacitus gives a considerable amount of space to an excursus[73] on the character and feelings of the Britons.[74] The division of subject-matter of the excursus resembles that of the *Germania*, where the description of the Germans is given in two sections, i.e. a discussion of origins is followed by a description of the German way of life.[75] In the *Agricola*, Tacitus' far fuller description of the Britons under the first head provides an indication of his principal interest. After demonstrating the probability that the Britons are descendants of conquering Gauls, Tacitus draws a moral: *plus tamen ferociae*[76]*Britanni praeferunt, ut quos nondum longa pax emollierit. nam Gallos quoque in bellis floruisse accepimus; mox segnitia cum otio intrauit, amissa uirtute partier ac libertate. quod Britannorum olim uictis euenit: ceteri manent quales Galli fuerunt,* 'but the Britons show more spirit, they have not yet been softened by protracted peace. The Gauls too, we have been told, once had a great military reputation, but then came sluggishness with peace, and valour was lost at the same time as liberty. The same fate has befallen such of the Britons as have long been conquered; the rest are still what the Gauls used to be' (*Agr.* 11.5). This passage shows that Tacitus was interested in the consequences of the loss of liberty.

---

[72] Hence the sketchiness of information in some respects compared with Caesar or Strabo. On Roman geographical descriptions, see Syme (1958a: 126). Sallust, although once proconsul of Africa, did not use personally gained information for his excursus (*Iug.* 17).

[73] For a literary interpretation of the excursus, see Clarke (2001) [Ch. 1 above]. On the place of the excursus in the work as a whole see Sailor (2008: 81–9).

[74] The excursus belongs to the genre of classical ethnography, whose traditionality, accuracy (or lack of it), and use by Greeks and Romans for self-definition and self-criticism has been much discussed recently. See e.g Thomas (1982); Clarke (1999). There has been considerable discussion particularly of the realism of Roman ethnography and the extent to which its conventional descriptions are merely a code to mark 'otherness'. See Shaw (2000).

[75] Tac. *G.* 2–4 (origin), *G.* 6ff. (customs, starting with military customs). Similarly Caesar, *BG* 5.12.1–2 (origins of Britons), *BG* 5.14 (customs). Ammianus on Gauls: 15.9.1 (origins), 15.12 (customs). For Gauls and Germans Caesar describes customs only, *BG* 6.11ff. Sall. *Iug.* 17–19 has only origins of peoples and cities of Africa. Strabo 4.5.2 deals only with customs of Britons.

[76] *Ferocia*; cf. Traub (1953: 252) on this passage and *Agr.* 37.6.

The continuation of the excursus confirms this. The derivation of the Britons from the Gauls is immediately followed by an account of the Britons' manner of waging war. This information would seem to belong to a description of the way of life of the Britons. But Tacitus has moved it forward because it illustrates the point just made: it describes the warlike behaviour which the conquered Gauls have been induced to give up. In addition, it makes a new point about the implications of freedom: disunity and internecine strife. For the tribes are torn by the conflicts of the factions of rival chiefs, and rarely do several tribes combine against a common enemy. Thus one by one they fall victims to the Romans (*Agr.* 12.1).

Next, Tacitus deals with climate and produce of Britain. Then he comes back to the people and with *ipsi Britanni* seems on the point of a full description of the Britons' way of life. But he reduces this to a minimum. There is nothing about religion or marriage customs, merely: *ipsi Britanni dilectum ac tributa et iniuncta imperii munia impigre obeunt, si iniuriae absint: has aegre tolerant, iam domiti ut pareant, nondum ut seruiant,* 'The Britons themselves submit to the levy, the tribute, and other charges of the empire with cheerful readiness provided there is no abuse. That they resent, for they are broken in to obedience, not to slavery' (*Agr.* 13.1).

This statement, the last part of which Tacitus was to use of the Romans themselves,[77] is significant. In its context at the head of the account of the Roman occupation of Britain it provides the psychological explanation of Boudicca's rebellion, as well as a practical justification of Agricola's policy of eliminating abuses from the administration. But it also reveals once again Tacitus' concern with the consequences of subjection, and the belief that in the long run it destroys in the subject people a sense of the justice which is their due.

The same concern is revealed in the two lengthy speeches given to Britons, the grievances that preceded the revolt of Boudicca (*Agr.* 15) and the speech with which Calgacus rallied his men to preserve their liberty in Scotland and to regain the liberty of the rest of Britain (*Agr.* 30–32). The Boudicca revolt is given a very prominent place in the account of the Roman occupation of Britain. This is not inappropriate in a biography of Agricola, because Agricola took part in

---

[77] *H.* 1.16: *imperaturus es hominibus qui nec totam seruitutem pati possunt, nec totam libertatem.* On Tacitus' views about the Roman Empire, see now Sailor (2008: 50–118).

this campaign on the staff of Suetonius Paulinus,[78] but, on the other hand, nothing is here said about Agricola's own experience in the rebellion. Instead, most space is given to the grievances of the Britons, which, however, are evidently not related to explain the circumstances of that particular rebellion. Comparison with the much fuller account in the *Annals* (*A.* 14.31) shows that in the *Agricola* the grievances have been generalized almost out of recognition.[79]

> *nihil profici patientia nisi ut grauiora tamquam ex facile tolerantibus imperentur . . . alterius manus centuriones, alterius seruos uim et contumelias miscere. nihil iam cupiditati, nihil libidini exceptum. in proelio fortiorem esse qui spoliet: nunc ab ignauis plerumque et imbellibus eripi domos, abstrahi liberos, iniungi delectus . . .*

> Nothing is gained by submission except that heavier burdens are imposed on men who seem willing to bear them. . . . Centurions, the instruments of the legate, and slaves, those of the procurator, mingle violence and cruelty. Nothing is any longer safe from their greed and lust. In war it is the brave who take the spoils; as things stand with us it is mostly the cowardly and unfit for war who rob our homes, kidnap our children, and conscript our men . . . (*Agr.* 15.1–3).

The grievances are not irrelevant to the theme of the biography, since they bring out the merits of the very different administration of Agricola. On the other hand, the strong impression remains that Tacitus has also recorded these grievances for their own sake. This impression is strengthened by the fact that within the comparatively short compass of the *Agricola* there is in Calgacus' speech a passage on the same theme: *auferre trucidare rapere falsis nominibus imperium, atque ubi solitudinem faciunt, pacem appellant*, 'They call plunder, murder, rapine, by the deceitful title of empire, and when they make a desert they call it peace' (*Agr.* 30.4), whereas *nos . . . in excidium petimur; neque enim arua nobis aut metalla aut portus sunt, quibus exercendis reseruemur*, 'we are sought only for extermination, for we have no fertile lands, mines, or harbours for the working of which we might be spared' (*Agr.* 31.2).

So far the picture is grim. But against this dark background the governorship of Agricola stands out all the more brightly. Agricola abolished those 'abuses' which the Britons resented, kept freedmen

---

[78] See above, n. 10.
[79] See the interpretation of Roberts (1988).

and slaves out of public business, and by various reforms enabled the Britons for the first time to appreciate that peace offered blessings (*Agr.* 19–20.1). But not content with redressing wrongs, Agricola instituted a policy of urbanization and Romanization, with a view to inducing the Britons to give up their warlike habits and accustoming them to *otium* and *quies*. Under his encouragement, the Britons began to live in cities built in the Roman manner, to have their children brought up in a Roman rhetorical education, and to enjoy 'the amenities which make vice agreeable', colonnades, baths, and luxurious banquets. Men who did not know better, we are told, called this civilization when in fact it was part of slavery (*Agr.* 21).

Taken together, these passages form a picture of the two extremes towards which Roman rule might tend. At the worst, the subject peoples are helplessly exposed to exploitation and every kind of evil. Under the most favourable conditions, they are accustomed to *quies* and *otium* and to the adoption of Roman civilization. This is not an unmixed good. As the subjects learn the Roman way of life, they lay aside the warlike spirit (*Agr.* 11.5) and the proud virtues that are related to it and take on the vices of civilization. Moreover, it can, I think, be assumed that Tacitus found truth in both extremes. The speeches admittedly are highly rhetorical, and closely resemble in general tone and contents speeches Tacitus put into the mouths of other freedom fighters in the *Annals*[80] and *Histories*.[81] But this does not mean that he did not intend them to express a degree of truth. In the case of the speeches in the *Agricola*, the fact that we know that the grievances of the followers of Boudicca were justified adds force to the arguments of Calgacus. Neither in the case of Calgacus nor in that of some of the other barbarian leaders does Tacitus insert any disparaging comments about the speaker which might detract from the effect of the speech, in the way in which he was to detract from the more moving speech of a leader of mutinous legionaries.[82]

Indeed, the aggressive imperialism which is attributed to the Romans in the first part of Calgacus' speech is the policy which Tacitus himself felt accorded best with the dignity of the Roman people, and

---

[80] Cf. the debate of Arminius and Flauus (*A.* 2.9–10); the speech of Arminius (*A.* 2.15); Caratacus (*A.* 12.34, 12.37).

[81] Ciuilis, *H.* 4.14, 4.17, 4.32.

[82] Notice the disparagement of Percennius and the discrediting of his arguments (*A.* 1.16). On this, see Auerbach (1957: 32).

whose relaxation under the influence of the Empire he regretted. Of course, this does not mean that he advocated or even condoned injustice in the treatment of the conquered. But even here he would surely have insisted that the interest of the Roman state should override all other considerations,[83] and he provides at least two examples which show that even the extreme charges of Calgacus are not without justification in Roman practice. The fate of the Ampsivarii proved that the Romans might indeed prefer maintaining a desert on their frontier to having it settled by an allied people,[84] and the story of the Friesians and the visit of their kings to Rome is evidence of the fact that admiration of the nobility of a barbarian tribe would not divert the Romans from sacrificing it to Roman interest.[85]

In the same way it can be shown that the criticism of Romanization represents a view deeply held by Tacitus. In the *Histories* he gives an eloquent speech to the Tencteri in which they ask the citizens of the Colonia Agrippinensis to return to the way of life of their fellow Germans,[86] and to reject those vices which are of greater use to the Romans even than arms in keeping their subjects in obedience (*H.* 4.64.). In the *Annals* too, Tacitus describes how a young Parthian prince educated at Rome became estranged from his people and lost his throne.[87] The *Germania*, which describes the virtues of a free

---

[83] e.g. *Agr.* 13.3, the ironical comment on the decision not to conquer Britain: *consilium id diuus Augustus uocabat, Tiberius praeceptum*; also *Agr.* 16, sneers at peaceful governor. *A.* 4.32.2: *nobis in arto et inglorius labor, immota quippe aut modice lacessita pax . . . princeps proferendi imperii incuriosus erat*; *A.* 14.38.3: *Iulius Classicianus . . . Suetonio discors, bonum publicum priuatis simultatibus impediebat*, on attempts to obtain more humane methods of pacification. Cf. also Agricola's view, *Agr.* 35.2: *ingens uictoriae decus citra Romanum sanguinem bellandi*. On the auxiliary nature of the battle of Mons Graupius, see now Gilliver (1996). The tactic of keeping legions in reserve was also employed by Trajan on his Dacian campaign (Richmond 1944: 43). Cf. also the callousness of *G.* 33.1: *seu fauore quodam erga nos deorum: nam ne spectaculo quidem proelii inuidere. super sexaginta milia non armis telisque Romanis, sed quod magnificentius est, oblectationi oculisque ceciderunt*.

[84] *A.* 13.55.2, request: *ne uastitatem et solitudinem mallent quam amicos populos*; their fate, *A.* 13.56.3: *errore longo hospites, egeni, hostes in alieno quod iuuentutis erat caeduntur, imbellis aetas in praedam diuisa est*.

[85] *A.* 13.54: *captis caesisue qui peruicacius resisterant*.

[86] Cf. *G.* 28.

[87] *A.* 2.2ff. For other accounts of failures of princes educated at Rome, see *A.* 11.16, 12.11, 12.29–30, 14.26.

people, is interspersed with comments which underline their moral superiority over the Romans.[88]

To conclude, there is a theme running through the whole of the *Agricola*: the consequences of the loss of liberty. This theme is not treated from the same point of view throughout. The sections centred on the career of Agricola treat the theme in the form of a thesis as to what constitutes a praiseworthy life under an emperor. The passages which focus attention on the Britons bring out the physical and moral consequences that follow loss of national independence, both when the foreign government is tyrannous and when it is fair and benevolent. But the conclusion that while the evils of subjection to a tyrannous overlord are all but unlimited, even benevolent rule entails moral degeneration is shown to be true at Rome as well as in Britain.

The question arises whether Tacitus deliberately set out to demonstrate the parallel between the rule of the Caesars over the Romans and of the Romans over their subjects, thus applying a common yardstick to the condition of both. The *Agricola* as a whole does not leave the impression that it was designed to bring out this parallel. It is more likely that Tacitus introduced the theme of liberty into the British section of the *Agricola* because it provided an issue which could be used to dramatize[89] his hero's achievements there. To assist him, there was in use at Rome a traditional stock of arguments that might be used to attack empires in general and that of Rome in particular.[90] But once Tacitus had decided to use the theme, he was faced with the task of adapting the arguments to the particular situation, and of making the total effect as convincing as possible. In doing this he could not help but draw on the Roman experience which so preoccupied him. Thus he has drawn a picture of the subjection of Britain which resembles his analysis of Roman conditions, not only in general pattern but also in points of detail. Close resemblances are to be found in the causes and consequences

---

[88] *libertas* among the Germans: *G.* 11, 21, 25, 28, 44, an exception 45; their morals, *G.* 18ff; the most difficult enemies of the Romans, *G.* 37.3: *quippe regno Arsacis acrior est Germanorum libertas.* Now see O'Gorman (1993) [Ch. 3 below].

[89] Cf. the speeches at Sallust, *Iug.* 14 and 24.

[90] *H.* 4.68.6: . . . *cuncta magnis imperiis est obiectari solita.* Originated by Carneades? Cic. *Rep.* (ed. C. F. W. Müller), 3.12.1, from Lact. *Inst. Diu.* 5.16.2–4; *Rep.* 3.14, 3.15. Used in resistance to Rome: Sallust, *Hist., Ep. Mith.* 17–21. Freedom fight of barbarians: Caesar, *BG* 7.77 (speech of Critognatus). See Fuchs (1938: 17 and 47).

assigned to *otium* and *quies*.[91] The hostility to virtue in the governed[92] and indifference to the sanctity of life are characteristic of tyrannous government at Rome and in Britain alike.[93] In both places subjects are forced to submit to slaves or freedmen, and rulers concerned to remove from sight anything that reminds subjects of better conditions.[94] Finally, in the *Histories* Tacitus was to apply to the Romans the verdict he had given on the Britons: that they were 'broken to obedience, not to slavery'.[95] Thus the parallel between Romans and barbarians, even if it is not part of the conscious design of the *Agricola*,[96] is nevertheless real, because a Roman senator's experience of subjection to an emperor lies behind every part of the work.

ADDENDUM

The majority of readers of the *Agricola* probably read it as the principal source on the Roman occupation of Britain, and its value as such is ever being reassessed in the light of new discoveries of archaeology.[97] Tony Woodman and Chris Kraus are preparing a new edition which will survey the current state of play. Recent excavations have suggested an earlier date for several Roman military sites in the north, with a clear implication that, contrary to the impression given by Tacitus, Roman occupation of this area preceded Agricola.[98] My article focused on the theme of liberty. There has been relatively little writing on this aspect of the *Agricola*, perhaps because many scholars now disqualify the ideal (or ideology) of *libertas* examined

---

[91] *Quies* and *otium* among barbarians: *Agr.* 21.1, *ut . . . quieti et otio per uoluptates adsuescerent*; *Agr.* 11.5: *mox segnitia cum otio intrauit amissa uirtute pariter ac libertate.* Among Romans, *D.* 41.5: *quoniam nemo eodem tempore adsequi potest magnam famam et magnam quietem. . . .* Tyrants enforce *quies* or *otium* on individuals: *Agr.* 6.3, 42.2. Cf. *A.* 1.2.6, 12.12.2.

[92] *Agr.* 31.4: *uirtus porro ac ferocia subiectorum ingrata imperantibus*; *Agr.* 41.1: *infensus uirtutibus princeps.*

[93] Cf. *Agr.* 31.3–4, with *Agr.* 44.5: *Domitianus non iam per interualla . . rem publicam exhausit.*

[94] *Agr.* 24.3: *et uelut e conspectu libertas tolleretur.* Similarly, Britons consider the sight of *seruitium* infectious, *Agr.* 30.3. Cf. at Rome: *Agr.* 2.2, 39.3.

[95] See above, n. 77.

[96] I now feel that the parallel must be deliberate, and an essential feature of Tacitus' design.

[97] e.g. Hanson (1991b: 174–88).

[98] Hoffmann (2004).

and promoted in the *Agricola* and other writings of Tacitus as a mere screen masking the clinging to power of the old senatorial elite. But Oswyn Murray has now edited *Peace and Liberty in the Ancient World*, a series of lectures delivered by Arnaldo Momigliano in March 1940.[99] These lectures are of course a product of their times. They represent a tradition of continental and particularly of Italian scholarship, and they also reflect a particular stage in the intellectual development of a great ancient historian. But they are nevertheless of great interest to the reader of Tacitus. Momigliano in deliberate opposition to Syme focuses on the power of ideas and ideals to shape history, and like Tacitus, in the *Agricola* and elsewhere, Momigliano was concerned with the problem of how freedom can be reconciled with civil order and peace.

[99] See Murray (forthcoming).

3

No Place Like Rome: Identity and Difference in the *Germania* of Tacitus

Ellen O'Gorman

The *Germania*, as its full title *de origine et situ Germanorum* implies, is about Rome. This is clearest from passages couched almost entirely in negative terms, as in *G.* 19.1–3:

> *ergo saepta pudicitia agunt, nullis spectaculorum illecebris, nullis con-*
> *uiuiorum irritationibus corruptae. litterarum secreta uiri pariter ac*
> *feminae ignorant . . . nemo enim illic uitia ridet, nec corrumpere et cor-*
> *rumpi saeculum uocatur.*

Therefore they live within the confines of chastity, uncorrupted by the enticements of the spectacle or the excitements of the banquet. Women and men alike are unaware of the use of secret letters . . . for there no-one finds vice a laughing matter, and they do not say that to corrupt or be corrupted is just a sign of the times.[1]

The Romanocentric focus has been recognized to varying degrees by every reader of the monograph who has written on the subject.[2] Here I intend to demonstrate that the *Germania* does more than examine Germany and Germans with the continual, more or less explicit, parallel of Rome and Romans; the text in my reading is an exploration of a country (Germany) in search of the ideological (Roman) self.[3] *Germania*,

---

[1] All references are to the edition of Anderson (1938).

[2] Five examples: ibid. ix; Syme (1958a: 48, 126); Dudley (1968: 221); Dorey (1969a: 12–14); Mellor (1993: 14–16, 62).

[3] For comparable readings of Tacitus' *Agricola*, see Clarke (2001), [Ch. 1 above]; Rutledge (2000).

in other words, is a creation of the Roman writer, through which vestiges of Rome are traced. First, therefore, I consider the creation of Germany, then the exploration of the textual country, and finally examine what is the purpose of the exploration, and the extent to which it succeeds or fails.

As should be evident from my use of the term 'textual country' or my placing of inverted commas around 'Germany', I am concerned with the representation or rather creation of Germany within the text,[4] and not with its relation to the physical country of Germany.[5] *Germania* is therefore read as a deliberately ambiguous term, in that it is the title of both country and monograph; I will be examining the literary implications of landscape at various points. In examining the relation of representation to the physical world, therefore, I will concentrate on the connection between the text's assertion of power over its subject, and the Roman military invasion of and (sometimes tenuous) control over Germany, which is manifested in a number of ways. One of my most pervasive assumptions is that the monograph, *Germania*, is never an innocent text.

The text falls into two halves;[6] the first half (*G.* 1–27) is a survey of the country as a whole, following the tradition of ethnographical and geographical writing. This is concerned with Germany and the Germans in general terms, covering physical geography, climate, agricultural produce, mineral resources, origins and features of inhabitants, political, social and military organization.[7] The second half moves from region to region, tribe to tribe, mentioning points of distinction or difference, usually interesting local customs. The narrative dynamic of the second half is, for the most part, spatial, while that of the first half is more thematic. These two halves tend to undermine each other, not least because the first half unifies Germany and the second divides it. Having followed the tribes of Germany to the farthest shore in the north, the text terminates at the boundaries

---

[4] 'The Romans created the enemy whom they could not overcome, but who was later on ready to overcome the Romans.' Sallman (1987: 125).

[5] Textual countries offer scope for playing with the boundaries/connections between representation and the physical world; examples abound, such as Salman Rushdie's Pakistan, David Lodge's Rummidge, or Caesar's Gaul. Cf. Krebs (2006).

[6] Rives (2002).

[7] This first half follows very closely the traditional structure of ethnography (as summarized by Thomas (1982: ch. 1), and mirrors the structure of the ethnographic digression in the *Agricola* (*Agr.* 10–13). On the ethnographic tradition in relation to *Germania* see Rives (1999: 11–21). On the uses of ethnography in *Agricola*, see Sailor (2008: 81–9).

between the extremes of barbarism (represented by the Fenni) and the beginnings of fable and legend.[8]

Germany is created by the text, but the author is interested in representing the country as being already there. On the surface of the text, Germany seems to be already in existence, a country to be discovered, visited, and translated. However, the representation of Germany is, from the outset, that of raw material, to be shaped as a Roman artefact.[9] A crucial descriptive term in this context is *informis*: *quis . . . Germaniam peteret, informem terris*? ('Who would want to go to Germany, ugly [or shapeless] as to its lands?', *G.* 2.2). The word recurs twice more in the monograph, in both cases reinforcing the role of the Roman as a shaping force. The first of these pertains to German houses—*materia ad omnia utuntur informi et citra speciem aut delectationem* ('for all of these things they use materials which are shapeless and have no beauty or attractiveness', *G.* 16.3)—and conveys the lack of recognition of shape on the part of the Roman, and the attendant value judgement of the materials: they are not beautiful. This is undermined immediately by the ensuing description of the Germans painting their houses. In other words, not only is the Roman implicitly imposing shape (and with it value) on the German material, but also he is represented as in some way misinterpreting what he sees.[10] This example serves to destabilize the opening judgement on Germany as being *informem terris*. Further, it demonstrates to the reader that the representation of Germany is, in a sense, contaminated by the Roman interpretation, and that the interpretation is represented as contaminated. In short, what the reader is

---

[8] Cf. Murphy (2004: 165–93).

[9] Edmundo O'Gorman (1972) discusses similar issues in the context of the Columbus journeys. His contention that America is invented rather than discovered is also concerned with the question of the recognition of (or refusal to recognize) shape.

[10] The Roman view of, or display to, the Germans is for the most part male and military/administrative: *ceteris gentibus arma modo castraque nostra ostendamus* ('we only show our armies and camps to the other tribes', 41.2). But in the *Annals* Agrippina shows her power to the Ubii: *Agrippina quo uim suam sociis quoque nationibus ostentaret in oppidum Ubiorum in quo genita erat ueteranos coloniamque deduci impetrat* ('Agrippina, in order to display her power to allied tribes as well, arranged for a colony of veterans to be established in the town of the Ubii where she had been born', *Ann.* 12.27.1). The gender distinction of spectator and viewed object is further problematized within the *Germania* by the parallel between the Roman presence as audience to the fighting Germans (*G.* 33; cf. p. 115 below) and that of the German women, who watch their men in battle (*G.* 7.3–8.1).

shown is a representation of Roman prejudice, which takes shape in the form of a country. The second instance of *informis* is more complex, discussing the collection of amber on the shores of the sea which rings the known world: *ipsis in nullo usu: rude legitur, informe perfertur, pretiumque mirantes accipiunt* ('they have no use for it: it is rough when they gather it, they bring it to us unshaped and are amazed to be paid for it', *G.* 45.5). This is at odds with what the elder Pliny tells us about the many uses of amber by local inhabitants;[11] once more Tacitus' representation of the Germans has a further point to make. The image is of the barbarian providing the raw material to which the Roman will give *forma*, but the representation of the amber trade has many more levels, which I will explore later. Where the word *forma* appears in its meaning of 'shape', two refer to German shaping[12] and two to Roman, first the Roman fashioning of coins, recognized by the Germans—*formas quasdam nostrae pecuniae agnoscunt atque eligunt* ('they recognize and choose certain shapes of our coinage', *G.* 5.4)—and secondly the Roman imposition of their own myth upon the sunrise in the far north: *sonum insuper emergentis audiri formasque equorum et radios capitis aspici persuasio adicit*[13] ('popular belief has it that you can hear the sound of the sunrise[14] and see the shapes of the horses and the rays of the god's head', *G.* 45.1). From the rough pieces of amber to the vast divinity of the sun, and from the German huts to the country as a whole, the Roman position in relation to the German is always the same, represented in terms of the shaping of raw matter.

The idea of Germany as a space to be described, therefore, is intertwined with the idea of Germany as a place to be remoulded, particularly when we recall that *forma* was the word used for a map drawn up by Roman *mensores*, for the eventual purpose of redistributing the land recorded.[15] The boundaries, then, are set down in

---

[11] Pliny *HN* 37.44.

[12] *Forma nauium eo differt quod utrimque prora paratam semper adpulsui frontem agit* ('the shape of their boats differs like this: they have a prow at both ends, with a front always ready to go forward', 44.1); *insigne superstitionis formas aprorum gestant* ('they carry representations of boars as their religious totems', 45.2).

[13] 'The sun-god with radiate head, driving a horse-drawn chariot, is an idea that belongs to Greek and Roman mythology but is not found in German' (Anderson 1938: 208).

[14] Cf. Rives (1999: 316).

[15] *OLD forma* 15a; Nicolet (1991: 152).

order to be re-created, and for a specifically possessive purpose. Boundaries are, of course, of immense importance, not only to the ethnographer and the historian.[16] The idea recurs, in various forms throughout the text, of a boundary's double significance: as a barrier between spaces and peoples, and as a medium through which another space and another people can be approached. The first of these is the physical boundary, the rivers, Ocean and mountains[17] (*G.* 1.1):

> *Germania omnis a Gallis Raetisque et Pannoniis Rheno et Danuuio fluminibus, a Sarmatis Dacisque mutuo metu aut montibus separatur: cetera Oceanus ambit.*

> All Germany is divided from the Gauls, Raetians and Pannonians by the rivers Rhine and Danube, and from the Sarmatians and the Dacians by mutual fear and mountains; the Ocean surrounds the rest.

The first role of a boundary is here stressed, with the word *separatur*; later when the rivers are repeatedly crossed and recrossed, the force of *separatur* is diminished, as the second role of the boundary comes into play.[18] Despite the use of natural boundaries here there is no indication of transgression in crossing them, as is often the case in references to boundaries.[19] Rather, crossing the boundary of a river seems to result in knowledge: self-knowledge in the case of the *Germani*, who acquire their national name through transgression and displacement (*G.* 2.5, discussed below). Later, transgression blurs the boundaries of ethnic distinction, when crossing and recrossing of a boundary homogenizes the neighbouring tribes and makes it impossible to determine their origin (*G.* 28.3).[20] There is here a sense of futility on the part of the reader, in that the boundary's existence is itself ineffective: it does not draw a distinction between one tribe and the next.

---

[16] 'The question of otherness raises that of frontiers. Where does the break dividing the same from the other occur?', Hartog (1988: 61).

[17] Murphy (2004: 138–48) and Salway (2004) analyse rivers as mediums of discovery.

[18] *Mutuo metu*, the psychological boundary, at first seems to operate only within the first role, that of a barrier. However, it does often lead to *bellum*, which can play both roles. Cf. Braund (1996b).

[19] See e.g. Thomas (1982) and Hartog (1988: 331).

[20] Whittaker (1983: 110–27), approaching from the archaeological viewpoint, arrives at similar conclusions about the role of boundaries between Roman and barbarian, particularly stressing the role of trade.

Ocean is immediately presented as being more complex than the other boundaries of Germany: whereas they separate, this surrounds and encircles, an image of far greater power. The Ocean is a more sinister boundary, by virtue of its size (*immensa spatia, G.* 1.1), ferocity (*aduersus Oceanus, G.* 2.1)[21] and position, at the edge of the *oikoumene.* For these reasons it is represented as a more resistant boundary than the rest, forbidding the more cursory crossings— *subitos hostium incursus prohibet Oceanus* ('the Ocean prohibits sudden, hostile invasions', *G.* 44.3). It is only in the case of the Ocean, furthermore, that the issue of transgression comes up (*G.* 34.2–3):

> *ipsum quin etiam Oceanum illa temptauimus . . . sed obstitit Oceanus in se simul atque in Herculem inquiri. mox nemo temptauit, sanctiusque ac reuerentius uisum de actis deorum credere quam scire.*

> There we have encroached upon the Ocean itself . . . but the Ocean resists enquiry of itself or of [the Pillars of] Hercules. No-one lately has made the attempt; it seems holier and more reverent to believe in divine deeds than to know them.

Here the boundary is not between space so much as between worlds; transgression is more religious than spatial. As we see, knowledge, the reason for both transgression and delineation of a boundary (but which comes first?), is no longer a sufficient reason, being replaced with belief, which requires no transgression. The effect is to place Rome and Germany on a more or less equal footing, on this side of the barrier—Ocean—between the worlds of men, whom it is possible to know, and gods. We see the Ocean operating within the second role, as mediator, from time to time, as when bringing Ulixes to Germany (*G.* 3.3), but it also opens up a new way of looking at a boundary, as a space in its own right. This is clear from the outset, when it is represented as holding islands, kings, and peoples (*G.* 1.1). Later, the states of the Suiones are said to exist *ipso in Oceano* ('in the very Ocean', *G.* 44.1).[22]

---

[21] The meaning of *aduersus* here is debated, whether it is purely spatial, meaning 'antipodal' (Anderson 1938: 38), or is personified as 'hostile' (see esp. Romm (1992: 142–9)). Since my contention is that meaning in the *Germania* is never simply spatial, both these interpretations can be incorporated.

[22] At a lesser level, we find the other boundaries of *G.* 1.1 operating as inhabitable spaces: *Bataui . . . insulam Rheni amnis colunt* ('the Batavi live on an island in the river Rhine', *G.* 29.1); *Veneti . . . inter Peucinos Fennosque siluarum ac montium erigitur*

We now turn from representation of shape as imposed (by nature or by Roman interpretation) to that of the Roman looking for shape or signs, which he can then interpret. The boundaries here come into their second role, as means of communication, through which the Roman can enter into the space of Germany. There is no point within the text at which the Roman is not present; the very existence of a monograph in Latin *de origine et situ Germanorum* makes this clear. However, there are points at which Roman presence becomes more intrusive, first by the implication of closer interaction with the Germans than is at first indicated by the language of isolation and exploration in the opening chapters, secondly by the division of Germany itself into what land is held by Rome, what tribes recognize *imperium Romanum*, and what lands and tribes are still independent: in short, the presence of the Romans in that part of Germany which is the Roman province, and their military and commercial encounters with the Germans. The role of the Roman in these explicit passages differs from the overall, implicit Roman presence as the norm, the centre, and the source of the text. It is, in a sense, the understood comparison made active, but it is more than a comparison. The Romans in these passages are effecting or attempting acts of possession, imposing value through shape, and thus expanding the centre. Thereby Germany and Germans are changed into something approaching the Roman. This is the story of Germany within the historical (chronological rather than spatial) framework, of Roman invasion and occupation. Denied full expression by the language of ethnography, it nevertheless remains as one of the assumptions from which the text acquires validity. The very study of Germany represents that country as passive, subject to scrutiny by the powerful, invasive Rome.[23] Therefore the implied Roman functions at two distances from Germany: as the occupant of the centre to which this periphery perpetually relates, and as an active participant in the implied invasion of the other country.

War is, of course, the most frequent medium by which the Roman approaches Germany, as indicated at the outset: *gentibus ac regibus, quos bellum aperuit* ('by peoples and kings whom war has discovered', G. 1.1). *Bellum* here at first seems to function as a mode

---

('the Veneti live between the Peucini and the Fenni in the woods and mountains', G. 46.2). Cf. Murphy (2004: 166–74) on Pliny's version of the Chauci.

[23] See Said (1985: ch. 1): 'Knowing the Oriental'.

of exploration, echoing the dual roles of Oceanus and the rivers as both barriers and bridges; war carries the Romans to Germany and leads to discovery of the Germans. However, the image of disclosing is strongly influenced by *bellum*; the kings and peoples are revealed to Rome within the discourse of war, and it is only through war that they can be understood or even recognized.[24] This makes sense if we ask what they are to be recognized as; the answer is, of course, as barbarians. The method of recognition of Roman or barbarian is essentially military. War is a way of establishing the ethnic boundary. The only Romans which the barbarians of the furthest shore are likely to encounter (with the exception of traders—see below) are the military.[25] Their recognition of what it is to be a Roman is, therefore, intrinsically warlike, and to this image they present a reflection—or, more to the point, to this image the Romans seek a reflection. The portrayal of the Germans in battle presents some of the most specific images in the monograph, combining authorial assertion with a wealth of detail.

The function of war in an ethnographic context, therefore, is both to discover and to confirm, to encounter and to keep distinct: a highly complex series of roles. At a narrative level, the process of battle is here presented without its temporal underpinning, as a series of iteratives (*G.* 6–8), concealing the historical context of the battle or battles. In other words, the statements which are here presented in a certain role, as 'information about Germany', occlude the source of this information—war between Rome and Germany—and its context—Rome's invasion of Germany. There is a vestige of this context at *G.* 8: *efficacius obligentur animi ciuitatum quibus inter obsides puellae quoque nobiles imperantur* ('obedience is most effectively enforced in states from which noble women are exacted as hostages', *G.* 8.1). The final *imperantur* betrays the occupation of power behind the seemingly innocent collection of facts.

---

[24] A comparable passage can be found in the elder Pliny, *HN* 5.51, where the source of the Nile is held to be uncertain because that area has only been discovered by explorers and not by war (*tantum inermi quaesitu sine bellis quae ceteras omnis terras inuenere*).War here functions as the criterion of discovery and of certainty (perhaps because of the origin of annalistic history as an account of wars, rather than the ethnographical link with the fabulous and ambiguous).

[25] *Ceteris gentibus arma modo castraque nostra ostendamus* ('we only show our armies and camps to the other tribes', 41.2). Said (1985) also refers to the Orientals' view of the British, when they see only male administrators under the age of 50.

The image of the German is once more a reflection of the Roman, in that it is a reaction to Roman action. It is possible to observe the fighting German because he has been provoked to fight. Further, he can be made to stop fighting, by the use of hostages. In this representation, the German is not even ultimately responsible for his actions, which have a Roman source and a Roman end: historically, conquest; ethnographically, knowledge. Nor is it possible to distinguish the two; historical conquest can be described as ethnographical knowledge and vice versa.[26] Further use of the German as a Roman reflection occurs in the represented Romanization of the German.[27] While the effect of these passages is to present an image of the pure German gradually being changed, it is worth noting that, if the antithesis to 'German' is 'Roman', it is impossible to present a 'pure German' in the text; such a creature could not be known.[28] In any case, Roman influence on German behaviour, as in the above example of war and hostages, is present at all times.

A less forceful manipulation of German-ness is evident in the instances of mercantile encounters between Rome and Germany. The first of these, at *G.* 5.4, represents the original, still generally prevalent German attitude to precious metal: *est uidere apud illos argentea uasa . . . non in alia uilitate quam quae humo finguntur* ('silver vases can be found in their possession . . . not held to be any more precious than those made from clay'). The Roman presence, indicated in two words, is then demonstrated in the act of changing: *quamquam proximi ob usum commerciorum aurum et argentum in pretio habent formasque quasdam nostrae pecuniae adgnoscunt atque eligunt* ('but those nearest our border, thanks to the regularity of trade, consider gold and silver to be of value, and they recognize and choose certain shapes of our coinage'). The invasive presence of the Romans is spatially indicated by the use of *proximi* and, later, *interiores*, and the temporal aspect in *pecuniam probant ueterem et diu notam* ('they prefer our older coins, known to them for a long time', *G.* 5.5). This is a gradual change, effected in the *Germani* by regular intercourse, *ob usum*. Interestingly, German awareness and

---

[26] 'Knowledge gives power, more power requires more knowledge, and so on in an increasingly profitable dialectic of information and control' (ibid. 36).

[27] See Balsdon (1979: 82): 'Roman history is in fact a story of continuous extension of the citizen body . . .'.

[28] 'What is the meaning of "difference" when the preposition "from" has dropped from sight altogether?' (Said 1985: 106).

recognition of the Roman presence is indicated by *adgnoscunt* and *diu notam*, and the collusive element in the Roman appropriation by *eligunt* and *probant*. The German presented here as willing and cooperative is a very different image from that of the following chapters, reflecting another face of Roman policy about barbarians. This is Romanization by stages: proximity, recognition, assimilation.

The second commercial meeting of Roman and German carries none of these stages. Chapter 45 deals with the exotic region to the right of the Suebian sea, where amber has its origin (*G.* 45.5):

> *nec quae natura quaeue ratio gignat, ut barbaris, quaesitum compertu-mue; diu quin etiam inter cetera eiectamenta maris iacebat, donec luxuria nostra dedit nomen. ipsis in nullo usu: rude legitur, informe perfertur, pretiumque mirantes accipiunt.*

> Being barbarians, they have not considered or discovered what is its nature or the reason for its existence; indeed for a long time it lay with the rest of the flotsam, until our luxury gave it a name. They have no use for it: it is rough when they gather it, they bring it to us unshaped and are amazed to be paid for it.

The distance between the Roman and German, spatial and moral, is seemingly impassable. The Germans have acquired no understanding of the substance, unlike the Romans (*G.* 45.8), nor do they recognize its worth, leaving it on the shore; even when receiving payment for it they are *mirantes*. They have a different name for amber, and they convey it to the Romans *informis*, not having a proper form; Roman *luxuria* gives it *forma* with its *nomen*.[29] However, the impact of Roman change on German values is still present, but hidden. Though Tacitus claims that the Germans do not recognize the worth of amber or the significance of the *pretium* they receive, nevertheless he portrays them collecting the amber for payment, whereas before it lay on the shore, *donec luxuria nostra dedit nomen* ('until our luxury gave it a name'). Also the Germans regularly accept this *pretium*, implying *usus commerciorum* ('regularity of trade'), although they are outsiders. The Roman assimilation is a more insidious process in this episode. The trade which is taking place has immense moral significance, for the Romans are not only trading amber but also attitudes to amber. The close identification of *luxuria* with the identity or

---

[29] 'If for eight hours a day you work as a cutter of agate, onyx, chrysoprase, your labour which gives form to desire takes from desire its form' (Calvino 1997): 14).

recognition of amber makes this clear.[30] As in the case of the coins (*G.* 5.4–5), the Romans are teaching the barbarians to recognize the value of things—*iam et pecuniam accipere docuimus* ('we have taught them now to accept money', *G.* 15.3)—although Tacitus shows awareness that value is not absolute. The *pretium* received for the amber is, in this sense, *luxuria.*[31]

An integral part of the Roman act of possessing another space is the act of naming. In this sense, the entire Latin text *de origine et situ Germanorum* (as well as being an approach, and a barrier, to Germany) is an act of possession by the Roman writer, as he names and makes comprehensible alien places and peoples. The words *nomen* ('name'), *uocare* ('call'), *uocabulum* ('word') recur throughout the text, explicitly appropriating German acts and artefacts, and serving as a lexicon to German attitudes, to which the Germani ostensibly apply names. Some of these seem straightforward enough; the spears used by the Germani in battle are in their language *frameae*, and thereafter are called by that name.[32] Other German names have more moral significance. Later in chapter 6 another military *nomen* occurs: *centeni ex singulis pagis sunt, idque ipsum inter suos uocantur, et quod primo numerus fuit, iam nomen et honor est* ('there are a hundred men from each canton, they are called among themselves the hundred, and what was originally a number is now a title and an honour', *G.* 6.5). The transition—*numerus* to *nomen* to *honor*—displays the shift in meaning within a single word, losing numerical and gaining titular significance. A similar example of a shift in meaning occurs at *G.* 36.1: *ubi manu agitur, modestia ac probitas nomina superioris sunt*

---

[30] Cf. Pliny, *HN* 37.30.

[31] Catharine Edwards has pointed out to me how the original sense of *luxuria* as excessive growth can echo here, so that *luxuria nostra dedit nomen* can be read in the wider sense of Germany as a whole. This, in conjunction with the occurrence of the word *informis*, implies amber as a synecdoche for Germany. The idea of Rome's expansion as excess does not seem consistent with the absence of any sense of transgression of boundaries, as noted in the previous chapter. However, the expansion of empire in the pursuit of *gloria* is here exploited for amber, a moral excess at Rome's centre which is articulated at the margin. We see this transgression from a slightly different angle in the *Annals*: *lapidum causa pecuniae nostrae ad externas aut hostiles gentes transferuntur* ('our money is handed over to foreigners and enemies to buy stones', *Ann.* 3.53.4).

[32] The use of *framea* rather than *hasta* seems to be an isolated resistance to Roman possession through naming. If it is a German act of invasion into Latin text, the author is certainly colluding by his recognition and choice of the word. Germanicized Latin or Latinized German?

('when there is conflict, the titles of moderation and honesty go to the victor').[33] The name is affected by power, a concept also inherent in *G.* 6.5; the *honor* of the *centeni* becomes inextricably linked with the *nomen* 'centeni'. Thus the *superiores* can claim *modestia ac probitas* by virtue of physical strength. The differentiation of tribes by name is linked to the same strength at *G.* 34.1: *maioribus minoribusque Frisiis uocabulum est ex modo uirium* ('the names of the greater and lesser Frisians are determined by their strength'). In this case the name of a tribe contributes to an understanding of its nature. At *G.* 28.2 the name of the Boiohaemi provides information *de origine et situ: significat loci ueterem memoriam quamuis mutatis cultoribus* ('it signifies the memory of their original homeland, although they have emigrated'). Other names clarify distinctions within tribes, as at *G.* 38.1, 43.3, and 45.1. The studied precision of the naming betrays its role in understanding, hence in possession and power. Yet the understanding to which the Romans aspire is frequently an invented understanding, by virtue of their practice of assimilation.

Intrinsic to the concept of naming is that of speaking and hearing, which is of more weight throughout the text than that of seeing.[34] Hence many chapters afford a more or less visual representation of a Germanic custom, followed by a naming of that custom, either directly authorial or nominally German, often in the form of a Tacitean epigram: *ea est in re praua peruicacia; ipsi fidem uocant* ('in such behaviour they demonstrate a vicious obstinacy which they would call integrity', *G.* 24.4). A conflict is set up between the Roman and German names; what the Romans would call *res praua* the Germani would call *fides*. This conflict recurs in the section on amber discussed above; the Romans call *sucinum* that which the Germans call *glesum* (*G.* 45.4). Unlike *hastas uel ipsorum uocabulo frameas* ('spears or in their own word "frameae"', *G.* 6.1), which remain *frameae* thereafter, *sucinum* does not become *glesum* (cf. *G.* 45.8), perhaps because it is named by Roman luxury. The question of which name to use seems to depend on the possession of the named object and the ability to shape; naming is itself a form of shaping.

---

[33] This reading is often contested; see e.g. Gilmore (1970) and Wellesley (1970).

[34] 'For the Roman, who attaches such importance to the utterance of solemn formulae, seeing is less important than hearing' (Benveniste (1971), quoted in Hartog (1988: 261). The text itself would be heard rather than seen, in the ancient practice of literary recitation.

The vocabulary of naming reaches its highest density at *G.* 2.3–3.4, dealing with the origin of the Germani, followed by the (apparent) digression on the presence of Hercules and Ulixes in Germania. It commences with an origin myth, involving a divine element. From this comes the names of tribes. Here, and at the beginning of chapter 3, the Germani themselves are explicitly referred to as sources for the information set out: *celebrant carminibus antiquis, quod unum apud illos memoriae et annalium genus est*[35] ('they celebrate [him] in ancient songs, which is their only form of record or annals', *G.* 2.3). The oral history appealed to in these two chapters is appropriate, given the emphasis on speaking, singing, sounding and naming. Tacitus then refers to other authorities: *quidam, ut in licentia uetustatis, pluris deo ortos plurisque gentis appellationes . . . adfirmant* ('certain writers, with the licence of antiquity, state that the god had more sons, who gave their names to more tribes', *G.* 2.4). These authorities (probably, as Anderson points out, Roman antiquaries) reverse the process of the *carmina antiqua*, which represent the name as shifting from semi-divine *conditor* to tribe.[36] Here, the existence of a tribal name is utilized to create other sons of Mannus. The conflict between Roman and German authorities over the origin (and therefore the legitimation) of the tribes is yet another occluded record of Roman invasion of the German sphere; the Romans evidently consider themselves entitled to make authoritative statements about the Germans, implying knowledge resulting from scrutiny (of the passive Germany) and superiority inherent in speaking for the barbarian. This is presented as something of an impertinence—*ut in licentia*—since the barbarian can speak and has spoken. Yet the point is that the Romans can presume to speak for the barbarian, can make authoritative statements, and can be given a hearing in the text.

In the ensuing account of German names, however, the Roman is both silent and largely absent, existing only as a spectator, or rather as

---

[35] This forms part of the representation of Germans as early Romans (and of the ethnography as a history of the early Romans). See Wiseman (1986: 86–100). Particularly interesting in this context are his comments on the proximity of history to *fabula* and the interpretation of early monuments (*licentia uetustatis*).

[36] Robinson (1935) has remarked how Mannus as *origo* and his sons as *conditores* (and source of names) evoke Aeneas and Romulus, who play the same roles in the Roman mythology (he cites also *origo Iuliae gentis Aeneas . . . et conditor urbis Romulus* ('Aeneas the origin of the Julian family . . . and Romulus founder of the city', *Ann.* 4.9.2).

a reader (audience) of early German history. The *nomina* of *G.* 2.3
and 2.4 are *uera et antiqua*, true and ancient. Some are linked with the
origin of the *gens*. They are the *nomina* which the Germani apply to
themselves (*G.* 2.5):

> *Ceterum Germaniae uocabulum recens et nuper additum, quoniam
> qui primi Rhenum transgressi Gallos expulerint ac nunc Tungri, tunc
> Germani uocati sint.*

> But the name of Germany is a recent addition, since those who first
> crossed the Rhine drove out the Gauls and are now called the Tungri,
> but were at that time called Germani.

The *nomen*, therefore, of the Germani is set in opposition to the *uera
et antiqua nomina* preceding it. Not only is it a new name, but it
comes from outside the space of Germania. However, it is not an
invented name; it comes originally from within Germania, though it
is not mentioned among the *uera et antiqua nomina*. Unlike the later
tribal names which break down into small groups (the Suebi, *G.* 38.1;
the Lugii, *G.* 43.3), 'Germani' is a tribal name applied to an entire
gens, a synecdochic naming (*G.* 2.5):

> *ita nationis nomen, non gentis, eualuisse paulatim, ut omnes primum a
> uictore ob metum,*[37] *mox etiam a se ipsis inuento nomine Germani
> uocarentur.*

> So as the name of the country, not the tribe, it gradually gained
> momentum, so that at first everyone was called by the victors' name
> from fear, then the Germani found out and picked up the name, which
> they had, after all, made up themselves in the first place.

Naming is once more linked to power and physical strength. The
interplay of power and possession in this naming process is interesting. The Tungri complete an invasive act of possession, crossing into
Gallic space and driving out its inhabitants. They call themselves, and
the Galli call them, Germani; thus they impose their naming system
on those they have invaded. They are *primi transgressi*, so the possessing of Gallia does not end with the Tungri. The other German tribes
which invade are called 'Germani' by the Tungri, to inspire fear. The
act of aggressive assimilation is not so much directed at the other
'Germani', the assimilated, as at the Galli, the object of aggression.

---

[37] For an alternative reading, see Hansen (1989).

This naming is then taken up by the other 'Germani'. As in 5.4, *adgnoscunt atque eligunt*; they recognize the name as applying/being applied to them, and choose to use it. Hence the name crosses back into Germania and is (re-)invented. As Anderson has remarked, the development of a tribal into a national name has always been due not to the tribe which bore the name but to its alien neighbours.[38] However, although the Tungri apply the name 'Germani' to the other tribes, they do so *ob metum*, both to inspire fear and for fear of not inspiring fear—a constraint placed upon the invaders' use of names by their own invasion. Thus the assumption of the name 'Germani' can be read not as an act of possession so much as an act of defence, picking up on the ambiguous nature of the relationship between invader and invaded, as represented also in the Roman–German encounter.

The invasion represented here is outward, for the Germans. Following this account there is mention of Hercules, as a hero rather than founder of a *gens* (such as of the Scythians in Herodotus). Strangely, instead, the narrative turns to Ulixes, another famed wanderer (*G.* 3.3):

> *ceterum et Ulixen quidam opinantur longo illo et fabuloso errore in hunc Oceanum delatum adisse Germaniae terras, Asciburgiumque, quod in ripa Rheni situm hodieque incolitur, ab illo constitutum nominatumque; aram quin etiam Ulixi consecratam, adiecto Laertae patris nomine, eodem loco olim repertam, monumentaque et tumulos quosdam Graecis litteris inscriptos in confinio Germaniae Raetiaeque adhuc extare.*[39]

> But also some people think that Ulixes, on that long and fabulous journey, being swept into this Ocean, came to the lands of Germany, and that Asciburgium, which even today is inhabited, situated on the banks of the Rhine, was founded and named by him; and also an altar was consecrated by Ulixes, which he inscribed with the name of his father Laertes. This altar was found in the same place, and monuments and tumuli inscribed with certain Greek letters still stand on the borders of Germania and Raetia.

The first question would seem to be why such activities would be ascribed to Ulixes, who is a traveller neither for the sake of travelling

---

[38] Anderson (1938: 45).

[39] It is interesting to note how the markers left by Ulixes serve to validate the boundaries drawn around Germany by the Latin text.

nor for the purpose of invasion. His appearance in the text ironically
harks back to the rhetorical question at *G.* 2.2: *quis porro, praeter
periculum horridi et ignoti maris, Asia aut Africa aut Italia relicta
Germaniam peteret, informem terris, asperam caelo, tristem cultu
aspectuque, nisi si patria sit?* ('but apart from the danger of a rough
and unknown sea, who would leave Asia or Africa or Italia and seek
Germania, ugly in its lands, harsh in its weather, gloomy to inhabit
and to view, unless it were his native land?'). This question as it stands
has seemed problematic, since the *quis* is presumably a German, for
whom the question's existence is completely unnecessary; the Roman,
for whom the question is necessary, knows that Germany is not his
patria, hence paradoxically his question is at the same time unnecessary. Pushing the question to any length reveals that for both Roman
and German this is a pointless question. If we examine the itinerary
postulated in the question—*Asia aut Africa aut Italia relicta*—we can
see its absurdity in relation to the German, but its peculiar aptness to
Ulixes himself, particularly since the reason for his long and fabulous
wanderings is the very reason stated: he seeks his *patria*.[40]

Aside from the absurdity of sailing up-river in search of Ithaca, the
deeds of Ulixes are more indicative of the explorer and possessor:
more reminiscent, in fact, of the deeds of Hercules, who appears in
this same passage, seemingly as a 'mere' war hero. Ulixes first founds
a city, not only a standard Herculean activity but also a deed wholly
unassociated with the Ulixes of myth and of the occasional hero cult.
The founding and naming of a city is an uncompromising act of
possession and power in a foreign land.[41] Secondly, he raises an altar
adiecto Laertae patris nomine ('which he inscribed with the name of
his father Laertes'). As Anderson has pointed out, both activities are
common, placing a marker at the limit of one's explorations and
including the father's name within the inscription. Once more they
are acts of possession. By marking out his personal boundary, Ulixes
is defining his personal space, the space he has travelled; by marking
his boundary with his father's name he is defining the centre of that

---

[40] However, the question is not answered satisfactorily even at this level.
Though it purports to answer itself, it is in effect unanswerable.

[41] D. C. Feeney has remarked that it is usual for Hercules not only to found a city,
but also to father a child or two (occasionally originating a race) on his travels,
whereas Ulixes only fathers once on foreign soil. Both actions, founding and fathering,
intensify the representation of the foreign land as a passive object before the active
invader, and confirm the female/male opposition mentioned in n. 10 above.

space, the source of the power by which he can effect possession. Anderson has remarked that the story of Ulixes must have reached the Rhine with the Roman soldiers; this presents Ulixes and his story as a Roman sign of invasion. Strangely, the physical and written signs at this point are all ascribed to non-Romans: the altar set up by the wandering Greek and the monuments of either Greek or Celtic work.[42] The Roman assertion here is verbal, or at any rate not specifically written—*quidam opinantur*—an inversion of the oral German vs. written Roman sources of *G.* 2.3–4.[43] The Roman markers of invasion and possession are here very subtle, easily ascribed elsewhere. Like the coins of *G.* 5.4, the Romans introduce symbols which are accepted and used by the barbarians, but which nevertheless operate as *uestigia* for the Roman presence. The effect is to give the impression that the Roman is acting merely as a reader or spectator of Germany, occluding his frequent operation as writer and actor.

The Roman historic presence, as reader, writer, or participant, is indispensable to ethnography, though fragmented and hidden. Just as the ethnographical digression is essential to a work of history, so too the historical superstructure is a necessary context to the ethnographical work. Their generic interdependence mirrors the dialectic of information and control inherent in Rome's dealings with the German barbarian. 'No representation of the world would be complete without a representation of power and no representation of power would be worth much without a representation of the world.'[44]

So far I have been examining the representation of the barbarian and the foreign land from the viewpoint of Roman ascendancy, as the norm, centre, and superior race. This hierarchy is, however, challenged by the text in two ways: first by demonstrating that Romans are not always in a position of moral superiority; secondly by presenting Rome as being in a precarious position of supremacy, from which it may at any point be toppled. This role of the barbarian, as 'noble savage', in opposition to the barbarian as the repository of all that is uncivilized and socially undesirable, is an ever-present tension

---

[42] The use of the Greek alphabet by Celts is not unheard of: Caesar, *BG* 6.14.3, cf. Anderson (1938: 52); Balsdon (1979: 118).

[43] There is a parallel patterning between *G.* 2.3–5 and *G.* 3.1–3 in the appeal first to German oral accounts (*celebrant carminibus antiquis; Herculem memorant, primumque canunt*) then to nameless authorities (*quidam opinantur; quidam adfirmant*).

[44] Hartog (1988: 360).

in any portrayal of the foreigner, particularly the primitive for-eigner.[45] In the description of the German as an unspoiled primitive there is evident a temporal distancing of Germany, as the primitive Roman is evoked. The historical pattern of decline from a morally upright past is the source of this representation. However, since the upright past is constructed by the degenerate present (standing in relation to the past as German to Roman in the text), ancient morality is the antithesis to the particular immoralities considered the bane of contemporary Rome. Hence, the depiction of the noble primitive as superior to the contemporary Roman focuses on the issues of materialism and sexual morality.[46]

The discourse of barbarian representation in the ancient world is very much a discourse of duality, polarity, of being either one or the other, although this is often masked by the assignation of otherness to elements of one's own society.[47] Three-way splitting does not, in practice, occur. In other words, if two types of barbarianism are represented, one will be assimilated to the Roman.[48] If, therefore, the morally superior German becomes the primitive Roman, what is the Roman? The answer may be sought in the implicit historical view, which can be read as a view of Rome in a state of moral decline. The usual marker date for this decline is around the time of Rome's emergence as dominant power in the Mediterranean, with the intro-duction of demoralizing eastern luxury.[49] The moral yardstick of Rome is polarized into desirable and undesirable, or, more bluntly, right and wrong. The former extreme is then projected into the past in order to give it the validity of tradition, while the latter is ascribed

---

[45] See e.g. Lovejoy and Boas (1973) on the alternating ascriptions of vegetarianism and cannibalism to primitives. Note also their distinction between cultural and chronological primitivism.

[46] German materialism is examined here. The main focus on sexual morality in the *Germania* occurs at chs 18–20. Anderson's (1938) commentary for these chapters charts the implied contrasts with contemporary Rome.

[47] 'The use of foreign terms emerges as one manifestation of a powerful ideological myth that whatever is viewed with anxiety has been brought in from outside' (Kennedy 1992: 29). See also Said (1985: 206).

[48] See Hartog (1988: 259) for an examination of Persians occupying the role of Greeks when they are portrayed in opposition to Scythians: 'The rhetoric of otherness thus tends to be dual and, as might be expected in this narrative, *alter* truly does mean the other one (of two).'

[49] See Earl (1967: 19ff.) for a selection of dates marking Rome's moral decline. All are associated with materialism and sexual licence issuing from the east. A crucial examination of Rome's encounter with the Greek East is Gruen (1992).

not only to recent times but to foreign influence. Since, therefore, the history of Roman values is constructed in terms of their present, this 'moral history' of Rome has its own role as an ideological barrier to Asiatic influences.[50] Thus the primitive Roman is evoked, not against the decadent Asian, but against the corrupted, contemporary, easternized Roman. This comparison frequently takes place in a rhetorical context, evoking the primitive Roman of the past; here it is spatial. The portrayal of Germany as similar to primitive Rome serves to align contemporary Rome with the east, which is represented as a foreign land more comprehensible and familiar to the Roman.

The primitive German/Roman prompts the calling into question of the absolute value of material things (*G.* 5.3–4):

> *argentum et aurum propitiine an irati di negauerint dubito . . . est uidere apud illos argentea uasa . . . non in alia uilitate quam quae humo finguntur.*[51]

I do not know whether the gods have denied them gold and silver as a favour or a punishment. . . . Silver vases can be found in their possession . . . not held to be any more precious than those made from clay.

Similarly, amber has meaning only in the eyes of the luxurious Romans (*G.* 45), and the Germans view the Roman meaning for amber with wonder: *pretiumque mirantes accipiunt* ('they are amazed to be paid for it', *G.* 45.5). As we have seen, the Romans appear to be in a position of superiority at this point, recognising amber's worth, giving it *forma* and *nomen*, teaching the barbarians to recognize amber in the Roman way, at any rate to the extent of gathering it rather than letting it lie. Of course, the words *nostra luxuria* are a strong indicator that Roman values are not going unchallenged by the text; in fact, by connecting amber to oriental incense and balsam at *G.* 45.7, Roman luxury is again aligned with the east. Furthermore, Roman shaping and understanding of amber is implicitly deflated. At first represented as superior—*nec quae natura quaeue ratio gignat, ut barbaris, quaesitum compertumue* ('being barbarians, they have not considered or discovered what is its nature or the reason for its existence', *G.* 45.5)—Roman enquiry into the nature of amber, we are told in neutral tones, merely results in the destruction of both

---

[50] Storoni Mazzolani (1972: ch. 9).

[51] It is worth noting that of the ten occasions in the text where Tacitus employs the first person singular, seven carry strong overtones of uncertainty.

natura and *forma*: *si naturam sucini admoto igne temptes, in modum taedae accenditur alitque flammam pinguem et olentem; mox ut in picem resinamue lentescit* ('if you test the nature of amber with fire, it burns like a torch, producing a thick, smoky flame; then it cools into pitch or resin', *G.* 45.8). The end of Roman luxury and enquiry is as rough and formless as the original, neglected amber, but through the medium of wasted labour and *pretium*. Identity and difference are here elided, by pursuing the amber from its original status as beach debris, through its pivotal position of negotiation between Roman (oriental) and German (Roman), to its final metamorphosis into a useless resin.

The melting of amber problematizes not only the imposition of shape (and name) but also the search for meaning, since the whole process of looking for amber results only in pointless destruction. The Roman search through Germany is further problematized when we consider the object of that search. The shape or meaning which is sought is inevitably a Roman one; as remarked at the start of this paper, specifically German shapes are denied meaning by the Roman interpretation. As I have discussed above, the position of Rome as the source of normal behaviour is destabilized by the assimilation of German morality to that of the early Romans. I have remarked on how Rome itself in these instances is linked to the East. This shifting of 'Roman-ness' serves also to undermine Rome's position at the centre of the world, by displacing the strong ideological underpinning which serves both to legitimize Roman expansion and to hold Rome together as a city. The shift of Roman morality into the German sphere is a product of the unsatisfactory political situation in Rome itself, leading to its portrayal as a city alien to its own inhabitants. This representation of Rome as strange and divergent is a strong feature of subsequent Tacitean writing,[52] and we see it here reflected in the representation of the foreign land, traditional repository of the strange and divergent, now a refuge for the familiar. The search through Germany, then, is a search for Rome and what are seen as Roman values.[53] The only reason for a Roman to visit Germany is to

---

[52] See Henderson (1992); Plass (1988); Woodman (1992) [Ch. 13 below].

[53] e.g., the search for *libertas*, which develops into a complex nexus of ideas integrally linked over the entire Tacitean corpus. Even within the *Germania*, tracking *libertas* through the markers of slaves, masters, and freedmen enmeshes the reader in the complexities of German religion viewed through the filter of Roman interpretation.

seek his native land.[54] This is what underpins the representation of Germany as a re-enactment of early Roman history, with the Roman as audience.[55] Thus the language of the 'gladiatorial show, of which the Romans were delighted spectators'[56] is used to describe the view of a battle between two German tribes (*G.* 33.2). The Romans here are watching a civil war, a characteristically Roman kind of war.[57] The idea of a spectacle is turned around at *G.* 37.6, where the Germans in turn act as spectators of Roman internal conflict and take the same opportunity to benefit from it: *inde otium, donec occasione discordiae nostrae et ciuilium armorum expugnatis legionum hibernis etiam Gallias adfectauere, ac rursus pulsi* ('then there was a lull, until with the opportunity offered by our discord and civil war, having taken over the legions' winter quarters they even threatened the Gauls, but then were driven back'). The use of imagery of the Roman as the audience at a gladiatorial show, and at the same time as the reader of early Roman history, seems temporarily to elide anxiety about transgression between the spheres of object and onlooker.[58] But it is also made clear that the Romans are delighted spectators of the German civil war because it deflects German aggression from them. Roman presence in Germania is hardly one of unchallenged supremacy; the invasive bearers of *imperium* not only risk repulsion but also are in danger of instability at the centre by German dissidence at the margin. This collapses the respective roles of Roman and German as onlooker and object, as they meet in the domain of war.

The search for a re-Romanized Rome in the exploration of Germany is foredoomed, not only because the German, however like the early Roman he is, will inevitably present himself in

---

[54] *Quis... Germaniam peteret... nisi si patria sit?* ('Who would want to go to Germany, unless it were his native land?', *G.* 2.2). This reminds us that Ulixes is not the only wanderer to move westwards from Asia. There is also Aeneas, an interesting model for the Roman in this text, since he seeks his *patria* elsewhere, having left it behind him, in ruins.

[55] 'Audience' combining the idea of the spectator at a show and of the 'reader' of the orally presented text.

[56] Anderson (1938: 162); cf. Murphy (2004: 158–9).

[57] The idea of civil war as spectacle is most particularly prevalent in Lucan's *Bellum Ciuile*.

[58] The use of two separate images here to represent the German, as gladiator or as early Roman (bound together by the same role for the contemporary Roman as audience), represents the conflict of the two roles of the barbarian, as noble or ignoble savage (see Lovejoy and Boas 1973). The ambiguous status of the gladiator (marginal and yet/therefore reaffirming Roman-ness) is examined in Wiedemann (1992).

opposition to Rome, but also because all the Roman can find in Germany is a reflection of the Roman condition, which itself is alien to 'Rome'. Further, the search itself, by acknowledging the de-Romanization of Rome, undermines the identity/difference distinction which informs the ethnographic text. Again this is articulated at margins and boundaries, which become sites of ambiguity. Germany's shape, when pressed, is revealed as shapeless (*informem terris*), much as the amber (which we have seen as synecdoche for the country), when tested by Roman *ratio*, collapses into formlessness.[59] The amber almost concludes the search through Germany, and, paradoxically, it is immediately followed by a strong statement of ethnic differentiation (*G.* 45.9):

> *Suionibus Sitonum gentes continuantur. cetera similes uno differunt, quod femina dominatur: in tantum non modo a libertate sed etiam a seruitute degenerant.*

> After the Suiones come the tribes of Sitones. They are similar to the rest but for one thing, that they are ruled by women: in this they sink not only below the standards of liberty but also beneath those of slavery.

The distinction between the tribes here seems clear, but parallels the distinction between early and imperial Rome.[60] Once more, identity and difference are confounded.

The final chapter of the *Germania* is pervaded with an atmosphere of doubt and disbelief. The last tribes of Germany are the Peucini, Veneti, and Fenni, but their status as Germans is questioned almost before they can be described: *Germanis an Sarmatis adscribam dubito* ('I hesitate as to whether I should put them in the category of Germans or Sarmatians', *G.* 46.1). The difficulty of determining German-ness destabilizes the text in two ways, first by undermining the nature of ethnic difference as a whole, and secondly by introducing the possibility that the text has strayed past its own boundaries, which coincide with the boundaries of the country. The Peucini, then, are first assigned to the 'right' side of the German boundary, by virtue of their language, *cultus*, and fixity of dwelling place. Then their

---

[59] Compare Nero's deformation in effigy: *effigiesque in eo Neronis ad informe aes liquefacta* ('and a statue of Nero therein was melted into shapeless bronze', *Ann.* 15.22.2).
[60] Not only the Rome of the younger Agrippina (*Ann.* 12.7.3) but even that of Livia Augusta (*Ann.* 1.10.5).

ethnic identity is blurred by mention of intermarriage with the Sarmatians. The Veneti receive similarly self-contradictory analysis, although in reverse. First they are ascribed Sarmatian qualities, and assigned to a marginal position both geographically (in the mountains) and morally (as thieves). For all that, they are defined as Germans, again because of the fixity of their homes. Interestingly, while the Peucini and Veneti represent ambiguity by combining qualities of both races, the Fenni are neither German nor Sarmatian, and their representation, couched in cumulative negatives, denies them the qualities either of sameness or of difference within the parameters already set up (and problematized) in the rest of the text. The Fenni represent the ultimate in barbarism, but not merely as nomads; the Sarmatians are nomads but, with carts and horses, allowed recognition by the Roman.[61] The Fenni, on the other hand, have nothing. They not only lack fixity but, are almost entirely free of the ability to impose shape (which the Sarmatians implicitly have by their construction of carts). The artefacts of the Fenni are so close to their raw material that they barely merit a change of name (*G.* 46.3–4):

uictui herba, uestitui pelles, cubile humus: solae in sagittis spes, quas inopia ferri ossibus asperant . . . in aliquo ramorum nexu contegantur.

For food they have plants, for clothes, hide, for beds, the ground: their one hope lies in arrows, which they tip with bones, lacking iron . . . they are sheltered by a sort of weaving of branches.

The instability and formlessness of the Fenni symbolizes the inevitable result of the Roman ethnographic search, which has collapsed identity and difference, and here begins to unravel the fabric of the Roman/German social structure, by the representation of a tribe which not only lacks that social structure, but chooses to reject it (*G.* 46.5):

sed beatius arbitrantur quam ingemere agris, inlaborare domibus, suas alienasque fortunas spe metuque uersare: securi aduersus homines, securi aduersus deos rem difficillimam adsecuti sunt, ut illis ne uoto quidem opus esset.

But they think that it is a better existence than to toil in the fields, labour over houses, hang all one's fortunes on hope and fear: safe from men

---

[61] Their similarity to the Scythians of Herodotus makes them a familiar sign of otherness.

and gods, they have achieved something very difficult, that they do not even need to pray.

Cetera iam fabulosa: Hellusios et Oxionas ora hominum uultusque, corpora atque artus ferarum gerere: quod ego ut incompertum in medio relinquam ('the rest is fable: the Hellusi and Oxionae who have the heads and faces of men, and the bodies and limbs of wild beasts: since it is not understood I will leave it there', *G.* 46.6). The fabulous marks the border of the ethnography, as has already been shown in relation to the Ocean and the Pillars of Hercules (*G.* 34.2–3, quoted above). The implication of the end of the monograph is that the text has reached the end of its space. Beyond the boundary the collapse of identity into difference continues, with the semi-bestial humans.[62] But the fabulous, as well as being a barrier, is also a means of reaching Germany; Ulixes discovers Germany on his long and fabulous journey (*longo illo et fabuloso errore*) towards the beginning of the text. The half-human animal is a figure of the same mythological world from which Ulixes emerges. The significance of this has to do with the origins of ethnography, in legend and tales of wonder.[63] The fabulous serves, therefore, as beginning and end, spatially and poetically, locating Germany in the middle, which is where Tacitus leaves it: *in medio relinquam*. In the context of the Roman search for 'Rome' through the text, the final words form the ultimate expression of abandonment, as the seeker finds only the all too familiar and the irremediably strange, which merge into one another and result not only in the failure of understanding (*ut incompertum*) but in its very futility.[64]

---

[62] See esp. Wiedemann (1986).

[63] Discussed in Gabba (1981); Romm (1992); Woodman (1992) [Ch. 13 below].

[64] I am grateful to David Braund, Sue Braund, Debra Hershkowitz, Duncan Kennedy, Charles Martindale, and most especially Catharine Edwards for their helpful criticism and advice during the initial drafting of this article. I am also very grateful to Rhiannon Ash for her help with revising and updating this for reprinting in the present volume.

4

Praise and Doublespeak: Tacitus' *Dialogus*

Shadi Bartsch

As Tacitus' *Dialogue on Orators* launches into the opening exchange between its dramatis personae, the worlds of poetry and oratory come into immediate, if exaggerated, contrast. It is the day after the dialogue's spokesperson for poetry, Curiatius Maternus, has recited his new drama, *Cato*; his interlocutors Marcus Aper and Iulius Secundus, in contrast, are well-known figures from the world of the forum, where their oratory has been the object of both admiration and criticism. Aper asks Maternus in some puzzlement why he would wish to devote himself to writing verse when unlike some poets he has talent enough for the law courts: it is through oratory that he can come to the rescue of friends in danger, terrorize his foes, succour the state, and win widespread fame—and even imperial favour. Maternus responds, however, by painting an idealized world of pastoral serenity in which he can roam as poet, unencumbered by the anxieties of the forum and at a distance from the vicious political intrigues of the day; as for fame, the public recitation of his tragedies has bestowed more upon him than his oratory.[1]

But Maternus' preference for poetry over oratory as the dialogue's first topic of contention should invite us to cast an appraising eye not only at the pretty defence of poetry that constitutes much of

This essay remains much the same as the original but for updated references in the notes. My gratitude is due to Rhiannon Ash for taking on much of this responsibility.

[1] As Levene (2004: 167) points out, 'The implication of both speakers is that the conditions for success in the two genres are so disparate that one cannot effectively obtain success in both.' On the characterization of poetry here, see also Penwill (2003: 124–5).

his response in the debate with Aper but also at his own practice as a dramatist, described in the build-up to this first debate. As the interchange between Maternus and Secundus makes clear, this practice is not pastoral so much as unambiguously political, anti-imperial, and dangerous to its author. In reciting his drama *Cato*, Maternus had offended the emperor and his court (*potentium animos*, 'the feelings of the powerful', *D.* 2.1) and forgotten his own safety (*sui oblitus*, 'forgetful of himself', *D.* 2.1).[2] Secundus expects that this turn of events will spur his friend's fear and perhaps lead to a revision before publication: let Maternus revise his play and publish a *Cato* that will be safer, although perhaps not better. Secundus even hints at a way out of the present predicament: he suggests that Maternus should lay the responsibility for the detection of offensive matter in his drama on those who attended the recitation rather than take it upon himself; let him cut from his work 'anything that supplied material for a *misguided* interpretation', *praua interpretatio* (*D.* 3.2). It is still possible for Maternus to disavow the apparently subversive content of his *Cato*.

Maternus not only rejects this option; he affirms that Aper will recognize in the published version what he heard in the recited one. His meaning is clear: any matter in the *Cato* that has given offence to powerful circles is there by choice. Anything omitted, he promises, will be found in the upcoming *Thyestes*. And even these two plays must take their place among others: Maternus has written a *Domitius* and a *Medea* as well.[3] The titles of these works and the reaction of the imperial court to the recent *Cato* make this much clear: Maternus is writing one play after another dealing with topics well suited to anti-imperial rhetoric; he is 'using tragic themes to reflect dramatically on tyranny and opposition to it; furthermore, it is clear from his offending powerful people that he was expressing in his dramatic tyrants an analogue to the imperial system'.[4] In so doing, he is putting himself at

---

[2] See Güngerich (1980: 10), who notes that *potentium* here designates the emperor and his court, as at Tac. *A.* 6.48.1 and 16.19.3; and also on *sui oblitus*: Maternus has failed to think of the possible consequences of his role for himself. Luce (1993: 23–4 with n. 42) (to whom I am greatly indebted for an advance copy of his article) and Bardon (1953: 174) interpret this passage in the same way. Gowing (2005: 112) stresses that Maternus is thereby virtually becoming Cato and forgetting himself.

[3] For speculation on the relationship of the subject-matter of these tragedies to political developments at Rome under Nero and Vespasian, see Bardon (1956: 215); Frank (1937); Syme (1958a: 104 n. 4).

[4] Williams (1978: 33). The point is widely recognized; see, besides the citations in n. 3 above, Bardon (1953: 174); Heldmann (1982: 256–7); Heubner in Güngerich

some personal risk—yet it is a risk he is fully aware of and even accepts as a duty (*D.* 3.3).

Political drama likewise emerges as Maternus' metier when he replies to Aper in his defence of poetry proper, at least while he remains on the topic of his own career. Aper has warned that in writing a *Cato*, Maternus is courting danger from high places, nor can he shield himself, once offence is taken, with excuses available to those pleading at the bar:

efferuescit enim uis pulcherrimae naturae tuae, nec pro amico aliquo, sed, quod periculosius est, pro Catone offendis. nec excusatur offensa necessitudine officii aut fide aduocationis aut fortuitae et subitae dictionis impetu: meditatus uideris [aut] elegisse personam notabilem et cum auctoritate dicturam. sentio quid responderi possit: hinc ingentis exis<tere> assensus, haec in ipsis auditoriis praecipue laudari et mox omnium sermonibus ferri. tolle igitur quietis et securitatis excusationem, cum tibi sumas aduersarium superiorem.

The force of that fine character of yours boils over in a flash, nor do you offend on behalf of a friend, but on behalf of Cato, which is more dangerous. Nor is your offense excusable by the obligation of doing a service or by the loyalty of an advocate or the inspiration of a chance and sudden phrase; you appear to have deliberately picked a noteworthy character and one whose words would carry weight. I realize what can be said in reply: it is from this that arises huge applause [with Muretus' conjecture *existere*]; it is this that is especially praised in the recitation halls themselves and soon is on everyone's lips. So out with your excuse of wanting quiet and safety, since you take on a more powerful adversary [*aduersarium superiorem*]. (*D.* 10.6–7)

Maternus' recitations are 'more dangerous' than a career at the bar; his dramas may create a stir among the audience, but they also alienate an ominously unnamed *aduersarius superior*, presumably because their content is readily interpretable as oppositional (again, an interpetation Maternus has refused to disavow). Here again appear two familiar features of Maternus' tragedies: their anti-imperial

(1980: 209); Kennedy (1972: 519); Luce (1993: 14 n.15); Michel (1962: 23 n.48); Syme (1958a: 104, 110). However, for a distinction between anti-imperial and anti-tyrannical, see Gallia (2009: 197), who points out that 'within the ideological framework of the early principate, an anti-tyrannical message was not necessarily the same thing as an anti-imperial one'. Obviously, any such argument must remain speculative in the absence of Maternus' plays. Keitel (1995: 275–88) considers Plutarch's deployment of models from tragedy in his *Galba* and *Otho*.

ideology and the consequent risk to the author. But even as he praises the poet's distance from the forum, Maternus' reply to Aper simultaneously confirms the political content and impact of his works and completely ignores the question of his present danger. It is through his dramatic recitations, not his efforts at the bar, that he has won the fame and reputation that Aper would make the reward of oratory alone; and this renown, moreover, has been the fruit of a poetic practice that has been anything but disengaged, for Maternus claims he broke the power of Nero's creature Vatinius through such a recitation.

> *ego autem sicut in causis agendis efficere aliquid et eniti fortasse possum,*
> *ita recitatione tragoediarum et ingredi famam auspicatus sum, cum*
> *quidem in Nerone improbam et studiorum quoque sacra profanantem*
> *Vatinii potentiam fregi, <et> hodie si quid in nobis notitiae ac nominis*
> *est, magis arbitror carminum quam orationum gloria partum.*

But for my part, although I may have the ability to accomplish something, though with effort, in pleading cases, I began to win a reputation through the recitation of tragedies, when I broke Vatinius' unholy power in my play the *Nero* [*in Nerone*]—that power which was violating even the sacred realm of literary studies; and in the present too, if I have any fame and repute at all, I think it has been gained more through the prestige of my poetry than of my oratory. (D. 11.2)[5]

The uncertain state of the text here has spawned debate and divergent conclusions about the chronology and literary locus of Maternus' attack on Vatinius;[6] nonetheless, these few words of the dramatist on his own career firmly establish him as a wielder of political barbs and an engagé whose life bears little similarity to his subsequent portrayal of the poet's secluded existence amidst the woods and glades.

Maternus ends his speech with words that hint ominously at his own death and disgrace. It is after all highly suggestive that Maternus appends to his impassioned defence of poetry a description of the way he does *not* want to die—a risk he has ostensibly avoided by choosing the life of a poet and steering clear of the forum and its dangers.

---

[5] Accepting *in Nerone*, the reading of Furneaux's Oxford text (3rd edn, 1952). The apparatus to lines 21–3 runs as follows: 21 *in Neronem* (*AB*, Gudeman) *imperante Nerone* (L. Müller), 22 *Vatinii* (J. F. Gronovius) *uaticinii* (*codd.*), 23 *et* (*add.* Lips.). For a discussion of the crux, see Kragelund (1987).

[6] See Bartsch (1994: 200–202).

Maternus at *Dialogus* 13.6 notes whimsically that some day his fatal hour too shall fall; may his death not bring with it the risk of imperial confiscation of his legacies; may the statue on his tomb be happy and garlanded, not downcast and grim; and may no one propose a motion in the senate or petition the emperor on behalf of his good name. In other words, Maternus raises the spectre of a series of circumstances that would normally accompany the death of a man whose fall had come through imperial opprobrium or formal condemnation.[7] That Maternus should speak of his death in this way in the context of a dialogue whose dramatic frame rests on his act of literary defiance and the offence it has occasioned suggests that the reader is to see his words as an unwitting prophecy, to fear, perhaps, the worst for his future. As T. J. Luce well concludes, 'The repeated references early in the *Dialogus* to the offense Maternus has given to the powerful and to the concern that his friends express for his safety, and, above all, this highly charged conclusion to his first speech strongly suggest that Maternus soon after met an untimely end.'[8]

Tacitus' contemporary readers may have known of Maternus and his fate for a fact; alternatively, they may have recognized the poet, or perhaps just his untimely end, as a pure figment of the author's imagination. Whichever was the case, for us moderns there can be no such certitude. Students of Tacitus have endowed the Curiatius Maternus of the *Dialogus de Oratoribus* with an array of identities: he is the Maternus who merits brief mention in Dio Cassius 67.12.5 as a 'sophist' put to death by Domitian in AD 91 or 92 for declaiming against tyrants;[9] he is an otherwise unknown poet who met his death

---

[7] Luce (1993: 24 with n.43) interprets *pro memoria mea nec consulat quisquam nec rogat* (*D.* 13.6) as 'should [Maternus] die condemned or under a cloud'. See also Barnes (1986: 238–40).

[8] Luce (1993: 24).

[9] As argued by Matthiessen (1970), with the qualification that Dio was probably mistaken in identifying the cause of death as a declamation; and already in Norden (1898: 324–5). (Norden retracts this view on p. 19 of the *Nachtrage zu S.* 322f in the second edition of 1909.) Barnes (1981) and (1986: 238–44) further identifies the Curiatius Maternus of Dio 67.12.5 with one M. Cornelius Nigrinus Curiatius Maternus, governor of Moesia and Syria, who figures in an inscription from the Spanish town of Liria, published in *AE* (1973: 283). However, the equation of Maternus with Dio's sophist seems to me untenable, and the standard objections to this point of view must prevail. Dio's passage refers to a *scholasticus* (in Greek *sophistes*) practising declamation. However, Maternus has explicitly renounced oratory at *Dialogus* 11.3 and 5.4; and as Bardon (1953: 172–3) observes, 'at the end of the *Dialogus* (chap. 42), Aper opposes Maternus "to the rhetoricians and teachers of declamation", and when

under Vespasian at the hands of the *delatores* ('informers');[10] he is a figure whose fictitious execution Tacitus hints at to serve the larger aims of the *Dialogus*.[11] But whatever the truth about Maternus' ultimately unrecoverable historical identity, the scholarly consensus over his portrayal by Tacitus itself provides the most important feature for our reading: Tacitus, within the bounds of the work, emphasizes Maternus' danger and hints at his death. A further factor contributes to this effect: as argued in particular by Cameron (1967) and Matthiessen (1970: 172ff.), a dialogue hinting at the imminent demise of its principal interlocutor would find numerous literary precedents in which the host or main interlocutor was known to have suffered a premature death shortly after the dramatic date— Socrates in Plato's *Phaedo*, Crassus in Cicero's *De Oratore*, and Scipio Aemilianus in his *De Republica*, to name only a few.[12] Finally, we

Maternus himself retraces his career (chap. 11), he says nothing about a rhetorician's activity.' Luce (1993: 24 n.44) offers agreement and points out further discrepancies: 'The worry repeatedly expressed by his friends seems premature for a death that was to come sixteen or seventeen years later, especially for a man already into middle age, as he seems to be in the *Dialogus*. Dio's language does not suggest to me a poet reciting tragedies but an orator declaiming a speech, an activity which Maternus is represented as renouncing in 75.' (As Syme (1958a: 799) notes, 'It was a little late in the day for Curiatius Maternus to be practicing the art of declamation'.) Moreover, Gudeman in his second edition of the *Dialogus* (1914: 38) notes the existence of some 159 Materni in the epigraphical evidence, among which number two Curiatii Materni who bear manifestly no relation to the poet of the dialogue. For further argument against the identification, see Gudeman's 1914 edition, 67; Güngerich (1955: 443 n.4); Heubner in Güngerich (1980: 199); Stroux (1931: 338); for recent bibliography on the question, see Matthiessen (1970: 171 nn. 8 and 9). Among other scholars who accept the identification, Hartman (1916: 365), who reads the textual variant 'witty', *asteion*, in the place of 'practicing declamation', *askon*, rejects Dio's reason for the death as anti-Domitianic propaganda; while Herrmann (1939) identifies Maternus with the Curiatius of Martial 4.60 and the Maternus of Martial 10.37, 2.74, and 1.96, and claims on this basis that Maternus died in fact a natural death around AD 88.

[10] Thus Cameron (1967); Kennedy (1972: 518); Luce (1993: 19 with n. 44); Martin (1981: 63); Michel (1962: 23); Murgia (1980: 122); Syme (1958a: 110–111); Williams (1978: 34). Köhnken (1973: 41) does not commit himself but emphasizes that Maternus' danger is very real, if we judge by the examples of Arulenus Rusticus, Herennius Senecio, and Cremutius Cordus. For my own suspicions about Maternus' historical identity, see below, note 77.

[11] As suggested by Duret (1986: 3207): 'It is clear that the character in the dialogue consents to the possibility of imminent death with the cheerfulness of Socrates in his prison. It appears more dubious that, historically, Maternus was executed.'

[12] For the comparison to the *De Oratore* and the *De Republica*, see also Michel (1962: 23) and Fantham (2004: 319–26). There is further discussion of the relationship between the *Dialogus* and the *de Oratore* (and ultimately Plato's *Symposium*) in Allison (1999: 479–92). *Contra* see Haß-von Reitzenstein (1970: 37–8), who notes the

should not discount the interest Tacitus shows elsewhere in the unpleasant fates of men whose literary output rubbed a ruler the wrong way, and who, as such, might provide historical parallels or models for Maternus' situation in the *Dialogus;* as Köhnken (1973: 41) observes, the danger that Maternus knowingly incurs with his dramatic recitations can be set beside the condemnation and death of Arulenus Rusticus and Herennius Senecio for their writings in Tacitus' *Agricola*, 2.1. Indeed, Tacitus sometimes magnifies the role that the victims' literary production has played in ensuring their punishment, as if to underline a connection between their writings and their ruin that, historically speaking, was less significant than he would have it. A notable example is his description in the *Annals* (4.34) of the prosecution of Cremutius Cordus in AD 25: Tacitus reports only that Cremutius was arraigned *nouo ac tunc primum audito crimine, quod editis annalibus laudatoque M. Bruto C. Cassium Romanorum ultimum dixisset,* 'on a new charge, heard then for the first time: that he had published a history in which he praised M. Brutus and called C. Cassius the last of the Romans' (*A.* 4.34.1); but as Ronald Syme remarks, 'Cremutius' writings were not the sole, or even the main charge against him.'[13] Similarly, it is Mamercus Aemilius Scaurus' tragic drama that is proffered as the real reason for his fall in AD 35 (*A.* 6.29.3), although Tacitus notes that the charges brought against him publicly were adultery with Tiberius' niece Livilla and the practice of magic rites. So too, reading the *Dialogus*, we come away with the impression that it is Maternus' poetry that has sealed his fate, presumably at the hands of the *maligni* and the *fabulae* they will carry to the ears of Vespasian.

This dramatic setting lays the foundation for a series of strange contradictions in the figure of Maternus. We may recall that the Cremutius of Tacitus' *Annals*, defending the praise of Brutus and

---

parallels but thinks they have little meaning for Maternus' situation. On the other hand, Matthiessen (1970: 172–6) accepts the identification with Dio's Maternus and argues that the late death of the principal, as well as the content of the Aper–Maternus debate, is modelled on Plato's *Gorgias,* with Aper as Callicles and Maternus as Socrates. On links to the *Gorgias* see also Häussler (1969: 65 n.2 with bibliography); and Egermann (1935: 424–30).

[13] Syme (1958a: 337 n.10). Syme adduces the testimony of Seneca, *Consolatio ad Marciam* 1.2ff; 22.4, and cites Rogers (1935: 86f.). See also Bartsch (1994: 243 n.50) and the detailed analysis of Moles (1998).

Cassius that supposedly procured his prosecution in AD 25, delivers a speech to the senate in which he denies that he has violated the *lex maiestatis* ('law of treason') and laments the death of freedom of speech (*A.* 4.35.1), finally forestalling his sentence by commiting suicide. Maternus, however, who seems to be similarly at risk for *his* work about yet another republican-hero-*cum*-ideological-figurehead—Cato—uses his second and closing speech in this dialogue to praise the political conditions of the present and the emperor himself even as he outlines in it his own reasons for the decline of contemporary oratory. And this second speech clashes not only with the implicit stance that must belong to any author of a *Cato* but also with the explicit content of Maternus' first speech in defence of poetry. These contradictions, long an obstacle to a complete under-standing of the *Dialogus*, are not to be decried or eliminated through compromise. Rather, they function as signposts for readers of the *Dialogus*; pinpointing attention upon themselves, they establish their own clash as the locus of meaning, while the figure of Maternus, poet and dissident encomiast, serves as the alembic from which this mean-ing emerges.

These contradictions inherent in Maternus' doings and sayings have been so labelled according to differing notions of what in fact constitutes a contradiction, but on certain points the discomfort has been pervasive. Apart from the problem of why the author of (dangerously) pro-republican plays would deliver a speech in praise of Vespasian and his regime in the first place, scholars have been particularly struck by the discrepancy in the two views of contem-porary political life that emerge from Maternus' first and second speeches in the *Dialogus*.[14] Justifying in the first his decision to abandon court oratory, Maternus describes the eloquence of the present day as stained with the blood of its victims, greedy for gain, a weapon used for the offence only. As he puts it, *nam lucrosae huius et sanguinantis eloquentiae usus recens et ex malis moribus natus atque, ut tu dicebas, Aper, in locum teli repertus*, 'The employment

---

[14] In what follows I am particularly indebted to Luce (1993), who offers the best analysis to date of the internal contradictions of the *Dialogus* (our conclusions, however, will differ considerably), and also to discussions such as those of Heldmann (1982) and Williams (1978: 33–4). The issue of these contradictions is much-travelled ground in the scholarship on the *Dialogus;* I offer here only another summation of problems long since identified.

of this profitable and bloodstained eloquence is a recent one, arising from men's evil natures, and, as you yourself were saying, Aper, it has been developed for use as a weapon' (*D.* 12.2).[15] Moreover, those who use it—such as the Crispus and Marcellus whom Aper has offered as the models of success—are themselves no better than slaves; although they are objects of fear to their victims, they live in fear for their own lives, and their vaunted power is precarious and little better than that of the imperial freedmen (*D.* 13.4).

Maternus never applies the term to the men he so describes, but these model orators of the present day are readily recognizable as the *delatores* ('informers') whose access to the emperor's ear culminated in the death of their senatorial victims.[16] Aper had picked out two for special praise, Vibius Crispus and Eprius Marcellus. Both, he noted, had risen from obscurity to immense wealth and renown, though originally pre-eminent neither in birth nor in fortune nor even (as he adds perhaps gratuitously) in moral character; now, however, they are chief among the emperor's friends and can obtain whatever they want (*D.* 8.3). So Aper describes contemporary oratory as the province of the informers, and the emperor as in their debt—nor, as it seems, was he exaggerating. As Winterbottom observes wryly of Aper's selected pair, 'Marcellus became proconsul of Asia, for three years, then, for a second time, consul, in 74. Vibius Crispus governed Africa and Tarraconensis, besides his *cura aquarum . . .* The *delatores* were now not merely powerful—they had long been that. Now they were positively members of the Establishment.'[17]

---

[15] Gallia (2009: 176) discusses the significance of Tacitus' continued use of military idioms in the *Dialogus*.

[16] See Luce (1993: 22 with n.34); Winterbottom (1964: 90–94); as Winterbottom remarks (90), 'Aper denies that oratorical glory is, in fact, dead. His main examples are Eprius Marcellus and Vibius Crispus (8.1). The choice is significant. For the outstanding fact about first-century oratory is that the only orators to achieve any prominence or influence *by means of their oratory* are the *delatores*. The rest were decorative but impotent.' Aper himself is described by Tacitus in terms not unlike those used for the *delatores* and their oratory; see Syme (1958a: 109 with n.4), and Winterbottom (1964: 94); see also Michel (1962: 38ff.). For a general study of the imperial informants, see Rutledge (2001).

[17] Winterbottom (1964: 93). Compare Tac. *H.* 2.95.3. On the careers of these two see also Brink (1989), 496; Güngerich (1980 21, 28); Syme (1958a: 594–5). For a different perspective, see Goldberg (1999) [Ch. 5 below], who not only comes to the defence of Crispus and Marcellus, but also finds Maternus' repudiation of public oratory a dubious moral stance. As he argues (1999: 230), 'The rash of senatorial prosecutions that we associate with the delators may well have been distasteful to a man

How is it, then, that in his second speech Maternus presents an entirely different picture of the contemporary political situation that he criticized in the first? Maternus here claims that what little forensic activity is still going on is merely a sign that the state is a step or two short of perfection: orators are still sometimes needed to represent the guilty and the oppressed; towns still need protection from aggression and civil strife; provinces may still be defrauded (*D*. 41.1–2). But the distance to the ideal state is but a short one, since, as Maternus asks, *quid enim opus est longis in senatu sententiis, cum optimi cito consentiant? quid multis apud populum contionibus, cum de re publica non imperiti et multi deliberent sed sapientissimus et unus? quid uoluntariis accusationibus, cum tam raro et tam parce peccetur?*, 'What need is there of long deliberations in the senate, when the best citizens quickly come to an agreement? What need of many speeches before the people, when it is not the ignorant masses who deliberate on state matters, but one man who is wisest of all? What need of prosecutions voluntarily undertaken, when crimes are so infrequent and so trivial?' (*D*. 41.4). We are far indeed here from the vision of a bloodstained oratory run amok that pervaded the debate with Aper;[18] the small scope for eloquence that Maternus now grants has nothing to do with the informers or their activity, and the present has changed from a time of horror to a time of near-idyllic peace.[19] And what of the figure of Vespasian himself? The man whom Aper describes as full of affection and even reverence for his friends Marcellus and Crispus (*D*. 8.3), Maternus here characterizes as *sapientissimus et unus*, the 'one man who is wisest of all', who single-handedly guides the state's policy and shows clemency in the courts. In light of the first speech, the second one takes on a peculiar tint, and it is difficult not to feel, with Townend, that 'the apparent

---

like Maternus, but such distaste does not justify abandoning the legitimate needs of clients and friends.' Despite Aper's taste in oratory Champion (1994: 152–63) argues against a wholly negative assessment of his character.

[18] Heldmann (1982: 283) draws attention to the contrast between bad and good character (*mali mores* and *boni mores*), the one emphasized at *D*. 12.2, the other at 41.3.

[19] Luce (1993: 22) focuses on this contradiction: how odd that 'in his final speech [Maternus] characterizes the political climate of the present day as one of peace, security, and good order'. As he goes on to point out, the peculiarities here are heightened by Tacitus' anti-imperial stance in his own works: 'Contrast, too, this rosy picture with Tacitus' unfavorable estimate of so many aspects of the principate in his historical writings.'

praise of Vespasian in *Dialogus* 41.4, as *sapientissimus et unus*, is robbed of almost all its effect by the frank admission in chapter 8 of the same work of the political prominence of Eprius Marcellus and Vibius Crispus, and their abuse of power despite their questionable characters'.[20]

As if to highlight the peculiar nature of such praise from the mouth of Maternus—that author of a *Cato*—and to cause still more readerly trepidation on behalf of the poet, Tacitus' Aper chooses to demonstrate the power of modern eloquence by recalling to his audience Marcellus' oratorical successes—despite the animosity of the senate—against the attacks of the Stoic philosopher Helvidius Priscus. *quid aliud infestis patribus nuper Eprius Marcellus quam eloquentiam suam opposuit, qua accinctus et minax disertam quidem, sed inexercitatam et eius modi certaminum rudem Helvidii sapientiam elusit?* 'What other than his eloquence did Eprius Marcellus recently wield against the hostile senators, when, fierce and ready for battle, he foiled Helvidius' philosophical wisdom—eloquent, to be sure, but unpracticed and inexperienced in that sort of confrontation?' (*D.* 5.7). Aper refers here to the events of AD 70 and the early days of Vespasian's principate, when a welling of senatorial indignation against the *delatores* ('informers') encouraged Helvidius to take up a daring but useless attack on Marcellus—useless, because the next meeting of the senate brought gentle but sinister reprimands by Vespasian and Licinius Mucianus that put a sudden end to this brief flowering of free speech. Such at any rate is Tacitus' account of the matter at *H.* 4.43–44 (see especially 4.44.1).[21] The significance of this incident for Maternus' poetic activity emerges from two crucial facts. For one, the Stoic Helvidius, as Tacitus' readers would know, had deliberately assumed the mantle of the younger Cato and the republican martyr's ideological stance—indeed, the Marcellus of the *Histories* calls him a *rediuiuus* Cato to his face.[22] And second, as Tacitus' readers would

---

[20] Townend (1973: 152).

[21] On the attack (disarmed in part by Mucianus' threatening wielding of the *S.C. Turpilianum*), see Levick (1999: 85). Wardle (1996: 208–22) talks (210) in terms of a 'power-struggle' between Vespasian and Helvidius, focused particularly on the restoration of the Capitol.

[22] At *H.* 4.8.3 Tacitus has Marcellus link Helvidius and Cato during a quarrel (occurring earlier, in AD 70) about the selection of envoys to be sent to Vespasian: Marcellus sneers in the senate, *denique constantia fortitudine Catonibus et Brutis aequaretur Heluidius: se unum esse ex illo senatu, qui simul seruierit*, 'Helvidius may

also be aware, Helvidius' exile and death occurred at approximately the dramatic date of the *Dialogus* itself.[23] Maternus' play about the Stoic hero Cato comes at a time when Cato's chief emulator is suffering, or has suffered, the penalty for his principles, and this at the hands of the emperor whom Maternus himself has offended and through the *delatores* ('informers') whose power he deplores.[24] As readers we are induced to recall Helvidius' death for his outspokenness, to see parallels in Maternus' behaviour, and to wonder perhaps at the content of the *Cato*—was it a response to, and a commemoration of, Helvidius' lot, clad in the guise of historical tragedy?[25]

Likewise provocative is Maternus' attitude toward the fallen Republic as he expresses it in his closing comments. Along with his praise for the present regime and the peace, order, and moral probity it stands for, Maternus decries the folly of the old order even as he acknowledges that it provided the conditions necessary for the flourishing of a great oratory. Fame and tranquillity cannot both come to citizens of the self-same epoch (*D.* 41.5), and the glory won by oratorical skill and influence, he claims, was possible only in the turbulent times of the republic: *non de otiosa et quieta re loquimur et quae probitate et modestia gaudeat, sed est magna illa et notabilis eloquentia alumna licentiae, quam stulti libertatem uocant, comes seditionum, effrenati populi incitamentum, sine obsequio, sine seueritate, contumax, temeraria, arrogans, quae in bene consitutis*

---

rival the Catos and the Bruti in resolution and bravery; I am only one man in this senate, which serves the emperor in tandem.' I hope no one will protest that Tacitus' rendition of these events in the *Histories* is marked by personal bias or distortion. Of course it is—and that is why it is a useful tool for understanding the more oblique viewpoint of the same author's *Dialogus*. See Michel (1962: 92) on Marcellus and Helvidius at *H.* 4.6ff., noting the similarities.

[23] As Michel (1962: 40) notes, 'The orator evokes the recent setback of the Stoic Helvidius Priscus, who had attacked the delator Eprius Marcellus . . . Through the *Histories,* we know of the debate which set Marcellus and Priscus in opposition . . . We have pointed out that the *Dialogus* is situated by its author in a time very close to the downfall of this hero, and in a setting of senators who admire him.' See also Heldmann (1982: 268); Martin (1981: 60).

[24] On Helvidius' downfall in AD 74 or 75, see Dio 65.12.2 and Suet. *Vesp.* 15.

[25] On this probability see Heldmann (1982: 268); Michel (1962: 24 n.53); Syme (1958a: 104 n.4, 211–12). On the importance of the dramatic date for our understanding of Maternus' danger, see Williams (1978: 34): 'The date AD 75 was certainly chosen by Tacitus because of the proximity of the exile and death of Helvidius Priscus, the first really sinister sign in the new regime. The reader has a nagging sense of dramatic irony in the contrast between Maternus' equanimity, even complacency, and the worries of his friends on his behalf.'

ciuitatibus non oritur, 'We are not discussing a leisured and peaceful activity and one which takes pleasure in morality and modesty; no, that great and noteworthy eloquence is the foster child of licence (which stupid men call freedom); it is the companion of sedition, the goad of a frenzied populace, a thing without deference, without discipline, brazen, rash, arrogant, which does not arise in well-ordered states' (*D*. 40.2). As is well known, Maternus here offers his interlocutors a slightly modified quotation from Cicero's *Brutus*.[26] Where Maternus maintains that eloquence is *alumna licentiae, quam stulti libertatem uocant*, 'the foster child of licence, which stupid men call freedom' (a reference to the political conditions of the republic), and that it *in bene constitutis ciuitatibus non oritur*, 'does not arise in well-ordered states', Cicero had claimed that eloquence is *pacis est comes otique socia et iam bene constitutae ciuitatis quasi alumna quaedam*, 'the companion of peace and leisure and the foster child, so to speak, of a well-ordered state' (*Brutus* 45)—precisely the situation that Maternus identifies as fatal for great oratory.[27] So it would seem that Cicero links eloquence to peace, Maternus to discord. It is a contradiction, however, that goes no deeper than the surface, for both Maternus and Cicero are agreed on one crucial fact:[28] great oratory goes hand in hand with conditions of political freedom (be it named

[26] On the relationship between the *Dialogus* and the *Brutus* see, most recently, Gowing (2005: 111–12) and Levene (2004: 191–3).

[27] On the verbal parallels, see e.g. Bringmann (1970: 171–4); Caplan (1944: 318 n. 21); Güngerich (1980: 176–7); Koestermann (1930: 415–21); Luce (1993: 26 n. 52); Martin (1981: 63–4). As these commentators note, Maternus is also evoking *De Oratore* 2.35, where Antonius praises the power of the orator to guide state policy, both stir and calm the people, and see that justice runs its course, while Maternus focuses only on the orator's role as a *effrenati populi incitamentum*, 'goad of a frenzied populace'. On this difference, see Michel (1962: 54–5). On parallels between Maternus' stance here and that of the anonymous philosopher in Longinus' *On the Sublime*, see Bartsch (1994: 203–6).

[28] Caplan (1944: 318) observes, 'Cicero's thought is not necessarily in conflict with that of Tacitus' interlocutor. Cicero is thinking of freedom from foreign wars, and his "well-regulated civic order" is opposed not to a state torn by dissensions, but to one whose institutions have not yet been firmly established.' But the point to be emphasized here is that Cicero is referring, naturally enough, to the Republic. It is interesting that Luce (1993: 26 n.52) rejects Caplan's statement as 'controverted by the facts and by the language'. The disagreement here must arise from a confusion over just what we designate as Cicero's basic 'thought'—that eloquence is the companion of peace (against Maternus), or that eloquence flourishes under a republican (or democratic) constitution (with Maternus). Most of the commentators emphasize the former and hence dwell on the dissimilitude of the two—Maternus' assertion 'is phrased in words deliberately chosen to contradict Cicero' (Martin 1981: 63).

peace or discord) and flourishes in the absence of absolute rule; Cicero's subjects here are nothing other than the Greek democracy and, in close parallel, the Roman Republic.[29] Why then should Maternus, or rather Tacitus, evoke this particular dictum of Cicero to buttress his point, given that those who recall Cicero's actual words will have to untangle what is apparently a confusing contradiction?[30] Surely because the reader will recall precisely this: that *Cicero's* 'well-ordered state' encompasses the Republic that Maternus faults for the opposite quality even as he appropriates Cicero's exact words (*bene constituta ciuitas*, 'a well-ordered state') to refer now, not to the Republic, but to the empire.[31] Maternus' description of Vespasian's regime comes in the borrowed language of Cicero's praise of the Republic, even as our poet repeats the apparent content of Cicero's association of freedom and eloquence. In short, Maternus' critique of freedom is a statement whose foundation rests on a view that radically denies the disjunction between liberty and order. Is Cicero then to be numbered, we ask, among the *stulti* ('stupid')?—a question that

---

[29] In the immediate context of the quotation from *Brutus* 45, Cicero is speaking of the development of the democracy at Athens, but the whole *Brutus* addresses the great orators of the Roman Republic from its inception to a period about ten years before the dramatic date of 46 BC, and Cicero thinks of Latin eloquence as reaching its apex during the decades before and up to his own day. Thus L. Licinius Crassus, familiar to us from the *De Oratore*, is twice referred to as the most accomplished of the orators of the recent past (*Brutus* 143, 296); for the present, we hear at *Brutus* 6 that Hortensius' death has saved him from seeing the Roman forum robbed of his eloquence, which was worthy of both Rome and Greece, by Julius Caesar's dictatorship. And of course Cicero's oratory had itself reached its peak in those better days of the Republic, which Cicero explicitly identifies as being, at that time, *bene moratae et bene consitutae ciuitatis*, 'a state with good morals and a good constitution' (*Brutus* 7). So here too is a precedent for Maternus' quotation, and one that links republican tranquillity to excellence in oratory. (On Cicero's own perfection, see *Brutus* 8 and Atticus' flattery in 296; also 321–2.) Note that Antonius in the *De Oratore* 2.33 says exactly the same thing with reference to the Roman Republic of his own day (the dramatic date is 91 BC); he describes the actual practice of oratory as *qui in omni pacata et libera ciuitate dominator*, 'that which holds sway in every peaceful and free state'. And Crassus likewise at *De Oratore* 1.30 observes that *haec una res in omni libero populo maximeque in pacatis tranquillisque ciuitatibus praecipue semper floruit semperque dominata est*, 'this one art has always thrived and always held sway among all free people, and most of all in peaceful and quiet states in particular'. See also Caplan (1944: 318).

[30] Güngerich (1980: 176) notes that Tacitus takes over the two Ciceronian passages with a reversal of meaning that is all the more striking for its lexical similarities.

[31] Köhnken (1973: 47) argues that Maternus refers only to the *final* years of the Republic in his critique, and so his comments on licence and disorder are to be taken at face value, if not his praise of the present regime. But Maternus criticizes the Gracchi too, at *D.* 40.4.

serves to render our acceptance of the surface meaning somewhat vulnerable to doubt. And the plot thickens: in drawing on the *Brutus*, Tacitus deploys a work that is framed by its author's lament over the lost opportunities for eloquence that have attended Julius Caesar's dictatorship at Rome.[32] It is a work in which Cicero openly mourns the death of Roman oratory since the passing of republican liberty—a liberty [which], we might say, the oppressed call licence.[33]

Is Maternus, then, sincere in his praise of a civic order that has stripped eloquence of its potential? His next comments make such a unitary reading virtually impossible. For he continues in his praise of Vespasian's principate by drawing an analogy with the political systems of Sparta, Crete, Macedonia, and Persia; eloquence, he says, was unknown in these states too, as indeed in any that was content with an established sovereignty (or a 'settled government'; the Latin is carefully ambiguous: *quae certo imperio contenta fuerit*, 'which was content with a settled government', *D*. 40.3). And yet, if anything, a Roman *princeps* would prefer to *dissociate* his regime from states mostly synonymous with despotism, so that Heldmann, for example, claims that this passage necessarily functions as a critique of the principate, and it is hard to recognize as such only because it is placed in the context of an ironic panegyric.[34] Other aspects of Maternus' behaviour have provoked similar conclusions about irony. In the same speech, he comments that the present is a time when oratory can have little scope because people have moral characters, willing to serve the ruler (*bonos mores et in obsequium regentis paratos*, 'well-behaved and ready to obey their rulers', *D*. 41.3); and yet this is strange praise from an author of a subversive drama about that

---

[32] Brutus' career too, says Cicero, has been thwarted by the dismal fate of the republic (*Brutus* 331), a time when *eloquentia obmutuit*, 'eloquence has fallen mute' (*Brutus* 22). And compare also *Brutus* 9, referring to orators who could use their skills freely when the republic was not undermined by the likes of a Julius Caesar.

[33] I believe that by this appropriation and alteration of Cicero's original statement, Tacitus is letting us uncover the way in which 'the language of false political reality moves in order to mask the truth, [as] epitomized by Orwell's "war is peace; freedom is slavery"'—just as he does more overtly at *Agr.* 30.4, where he has the Briton Calgacus comment of the Romans that 'where they make devastation, they call it peace' (discussed by Plass 1988: 44). See similarly Petillius Cerialis' speech at *Hist.* 4.73.2.

[34] Heldmann (1982: 281); see Martin (1981: 64).

rebel Cato, even if we dilute *obsequium* to the most innocuous of its meanings, from 'servility' to 'deference'.[35]

In any case it seems that freedom, which Maternus calls licence in his final speech, is gone; and earlier in the *Dialogus* he is less reticent about naming the same word in more favourable terms, albeit narrowed to its sense of freedom of speech,[36] and calling its loss a sign of degeneration. Asking Messalla to continue with his reasons for the decline of eloquence, he boldly bids him to *utere antiqua libertate, a qua uel magis degenerauimus quam ab eloquentia*, 'use that old-time freedom from which we have degenerated even more than from eloquence' (*D.* 27.3). This injunction too could provide a striking enough comment on the oppressive climate of Vespasian's principate.[37] In short, by problematizing the relation of this final eulogy to

---

[35] Williams (1978: 41 with n.81), argues against this reading, emphasizing the phrase *bonos mores* and downplaying the interpretation of Köhnken (1973: 49); in Williams' view, 'it is wrong to treat that last phrase . . . as equivalent to *seruitium* and refer to Maternus' words in 13.4, where he characterizes *delatores* like Eprius Marcellus as "insufficiently servile in the views of their masters but insufficiently free in ours". Many points of view are possible on freedom: one when you think of sensible political behaviour, another when you think of extremists.' But this is not very convincing unless one has already accepted his view of Maternus' last speech as referring to the conditions of AD 102. See below, n.42. Williams takes the same stance on Maternus' adaptation of Cicero's views from the *Brutus*; citing *D* 40.2, he comments (41) that Maternus 'refers to extreme republicans, among them the Stoic opposition for whose political sense Tacitus sometimes showed scant respect'. But Maternus seems to be referring rather to the republican constitution itself (as suggested by *nostra quoque ciuitas, donec errauit*, 'our state too, as long as the constitution was unsettled', *D.* 40.4), and the conditions he describes at 40.4 disappear only with the establishment of the principate, which he himself has claimed brings with it respect for authority, harmony in the senate, peace in the forum, etc. In any case, can we really say of Cicero, whose case Maternus brings up in *D.* 40.4, that he falls into the category of an 'extreme republican' as we might, for example, of the Gracchi? Note that on *Dialogus* 13.4, Winterbottom (1999: 338) tentatively suggests adding *metu tum* between *cum* and *adulatione*.

[36] Not sufficient reason, as Williams (1978: 41 with n.83) claims yet again, to downplay the incendiary quality of this comment by translating it as 'the freedom to speak freely' rather than 'freedom of speech'—i.e. by translating it in a sense 'limited by social convention as well as by imperial censorship' and thus removing its barb.

[37] Williams (1978: 33) identifies this statement as the source of another of the *Dialogus*' internal contradictions: although Maternus 'makes the point that *libertas* in the sense of "freedom of speech" is inconsistent with strong central government', this view 'takes not the slightest account of Maternus' own activity' as playwright. But implicit criticism of the regime in a historical drama is not the same thing as freedom of speech, and in any case an outspokenness that brings down upon its head the danger that his friends fear for Maternus is not in fact freedom of speech, but rather its opposite.

the rest of the dialogue in the ways laid out above, Tacitus effectively destabilizes its content:[38] we find suddenly and necessarily foregrounded at this moment of praise the question of Maternus' sincerity. Quite simply, Maternus appears to be mouthing an encomium in which he *may* be ironic, given his characterization in what has preceded and given, too, the dramatic frame of the work.

One course of argument at this point is to explain away the difficulty by positing solutions of varying credibility.[39] We (and the original audience) could ascribe these contradictions not to irony but to the riven soul of the poet, torn between a longing for the artistic and political freedom of the Republic and an appreciation of the peace of the present;[40] to the riven soul of the historian, split along approximately the same fault line;[41] to the author's incorporation of two different historical periods into a single dialogue, so that

---

[38] I cannot agree with the position of Williams (1978: 40): 'The degree of this contradiction can be (and often is) exaggerated and Maternus' speech therefore interpreted as deeply ironic. The degree of contradiction needs careful definition. It is less than it seems, for Maternus is speaking about oratory (not any other branch of literature), he is speaking to men who consider themselves orators, and he is speaking in the character of a poet who has been urged to return to oratory. From this point of view, society and politics exhibit certain characteristics that Maternus himself may well regret (and attack) but that are not only valued by most people but are most relevant to the condition of oratory: these are peace, security, and obedience on the part of the governed.' This does not address the problems we have been considering here (the issue of the informers, for example—although Williams can always say that this is a feature of the dramatic date of AD 75 and not of the time of Maternus' last speech, supposedly AD 102). Moreover, the distinction between poetry and oratory in this dialogue is not so clear-cut as Williams would have it, as even he concedes later (47): 'Aper made a very important point when he defined *eloquentia* (10) as a concept wide enough to accommodate any and every kind of literature...[The concept] opens the way, in fact, for Maternus to assert an equally proper, but entirely different, sense of values, embodied in a quite different literary activity.' See below, n.61.

[39] The best discussion of the scholarship on this question is in Luce (1993: 22-5).

[40] The principal suscribers to this theory of a 'Zwiespalt in Denken und Fuhlen', or split between heart and intellect, in Maternus are Keyssner (1936: 104, with further bibliography), and Klingner (1932). Klingner (1932: 153-4) does acknowledge that Maternus, who makes no mention in his last speech of words like *gloria*, *libertas*, and *uirtus*, 'cannot speak out his whole conviction and less still that of Tacitus'. But for Klingner this is a function of Maternus'—and Tacitus'—recognition that it is impossible to reconcile the 'Antinomic' between the values of republic and empire. See similarly Barwick (1954: 27). Heubner in Güngerich (1980: 208) objects with justification that this view is not supported by Tacitus' portrayal of the self-assured and courageous Maternus.

[41] Along with the scholars of n. 40 above, see Häussler (1969: 194-6 with n.8), who distributes the 'real' Tacitus among the three interlocutors, each of whom represents an aspect of his viewpoint but not its totality. Luce (1993: 24-5) has a good discussion

Maternus' pair of speeches describe respectively the conditions of AD 75 and AD 102;[42] or to the nature of the dialogue form itself, with its eristic paired debates that are not meant to be evaluated in terms of comprehensive consistency.[43] The third of these suggestions has been dismantled by the proponent of the fourth (see n.42); this solution in turn, while it has the advantage of respecting the limits of the text and steering clear of the psychoanalytic speculation common to the first two, still leaves unanswered the problem of Maternus' situation as portrayed in the dialogue's setting. Let us grant that

of the 'split consciousness' interpretation of the work, which consists of the first two positions mentioned in the text. His own approach is to subdivide these into theories about the 'psychological factor' ('the conflicted and conflicting facets of Tacitus' own personality are mirrored in the opposing interlocutors and the opposing arguments') and the 'ambivalence factor' (citing Goodyear 1970b: 16 as an example: Tacitus 'wavers between nostalgia for the past and realistic acceptance of the present').

[42] This is the argument of Williams (1978: 35), who suggests that 'Maternus' final speech reflects the political situation of about AD 102, and the terms of his analysis are close to those that Tacitus himself uses when he speaks in other works of the period at which he was writing—i.e. the time of Trajan. Aper's speech, in contrast, is directed to setting the oratory of his own particular time in a historical framework extending from Cicero's time to AD 75,' a temporal disjunction highlighted by the attention paid to the *delatores* in the early part of the dialogue versus their absence from Maternus' final speech. But Williams' analysis, which rests largely on the claim (37) that references to the dramatic date of AD 75 occur only in the first section of the work and before *D.* 15, is effectively refuted by Luce (1993: 22–3), who demonstrates that Maternus' reference to the literary output of one Licinius Mucianus as late as *D.* 37.2 must fix this final speech in the 70s and not in AD 102. Moreover, Williams' analysis falls apart on entirely different grounds if we accept the dating of the *Dialogus* to the reign of Nerva rather than that of Trajan, as we must, I think, after the canny analyses of Murgia (1980) and (1985). For further arguments against Williams' position, see also Murgia (1980: 118, 122). Beck (2001: 159–71) also argues for AD 75.

[43] Thus Luce (1993), 26–38, in an astute and meticulous article whose strong arguments, to my mind, do not quite clear away all the cobwebs. Luce would suggest (33) that 'the concentration by scholars on the individuals in the *Dialogus* has created much needless confusion because of the twentieth-century assumption that, in order for each interlocutor to be consistently characterized, the arguments given to him must be consistent also. The characters are indeed "consistent", but in ancient, not modern, terms. By training, habit, and volition the speakers aim to present the strongest case they can for a particular point of view. This results in what moderns perceive to be exaggeration and contradictions, but what the ancients would have regarded as a natural and obligatory result for any speaker worth his salt. Thus, when Maternus gives two quite dissimilar pictures of contemporary public life, the differences are due chiefly—probably wholly—to the different rhetorical aims of his two speeches.' I can agree that the reader is to draw her own conclusions from the contradictions inherent in each debate, but it seems to me that Tacitus has 'stacked the deck' to influence our reading. The hints about Maternus' death are hardly conducive to a purely rhetorical understanding of his two speeches.

the interlocutors make the strongest possible argument for their respective positions, even if this eventually involves them in self-contradiction; the fact remains that *Maternus is in danger for his literary outspokenness*, that this danger is not dependent on the context of the paired debates, and that it is this same Maternus whose fulsome encomium of the present regime in the last debate brings the dialogue to a close. In short, we can do nothing to mitigate the fact that Tacitus ascribes this praise to the one character from whose mouth it will have the least credibility.

So it seems we must abandon the one assumption common to all these explanations: that Maternus speaks with what can be understood *only* as an essential sincerity, even if (as the first two views would have it) his perspective is complicated by an element of personal confusion and nostalgia for the past.[44] This compels us to include *as an equally valid interpretive option* the insincerity of the last speech—indeed, an option Maternus himself encourages us to adopt when he announces at *D.* 27.3, some time before launching into his effusive speech on the present emperor, that the old freedom of speech is dead. For if freedom of speech is dead, what is left but a kind of speech that conforms to external political exigencies? However, to ask the simple question—is Maternus sincere or not?—is to ask the wrong question. It is true that to read Maternus' praise of the principate as insincere is an approach that has found a number of adherents in recent German scholarship, where it is generally treated under the rubric of his *irony*; as most notably argued by Köhnken (1973), the problems posed by Maternus' curious blend of anti-imperial and pro-imperial stances, together with the aforementioned

---

[44] So also Winterbottom (1964: 97 n.29), who calls Maternus' encomium of Vespasian and the principate 'wistful' and observes that 'Maternus' final speech, filled with the vague nostalgia of the early Trajanic period, dispels the different optimisms of Aper and Messalla'. Goodyear (1970b: 66) thinks Maternus is sincere but somewhat blind to his own situation. Luce (1993: 22) draws attention to Reitzenstein (1915), who argues that at the time of the composition of the *Dialogus* Tacitus felt an optimism about the principate, reflected in Maternus' second speech, that left him in his later years. Flach (1973: 205–7) claims that Maternus' picture of the principate represents an ideal, not the present situation, and so he is not being ironic (however, Maternus' picture of the present in his last speech is glowing enough to disarm this view). Finally, Maternus' sincerity is taken for granted by a large field of scholars who do not discuss the issue *per se*: see e.g. Bardon (1940: 380); Barnes (1986); Barwick (1954: 18–21); Bringmann (1970: 173ff.); Brink (1989: 496–7); Haß-von Reitzenstein (1970: 154–5).

comment on the degeneracy of contemporary freedom of speech, encourage us to read his praise as ironic—a dispraise only half-hidden by its veil of words. Köhnken would therefore urge that 'Maternus is neither a "hypocrite" nor a "hair-splitting dialectician"... Rather, the hearer must understand, on the basis of the context and the characterization of Maternus in the *Dialogus,* that a praise of the principate that comes from him can only be meant ironically.'[45] Similarly, but with a slightly different emphasis, Matthiessen argues that the intimations of Maternus' death in the work and the evidence of the continuing influence of Nero's informers under Vespasian give a bitterly ironic undertone to his final speech.[46] This focus on Maternus' irony, or even his sarcasm, is common also to the subsequent work of Heldmann and Heubner, who argue with their predecessors that Maternus' praise can be read only as its own opposite.[47]

But if this is viable as the only reading pressed upon us by the text's own contradictions, what of the effect of Maternus' epiphany as an oily-tongued ironist at the end of the dialogue in which he has made so clear his reservations about the abuses of power and privilege endemic in his day, and in which we hear he recited his *Cato* with a single-mindedness that was oblivious to considerations of personal safety? There are several answers here, all pointing to a context broader than simple irony. For one, Maternus' praise now becomes a praise that simultaneously reveals something about the conditions of its own production: we see that it is precisely the inconsistencies

---

[45] Köhnken (1973: 46), responding to the two choices (hypocrite, hair-splitter) 'which Klingner seems to presume are the only alternatives to the explanation he proposes'.

[46] Matthiessen (1970: 177): 'In the dialogue Nero's rule is still all too much in everyone's memory, and his creatures like Vibius Crispus and Eprius Marcellus are still too influential, for us to be able to take Maternus' hymn of praise to the present-day system of government at face value.'

[47] See Heldmann (1982: 383), and Heubner in Güngerich (1980: 208), who has dismissed the other possibilities to state his support for Köhnken. Even Williams (1978: 41–2) must acknowledge the strange effect of Maternus' praise, although his explanation for its existence cannot be accepted: 'There is nevertheless an element of exaggeration or elevation in the way Maternus speaks of the regime, particularly in his description (41.4) of the emperor and his *dementia* ... The effect of this exaggeration or elevation on the part of Maternus is more that of slightly rueful good humour than of irony; but, however one defines it, this tonal nuance bridges the separation between the Maternus of AD 75 and the views for which he is made the vehicle by Tacitus at the end of the final speech, and which belong firmly to about AD 102.' Williams likens Maternus' sentiments to those of Tacitus himself in the *Agricola* and *Histories*—as we shall see, a risky procedure.

that give rise to the problem of Maternus' sincerity in his final speech that also explain the *need* for that final speech at all. In other words, it is precisely the fact that Maternus' perspective in his first speech can be interpreted as critical (and that he is happy to have his play be so interpreted) that simultaneously gives rise to our uneasiness with Maternus' final encomium *and* offers us something with which to explain his recourse to it, and indeed interpret it as a 'recourse' in the first place: it would not be necessary for him to utter anything of the sort had he not first voiced opinions that, in a situation in which free speech is curtailed, might have unpleasant repercussions. Understanding Maternus' praise as ironic is only the first step to seeing how the same feature of the *Dialogus* that makes this praise so problematic at its late appearance—that is, Maternus' implicit critique of Vespasian's rule—does double duty in the text as the motivating force that necessitates the inclusion of an encomium— even as this praise works on another level altogether to make the work acceptable to that element of the audience that would rather see it as *not* critical. For let us not forget the role of Maternus' audience. Present for his speech are a man whose models for success are informers and who has nothing but praise for the current regime, and another who is half-brother to the infamous Regulus.[48] For this audience, and presumably for a select audience outside the text in Tacitus' own day, Maternus' eulogy will seem only appropriate.

Given this situation, a more informative concept than 'irony' for what Maternus is doing in offering a praise that asks not to be taken only at face value is that of 'doublespeak'.[49] For characteristic of doublespeak is the appropriation of the ideological language of the court in such a way that, thanks to the peculiarities of the context in which it appears, allows its use to be understood as its opposite or at least as an uncomplimentary version of the original[50] *although* this

---

[48] Penwill (2003: 130–32) suggests that Maternus turns to this peculiar encomium precisely because of the arrival of Messala.

[49] A word to all extents synonymous with the term applied to Maternus by Murgia (1980: 123): 'Maternus gives an example of the kind of double-talk that was essential under the empire for personal safety, and which normally communicated one thing to supporters of the emperor, another to his opponents.' Murgia has it exactly right.

[50] For discussion of this phenomenon in the *Dialogus*, see Köhnken (1973: 34–6), and Heldmann (1982: 280) (who, like Köhnken, directs his comments to irony): 'An essential means of irony is, as has long been recognized, the uncritical and often exaggerated use of the language of state ideology.' Köhnken pairs passages such as Tac. *A.* 11.3.1 and *D.* 41.4 (on imperial *dementia*) and *A.* 13.3.1 and *D.* 41.4 (on

context does not irrefutably fix the content of what is said in one way or another for its audience. For if it is true that irony 'describes a statement of an ambiguous character, which includes a code containing two (or more) messages, one of which is the message of the ironist to his "initiated" audience and the other the "ironically meant" decoy message',[51] still, the nature of irony is to reveal itself as such, and the decoy message generally does *not* deceive any of its audiences.[52] But Maternus' praise does not imply only, *in bitterironischer Weise*, the opposite of what it says; it offers dual meanings to its different audiences, pro- and anti-imperial.[53] The close of the *Dialogus* figures forth Maternus as a poet whose flattering last words let themselves be read as ironic but do not compel it; such determinacy would defeat the very purpose for which his praise was tendered, and is moreover counterindicated by the critical reception of the work. In sum, if leeway for interpretive choice were absent, then we might call Maternus' last speech irony, but because his speech carries different meanings according to the nature of its audience, doublespeak is a more exact description of it, since it encompasses, even demands, indeterminacy. Doublespeak depends only on the existence of one element of the audience who will suspect the presence of double

imperial *sapientia*) and argues that Maternus uses the ideological buzzwords of the principate in his final praise of empire to point up more severely the contrast between propaganda and reality, as Tacitus does in the *Annals*.

[51] The definition is that of Rose (1979: 51), cited in Plass (1988: 30 n.9). Plass (32) comments, '*If* Tacitus is inviting a parodic reading of this declaration, it is a stellar example of the techniques of ironic wit we have been examining: political jargon quoted to be contradicted by the veiled contrary intention that frames and thus transforms it into clever self-refutation' (my emphasis). The presence of that 'if' in Plass's analysis is telling: the element of uncertainty, of *in utramque partem*, nudges the passage over from his diagnosis of irony to one of doublespeak.

[52] The limitation of the 'ironic' point of view is that it cannot always include the possibility of two valid meanings in its analysis of Maternus' praise-speech; Köhnken (1973: 40–41), for example, emphasizes that this speech can in no way be thought of as simultaneously fulfilling the function of an imperial *adulatio*. But indeed it must. Compare the doublespeak in which Pliny engages in the anecdote about Regulus (*Ep.* 1.5.5–7); there too, the speaker's words mean different things to their different audiences but can also be understood as betraying the constraints of his circumstances.

[53] Of course, both meanings may be available to both audiences at the same time, but this feature tends not to be problematic for either. There are no actual (as opposed to theoretical) cases that I know of in which the recipient of the praise chooses to 'hear' the other available meaning.

meaning and understand its strategic value. Such an audience, I would argue, the *Dialogus* works to render *us*.[54]

Further implications for our interpretation of the work follow close upon this one. It has not gone unnoticed that the only political risk-taker of the *Dialogus* is the one man who has professed to give up court oratory and the political hazards attendant upon it; the poet Maternus uses his medium to take on the imperial court and, presumably, to give voice to the sentiments of senators nostalgic for the republic, although these were sentiments normally muted by the dangers of free speech and recently hushed altogether by the end that befell the excesses of a Helvidius Priscus.[55] We recall that Maternus' *Cato* was a work in which he deliberately confronted an adversary more powerful than himself, as Aper complained (*aduersarium superiorem*, 'more powerful adversary', *D.* 10.7). How curious, then, that in so doing Maternus was carrying out the very function he himself later ascribes to the eloquence of the lost days of *libertas*, when orators had a free field to issue political challenges:

> *iam uero contiones assiduae et datum ius potentissimum quemque uexandi atque ipsa inimicitiarum gloria, cum se plurimi disertorum ne a P. quidem Scipione aut L. Sulla aut Cn. Pompeio abstinerent et ad incessendos principes uiros, ut est natura inuidiae, populi quoque ut histriones auribus uterentur, quantum ardorem ingeniis, quas oratoribus faces admouebant!*

And in truth, what a flame was set to genius, what a torch to the orators, by the constant public meetings and the free privilege of harrassing the most powerful individuals and the glory too that came from these feuds, when the majority of the eloquent did not even keep their hands off Publius Scipio or L. Sulla or Gnaeus Pompeius and just like actors, were

---

[54] Williams (1978: 40 n.80) protests that 'Köhnken's examples of Tacitean irony... demonstrate conclusively that Tacitus lets his irony appear quite clearly in the sarcastic tone which is betrayed by the unexpected vocabulary. The essential straightfacedness of Maternus' speech is not paralleled elsewhere.' Williams' view is affected by his dating of the *Dialogus* to AD 102, but this point aside, the fact remains that doublespeak and irony are not the same thing; Maternus' final speech is not meant to be, in isolation, a clear specimen of irony. It is meant to be taken with Maternus' first speech and thus understood as a comment on the circumstances of imperial eulogy. And comparanda do exist: those passages where Maternus' 'essential straightfacedness' *is* in fact paralleled, namely, the introductory passages to the *Agricola* and *Histories*.

[55] Once again, the perspective here is taken from Tacitus' own *Histories*, 4.4–10 and 43–4.

using the ears of the public as well to assail the leading men, as is characteristic of ill will! (Dial. 40.1)[56]

The privilege of harassing the powerful and the glory gained thereby: the *Lebensraum* of the republican orator, so characterized, echoes meaningfully in our ears after Aper's description of Maternus' dramatic recitation of the day before. Maternus has assumed this privilege, and he has, it seems, taken considerations of glory into account as well, for Aper has not only criticized the poet for his choice of target but also for his motivation. Reproaching Maternus for using a character like Cato and risking imperial offence, he has then answered his own objections: *sentio quid responderi possit: hinc ingentis exis<tere> assensus, haec in ipsis auditoriis praecipue laudari et mox omnium sermonibus ferri. tolle igitur quietis et securitatis excusationem* . . . . 'I realize what can be said in reply: it is from this that arises huge applause, it is this that is especially praised in the lecture halls themselves and soon is on everyone's lips. So out with your excuse of wanting quiet and safety . . .' (*D.* 10.6–7, with Muretus' *existere*). And indeed, whether or not Maternus has so wished it, he is the talk of the town. Already the roles of imperial poet and republican orator seem to be merging; how much more so when we consider that Maternus, who has thrown himself into the role of Cato (all too literally here, he is *just like an actor*), is *ad incessendos principes uiros . . . populi . . . auribus uterentur,* 'using the ears of the public to assail the leading men' (*D.* 40.1): the *principes* targeted by the republican orator before the crowds in the forum are now the single *princeps* whom Maternus can be read as attacking before his own audience.

In fact, Maternus is quite the sensation at Rome: a glory meted only it seems, to his own field of activity. We hear of no *orators* winning such fevered applause and acclaim; as observes even the one interlocutor who feels that contemporary oratory has suffered no decline—and he does so immediately after commenting on the enthusiastic clapping and widespread talk [which] Maternus' performance provoked—*nobis satis sit priuatas et nostri saeculi controuersias tueri, in quibus si quando necesse sit pro periclitante amico potentiorum aures offendere, et probata sit fides et libertas excusata,* 'Let it be enough for us orators to take on the defense in private

---

[56] In the phrase 'just like actors' (*ut histriones*), I have read Halm's conjecture *ut* for the daggered *et.*

controversies typical of our times, in which, if it is ever necessary to offend the ears of the powerful on behalf of a friend who is in danger, our loyalty would find approval and our outspokenness forgiveness' (*D.* 10.8).[57] The oratory of the present takes place on a smaller scale than that of the past. Yet, as Maternus notes, great oratory must have the applause that is its lifeblood: *oratori autem clamore plausuque opus est et uelut quodam theatro; qualia cotidie antiquis oratoribus contingebant,* 'The orator needs hubbub and applause, and a theatre, so to speak; things that befell the orators of old on a daily basis' (*D.* 39.4). None of these things enters the province of the strait-jacketed oratory of his own time, but we see that there is another field where popular glory and political outspokenness are yet possible, where the speaker will win huge acclaim, where, as with Maternus, his performance will become the talk of the town.[58]

Now, we know that Maternus is not indifferent to the principate's restriction of the freedom of its subjects, a freedom he equivocally calls 'license' in his final speech in such a way that the use of such a euphemism itself shows that frankness is dead. Elsewhere, before he launches into his encomium, he is not so careful: what oratory exists today is the bloodstained variety wielded by the informers, and the old freedom, along with the old eloquence, is a past ideal only, one from which present speakers have degenerated (*D.* 27.3). But the *Dialogus* seems to show that the Maternus who feels freedom of speech is gone and who has abandoned oratory for poetry has merely found a new medium for the old functions of republican free speech, a way to speak his mind behind the veil of fiction or history. As Kennedy notes, 'Maternus' oratory is not being silenced by fear, but he has discovered that his point of view can find an expression in poetry, as Tacitus found in history'.[59] Similarly, Duret voices his suspicions about Maternus' preferred field of activity; this 'false playwright's' true interest was neither poetry nor drama 'but the only

---

[57] As Luce (1993: 30) notes, 'This concession does not fit well with the picture of oratory that [Aper] sketched earlier in his speech.'

[58] Emphatic on this point are Luce (1993: 32): 'Praise for a poet is weak and evanescent, Aper declares. Yet sitting beside him is proof to the contrary: Maternus, holding the manuscript of the offending *Cato* in his hands, and with *Thyestes* in the works'; Häussler (1969: 57–8); Heldmann (1982: 261–2); Williams (1978: 46).

[59] Kennedy (1972: 519).

refuge possible for freedom of speech. In his plays, the characters of Jason and Agamemnon spoke like orators (9.2)'.[60]

In short, the imperial poet, with his theatre and his audience, is the closest approximation to the republican orator.[61] It is a reading of the *Dialogus* that is made all the stronger by the choice of Maternus, apostate orator and earnest poet, as spokesperson,[62] and also by the identification of poetry as a form of eloquence by both Aper at *D.* 10.4 and Maternus himself, who explains that he has abandoned forensic oratory *ut . . . sanctiorem illam et augustiorem eloquentiam colam*, 'to practise that holier and more venerable eloquence' (*D.* 4.2). Both oratory and poetry, then, belong to that realm of eloquence about whose decline Tacitus poses the opening question of the dialogue, and there is a sense in which the *Dialogus* is *about* this transition of political comment from one realm to another: it is about how the conditions of the principate have encouraged the indirect medium of poetry to take over from the forthright voice of oratory.[63] Certainly Maternus' plays as the *Dialogus* represents them have done so. Historical or mythical though they be, they lend themselves to interpretation as a comment on the present—and an effective comment at that. As we might recall, it was through his poetry, at some date before the dramatic present, that Maternus actually broke the political influence of the hated Vatinius.

Such an understanding of the *Dialogus* recasts entirely the well-aired question of the relevance of the first debate to a work that purports to be about oratory.[64] It may also throw some light on a final contradiction between what Maternus says and what he does. Much of Maternus' first speech is given over to a description of the

---

[60] Duret (1986: 3210).

[61] This is also the conclusion of Heldmann (1982: 286), who sees that the tragedies have taken over the former role of oratory as the expression of political opinion; likewise Heubner in Güngerich (1980: 209).

[62] Cf. Williams (1978: 47): 'Maternus is given so important a part in the *Dialogus* because . . . he has been an orator and knows what they are talking about but is now a poet and represents an attitude to literary composition that is pretty well the opposite of the orator's.' See also Heubner in Güngerich (1980: 203); Kennedy (1972: 518).

[63] See also Güngerich (1980: 16). A Renaissance note: Kahn (1985: 188–9) observes of Sidney's *Apology for Poetry* that a familiarity with contemporary arguments *in utramque partem* 'allows us to see not only that Sidney's defense is structured as public oration, but also that the thematic contradictions and inconsistencies are part of a rhetorical strategy to engage the reader in a process of judgment that is itself instructive'.

[64] See also below, n. 70.

quiet life of the poet, who withdraws for inspiration to the woods and groves of the countryside; his art once held sway in a golden age free from accusers and accusations, his life is a happy literary fellowship which Maternus contrasts to the anxious life of the orator (*D.* 12.1–13.1). By his own account, Maternus would rather be a poet than an orator because he prefers to the treacherous turmoil of the forum *securum et quietum Vergilii secessum, in quo tamen neque apud diuum Augustum gratia caruit,* 'the safe and quiet seclusion of Vergil, in which the poet nonetheless did not forsake the favour of the divine Augustus' (*D.* 13.1). But this is emphatically not Maternus' choice, to pick a safe seclusion from which to seek the favour of the emperor;[65] and it may be that what Maternus says about the poet's life and aims is disconsonant with his own because Maternus here is voicing the disclaimer typical of those engaging in a political poetry— even as it jars oddly with his recent comments on his old success against Vatinius. For no practising poet will say of his poetry point-blank that it is a site for criticism of the *present* ruler; under circumstances such as prevail in the *Dialogus* itself, the practice and claims of poetry remain always at odds. Significantly, Maternus' sanitized poet, the subject of his description but not the representative of his activity, the poet who abstains from political invective and seeks in his seclusion the favour of the *princeps,* is the model for the writer on whom Aper chooses to focus in his denigration of poetry in general, the contemporary poet Saleius Bassus. Saleius' verses are pretty, Aper concedes, but he has no influence and personal standing to speak of. When he offers a reading of his poetry he is obliged to beg people to attend, and the applause he wins is fleeting and empty:

hic exitus est, ut cum toto anno, per omnes dies, magna noctium parte unum librum excudit et elucubrauit, rogare ultro et ambire cogatur, ut sint qui dignentur audire, et ne id quidem gratis; nam et domum

---

[65] The contradiction has often been noted but not yet so resolved. See e.g. Luce (1993: 23–4, 31): '[Maternus' choice] is a retreat not from danger, but into it. The Utopian world of the poet seems particularly unreal in the face of the perilous situation his poetry has put him in at the present moment.' Bringmann (1970: 167–75) argues that Maternus' idyllic view of the poet's habitat uses the language of golden age descriptions typical of court poetry to depict an ideal of which the principate, for all its propaganda, falls short. On the other hand, Haß-von Reitzenstein (1970: 151–5) takes the idealism here as a foil for the critique of oratory, which not only is bloodstained in the present (she argues) but has been so since the past days of the republic.

mutuatur et auditorium exstruit et subsellia conducit et libellos dispergit.
et ut beatissimus recitationem eius euentus prosequatur, omnis illa laus
intra unum aut alterum diem, uelut in herba uel flore praecerpta, ad
nullam certam et solidam peruenit frugem, nec aut amicitiam inde refert
aut clientelam aut mansurum in animo cuiusquam beneficium, sed
clamorem uagum et uoces inanes et gaudium uolucre.

This is the upshot, that when over a whole year, for every day and most
of the nights, he has hammered out and lost sleep over a single book, he
is obliged to invite people himself and solicit them so that they will
deign to come listen, and not even that is for free: for he borrows a home
and prepares a recitation room and hires chairs and dispenses pro-
grammes. And even if a great success attends the recitation, all that praise,
after a day or two, comes to no fixed and solid benefit, like a plant or
flower plucked too early, nor does he carry off from it a friendship or client
or gratitude for a service that will last in anyone's heart, but an inconstant
acclaim and empty shouts and a fleeting pleasure. (D. 9.3–4)

To be sure, says Aper, Vespasian recently awarded Saleius 500,000
sesterces in a much-praised act of generosity; well, *pulchrum id*
quidem, indulgentiam principis ingenio mereri: quanto tamen pul-
chrius . . . se ipsum colere, 'it's a fine thing to earn the favour of the
emperor by one's talent; but how much finer . . . to pay court to
oneself!' (*D.* 9.5). Saleius, we see, is a court poet, maintained by
Vespasian, harmless, charming, and apolitical. Is it coincidence that
he is attended by an audience that is desultory at best?[66] Aper's
description of Saleius' efforts to cull hearers for his recitation provides
a vivid contrast to the excitement and hubbub at Maternus' performance, and while Saleius may be the kind of poet Maternus describes,
it cannot be chance that the man Maternus names in passing as proof
of a poet's ability to win high standing and reputation is one Pomponius Secundus (*D.* 13.3). Pomponius was a consular writer of
tragedies whom we know to have skirted the fate of banishment
under Tiberius[67]—and given his *métier*, the possibilities for speculation are ripe, as Heldmann notes.[68] The only poet Maternus mentions

[66] Luce (1993: 30 n.63): 'Aper's language implies that the poet must play up to the emperor from a position of dependency.'
[67] Pomponius Secundus is identified as a playwright at Quint. *Inst. Orat.* 10.1.98; Tac. *A.* 11.13.1; Pliny *Epist.* 7.17.11. For his chequered career under Tiberius, see Tac. *A.* 5.8 and 6.18.1; under Claudius, *A.* 12.28. For further biographical information see Duret (1986: 3163–71) and Güngerich (1980: 54).
[68] Heldmann (1982: 266).

is one far removed from Aper's Saleius Bassus: a poet, perhaps, in his own image, and in any case not a man to write pleasant verses for the *princeps* in the hopes of an imperial handout.

It is easy enough to answer now the question of why the first debate takes place at all, given that the professed topic of the dialogue is the decline of oratory:[69] the first debate is a debate for the soul and heart of the dialogue, although we do not realize it until we reflect on the significance of Maternus' doublespeak. Poetry, as we realize at the end, is in fact not only an alternative but a substitute for the defunct freespoken oratory of the Republic. For the fact that Maternus delivers an encomium of Vespasian that is equivocal is proof of the effects of the imperial regime on the old free speech, while the potential for Maternus' *Cato* to be interpreted subversively shows where the old function of republican outspokenness has ended up, albeit in disguised form. The contradictions of the *Dialogus* stand revealed as its praxis, as the site of what it *says*: the first debate, which reveals so tellingly the political conditions of the times, is needed in order to show up Maternus' final speech as doublespeak; and it is because this final speech is shown up as such that readers are led to the connection between the need for imperial encomia, the lack of freedom under the principate, and the possibility of dual readings thanks to those two factors. Without the first debate, the final speech could not be read as a damning comment (as well as a simple act of praise) about what Roman senators and writers were compelled to say of their rulers in order to gain the space to say other things liable to less charitable interpretation.[70]

---

[69] It is a question posed with some frequency in the scholarship; see e.g. Gugel (1964: 241ff.); Häussler (1969: 50–67), with extensive bibliography in the notes; Heldmann (1982: 272ff.); Heubner in Güngerich (1980: 203); Martin (1981: 61); Williams (1978: 29, 47). Heubner in Güngerich (1980: 203 nn. 1 and 2) also lists scholars who think that the content of the first debate has nothing to do with the main topic of the *Dialogus* or that it is simply a subordinate theme.

[70] The fullest attempt to answer the question of what the first debate is doing in a dialogue that professes to be about the decline of oratory is that of Häussler (1969). Häussler criticizes other readings of the *Dialogus* because they can argue only that the first debate is relevant, not that it is necessary (e.g. Gugel 1964: 249, who says of Maternus' final speech on why oratory *has* declined that it is there to justify Maternus' poetic career; only when Maternus has shown that great oratory is no longer extant does he show he had the right to turn to poetry, and the first speech receives its justification retroactively from the second. And only at a historical time such as that revealed to us by the first speech is it possible to speak—as in the final debate—about the decline of oratory at all). Häussler (1969: 54) protests that the confrontation

What is the point of such a dialogue, from the perspective now of its author's own agenda? Those answering this question have often enough tripped over the distorting assumption of Maternus' sincerity in praising the regime. In fact the meaning of the *Dialogus* veers wildly about this pole: because those who would read Maternus' speech as sincere see it as running parallel to similar passages in the *Agricola* and *Histories*, where Tacitus offers first-person praise for the reigning emperors Nerva and Trajan respectively, these readers are then left with solutions that involve splits along a spiritual or chronological fault line.[71] But such comparisons of Maternus' eulogy with Tacitus' compliments to the ruling emperor rely on two untenable assumptions: first, that the *Dialogus* was composed under Trajan in or around AD 102, when the political context was different from that of AD 97 and Nerva's principate; second, that Tacitus' own words of praise at the openings of the *Agricola* and the *Histories* were not themselves motivated by the same considerations we see at work for Tacitus' character Maternus.[72] This latter is a dangerous assumption

---

between oratory and poetry in the first debate is not the enabling condition for the final debate, for to hint that a poetic *otium* can be condoned is an argument also possible in republican times, and himself (1969: 57) resolves the issue by suggesting that the *Dialogus* is really about poetry's eternal life in contrast to the transitory nature of oratory. This argument is supported (he says) by the fact that poetry's fame is longer-lived than that of oratory; consider how the points of Maternus at *D.* 12.5 and 13.3 overturn Aper's view at *D.* 9.4. So his conclusion (1969: 67) is that the *Dialogus* follows a progression of thought: oratory is mortal; it is dying; it in fact has to have died. I am not convinced that Häussler actually escapes his own strictures, but at any rate his argument does not contradict the view I advance in the text, although it shows a very different emphasis. For a discussion of other views, see Haß-von Reitzenstein (1970: 144–58); she herself (152) takes the simpler view that the first debate is there to supply material on which to base the critique of oratory in the third.

[71]   A good example of this problem is Klingner (1932: 155), who identifies Maternus with Tacitus precisely in their approval of the new emperor. Similarly Keyssner (1936: 106).

[72]   Cf. Tac. *Agr.* 3.1: *nunc demum redit animus; sed quamquam primo statim beatissimi saeculi ortu Nerua Caesar res olim dissociabiles miscuerit, principatum et libertatem, augeatque cotidie felicitatem temporum Nerua Traianus . . . natura tamen infirmitatis humanae tardiora sunt remedia quam mala . . . .* 'Now, late in the day, morale is returning; but although from the earliest inception of this blessed age the emperor Nerva has united things formerly irreconcilable, the principate and freedom, and Trajan is every day increasing the happiness of the times . . . nonetheless by the nature of human weakness the remedies are slower than our sufferings.' And Tac. *H.* 1.4, on his intention to write of the present times at some future date: *quod si uita suppeditet, principatum diui Neruae et imperium Traiani, uberiorem securioremque materiam, senectuti seposui, rara temporum felicitate, ubi sentire quae uelis et quae sentias dicere licet,* 'If my life's length should suffice, I have set aside for old age the

and can by no means be blithely deployed as a tool for reading: given that Tacitus' historical works are in an important sense *about* the way political language masks its opposite and can almost be read as a glossary of the false official language of virtue imposed by imperial ideology upon its subjects, his own use of terms like *freedom, happiness*, and *safety* are always already undermined by their unveiling as hollow in the very works in which they appear.[73] If on the other hand we reserve judgement on the question, a new way of posing it comes into view with the end of the *Dialogus*: no longer is it axiomatic that Maternus' praise of Vespasian *must* be sincere because Tacitus himself wrote similar passages in praise of Nerva and Trajan;[74] rather we may ask, reversing the interpretive logic, whether Maternus' praise of Vespasian does not change the way we must read Tacitus' own imperial eulogies. The texts we privilege as the keys to the *Dialogus* may be none other than the texts that the *Dialogus* itself brings into better focus—as I hope will become more clear by the end of this discussion.

As to the first issue, the question of when the *Dialogus* was composed, this must be reconsidered, I think, on the basis of Charles E. Murgia (1980), who argues on literary grounds for an ascription to Nerva's reign.[75] As Murgia illustrates, the usual evidence for AD 102 is seriously flawed. Those supporting this date do so on the ground that

---

principate of the divine Nerva and the rule of Trajan, a richer and safer topic, thanks to the rare happiness of the times, when you can feel what you wish and say what you feel.'

[73] See esp. the insightful discussion in Plass (1988: 26–55). Plass aptly cites (32) Tac. *A.* 3.28.2 ... *pace et principe uteremur* ('under Augustus, "we had peace and—a master"') as an epigram that parallels the technique of the *Dialogus* itself: 'Long debates are indeed "unnecessary" when there is no real freedom, and the judge's clemency is naturally "ready" when it is wholly arbitrary. Both in logical structure and in the point it makes this comes close to the witty self-refutation of the formal epigram like the one at *A.* 3.28.3 [*sic*] ... "Master" works by *para prosdokian* to frame and parody "peace" and thus produce a sour joke given added edge by the derisive jingle in *pace et principe*.'

[74] As Keyssner (1936: 107) and Williams (1978: 35, 41, 50) would claim. See also Bardon (1940: 380).

[75] Supported by Barnes (1986: 230). Moreover, after the arguments of Bruère (1954) and Güngerich (1956), it is clear that Pliny's *Panegyricus* contains imitations of the *Dialogus*, so that it is likely but not certain that the latter antedates AD 101 and Pliny's revisions of his work. Also dating at AD 96–97 are Bardon (1940: 379), and (1953: 179). The competing view locates the work in or around AD 102; see Cameron (1967: 260); Güngerich (1956); Syme (1958a: 672); Williams (1978: 26–7); originally the view of Kappelmacher (1932: 121–9). Heubner in Güngerich (1980: 195–7) and

Fabius Iustus, to whom the *Dialogus* is dedicated, reached the suffect consulship in that year. But Tacitus does not mention this consulship, an omission that violates precedent (1980: 100). Nor does his bitter comment at *Agricola* 3.2 to the effect that he and his fellow countrymen passed fifteen years in silence under Domitian have any bearing on the *Dialogus'* possible priority over the *Agricola*—compare Pliny's *Panegyricus* 66.4–5, with the same theme and plenty of prior literary output on the speaker's part (1980: 101–2). Finally and most important, Murgia demonstrates (to my mind irrefutably) that the literary commonplaces from Cicero and Quintilian that appear in the *Agricola* and *Germania* travel by way of the *Dialogus*, which must therefore precede these two works (1980: 104–6). When we then consider that Nerva's brief principate was a time in which the *delatores* continued to hold their high position for the most part unpunished and much to the dismay of those among the senators who would have been all too happy to see their downfall, a final piece of the dialogue falls into place. Maternus' damning appraisal of the influence over Vespasian of the bloodthirsty informers who had been so powerful during the principate of that emperor's predecessor, Nero, together with the setting of the *Dialogus* in the time of Helvidius Priscus' attack on Eprius Marcellus and the short-lived blossoming of senatorial free speech in that year, have immediate relevance for Nerva's deplored complaisance toward the hated *delatores* of the former Domitianic regime.[76] Eprius and Vibius become representative not only of the informers as a group, of their immunity to senatorial attack, and of the dangers of free speech under any regime in which the emperor

---

Kennedy (1972: 516–17) date the work to AD 101; Martin (1981: 60) to some time between AD 102 and 109. No one any longer maintains, as far as I am aware, that the work antedates the reign of Domitian (AD 81–96); this view, based largely on stylistic considerations, was decisively overturned by Leo (1898), reviewing Gudeman's edition of Tacitus' *Dialogus* (Boston, 1894). For further bibliography see Barnes (1986: 229–32); Murgia (1980: 99–100).

[76] As Murgia (1980: 117) points out of the *Dialogus'* introduction, 'The implication is that the reasons set forth [sc. for the decline of eloquence] at the dramatic date (AD 75) are still relevant at the time of writing and publication. But in fact there were substantial differences in the circumstances of AD 102 and even more radical differences in the propaganda of the times.' Besides the fact that Trajan suppressed the *delatores*, Murgia notes that the speeches of this period were long rather than short (vs. *D.* 19.2, 20.1, 38, 41.4) and that parts of the *Dialogus* are insulting to Pliny if they come after the *Panegyricus* (cf. *D.* 20, 41.4 vs. *Paneg.* 76.1); see also the further arguments in Murgia (1985), where he suggests that the first book of Pliny's letters, dating mostly from the time of Nerva, shows the literary influence of the *Dialogus*.

grants them hearing, but also of the unhappy phenomenon of their continuing influence from the reign of one hated emperor to that of his supposedly reformist successor.[77] Such was the situation under the emperor Nerva, graphically related in a famous letter of Pliny the Younger: Pliny tells of a dinner party of Nerva's at which the *delator* Fabricius Veiento, notorious for his activities in the days of Domitian, was ingratiating himself with the emperor to the great distaste of the other guests present. The conversation turned to yet another informer, the deceased Catullus Messalinus; when the emperor wondered aloud what would have happened to him if he had survived, Iunius Mauricus ventured to opine that Messalinus too would have been a

---

[77] On Vespasian's attitude toward the *delatores*, and the flaws in propaganda about 'good' emperors, see the daring words of Curtius Montanus to the senate in AD 70 as presented in Tac. *H.* 4.42.5–6: *an Neronem extremum dominorum putatis? idem crediderant qui Tiberio, qui Gaio superstites fuerunt, cum interim intestabilior et saeuior exortus est. non timemus Vespasianum; ea principis aetas, ea moderatio: sed diutius durant exempla quam mores. elanguimus, patres conscripti, nec iam ille senatus sumus qui occiso Nerone delatores et ministros more maiorum puniendos flagitabat. optimus est post malum principem dies primus,* 'Do you think Nero was the last of the tyrants? So they too had believed, who survived Tiberius and Caligula, when meanwhile a more abominable and savage man arose. We do not fear Vespasian; such is the age, such the moderation of our *princeps;* but precedents endure longer than stability of character. We have become weak, conscript fathers, nor are we any longer that senate which in accordance with tradition demanded punishment for Nero's informers and satellites once he was dead. The best day after the death of a bad ruler is the first.' The informers continue their influence; the good emperor becomes the bad; and, as Michel (1962: 95) comments, these cynical words were written under Trajan, that recipient of praise in the introduction to the *Histories.* And an incidental comment on my part: the similarity of the names Curtius Montanus and Curiatius Maternus, their common outspokenness against the Neronian informers, and the associations both share with Helvidius Priscus have often spurred me to the bold thought that the poet of the *Dialogus* may be no other than a fictional character meant to evoke his parallel from the *Histories* who turns up there, oddly enough, in the same paragraph as Vipstanus Messala, our friend from the *Dialogus*, now defending his *delator* half-brother Regulus. Of course, an unprovable hypothesis: but how very odd that in the *Annals* the same Montanus is criticized in AD 66 by Eprius Marcellus as a writer of 'damnable poetry' who has mocked the ruler with impunity *(carmina* can refer to tragedy) and that, exiled for precisely this poetry, he is offered an imperial pardon by Nero *on the condition that he withdraw from his public career* (Tac. *A.* 16.28.1, 29.2, 33.2). This is Maternus' own trajectory in the *Dialogus*. Cf. also Michel (1962: 95), who thinks the *Dialogus* contains an allusion to Montanus. Along the same lines, Marcus Aper, who has no existence outside the *Dialogus*, seems curiously evocative of the *delator* Domitius Afer, both men marked by Gallic birth (cf. *Dial.* 10.2) and a vehement speaking style; and, as Andrew Riggsby points out to me (personal correspondence, August 1992), Afer appears in the company of Julius Secundus and Vibius Crispus at Quint. *Inst.* 10.1.118–19 and 12.10.11.

guest at this dinner (*Ep.* 4.22.4–6).[78] So was it that Nerva, torn between the demands of the dead Domitian's detractors and his supporters, adopted a dangerous moderation: as Cizek comments, 'The exiles, the old-fashioned senators, the representatives of the circle around the Helvidii were demanding vengeance; they wanted the head of the *delatores* who did service to Domitian. Yet, prudent, Nerva punished only the minor informers and very few *delatores* of middling rank. The main partisans of Domitian were spared and even treated with deference.'[79]

If this, however, is a subtext of the *Dialogus,* it is not only Maternus but the author who needs to leave himself room to claim that his criticism of Vespasian's regime is not in fact a critique of the situation in his own day. Certainly readers in positions of power as well as the particular interpretive community that was intended to grasp what was going unsaid would know how to read for such criticism—a fact of which Tacitus elsewhere shows himself entirely cognizant, especially in his disclaimer of intent in the *Annals,* where he comments that readers are always to be found to *ob similitudinem morum aliena malefacta sibi obiectari putent,* 'think they are being charged with

---

[78] See also Ps.-Aurelius Victor, *Epitome de Caesaribus* 12.5. Pliny *Epist.* 1.5 shows an M. Aquilius Regulus who is timid and humble after Domitian's death, but nonetheless Regulus lived unscathed to AD 104. Nerva may have taken measures of some sort against a few less consequential informers; see Dio Cassius 68.1.2 and Pliny's *Paneg.* 35.4.

[79] See also Cizek (1983: 106, 147–50). And so those who argue that the compositional date of AD 102 is evidence for Maternus' sincerity would seem to have it exactly backward. See esp, Williams (1978: 36): 'When Maternus in his final speech asserts conclusively that good government by one man does not need oratory, the oratory it most conspicuously does not need was that on which all emperors from Tiberius to Domitian had most heavily relied for the protection of the regime, the oratory of the great *delatores*. But the most decisive difference between the situation of AD 75 and AD 102 lay in the fact that Trajan had once for all (following a brief initiative by Titus, reversed by Domitian) abolished *delatores* [Suet. *Titus* 8.5; Pliny *Paneg.* 34–5] . . . Maternus' final speech is designed to be an analysis of the immediate situation of AD 102 and so must omit all consideration of that type of oratory.' Williams adduces this fact to argue that Maternus' final speech must refer to AD 102 and not the dramatic date of AD 75, thus using the point to support his theory of a temporal shift within the dialogue. But the question he claims to have answered (32)—'how could Tacitus, without gross anachronism, set a debate in AD 75 that would still be relevant to the situation of AD 102?'—is itself wrongly formulated. For other reasons Williams is demonstrably in error, see above, n. 42. Against the claim of Paratore (1951) that Tacitus shows himself benign to Vespasian in his other works, see Bardon (1953: 173–4), citing *H.* 2.84—not to mention the unsavoury account of the Priscus–Marcellus feud, also in the *Histories.*

other people's crimes because of the similarity to their own character' (*A.* 4.33.4).[80] That Tacitus should write a dialogue in which a poet is using tragic drama to criticize the regime is potentially problematic for the author because it suggests there are grounds for complaint in the first place, that freedom of speech is gone. That Tacitus should imply that this same playwright is in trouble for his drama is also problematic, for it suggests that even a poet using mythology and history as the subject of his play may feel the dangerous weight of the imperial ire. And that Tacitus should comment obliquely on the continuing influence of the *delatores* under Vespasian while writing under Nerva is yet again problematic, because it lends itself to a translation into terms relevant to the present much as did Maternus' *Cato*.[81] Hence perhaps the many removes between the text's content and the author's voice: they are there to make the question of intent slippery enough to be safe. Tacitus insists that he is reporting a conversation he heard as a youth, emphatically denying originality and intervention (*D.* 1.2–3);[82] he situates the dialogue in the past of some twenty years ago, long before Nerva's time (*D.* 1.2, 17.3, 24.3); and he carefully emphasizes that the peculiarites of the interlocutors' viewpoints are the product of their different characters (*D.* 1.3).[83] Most of all, Maternus' praise of Vespasian functions as just such a safety-catch. With this move, Tacitus can deny both the poet's critical

---

[80] Cf. Bartsch (1994: 244 n.59).

[81] Obviously such an argument suggests that Tacitus shares Maternus' views, at least to the extent that he employs the figure of the poet to make a comment on praise, poetry, and free speech. Some scholars have seen a close correspondence between the two figures, both of whom abandon careers in oratory for a more literary occupation through which they can voice their true views on the principate: see Bardon (1940: 380); Barwick (1954: 30); Heldmann (1982: 286); Kennedy (1972: 518); Keyssner (1936: 107–10); Williams (1978: 47). There are a good discussion and further biblio-graphical information in Heubner in Güngerich (1980: 207–8).

[82] Haß-von Reitzenstein (1970: 18–19 and 96–100) has an illuminating discussion of what she identifies as Tacitus' distancing techniques here, and emphasizes the contrast to the Ciceronian dialogues, where the author does participate in the con-versation which he later records. As she notes, the suggestion that the author speaks from memory is to some extent paralleled in those dialogues (cf. *De Or.* 1.4, 1.23; *De Rep.* 1.13; see also the comments of Bardon (1953: 179), but Tacitus' insistence is singular.

[83] For a different interpretation, see Haß-von Reitzenstein (1970: 28–31). Murgia (personal communication, May 1992) would argue that the convention of placing the dialogue in the past works only if Maternus is a genuine historical figure; for if not, why the elaborate hints at the date at *Dial.* 2.1? But perhaps the Maternus–Montanus link offers a way out here.

intent and his own at the same time, leaving room for doublespeak even as he makes the point that makes doublespeak necessary.[84]

This, then, is what we are left with as we reach the end of the *Dialogus* and reflect on its content: Maternus the poet can be nothing other than a paradigm for the loss of freedom which he talks about in such positive terms in his final speech. By showing us the risk Maternus runs and by putting in his mouth words of praise about the emperor which others could reinterpret in a negative light, Tacitus makes of this figure an *exemplum* of the lost *libertas* of the principate and of its replacement by a different kind of discourse, even as Maternus speaks the flattering words that deny to that *libertas* any nature but that of *licentia*. And Maternus' praise of Vespasian does change the way we read Tacitus' own imperial eulogies. They are not there to be taken as sincere testimonials but to create room for the voice of an author who utters them for diverse audiences to understand diversely.

---

[84] It is suggestive to find that Maternus' political explanation for the decline of oratory finds an almost exact parallel in another writer who found it equally necessary to handle gingerly so incendiary a topic—the author of *On the Sublime*. See Bartsch (1994: 203–6).

5

Appreciating Aper: The Defence of Modernity in Tacitus' *Dialogus de Oratoribus*

Sander M. Goldberg

Nearly a century ago, Friedrich Leo argued with his characteristic acumen that the neo-Ciceronian style of Tacitus' *Dialogus de oratoribus* was as much a function of its genre as its subject. 'The genre', he observed, 'demands its style. One who deals with different genres must write in different styles.'[1] Alfred Gudeman, the target of Leo's review, had therefore missed a key step in the argument for Tacitean authorship when he invoked 'the influence of subject-matter' without considering the demands of genre. In hindsight, the point seems almost obvious, and the sophistication of recent work on the date and style of the *Dialogus* has left Gudeman's discussion far behind. The advance in method—if not necessarily in results—has been profound.[2] Leo's success in linking genre and style, however, has also had a second, less happy result: it has encouraged belief in a corresponding link between genre and content, as if Tacitus necessarily embraced Ciceronian values along with his Ciceronian forms.

This essay owes much to audiences in California and Colorado, to *CQ*'s editor and referees, to Charles Murgia, ever a keen but fair-minded critic of my views, and to Charles McNelis, who first pointed me toward the *Dialogus*.

[1] Leo (1960: 285): 'Die Gattung erfordert ihren Stil, wer verschiedene Gattungen behandelt, muss in verschiedenen Stilen schreiben.' Gudeman's revised and expanded edition of the *Dialogus* (Berlin, 1914: 21–3) still missed the point of this observation. For the context of Leo's contribution to the study of the *Dialogus*, see Bo (1993: 250–63).

[2] In particular, Güngerich (1951); Murgia (1980; 1985); Brink (1989). See now the summary and critique in Brink (1994: 253–75).

The *Dialogus* is often thought to accept Cicero's aesthetic agenda and to examine why the orators of succeeding generations failed to maintain its ideals and standards. Perhaps inevitably, its analysis is then read as a rather depressing tale of oratory's literary, social, and moral decline. This view demands reconsideration. To explore, as the *Dialogus* certainly does, the collapse of Ciceronian values is not necessarily to regret that collapse. We have, I think, too often read our own prejudices into the *Dialogus* by presuming a post-Augustan decline in oratorical standards and, in the process, reducing our sensitivity to important variations in and departures from the generic conventions that Tacitus so deliberately recalls. The result is a significant distortion of the *Dialogus'* view of oratory under the empire.

The first sign of this distortion involves the statement of its subject. The title promises, and the text delivers, a discussion of Roman orators, but there is little basis for the frequent claim that in it, Tacitus clearly asserted the decline, even the death, of oratory.[3] The work makes only one unqualified statement of oratory's decline. It appears in the very first sentence: *saepe ex me requiris, Iuste Fabi, cur, cum priora saecula tot eminentium oratorum ingeniis gloriaque floruerint, nostra potissimum aetas deserta et laude eloquentiae orbata uix nomen ipsum oratoris retineat.* ('You often ask me, Justus Fabius, why, although earlier epochs teemed with the talents and fame of so many distinguished orators, our own age, especially barren and bereft of praise for eloquence, barely retains even the name "orator".'). The statement is as clear as the theme is familiar, but a conventional opening does not necessitate a conventional thought. In this case, we need to consider who is speaking and to what purpose.

The feigned reluctance of an author to respond to the repeated requests of a friend or patron is a pose with a long history in Roman letters. To announce a subject in this elegant and economical way while simultaneously making a dedication became a favourite device of poets and prose writers alike. The injunction to which they purport to yield often takes the form of a reported command. Both the Republican *Rhetorica ad Herennium* and Quintilian's *Institutio oratoria* employ this conceit:

---

[3] Williams (1978: 49). Cf. Barnes (1986: 232): 'The *Dialogus* does not discuss the decline of oratory: it assumes it.' Similar statements by e.g. Luce (1993: 19); Brink (1989: 490); Heldmann (1982: 163).

. . . tamen tua nos, Gai Herenni, uoluntas commouit ut de ratione dicendi conscriberemus, ne aut tua causa noluisse aut fugisse nos laborem putares.

Your desire, Gaius Herennius, has nevertheless moved me to write about the practice of public speaking so you will not think I have ignored your request or avoided the trouble of fulfilling it. (*Rhet. Ad Her.* 1).

efflagitasti cotidiano conuicio ut libros quos ad Marcellum meum de institutione oratoria scripseram iam emittere inciperem.

You have been pressing me daily and insistently to begin publishing those books on the education of orators that I had written for my friend Marcellus. (Quint. *Inst. Or.* 1.1 *Ep. ad Tryphonem*).

The pose, though adroit, could be risky in public. The *quondam* elegist Passenus Paulus, for example, once opened a recitation with the words *Prisce, iubes,* ('Priscus, you order') and found himself unable to continue when his friend Javolenus Priscus was heard to remark, *ego uero non iubeo* ('Indeed I do not order').[4] Most poets were therefore more subtle in using the convention, as Vergil was in refer- ring to a 'poem begun at your request' (*iussis carmina coepta tuis, Ecl.* 8.11–12). Another variant substitutes an indirect question for the clause of command. Cicero does this at the beginning of *Orator.*

utrum difficilius aut maius esset negare tibi saepius idem roganti an efficere id quod rogares diu multumque, Brute, dubitaui. . . . Quod quo- niam me saepius rogas, aggrediar non tam perficiendi spe quam experi- endi uoluntate. . . . Quaeris igitur idque iam saepius quod eloquentiae genus probem maxime et quale mihi uideatur illud, quo nihil addi possit, quod ego summum et perfectissimum iudicem.

Whether it is more serious and more difficult to refuse what you are so often requesting or to produce what you request is something, Brutus, I have considered long and hard . . . But since you ask so often, I shall approach the task not so much in hope of succeeding as from a will- ingness to try . . . You ask, then, and have asked repeatedly what type of oratory I most approve and what the nature of that oratory seems to me to be to which nothing can be added and which I think the best and most perfect. (*Orator* 1–3)

---

[4] Plin. *Ep.* 6.15. On Priscus' interruption, see Hiltbrunner (1979). *iubere* is a very weak imperative (cf. White 1993: 266–8), which doubtless facilitated the lexical and syntactic variants so common within this convention.

The similarity of his *me saepius rogas* to Tacitus' *saepe ex me requiris* led Janson to conclude as a matter of course that Tacitus is quite simply employing a formula, a generally self-deprecatory form of expression that had been used so often that its real content had become diluted.[5]

Janson is certainly right about the *Orator*: its preface is strikingly thin in content. The request it reports is a characteristically vague and open-ended wish for an opinion without the offering of one.[6] This is where Tacitus departs from his predecessors. Only here, in the preface to the *Dialogus*, do we find an expository question that itself advances a proposition of substance—the decline of contemporary oratory—and only in the *Dialogus* is the author reluctant not only to reply (that reluctance is traditional) but to endorse the thesis being advanced: *cui percontationi tuae respondere, et tam magnae quaestionis pondus excipere . . . uix hercule auderem si mihi mea sententia proferenda* ('I would scarcely dare respond to your query and take up the burden of so great a question, if I had to make public my own opinion', 1.2). The decline of oratory becomes a question which Tacitus never answers in his own voice, and his reluctance to do so is not the result of false modesty. He instead is putting distance between what has become Fabius' statement of the theme and what might be his own opinion on the subject. Indeed, the last we actually hear from Tacitus *in propria persona* is a reminder to Fabius that an opposing view is also possible: 'nor was someone lacking to take up the other side, too, and by ridiculing and mocking old times to champion the eloquence of our own day over the talents of our ancestors' (*D.* 1.4). The proemium thus introduces without endorsing the thesis of oratorical decline.[7] The conventional opening does not commit itself to the conventional value.

What it offers instead is the report of a conversation which Tacitus sets back to the early 70s. Leading orators of the time have gathered at

---

[5] Janson (1964: 62).

[6] Especially clear at *Or.* 3: similar effects at Cic. *Top.* 4–5; Col. 2.1; Sen. *Ep.* 7.1, 22.1. The form recalls the neutrality of Roman comedy's expository questions, where one character simply calls upon another to explain his behaviour or his condition (e.g. Pl. *Cur.* 1–2).

[7] Charles Murgia points out to me that this distancing would also insulate Tacitus from the political implications of the arguments advanced, a particularly valuable protection if, as Murgia has argued (1980), endorsed with further arguments by Barnes (1986: 229–3), the *Dialogus* dates from the time of Nerva, when the promise of a restored *libertas* might easily have outstripped the reality. I find the argument of Brink (1994) for an early Trajanic date, i.e. *c.*99–101, much less compelling.

the house of Curiatius Maternus to urge him to abandon the writing of tragedies and return to his career as a legal advocate. Such an invocation of past luminaries was itself a conventional device of literary dialogue, but the convention Cicero used to lend authority to the argument he advances becomes another distancing device for Tacitus. He conjures up a previous generation of speakers in order to avoid responsibility for what they say.[8] The result is a dialogue of shifting values and perspectives that 'pursues no thesis, single or composite, nor does it answer a particular question, not even very fully the question posed at the outset'.[9] Rather, the discussion moves through three interconnected phases: the relevant virtues of poetry and oratory, the relevant virtues of oratory's ancient and modern practitioners, and the best training and environment for nurturing their skills. All the speakers will agree that oratory has changed with time. Whether that change constitutes a decline, i.e. whether the change has been for the worse and if so, in what respects, is among the issues they debate. And debate it is, for key aspects of the question raised in the preface remain open to the end.

The openness of the question should not be a surprise. Discussions of oratory in the early Empire did not universally assume decline from some earlier age of greatness. There were indeed Romans—the elder Seneca was one—who thought that eloquence had peaked with Cicero,[10] but glorifying the past beyond its deserts was also a critical topos of some standing (Lucr. 3.956, Prop. 3.1.23, Vell. Pat. 2.92.5, Sen. *Ep.* 16.9, Tac. *D.* 18.3). Velleius Paterculus found distinguished predecessors an intimidating bar to progress (1.17.7), which is perhaps one reason why Quintilian made a point of praising his contemporaries (10.1.122) and their achievements (12.11.28)

---

[8] So, rightly, Haß-von Reitzenstein (1970: 12–17). Contrast Cicero's straightforward declaration at *Sen.* 3: *omnem autem sermonem tribuimus . . . Marco Catoni seni, quo maiorem auctoritatem haberet oratio.* (Cf. *de Or.* 1.23, *Rep.* 1.12). The historicity of Tacitus' speakers is widely assumed, though Aper and Maternus are known only from this work. They were probably real people, but Bartsch (1994: 260, n.68) is right to raise the possibility that Maternus may be a fictional composite.

[9] Brink (1994: 276–7).

[10] *Con.* 1 Prf. 6–7: *quidquid Romana facundia habet . . . circa Ciceronem effloruit; omnia ingenia, quae lucem studiis nostris attulerunt, tunc nata sunt. in deterius deinde cotidie data est . . .* Similar views in Sen. *Ep.* 114.1–2; Petron. 1ff., 88; Plin. *N.H.* 14.1.3–7. See Caplan (1970: 176–89); Kennedy (1972: 446–64); Heldmann (1982: 131–98). The very commonplace, however, might itself tell against Tacitus' interest in it. See Bo (1993: 342–5).

while predicating his entire educational programme upon the undi-
minished prestige of the orator's calling.[11] Tacitus, of course, was
himself one of those distinguished imperial orators, and the record
of his career, however murky and incomplete, provides no external
reason to attribute an argument for decline to him here. What seems
to fuel a modern tendency to do so is something rather different, a
widespread distaste for his champion of modernity.

This champion is the orator M. Aper, who has two substantial
speeches. The first argues forcefully and unashamedly for the utility,
pleasure, and power that oratory confers on its practitioners
(*D.* 5.3–10). Orators, by which he means courtroom pleaders, are
men of status and influence, and Curiatius Maternus is therefore
foolish to sacrifice that prestige on the altar of poetry. Aper's second
speech argues that eloquence is a relative concept (*D.* 16.4–23).
Speakers should be judged only by their effectiveness in their own
time, and modern times present special challenges. What can be
expected of an orator when everyone knows the same rhetorical
tricks, and when courts have become places of business, not public
attractions? Arguments like these have not won the admiration of
classicizing readers, who adopt two strategies for dismissing Aper's
message. One, focusing on the first speech, assaults his character. The
second assaults his seriousness. Let us take these in turn.

THE ASSAULT ON CHARACTER

Aper's first speech, says Williams, reveals his 'brashness and pragmatism and his vulgar sense of values'.[12] By brashness and vulgarity
Williams presumably means Aper's self-evident pride at his own rise
from obscure origins in Gaul to high position at Rome (*D.* 7.1, 10.2).
The man is thus a shameless parvenu. As for pragmatism, clearly a
negative trait in this context, 'he betrays himself completely', writes
Barnes, 'when he names his oratorical heroes: they are Eprius Marcellus and Vibius Crispus (*D.* 8.1–4), who stand for the class of
delatores'.[13] All the odious connotations of that group, as infamous
for the 'strong, savage, and unbridled' viciousness of their oratory as

---

[11] Cf. Heldmann (1982: 170).   [12] Williams (1978: 28).
[13] Barnes (1986: 237).

for the immorality of their prosecutions, are thus imputed to their fellow-traveller, M. Aper.[14] Dismissing him in this way, however, conflates issues of style and morals that are better kept separate.[15]

The self-serving accusers (*delatores*) of the first century are widely reviled by ancient and modern authorities alike for the immorality of their prosecutions, while their manner of speaking has been condemned for its lack of discipline. M. Aquilius Regulus' famous contrast between his own oratory and Pliny's is often cited in this context: 'you think all aspects of a case must be pursued; I spot the throat at once and grab it' (*tu omnia quae sunt in causa putas exsequenda; ego iugulum statim uideo, hunc premo*, Plin. *Ep.* 1.20.14). 'There, uniquely and memorably,' comments Winterbottom, 'speaks the violent oratory of the *delatores*.'[16] The imagery is undoubtedly violent, but the chronology should give us pause. Regulus prosecuted three consulars under Nero and grew rich in the process, but his career as a *delator* ended in 70, when Pliny was still a boy. After Nero's death, Regulus spoke only for the defence in criminal cases and devoted most of his effort to the civil law. By the 90s he had become the leading advocate of the Centumviral court.[17] His prosecutorial career was thus long over by the time Pliny shared a court with him. The context of Regulus' remark—the letter dates from the late 90s—must be the Centumviral court, where speeches were normally limited to an hour or two. Its meaning is plain: 'You beat around the bush. I get straight to the point.' This is not necessarily a vice. Pliny, who once spoke in court for a full seven-hour sitting (*Ep.* 4.16.2–3), might demur, but that is precisely the issue. On what basis should we champion Pliny's rhetorical values? When he faults Regulus for

---

[14] This characterization, which makes the delators' style of speaking as unsavoury as their motives for doing so, was constructed by Syme (1958a: 331–3) and is adopted by e.g. Winterbottom (1964: 90–94) and Kennedy (1972: 440–42). The more balanced view of delation in Sherwin-White (1966: 93–5) deserves wider attention. Aper's biography must be deduced from the *Dialogus* itself. See Gudeman (1914: 68–70) and Syme (1958a: 799–800).

[15] So Luce (1993: 34 n. 74), of Williams (1978), Barnes (1986), et al.: 'The values by and large are those of the twentieth century, not first-century Rome.' Aper's anticlassical sensibility is a frequent source of discomfort. For the range of opinion, see Bo (1993: 222–7).

[16] Winterbottom (1964: 94).

[17] Tac. *H.* 4.42; Plin. *Ep.* 4.7.3–5, 6.2; Mart. 6.38. Cf. Syme (1958a: 101–2) (recasting Pliny's personal opinion as historical fact) and (more circumspectly) Duret (1986: 3268–70).

having only unrestrained genius (*nihil denique praeter ingenium
insanum, Ep.* 4.7.4), he is writing not of an orator without skills
(Regulus' formidable success at the bar proves the contrary) but of
an orator who does not value *his* skills. That too is not the same thing
and not necessarily a bad thing, as modern readers of the *Panegyricus*
ought to know.[18] If given a choice between hearing Regulus plead a
case and hearing Pliny, anyone about to sit on a courtroom bench
might well think twice before choosing the latter. Much of what is
said about Regulus' oratory is doubtless true, but it does not necessarily amount to bad oratory, nor is it inexorably bound to the immorality of delation.

Aper's two oratorical ideals, Eprius Marcellus and Vibius Crispus,
are even more difficult to characterize simply. Or to blend into one.
Marcellus first achieved oratorical prominence as one of the prosecutors of Thrasea Paetus in 66, when he displayed that ferocity in
attack which Syme would make central to his stereotype of the
delators. On that occasion, says Tacitus, he practically glowed with
his natural savagery and menace (*ut erat toruus ac minax, uoce uultu
oculis ardesceret, A.* 16.29.1, cf. 22.6). Upon Paetus' condemnation,
Marcellus received five million sesterces. He then remade himself
under Vespasian, however, becoming proconsul of Asia (70–73)
and suffect consul for a second time (May 74). He held three priest-
hoods and was a trusted adviser to the emperor throughout the 70s.
Vibius Crispus had an even more distinguished career: suffect consul
three times, *curator aquarum*, proconsul, and Imperial legate. As an
orator, he was not an attacker by nature and made his reputation in
civil cases. Both Quintilian and Juvenal call him *iucundus* ('pleasant'),
to which Quintilian adds *elegans* ('suave') and *delectationi natus*
('born to charm', Quint. 5.13.48, 10.1.119; Juv. 4.81–3). His wit, gentle
rather than biting, was famous (Quint. 8.15.3; Suet. *Dom.* 3; Dio
64.2.3). Tacitus, as is his wont, comments darkly on Crispus' prosecution of the Neronian *delator* Annius Faustus, who had destroyed
his brother (*H.* 2.10), but it is at least clear from the ancient testimony
that Crispus and Marcellus had quite different personalities and styles

---

[18] The published *Panegyricus* was in fact an expansion of the speech delivered
in September 100. The captive audience on that occasion restrained Pliny's
natural exuberance: *animaduerti enim seuerissima quaeque uel maxime satisfacere*
(Pl. *Ep.* 3.18.8–9 and Sherwin-White 1966). For a taste of Regulus' aggressive style, in
court and out, see Plin. *Ep.* 1.5, itself a deft exercise in character assassination.

of speaking.[19] What they shared was success and the pragmatism that made success possible. 'I may regard with admiration an earlier period,' Tacitus has Marcellus say, 'but I acquiesce in the present, and, while I pray for good emperors, I endure whatever comes our way' (*H.* 4.8.2). Who in this period could claim more? Even Vipstanus Messala, the somewhat complacent *laudator temporis acti* of the *Dialogus*, saved his half-brother Regulus in 70 when Vespasian shifted the ground under the informers' feet (*H.*4.42). Vespasian himself was a man who Tacitus thought changed for the better when circumstances allowed (*H.*1.50), and Tacitus' own public career soared highest under Titus and Domitian (*H.*1.1.3). Pragmatism of the kind Aper would admire is not in itself sufficient grounds for moral condemnation.

Yet Marcellus and Crispus were hardly moral innocents. Though we may soften our opinion of them by appeal to their subsequent careers, the *Dialogus* is deliberately set in the 70s, when memories of Neronian delation were still fresh and its emerging variant under the Flavians a source of anxiety. Not long before its dramatic date, Marcellus was attacked in the senate by Helvidius Priscus: he walked out in company with Crispus, the one with a scowl and the other with a smirk.[20] Not until the next session did the extent of their imperial protection become clear to all. Aper deliberately and favourably recalls this very scene just before citing Marcellus and Crispus as positive examples of self-made men (*D.* 5.7). Their great wealth, he continues, is the reward of their oratory (*ad has ipsas opes possunt uideri eloquentiae beneficio uenisse*, *D.* 8.2), and they have gained it without the concomitant gifts of birth, talent, or good character (*sine commendatione natalium, sine substantia facultatum, neuter moribus egregius*, *D.* 8.3). Maternus promptly shows the ambiguity of such praise by disavowing 'the practice of this profitable and bloody eloquence, new and born from bad character' (*lucrosae*

---

[19] *Pace* Winterbottom (1964), who, like Syme, makes Tacitus' bias against them his own. The great difficulty in assessing such figures lies in distinguishing matters of fact in the record from matters of taste. As Duret (1986: 3270) observes of Tacitus and Pliny, 'En fait, l'unité de ce "style de la délation" risque d'avoir existé surtout dans l'esprit des auteurs classicisants.'

[20] *H.* 4.43.2: *ambo infensi, uoltu diuerso, Marcellus minacibus oculis, Crispus renidens...* The description is a masterpiece of innuendo but also true to their separate natures as Tacitus records them. Winterbottom (1964: 93) accepts the narrative at face value.

huius et sanguinantis eloquentiae usus recens et ex malis moribus natus, D. 12.2). The *eloquentia* to which he refers is clearly that of the *delatores*. Is he not then also repudiating the men Aper admires and thus the values he represents?

It would be easier to accept Maternus' remark as a sweeping repudiation of the delators' *lucrosa eloquentia* ('profitable eloquence') and to join him in that condemnation if he were distinguishing between their oratory and some other, better kind of oratory. His distinction, however, is simply between oratory and poetry, as if all oratory that is *recens* ('new') is necessarily *ex malis moribus natus* ('born from bad character'). He speaks as if his choice lies between becoming a poet and becoming a delator. This is a false division, dismissing at a stroke both the pleasure Aper takes in the orator's power and that power itself. Maternus prefers the poet's life. Where Aper delights in the clamour of litigants, he seeks only quiet and seclusion and looks to a Golden Age teeming not with advocates and accusations, but with poets and seers (*et oratorum et criminum inops, poetis et uatibus abundabat, D.* 12.3). His language at this point is highly wrought—Maternus' poetic temperament perhaps gets the better of him[21]—but we should not follow his lead, for the position he advocates is as morally difficult as Aper's.

Aper had made his case for the utility of oratory in broad social terms. A man like Maternus, he says, is 'born to that manly eloquence and oratory, with which he can simultaneously secure and protect friendships, assume obligations, champion provinces' (*D.* 5.4). These were the obligations immortalized by Cicero, which is why Aper sketches the orator's power in deliberately Ciceronian terms.

quid est tutius quam eam exercere artem qua semper armatus praesidium amicis, opem alienis, salutem periclitantibus, inuidis uero et inimicis metum et terrorem ultro ferat, ipse securus et uelut quadam	*quid tam porro regium, tam liberale, tam munificum, quam opem ferre supplicibus, excitare adflictos, dare salutem, liberare periculis, retinere homines in ciuitate? quid autem tam necessarium, quam tenere*

---

[21] Note the invidious balance of *inops . . . abundabat* and the clichéd redundancy of *poetis et uatibus*. *Sanguinans* (*D.* 12.2) is a very unusual word. Even *sanguineus* would be unexpected: the normal word in prose is *cruentus*, e.g. Cic. *Har.* 3, *imperio cruento illo*; *Phil.* 1.17, *pecunia cruenta illa*. Cf. Sal. *Cat.* 58.21, *cruentam ac luctuosam uictoriam*. Maternus' cretic rhythm is also striking.

perpetua potentia ac potestate munitus?	*semper arma quibus uel tectus ipse esse possis uel prouocare improbos uel te ulcisci lacessitus?*
What is more secure than to practice an art by which one is always armed to bring protection to friends, aid to strangers, safety to those in danger, yet also fear and terror to the envious and the hostile, while you yourself are safe and fortified as if by some everlasting power and authority? (*D*.5.5)	What is as regal, as humane, as generous as bringing aid to the distressed, rescuing the afflicted, providing safety, freeing from danger, saving men from exile? What is as essential as always holding weapons with which you can defend yourself or challenge the wicked or take revenge when provoked? (*de Or.* 1.32)

Even the sinister enthusiasm of Aper's *metum et terrorem ferat* finds an equivalent in Cicero's *tenere semper arma*. This correspondence is entirely apposite, since the social functions of the orator as Cicero describes them were hardly out of date under the emperors. Precisely this kind of obligation to clients and friends led Pliny and Tacitus not only to prosecute Marius Priscus for corruption and extortion when he was proconsul of Africa, but to refuse mere restitution to his victims, instead pressing remorselessly for a sentence of exile. It was, or so Pliny would claim, an action in the old republican style.[22] Even the whiff of vainglory and corruption in Aper's declaration of oratory's rewards ('what is sweeter . . . than to see one's house always crowded, filled with an assembly of very distinguished men?', *D.* 6.2) recalls a pleasure known and valued under Republic and Empire alike. When, for example, Pliny reminds Tacitus of the students who flock to him, drawn by his oratorical brilliance (*copia studiosorum, quae ad te ex admiratione ingenii tui conuenit*), he hardly intends to arouse an unpleasant memory in his consular friend (*Ep.* 4.13.10, cf. *Ep.* 7.20). For Maternus to repudiate the oratorical enterprise itself, which is what he does in preferring silence to the clamour of litigants at his door (*D.* 12.1), is therefore to turn his back not just on vanity and avarice but on the very obligations of his class to his society.[23] How

---

[22] Plin. *Pan.* 76.1–2. The prosecution was complex and probably extended from a first indictment in 98 to final judgement in 100. See Syme (1958a: 70–71); Sherwin-White (1966: 56–8); Brink (1994: 277–8).

[23] Thus, in defending Aper, Champion (1994: 155) stresses the social context of his first argument: 'Aper's concern with the public recognition of status lay at the core of the Roman aristocratic mentality.'

high a moral position is that? The rash of senatorial prosecutions that we associate with the delators may well have been distasteful to a man like Maternus, but such distaste does not justify abandoning the legitimate needs of clients and friends. He is admittedly no coward—his plays are themselves acts of courage (*D.* 3.3) and he maintains his readiness to defend any senatorial colleague in need (*D.* 11.4)—but the strength of Aper's argument lies not with such extraordinary demands as these but in the ordinary press of business that marks, and even justifies, the aristocrat's place in the society that supports him. Maternus' withdrawal from such traditional civic duties when he still has much to accomplish (*D.* 5.4) is thus fraught with moral ambiguities.[24]

After all, it remained well within an aristocrat's power to fulfil these obligations, even the obligation to prosecute, without becoming a *delator*. The administration of justice at Rome depended on the expertise of what, in modern terms, were always private advocates. Claiming the right to legal redress (*postulatio*), filing an indictment (*delatio nominis*), and speaking as *accusator* in family matters were traditionally domestic responsibilities. The prosecution by individuals of offences alleged in the public domain also had a long history, though the distinction between prosecution as a political weapon and as an exercise in civic responsibility was sometimes difficult to see.[25] Cicero struck a particularly high-minded pose when asserting his right to prosecute Verres (*Diu. Caec.* 27–47), though his motives were not entirely unselfish. Nearly two centuries later, Quintilian was still reminding readers that rooting out corruption through legal action remained a patriot's duty (*Inst.* 12.7.1–5). The evil that arose under Tiberius was not an increase in prosecutions *per se* but something much more specific, the use of prosecution for private gain, which did not really cease until the time of Trajan. Delation was

---

[24] Neither Thrasea Paetus' withdrawal under pressure from public affairs in 65 nor Tacitus' own apparent retirement after the prosecution of Marius Priscus is quite comparable. Cf. Luce (1993: 17, n.20): 'Maternus' decision to abandon public life seems particularly at odds with Tacitus' praise for those who serve the state well, despite the dangers and difficulties: *Agr.* 42.4, *Ann.* 4.20.2.'

[25] Cf. Gruen (1968: 6): 'The criminal prosecution as a political weapon . . . occurs with such frequency and regularity that it may legitimately be regarded almost as an institution. To a surprisingly, perhaps alarmingly, large extent, the business of politics was carried out not in the *comitia* or in the *curia,* but in the courts.' Politically motivated trials of course remained familiar to later generations as well.

Sander M. Goldberg 167

no simple phenomenon to be roused or abolished at will.[26] The legal waters could be murky, but not murky enough to justify Maternus for staying aloof or to justify the condemnation of Aper for plunging in.

THE ASSAULT ON SERIOUSNESS

The second assault on Aper's credibility takes two forms. The first trivializes his argument. In his second speech, Aper objects to applying the term *antiqui* ('ancients') to Cicero and his contemporaries. Only 120 years, the span of a single generation's memory, separates him from Cicero. Old men he had heard in his youth could have heard Cicero in *their* youth: 'You can't split up time like this, and go on using "ancient" and "old-timers" of men whom the same hearers could have recognized and thus joined to us in a single life-span' (*D.* 17.6). His opponent Messala dismisses this line of argument as a quibble—'I am not fighting about a word,' says he (*D.* 25.2)—and some moderns share his view, but the point at issue is not simply a matter of labels. Aper's defence of modernism is also an attack on the retrospective admiration of past performances that encourages the creation of a canon of orators. Because good oratory is simply effective oratory, resistance to the formation of a canon is central to the pragmatist's case. Eloquence, he will say, 'does not have a single face' (*non esse unum eloquentiae uultum, D.* 18.3). Not even the 'ancients' Cicero, Brutus, and Calvus agreed among themselves on such matters (*D.* 18.5–6). All we can do is judge speeches on their own merits and understand them within the context of their own time and situation. Where Aper will concede a turning point in the history of oratory therefore does not come with Cicero, however high he raised the standards of Roman *eloquentia*. This is why, though acknowledging Cicero's greatness, Aper treats him outside the basically chronological

---

[26] So, rightly, Luce (1993: 23 n.40). This was probably why Quintilian had to point out that prosecution in the expectation of gain was a kind of larceny: *itaque ut accusatoriam uitam uiuere et ad deferendos reos praemio duci proximum latrocinio est, ita pestem intestinam propulsare cum propugnatoribus patriae comparandum* (*Inst.* 12.7.3). Cf. Plin. *Pan.* 34 on the *delatorum agmen . . . quasi grassatorum quasi latronum* rooted out by Trajan. Yet as Sherwin-White (1966: 95) observes: 'the professional *delator* could not be eliminated, because the Roman state had no other means of enforcing its laws'.

order of his survey and emphasizes the faults of Cicero's early speeches ('slow in his openings, prolix in his narratives, lax in his digressions', *D.* 22.3) over the brilliance of his eventual achievement. When viewed from the perspective of the later first century AD, Cicero's world was still essentially the world of Licinius Crassus, the Gracchi, and the elder Cato, a world that gave extraordinary licence to the orator. For Aper, the significant change came a generation later with Cassius Severus (d. *c.* AD 34), because he was the first orator to face judges and juries lacking the patience for rhetorical display.

Cicero and his contemporaries treated persuasion as 'a function more of emotion than of fact, but the Centumviral court of Cassius' day had become a place of business. Judges who know the law create neither the need nor the opportunity for technical proofs or complex (and potentially tendentious) legal explications. The one passage in the *Dialogus* that deals with the orator's *ars* is thus a telling attack on rhetorical technique as Aper ridicules the arid precepts to be found in the manuals of Hermagoras and Apollodorus. His criticism of them is not misplaced, nor is his impatience with the self-serving convolutions of a speech like Cicero's *Pro Caecina.*[27] Aper here is championing the legal rationality that in fact brought about a marked improvement in the administration of justice at Rome. From the standpoint of purely legal history, the 'decline' of oratory was a very good thing, a final tipping of the balance between advocates and jurists in the latter's favour.[28]

Messala in turn will grant Cassius the title *orator*, at least in contrast to his successors, but will also criticize him as crude and unsophisticated: his vehemence is unrefined (*plus bilis habeat quam sanguinis*, 'he has more bile than vitality', *D.* 26.4) and he lacks

---

[27] *D.* 19.3–20.4 with the comments of Gudeman (1914: 323–34). Contrast such passages as Cic. *de Or.* 2.178: *ipse [qui audiet] sic moueatur, ut impetu quodam animi et perturbatione magis quam iudicio aut consilio regatur* and *de Rep.* 59: *apud me, ut apud bonum iudicem, argumenta plus quam testes ualent.* This was the style of presentation that could lead a jurist like C. Aquilius Gallus to remark (with some impatience?), *nihil hoc ad ius; ad Ciceronem* (*Top.* 51). The dilemma presented at *Quint.* 78–83, a case heard by Aquilius as *iudex*, is a nice example of a proof that Aper would doubtless find both *longus* and *otiosus.*

[28] Cf. Frier (1985: 266), and for the deliberate obscurity of legal issues in a Ciceronian speech, Brunt (1982). Given these advances in the judicial system, it is difficult to know what Pliny meant in professing his *cum Cicerone aemulatio* (*Ep.* 1.5.12) or how Cicero would have been a good model for advocates before the Centumviral Court of the mid-90s.

technique (*non pugnat sed rixatur*, 'he does not fight, but brawls', *D.* 26.4). This stylistic judgement also appears in Quintilian, but it is not entirely fair to Cassius.[29] We know him best from the elder Seneca, who devoted the preface of *Controuersiae* 3 to discussing why Cassius was a better advocate than declaimer. Seneca describes a dignified and powerful court speaker, straightforward in both argument and language (cf. Quint. *Inst.* 8.2.2). His speeches contained nothing extraneous (*nihil in quo auditor sine damno aliud ageret*, 'there was no place where the listener could afford to let his attention drift', Sen. *Contr.* 3 preface 2) and were short enough that he could plead two private cases in a single day.[30] His greatness as an orator, however, did not rest solely on his words. It was inseparable from his impressive physique, his noble bearing, and the resonance and range of his voice. He was also a great improviser, playing to the needs of the moment and always with an eye on the judge (7). None of these gifts translates well to a published text, which is why, says Seneca, 'It is impossible to judge him from his publications . . . he was far greater heard than read.'[31] Aper aside, Seneca is our one great admirer of Cassius precisely because he is the only one of our sources to have heard him speak. The key point about Cassius Severus, then, is that with him oratory continued to be oratorical, but it ceased to be literary.[32]

The second prong of the assault on Aper's seriousness questions the sincerity of his argument: his position is easier to dismiss if he does not believe it himself. So Maternus seeks to soften the vehemence of Aper's speech (*quo torrente, quo impetu saeculum nostrum defendit!*, 'With what a torrent of words, with what energy did he defend the age in which we live!', *D.* 24.1) by suggesting that he speaks less for himself than for the sake of the argument. Such posturing was one way Cicero represented argument *in utramque partem*, and

---

[29] *D.* 26.4; Quint. 10.1.116–17, 12.10.11. Brink (1989: 484–94) detects in Messala's speech strong echoes of Quintilian's lost *De causis corruptae eloquentiae*. For Cassius, see Bornecque (1902: 157–9); Winterbottom (1964: 90–92); Heldmann (1982: 163–98).

[30] Sen. *Contr.* 3 Pr. 5. Cassius almost invariably prosecuted, though not often successfully. Cf. his revenge on Cestius, the Cloaca Maxima of declamation, as reported at Sen. *Contr.* 3 Pr. 17 and the story in Macr. *Sat.* 2.4.9.

[31] Sen. *Contr.* 3 Pr. 3. Cf. 4: *deinde ipsa quae dicebat meliora erant quam quae scribebat.*

[32] This is itself no mere quibble over 'the literary', since the point at issue between Aper and Maternus is less the quality of modern oratory than whether to be an orator at all under modern conditions.

Maternus imputes this role to Aper in language calculated to recall the Ciceronian precedent.[33]

Quae cum Aper dixisset, 'agnoscitisne', inquit Maternus 'uim et ardorem Apri nostri?...ac ne ipse quidem ita sentit, sed more ueteri et a nostris philosophis saepe celebrato sumpsit sibi contra dicendi partes'.

Haec cum Antonius dixisset...Tum Crassus 'operarium nobis quendam, Antoni, oratorem facis atque haud scio an aliter sentias et utare tua illa mirifica ad refellendum consuetudine, qua tibi nemo umquam praestitit; cuius quidem ipsius facultatis exercitatio oratorum propria est, sed iam in philosophorum consuetudine uersatur maximeque eorum, qui de omni re proposita in utramque partem solent copiosissime dicere...'

...neque aut Secundum aut Maternum aut te ipsum, Aper, quamquam interdum in contrarium disputes, aliter sentire credo.

After Aper had said these things, Maternus spoke: 'Do you recognize our friend Aper's power and zeal?...yet not even he believes this, but following in the old way often championed by our friends the philosophers, he has taken on himself the task of speaking in opposition.' (*D.*24.1–2)

After Antonius had said these things...Then Crassus: 'You are making our orator into some kind of labourer, Antonius, but I suspect you think otherwise and are employing that remarkable taste of yours for refutation, at which nobody has ever excelled you. The exercise of that ability certainly belongs to the orators, but now it is utilized most particularly by those philosophers, who are accustomed to argue with great fluency on both sides of every proposition...' (*de Or.* 1.263)

(cf. *D.* 15.2, Messala speaking): I don't believe Secundus or Maternus or even you, Aper, think otherwise, despite your occasional arguments to the contrary.

---

[33] The formal debt to *de Oratore* is very well analysed by Haß-von Reitzenstein (1970: 131–43). Deuse (1975: 51–68) rightly wonders how readers are meant to

Why does Tacitus create this deliberate echo? It is not sufficient to claim on structural grounds that Tacitus associates Antonius and Aper in order to repudiate Aper's position. As we have seen in the proemium, similar form does not guarantee similar content. It may help to put the question a slightly different way: why does Tacitus direct attention to this particular passage at the end of the first book of *de Oratore*?

Antonius there has just finished arguing against Crassus' famous notion that the true orator is one who can speak effectively on any subject: *quaecumque res inciderit, quae sit dictione explicanda, prudenter et composite et ornate et memoriter dicet* ('whatever matters crop up which must be unfurled in dialogue, he will speak wisely, methodically, charmingly and with a ready recollection', *de Or.* 1.64). That demand for universal knowledge, countered Antonius, requires of the orator unnecessary and unrealistic skills. An orator is simply an effective speaker: he needs broad but not particularly deep knowledge (*de Or.* 1.213–18). This refutation is often dismissed because Cicero in his own voice seems to endorse Crassus' position early in the next book (*de Or.* 2.5). Critics who treat Crassus as Cicero's spokesman therefore discount Antonius' reply and point to his own more accommodating stance later in the dialogue (cf. *de Or.* 2.40ff.). There are two reasons, however, not to ignore Antonius' initial argument. First, he is probably right in what he says. Take knowledge of the law, so central to modern ideas of courtroom pleading but so oddly peripheral to Republican Roman practice. Antonius' cavalier attitude toward civil law throughout the dialogue (*de Or.* 1.234–55, cf. 2.142–5) belittles Crassus' recommendation that the orator make an extensive study of Greek and Roman law (*de Or.* 1.57–9, 165–200). He does so not as devil's advocate but as spokesman for his time and place: *Crassus'* view is the exceptional one.

Advocacy and jurisprudence stood in uneasy alliance throughout the Republican period.[34] Advocates of the late Republic were not jurists and had only limited respect for the men who were. Though pleading a case would, as a practical matter, require some knowledge

---

respond to Aper, but his answer to that question is unconvincing. See Luce (1993: 19–20). Similar claims for Aper as devil's advocate are made at *D.* 16.3 by Maternus and at *D.* 15.2 and 28.1 by Messala, but as Williams (1978: 43) observes, 'Aper never gives the slightest hint that the views he expresses are not his own.'

[34] Frier (1985: 252–4), and, more generally, Rawson (1985: 201–14).

of legal procedure (*Part.* 99–100), there was a common belief that only failed orators actually became jurists (Cic. *Mur.* 29, Quint. 12.3.9, 11). Crassus himself was self-trained in the law and never gave *responsa*.[35] Neither did Cicero. When forced to give up oratory in the 40s, he would reflect proudly on his early study with the jurist Scaevola (*Amic.* 1.1) and on the social significance of the jurisconsult (*Off.* 2.65); but as consul in his prime, Cicero's public attitude was quite different. In *Pro Murena*, for example, he played off the traditional Roman distrust of 'experts' by gently mocking the prosecutor Sulpicius, a jurist of note, as a well-meaning but impractical legal theorist lost in the public arena (*Mur.* 19–30). What legal knowledge an advocate needs, Cicero claimed, could be acquired at will: 'If you provoked me, a very busy man, would I not turn myself into a legal authority within three days?'[36] This is precisely Antonius' point. Like M. Aper after him, he is a practical man and talks sense.

Second, privileging Crassus' argument at the expense of his opponent is not fair to the nature of *de Oratore* and not a good strategy for reading it. Cicero's own voice is not to be heard in any one of its characters to the exclusion of others. Back in 155 BC, the elder Cato may have been genuinely puzzled over the philosopher Carneades' ability to argue opposite sides of a proposition with equal conviction, but by Cicero's day Romans understood both the technique and the point of arguing *in utramque partem*. A didactic handbook like the *Partitiones oratoriae* would employ an authoritative voice, but the exploration of theoretical concerns in the first book of *de Oratore* requires something quite different. It is not an explication but a deliberately contentious, unresolved debate offering not 'a straight-

---

[35] Cic. *Off.* 2.43; *Brut.* 155. Whether the historical Antonius hid his learning or was in fact comparatively unschooled remains unclear. Cic. *de Or.* 2.4 and 2.153 suggest a pose; *Brut.* 139–42 is deliberately vague on the point. See Leeman and Pinkster (1985: 187–8) and Hall (1994: 211–16).

[36] *Mur.* 28: *itaque si mihi, homini uehementer occupato, stomachum moueritis, triduo me iuris consultum esse profitebor?* For Cicero's strategy, see Kennedy (1972: 181–6). Note that, although the *praetor urbanus* was the Republic's chief legal officer, no urban praetor of the late Republic is known to have had more than a layman's knowledge of law (Frier 1985: 47–8). At *Mur.* 54–85 Cicero metes out similar treatment to the second prosecutor, Cato, casting him as an impractical philosopher. Cato was not amused ('What a witty consul, we have!', Plut. *Cat. Min.* 21.5–6), but the strategy clearly paid off. As Gruen (1984: 247) observes in the diplomatic context, 'Specific credentials were unsought and unneeded. Indeed, they would go against the grain of an aristocratic society whose leaders asserted capacity in every aspect of public life.'

forward argument resulting in a fixed conception, but rather a grop-
ing for probabilities, attitudes and points of view'.[37] To dismiss
Antonius' speech in this theoretical part of the work because he will
concede its limits at the beginning of its technical exposition (*de Or.*
2.41) or because Cicero will echo his opponent (*de Or.* 2.5) is to
seek—wrongly—just such a fixed conception.[38] Yet Tacitus is not
pointing to *de Oratore* simply to recall Cicero's complexity. He adds
a still richer complexity of his own.

Messala follows Aper's second speech with an argument for the
virtues of full and old-fashioned education. Modernity, he says, is
only an excuse for expedience and lack of discipline. An orator of
Cicero's success must have had extensive knowledge of all subjects
(*non denique ullius ingenuae artis scientiam ei defuisse*, 'in short he
was not lacking knowledge in any area of higher learning', *D.* 30.4),
needed knowledge of human nature to argue his cases successfully (*de
quibus copiose et uarie et ornate nemo dicere potest nisi qui cognouit
naturam humanam*, 'nobody can speak about such things with full-
ness, variety and elegance unless he has come to know human nature',
D. 31.2), and could not simply have acquired all that knowledge as the
need arose (*nec quisquam respondeat sufficere ut ad tempus simplex
quiddam et uniforme doceamur*, 'Let nobody argue in response that it
is enough for us to learn for the occasion some simple issue of a single
kind', *D.* 32.1). Both the argument and its expression are meant to be
familiar. Having sent us back to *de Oratore* by echoing its structural
formulae, Tacitus has made it all the easier for readers to recognize
Messala's speech for what it is, a somewhat complacent and jejune
version of the argument that Crassus had made and Antonius refuted.
Tacitus' allusion invites us to hear Messala's speech in the context of
their exchange. He has several ways to undercut Messala—the very
mise en scène of the *Dialogus,* for example, contradicts Messala's
claim that the *tirocinium fori* ('training-ground of the forum') is a
dead institution—but none is more effective than this intertextual

---

[37] Leeman (1975: 146). For the importance of the Academic style of argument to
Cicero, see Hall (1994: 222–3). Here too Tacitus follows Ciceronian precedent: 'The
real Tacitus is not to be found in any one character's *ipsissima uerba*, but must be
deduced from them all' (Murgia 1980: 111; cf. Brink 1993: 34 and *D.* 1.3). Haß-von
Reitzenstein (1970: 34) is therefore not quite correct to call the *Dialogus* the first
Roman dialogue to be something more than a textbook in disguise. For the famous
Carneades episode, see Plin. *N.H.* 7.112; Plut. *Cat. Mai.* 22.2–5; Cic. *Rep.* 3.8–12.

[38] For the bipartite structure of *de Oratore,* see Cic. *Att.* 4.16.3.

refutation of Messala's speech by M. Antonius. Tacitus gives Aper a potent ally.

He finds additional support within the *Dialogus* itself, though it comes from an unexpected quarter. The very last speech brings us back to the beliefs of Curiatius Maternus. He had begun the discussion by announcing that he would turn his back on the orators' kind of eloquence: 'I chose some time ago . . . to give up the narrow squabbles of forensic cases, over which I have sweated more than enough, and to cultivate that more sacred and revered eloquence' (*ut omissis forensium causarum angustiis, in quibus mihi satis superque sudatum est, sanctiorem illam et augustiorem eloquentiam colam, D. 4.2*). Now he returns to the nature of *eloquentia*, this time with an echo and a confirmation of Aper's central points: that legal arguments do not encourage fulsome oratory, and that modern taste does not tolerate histrionics. It is no longer necessary to interpret a praetor's interdict for the benefit of an untrained judge, or to turn a speech into a performance. As courts have become places of business, oratory must yield to argument.

Aper	Maternus
20.1: *quis <de> exceptione et formula perpetietur illa inmensa uolumina quae pro M. Tullio aut Aulo Caecina legimus?*	37.4: *nam multum interest utrumne de furto aut formula et interdicto dicendum habeas an de ambitu comitiorum, de expilatis sociis et ciuibus trucidatis.*
20.3: *nec magis perfert* [sc. *uulgus*] *in iudiciis tristem et inpexam antiquitatem quam si quis in scaena Roscii aut Turpionis Ambiuii exprimere gestus uelit.*	39.4: *oratori autem clamore plausuque opus est et uelut quodam theatro, qualia cotidie antiquis oratoribus contingebant.*
20.1: Who endures those immense volumes about counterpleas and stipulations that we read on behalf of M. Tullius or Aulus Caecina?	37.4: It makes a considerable difference whether you must speak about a theft or a ruling or an injunction or about electoral fraud, the pillage of allies, or the slaughter of citizens.
20.3: Nor does the crowd tolerate that grim and unshaven antiquity in trials any more than if someone wished to copy the gestures of Roscius or Ambivius Turpio on the stage.	39.4: An orator needs noise and applause and a kind of theatre, such as the ancient orators encountered every day.

What is new this time around is Maternus' emphasis on the cost of the old eloquence, nourished as it was by the social strife of the dying Republic: 'great eloquence, like a flame, is nourished by fuel and flares up with movement and brightens as it burns' (*magna eloquentia, sicut flamma, materia alitur et motibus excitatur et urendo clarescit, D.* 36.1). Unlike Aper, he tacitly assumes Messala's distinction between 'ancients' and 'moderns' (*D.* 36.2), but not to canonize the *antique* ('ancients'). Maternus accepts Aper's view that the old eloquence is dead as nails, and he does not want it back.

Aper	Maternus
23.5–6: *uos uero, disertissimi <uiri>, ut potestis, ut facitis, inlustrate saeculum nostrum pulcherrimo genere dicendi. . . . sic exprimitis adfectus, sic libertatem temperatis, ut etiam si nostra iudicia malignitas et inuidia tardauerit, uerum de uobis dicturi sint posteri nostri.*	40.2: *non de otiosa et quieta re loquimur et quae probitate et modestia gaudeat, sed est magna illa notabilis eloquentia alumna licentiae, quam stulti libertatem uocant, comes seditionum, effrenati populi incitamentum sine obsequio, sine seueritate, contumax temeraria adrogans, quae in bene constitutis ciuitatibus non oritur.*
23.5–6: Distinguish our age, my very eloquent friends, as you can, as you do, with the most handsome kind of speaking . . . You produce such emotion, you so moderate freedom that even if our own judgements are dulled by envy and jealousy, our posterity will speak the truth about you.	40.2: We are not speaking about some casual and calm thing that rejoices in probity and modesty, but that great and famous eloquence, the nursling of license, which fools call liberty, the companion of sedition, the goad of an unbridled populace, without submission, without dignity, insolent, rash, arrogant, such as does not arise in a well-organized state.

Aper's view of eloquence could be pragmatic (*ut potestis, ut facitis*) because he accepts present conditions at face value. Like Quintilian, he is comfortable in his world and not intimidated by its memories (cf. *Inst.* 12.11.28: 'if there is no expectation of surpassing the great, there is nevertheless great honour in following them'). Aper willingly accepts any oratory that has lost neither its utility nor its reward. Maternus accepts the new style for a much bleaker reason: the price of the old one was too high. The eloquence of the Gracchi or of Cicero was too dearly bought (*D.* 40.4). He therefore repudiates the old *eloquentia* in almost a parody of Cicero's own formulation: 'not among those organizing a government or waging wars or hampered and bound by the tyranny of kings is the passion for speaking accustomed to be born. Eloquence is the companion of peace, the ally of leisure and like a kind of nursling of a well-organized state' (*nec enim in constituentibus rem publicam nec in bella gerentibus nec in impeditis ac regum dominatione deuinctis nasci cupiditas dicendi solet. pacis est comes otique socia et iam bene constitutae ciuitatis quasi alumna quaedam eloquentia, Brut.* 45). Like Aper, Maternus finds his contemporaries as eloquent as conditions require. And he is glad they have no need for greater eloquence.[39] The discussion has made him no more willing to resume his oratorical career but much clearer about his reasons for refusing to do so.

His acceptance of the new condition of oratory often disconcerts and disturbs modern readers. It may be too tinged by vanity (*D.* 39.3). It is certainly too acceptive of the Imperial system: 'What need is there for long speeches in the senate, when the best men immediately agree? Why have great assemblies before the people, when not the inexperienced and the many decide affairs of state but the wisest man alone?' (*quid enim opus est longis in senatu sententiis cum optimi cito consentiant? quid multis apud populum contionibus cum de re publica non imperiti et multi deliberent sed sapientissimus et unus?, D.* 41.4). How can the man whose outspokenness provided the very occasion for this discussion now speak so submissively? Surely, Maternus, like Aper, cannot mean what he says. His speech must be either an ironic 'accommodation' to political realities or some kind of 'doublespeak'.[40] Taken by themselves, Maternus' words may well strike a reader this way, but they should not be isolated from their cultural context. Maternus' sentiments are hardly unique. Quintilian used very similar words, without irony and possibly even with relief, in observing that modern orators no longer required the kind of urgent appeal found in Cicero's *Pro Murena*: 'that kind of thing is almost completely gone in

---

[39] *D.* 41.5. Maternus thus puts in a favourable light the topos also found in the roughly contemporary *de Sublim.* that great writers flourished with democracy and died with it (44.2–12).

[40] So, respectively, Rudich (1985: 95–100) and Bartsch (1994). Bartsch (1994: 110–16) is especially good on the tensions within Maternus' last speech, but I remain sceptical of any argument that denies to Tacitus the ability to mean what the critic does not want him to mean.

our day, since everything rests on the care and protection of a single man and cannot be endangered by the outcome of a trial', (*quod genus nostris temporibus totum paene sublatum est, cum omnia curae tutelaeque unius innixa periclitari nullo iudicii exitu possint, Inst.* 6.1.35). Pliny was certainly relieved to find in Trajan an emperor 'in whose hands both the state and ourselves rest' (*in quo et res publica et nos sumus*).[41] There is no reason for Maternus, early in Vespasian's Principate, to be any less sincere in expressing these sentiments than Pliny was early in the reign of Trajan or, for that matter, Tacitus was when writing them for Maternus in the time of Nerva. Ironic readings of Maternus' words are predicated on (and necessitated by) not so much the argument of the *Dialogus* itself as too sweeping a sense of oratory's 'decline'. Accept a more nuanced view of decline, a view that finds a place for Maternus' equation of eloquence with verbosity and liberty with civil strife, and we are free to take his speech, like Aper's, at face value.

This is not a reductive or simplistic reading, but it does suggest a somewhat *different* reading of the *Dialogus*. Restoring Aper's role to seriousness and respectability forces us to recognize in his two speeches a shrewd, progressive, and fundamentally receptive analysis of contemporary literature. Aper brings to the centre of the debate those changed circumstances which both redefined the practice of Roman oratory in the early Empire and established the governing aesthetic of the period.[42] As Williams observes,[43] Aper is never refuted, and the fact that Maternus himself, with all the weight of the closing speaker, eventually defines a place for oratory in terms very like Aper's shows the power and, I would say, the fundamental accuracy of his sense of modernity. The real point of the *Dialogus* is thus not to retell an old and presumably sad tale of oratory's decline. The direction oratory should take—what of the old style was worth

---

[41] *Pan.* 72.1. Cf. Plin. *Ep.* 3.20.12 (*sunt quidem cuncta sub unius arbitrio*), leading Sherwin-White (1966: 262) to observe, 'The position must have been generally recognized for Pliny to state it so frankly.' Brink (1993: 347) stresses the relevance of all these passages to Maternus' speech.

[42] Costa (1969: 31): 'May we not then see behind those parts of the treatise which defend contemporary oratory a wider defence of Silver Latin prose style, of which Tacitus himself was to become the most notable exponent?'. Costa's distinction (27–31) between the 'ostensible subject' of the *Dialogus* and its wider ramifications deserves more serious consideration.

[43] Williams (1978: 43).

restoring and what of the new was right to maintain—was a matter of real interest (and uncertainty) after the death of Domitian. By exploring this question in all its complexity, Tacitus suggests a new, not necessarily inferior, definition of Roman *eloquentia*. As a meditation on the dynamics of literary change, the *Dialogus* thus emerges as a key work for recovering not just the literary values of the so-called Silver Age, but the forces at work in generating those values.

ADDENDUM, 2009

Students of the *Dialogus* have much to gain from Mayer (2001), the first full commentary to appear in nearly a century. Its sensitivity to stylistic nuance and Ciceronian echo leads to many fine insights, though Mayer's reading of the work is very dark and reviewers have chided him for suppressing alternative views.[44]

Issues raised here remain central to scholarly discussion. The traditional view of oratorical decline, given a thoughtful, measured defence by Reinhardt and Winterbottom (2006: xxxiv–xxxvii), maintains its appeal among philologically oriented critics such as Dammer (2005). The more positive view of Imperial oratory advanced here draws support from other quarters. Crook (1995: 172–97) set the tone by stressing the continued vitality of legal advocacy under the emperors. So too Bablitz (2007), and recent studies of Quintilian, e.g. Hall (2004) and Leigh (2004), are consistent with that view. Rutledge (1999) specifically challenges the stereotype of the *delatores*' 'violent' oratory, and the biographical data in Rutledge (2001) further complicates the picture by cataloguing the many legitimate civic achievements of men like Eprius Marcellus (225–8), Vibius Crispus (278–82), and Aquilius Regulus (192–8). For the career of Cassius Severus, see Kaster (1995: 225–6). There is also growing recognition that Romans of Tacitus' generation did not necessarily see the *libertas* of the late Republic as a virtue: Fantham (2004: 319–26) and Gowing (2005: 109–20) address the shifting memory of the Republic in the later Principate and the implications of that revalued memory for interpretation of the *Dialogus*. Their arguments are part of a larger movement to set the *Dialogus* within the broader context of Roman struggles with literary history, in particular the problems of periodization and canon formation familiar to historians of all literatures. Schwindt (2000: 196–206) and Levene (2004) make important contributions to this approach.

---

[44] *BMCR* 2002.03.05 (Goldberg), *Phoenix* 57 (2003) 351–3 (Barnes), *CR* 54 (2004) 410–12 (Corbeill).

Ironic readings of Maternus' last speech thus continue to be challenged as broader views of the Imperial system develop, e.g. Lier (1996), Winterbottom (2001), Gallia (2009). The great distinction of Tacitus' public career into the second century, conveniently traced by Birley (2000), also remains to be reconciled with the persona of the brooding ironist familiar from the *Histories* and *Annals*, while renewed interest in Pliny as a significant public and literary figure in his own right has encouraged reassessment of their friendship, the significance of their oratorical careers, and thus the health of oratory in Trajan's Rome: Griffin (1999), Dominik (2007), Edwards (2008).

These, along with other issues in what has become a rich and productive debate, are surveyed in detail by Goldberg (2009: 73–84).

6

The *Agricola*: Stepping-stone to History

Ettore Paratore

It is clear that the *Agricola*, as the first external manifestation of Tacitus' impulse towards historiography, and also—in line with the fixed characteristics we have detected in our author's early production—dealing with the same historical period that Tacitus was about to study in depth, shows material points of contact with the *Histories* and, to a lesser degree, even with the *Annals*. Anyone who is willing to dwell upon these substantive analogies will discover something which is hardly surprising, but which in fact confirms the line of development we have already begun to trace in Tacitus's work and thinking: the points of contact with the *Histories* do not show any considerable discordance, but those with the *Annals* denote an imperfect correspondence.

The most conspicuous example of the latter is found in *Agricola* 14–16, which narrates the history of Britain in the period preceding Agricola's government. This is a subject to which Tacitus will return at *Annals* 14.29–39. A comparison with these chapters shows that the main storyline remains identical: the leaders named are the same, Didius Gallus, Veranius, Suetonius Paulinus. However, in the *Agricola*, although there is mention of the attack on the island of Mona in AD 61 (*Agr.* 14), there is silence about the excesses committed by the Romans (*Annals* 14.30). Even there he justifies them by reference to the Druids' *saeuae superstitiones*, 'savage superstitions', to which the island was stage, so much so that, in the Christian era, it witnessed a second massacre for the same reasons, this being the subject of one of Leconte de Lisle's *Poèmes barbares*.

[I am extremely grateful to Francesca Albini for translating this extract from Paratore's monumental study of Tacitus (1962).]

Again, at *Agricola* 16 we find mention of Boudicca, but not a word about the atrocious offences she suffered at the hands of the Romans (*Ann.* 14.31) or about her spirited suicide (*Ann.* 14.37). On the contrary, precisely because there is no concrete discussion of the copious reasons for rebellion supplied to the Britons by the Romans, the whole of *Agricola* 15 is dedicated (in an incomparably more extensive way than in the corresponding passages of the *Annals*) to the considerations which brought the Britons to revolt: there is generic reference to *iniuriae*, 'injuries', to the Romans' excesses *in sanguinem* ('against their lives') and *in bona* ('against property'), to sons taken away, to the necessity of defending *coniuges parentes* ('wives, parents'), to the *auaritia* ('greed') and *luxuria* ('luxurious living') of the rulers, but no specific fact is cited, almost so as to minimize through generalization the factors which were stirring the rebels.[1] This is even more worthy of note because at *Agricola* 15 there is phrasing very similar to that at *Annals* 14.31, where mention is made of the outrage suffered by Boudicca and her daughters: *alterius manus centuriones,*[2] *alterius seruos uim et contumelias miscere,*[3] 'the instruments of one, the centurions, and those of the other, the slaves, mingle violence with insults' (*Agr.* 15.2); *adeo ut regnum per centuriones, domus per seruos, uelut capta uastarentur,* 'so much so that his kingdom was devastated by centurions, his household by slaves—as though both were captured property' (*Ann.* 14.31.1). We can almost infer that in the *Agricola*, Tacitus holds back from colouring the Britons' complaints with concrete references: such a comparison and, even more importantly, the simple consideration that on Britain's affairs Tacitus must have already been well informed by his father-in-law[4] are enough to eliminate the possibility that the discrepancies in the narration of the events between the *Agricola* and

---

[1] This general attitude recurs in Calgacus's words at *Agr.* 31; it is symptomatic that Boudicca is again remembered there (*Brigantes femina duce exurere coloniam, expugnare castra . . . potuere,* 'the Brigantes, under a female general could burn down a colony and storm a camp') and with the same suggestive *iunctura* (*femina duce,* 'under a female general') of *Agr.* 16. This shows the 'symphonic' character that repeated patterns have in Tacitus, as well as in Virgil, and the subtly allusive manner with which sometimes Tacitus likes to underline it. Cf. also n. 6 below.

[2] This is the emendation by Beatus Rhenanus: the manuscript reads *centurionis*.

[3] The *secunda manus* in the *Hersfeldensis* has the emendation *ciere* in the margin.

[4] As early as *Agr.* 4.3, Tacitus makes reference to personal confidences made to him by Agricola: *memoria teneo solitum ipsum narrare,* 'I remember how he himself used to relate'. Cf. also *Agr.* 24.3, *saepe ex eo audiui,* 'I often heard from him'.

book 14 of the *Annals* should generally be attributed to the fact that when writing the *Agricola*, Tacitus had not as yet consulted the sources later used for the *Annals*. The real reason for the difference is to be found in the fact that at this point, Tacitus still has confidence in the goodness and validity of Roman rule,[5] while in the *Annals*, as we shall see, his pessimism undermines even his trust in the legitimacy and capability of Rome's administration over the barbarians. Here, if anything, the description of Boudicca at *Agricola* 16 is a first example of the suggestive manner in which Tacitus will describe barbarian women in the *Germania*: it is underlined by the meaningful juxtaposition *femina duce*, 'under a female general' (*Agr.* 16.1), and by the consistent comment *neque enim sexum in imperiis discernunt*, 'for they make no distinction between the sexes in their rulers' (*Agr.* 16.1).[6] A peculiar parallel is found at *Annals* 14.35.1, where the same observation is backed, as usual, by the concrete arguments silenced in the *Agricola*: *Boudicca curru filias prae se uehens, ut quamque nationem accesserat, solitum quidem Britannis feminarum*

---

[5] Arnaldi (1945: 32–3) rightly notices in this respect that in the *Agricola* Tacitus shows more optimism than in the *Annals*, but I am not sure he sees the true reason for this difference when he ascribes it to the fact that then Tacitus was in a state of euphoria, having just emerged from the Domitianic tyranny. Recently, Walser (1951: 128–36) has analysed the chapters of *Annals* 14 relating to Boudicca's revolt, but mainly in order to compare them with Cassius Dio 62.1–12, to deduce the plurality of the sources used by Tacitus (Pliny the Elder, Fabius Rusticus), and to point out the poor credibility of the Tacitean narrative which in his opinion does not reveal anything of the true causes and purposes of the revolt, but indulges only in rhetorical representation. It is undeniable that in the *Annals* Tacitus' historical sense appears somewhat blurred, but Walser's point of view does not seem correct to me. It is not a taste for rhetoric which prompts Tacitus to make use of anti-Roman topoi; it is instead his evolving distrust in the validity of the Empire which prompts him to indulge in those topoi. Walser's work, informed as it is by the traditional criterion of a Tacitus who is pure artist and by definition unreliable, appears to me peculiarly straggling behind. Of the difference in tone between the narrative in the *Agricola* and the one in the *Annals*, Walser does not show any inkling: he merely points out (1951: 134 n. 582) that the same 'untechnical' formula (*in formam prouinciae*, 'to the condition of a provice') which is already used at *Agr.* 14 then returns at *Ann.* 14.31. He also notes (1951: 135) that the topical description of the *mala seruitutis* ('evils of slavery') already appears at *Agr.* 14—but the fact that the description in the *Agricola* is generic, while the one in the *Annals* is based on concrete facts, escapes him, unless we are to find a trace of such intuition in the fact that he calls the former *Darstellung*, 'representation' and the latter *Beschreibung*, 'description'.

[6] Through this feature too Calgacus's speech is linked to *Agr.* 16: cf. *Agr.* 32.2, *nullae Romanos coniuges accendunt, nulli parentes fugam exprobaturi sunt*, 'there are no wives to fire up the Romans, no parents to reproach their flight'. Similar content features at *Germ.* 7–8.

ductu bellare testabatur,[7] *sed tunc non ut tantis maioribus ortam regnum et opes, uerum ut unam e uulgo libertatem amissam, confectum uerberibus corpus, contrectatam filiarum pudicitiam ulcisci,* 'As Boudicca, carrying her daughters before her in a chariot, approached each tribe, she testified that it was of course customary for the Britons to take to the field under female leadership; yet now she was not, as one sprung from great ancestors, avenging her kingdom and wealth but, as one of the people, her lost freedom, her body battered by beatings, and the abused chastity of her daughters.' Only after these fundamental introductory considerations does Boudicca's speech, reported in indirect form, takes up some of the considerations already developed at *Agricola* 15.

The difference between the *Agricola* and the *Annals*, therefore, resides in the fact that the *Agricola* shows a Tacitus who has not as yet developed the lucid exposition of political problems typical of the *Histories*, but lives some of its premises in a form that is still more emotional than intellectual; while the *Annals* is the expression of a Tacitus who has abandoned the equilibrium of the time of the *Histories* and veers more and more towards a dark vision, thus introducing into his narrative even details that are very discouraging about the positive vitality of the Empire. Besides, the tendency to translate the mention of barbarian customs in the form of an epic, artistic vision, almost happily indulging in the thrill created by a disinterested, fantastic recreation, complete with characters of evocative exoticism—this is perhaps the first manifestation in the whole of western literature of conscious exoticism in contact with the mysterious north—is a sign that Tacitus has not as yet reached political maturity in the way he deals with these problems concerning the future of Rome, which he already feels are the most serious of all. In the *Germania*, the two tendencies (political concern and a taste for poetically reliving the fascination of those remote lands) will find their highest explication and a way of coexisting without disturbing each other: here we already notice the first manifestation of that technique.

The *Agricola* and the *Histories* have a much closer relationship with one another in particular points of detail as well. At *Agricola* 16, in continuing the list of leaders in Britain, after Petronius Turpilianus,

---

[7] Muretus tried to regularize the construction introducing *se* after *sed*, which would be easy to explain paleographically as a haplography.

Tacitus mentions Trebellius Maximus and Vettius Bolanus: the former is *segnior et nullis castrorum experimentis*, 'less energetic and having no experience of the camp' (*Agr.* 16.3), and provokes a sedition among his own soldiers, so that *fuga ac latebris uitata exercitus ira, indecorus atque humilis precario mox praefuit*, 'after avoiding the army's anger by escaping and finding a hiding-place, undignified and humiliated, he was permitted to govern on sufferance' (*Agr.* 16.4); under the latter *eadem inertia erga hostes, similis petulantia castrorum, nisi quod innocens Bolanus et nullis delictis inuisus caritatem parauerat loco auctoritatis*, 'there was the same apathy towards the enemies, the same disobedience in camp, except that Bolanus, who was inoffensive and had done nothing to earn hatred, procured affection, rather than exercising authority over his men' (*Agr.* 16.5). At *Histories* 1.60 the army's mutiny against Trebellius Maximus is mentioned again. Yet the visible difference is that here Tacitus dwells on the contrast between the proconsul and the legate Roscius Coelius. We also find the additional information that the abandoned Trebellius took refuge with Vitellius and that the legionary legates controlled the province.

However, this divergence is of a very different nature from the one between *Agricola* 15 and *Annals* 14.29–39: in the *Agricola* we do not find an omission that distorts the entire tone of the narration as we do in the *Annals* passage, but only an omission of secondary details in a fabric that is entirely interwoven, in both works, with concrete details, while at *Agricola* 15, abstract considerations prevail over the concrete details of *Annals* 14.29–39. This discrepancy therefore only serves to confirm the view that, unlike the *Germania*, the *Agricola* cannot be considered as a detached section of the *Histories*, at least for the most part (the central part in narrative style), but rather only the remote, provisional anticipation of certain data contained in the major work. Likewise, at *Histories* 2.65.2, Tacitus again recalls the shame imposed on the character of Trebellius Maximus, who *profugerat Britannia ob iracundiam militum*, 'had fled from Britain because of his soldiers' resentment', but then adds a detail already recorded at *Agricola* 16: *missus est in locum eius Vettius Bolanus*, 'Vettius Bolanus was sent to replace him'. It is just a fleeting mention, as is the other one at 2.97.1, that Vettius Bolanus moved slowly, *numquam satis quieta Britannia*, 'as Britain was never settled enough'. In any case, even these two brief references are perfectly consistent with the ending of *Agricola* 16 and, if anything, they demonstrate how the same material, with the same spirit, has been elaborated in the two works into two different narrative perspectives: this is entirely natural, given that, in its central part, the *Agricola* focuses particularly on events in Britain, while in the first part of the *Histories* these events are, and must be, seen only in passing.[8] And if in the *Histories* a detail is added (the contrast of Trebellius Maximus with a legionary legate and his flight from Britain), this is in order to throw better light on one of the most painful phenomena of the crisis of the year 69: the lack of discipline within the legions. For that matter, this theme is already anticipated in the *Agricola* (and it is a crucial element to establish the close relationship between the *Agricola* and the *Histories*) as early as *Agricola* 16 (*miles otio lasciueret*, 'the soldiery became lax through idleness', *Agr.* 16.3; *petulantia castrorum*, 'the boisterousness of the camp', *Agr.* 16.5) and finds acute expression at *Agricola* 27.1, where Tacitus' tendency towards bitter derision flares up, as it often does in the *Histories*, with a bright and witty tinge: here it is said that Agricola's soldiers were *modo cauti ac sapientes prompti post euentum ac magniloqui erant*, 'recently cautious and prudent, but after the outcome they were ready for action and boastful', and there then follows the classic reflection: *iniquissima haec bellorum conditio est: prospera omnes sibi uindicant, aduersa uni imputantur*, 'this is the most unfair feature of wars: everybody claims the successes for themselves, but setbacks are laid at the door of one man only'.

Similarly, at *Agricola* 5.1, Suetonius Paulinus' personality (*diligenti ac moderato duci*, 'a careful and restrained general') is sketched in a manner perfectly consistent with the portrait found in the *Histories* (2.25.2, *cunctator natura et cui cauta potius consilia cum ratione*[9] *quam prospera ex casu placerent*, 'a dawdler by nature and the sort of man who liked cautiously reasoned measures rather than accidental success'; 2.32.1, *tunc Suetonius Paulinus dignum fama sua ratus, qua*[10] *nemo illa tempestate militaris rei callidior habebatur, de toto genere belli censere, festinationem hostibus, moram ipsis utilem disseruit*, 'then Suetonius Paulinus, thinking that it suited his reputation—nobody at that time was considered more skilful in military science—to express his view about the general conduct of the war,

---

[8] Therefore it seems even stranger that in these books of the *Histories* there is no mention of Agricola. Cf. earlier at Paratore (1962: 39, n.19).

[9] Nóvak expunges *cum ratione*.

[10] Some humanistic hapographs read *quia*, of which Andresen approves.

argued that haste served the enemy, but delay was useful to their own side'; 2.37.2, *Paulinum, qua prudentia fuit*, 'Paulinus, with his practical good sense'; 2.39.1, *Celsus et Paulinus, cum prudentia eorum nemo uteretur*, 'since nobody made any use of the proficiency of Celsus and Paulinus'); furthermore, at 2.37.1 we are reminded of how *militia clarus gloriam nomenque Britannicis expeditionibus meruisset*, 'by his distinguished service he had won glory and reputation in his British campaigns'. So, at *Agricola* 17, the figures of Petilius Cerialis and Frontinus take centre stage: the former will fill books 4 and 5 of the *Histories*, as the man who resolved the Batavian rebellion led by Civilis; the latter is presented at *Histories* 4.39 as the man who summons the Senate, in his capacity as urban praetor, for the first regular commencement of the regime after the Flavian victory, and who, by resigning from the office of praetor, allows Domitian access to the post.

The fact that the mention of Frontinus here sets up a reconnection with the *Agricola* is demonstrated by a very suggestive sentence which follows immediately: *uis penes Mucianum erat, nisi quod pleraque Domitianus instigantibus amicis aut propria libidine audebat*, 'real power lay with Mucianus, except that Domitian dared to carry out many acts at his friends' instigation or through his own whims' (*H.* 4.39.2). It offers a precise parallel with *Agricola* 7.2, *initia principatus ac statum urbis Mucianus regebat, iuuene admodum Domitiano et ex paterna fortuna tantum licentiam usurpante*, 'Mucianus controlled the initial affairs of the principate and the business of the city, since Domitian was still a very young man who claimed from his father's elevation only the freedom to do as he liked'. We have already noticed[11] how this passage in the *Agricola* does not correspond exactly with the manner in which Tacitus in the *Histories* depicts the power-sharing of Mucianus and Domitian before Vespasian's arrival: cf. 4.40 (the first speech, decorous and modest, by Domitian in the Senate); 4.46 (Domitian wisely meets the demands of the mutinous soldiers); 4.47 (Domitian proposes essential measures)— so much so that when at 4.51.2 we read that Vespasian hears an unfavourable report about Domitian *tamquam terminos aetatis et concessa filio egrederetur*, 'on the grounds that he was transgressing the boundaries appropriate to his age and what was permissible for a

---

[11] Paratore (1962: 38).

son', it is easy to interpret this detail in the sense that Domitian's fervid activity[12] might have provoked the jealousy of the parvenus and therefore inspired their slanderous words against him to the Emperor. Therefore, at 4.68 it becomes clear that there is a palpable contradiction between Tacitus' more considered and understanding way of depicting the young Domitian's activity and its more negative interpretation inherited from the *Agricola*. The reason is that on the one hand we see that, in order to get rid of Arrius Varus, Mucianus has to appoint as praetorian prefect Arrecinus Clemens, a man liked by Domitian and belonging to the senatorial order, and so the picture takes shape of a Mucianus who vents his hatreds and jealousies, while Domitian demands in return from him the appointment of illustrious and moderate individuals; on the other hand, Mucianus is presented as *moras nectens quis flagrantem* [sc. *Domitianum*] *retineret, ne ferocia aetatis et prauis impulsoribus, si exercitum inuasisset, paci belloque male consuleret*, 'contriving delays to restrain [Domitian's] ardour, in case through his youthful ferocity and wicked instigators, having gained control of the army, he would become a liability in peace and war alike' (*H.* 4.68.3). From all of this we can also infer that Frontinus, who had 'baptized' Domitian in the office of praetor, was somebody close to him; and therefore we find confirmation of our conjecture[13] that, when Agricola was sent to Britain to succeed Frontinus himself, this was not out of tune with the provision of Domitian, who perhaps had been accepted back into his father's good books, and who was keen that in Britain a person close to him would succeed another equally appreciated man.

Similar considerations of the affinities of tone between the *Agricola* and the *Histories*, which outline the former as a fervent precursor to the latter, are suggested by *Agricola* 30–34—the apex of this work—through the two opposing speeches of Calgacus and Agricola. Already in this surprising insertion of two speeches within a minor work which is itself a speech, as previously noted,[14] we see a disruption of the *Agricola*'s structure: a valid explanation of this could be that here

---

[12] Also note that at *Hist.* 4.39.2, it is said that Domitian *pleraque . . . audebat*, 'ventured a number of measures', while at *Agr.* 7.2 we had read that Domitian took upon himself *tantum licentiam*, 'great licence': it is not a negligible nuance, as it confirms how in book four of the *Histories* Domitian appears in a more dignified light. From Cassius Dio (66.2–3 and 10) little can be deduced.

[13] Paratore (1962: 61–2).

[14] Ibid. 118.

historiographical concerns have taken over the attention of Tacitus, who perhaps was already oriented towards and practising the technique of the *Histories*. From a rhetorical and artistic point of view, Calgacus' and Agricola's speeches are perhaps the most beautiful written by Tacitus: we can see that he is still in the full bloom of his activities as an orator, at the time when he was writing the eulogy for Verginius Rufus (Pliny *Epistle* 2.1) and the closing prosecution speech against Marius Priscus (Pliny *Epistle* 2.11). And these are original models of oratory, in which the redundant elements are naturally determined by the fact that they are speeches, aimed at an effective stirring of the emotions. These are the rhetorical colourings we constantly come across in the speeches—and not only in the speeches—of the *Histories*, even though they have nothing in common with the Ciceronianism of the *Dialogus*. Equally, not only in the speeches of the *Agricola* but also in other passages of the same work we find, for instance, tricolic forms typical of the style of the *Histories*: cf. e.g. *Agr.* 18.4, *qui classem, qui nauis, qui mare exspectabant*, 'who were looking for a fleet, for ships, for [an attack by] sea', where, in any case, the redundancy can also be explained with the fact that in the *Agricola* Tacitus has sprinkled his writing with stronger rhetorical colourings for the purpose of *recitatio*.

It has not escaped Arnaldi[15] that at *Histories* 4.68–74, the same situation as *Agricola* 30–34 recurs, with the opposing addresses of a barbarian leader, Julius Valentinus, and a Roman general, Petilius Cerialis. However, Tacitus is not repeating himself because at *Histories* 4.68, he has given us only a summary of Valentinus' speech, from which it appears to have been quite similar to that of Calgacus. Nevertheless, it has escaped Arnaldi that, although we have not listened to Valentinus' voice, a little earlier (4.64) we did listen to the voice of the *ferocissimus e legatis*, 'most violent of the legates', of the Tencteri, which ended with exhortations and remarks very similar to those in Calgacus' speech. Furthermore, Valentinus' and Petilius Cerialis' speeches are separated by *Histories* 4.69–72, which contain the narrative of intervening events. In the case of Petilius Cerialis, as Arnaldi himself notices, we do listen to his voice, as we do with Agricola's at *Agricola* 33–4; but we listen to it because the audience, and thus the content, of Cerialis' speech are very different from those

---

[15] Arnaldi (1945: 44).

of Agricola's speech: Agricola was addressing his soldiers to urge them to fight against the barbarians, while Cerialis talks to the barbarians themselves to reassure them about Rome's intentions and to extol the ways, the fruits, and the purposes of Roman rule. If anything, a bridging speech between Agricola's and Cerialis' is represented by Dillius Vocula's address at *Histories* 4.58: this is a speech, unique in its genre, of a Roman commander who has to beg his troops not to go and fatten the ranks of the barbarians.[16] Therefore, the comparison between *Agricola* 30–34 and *Histories* 4.58, 68, 73–4 is one of the most striking examples of Tacitean *uariatio* within the structure of a work. Yet it is undeniable that in sketching the rhetorical contrast in book 4 of the *Histories* between a barbarian leader and the Roman generals, Tacitus has remembered the precedent in the *Agricola*, to the point that he does not want to give Valentinus a long speech, in order to avoid virtually repeating that of Calgacus. At the same time, this proves that already in the *Agricola*, applying the classical scheme of the speeches of the two generals before battle,[17] Tacitus revisits, under the rhetorical packaging with which it had been covered for some time, the original Thucydidean style of setting opposing points of view against each other, in order to better clarify a situation. Indeed, in the two speeches of Calgacus and Agricola, we do not so much feel the character of the two leaders, we do not perceive the prevailing of an interest, of a research into their psychological nature, as much as the need to dissect the opposing reasons of the Britons and the Romans (Calgacus: *neque enim arua nobis aut metalla aut portus sunt, quibus exercendis reseruemur,* 'we have no fields, or mines, or ports for the working of which we might be set aside' (*Agr.* 31.2); Agricola: *transigite cum expeditionibus, imponite quinquaginta annis magnum diem, adprobate rei publicae numquam exercitui imputari potuisse aut moras belli*[18] *aut causas rebellandi,*[19] 'Have done with expeditions, crown fifty years with one

---

[16] [See Ash (2010b) for a discussion of Vocula's speech.]

[17] A typical example is that of Hannibal's and Scipio's speeches in their meeting before Zama at Livy 30.30–31, with the appendix containing the exhortation to the troops at 30.33.

[18] But *bellandi* in marginal correction of the *seconda manus* in the *Hersfeldensis* (*Aesinas*), by influence of the following *rebellandi*.

[19] These are not just beautiful exhortative phrases as in all the generals' speeches before a decisive action: they are the acute denunciation of a chronic malaise of the Roman state.

great day, prove to the state that the army could never have been to blame, either for the war dragging on or for the causes of the rebellion' (*Agr.* 34.3). The future author of the *Histories* has here made his first foray, and even done a little more, showing us even at this point another very interesting sign of maturity, the sign of the real Tacitus emerging above the surface of the traditional rhetorical repertoire. And, in a similar situation in the *Histories*, in the most tragic situation in which the Roman empire, exhausted by the civil war, had ever found itself (the Batavian revolt), he has remembered this, avoiding repetition of the classic contrast of *Agricola* 30–34 and varying it in a deft manner.

It is therefore clear that the *Agricola*, even with regard to the most typical essence of its style, prefigures the *Histories*. In this sense, the fundamental characteristic of this work is the mastery of crowd scenes: at *Agricola* 37–8, Tacitus presents the first great example of this technique. We have already said that in the description of the rout of the Britons it is reasonable to find traces of Sallust.[20] Notwithstanding, Tacitean description already shows a desire to broaden the horizon as widely as possible and, above all, a tendency to convey the most subtle and deep shiver from a picture (*uastum ubique silentium, secreti*[21] *colles, fumantia procul tecta, nemo exploratoribus obuius*, 'everywhere there was desolate silence, secluded hills, houses giving off smoke in the distance, not a soul encountering the scouts', *Agr.* 38.2). This is not found in the corresponding Sallustian scenes. Sallust handles the crowd wonderfully, but as a politically fluid element, in its blind, fickle reactions to the events: his *de Coniuratione Catilinae* is a particularly marvellous example of this ability. As a tribune and a man politically accustomed to firing up the people (as in the famous episode of Clodius' funeral), Sallust must have been deeply aware of this function of the crowd, in an age still shaken by the furious disputes of the traditional kind, those linked to the activity of the Senate and of the assemblies. Tacitus, instead, being much less experienced in the kind of active political life to which Sallust was accustomed, does not restrict his focus to the agitation of the Roman plebs, but extends it to the crowds of the provinces and the masses of the barbarians, or to the riotous and overbearing troops, in

---

[20] Paratore (1962: 178 n.17).
[21] In his edition of Tacitus (Leipzig, 1752), I. A. Ernesti proposed the emendation *deserti*.

the new perspective revealed by his view of history and of the Empire. Out of this, through his artistic instinct, newer pictures are born, original scenes of error, violence, dismay, religious astonishment or sullen mystery, all forming the seductive background in which the clash of opposing political forces unfolds. In these chapters of the *Agricola* and in almost the whole of the *Germania*, this very particular nature of the Tacitean palette establishes itself, so that, when we find its nuances in the *Histories* and in the *Annals*, we can be certain that we are faced with one of Tacitus' idiosyncracies.

Therefore, we have laid another firm foundation in our investigation.[22] Not even the question of the *Germania*'s sources affects such considerations, because an almost sacral thrill of mysterious barbarism is so skilfully diffused throughout the work and gushes out so consistently from all the details arranged with subtle harmony that we cannot fail to recognize in it the sign of a conscious, profound reworking on Tacitus' part. As with the problem of the administration of the provinces, so too with the theme of representing crowds in motion, we can therefore conclude that the *Agricola* and *Germania* (especially the former) embody an initial burst, in which sentimental and artistic interest prevails over the political and speculative: it seems that at first Tacitus wanted to dip his toes in the water in order to check how far he could express in suggestive forms the forces to which the great historiographical theme (which he was already starting to cherish) was driving him to direct his attention. Once his muscles were warmed up, in his major works he was able to find a better balance between the purely artistic suggestions of the great crowd scenes and the political considerations that had to underlie such scenes, in order to shed light on the deeper reason for the phenomenon.

---

[22] We have at any rate detected other extremely important details about the first ripening of Tacitus' political thoughts in the speeches of Calgacus and Agricola. This analysis has confirmed the effectiveness of the methodical principles enunciated in the introduction: in Tacitus' work there are parts that are certainly original, a safe and solid ground for any attempt to establish the true individuality of the writer; and precisely in these parts Tacitus' political thought begins to manifest itself, thus revealing itself as an original κτῆμα of the author.

7

Critical Appreciations III: Tacitus, *Histories* 3.38–9

N. P. Miller and P. V. Jones

I

[38] *Nota per eos dies Iunii Blaesi mors et famosa fuit, de qua sic accepimus. graui corporis morbo aeger Vitellius Seruilianis hortis turrim uicino sitam conlucere per noctem crebris luminibus animaduertit. sciscitani causam apud Caecinam Tuscum epulari multos, praecipuum honore Iunium Blaesum nuntiatur; cetera in maius, de apparatu et solutis in lasciuiam animis. nec defuere qui ipsum Tuscum et alios, sed criminosius Blaesum incusarent, quod aegro principe laetos dies ageret. ubi asperatum Vitellium et posse Blaesum peruerti satis patuit iis qui principum offensas acriter speculantur, datae L. Vitellio delationis partes. ille infensus Blaeso aemulatione praua, quod eum omni dedecore maculosum egregia fama anteibat, cubiculum imperatoris reserat, filium eius sinu complexus et genibus accidens. causam confusionis quaerenti, non se proprio metu nec sui anxium, sed pro fratre, pro liberis fratris preces lacrimasque attulisse. frustra Vespasianum timeri, quem tot Germanicae legiones, tot prouinciae uirtute ac fide, tantum denique terrarum ac maris immensis spatiis arceat: in urbe ac sinu cauendum hostem, Iunios Antoniosque auos iactantem, qui se stirpe imperatoria comem ac*

[The following 'duet' was the third of a regular (but now defunct) series in the journal *Greece & Rome*. It began with Bramble (1973) and Lyne and Morwood (1973) on Propertius 3.10, continued with Williams and Carter (1974) on Virgil *Aeneid* 12.843–86, Miller and Jones (1978) on Tacitus *Histories* 3.38–9, Booth and Verity (1978) on Ovid *Amores* 2.10, Williams and Kelsall (1980) on Joseph Addison, *Pax Gulielmi Auspiciis Europae Reddita*, and culminated with Griffin and Hammond (1982) on Homer *Iliad* 1.1–52.]

magnificum militibus ostentet. uersas illuc omnium mentis, dum Vitellius amicorum inimicorumque neglegens fouet aemulum principis labores e conuiuio prospectantem. reddendam pro intempestiua laetitia maestam et funebrem noctem, qua sciat et sentiat uiuere Vitellium et imperare et, si quid fato accidat, filium habere.

[39] *Trepidanti inter scelus metumque, ne dilata Blaesi mors maturam perniciem, palam iussa atrocem inuidiam ferret, placuit ueneno grassari; addidit facinori fidem notabili gaudio, Blaesum uisendo. quin et audita est saeuissima Vitellii uox qua se (ipsa enim uerba referam) pauisse oculos spectata inimici morte iactauit.*

Blaeso super claritatem natalium et elegantiam morum fidei obstinatio fuit. integris quoque rebus a Caecina et primoribus partium iam Vitellium aspernantibus ambitus abnuere perseuerauit. sanctus, inturbidus, nullius repentini honoris, adeo non principatus adpetens, parum effugerat ne dignus crederetur.

[38] Around that time, the fact that Junius Blaesus had died became known and generated much talk. This is what I have heard about it. Vitellius was lying seriously ill at his house in the Servilian Park when he noticed that a lofty neighbouring dwelling was ablaze with umpteen lights which shone through the night. On enquiring the reason, he was told that Caecina Tuscus was holding a large dinner party, and that the guest of honour was Junius Blaesus. His informants gave an exaggerated account of lavish display and a relaxed and convivial atmosphere. Critics readily came forward to denounce Tuscus himself and others, but more venomous charges were laid against Blaesus for spending his days in merriment while the emperor was ill. There are always people who keep a sharp lookout for signs of an emperor's displeasure. When it became clear enough to them that Vitellius had been provoked and that Blaesus could be ruined, they assigned the role of informer to Lucius Vitellius. He was Blaesus' enemy, bitterly jealous of a man whose excellent reputation towered above his own life, sordidly marked by every type of scandal. Lucius suddenly flung open the door of the emperor's bedroom and knelt down before him, clasping Vitellius' young son in his arms. When Vitellius asked him what the trouble was, he said that it was not because of his own personal fears and private anxieties that he had brought his tearful appeals, but from concern for his brother and his brother's children. There was no point in fearing Vespasian: all those German legions, all those brave and loyal provinces, a huge and immeasurable sweep of land and sea served as a defence against him. It was in Rome and in his own intimate circle where the emperor must guard against an enemy who boasted the Junii and Antonii as his ancestors, and who sought to show himself off to the

soldiers as an affable and generous member of a ruling family. All public thoughts turned in that direction, while Vitellius, paying no attention to who were his friends and who were his enemies, was nurturing a rival who was contemplating the emperor's sufferings from a banqueting table. This man should pay the price for such untimely festivity by a night of misery and death, in which he would learn to his cost that Vitellius was still alive and still emperor, with a son to succeed him in the event of his death.

[39] Vitellius was hesitating between murder and his fear that if he postponed Blaesus' execution, his own ruin might soon follow; but to order it openly would cause a terrible scandal, so he decided it was best to use poison. What made people believe him guilty was the conspicuous pleasure he took in visiting Blaesus. Indeed, Vitellius was heard to make a most vicious remark, boasting that 'he had feasted his eyes on the spectacle of his enemy's death'. I quote his actual words.

Blaesus not only came from an illustrious family and possessed gracious ways, but he was also stubbornly loyal. Even while Vitellius' position was still sound, he was approached by Caecina and other prominent members of the party who were already turning against the emperor, but he persisted in refusing to join any plot. Despite being a model of goodness and a calm man who turned his back on any sudden promotion, let alone the principate, he had not been able to avoid being thought worthy of it.

II

At first sight, this self-contained account of the death of Junius Blaesus seems rather oddly placed at a crisis of Vitellius' fortunes. The second battle of Bedriacum has been lost, and Cremona sacked: one of Vitellius' generals[1] has defected, and the other,[2] now proceeding northwards in reluctant and unsoldierly fashion, is soon to be captured and rendered useless: the immediate context has indicated the sloth and weak vindictiveness of Vitellius, and wryly pointed the self-absorption of senators, collective and singular. The insertion of the story of Blaesus' end is interesting: and so is its presentation.

---

[1] Alienus Caecina: see *H.* 3.36.2.　　[2] Fabius Valens: see *H.* 3.36, 40; 43.

A rather vague temporal connection (*per eos dies*, 'around that time') provides the necessary formal link, and the new subject is correctly and precisely indicated. But the stylistic stress of the opening phrase is on *nota . . . et famosa*, 'became known and generated much talk', as is shown by the doubling, separation, and placing of the adjectives, and also by their possibly ambiguous meaning: 'talk' which is 'caused' is not always laudatory.[3] The next phrase is a source reference. Tacitus' source may have been personal and verbal, but is more likely to have been one of the 'Death-Scenes of Famous Men' which we know[4] to have been a popular literary form at the time he was writing. Like many of Tacitus' source references,[5] this serves a double purpose: it proffers a guarantee that he has not invented the story, and it does not commit him to belief in its accuracy. This suggests that, as with his use of rumour in the Tiberian books, Tacitus finds the story a convenient illustration of some general point.[6] What this point is, is first indicated by the opening words of the story proper. Death and a serious illness are a natural connection: but it is not Blaesus who is ill, and the unexpected appearance of the name Vitellius is therefore striking, and suggests that here is the focus of the historian's interest.

The movement of the narrative underlines that interest. It is terse and economical in its presentation of necessary background, and more elaborate where the emperor's emotions are involved. *Seruilianis . . . sitam* contains no unnecessary word (and two simple local ablatives),[7] while the blaze of light,[8] its duration, and its intensity combine to make a vivid vignette of a sick emperor's restlessly wandering gaze. Question and answer bracket the next sentence, whose information is rapid, but climactic: the sequence of dinner party, large dinner party, large dinner party in honour of Blaesus, is neatly conveyed, and the more sinister elements of exaggeration,

---

[3] It is clear from Gerber and Greef (1962) that Tacitus most frequently uses both adjectives in the derogatory sense.

[4] Pliny, *Epp.* 5.5.3 and 8.12.4. [On such death-scenes, see further Ash (2003).]

[5] Cf. *H.* 2.37: *A.* 12.67, 14.2, 14.9, 15.38.

[6] [On Tacitus' use of rumours, see Shatzman (1974) and Gibson (1998); and more generally, Laurence (1994).]

[7] The style of the sentence makes it very unlikely that the omission of *in* before *uicino* is the responsibility of anyone other than Tacitus himself. [On Tacitus' style in the *Histories* more generally, see Ash (2007a: 14–21).]

[8] *Conlucere* is emphatically placed, an intensive form, and a word mostly found in poetic/descriptive contexts.

ostentation, and orgy are presented in a laconic Tacitean tail-piece.[9] The move to direct slander, and its concentration on Blaesus, is pointed by *nec defuere qui* ('Critics readily came forward . . .', a favourite form of Tacitean emphasis),[10] and by the placing of Blaesus' name at the climax of the series, immediately preceded by the adverb *criminosius* ('more venomously'). The accusation, when it comes, is further focused on him by its singular verb, and its substance is presented in the prominent adjectives.

The stylistic texture of the next sentence in this economical narrative is very close and complex. Vitellius' (deliberately?) ruffled feelings are pointed by the placing of the passive participle *asperatum* ('provoked'), and by the word itself,[11] which in this meaning is rare enough to be noticeable: the possibility of making Blaesus a victim is indicated by word-order and passive verb: the interconnection between these two facts is mirrored in the balanced presentation of the clauses: the sort of people who make such connections, and the fact that they are a continuing product of Empire, is economically indicated by the use of the generalizing present tense: and without further ado we move to action, an action on which Tacitus' judgement is made clear by his use of *delationis partes*, 'the role of informer'. Informers are anathema, and L. Vitellius is putting on an act.[12]

It is also clear that the preliminaries are over, and the real action about to start. From this point on, the narrative presentation is more expansive and elaborate, indicating that here is, for Tacitus, the essence of the story. The discreditable motive of the emperor's brother is not only pointed by the employment and placing of *praua* ('wicked'); it is expanded in a causal clause which *eum* ('him') and the indicative verb *anteibat* ('towered above') make, not an expression of L. Vitellius' feeling, but a statement of fact. His irruption into the emperor's private room, his emotive use of the emperor's young son, and his theatrical gesture in falling at the emperor's feet are vividly

---

[9] [Gowers (1993) offers a wide-ranging study of food and banqueting (traditionally having rich scope for invective).]

[10] Cf. *H.* 3.37.2, 78.1, etc.

[11] For this metaphorical meaning of *aspero*, the Thesaurus cites only Tacitus, Ammianus, and a few late writers. Tacitus so uses the word five times. Cf. *H.* 2.48.1, 3.82; *A.* 1.72, 2.29, 3.12.1. [The metaphor derives from the sharpening of weapons: see Woodman and Martin (1996: 142) and Ash (2007a: 207). Woodman (2006b) offers helpful discussion of Tacitus' creative use of metaphorical language.]

[12] [Rutledge (1999; 2001) considers *delatores* more generally.]

evoked by the historical present *reserat* ('opens'), the vocabulary of *sinu complexus* ('clasping in his arms'), and the final phrase which combines a dative of goal (*genibus*, 'knees') and an extended use of the present participle (*accidens*, 'falling at'): neither construction is new in Silver Latin prose, but the combination is still sufficiently striking. The emperor not unnaturally inquires what all the noise is about, and the rest of the chapter (amounting to nearly half) is occupied by his brother's reply, presented in dramatic, though indirect, speech.

The length and elaboration of this speech, in such a context, is noteworthy. It plunges straight in, the *se* and *sui* after *quaerenti* ('When Vitellius asked') sufficiently indicating that this is speech: and it makes its point with the aid of balance (*non se . . . nec sui*), anaphora (*pro . . . pro, tot . . . tot*), climax (*tot . . . tot . . . tantum denique*), emotional vocabulary (*in urbe ac sinu*, 'in Rome and in his own intimate circle'; *stirpe imperatoria*, 'ruling family'; *principis labores e conuiuio prospectantem*, 'contemplating the emperor's sufferings from a banqueting table'), significant juxtaposition (*urbe/sinu/hostem, laetitia/maestam*), alliteration (*sciat et sentiat uiuere Vitellium*), and vivid syntax (all the subjunctive verbs are present: and *dum . . . fouet* is preserved in its original indicative[13] to keep its meaning beyond dispute). The speech is allotted to L. Vitellius, but the words are the words of Tacitus, and such words are usually selected and presented with deliberate care.[14] What is the speech telling us?

The first point of emphasis is that Vitellius is being told of a threat to himself and his family: this emphasis is produced by the *sed* ('but') clause, with its repeated *pro* and *fratre/fratris* ('brother'), which answers the initial negative phrases. The next climax is more elaborate and exaggerated. The basic structure is still that of the negative opening which throws emphasis on the positive statement which follows. But this time the name of Vitellius' immediate rival is emotively introduced, and the negative phrase is reinforced by a soaring rhetorical tricolon, whose forceful assertions about German legions, loyal provinces, and vast distances between Vitellius and his opponents ring very oddly in the ears of those who have just read the first thirty-five chapters of this book. The positive statement which

---

[13] This construction is occasionally found in Golden Latin, but more often in Tacitus. It combines archaism, accuracy, and novelty.

[14] [There has been much discussion of the language of Tacitus' speeches: see Adams (1973), Adler (2008), Ash (2010b), Brock (1995), and Keitel (1991; 1993).]

they are designed to highlight, and which is the heart and climax of the accusation, is presented in a sentence as compact and close-textured as any Tacitus ever wrote. Capital, court, precaution, public enemy: distinguished descent (partly from an emperor's opponent) and open pride in it: a family line with military and imperial[15] connections backing deliberate display, to the army, of qualities useful in emperors—the reverberations of the words so starkly presented are almost endless. Fancy finally takes flight into *uersas illuc omnium mentis* ('All public thoughts turned in that direction'), then descends, via a reference to Vitellius which hardly flatters his intelligence, to something more approximating to reality. *Prospectantem* ('contemplating') gives a nasty twist to the facts as they have been presented to us, and the phrase is surely a bathetic end to a sentence which started with a charge of universal disaffection. The bathos is, I think, deliberate, as is the rather clumsy *si quid fato accidat* ('in the event of his death') in the next sentence: L. Vitellius is perhaps having difficulty in concocting a plausible charge, but he knows how to work on his brother's feelings.[16] And these, surely, are the points which the speech is really making: the elaborate rhetoric and its occasional lapses throw into relief both the ridiculous nature of the charges and the character of the emperor who believed them. In any reasonable society, a *maestam et funebrem noctem* ('a night of misery and death') seems a high price to pay *pro intempestiua laetitia* ('for such untimely festivity'), and the proposed lesson about the emperor's life, power, and succession an illogical one.

But it worked. The opening words of *H.* 3.39 emphatically present a characteristically fearful hesitation between discreditable alternatives, which are spelled out in a suitably balanced structure. The decision to proceed by poison seems appropriate for one in such straits, and it appropriately closes the sentence which began with *trepidanti* ('hesitating'). We then have the final climax of the story, and it is not, significantly, a description of the death-scene (*ueneno*, 'poison', *facinori*, 'crime', and *morte*, 'death' are all we get of that), but a picture

---

[15] Blaesus was presumably a descendant (son? grandson? nephew?) of the Junius Blaesus of *A.* 1.16, who was the last non-member of the imperial family to be awarded the title *imperator* (*A.* 3.74). [See Woodman and Martin (1996: 488–9).] His connection with the Antonii is unknown: but Mark Antony, as well as being a rival of Augustus, was also married to his sister Octavia.

[16] [See Bannon (1997) for a study of fraternal *pietas* (whose ideal standards Lucius fails to meet in his exploitation of his own brother).]

of the emperor Vitellius. The alliterative *facinori fidem* effectively juxtaposes charge and corroborative evidence: the adjective *notabili* means both noticeable and noteworthy: and finally, Vitellius is allowed to condemn himself in words whose savagery is specifically guaranteed as genuine.[17] He not only says them, he revels in them (*iactauit,* 'boasted'): and with this word the narrative abandons him, and ends with an obituary notice for Blaesus.[18]

The placing of his name indicates the change of topic. His recorded qualities are not only such as Tacitus approves,[19] they are presented so as to emphasize his steadfast integrity. *fidei obstinatio* ('stubbornly loyal') is pointed by its position, by the *super* construction which precedes it, by the abstract noun which almost personifies the steadfastness, and by its expansion in the following sentence. It is not a quality which has been at all evident in the recently recorded activities of Vitellius and his court. In the historian's measured judgement, Blaesus was *sanctus* ('a model of goodness', a word with impressive overtones), *inturbidus* ('calm', which seems to be a Tacitean coinage), and not the sort of man (the genitive with the participle expressing a permanent characteristic) to seek any sudden preferment, much less the principate. Not Guilty, in fact: his only mistake (a typically Tacitean twist, this) was his failure to ensure that he be thought undeserving of the office.

The passage thus begins and ends with Blaesus. But there is surprisingly little hard information about him in between. This is the first mention of him since *H.* 2.59, where his qualities and Vitellius' instinctive dislike of them were pointedly presented. Tacitus makes no attempt to recall these qualities, or Vitellius' dislike, at the start of our passage: this story is to make its own point in its own way. The story is ostensibly about the death of Blaesus, but the death is not related. The crescendo from guest of honour to inconsiderate courtier to rival for the principate is presented in a series of increasingly elaborate and fantastic allegations, which tell us little about Blaesus,

---

[17] Cf. *A.* 14.59, 15.67. Tacitus rarely quotes directly: when he does, his reasons are clear (in *A.* 15.67 they are specific): we need not therefore doubt that he found the words in a source. They are also attributed to Vitellius by Suetonius (*Vit.* 14.2), but associated with a different occasion. Which author mistook or misused his source cannot be proven: but Suetonius' collection of scurrilous and quite unspecific gossip ('one of these'. . . 'two sons'. . . 'a Roman knight') is unimpressive.

[18] [On death notices in Tacitus and other Roman historians, see Pomeroy (1991).]

[19] Cf. *A.* 5.8, 14.9.

but a good deal about Tacitus' opinion of Vitellius and his court. And that, surely, is the point of the story's use and presentation.[20] Things were falling apart in Vitellius' Rome, and the tale of Junius Blaesus' death was a good illustration of that fact, and of what Tacitus considers to be some of the reasons for it.

N. P. MILLER

III

This passage is an exercise in paradox and irony.[21] The very first sentence warns us of the element of paradox. The death of Junius Blaesus was, we are told, *nota* (a *cause célèbre*), but equally it was also *famosa* ('subject of many stories'). Since everyone had heard about it, but no one appeared to know the truth, Tacitus gives us his version (*de qua sic accepimus*, 'This is what I have heard about it'). This is an important point, and one to which I shall have to return when the text has been analysed.

We are plunged *in medias res*. Vitellius is sick, and dangerously sick as well (*graui*). Since Vitellius' illness is central to the episode, the fact comes first in the sentence. Now follows the sequence of words: in the 'Servilian gardens' (*Seruilianis hortis*) there is a millionaire's tower-block apartment (*turrim uicino sitam*) which is (naturally) lit up at night (*conlucere per noctem*) . . . but *crebris luminibus* ('with umpteen lights')? A party! The scene appears to unfold before the sick Vitellius' mind, and it is only with the last words, *crebris luminibus* ('with umpteen lights'), that realization dawns on him that his normal night-time viewing (the ill sleep little at night) is suddenly different. Note also, and retain, *uicino* ('nearby'). So Vitellius is not so ill that he cannot spot signs of revelry, nor is he so indifferent that he forgets to inquire the reason (*sciscitanti causam* . . . , 'on enquiring the reason'). One would really have thought that a seriously ill man would have

---

[20] For Tacitus' careful selection of candidates for obituary notices in the *Annals*, see Syme (1958a: 312–13), and (1958b) [Ch. 10 below].

[21] A version of III was given to the London Classical Association. Keith Sidwell and Frances Corrie are responsible for considerable tightening and improvement of the argument, particularly at the end. [On the phenomenon of irony in Tacitus, see Köhnken (1973), Robin (1973), and O'Gorman (2000); Plass (1988) is also relevant. The study of Bartsch (1994) is illuminating.]

better things to do than to inquire after his neighbour's nocturnal junketings. But then again, if Vitellius is ill he is still emperor, and the price of tyranny is eternal vigilance.[22]

Back comes the news that Caecina Tuscus is holding a party, and that the guest of honour is Junius Blaesus (*sciscitanti . . . nuntiatur*, 'On enquiring . . . he was told'). And then, we are at once told, everything about the party was exaggerated (*cetera . . . animis*). This seems rather odd. Why on earth should everything be exaggerated? However much Vitellius may have enjoyed details of *lasciuia* ('licentiousness'), he was, after all, on his bed of pain, when these things appeal less than they might have done in normal circumstances. Unless, of course, people were gunning for Blaesus and wanted to prompt an adverse reaction in Vitellius . . . (One is forcibly reminded of the exploitations of the gutter press: I think especially of *The Times* and its righteous proclamation in a leader of its refusal to print pictures of a prominent politician who had fallen into a gutter in a paralytic stupor. The leader's description was infinitely more degrading and titillating than the pictures.)[23] That this suggestion is on the right lines is immediately confirmed by what follows: *nec defuere qui . . . ageret* confirms that there were people prepared to make accusations against everyone implicated in the party, but especially Blaesus. It really does look as if there is a group of people out to exploit the emperor's whimsy with a view to getting rid of Blaesus. And what a whimsy: the only point they have to exploit is that Blaesus was enjoying himself while the emperor was ill (*quod . . . ageret*). Yet it cannot have been an accusation which Vitellius was going to laugh out of court, since the inquiry originated from him in the first place. The next sentence—*ubi asperatum . . . partes*—clinches it: there were those on the look-out for *principum offensas* ('signs of an emperor's displeasure'). It was only a party, but observe that now it has become an *offensa* ('an affront'; Thucydides would have applauded that deadly change of terminology). It is by now clear that the anti-Blaesus

---

[22] [The motif of the menacing gaze is one component of the stereotypical tyrant in ancient literature, but see especially Keitel (2007) for its application to Vitellius. We have already seen a disturbing instance when Vitellius gazes at the gory aftermath of the civil war battle which brought him to power (*H*. 2.70.4, with Ash (2007a: 275–6).]

[23] [Newspaper practice in publishing pictures of prominent people (or not) has undergone some interesting changes since the original publication of this article in 1978, particularly since there is always the risk now that 'photographs' can be high-quality fakes.]

faction (whoever they were) is winning its battle for the emperor's mind. Vitellius is *asperatum* ('provoked'), and they are satisfied that Blaesus *posse peruerti* ('could be tripped and thrown', a wrestling metaphor entirely in keeping with *offensa*, which is something you trip over, a stumbling-block. We might be tempted to change the event and say that Blaesus was for the high-jump). *Acriter* ('sharply') is final confirmation of our suspicions: yielding to, or exploiting, the emperor's whim was a deadly serious business.

The emperor, then, is ready. Since the whole affair is a set-up, someone has to be found to make the most of it. The task is given to the emperor's brother, Lucius. We are not told whether it was Lucius who started the whole intrigue. Tacitus imputes a motive to Lucius for accepting the task of revealing all to the emperor (*ille infensus . . . anteibat*), but this seems to me to ring rather hollow. In this shadowy world of intrigue, of suggestion, and of counter-suggestion, there is no need for the black-hearted villain envious of the spotless hero. To introduce an element of personal motivation seems to me out of place.

Lucius' performance is brilliant. First, the striking entry (*reserat*); and then, the tableau—Vitellius' son clasped to his bosom and the posture on the knees (*filium . . . accidens*). All this is straight out of *The Sound of Music*. One expects Lucius to clutch his free hand to his heart and burst into song. One may imagine the ill Vitellius struggling up on his cushions and kindly inquiring what on earth is happening (as indeed he does—*causam confusionis quaerenti*, where *confusio* means 'disorder, all things being mixed up'). It is plain that Lucius has calculated that a little high drama may be needed in front of his sick brother if he is to win him round. After all, the conclusion was that Blaesus *posse peruerti* ('could be tripped and thrown')—it was by no means an 'open and shut' case; the ill Vitellius may well have forgotten about the whole thing; and, as we shall soon read, Blaesus was sickeningly loyal. Consequently, Lucius is going to have to wring a few brotherly withers pretty hard to win his case. Besides, his case is not the strongest. A prosecution which demands the death penalty for going to a party will need to rely on more than a little circumstantial evidence if it is to succeed.

But Lucius is equal to the occasion. Realizing the weakness of his case he opens, like any well-trained barrister, with a string of avowals of disinterestedness (*non se . . . attulisse*), without revealing in any way what it is in which he is so disinterested. He then makes an arcane reference to Vespasian (*frustra . . . arceat*); hints darkly at an enemy with powerful connections (*in urbe . . ostentet*); suggests that Vitellius does not realize the danger he is in (*uersas . . . prospectantem*); and closes with a veiled threat against Vitellius' safety if he does not act (*reddendam . . habere*). What on earth would Vitellius, nightcap on head, have made of this? Quite a lot—as a closer inspection of Lucius' brilliant appeal makes clear.

Bear in mind that, all the time, Lucius is on his knees in a suppliant position, in tears, and clutching Vitellius' child to his heaving bosom (*filium . . . accidens*; *preces . . . attulisse*). Lucius is playing on the upper registers of his emotional range. His opening appeal (*non se . . . attulisse*) avers his disinterested loyalty to his brother and to his brother's family.[24] This is an important start to make because family interests are immediately implicated. The importance of that suggestion will not have been lost on the gravely ill Vitellius. The appeal will carry double weight since Lucius has Vitellius' son in his arms (heaven knows what he made of it all).[25] Lucius continues that there is no need to fear Vespasian, for a number of very good reasons (*frustra . . . arceat*—note the dramatic ascending tricolon with anaphora in *tot . . . tot . . . tantum*), an assertion which at once demonstrates Lucius' implicit trust in his brother's management of the Empire. It is obvious what Lucius is after. He has demonstrated his loyalty to and faith in Vitellius—he can reciprocally claim Vitellius' loyalty and faith in him. That relationship established, Lucius can move onto the charge. The tone now changes (*in urbe . . . ostentet*) to one of conspiratorial innuendo. There are no names, only hints and suggestions and implied threats—*Iunios . . . iactantem . . . stirpe imperatoria*, and so on. One can almost feel Vitellius' attention being drawn into the web Lucius is spinning. 'But whom on earth is Lucius referring to?', one can see Vitellius thinking. *Versas . . . prospectantem* tells him. It is a brilliant stroke. There are still no names, but there are gestures. Remember *turrim uicino sitam* ('lofty neighbouring dwelling'), viewable from Vitellius' bed? *Illuc* ('in that direction') must

---

[24] [Levene (1997: 143) [Ch. 8 below] observes that in Tacitus' account, 'Vitellius' love for his family has consistently been his one attractive trait'. Thus Lucius' exploitation of this trait to manipulate his brother seems especially predatory.]

[25] [Morgan (1991) explores other instances of the emotive impact of this boy on Tacitus' text.]

indicate a gesture to it by Lucius.[26] At a stroke, Lucius has recovered the whole memory of the incident for Vitellius, in precisely the same terms as Vitellius observed it in the first place—from his bed of pain, overlooking the Servilian gardens. Now Lucius pushes the knife in. Vitellius is incapable of distinguishing friends from enemies (*amicorum inimicorumque neglegens*, 'paying no attention to who were his friends and who were his enemies'), he is actually encouraging a rival (*fouet*, 'nurtures'), whose pleasures in parties are in stark contrast to Vitellius' agonies (*labores . . . conuiuio*), and who watches over Vitellius (*prospectantem*—it was after all a *turris*) as if master of him, and, naturally, with all the right contacts (previous sentence). All the circumstances of Vitellius' illness which make him so vulnerable are directly related to Blaesus' activities and set in the context which precisely recreates the circumstances of Vitellius' original inquiry.

But if this is not enough, the final sentence is a masterpiece (*reddendam . . . habere*). Still no names, but instead the incriminating party is brought directly out into the open for the first time. Now that party was, as a matter of fact, the beginning and ending of the whole case against Blaesus. But Lucius makes it appear to be the straw that broke the camel's back, the final piece of intolerable behaviour on Blaesus' part that made his guilt certain and his punishment assured. Finally, the threat. Lucius, stressing the power of the living Vitellius (*uiuere . . . imperare*), destroys the whole edifice with the possibility of his death. The understated *si quid fato accidat* ('in the event of his death')—and he was seriously ill too, as well as seriously 'threatened' by Blaesus—must have grated harshly against the confident *qua sciat* ('in which he would learn') . . . . *imperare*, and the final stroke, *filium habere* ('that he had a son'; surely another gesture to the child in his arms), must have sounded as false to Vitellius as it was meant to. Vitellius knew as well as anyone that if he, Vitellius, was killed or died, his son's status was, in those times, irrelevant to the question of succession. Indeed, being son of the emperor was probably the most dangerous qualification on earth at that time, a sure guarantee of instant fatality.

The flattery, the protestations of loyalty, the innuendoes, the final threat stabbing out like a knife under the cloak of Lucius' winning

---

[26] [The topic of gestures and non-verbal rhetoric in the Roman world has understandably attracted scholarly attention more generally: see Edwards (1993); Corbeill (2004).]

words, carry the day (*trepidanti . . . grassari*). The conviction which
Lucius carried is nicely pointed by the observation that Blaesus had
started out as a *hostis* (*in urbe ac sinu cauendum hostem,* 'It was in
Rome and in his own intimate circle where the emperor must guard
against an enemy'), but had turned into an *inimicus,* a personal
enemy, by the time Lucius had finished with him (cf. *amicorum
inimicorumque neglegens,* 'paying no attention to who were his
friends and who were his enemies', with *spectata inimici morte,* 'on
the spectacle of his enemy's death'). We are left with a typical
Tacitean valediction. Blaesus was as loyal and as safe as any man
could possibly have been. But even that can be turned against a man
in the court of Vitellius.

I began by saying that this passage was an exercise in paradox and
irony. Both are intentional, both part of the effect Tacitus is trying to
create by writing as he does. First, and most obvious, the paradox.
The fact is that Tacitus, as he tells us, did not know the truth behind
this episode: nobody did. Consequently, Tacitus is unable to answer
the traditionally 'historical' questions—Who was responsible for the
attempt on Blaesus? How was the opposition organized? Why was the
attempt made anyway? *Cui bono?*, and so on. But the fact that Tacitus
cannot answer them is in itself a significant and important observation about the nature of Vitellius' court at that time. The paradox is
that Tacitus' confessed ignorance of the nature of the plot does not
prevent him using the episode as a medium for historical insight.[27]
This raises very sharply the question of what we mean by historical
truth, and it is worth observing that Lucius' 'speech' to Vitellius
occupies almost half the episode. How far can a historian take this
kind of novelistic device and still claim to be writing history? In other
words, is Tacitus justified in using this incident in this way to create a
feeling for the mood of Vitellius' court? How can we tell it is true?

Second, the irony. This has its origins in the paradox, and it is this
irony which gives the passage its terrifying power. The irony resides
in the utter absurdity of the whole case against Blaesus (the charge
itself and the attempts made to convince Vitellius of its significance),
and the cast-iron certainty that Blaesus will be found guilty of it. As
the 'historical' questions—who? why? how?—gather thick and fast
and fail to be answered, so the incredulous reader is made more and

---

[27] [For a study of conspiracy narratives large and small, see Pagán (2004a).]

more certain that Blaesus is done for. This creates an almost un-bearable tension in the narrative. There is another important consequence. As the episode becomes more and more irrational, so the pathos engendered by the innocent Blaesus' inevitable demise is heightened. The passage possesses almost tragic power.[28] This is why I said earlier on that the ascription of human motive to Lucius seemed to be out of place. It is the faceless irrationality of the unseen powers at work which gives the passage its intensity. Paradoxically, of course, Lucius' involvement may have been the one solid piece of evidence for the cause of the whole enterprise.

Whether the episode is treated novelistically by Tacitus or not, comparison with a novelist such as Kafka is irresistible (*The Trial* springs to mind at once). Solzhenitsyn, too, before he became a figure of internationally acclaimed righteousness, was able, over the spread of a whole novel, to create precisely the sense of helpless futility in the face of irrational powers that Tacitus encapsulates here. One wonders how Tacitus would have described the fate of the luckless Dyrsin, imprisoned under the following circumstances:

> At the beginning of the war he had been denounced for 'anti-Soviet propaganda' by his neighbours who wanted—and were subsequently given—his flat. When the investigation showed that he had not been guilty of any such thing, it was then alleged that since he listened to German broadcasts he would have been capable of carrying on 'anti-Soviet propaganda'. He didn't, it was true, actually listen to German broadcasts, but since he was in possession of a radio set despite the ban, he could have done so. Finally, although he didn't in fact have a radio set, it was alleged that he could have had one, since he was a radio engineer by training, and hadn't a box containing two valves been found during the search of his flat? (from *The First Circle*)

P. V. JONES

---

[28] [Santoro l'hoir (2006) explores Tacitus' use of tragic motifs in the *Annals*.]

8

Pity, Fear, and the Historical Audience: Tacitus on the Fall of Vitellius

D. S. Levene

I

For the Roman historians, no passion is more prominent than fear. Fear for them is perhaps the single most important influence on the behaviour of individuals and states. It is often a negative force, deterring people from courses of action that they might otherwise entertain. But it can sometimes cause activity too. A country may be led to attack its neighbour through fear; fear can decide the outcome of a battle or a siege. Fear of assassination may lead a ruler into tyranny; yet it may be fear that drives the hand of the assassin.[1] When a historian wishes to analyse a situation, or explain a policy, he will very often do so at least partly in terms of fear.

Pity is less central. It probably appears less often than, say, anger or hatred as an explanation for action. Yet it too has an important role to play when, for example, people consider whether defeated opponents should be spared, with the concomitant idea that, if so, they may live to fight again or, alternatively, may transfer their allegiance to the victor out of gratitude. Here pity or the absence of pity may be presented as the key that will change the course of history.

Does the portrayal of these emotions in the Roman historians owe anything to philosophy? Many of the papers in this volume[2] are

[1] See Martin and Woodman (1989: 253) on the way in which rulers' and subjects' fears are bound together; more generally Heinz (1975: 30–73).
[2] Braund and Gill (1997).

concerned with philosophical influences on Roman literature, and one might hope to find such connections here. Stoicism, in particular, has a distinctive attitude towards the passions, is certainly important for understanding many Roman writers, and has indeed at times been claimed to have influenced various of the major historians.[3] Is there anything of Stoicism in their accounts of pity and fear?

It is hard to find it. Both pity and fear were roundly condemned by the Stoics.[4] For Roman historians, however, pity is almost always a positive trait.[5] With fear, of course, they are closer to Stoic views. It is hardly surprising that historians writing in a culture that set a high premium on military virtues should often present fear as something to be condemned. Yet such condemnation is far from universal. Fear is frequently attributed to characters in what seem quite neutral contexts, without any obvious indication that it is a defect. Still more significantly, historians will sometimes present fear as something explicitly positive. Most famous, for example, is Sallust's account of 'fear of the enemy' (*metus hostilis*) as something that kept the early Romans virtuous.[6] Livy takes this theme up at 1.19.4, with the additional twist that he there presents 'fear of the gods' (*metus deorum*) as a desirable alternative;[7] while Tacitus (*A.* 6.51.3) applies a similar idea to Tiberius, and claims that it was fear that until the end of his life kept him from indulging his vicious character.[8]

Thus there seems to be little influence of Stoicism; but what of other philosophical schools? Epicurean theories of the passions are less prominent in surviving accounts of their doctrines, but one can piece together evidence for their views. They seem to have applauded pity, and to this extent are similar to the historians (Diogenes Laertius 10.118). However, they, like the Stoics, generally condemned fear, as not being

---

[3] e.g. Pantzerhielm-Thomas (1936); Walsh (1958; 1961: 46–81); cf. André (1991).

[4] On fear, see e.g. Cicero *Tusc.* 2.11, 4.64, Epictetus 4.7, Diogenes Laertius 7.112–13; on pity e.g. Cicero *Mur.* 62–3, *Tusc.* 4.56, Seneca *Clem.* 2.4–6, Diogenes Laertius 7.111, 7.123. See Sandbach (1975: 59–62).

[5] A general condemnation of pity is put into the mouth of Caesar by Sallust (*Cat.* 51.1–4); but this is a deliberately paradoxical passage, which can hardly be accepted at face value; it is moreover subsequently undermined by the author (*Cat.* 54.2–3).

[6] *Jug.* 41.2; *Hist.* 1.11–12; the idea itself is, of course, an ancient commonplace (Earl 1961: 47–9).

[7] Ogilvie (1965: 94–5); cf. Levene (1993: 136).

[8] 'Finally, with shame and fear gone, he simply followed his own character, and abandoned himself to both crime and disgrace.' See also Heinz (1975: 42–53).

conducive to *ataraxia*;[9] hence the reasons that led us to discount Stoicism as an influence should lead us similarly to reject Epicureanism.

Much closer is Aristotle. Though there is no clear account of pity in his ethical writings, there is a famous discussion of courage and fear at *NE* 3.6–9. The details are not always coherent,[10] but Aristotle certainly believes that true courage does not involve the total absence of fear; rather the brave man fears only those things that it is appropriate to fear, and reacts to those things in an appropriate manner (*NE* 1115b15–19). This doctrine of the mean can be applied to other qualities, including some (such as pity) that Aristotle does not treat in detail.[11] All of this seems closer to the Roman historians' pragmatic approach to pity and fear than does any other doctrine so far considered.

However, we should not deduce from this that the historians were influenced by Aristotelian ethics directly. True, from the first century BC onwards Romans were acquainted with Peripatetics.[12] Whether the actual writings of Aristotle were much studied by Romans is more dubious: Cicero *Top*. 3 says not, and there is little in the Latin writers of the next hundred years to suggest that things changed later. Even Seneca does not show any deep acquaintance with Aristotelian philosophy.[13] For our purposes, it is especially noteworthy that Cicero, even when purporting to give an account of Peripatetic ethics in *Fin*. 5, does not refer to the doctrine of the mean. Admittedly, Cicero's account is based not on mainstream Peripatetic thought but on the syncretic account of Antiochus of Ascalon (*Fin*. 5.8, 5.75), but this may itself suggest that Aristotle's own thinking on the subject was relatively unfamiliar.[14] We may add that, while Aristotle's broad approach is fairly similar to those of the historians, the detailed examples that he provides of appropriate and inappropriate types of fear are not correlated especially closely to the attitudes of their narratives.[15]

---

[9] Epicurus *Sent*. 10; Lucretius 2.16–19; Cicero *Fin*. 1.49. Cf. Bailey (1947: 796–7); Mitsis (1988: 71–4, 90–91).

[10] The problem arises not least because Aristotle seems to wish to treat courage as a 'mean' of two separate passions, fear and confidence. See Pears (1978); Urmson (1988: 63–5).

[11] *NE* 1106b18–23. However, at 1115a5 he inconsistently implies that all the virtues will receive a detailed treatment, something that is not true of pity.

[12] Griffin (1989: 7) in Griffin and Barnes (1989).

[13] Gottschalk (1987: 1140–41).

[14] Barnes (1989: 86–9).

[15] e.g. the popular notion of 'fear of the enemy/gods' (text to nn. 6 and 7 above) have no place in Aristotle. On the other hand, Aristotle's precise distinction of various incomplete types of courage at *NE* 3.8 is hard to trace in the historians.

It is more likely, therefore, that such views are part of a general cultural complex that is emerging separately in Aristotle and the Roman historians. It may be that this part of Aristotle's ethical doctrine is attempting to provide a philosophical grounding for non-philosophical views;[16] but it is also the case that aspects of Peripatetic ideas filtered into wider culture via their influential work on rhetorical theory.[17] This, however, introduces a further consideration. Up to now we have been treating pity and fear solely as qualities by which we can analyse characters' motives and judge them morally. But in rhetorical theory an additional element is highlighted: the emotions of the audience itself. Aristotle gives an extremely precise dissection of fear and pity (among other emotions) in the *Rhetoric* (2.5, 2.8); and the avowed aim is to explain how they may be aroused in the listeners (*Rhet.* 1383a8–12.). The arousal of emotions in the audience likewise becomes a major theme of later rhetorical writings; Cicero and Quintilian are especially clear examples.[18] All of this is well known, and has been much discussed; as too has the even more famous application of similar criteria to poetic criticism by Aristotle in the *Poetics*, where, of course, it is precisely pity and fear that are identified as the emotions that it is characteristically tragedy's object to arouse.[19]

How do the ancient theorists believe that these emotions are to be induced in the audience? Once again, the answer is famous: the hearers are to be encouraged to identify with the emotions experienced by the participants in the events about which they are hearing. In the case of oratory, Aristotle suggests that the audience should imagine itself as directly affected by what is described.[20] This will often mean taking over the emotions of the orator.[21] Oratory is by its very nature generally concerned with real people, and it is relatively easy to see how an audience might find the situation personally

---

[16] Fortenbaugh (1975: 12–16).

[17] Solmsen (1941).

[18] See e.g. Cicero *de Or.* 2.185–216; Quintilian 6.1–2.

[19] *Poet.* 13–14. Pity and fear were regularly linked together, especially in discussions of literature: see Halliwell (1986: 170); also Nehemas (1992).

[20] See e.g. *Rhet.* 1382a24–32 (on fear); 1385b15–19 (on pity). Also Cicero *de Or.* 2.211; Quintilian 6.2.34.

[21] This does not often emerge in Aristotle, who seems rather to envisage the speaker himself remaining calm while inducing emotion in the audience (see Gill 1984: 151–5), but it is important in later theory: e.g. Cicero *de Or.* 2.189–90; Quintilian 6.2.3, 6.2.26–36.

affecting. But in less topical genres, such as tragedy, and even in narrative genres, a similar effect can be achieved. *Enargeia* often performs a central role here: the vivid description breaks down the barriers between the audience and the characters and encourages the former to share the viewpoint of, and hence to empathize with, the latter.[22]

This account, however, needs a certain qualification: pity and fear do not seem to be emotions that are aroused in an identical manner in an audience. The most plausible account of what it is for members of an audience to fear is, as discussed above, for them to place themselves imaginatively in the position of a character, who either actually does fear for himself or at least is in a position where such fear would be appropriate. But for an audience to pity, no such emotion need be experienced by any character in the work at all: one can respond directly to the portrayal of the fearful (or otherwise wretched) character's plight.[23] The two emotions are still, of course, closely related, and the one will often lead to the other (a point well brought out by Halliwell). But the methods by which they are aroused in the audience would appear to be fundamentally different: with fear, one takes over a character's emotion directly, with pity, one responds to his plight sympathetically—but from the standpoint of an observer.

However, there is a further consideration, which is sometimes overlooked. Writers on rhetoric, as was pointed out above, often argue that the best way to induce emotions in an audience is for the orator himself to display those emotions: and this is true of pity as well as of fear.[24] This may suggest that, even in narrative genres, pity may be aroused in an audience by similar methods to that of fear: namely, by persuading them to take over the emotions of a character who is pitying another character. As I shall show later, this method may become especially desirable when the character to be pitied is one to whose plight the audience might not automatically respond with sympathy. By showing him through the eyes of someone who is actually pitying him, one can instil in the audience a similar emotion.

This type of pity and fear may be described as 'audience-based'. We may distinguish it from the type discussed at the start of the paper,

---

[22] Gorgias *Helen* 9; Aristotle *Poet.* 1462a14–18 (cf. *Rhet.* 1386a32–5); *Rhet. ad Her.* 4.68–9; Horace *A.P.* 99–104; Quintilian 6.1.31–2, 6.2.29–36.

[23] On this analysis of 'audience-based' fear, and its consequent asymmetry with pity, see Lucas (1968: 273–5); Russell and Winterbottom (1972: 87); and esp. Halliwell (1986: 175–9).

[24] e.g. Cicero *de Or.* 2.189–90; cf. *Rhet. ad Her.* 2.50.

which is essentially concerned with explaining and evaluating the behaviour of those who are subject to these emotions, and which may be called 'analytic'. The importance of the latter in the historians was described above; but the presentation of history in a 'tragic' fashion, which meant above all the describing of events in a sensationalist manner likely to arouse the 'tragic' emotions of pity and fear in the audience, was, plainly, also a widely accepted technique;[25] it is indeed used by some as a criterion of good historical writing.[26]

But what precisely is the relationship between these two forms of emotional presentation? Some might think that the two are most likely to be operating at different times, and that primarily 'analytic' passages are not those which are aimed at generating emotions in the audience. Thus Christopher Gill, in a series of articles, distinguishes what he calls 'character viewpoints' from 'personality viewpoints', and argues that they have broadly different and indeed contradictory effects.[27] The former entail looking at a character from outside, and detailing his traits in a clinical and often moralistic fashion; the latter approach is more psychological, and involves the adoption of a character's viewpoint, without judging him according to external standards. A treatment of pity and fear that encourages an audience to take over those emotions can be seen as a particular example of Gill's 'personality viewpoint'. On the face of it, such a treatment seems unlikely to encourage that same audience to engage at the same time in an analysis of historical causation.[28]

However, the ancient sources do not support such a clear-cut distinction. When Aristotle in the *Poetics* speaks of the arousal of emotion in the audience, his fundamental assumption is that it is primarily generated by the audience's perceptions of the moral qualities of the story.[29] This view is implied in the *Rhetoric* also, and derives more generally from Aristotle's broadly 'cognitivist' account of emotion. Emotions are based on one's analysis of the situation: if that analysis is accurate, one's emotions are appropriate and justified;

---

[25] So much is uncontroversial; for the more difficult problem of whether there was actually a school of 'tragic history' see e.g. Walbank (1972: 34–40); Fornara (1983: 120–34).

[26] e.g. Cicero *Fam.* 5.12.4–5; Dion. Hal. *Thuc.* 15; Plutarch *De glor. Ath.* 347A-C.

[27] Gill (1986; 1990); cf. also (1983; 1984).

[28] See esp. Gill (1990: 2–8).

[29] Aristotle *Poetics* 1452b28–1453a22; cf. Fortenbaugh (1975: 35, 50–53); Halliwell (1986: 158–9, 162–7).

an inaccurate assessment of the situation would lead to inappropriate and unjustified emotions.[30] But in either case emotion may be seen as firmly rooted in reasoned perception of the sort that I have associated with an 'analytic' approach. Such a 'cognitivist' account was adopted by other philosophers, notably the Stoics, who (with the distinguished exception of Posidonius) saw the passions as arising from reason— albeit mistaken reason; and this view of emotion often appears to underlie non-philosophical discussions of literature also.[31]

Looking specifically at historiography, a comparable point emerges from Polybius' criticisms of Phylarchus (Polybius 2.56.7–10):

> He is keen to excite his readers' pity and make them sympathize with what he describes; so he introduces women embracing altars, with hair dishevelled and breasts bare, and moreover the tears and laments of men and women being led away in the company of their children and aged parents. He does this through his whole history, trying always at every point to make us visualize dreadful scenes . . . A historian ought not to be shocking his readers by telling tall tales through his histories.

At first sight it might seem as if Polybius is making a point similar to that of those theorists who claimed that the arousal of emotion is liable to interfere with the audience's rational judgement.[32] But in fact this is not the chief thrust of his attack. It is not that emotion *per se* is inimical to rational analysis, but rather that the attempt to excite emotion is liable to lead a writer into falsehood; in a subsequent comment he does seem to allow that 'tragic emotions' can sometimes play a useful role for the historian (Polybius 2.56.13):

> In any case, with most of his tragic reversals, Phylarchus just tells us the story, without suggesting why things are done and to what end; and without this it is impossible to feel either legitimate pity or proper anger about any events.

This has various implications. First, it confirms that Polybius, like Aristotle, is adopting a broadly 'cognitive' approach to emotion. His distinction between 'legitimate' and 'illegitimate' emotions, as he later makes clear, is that the former are based on a complete understanding

---

[30] Cf. Aristotle *NE* 1106b21–3; see Halliwell (1986: 195–6). The analysis need not be conscious; on the contrary, the mark of a virtuous man for Aristotle is his ability automatically to perceive the situation and to feel the appropriate emotion. See Fortenbaugh (1975: 70–75).

[31] See Lada (1993: 113–19).

[32] See e.g. Gorgias *Palamedes* 33; Quintilian 6.2.5–6.

of the circumstances of the case, the latter on a partial view only. But, more interestingly, he also appears to suggest that these 'audience-based' emotions have in themselves a valid role to play in historiography. Provided that the author arouses *appropriate* emotions in the audience, by ensuring that the characters with whom they are encouraged to sympathize actually deserve their sympathy, 'audience-based' emotions are not only derived from, but may reinforce and underpin, the moral and historical analysis.

But Gill's arguments still have something to offer. Implicit in them is the claim that it is not *only* analysis of morals and causes in the Aristotelian or Polybian sense that can generate an emotional response in the audience: such 'audience-based' emotions can also be aroused independently of the 'analytic', for example, by a narrative method that leads one to identify with a particular character.[33] Indeed, this can itself be supported from the ancient critics: note, for example, the important role allotted to *enargeia* ('vivid illustration'), or the possibility of audience identification with a character who is pitying another leading to sympathy with the character pitied (both discussed in text to nn. 22–3 above). We may also observe the significant distinction at Aristotle *Poetics* 1453b1–3 between pity and fear that arise 'from the spectacle', and those which derive from the 'arrangement of events'—the former category suggesting that Aristotle (though disapproving of it) sees the possibility that the method of presentation may alone suffice to produce emotions in the audience.[34] 'Audience-based' pity and fear, then, sometimes derive from 'analytic' emotions, but sometimes also emerge independently; likewise, naturally, not *all* 'analytic' presentations of these emotions are such as to invite audiences to take on the emotions themselves. Therefore such an external, 'analytic' viewpoint can indeed, as Gill argues, conflict with independently derived 'audience-based' emotions.

But one further point should be considered. Polybius' account has shown 'audience-based' emotions that are not only derived from cognition, but actually influence it, by supporting the 'proper' picture of historical events. What then of independently derived 'audience-

---

[33] One might argue that, even in such cases, emotions are still based in cognitive perception, as they are connected with the adoption of a particular viewpoint; however, it is a rather different sort of cognitive perception from the essentially explanatory and moral analysis discussed so far, which usually seems to be assumed by both Aristotle and Polybius.

[34] See Halliwell (1986: 64–5).

based' emotions? It can be plausibly argued that these, too, have 'analytic' implications, inducing a particular picture of the moral circumstances.[35] For example, the fact that a character attracts audience sympathy may itself be taken to imply that his moral position is such as to deserve sympathy; this may imply a particular 'external' assessment of the situation.[36] If a historian sets this approach, with its own analytic force, against a straightforwardly 'analytic' approach, he can exploit the tension between these two modes of presentation, either to show one or other as ultimately inadequate, or even to leave the 'correct' analysis open. In the second half of this paper I shall seek to demonstrate that Roman historians did indeed exploit these two modes of presentation for the purposes of complex analysis, taking as a case study Tacitus, *Histories* 3.36–86.

II

Both fear and pity play a prominent role in the second part of Tacitus *Histories* 3. This is partly due to the fact that fear is one of the chief characteristics of Vitellius, as Tacitus presents him; Suetonius, by contrast, has little or nothing of this, and indeed is even ready to show Vitellius as unreasonably confident (e.g. *Vit.* 8). But Tacitus does not limit himself to giving an account of Vitellius' fear. As we shall see, he goes further still, and sets the whole action surrounding the fall of Vitellius against an intricate network of both fear and pity involving all the participants.

The sequence begins with the immediate aftermath of the Flavians' sack of Cremona. The scene now moves to Vitellius (*H.* 3.36–9), but at a time before he hears about this major blow to his cause. The result

---

[35] This is in fact implicit in some of Gill's discussion: e.g. his idea that a 'personality viewpoint' is associated especially with the expression of 'morally non-standard and problematic' views (Gill 1990: 6–7, 30–31). But, as Polybius suggests, and as I hope to demonstrate, 'personality viewpoints' need not only be questioning: they can encode positive and indeed quite conservative values, and the questions, if any, arise only if those values clash with others in the work.

[36] For a more extended discussion of the derivation of cognition from emotion, see Lada (1993: 116–19), citing both ancient sources and modern psychological theory. Nussbaum's controversial interpretation of Aristotelian *katharsis* as a cognitive clarification produced by pity and fear (Nussbaum 1986: 388–91; cf. 1992: 143–50) would point to a similar conclusion; but see *contra* e.g. Lear (1988).

is that the reader sees his behaviour here in an ironic light: the danger facing him is far greater than he realizes.[37] Fear and pity only enter the picture in *H*. 3.38–9, where his brother Lucius persuades him to take action against Junius Blaesus. Here the two emotions combine to explain Vitellius' murder of Blaesus. The fear is explicit,[38] the latter implicit in his brother's appeal on behalf of his son. But both emotions are shown as utterly misplaced. Blaesus, as Tacitus explicitly tells us, is not a threat to Vitellius (*H*. 3.39.2). Despite what Lucius says here, Vespasian is; and Vitellius' ignoring of this threat, as was said above, looks particularly ironic in the light of the defeat at Cremona, and in conjunction with his failure to take the recent defections from his forces seriously.[39] That this shows Vitellius in a poor light is undeniable, especially when we add that the murder of Blaesus to which these misplaced emotions lead is so clearly presented as an atrocious abuse of power.

Additional interest is provided by one striking sentence (*H*. 3.39.1):

> *trepidanti inter scelus metumque, ne dilata Blaesi mors maturam perniciem, palam iussa atrocem inuidiam ferret, placuit ueneno grassari.*

> The Emperor nervously hesitated between crime and terror. On the one hand, putting off Blaesus' death might bring on him swift ruin; but on the other to order it openly might cause dreadful resentment. So he decided to employ poison.

Tacitus' phrasing here is complicated and initially misleading. The implication of *inter scelus metumque* seems at first sight to be that fear might keep Vitellius from crime. This reminds us of the more positive forms of the emotion in the Roman historians, where people are deterred by fear from immoral actions (text to nn. 5–7 above). But, as is indicated by the word 'hesitated' (*trepidanti*) and the first part of the 'might' (*ne*) clause indicate, Vitellius is fearful either way: he has

---

[37] Dio, by contrast (if Xiphilinus' summary is to be believed), moved directly from the battle to Vitellius' reaction to it (64.15–16).

[38] *H*. 3.38.3–39.1: 'He [sc. Lucius] was not afraid or nervous for himself, but was begging and weeping on behalf of his brother and his brother's children. There was nothing to fear in Vespasian . . . the enemy to beware was in the city and their very bosoms . . . The Emperor nervously hesitated between crime and terror . . . so he decided to employ poison.' *non se proprio metu nec sui anxium, sed pro fratre, pro liberis fratris preces lacrimasque attulisse. frustra Vespasianum timeri . . . in urbe ac sinu cauendum hostem . . . trepidanti inter scelus metumque . . . placuit ueneno grassari.*

[39] Fuhrmann (1960: 271–2).

been affected by Lucius' speech, and is afraid not to commit the crime, as well as to commit it. Ultimately, fear simply leads him to commit the crime covertly, rather than openly. The reader is once again invited to analyse and judge Vitellius; and his fear is seen as all the worse through being a perverted version of the familiar moral deterrent.

Overall, therefore, this is an example of an 'analytic' treatment of pity and fear, combining explanation and evaluation. There is no idea that the audience might sympathize with emotions that are presented as so plainly out of place and immoral. It is true that there is a strong rhetorical context: as with the textbook rhetorical audience, pity and fear are awakened in Vitellius by Lucius' speech, which even employs the orator's standard trick of introducing a child.[40] But the readers are distanced from any direct access to the emotional effect of such a speech, partly by the fact that it is in *oratio obliqua*, but more importantly by the fact that, before it begins, Tacitus has told us that Lucius had ulterior motives in making it, and that Vitellius was already predisposed to accept its conclusions. Both orator and hearer are compromised in our eyes from the start.

At *H.* 3.54 we return to Vitellius, who has now learned of the Cremona disaster. Tacitus treats his response with great and ironic detail: Vitellius suppresses the report of the defeat, even killing the spies who tell him the truth, and fatally damages his own cause in the process (*H.* 3.54). At last he accepts the situation, and acts—but his actions are again shown as quite inappropriate (*H.* 3.55–6). In the course of this Tacitus describes his fear:

uoltu quoque et incessu trepidus . . . recentissimum quodque uulnus pauens, summi discriminis incuriosus. nam cum transgredi Appenninum integro exercitus sui robore et fessos hieme atque inopia hostes adgredi in aperto foret, dum dispergit uires, acerrimum militem et usque in extrema obstinatum trucidandum capiendumque tradidit . . .

Moreover, panic showed in his face and walk . . . He was terrified at every new setback, but was indifferent to the supreme crisis. It was open to him to cross the Apennines with his army's strength undivided, and to attack the enemy while they were exhausted by the winter and their lack of supplies. Instead he wasted his forces, and surrendered his

---

[40] *H.* 3.38.2: 'Clasping his [sc. the emperor's] son to his bosom'.

soldiers, who were fiercely ready to resist to the last, to slaughter or capture. (*H.* 3.56.2–3)

Just as before, this fear is misplaced, and ignores the real danger, an understanding of which could have led Vitellius to act more rationally. This time it does not have as strong an explanatory role—it is clear that, even before he is shown as afraid, Vitellius is behaving irrationally and failing to see what is in his best interests. But it is still fundamentally an 'analytic' treatment: if we do not see the·fear as the cause of his irrational behaviour, it is still a close concomitant of that behaviour, the unreasonableness of which is the chief focus of the passage. With Tacitus' ironic dissection of Vitellius' faults to the fore, there is yet again no idea that he might be an object of sympathy.

Yet not only Vitellius himself but also his followers are of interest here. At *H.* 3.55.3, his senatorial supporters are described as being afraid of him ('many were attracted through ambition, more through fear'); but at *H.* 3.58.2–3 the situation changes:

ea simulatio officii a metu profecta uerterat in favorem; ac plerique haud proinde Vitellium quam casum locumque principatus miserabantur. nec deerat ipse uultu uoce lacrimis misericordiam elicere, largus promissis, et quae natura trepidantium est, immodicus. quin et Caesarem se dici uoluit, aspernatus antea, sed tunc superstitione nominis, et quia in metu consilia prudentium et uulgi rumor iuxta audiuntur.

Their pretence of duty, which originated in their fear, had turned into real support. Most of them pitied not Vitellius, but the calamitous position of the Emperor. But he was there himself to work on their sympathies with his looks, words and tears. He was lavish with his promises and knew no restraint, as is typical of a man in a panic. He even wanted to be called 'Caesar' although he had previously scorned the title. But now he was attracted by the superstition of the name, and when one is afraid one is unable to distinguish sensible advice from vulgar gossip.

The first point to make is that Tacitus is using pity and fear to demonstrate Vitellius' progressive loss of control. His followers move from fearing him to pitying him, and he correspondingly is shown as increasingly subject to fear. It is less and less the case that Vitellius is capable of exciting terror in others, and more and more that he is in a position where he needs to be afraid, and where he is thus an appropriate recipient of compassion. A similar idea appears at *H.* 3.59.1:

ut terrorem Italiae possessa Meuania ac uelut regnatum ex integro bellum intulerat, ita haud dubium erga Flauianas partes studium tam pauidus Vitellii discessus addidit.

The capture of Mevania terrified Italy, because the war seemed to be beginning anew; but the panicky departure of Vitellius solidified support for the Flavian party.

The Italians' fear of Vitellius' forces is counteracted by Vitellius' own terror, which makes his weakness apparent, which in turn explains the general move to support Vespasian.

But there is another aspect to this passage. While Vitellius' fear, as presented above, is treated by Tacitus in an 'analytic' manner, his followers introduce a further consideration. For the first time, we see Vitellius through the eyes of other people who are sympathizing with him, and this is a viewpoint that it is possible to share, at least partially. It is true that Tacitus is still treating Vitellius' fears in an ironic manner. As in *H.* 3.38, there is a rhetorical context that is undermined by its presentation. Vitellius' speech is described rather than being shown directly; as a result his attempt to gain sympathy looks excessively calculating. Moreover, his promises, and his acceptance of the name 'Caesar', are clearly presented as the irrational products of his fear.

Likewise, his followers are not presented in a wholly attractive manner. The senators in particular are initially reluctant followers (*H.* 3.55.3), and have their contributions imposed on them (*H.* 3.58.2); and they, along with the knights, are the ones who soon lose their enthusiasm for him and drift away after his speech—their pity is suggested by Tacitus to be an 'ill-considered impulse' (*H.* 3.58.4). The knights come across slightly better, in that their contributions are voluntary. However, although Tacitus expresses contempt for the mob,[41] when it comes to Vitellius' freedmen he shows them in a far better light: he indirectly praises their support (*amicorum quanto quis clarior, minus fidus*—'the more distinguished the friend, the less loyal'),[42] and describes their spontaneous offers of

---

[41] Also *H.* 3.58.1: 'He was deceived by appearances into calling a craven mob (who were not going to dare anything more than words) "an army" and "legions".'

[42] Wellesley (1972: 155–6) claims that we should understand 'he was thought to be' (*habebatur*) here, and that this represents not Tacitus' view of the imperial freedmen, but rather Vitellius' mistaken view. Such a reading is, however, difficult to sustain when 'he was' (*erat*) would make equally good sense (Kühner and Stegmann 1955: 551).

money and help (*H.* 3.58.2); and the latter comes immediately prior to his description of the growing sympathy for Vitellius in the passage above. There is likewise no suggestion here that these supporters, unlike the upper-class ones, are subject only to a temporary passion in their pity for Vitellius.

The result is that the 'internal audience', composed of observers within the work, the people through whose eyes we view Vitellius here, are at least partly ones whose point of view we have no reason to reject: we can see Vitellius as genuinely deserving of pity, since they pity him. In effect, *this* audience is adopting an 'audience-based' viewpoint, and since our picture of Vitellius is partially mediated via them, we may begin to do the same.

How does this relate to the 'analytic' view of Vitellius that Tacitus has been establishing until now, and which, as I argued above, he continues to establish even in this passage? In one way it reinforces it, by emphasizing the weakness that leads his followers to drift away. But in another respect it jars slightly: by showing Vitellius as relatively sympathetic, it works against the 'analytic' viewpoint, which has been treating him entirely critically. However, Tacitus smooths over the potential clash by making it clear that the sympathy that Vitellius' supporters feel for him is limited to the office, not the man; this draws on the common feeling in the ancient world that a great fall from power is in itself deserving of pity.[43] In this way it is possible, it seems, to despise Vitellius for his fear, while sympathizing with him as a falling emperor. But this is always vulnerable to the objection that Vitellius the man and Vitellius the emperor are not separable; and Tacitus introduces an element that brings that problem to our attention, as he shows Vitellius now through his cowardice taking on the imperial title that he had previously rejected. How far audience sympathy for Vitellius can potentially extend is still left open.

Shortly after this, we are returned far more insistently to the idea of Vitellius as an object of pity. The theme is brought in at *H.* 3.65.2: *uultus procul uisentibus notabantur, Vitellii proiectus et degener, Sabinus non insultans et miseranti propior* ('their expressions were witnessed by those watching at a distance, Vitellius' downcast and degenerate, but Sabinus seemed not scornful, but closer to compassion'). It might seem that Sabinus' viewpoint is one that we are

---

[43] Dover (1974: 197).

disposed to accept, even though the actual description of Vitellius as 'degenerate' (*degener*) carries moralistic overtones that would seem to make him an inappropriate object of pity. However, we do not see Vitellius through Sabinus' eyes as he pities him; rather we see both of them from the point of view of observers, who regard Sabinus as 'closer to compassion', but whose view of Vitellius is the moralistic one mentioned above. Hence there is no invitation to the readers that they themselves should pity Vitellius.

Yet the idea that he is pitied is now there; it is continued by *H*. 3.66.1–2, where he is advised that Vespasian would not spare him even were he to surrender, and Tacitus sums up with the key phrase *ita periculum ex misericordia* ('so danger comes from pity'). As Wellesley says, 'the phrase is excessively obscure'; the most likely sense is 'danger from throwing himself on Vespasian's mercy'.[44] Tacitus is insisting more and more on the idea of Vitellius as an object of pity, even at the cost of straining the Latin. As in *H*. 3.65, there is no suggestion that this pity is to be taken over by the reader, as the thought is only coming up in *oratio obliqua* as part of a potential strategy to be rejected. But Tacitus has just before shown us Vitellius' weakness and lack of direction,[45] and the treatment of pity reinforces this. As before, we see more and more the diminution of Vitellius' status, as he becomes a person to whom pity might be applied.

But in the following sections (*H*. 3.67–8) the idea of pity is taken up by Tacitus with much greater length and complexity, when Vitellius attempts to abdicate his power. Here, once again, he is pitied, and we see in this his weakness and powerlessness (a theme ironically reinforced by *H*. 3.68.3, where his followers will not allow him to abdicate, and instead force him to return to the palace). But Tacitus' handling of the theme of pity moves the passage far more strongly in the direction of an 'audience-based' approach. Again, we have a rhetorical context, with Vitellius addressing the crowd; again, we see him through the eyes of the bystanders. But, much more than any passage that we have considered so far, the reader is encouraged to identify fully with those bystanders and to share their pity for Vitellius. Although the Romans often reacted to changes of fortune such as Vitellius' with, for example, ridicule or amazement (cf. *H*. 3.84.5 and text to n. 65 below), Tacitus does not allow

---

[44] Wellesley (1972: 163); cf. *OLD* s.v. *misericordia* 2.
[45] Esp. *H*. 3.63.2: 'He was so overcome by sloth that, if others had not remembered that he was Emperor, he himself would have forgotten it.'

for such a reaction here. *nec quisquam adeo rerum humanarum im-memor quem non commoueret illa facies* ('No one could have been so indifferent to human tragedy as to be unmoved by that scene', *H.* 3.69.1); the reader is implicitly included. Moreover, the description stresses the *appearance* of the scene—note *illa facies* ('that scene')–and this *enargeia* (text to n. 22 above) encourages audience involvement with the characters. And the word *facies* and the phrase *nihil tale uiderant, nihil audierant* ('they had never seen or heard of such a thing') help emphasize that the bystanders are an audience, rather than actors (they are, rather oddly, implicitly distanced from the sol-diers and people, who behave rather differently);[46] the readers conse-quently will merge this position with their own, since they can see both themselves and the internal audience as pure observers.[47] It is true that the people are said to react inappropriately to Vitellius' departure—but their inappropriate reaction is not pity, which is thus confirmed as an appropriate reaction.

The position of Vitellius here reinforces this. He is explicitly said (unlike at *H.* 3.58) to be saying things appropriate to the situation.[48] More importantly, in both his departure from the palace and his speech, he is linked as an object of pity with his family, and in particular with his mother and children, the only members of it who get any detailed description, and who are clearly deserving of total sympathy; we may compare *H.* 2.64, and indeed *H.* 3.66 just before this passage, where it is made clear to Vitellius that his son has nothing to hope for in the event of Vespasian's victory. The doom that hangs over them is plain from the reference to his mother's timely death,[49] and from the funeral imagery describing their depar-ture; the pathos of the diminutives referring to his son is also striking (the boy was in fact killed by Mucianus shortly after the Flavian victory (*H.* 4.80.1)).[50] Vitellius' family, and hence Vitellius himself,

---

[46]   The response of the soldiers and people has been shown at *H.* 3.67.2 just before: 'The people shouted words of inappropriate flattery; the soldiers maintained a threat-ening silence.' Cf. also *H.* 3.68.2: 'with even women watching'. On the 'audience' theme in general, see Borzsák (1973: esp. 65–6).

[47]   Compare Davidson (1991: esp. 14–16) on the way in which Polybius' readers' view of events merges into that of the internal audience.

[48]   *H.* 3.68.2: 'He said a few words suited to the sad occasion'.

[49]   *H.* 3.67.1: 'She had the good fortune to die a few days before the destruction of her family.'

[50]   Wellesley (1972: 164). *H.* 3.67.2: *pullo amictu Palatio degreditur, maesta circum familia; ferebatur lecticula paruulus filius uelut in funebrem pompam* ('He descended

are to be seen here as rightly pitied by the internal audience, and hence by the readers.

But Tacitus pulls us still closer towards an 'audience-based' treatment of Vitellius here; because the emperor is not only appealing for pity, but is himself one of those who are pitying his family.[51] That pity is shown as his private reaction, not simply as part of his speech, and hence is treated as genuine.[52] Vitellius' love for his family has consistently been his one attractive trait; Tacitus has made relatively little of it before now, but here it dominates the picture of him.[53] As we adopt the viewpoint of the internal audience, as set out above, we also adopt the near-identical viewpoint of Vitellius himself. The pity for him that has been built up as a result of seeing him through the eyes of pitying observers is now turned into a more direct and unmediated sympathy.

As before (p. 222 above), sympathy with Vitellius is tied to the idea of him as a falling emperor. What is said to excite the bystanders' pity is the idea of the former master of the world reduced to such ignominy;[54] and they contrast his public abdication with the violent ends of Julius Caesar, Gaius, Nero, Galba, and his heir, Piso (*H.* 3.68.1). However, this time it is in practice impossible to distinguish the man from the office, since the whole presentation of Vitellius here is such as to invite sympathy for him. To sympathize with Vitellius as emperor is now to sympathize with him as a man.[55]

from the palace wearing a black cloak, with his sorrowing household around. His little son was borne in his litter as if in a funeral procession').

[51] *H.* 3.67.1: *obruebatur animus miseratione curaque, ne pertinacibus armis minus placabilem uictorem relinqueret coniugi ac liberis. erat illi et fessa aetate parens* ('His mind was crushed by pity and concern that by persisting in warfare he would leave the victor less well-disposed towards his wife and children. He also had a mother who was old and weak'). *H.* 3.68.2 (Vitellius speaking): *retinerent tantum memoriam sui fratremque et coniugem et innoxiam liberorum aetatem miserarentur—simul filium protendens, modo singulis modo universis commendans* ('Let them only remember him, and pity his brother, his wife, and his children of tender years. As he spoke he held out his son, commending him to them individually and collectively').

[52] Contrast Dio/Xiphilinus 64.16.5, for whom this scene is described only to demonstrate Vitellius' inconsistency, and who of his pity for his son says only 'he held him out to them as if to invite pity'.

[53] Vitellius has earlier acted to protect or honour his family at *H.* 1.75.2, 2.59.3, 2.89.2, 3.38; Suetonius by contrast removes any indication of this attractive side to Vitellius, and actually shows him as cruel towards his family (*Vit.* 6, 7, 14).

[54] *H.* 3.68.1: 'The Roman emperor, until recently the master of the whole human race, was leaving the house of his power and departing from the principate through the people and the city.'

[55] Briessmann (1955: 80).

It is against this background that we reach the famous scene of Vitellius' death (*H*. 3.84–5). The most striking aspect of Tacitus' account here is the extent to which he uses *enargeia* to present Vitellius' fears in the most vivid light—especially at *H*. 3.84.4:

> *in Palatium regreditur uastum desertumque, dilapsis etiam infimis ser-uitiorum aut occursum eius declinantibus. terret solitudo et tacentes loci; temptat clausa, inhorrescit uacuis.*

> He returned to the huge, deserted palace. Even the lowliest slaves had slipped away, or else were avoiding meeting him. The loneliness and the silent rooms terrified him; he tried locks, he shuddered at the emptiness.

The reader is invited in effect to look at things through Vitellius' eyes, and hence to adopt his fearful viewpoint. The scene is dramatic and affecting, and clearly follows up the 'audience-based' approach to Vitellius: the audience empathizes with his fears, and pities him.

Added to this are various indications that Tacitus is, even in the humiliation of Vitellius' death, seeking to remove the worst indignity. In comparison with the accounts of Suetonius *Vit.* 16–17, Dio/Xiphilinus 64.20–21, and Josephus *BJ* 4.651–2, Tacitus softens the sense of moral degradation with which they surround his person. Although Tacitus has earlier made a good deal of his gluttony,[56] he now, unlike the other writers, does not refer to it.[57] Suetonius and Dio/Xiphilinus both describe his sordid hiding-place in some detail (the former has him hiding in the porter's lodge (*Vit.* 16), the latter in with the dogs (64.20.1–2)); Tacitus calls it only a *pudenda latebra* ('shameful hiding-place', *H*. 3.84.4). Tacitus does not show anything of his calculating and degrading attempts to avoid capture by disguising himself. He says nothing of his fortifying himself with a money-belt, pretending to be someone else, and then claiming to have information 'vital to Vespasian's safety' (Suetonius); nothing of his deliberately dressing in rags (Dio)—Tacitus refers to his *laniata ueste* ('clothes in tatters', *H*. 3.84.5) while he is dragged to execution, but the implication is that they were torn in the course of his flight or arrest. Such episodes would involve an overtly moralistic approach to

---

[56] e.g. *H*. 1.62.2, 2.31.1, 2.62.1, 2.71.1.

[57] Josephus *BJ* 4.651 actually describes him going to his death after emerging drunk from a lavish banquet; Suetonius does not have him initially wandering around alone, but accompanied by his pastry-cook and chef (*Vit.* 16); both Suetonius *Vit.* 17 and Dio/Xiphilinus 64.20.3 have him mocked for his fat stomach.

Vitellius that would hinder the audience from sharing his fears and pitying him.

In fact Tacitus even includes the occasional element that might positively justify a favourable moral reaction. Vitellius' final words are one example, which not only remind us of his earlier imperial status, but also are presented as having a certain nobility of their own.[58] Another is the account of the route he took to his death, in which he is implicitly linked to the deaths of Galba and Sabinus.[59] Although Vitellius had opposed both men, Tacitus did not show him as directly implicated in the deaths of either: the dominant impression is thus the link between their unjust deaths and Vitellius' own impending doom.[60] We can contrast Dio/Xiphilinus 64.20.2–3, who uses a similar effect partly to set Vitellius' degradation against his earlier glory, but also to remind us of his vices ('They led out of the palace the man who had revelled there').[61]

But also found in the passage are occasional hints at moral criticism of Vitellius from a more 'analytic' standpoint. These consequently jar against the 'audience-based' approach which the bulk of the passage is establishing; they are more like Tacitus' adverse comparison of Vitellius' death with Otho's in Book 2.[62] We can see this at *H.* 3.84.4 in the phrases *mobilitate ingenii* ('endemic restlessness'), *cum omnia metuenti praesentia maxime displicerent* ('he feared

---

[58] *H.* 3.85: *una uox non degeneris animi excepta, cum tribuno insultanti se tamen imperatorem eius fuisse respondit* ('One comment he made showed a mind not entirely degraded: as a tribune mocked him he replied that even so, he had been his emperor'). This is also found in Dio/Xiphilinus 64.21.2—but not Suetonius, despite his usual interest in 'last words' (apart from *Vit.*, only *Tib.*, *Claud.*, and *Dom.* lack this information). Doubtless Suetonius did not wish to include anything that would conflict with his picture of Vitellius as totally vicious.

[59] *H.* 3.85: 'Vitellius was compelled by his enemies' swords to lift his head and face the insults; then to watch his statues as they fell, and above all the rostra or the place of Galba's murder. Finally they forced him to the Gemonian Steps, where the body of Flavius Sabinus had lain.'

[60] See *H.* 1.41, 49, 3.74–5. Rademacher (1975: 248–9) argues that the description of the death of Vitellius in general recalls that of Galba. Cf. also *H.* 3.86, 'People cannot claim credit for their treachery who betrayed Vitellius to Vespasian after earlier deserting Galba.'

[61] Baxter (1971: 105–7) argues that the whole of the last section of the book is set up so as to recall the fall of Troy in *Aeneid* 2. By linking Vitellius to Priam, Aeneas, and the Trojans in general, Tacitus reinforces his presentation of him as a sympathetic figure of tragic stature.

[62] *H.* 2.31.1: 'Their deaths, for which Otho won a splendid reputation, but Vitellius a most infamous one'.

everything, but distrusted most his immediate surroundings') and especially *quae natura pauoris est* ('typically of one in a panic'), which suggests a rather clinical, external view of Vitellius' fear. 'Shameful hiding-place' is similarly moralistic; so too the phrase 'one comment he made showed a mind not entirely degraded' implies a general criticism of Vitellius—the clear suggestion is that degeneracy was more typical of his character. We may add that directly before this passage Tacitus has shown the heroic last stand of Vitellius' soldiers, and the implicit contrast is not to Vitellius' credit.[63] These factors are not prominent enough to wipe out the audience's sympathy, but they do raise the idea that there is something problematic about an 'audience-based' approach to such a fundamentally unattractive figure.

There is moreover a further complicating element. Here, as before, Vitellius is seen through the eyes of an internal audience. But whereas previously the internal audience pitied him, and hence encouraged readers to adopt the same viewpoint and do the same, now Tacitus tells us that Vitellius' degradation was so great that there was no place for pity; instead the onlookers taunted him.[64] The fact that Vitellius is described as a 'spectacle' (*H.* 3.84.5) might seem to suggest that we are once again (cf. text to n. 47 above) to see this internal audience as pure observers like ourselves, and consequently merge our viewpoint into theirs, which is fundamentally an 'analytic' one.[65] Against this might be the ironic comment on the mob with which Tacitus concludes the scene (*H.* 3.85): *et uulgus eadem prauitate insectabatur interfectum qua fouerat uiuentem* ('and the mob reviled him when killed with the same perversity that had led them to support him when alive')—this might lead us to see the internal audience's own viewpoint as flawed. True, we have already seen (text to n. 46 above) that Tacitus' internal audiences are not necessarily identical with any particular group of onlookers, even if that group is referred to in the same passage; but one could argue that here the fact that both the internal audience and the mob are described in comparable fashions

---

[63] The final sentence, directly before this passage, particularly points the contrast: 'even as they fell they were concerned to die honourably' (*H.* 3.84.3). Cf. Wellesley (1972: 186).

[64] *H.* 3.84.5: *multis increpantibus, nullo inlacrimante: deformitas exitus misericordiam abstulerat* ('Many taunted him, no one wept: the disfigurement of his death had wiped out pity').

[65] Cf. also Keitel (1992) for the general significance of the theme of 'spectacle' in Vitellius' story.

as hostile to Vitellius means that it is difficult to separate them from each other.

But more significant still is that just a few lines earlier Tacitus has presented the viewpoint of a similar internal audience as highly questionable (*H.* 3.83):

> *aderat pugnantibus spectator populus, utque in ludicro certamine, hos, rursus illos clamore et plausu fouebat. quotiens pars altera inclinasset, abditos in tabernis aut si quam in domum perfugerant, erui iugularique expostulantes parte maiore praedae potiebantur . . . saeua ac deformis urbe tota facies . . . quantum in luxurioso otio libidinum, quidquid in acerbissima captiuitate scelerum, prorsus ut eandem ciuitatem et furere crederes et lasciuire . . . uelut festis diebus id quoque gaudium accederet, exultabant, fruebantur, nulla partium cura, malis publicis laeti.*

The people stood by as spectators to the fighting; just like in a show in the arena, they supported first one side, then the other with cheers and applause. Whenever one side went under, the onlookers demanded that those who had hidden in shops or had taken refuge in houses be dragged out and slaughtered; and they themselves kept most of the booty . . . The whole city's appearance was cruel and distorted . . . You would believe that the city was simultaneously in the grip of rage and lust: there was every vice of luxurious living, every crime of the most brutal sack . . . It was as if this were an extra Saturnalian festivity: they rioted and revelled, caring nothing for either side, but rejoicing in their country's ruin.

Here the people of Rome are seen in an extended image as an audience; but to be an audience when atrocities are actually being performed in front of one's eyes is clearly presented as an abominable thing. Moreover, such audiences do not limit themselves simply to spectating, but also egg on the participants,[66] and even seek to profit by the destruction. And Tacitus implicitly confirms that the reader should not seek to identify with such internal viewpoints by using the second person 'you would believe' (*crederes*): the reader's view of such events ought to be very different.[67] Specifically, the *enargeia* and the stress on the appearance of the scene, once again, invite the reader to feel the sympathy that the internal audience do not. When Tacitus then treats Vitellius' humiliation, likewise, as a spectacle observed by an audience, this continues the same theme; given that an internal audience composed of the citizens of

---

[66] A touch manifestly derived from the behaviour of real Roman audiences, especially at gladiatorial contests; cf. Seneca *Ep.* 7.2–5, taken with Ville (1981: 442–5).

[67] Cf. 'Longinus' *On the Sublime* 26.1; see Gilmartin (1975: 116).

Rome has so recently been shown as corrupt, the idea of accepting as valid another such audience's view of Vitellius (especially in the context of a largely sympathetic presentation) can only jar.

III

So through Tacitus' handling of pity and fear, two very different pictures of Vitellius dominate at different times, but are finally brought into direct conflict. One is the 'analytic' picture, treating his fears as part of the explanation for his cruel and ineffectual behaviour, and implicitly or explicitly criticizing them in a moralistic fashion. The other is the 'audience-based' picture, which leads us to sympathize with those fears and pity him. We adopt the latter not least through accepting the viewpoint of the internal audience; at the end that internal audience would seem to turn us back towards the 'analytic' picture, but only at a time when its own status has been rendered problematic.

Moreover, as was argued earlier, the 'audience-based' treatment has an analytic force of its own: by suggesting that Vitellius is a character to whom pity may legitimately be given, Tacitus indicates that his fears do not set him as far beyond the pale as the 'analytic' treatment implied. In addition, the 'audience-based' mode is linked to the idea that Vitellius deserves sympathy as a falling emperor. This attitude is a traditional one in historians faced with a leader's demise (p. 222 above);[68] at the same time, it can hardly be divorced from its contemporary political resonances, encoding as it does the status of the emperor and his significance for the Roman world. But Tacitus blurs the distinction between sympathy for Vitellius as emperor and sympathy for him personally; and he then sets the 'analytic' against the 'audience-based' mode at the end, placing such an attitude in opposition to the highly undeserving character of Vitellius himself. The problem of the 'bad emperor' is thus starkly raised.

What, then, does this case study tell us about historians' use of pity and fear? To begin with, it seems broadly 'Aristotelian', in that the arousal of emotions in the audience is not opposed to a moralistic,

---

[68] Ancient writers tended to present the fall of even morally dubious leaders in 'tragic' guise. See e.g. Polybius on the fall of Philip V (23.10–11, followed by Livy 40.3–24); cf. Walbank (1938).

'analytic' treatment, but may form part of it. As before, however, we should not assume that this is due to direct philosophical influence on historians (text to n. 15 above). Nor should one even deduce from this some Hellenistic school of 'Peripatetic historiography':[69] many historians, including Thucydides well before the Peripatetics, can be argued to exhibit similar traits, and once again, it may well be that the Peripetatics were seeking to give a philosophical form to non-philosophical beliefs.

But perhaps the most significant conclusion, if Tacitus here is taken as representative, is that historians linked emotion to reason more closely than simply deriving the former from the latter. For while it is true that, as he moves towards an 'audience-based' portrayal of Vitellius, he excludes some of the negative features found in other versions of the story, he does relatively little to provide a positive reason in the 'analytic' sense for audience sympathy—this sympathy may encode political attitudes, as was argued above, but it is not fundamentally determined by external moral criteria. Rather, Tacitus approaches the issue in the opposite way: instead of establishing Vitellius as a character of greater stature than might originally have been implied, and allowing our sympathies to follow this revised perception of him, he arouses our sympathies in ways that are not primarily related to a reasoned morality at all, by the use of the internal audience and *enargeia*; and Vitellius' standing is improved in our eyes precisely because of the sympathy that has been generated for him.

Such a technique is found in other literary genres also (and indeed may even be implicit in Aristotle);[70] but to discover it in historians is especially noteworthy. A principal aim of historiography is the explanation, interpretation, and understanding of the world of the past. The arousal of the 'tragic emotions' in historical works has often been treated as something essentially divorced from this: a purely literary matter which, while making those works more attractive to read, interferes with or at best is irrelevant to the rational part of an historian's work. We can now see that the 'audience-based' approach to the passions is far from being inimical to historical analysis: it can lie at its very heart.[71]

---

[69] Cf. the debate on 'tragic history' (n. 25 above), and specifically Walbank (1972: 34–7).

[70] Lada (1993: 116–19).

[71] I should like to thank for their help Helen DeWitt, Andrew Laird, John Moles, Leighton Reynolds, Tony Woodman, the late Michael Woods, the participants in the Newcastle Narrative Seminar, and above all Chris Pelling and the Editors.

ADDENDUM

This paper, although not published until 1997, was completed towards the end of 1993. More than fifteen years have passed since then, and scholarship has significantly advanced on all of the topics the paper touches on; were I writing it today, I would certainly have couched my argument in somewhat different terms. Nevertheless, with one small exception (see below), nothing that has appeared has led me to change my mind, certainly with regard to the main issues I addressed. I have therefore left the article unchanged: my belief is that while much important and sophisticated work has been done since I wrote it, that work complements rather than undermines my main contentions.

The field covered by the article falls into three separate (but interlocking) areas. First is the study of emotions in Latin literature and in the ancient world more broadly. Not least in importance here are the other essays in the volume in which my paper was first published, namely Braund and Gill (1997); but many other powerful and sophisticated studies have been done. The bibliography is too vast to list in detail, but I should single out the insightful work of David Konstan (esp. Konstan 2001) and Robert Kaster (esp. Kaster 2007), as well as the essays in Sternberg (2005). Marincola (2003) addresses the specific topic of emotions in historiography, building partly on my piece while also (p. 301) correcting one apparently small but quite revealing error I made in it (p. 215), when I spoke of Polybius 2.56 as addressing 'the tragic emotions'. As Marincola rightly notes, Polybius speaks not of the 'tragic emotions' of pity and fear, but 'pity and *anger*'. This error does not (I think) affect the substance of my argument, but it does lead to a distortion of the Polybian evidence, since it has a less direct bearing on the dynamic interrelation between pity and fear than I implied. My discussion of the representation of emotion also drew on questions of characterization, especially as set out in an important series of articles by Christopher Gill, and here too significant developments have occurred. In particular Gill has substantially modified his earlier treatments in Gill (1996) and (2006); cf. also the critique by Pelling (2002: 321–9).

The second area with which my article deals is the role of internal audiences in historiography, and the various ways in which the reader's identification with (or failure to identify with) the perspective of those audiences can instil particular interpretations of the text. I returned to this topic myself in the context of Livy (Levene 2006), but there have been many other studies. Especially important here are Walker (1993) and Zangara (2007: 55–89 and 229–307) on the phenomenon in general; also Rood (1998: esp. 61–9) and Greenwood (2006: 19–41) on Thucydides, Feldherr (1998) on Livy, and Shumate (1997) and Manolaraki (2005) on Tacitus.

Thirdly, and finally, there have been a number of recent studies of the *Histories* which examine the portrait of Vitellius in the second half of Book 3, the passage I used as a case study. Haynes (2003: 71–111) provides a complex synoptic analysis of Vitellius as a weak emperor unable to manipulate an imperial world where power depends on the maintenance of illusion. Ash (1999: 118–25) offers a systematic discussion of the narrative of Vitellius in his decline. Pomeroy (2006: 184–9) builds on my treatment of Vitellius as an object of spectacle; Galtier (2001) focuses on the death of Blaesus as a tragedy in miniature, while Keitel (2007), concentrating on the same scene, looks at the image of Vitellius as a stock tyrant. Damon (2006: 252–4 and 264–5) treats Vitellius as an example of a failed emperor. Keitel (2008) examines his death scene in the context of its allusions to Virgil; Babcock (2000) treats the same scene as part of the series of emperors' deaths in the *Histories*.

9

Tacitus and the Death of Augustus

Ronald Martin

Tacitus' use and adaptation of phrases from earlier Latin writers is well known. By this means he adds to his own context something of the atmosphere belonging to the context from which the phrase is borrowed. So, for example, when at *A.* 4.1 he describes Sejanus in language modelled on Sallust's description of Catiline (*Cat.* 5), the reader is immediately made aware that he is to expect Sejanus to display the same resolute villainy that Catiline had shown.[1]

A similar effect may be obtained—as it often is in Virgil—when the author echoes his own language to stress the parallelism between two passages. The resemblance between *A.* 1.6.1 *primum facinus noui principatus fuit Postumi Agrippae caedes* ('The first act of the new principate was the slaughter of Postumus Agrippa') and 13.1.1 *prima nouo principatu mors Iunii Silani proconsulis Asiae* ('The first death in the new principate was that of Junius Silanus, proconsul of Asia') has often been noted, and the anachronistic use at the end of *A.*1.5.4 of *Neronem* to describe Tiberius (the cognomen is strictly applicable only before Tiberius' adoption by Augustus in AD 4) is probably[2]

---

[1] [For elaboration of these Sallustian parallels, see Martin and Woodman (1989: 77–87).]

[2] Professor C. O. Brink reminds me that Sörbom (1935: 4), among examples of *uariatio* in the use of proper names, quotes *A.* 3.56: *Tiberium—Neronem—Neronem—Tiberius.* Similarly, at *A.* 1.4–5 we have: *Tiberium Neronem—Tiberius—Neronem.* Since in the former case there is nothing more than a literary variation, it cannot be assumed without argument that *Neronem* at *A.* 1.5 is anything more. But at *A.* 3.56, the reference is to the tribunician power first conferred on Tiberius in 6 BC; there is thus no anachronism in the use of *Neronem* there. Similarly, at *A.* 1.3, *Nero*, used of Tiberius immediately prior to his adoption by Augustus, is legitimate. *Neronem* at *A.* 1.5.4 is different in being an

employed to stress that the circumstances of Tiberius' accession were as dubious as those surrounding the accession of Nero. The parallelism of the incidents which Tacitus records in the two cases has been well brought out by M. P. Charlesworth:

> The similarity is so great that it can scarcely be regarded as accidental; the reigning emperor (Augustus, Claudius) has been persuaded to adopt a stepson (Tiberius, Nero) as his heir: towards the end of his reign he appears to show signs of remorse and a desire to reinstate the dispossessed heir (Agrippa Postumus, Britannicus); the empress-mother (Livia, Agrippina the Younger) is alarmed for the safety of the scheme for which she has so long planned, and decides to put her husband out of the way; the emperor dies suddenly, but the news of his death is kept concealed until the accession of the stepson has been made certain'.[3]

But not only is there this considerable resemblance between the incidents enumerated in either case: there is a much greater degree of verbal correspondence than has yet been noted. The correspondence can best be illustrated by the use of letters in brackets[4] to indicate the beginning and end of each group of words where there is a significant degree of parallelism in thought or language.

> [(a) *grauescere ualetudo Augusti* (a)], *et quidam* [(b) *scelus uxoris suspectabant* (b)]. . . . *neque satis compertum est* [(c) *spirantem adhuc Augustum* (c) . . . *an* [(e) *exanimem* (e)] (sc. Tiberius) (c) *reppererit* (c)]. [(f) *acribus namque custodiis domum et uias saepserat Liuia* (f)], [(g) *laetique interdum nuntii uulgabantur* (g)], [(h) *donec prouisis quae tempus monebat* (h)] *simul excessisse Augustum et* [(i) *rerum potiri Neronem* (i)] *fama eadem tulit.* [(k) *primum facinus noui principatus fuit Postumi Agrippae caedes* (k)] . . . (*A.* 1.5–6)

[(a) there was a deterioration in Augustus' health (a)], and some [(b) suspected crime on the part of his wife (b)] . . . but it has not been satisfactorily uncovered whether [(c) he discovered Augustus still

---

anachronism (an unparalleled one, I think), and it is accordingly reasonable to believe that its employment in that passage is deliberate.

[3] Charlesworth (1927: 55a). [For more on Livia and Tanaquil, see Santoro l'hoir (2006: 48–9).]

[4] The letters (a), (c), (d) should be ignored for the present. They do not mark Tacitean parallels but represent correspondence between the versions of Tacitus and one or both of Suetonius and Dio Cassius; their significance is discussed later. The square brackets in bold are intended to distinguish individual units of text where parallels cluster.

breathing (c)] ... or [(e) lifeless (e)]. [(f) For Livia had cordoned off the house and streets with fierce guards (f)], [(g) and from time to time favourable news was published (g)] [(h) until, after provision for what the occasion demanded (h)], a single report carried the simultaneous announcement that Augustus had passed away and [(i) that Nero was in control of affairs (i)]. [(k) The first act of the new principate was the slaughter of Postumus Agrippa (k)] ... '

tum [(b) *Agrippina sceleris olim certa* (b)] ... *de genere ueneni consul-tauit.* ... [(d) *uocabatur interim senatus uotaque pro incolumitate prin-cipis consules et sacerdotes nuncupabant* (d)], *cum iam* [(e) *exanimis* (e)] *uestibus et fomentis obtegeretur,* [(h–i) *dum quae res forent firmando Neronis imperio componuntur* (h–i)]. *iam primum* [(f) *Agrippina...* *cunctos aditus custodiis clauserat* (f)], [(g) *crebroque uulgabat ire in melius ualetudinem principis* (g)] ... [(k) *prima nouo principatu mors Iunii Silani* (k)] ... (*A.* 12.66–13.1).

It was then that [(b) Agrippina, long determined on her crime (b)] ... debated about the type of poison ... [(d) In the meantime the senate was being summoned and the consuls and priests were enunciating vows for the princeps' preservation (d)], since, though already [(e) lifeless (e)], he was being covered with clothing and dressings—[(h–i) while matters for confirming Nero's command were being settled (h–i)]. First of all [(f) Agrippina ... had closed off all the approaches with guards (f)], [(g) and she frequently made it public that the princeps's health was getting better (g)] ... [(k) The first death in the new principate was that of Junius Silanus (k)] ...

Tacitus' intention is unmistakable: it is to use the suggestive power of words to invest the accession of Tiberius with the same air of questionable legitimacy that attended Nero's accession, and to stress how Tiberius, in just the same way as Nero, owed his position to the machinations of the emperor's widow.[5] The purely fictitious nature of the allegations against Livia has been demonstrated in another paper by M. P. Charlesworth.[6] Of the episode the Cambridge Ancient History says, 'the malicious gossip retailed by Tacitus (*A.* 1.15) and Dio (56. 31.1) at Livia's expense is unworthy of mention'.

[5] [Martin (1981: 162) argues that the parallelism in language is designed to catch the reader's attention, but also draws out the importance of the differences between the two situations.]

[6] Charlesworth (1923).

It is clear then that the factual ingredients of Tacitus' account of the *Tiberius* episode[7] derive principally from the account of *Nero's* accession (an account common to Tacitus, Suetonius, and Dio). But the borrowing of language is in the reverse direction, i.e. Tacitus' *Nero* passage depends upon what he had already written of Tiberius. It will not do, however, to leave the matter there, for it is well known that for much of the period under discussion[8] the three main authors (Tacitus, Suetonius, Dio) are dependent principally on the same literary source.[9] Since the dependence on a common source extends at times to the reproduction of close verbal parallels, some attempt must be made to show whether the parallels that have been noted in the two passages from Tacitus are the work of Tacitus himself, or whether he is merely reproducing parallels that already existed in his source. In attempting to answer this question it will be convenient to take first the accounts in Suetonius and Dio of the Claudius–Agrippina–Nero episode: the letters in brackets indicate the themes corresponding to those similarly designated in the passage from Tacitus.

> *prius igitur quam ultra progrederetur,* [(b) *praeuentus est ab Agrippina* (b)] . . . *et ueneno quidem occisum conuenit; ubi autem et per quem dato, discrepat.* . . . [(e) *mors eius* (e)] *celata est,* [(h–i) *donec circa successorem omnia ordinarentur* (h–i)]. *itaque et* [(d) *quasi pro aegro adhuc uota suscepta sunt* (d)], *et inducti per simulationem comoedi, qui uelut desiderantem oblectarent.* (Suetonius, *Claudius* 44–5)

> Then before he could proceed any further, [(b) he was stopped by Agrippina (b)] . . . There is agreement that he was killed by poison; but when and by whom it was administered is disputed . . . [(e) His death (e)] was concealed, [(h–i) until all the arrangements were set in place around his successor (h–i)]. Accordingly [(d) vows were undertaken for his safety, as if he were still a sick man (d)], and comic actors were brought under the pretence that he wanted them to entertain him.

---

[7] Dio also, it will be seen, has the same basic story; it follows that the factual parallelism is not the creation of Tacitus, but goes back to the source that both he and Dio used.

[8] There are some differences of detail in their account of the time and manner in which the poison was given to Claudius; for their significance cf. Momigliano (1932). But since Tacitus gives no details of the alleged poisoning of Augustus, this portion of the story does not concern us here.

[9] [For more on Tacitus' sources in the *Annals*, see Martin (1981: 199–213) and Devillers (2003).]

The thought of (b) corresponds approximately to (b) in Tacitus, but is much nearer to Dio (b) (see below), with which it has a close verbal affinity. Items (e), (h–i), (d) are consecutive in Suetonius, as are (d), (e), (h–i) in Tacitus: Suetonius lacks items (f), (g), (k). The verbal correspondence between Tacitus (d), (h–i) and Suetonius (h–i), (d) is striking and must derive from their joint source. If it is allowed that (h) (i) in *Annals* 1 corresponds to (h–i) in *Annals* 12 (the correspondence may be disputed, but seems probable),[10] it follows that items (h) (i) in Tacitus' account of *Tiberius*' succession, like items (h-i) in *A*. 12, must derive from Tacitus' source for *Nero*. This would confirm the opinion of Charlesworth that Tacitus, when he wrote his account of the death of Augustus, was influenced by what he had already read about the actions of the younger Agrippina.

[(b) ἡ Ἀγριππῖνα ... αὐτὸν προκαταλαβεῖν φαρμάκῳ ... ἐσπούδασεν (b)]. [(k) ἡ Ἀγριππῖνα οὕτω καὶ τὰ μέγιστα πράττειν ἐπεχείρει ὥστε Μᾶρκον Ἰούνιον Σιλανὸν ἀπέκτεινε, πέμψασα αὐτῷ τοῦ φαρμάκου ᾧ τὸν ἄνδρα ἐδεδολοφονήκει (k)]. (Dio 60.34.2; 61.6.4–5)

[(b) Agrippina ... hurried to get the better of him first by poison (b)].
[(k) Agrippina was always ready to undertake the most momentous deeds, with the result that she killed Marcus Junius Silanus by sending him some of the poison with which she had treacherously murdered her husband (k)].

We have only Dio's epitome for the period, and he lacks items (d), (e), (h–i), (f), (g). The verbal resemblance between Suetonius (b) and Dio (b) has already been noted. Dio (k) records the circumstances surrounding Silanus' death, but without any verbal resemblance to Tacitus (k).

---

[10] Since it is quite unlikely that the correspondence already existed in Tacitus' source(s) for the two reigns, there are two alternatives: (i) that the apparent correspondence is illusory, (ii) that the correspondence is of Tacitus' making. Exact parallelism between the two occasions is precluded by the fact that, whereas Tiberius' accession was effective from the time of the announcement from the house at Nola, the significant moment in Nero's case was his proclamation as *imperator* in the praetorian camp (*A*. 12.69); cf. Ramsay's translation (1909: 115, n. 3) for the increasing importance of the military in the appointment of a new emperor). In view of the difference in the circumstances, it may be argued that the degree of verbal correspondence is too great to be accidental. If *Neronem* at *A*. 1.5.4 is deliberate (cf. text at n. 2 above), an intentional correspondence between the two passages is perhaps made more likely. However, even if a resemblance between themes (h) and (i) in *A*. 1 and 12 is denied, it does not invalidate the other conclusions suggested in this paper.

Next we may take the Augustus–Livia–Tiberius episode in both Suetonius and Dio.

[(a) *adgrauata ualetudine* (a)], ... *Tiberium diu secreto sermone detinuit* .... (Suetonius, *Augustus* 98).

[(a) After his illness had grown more serious (a)], ... Augustus detained Tiberius for a long while in private conversation ...

... [(c) *sed tamen spirantem adhuc Augustum repperit* (c)] *fuitque una secreto per totum diem*.... (Suetonius, *Tiberius* 21).

... [(c) but Tiberius found Augustus still breathing (c)] and spent the whole day together with him in private ...

[(i?–k) *excessum Augusti non prius palam fecit quam Agrippa iuuene interempto* (i?–k)]. (Suetonius, *Tiberius* 22).

[(i?–k) Tiberius did not make the death of Augustus public before the young man Agrippa had been killed (i?–k)]

Suetonius states unequivocally that Augustus was still alive when Tiberius reached him, and disdains to record the allegations that he was poisoned by Livia. Parallels with Tacitus are therefore necessarily confined to (a), (c), (i?–k), but the verbal resemblance between (a) and (c) in the two authors is striking—(the Tacitean phrase is given first in both cases) (a) *grauescere ualetudo/adgrauata ualetudine*, (c) *spirantem adhuc Augustum ... reppererit/spirantem adhuc Augustum repperit*—and must surely derive from their common source. The correspondence of (i?–k) in Suetonius is debatable (*excessisse Augustum/excessum Augusti* scarcely clinches it). Suetonius has rejected the alternative that Augustus was dead before Tiberius arrived; but, having accepted the view that the announcement of the death *was* delayed, he requires a new motive for it, and finds it in the need to secure Agrippa's death first.[11]

[(a) ὁ δ' οὖν Αὔγουστος νοσήσας (a)] μετήλλαξε· καί [(b) τινα ὑποψίαν τοῦ θανάτου αὐτοῦ ἡ Λιουία ἔλαβεν (b)]. ἐπειδὴ πρὸς τὸν Ἀγρίππαν κρύφα ἐς τὴν νῆσον διέπλευσε ... (Dio 56.30.1)

[(a) So Augustus fell ill (a)] and died. Indeed, [(b) Livia met with some suspicion regarding his death (b)], in view of the fact that he had secretly sailed over to the island to see Agrippa ...

---

[11] [See further Woodman (1998: 23–39) on Tacitus' presentation of Agrippa Postumus' death.]

οὐ μέντοι καὶ ἐκφανὴς εὐθὺς ὁ θάνατος αὐτοῦ ἐγένετο· ἡ γὰρ Λιουία, φοβηθεῖσα μὴ τοῦ Τιβερίου ἐν τῇ Δελματίᾳ ἔτ᾽ ὄντος νεωτερισθῇ τι, συνέκρυψεν αὐτὸν μέχρις οὗ ἐκεῖνος ἀφίκετο. ταῦτα γὰρ οὕτω τοῖς τε πλείοσι καὶ <τοῖς> ἀξιοπιστοτέροις γέγραπται· εἰσὶ γάρ τινες οἳ καὶ παραγενέσθαι τὸν Τιβέριον τῇ νόσῳ αὐτοῦ καὶ ἐπισκήψεις τινὰς παρ᾽ αὐτοῦ λαβεῖν ἔφασαν. (Dio 56.31.1)

However, his death was not immediately made public. For Livia, fearing that, as Tiberius was still in Dalmatia, there might be some trouble, concealed the death until he arrived. This is the account of most writers, including the most trustworthy. Yet there are some who say that Tiberius was at hand during Augustus' illness and received some instructions from him.

[(k) τὸν μὲν γὰρ ᾿Αγρίππαν παραχρῆμα ἀπὸ τῆς Νώλης πέμψας τινὰ ἀπέκτεινε· (k)] (Dio 57.3.5)

'[(k) For Tiberius, having immediately sent someone from Nola, had Agrippa put to death (k)]'

The main outline of the alternatives given in Tacitus (c) and (e) is covered by Dio (who alone has the full story of the alleged poisoning of Augustus by figs), and is therefore to be ascribed to their joint source, but Dio has no resemblance to Tacitus in vocabulary, turn of phrase, or grouping of incidents.

The comparison of the versions of both anecdotes in all three authors has shown that for the parallel items he uses in *Annals* 1 and 12–13 Tacitus draws upon different sources. Among the probable sources three are specially worthy of note:

1. Items (b) [the empress-mother (Livia/Agrippina the younger) decides to poison her husband] and (k) [the deaths of Agrippa Postumus and Iunius Silanus] derive from the primary source, but (i) *scelus*, 'crime', occurring in both Tacitean passages alone, is probably Tacitus' own choice of word. He has chosen it, however, not in order to draw attention to a specific correspondence between the two passages, but because of the general associations that the word bears for him—*scelus* is a favourite word of Tacitus for describing poisoning (cf. Furneaux on *A.* 1.5); (ii) though the fact of Agrippa Postumus' death is recorded by all three authors, the verbal parallelism of *primum facinus noui principatus/prima nouo principatu mors* is in Tacitus

alone. It is unquestionable that this is Tacitus' own touch, and that it is designed specifically to stress the parallelism of the two situations.

2. Themes (h) (i) [the emperor's death (Augustus/Claudius) is concealed until all necessary steps have been taken to ensure the stepson's accession] may possibly in both *A*. 1 and *A*. 12 derive from the primary source for *Nero*. The significance that this hypothesis, if true, has for Tacitus' method of composition has been commented on above. The use of *Neronem* for Tiberius in item (i) of *A*. 1 is probably due to Tacitus himself.[12]

3. There still remain two themes, (f) and (g) [the empress-mother barricades the house in which the dead emperor lies, and issues reassuring reports about his health], which recur in both passages of Tacitus and nowhere else. In both passages they occur side by side,[13] coupled by -*que*. There can surely be little doubt that these two details are to be ascribed to Tacitus? They are the graphic, circumstantial details added to corroborate the rest of the story. One cannot be certain what suggested these two details to Tacitus' mind, but it is perhaps worth pointing out that precisely these two details are a conspicuous feature of Livy's account (1.41) of the concealment of Tarquinius' death by Tanaquil.[14] The parallel is not a verbal one—the broader canvas that Livy allows himself for the episode makes that understandable—but the following extracts from Livy's narrative are worth noting:

Tanaquil inter tumultum claudi regiam iubet, arbitros eicit … iubet bono animo esse; sopitum fuisse regem subito ictu; … iam ad se redisse; … omnia salubria esse; confidere propediem ipsum eos uisuros. (Livy 1.41)

---

[12] See text at n.2 above.

[13] Whereas (h–i), which, it has been suggested (see §2 above), have a different origin, are continuous with (f) and (g) in *A*. 1, but separated from them in *A*. 12.

[14] The parallel is already noted in Aurelius Victor, *de Caesaribus* 4.15: *ceterum funus* [sc. *Claudii*], *uti quondam in Prisco Tarquinio, diu occultatum, dum arte mulieris corrupti custodes aegrum simulant atque ab eo mandatam interim priuigno, quem paulo ante in liberos asciuerat, curam rei publicae*, 'However, as happened long ago with Tarquinius Priscus, the death [sc. of Claudius] was long concealed while the bodyguards, tainted by a woman's wiles, pretended that he was ill and that he had entrusted the care of the the state to his stepson, whom he adopted shortly beforehand as one of his children.'

Amidst the chaos, Tanaquil ordered the palace to be barricaded and she threw out any witnesses ... She urged the people to be confident, saying that the king had been stunned by a sudden blow ... but that he had already come back to consciousness; all the signs were favourable and she was sure that they would soon see Tarquin himself.

Though there is, I think, no other case in Tacitus where verbal echoes and parallelism of incidents extend over so considerable a portion of continuous narrative, the method of composition in the two passages is basically that which Tacitus uses on many other occasions. Starting with a core of factual detail, he works it into a context where 'nonfactual material'[15] establishes the emotional or moral tone that he wishes to evoke in the reader. At times—as, for instance, in much of the account of Nero's principate—the 'nonfactual material' merely strengthens the impression that is already implicit in the facts themselves: but where the interpretation of the facts is obscure or does not automatically support the view that Tacitus wishes his reader to take, it is the function of the 'nonfactual material' to ensure that the reader accepts Tacitus' interpretation of the events; this is particularly the case in *Annals* 1–6, where Tacitus' portrait of Tiberius' character depends less upon the record of his actions than upon the interpretation put upon them. Two of the three devices that Pippidi[16] mentions as being used by Tacitus in his portrayal of Tiberius' character are used in *Annals* 1.5–6. The suggestion of Livia's responsibility for the death of Augustus is given merely as a rumour (*quidam scelus uxoris suspectabant. quippe rumor incesserat*, 'some suspected crime on the part of his wife. A rumour had started ...', 1.5.1). But after the rumour has been given in oratio obliqua, Tacitus resumes with a telling phrase (*utcumque se ea res habuit*, 'Whether or not that was the case', 1.5.3) which serves as a 'gloss': its effect is 'I do not positively assert Livia's guilt, but her subsequent actions show that she was undeniably involved in the intrigue to secure Tiberius' succession'. The phrase *primum facinus* also functions as a 'gloss': it implies both that Agrippa Postumus' death was a crime for which the new regime was responsible and that it was only the first of many such crimes.

---

[15] The phrase is taken from Walker (1952: see ch. 4, esp. 33–4, and ch. 8, 158).

[16] Pippidi (1944), with an important review by Balsdon (1946): the three devices are (i) general psychological affirmations—this does not concern us here, (ii) 'glosses' (*gloses, éclaircissements*), (iii) *rumores*.

Once the pattern had been built up for the Livia–Tiberius episode, it was a simple thing to make use of its incident and language when Tacitus came to write the account of Claudius' death and Nero's accession. The sequence of incidents corresponded closely—this is not surprising, since the Livia episode was probably first fabricated on the basis of the traditional account of Claudius' death; as a result much of the phraseology could be taken over from the earlier passage without losing its appropriateness to the context. Two points only need comment. Whereas the allegation of the poisoning of Augustus is quoted only as a rumour, in the case of Claudius, Tacitus could state the poisoning as a fact, because it was universally believed to be so. In the second place, the barricading of the royal house and the issuing of reports of the (already dead) emperor's improving health, which Tacitus had added in *Annals* 1.5 (probably, as we have seen, from Livy's account of Tarquinius and Tanaquil) as corroborative detail, is inserted also into the account of Claudius' death.

It would be unwise from two passages to try to draw far-reaching conclusions about Tacitus' method of composition, but about the passages themselves two general points are clear. First, although there is little in them that is entirely original, the material is drawn, not from one source only, but from several; here, at least, Tacitus does not observe 'Nissen's law'.[17] Secondly, it is clear that, even if the probable sources of most of the material can be traced, the composite picture has a unity, bearing the imprint of Tacitus' own personality, that enables us significantly to describe the narrative as 'Tacitean'; by that word is meant something more than merely the narrative 'which Tacitus took over from the authors he copied'.

---

[17] [The ideas behind this contentious 'law' were formulated by the nineteenth-century historian Nissen, based on his view of how Livy used Polybius as a source. See Nissen (1863) and the introduction to this volume, p. 5 above. 'Nissen's law' implies that ancient historical writers tended to select a single main source, rather than fusing together a variety of previous accounts in a critical way, and that modern historians' rigorous notions of source criticism simply did not apply in the ancient world. Wilkes (1972: 179–81) offers a helpful critique.]

10

Obituaries in Tacitus

Sir Ronald Syme

Nothing could touch the pomp and splendour of a Roman funeral: the portraits of ancestors carried on parade, the emblems of magistracy, and the ultimate laudation. The thing was pageant, and history, and the material for history.[1]

When by decree of the senate it was ordained that the obsequies of some person of mark should be celebrated as act and homage of the community, at public expense and with a selected speaker, the item passed into the record and archives of the high assembly. Often no doubt there to be buried and forgotten (if there were no curious and competent enquirer), but the occasion might be retained in memory, the oration preserved by the author or by the family. Apart from that, a long tradition in literature enjoined the appraisement of a man's actions and virtues at the end. Among the Roman historians not often in Sallust, but Livy was amicable and generous, subsequent historians quite lavish.[2]

The two streams of derivation meet and mix in Cornelius Tacitus, with the senatorial and documentary in preponderance. His procedure will prove instructive, for more reasons than one.

---

[1] [On Roman funerals in general, and *imagines* in particular, see Flower (1996).]

[2] Seneca, *Suas.*, 6.21: *quotiens magni alicuius <uiri> mors ab historicis narrata est, totiens fere consummatio totius uitae et quasi funebris laudatio redditur. hoc semel aut iterum a Thucydide factum, item in paucissimis personis usurpatum a Sallustio, T. Livius benignius omnibus magnis uiris praestitit: sequentes historici multo id effusius fecerunt,* 'Whenever the death of some great man has been narrated by historians, almost always an overview of his whole life and, as it were, a funeral laudation are produced. After this was done once or twice by Thucydides, and the technique was likewise used by Sallust for a very few protagonists, Livy generously deployed it for all great men. His successors have used it much more effusively.'

On a surface view, the recording of events in strict order of time, year by year, constrained and hampered a historian. The author of the *Annales* himself bears witness, several times. It does not appear that he was unduly incommoded. Various devices offered. He might discover where he pleased some subject for an oration, he could turn aside and digress. Those portions of the work confirm his autonomy, reveal his predilections, and permit an approach to his character and opinions. The obituary notices are likewise the product of will and choice. The *Annales* present twelve entries of this type, embracing twenty men.[3] They tend to be put at the end of the annual chronicle. Four are registered explicitly as the last events of a year, two are in fact the last items, four penultimate. Hence only two in the body of the narrative.[4] A certain artifice might be suspected. Of the men commemorated, five stand alone, one entry groups three persons, the rest are disposed in pairs.[5] In four instances the vote of a public funeral is specified, and in two of them that ceremony is styled *censorium funus*, 'censorial funeral'.[6] Some of the other personages may in fact have been accorded that supreme honour. For example, the *nobiles* Cn. Cornelius Lentulus (consul 14 BC) and L. Domitius Ahenobarbus (consul 16 BC) whose decease is recorded (conjointly and in that order) under the year 25 (*A.* 4.44). Each had earned the *ornamenta triumphalia*, 'insignia of a triumph', and Ahenobarbus was close kin to the dynasty, having married Antonia, the niece of Caesar Augustus.

Not all *uiri triumphales*, 'men worthy of a triumph', of the Empire can be deemed to have a claim. The award, which Augustus invented as substitute and consolation for a triumph, was granted quite frequently. With Claudius, it became cheap and was vulgarized. However that may be, persons of high public station like the prefects for the city and the holders of a second consulship cannot easily have been denied a public funeral.

---

[3] *A.* 3.30, 48, 75; 4.15, 44, 61; 6.10, 27, 39; 13.30; 14.19, 47. Not taking into account the remarks on Tiberius (*A.* 6.51), Livia (*A.* 5.1), Julia (*A.* 1.53), the younger Julia (*A.* 4.71), and the funeral of Cassius' widow (*A.* 3.76); or, for that matter, comment on sundry deaths that belong to the narration.

[4] *A.* 4.15 (Lucilius Longus); *A.* 6.10 (L. Piso). Each had a public funeral.

[5] Standing alone, *A.* 3.48 (Sulpicius Quirinius); *A.* 4.15 (Lucilius Longus); *A.* 6.10 (L. Piso); *A.* 6.39 (Poppaeus Sabinus); *A.* 14.47 (Memmius Regulus). A group of three, *A.* 4.44 (Cn. Lentulus, Domitius Ahenobarbus, L. Antonius).

[6] Public funerals, *A.* 3.48 (Sulpicius Quirinius); *A.* 6.11 (L. Piso); *funus censorium*, 'censorial funeral', *A.* 4.15 (Lucilius Longus); *A.* 6.27 (Aelius Lamia). For that phrase, cf. *A.* 13.2 (the obsequies of Claudius Caesar); *H.* 4.47 (Flavius Sabinus).

Of the twenty characters singled out by the historian, all but three are senators of consular rank. Tacitus has quietly and artfully extended the category to take in these three anomalies. Namely, Asinius Saloninus (otherwise unknown), who was betrothed to a daughter of Germanicus Caesar (*A.* 3.75); the Roman knight Sallustius Crispus, the minister of Augustus and Tiberius (*A.* 3.30); and L. Antonius (son of the ill-starred Iullus), who died in reclusion at the university city of Massilia (*A.* 4.44).

The emergence and distribution of these necrological notices demands attention: nine of the twelve in the first hexad of the *Annales*, but none in the second (as extant), while the third has only three (registering five persons).

The earliest of them is peculiar and significant. It comes nearly halfway through Book 3. Had no person of due consequence in the Roman state passed away in the course of the six years preceding? Notable *uiri triumphales* such as M. Vinicius (suffect consul 19 BC) or M. Plautius Silvanus (consul 2 BC), it may well be, outlived Augustus.[7] Of them, or of certain others, no record. Perhaps the historian was slow to see the value of the device. Once aware, he exploits it to the full. The occasion is the decease of a consular, L. Volusius Saturninus (suffect consul 12 BC, *A.* 3.30). It is not only, or mainly, for his sake that Tacitus operates. A few words for Volusius, and he goes on to Sallustius Crispus, recounting his parentage (he was adopted by the historian, his great-uncle), the paradox of great ability under the show of indolence, the parallel with Maecenas; and he concludes with general reflections on princes and their favourites, on the transience of power and influence.

The next entry comes soon after, in the next year. It is devoted to P. Sulpicius Quirinius (consul 12 BC, *A.* 3.48). That the great majority should congregate in the Tiberian books is no surprise. The author had a purpose. He wanted to show that the matter of Roman history was not yet as dynastic and monarchic as it later became, that there still subsisted *quaedam imago rei publicae,* 'a certain image of the Republic'. And (it can be contended in face of confident doctrines), Tacitus paid little attention to the written authorities for the period, doubting their veracity and insight, but preferred to build up his narrative mainly on the basis of the *acta senatus,* 'acts of the senate'. Further, as he went on he discovered more and more transactions that

---

[7] *PIR*[1] V 444 (to whom should be assigned the anonymous *elogium* at Tusculum, *ILS* 8965); P 361.

evoked the previous reign (or ran continuous from its main themes, domestic or foreign), until before long he was impelled to announce that, if life was vouchsafed, he would turn back and narrate the times of Caesar Augustus (*A.* 3.24). The episode in question (the return to Rome of D. Junius Silanus) called up to renewed notoriety one of the scandals of the dynasty: the affair of Julia, the granddaughter of the Princeps. The decease of illustrious survivors (among them relatives of the reigning house, or involved in its vicissitudes) will have contributed to sharpen the historian's curiosity about that earlier and obscure epoch which (it appears) he had not studied with sufficient care when he decided to begin his imperial annals with the accession of Tiberius.

The second hexad of the *Annales* (as extant) is truncated, Caligula being lost, and also Claudius down to a point in the year 47 (subsequent to the beginning of Book 11). The missing books must be allowed for. Two men are known whom other sources credit with a public funeral, namely M. Vinicius and Passienus Crispus.[8] Each has a place in the sequence of second consulates with which Claudius Caesar embellished the early years of his reign, from 43 to 46, and both stand close to the dynasty. M. Vinicius (consul 30, II consul *ordinarius* 45) had been married to a princess, Julia Livilla, the daughter of Germanicus.[9] Passienus (suffect consul 27, II consul *ordinarius* 45]), who inherited the name and the wealth of Sallustius Crispus, was a wit and an orator of high celebrity. He must have been mentioned more than once in those books—and he was the husband of two princesses in succession, Nero's aunt Domitia and Nero's mother.[10] Nor would it have passed the knowledge and ingenuity of the historian to discover other persons fit for commemoration (if he needed them).

---

[8] Dio, 60.27.4; *Schol.* on Juvenal, 4.81. It would take too long to discuss the opulent Pompeius, starved to death by his kinsman Caligula—*fame ac siti periit in palatio cognati, dum illi heres publicum funus esurienti locat*, 'In the palace of his kinsman, he died from hunger and thirst, and his heir was setting in place the arrangements for a public funeral for him as he was starving' (Seneca, *De tranquillitate animi*, 11.10). Generally (but I suspect wrongly) identified as Sex. Pompeius, the consul of 14 (*PIR*[1] P 450). The recent treatment in *RE* XXI, cols. 2265ff. is not satisfactory. [*Addendum* from Syme's revised version of this piece from 1970: For Sex. Pompeius (*cos.* 14), see Syme (1970: 36–41). He is mentioned as dead by Valerius Maximus (4.7, *Ext.* 2)—and might therefore have qualified for an obituary notice in the *Annales*, book 5. The person alluded to by Seneca is presumably a son, not otherwise attested.]

[9] *A.* 6.30; cf. *PIR*[1] V 445.

[10] *Schol.* on Juvenal, 4.81, with the allegation *periit per fraudem Agrippinae*, 'he died by a scheme of Agrippina'. The previous wife is *PIR*[2] D 171.

As for Books 11 and 12, to palliate their apparent void, it can be pointed out that they contain two concealed obituaries, which happen to furnish sharply contrasted portraits of two successive legates of Germania Superior. Recording the *ornamenta triumphalia*, 'insignia of a triumph', of Curtius Rufus (suffect consul *c*.43)—not for any action in the field but for opening a mine in the territory of the Mattiaci—the historian subjoins an anecdote about the surprising career of that person (humble beginnings, a miraculous prophecy of future greatness, and the emperor Tiberius' support and testimonial), and terminates with a damning character sketch of the detestable *parvenu*—subservient though surly towards superiors, oppressive to those beneath, and not easy with equals (*A.* 11.21). Pomponius Secundus, however (suffect consul 44), is accorded a handsome farewell after his campaign against the Chatti: the *ornamenta triumphalia*, 'insignia of a triumph', are but a small portion of his renown, for posterity remembers Pomponius as a poet (*A*.12.28). It can be taken that the consular dramatist died not long after—and nothing more was going to be said about Curtius Rufus.

Finally, Books 13–16. Two pairs and one single entry: all persons who had not found mention hitherto in this section of the work. They exhibit sundry peculiarities. The first chronicles the decease of C. Caninius Rebilus (suffect consul 37, *A.* 13.30.2) and L. Volusius Saturninus (suffect consul 3, *A.* 13.30.2), the latter dying at the age of 90.[11] Caninius is here described as outstanding in the science of law. No other source knows him as a jurist, and it is not clear that he was a notable personage. Further, the kind of treatment he gets. The necrology is normally benevolent, though Tacitus is ready with derogatory comment (social or moral) on several persons, such as Sulpicius Quirinius, Ateius Capito, and Domitius Afer (*A.* 3.48, 3.75, 14.19). Of Caninius, who committed suicide (unique among these entries), he says that nobody thought he had the courage for it, such was his vicious effeminacy.[12] Adventitious and undisclosed reasons (it can be divined) go to explain the introduction of Caninius (see below). As for Volusius, a strange omission. Tacitus neglects to put on record the important fact that he was *praefectus urbi*, 'prefect for the city'. He

---

[11] *A.* 3.48, 75; 14.19.
[12] *A.* 13.30: *haud creditus sufficere ad constantiam sumendae mortis ob libidines muliebriter infamis,* 'he was not believed capable of the steadfastness needed for choosing death, owing to the womanly disreputableness of his lusts.'

was appointed under Caligula, presumably in succession to the mysterious Q. Sanquinius Maximus (suffect consul for the second time, 39); and he held that post to the day of his death.[13]
The next pair briefly couples two orators, Cn. Domitius Afer (suffect consul 39), and M. Servilius Nonianus (consul 35)—but Nonianus was also a historian, and he comes off best in the confrontation (*A.* 14.19).

Afer, whom Quintilian reckoned the greatest orator he had heard and worthy to take rank with the classic performers, had no doubt earned a mention several times in the missing books; and Tacitus, presenting Afer for the first time (in 26), went on to allude to the decline of his oratorical powers in old age (*A.* 4.52). That was early in the *Annales*. Some recapitulatory remarks would have been pertinent and helpful. By various devices and annotation Tacitus in the exordium of Book 13 indicates that he is making a fresh start and beginning a new section. Thus Annaeus Seneca and Afranius Burrus are introduced as though for the first time, their personalities and functions being deftly characterized (*A.* 13.2). Tacitus on Afer and Nonianus seems cursory or unduly concise: a revision might have expanded.

Nor is everything plain and easy about the last item of all, the death of P. Memmius Regulus (suffect consul 31) in 61 (*A.* 14.47).[14] Tacitus appends an anecdote. Nero fell ill, the courtiers were full of alarm and foreboding for Rome, but Nero reassured them. The *res publica*, he said, could look for stay and support to Memmius Regulus. If Nero's illness is the *anceps ualetudo*, 'ambiguous health', described in the previous year (*A.* 14.22.4), there is not much point in the comment added by Tacitus: *uixit tamen post haec Regulus quiete defensus*, 'Regulus nevertheless survived after this, protected by his quietitude' (*A.* 14.47.1). Now Regulus since his consulship had not been named in the *Annales* (as extant), apart from a piece of annotation on Lollia Paulina (he had been one of her husbands, *A.* 12.22). Tacitus pays generous tribute to the virtues and public renown of Memmius Regulus. To make things clear to the reader, ought he not perhaps to have stated that Regulus was the loyal and exemplary *nouus homo*, 'new man', who as consul had managed the destruction of Sejanus?

Various phenomena in the latest books of the *Annales* provoke reflection. On the lowest count they inspire a doubt whether the

---

[13] Pliny *NH* 7.62. For the date of his appointment, see *PIR*[1], V 661.
[14] [*Addendum* from Syme's revised version of 1970: For peculiarities in the treatment of Memmius Regulus, see Syme (1958a: 486, 743–4, 787).]

author revised those books. One might also be impelled to wonder whether he lived to complete the work, down to Book 18 (for that is clearly the design and structure, three hexads).[15]

Not that the relative poverty of the necrological rubric in the third hexad need in itself be a cause for surprise. The texture of history had changed since the days of Tiberius (less for the senate and more for the palace), and with it the historian's method (and in great part his sources also). He is far less preoccupied with the annalistic schema. Further, a number of the men commemorated in the Tiberian books were relics of an earlier age, whereas the consulars in prominence under Caligula, Claudius, and Nero (few of them comparable in fame) could be adequately depicted through the actions and performance of their prime.

The author may (it is true) have been guilty of inadvertence here or there throughout the work. In conformity with his keen interest in the history of Roman oratory, Tacitus allots not less than their due to the descendants of Asinius Pollio and Messalla Corvinus, the dominant speakers in the time of Augustus.[16] Messallinus (consul 3 BC), the elder son of Corvinus, delivers an oration marked by grace, candour, and tolerance, reflecting (it may be surmised) the manner of his parent (*A.* 3.34). The historian does not report his death—perhaps the oration was honour enough. The younger son, Cotta Messallinus (consul 20), may have survived Tiberius.[17] A speaker of great promise was heralded in the person of M. Claudius Marcellus Aeserninus, one of the five men (the others ex-consuls) whom Cn. Piso the legate of Syria asked to undertake his defence.[18] He does not recur in the narrative. Praetor in 19, Aeserninus should have had quick access to the consulate. It will therefore be inferred that he died not long after 19.[19]

---

[15] [*Addendum* from Syme's revised version of 1970: For the notion that the historian did not survive to complete the work, cf. Syme (1958a: 361, 742–5); Koestermann (1963–8) in his annotation on *A.* 16.35.2.]

[16] For the descendants of Pollio, who present sundry problems, see Oliver (1947: 147–60).

[17] Last mentioned in 32 (*A.* 6.5 and 6.7), but his proconsulate of Asia should fall in 35/6. By his full name, M. Aurelius Cotta Maximus Messallinus (*PIR*², A 1488), to be identified with M. Aurelius Cotta the consul of 20 (A 1487). For a fresh proof, see Syme (1956a: 18).

[18] *A.* 3.11. For his fame, see *A.* 11.6–7, where he is named in the company of consular orators.

[19] Groag, invoking *A.* 11.6, argues that he reached the consulate (*PIR*², C 928). Against, see Degrassi (1946: 38). Nor does Degrassi (1952) allow him to appear 'below the line'.

Aeserninus was a grandson of Pollio on the maternal side: also the last of the Claudii Marcelli.

Again, Cossus Cornelius Lentulus (consul AD. 1), *praefectus urbi* 'prefect for the city' after L. Aelius Lamia (consul 3): Lamia's decease at the end of 32 is registered by the historian, and another prefect was in office in 37.[20] Cossus is not only known to fame as the general who terminated the Gaetulian War in AD 6.[21] Somnolent though he seemed and bibulous, he had the trust of Tiberius Caesar, and he never let out a secret: like L. Piso the Pontifex (consul 15 BC), a rebuke and a warning to superficial moralists, as Seneca is careful to point out (*Epistulae Morales* 88.14).

As for the reigns of Claudius and Nero, three or four men can be named who might be thought to deserve an entry. Last heard of in 51 (*A.* 12.42), the great L. Vitellius, consul three times (as had been nobody since M. Agrippa), fades from the pages of the *Annales*: yet he was not defrauded of a public funeral (*A.* 6.32). Perhaps his activities (abundantly chronicled) had said enough—and the portrait at his first presentation in Book 6 could not have been improved upon (Suet. *Vit.* 3). L. Salvius Otho (suffect consul 33), a close and loyal friend of the dynasty (Tiberius liked him, and their physical resemblance excited surmise and suspicion), had rendered unusual services to Claudius, among them a conspiracy unmasked, in recognition of which his statue was set up on the Palatine (Suet. *Otho* 1). Legates of Britain naturally attract the attention of the man who married the daughter of Julius Agricola. A. Plautius (suffect consul 29), who led the invasion of Britain for Claudius Caesar, returning to Rome in 47, was allowed to celebrate an ovation (a distinction without parallel under the Empire). But Tacitus in a remark about Plautius under the year 57 had already referred to that ovation (*A.* 13.32).

A. Messalla, consul with Nero in 58, put old men in mind of Corvinus, colleague of Augustus (i.e. in 31 BC), so Tacitus affirms (*A.* 13.34). The family was in decay—this man took financial subsidy from Nero (without, however, incurring censure from Tacitus). He was also (it appears) the last consul in the direct line of the patrician Valerii. Again, ought not Tacitus to have set on prominent record the demise of that Paullus Fabius Persicus (consul 34), whom Claudius

---

[20] *A.* 6.27 (Aelius Lamia). The prefect in 36/7 was L. Calpurnius Piso (consul 27), cf. *PIR*², C 293.

[21] Dio 65.28.3; cf. *AE* 1940, 68 = *IRT* 301.

Caesar (irony rather than amity) styled *nobilissimum uirum, amicum meum*, 'a most noble man and my friend'?[22] He was a man of evil living, and, along with Caninius Rebilus, comes into the family history of the historian's wife. They offered to contribute towards the cost of games which her grandfather, L. Julius Graecinus, had to celebrate. That excellent man rejected help from the infamous pair.[23] Persicus was the last consul of the *gens Fabia*. The decline and fall of the *nobilitas* is one of the main themes of the *Annales*—brought down by and with the aristocratic dynasty of Julii and Claudii, but perishing through its own vices also.

The obituary satisfied various needs and aspirations in the historian. The longer a man went on living, the more he was struck by the paradoxes of fame and survival, the operations of fate or hazard, the *ludibria rerum mortalium cunctis in negotiis*, 'the mockeries made of mortal affairs in every activity' (*A.* 3.18.4). Tacitus is preoccupied with the vicissitudes of the governing order, and he insists on making it clear that he writes according to the manner and categories of the Roman past. The obituaries reinforce his design, and they proclaim his employment of the senate's archives (not that all the items are thence derived). Tradition and the Republic can be suggested in diverse fashions. Dying in 32 at the age of 80, L. Piso the Pontifex is in his own person a memorial of history: the son of Caesoninus, consul in 58 BC and censor. Choice language contributes to the effect: Piso's titles to renown stand in a sequence of bare, disconnected phrases, reproducing the old annalistic manner.[24] Similarly, the death of the excellent M. Lepidus (consul 6) is adorned with comments archaic and Sallustian on the Aemilii of ancient days.[25]

Furthermore, Tacitus is able to bring in episodes of Augustan history, as when the aristocratic generals Cn. Lentulus the Augur and L. Domitius Ahenobarbus, victorious beyond the great rivers,

---

[22] *ILS* 212, Col. II.1.25 (Lugdunum).

[23] Seneca *de Ben.*, 2.21.5. For the vices of Persicus, Seneca *de Ben.*, 4.30.2.

[24] *A.* 6.10.3: *patrem ei censorium fuisse memoraui; aetas ad octogesimum annum processit; decus triumphale in Thracia meruerat*, 'That his father had been censorial I have recalled; his age reached its eightieth year; he had won triumphal prestige in Thrace.'

[25] *A.* 6.27.4: *quippe Aemilium genus fecundum bonorum ciuium, et qui eadem familia corruptis moribus, inlustri tamen fortuna egere*, 'the Aemilian lineage was prolific of good citizens, and those from the same family whose behaviour was corrupt nevertheless enjoyed illustrious fortune.'

echo back to a more expansive epoch, evoking nostalgia and pointing the contrast with the deep peace of Tiberius' reign. Not only that. Ahenobarbus' father will be named, the admiral of the Republic and partisan of Marcus Antonius. By a felicitous coincidence the historian can go on to chronicle the death of L. Antonius at Massilia—hence a mention of his father Iullus, the paramour of Julia, the daughter of the princeps (*A.* 4.44).

It was the scandal of the younger Julia, brought to notice a number of years later, that prompted Tacitus to announce the project of a future history (above). A connected theme was Tiberius Caesar in his earlier discomforts and vicissitudes—friction with the daughter of Caesar Augustus, the clash with the princeps, the wilful retreat to an island.

The significance of Tiberius' sojourn on Rhodes was not properly estimated by Tacitus (it can be argued) when he began to compose the *Annales*: a passage alluding to it in Book 1 may not have been there inserted until the historian had come to speculate about the reasons that induced the emperor to go away to Capri.[26] Two of the necrological notices cannot have failed to stimulate his curiosity. In the year 21 Tiberius requested that the Senate vote a public funeral for P. Sulpicius Quirinius (consul 12 BC, *A.* 3.48). Among the reasons he adduced was the loyalty and good sense of Quirinius. When in official employment in the eastern lands, Quirinius had not neglected to show respect to Tiberius in reclusion at Rhodes—and Tiberius, reminded of those painful years, deviated into a bitter attack on another man, M. Lollius, the author of feud and discord.[27] Then, in 23, came the death of Lucilius Longus (suffect consul 7). No superior public offices or provincial commands explain this man (who, but for Tacitus, is only a name and date on the consular *Fasti*). But Lucilius Longus had been a personal friend of Tiberius all through—in fact the only senator who went with him to Rhodes. Wherefore a public funeral and a statue in the Forum of Augustus. The abnormal honour caught the attention of Tacitus.[28]

---

[26] The reference to Rhodes in *A.* 4.57, itself not well fitted in its near context, may have prompted the similar piece of annotation at *A.* 1.4. [*Addendum* from Syme's revised version of 1970: for Tiberius on Rhodes, see Syme (1970: 142; 1958a: 695–6).]

[27] *A.* 3.48.2: *incusato M. Lollio, quem auctorem Gaio Caesari prauitatis et discordiarum arguebat*, 'censuring M. Lollius, whom he criticized as being responsible for C. Caesar's prevarication and disaffection'.

[28] *A.* 4.15.2: *ita quamquam nouo homini censorium funus*, 'So, despite being a new man, a censorial funeral'.

Scepticism, experience of affairs, and hostility to consecrated opinions predisposed the historian to take an unfavourable view of Augustus, which was reinforced by pieces of forgotten knowledge that came to his notice when he studied the reign of Tiberius. Too late, however, to subvert the standard historical tradition or play Tiberius against Augustus.

The facts emerging about certain consular worthies cast a dubious light on patronage and honours in the Republic of Caesar Augustus. For the senator lacking benefit of birth, advancement accrued (as before) from military merit, from oratory, or from science of the law.[29] The standard and colourless paragon of the *nouus homo*, 'new man', was C. Poppaeus Sabinus (consul 9), enjoying the confidence of the government and kept in a provincial command for twenty-four years on end: the obituary quietly and suitably hits him off as *par negotiis neque supra*, 'equal to his business and no more' (*A.* 6.39.3). The historian, however, goes deeper in his revelations. Three detestable *noui homines*, 'new men', characterized in the ultimate verdict, exemplify the three types of promotion, soldier, orator, and jurist: P. Sulpicius Quirinius (consul 12 BC, *A.* 3.48), grasping and much disliked in his old age, Q. Haterius (suffect consul 5 BC, *A.* 4.61), voluble and adulatory, and C. Ateius Capito (suffect consul 5, *A.* 3.75), the lawyer subservient to power. The obituaries have their own validity. But the author was in a fortunate position—he had been able to display two of these three consulars in action, performing to character.[30]

But not all was evil and sinister. Men whom Tacitus approves for sagacity, moderation, and civic wisdom can stand as testimony. Thus L. Piso the Pontifex, *nullius seruilis sententiae sponte auctor*, 'having spontaneously initiated no servile proposal' (*A.* 6.10.3); M. Lepidus, whose virtues the narrative had adequately attested;[31] and old Volusius Saturninus, unharmed and unimpaired by the friendship and favour of a whole sequence of rulers (*A.* 13.30).

---

[29] *A.* 4.6 (Tiberius' principles in the award of *honores*).

[30] *A.* 1.13 and 3.57 (Haterius); 3.70 (Ateius). [*Addendum* from Syme's revised version of 1970: For obituary notices on Augustan *noui homines*, see Syme (1970: 580–81).]

[31] *A.* 6.27.4: *M. Lepidus, de cuius moderatione atque sapientia in prioribus libris satis conlocaui*, 'Marcus Lepidus, concerning whose moderation and wisdom I allocated sufficient space in earlier books'. Marcus (consul 6), not Manius (consul 11), cf. Syme (1955).

Good and bad stand in contrasted pairs. On the unsavoury Caninius Rebilus follows the venerable Volusius Saturninus (*A.* 13.30); and Domitius Afer is matched and mastered by Servilius Nonianus (*A.* 14.19). Further, the selection of entries for the necrological rubric indicates a preoccupation with families whose members were known to Cornelius Tacitus. The descendants of Messalla and Pollio concerned not past history and the annals of Roman eloquence only. The direct line of the patrician Valerii had lapsed—but Vipstanus Messalla carried their blood through descent on the female side, the friend of Tacitus' youth, and one of the four interlocutors of the *Dialogus*.[32] The Asinii show several consuls more or less contemporaneous with the historian,[33] and Asinii in the obituaries ought to be closely scrutinized. One is there though only a name and a prospect frustrated—Saloninus who was betrothed to a princess (*A.* 3.75). Another, M. Asinius Agrippa (consul 25), earns a generous laudation for virtue as well as pedigree—*claris maioribus quam uetustis uitaque non degener*, 'of brilliant rather than olden ancestors, and in his own life not their inferior' (*A.* 4.61). No word or act of his had been found worth a mention by the author of the *Annales*. As for the Volusii, the suffect consul of 12 BC hardly seems distinctive enough to inaugurate the first of the obituaries (and, as has been shown, he serves to bring in Sallustius Crispus). But Tacitus betrays some interest in the family, and in its opulence. This Volusius was the *primus adcumulator*, 'first accumulator' (*A.* 3.30.1), as he observes in a striking phrase.[34] There were two Volusii close coevals of Tacitus, the consuls of 87 and of 92:[35] quiet men, it may be presumed, and, like their old grandfather, not involved in politics or molested by a despot.

And, to conclude. Like the speeches and the digressions, the obituaries may convey personal disclosures about Cornelius Tacitus, consul, orator and historian. What he has to say about Q. Haterius shows up the fluent facile speaker who enjoyed an enormous vogue in his lifetime, and left nothing behind: it is style that matters, and the effort

---

[32] *PIR*[1] V 468.

[33] Asinius Pollio Verrucosus (consul 81), [*Po*]*llio filius* (suffect consul 85), M. Asinius Marcellus (consul 104), Q. Asinius Marcellus (*suff. anno incerto*, cf. *PIR*[2], A 1235).

[34] Observe that Nero in his reply to Seneca is made to adduce a Volusius: *nisi … quantum Volusio longa parsimonia quaesiuit, tantum in te mea liberalitas explere non potest*, 'unless my lavishness to you is unable to match the fulfilment which lifelong frugality brought to Volusius' (*A.* 14.56.1). Presumably the long-lived suffect consul of AD 3.

[35] *PIR*[2], V 663; 665.

of style.[36] Matched with the great Domitius Afer, Servilius Nonianus earns the primacy, an orator who passed on from eloquence to the writing of history: equal in talent to Afer, but a better man, and commended for grace of living.[37]

Not that the literary and structural value of the obituary should be neglected. Like the historical excursus, it can supply variety, tighten a link, or permit a transition most elegant and insidious. Reporting the decease of Ateius Capito, Tacitus inserts a reference to his rival in mastery of the law, the highly respectable Antistius Labeo, who was Republican by family, sentiment and doctrine—and not liked by the government. The pliant Capito won preferment and the consulate (*A.* 3.75). The next item is the funeral of Cassius' widow, the sister of Marcus Brutus, concluding Book 3 in splendour and power and evoking the Republic. The *imagines* of twenty-four noble families adorned that ceremony, but not those of the Liberators: *sed praefulgebant Cassius atque Brutus eo ipso quod effigies eorum non uisebantur*, 'but outshining all were Cassius and Brutus, for the very reason that likenesses of them were not on view' (*A.* 3.76.2).[38]

During his apprenticeship to public life in the reign of Vespasian Tacitus will have attended the obsequies of illustrious survivors, not neglecting the matter and quality of the laudation or the informed commentary of old men there present. L. Piso wound up his life at last (suffect consul 27), the son of Germanicus' enemy and *praefectus urbi* 'prefect for the city' in the last year of Tiberius;[39] also C. Cassius Longinus (suffect consul 30), the great jurist, who had come back from exile.[40]

---

[36] *A.* 4.61: *utque aliorum meditatio et labor in posterum ualescit, sic Haterii canorum illud et profluens cum ipso simul exstinctum est*, 'and, whereas the laborious deliberation of others continues to be effective in the future, that resonant flow of Haterius was extinguished along with himself.'

[37] *A.* 14.19: *Domitii Afri et M. Seruilii, qui summis honoribus et multa eloquentia uiguerant, ille orando causas, Seruilius diu foro, mox tradendis rebus Romanis celebris et elegantia uitae quod clariorem effecit, ut par ingenio ita morum diuersus*, 'Domitius Afer and M. Servilius, who had thrived in the highest offices and by considerable eloquence, the former in pleading cases, Servilius for a long time in the forum but later celebrated for transmitting Roman affairs and for the elegance of a life which he made more brilliant in that the equality of his talent was matched by the dissimilarity of his behaviour.' [*Addendum* from Syme's revised version of 1970: See further on Servilius Nonianus Syme (1970: 91–109 esp. 107).]

[38] [Flower (1996: 99) sees Tiberius' arrangements for the funeral of his son Drusus the following year as a 'reply' to Junia.]

[39] *PIR*², C 293. For his survival, see Pliny *Ep.* 3.7.12.

[40] *Dig.* 1, 2, 2, 52.

Consul himself in the year 97, Tacitus was chosen to deliver the laudation on Verginius Rufus, within reach of the purple in the crisis that brought down Nero, and surviving the emperors who feared and suspected him: Verginius was born in the year of Augustus' death (Pliny *Ep.* 2.1).

Tacitus had witnessed the obsequies of several rulers. When he came to chronicle the end of Caesar Augustus, no word of all the elaborate ceremonial, no oration. Instead, malice or a subversive equity. The spectacle of soldiers on guard excites derision—how superfluous and anachronistic! An age had lapsed since the tumultuous funeral of Caesar the Dictator (*A.* 1.8). And abundant comment is served up from the bystanders. That earlier historian, whom Cassius Dio copied and followed, and whose traces can be intermittently detected in the opening chapters of Book 1, duly equipped the spectators with eulogistic reflections on their dead ruler (Dio 56.43). Tacitus took over those reflections, modifying and abbreviating (*A.* 1.9). But Tacitus goes further. He makes the men of understanding, the *prudentes*, diverge into another track. They add the other side, detrimentally. More of it, and with more relish (*A.* 1.10).

[POSTSCRIPT

For an extensive study of obituary notices in Tacitus, see Pomeroy (1991). The most contentious of these is arguably Tacitus' assessment of Tiberius at *A.* 6.51, on which see Woodman (1989) and the commentary of Martin (2001). Ash (2003) considers the 'embedded' historiographical obituaries in Pliny's *Epistles*. Flower (1996) enriches our understanding of the historial context of Roman funerals. For a wide-reaching study of the cultural legacy of the republic viewed through the prism of the principate (particularly under Tiberius), see Gowing (2005).]

11

The Beginning of the Year in Tacitus

Judith Ginsburg

The White Rabbit put on his spectacles. 'Where shall I begin, please your Majesty?' he asked. 'Begin at the beginning,' the King said, gravely, 'and go on till you come to the end: then stop.' Lewis Carroll, *Alice's Adventures in Wonderland*

An analysis of Tacitus' use of the annalistic method may profitably begin with his answer to the question posed above. The focus of our attention will be the material Tacitus places at the opening of the annual account in the twenty-one years of *Annals* 1–6 for which the beginning is extant.[1] The aim of this chapter is to examine Tacitus' selection and treatment of his material at the beginning of the year's narrative. In doing so, we will have occasion to compare the historian's approach to the beginning of the year with traditional annalistic practice—a process which will elucidate not only Tacitus' methodology but his attitude toward the annalistic method as well.

THE OPENING FORMULA

At the very inception of the annual account Tacitus lays claim to belonging to the annalistic tradition by marking the transition from one year to the next with the names of the *consules ordinarii* ('normally appointed consuls') of the new year. This, we are told, was the procedure used to set off individual years in the *tabulae Pontificales*

[1] The years AD 15–29, 32–7.

('Priestly tablets'), where the new year began with the names of the consuls and other magistrates,[2] and it is well evidenced in the extant portions of Livy.

While Livy employs a variety of formulae to introduce the names of the consuls of the year, however, Tacitus chooses one of these, the ablative absolute construction (*x, y consulibus,* 'while *x* and *y* were consuls'), and makes it the regular form of expression at the beginning of the year's account. If we omit the year 20, which has no introductory formula,[3] the ablative absolute construction opens 14 of 20 years (70%) in *Annals* 1–6; Livy, by contrast, begins only 12 out of 48 years (25%) in Books 21–45 with the ablative absolute formula.[4]

Tacitus' preference for the ablative absolute construction attests an approach to the beginning of the annual account fundamentally different from that of Livy. If we examine briefly the various annalistic formulae employed by Livy, we will see that Tacitus, by making the ablative absolute construction the regular introductory formula for the year, chose the least specific of all the opening formulae available within the annalistic tradition, and one which would allow him great flexibility in the selection of material for the beginning of the annual narrative. For while Livy uses his opening formulae to introduce the early events of the year—the inauguration of the magistrates and their first functions—Tacitus employs the ablative construction simply to date the year. His approach, in contrast to that of Livy, is to single out an event which he considers important and to begin with that.

When Livy begins using the names of the consuls to open the year's account in Book 2, the most frequent formula employed is *x, y*

---

[2] Cf. Servius, *In Aen.* 1.373: *tabulam dealbatam quotannis pontifex maximus habuit, in qua praescriptis consulum nominibus et aliorum magistratuum digna memoratu notare consueuerat domi militiaeque terra marique gesta per singulos dies,* 'Each year the *pontifex maximus* had the whitewashed board on which, besides writing down the names of the consuls and the other magistrates, he also used to take note of the deeds worthy of being remembered, accomplished at home and in military campaigns on land and at sea, on a day by day basis.'

[3] The normal consular dating is missing at the beginning of the year 20. Tacitus takes up this year's narrative where he had left off in *A.* 2.75, with Agrippina's voyage to Rome with the ashes of Germanicus (*A.* 3.1). Only incidentally are the consuls identified by name a chapter later as the historian describes Agrippina's procession through Italy to Rome and the crowds which accompanied her on the way: *consules M. Valerius et M. Aurelius (iam enim magistratum occeperant) et senatus ac magna pars populi uiam compleuere,* 'The consuls M. Valerius and M. Aurelius (they had already commenced their magistracy) and the senate and a large section of the people filled the route' (*A.* 3.2.3).

[4] The years 218–179, 177–176, 169–167 BC.

consules facti,[5] '*x, y* became consuls', an expression which serves, in a narrative of the early Republic, to stress the annual election of the newly instituted chief magistrates. In the later books (21–45), where the narrative of individual years becomes more detailed and where an account of the consular elections occurs already at the end of the previous year, Livy employs other formulae which emphasize instead the first events of the new year.[6] These introductory formulae may be represented schematically as follows:

1. *magistratum* (*consulatum*) *inire,* 'entered the magistracy (consulship)'.
   (a) *anno Punici belli,* 'in the [*x*th] year of the Punic war'.
       e.g. (23.30.18) *circumacto tertio anno Punici belli, Ti. Sempronius consul idibus Martiis magistratum init,* 'The third year of the Punic war was now at an end, and on the Ides of March Tiberius Sempronius entered office as consul'.
   (b) *x, y consulatum inire* '*x, y* entered the consulship'.
       e.g. (25.3.1) *Q. Fulvius Flaccus tertium, Ap. Claudius consulatum ineunt,* 'Quintus Fulvius Flaccus and Appius Claudius entered their consulships, Flaccus for the third time'.
   (c) *idibus Martiis, quo die magistratum inierunt,* 'the Ides of March, the day on which they entered the consulship'.
       e.g. (33.43.1) *L. Valerius Flaccus et M. Porcius Cato consules idibus Martiis, quo die magistratum inierunt, de prouinciis cum ad senatum rettulissent, patres censuerunt. . .* 'When the consuls Lucius Valerius Flaccus and Marcus Porcius Cato on the Ides of March (the day on which they entered the magistracy) raised in the senate the question of the provinces, the senators decided . . .'
   (d) *cum idibus Martiis magistratum inissent,* 'when they had entered the magistracy on the Ides of March'.
       e.g. (26.1.1) *Cn. Fulvius Centumalus P. Sulpicius Galba consules cum idibus Martiis magistratum inissent, . . . de re publica, de administratione belli, de prouinciis exercitibusque patres*

---

[5] Cf. 2.9.1 (508), 2.41.1 (486), 2.63.1 (469). Sometimes *facti,* 'became', is omitted (e.g. 2.16.1, 2.54.1) or replaced by *fiunt,* 'become' (e.g. 2.43.1, 2.51.4). Other expressions found less frequently in the early books are *secuti consules,* 'followed as consuls' (e.g. 2.17.1, 3.30.1), *annus . . . consules habuit,* 'the year had as its consuls' (e.g. 2.18.1, 4.35.1) and *. . . consulibus,* 'While the consuls were . . .' (e.g. 2.34.7, 10.1.1).

[6] [On the consular year and the Roman historical tradition, see further Rich (1996), reprinted with some revisions in Chaplin and Kraus (2009: 118–47).]

consulerunt, 'When on March 15th, the consuls Gnaeus Fulvius
Centumalus and Publius Sulpicius Galba began their terms of
office, they consulted the senators on matters of state, the
management of the war, and the question of the provinces.'

(e) *magistratu inito*, 'after beginning the magistracy'.
e.g. (32.8.1) *Sex. Aelius Paetus T. Quinctius Flamininus consules
magistratu inito senatum in Capitolio cum habuissent, decreue-
runt patres*, 'When the consuls Sextus Aelius Paetus and Titus
Quinctius Flamininus, after beginning their magistracy, held a
meeting of the senate on the Capitol, the senators decided . . . '

2. *x, y consules cum . . . ad senatum rettulissent . . .*, 'When the
consuls *x* and *y* had raised in the senate . . . '
e.g. (30.1.1) *Cn. Seruilius et C. Seruilius consules—sextus deci-
mus is annus belli Punici erat—cum de re publica belloque et
prouinciis ad senatum rettulissent, censuerunt patres . . .*, 'It was
now the sixteenth year of the Punic War, and the consuls
Gnaeus Servilius and Gaius Servilius raised in the senate the
question of the state of the republic, the conduct of the war, and
the assignment of the province. The senators decided . . . '

3. *principio anni*, 'at the start of the year'.
(a) *principio insequentis anni (consules* or *cum consules) . . .*, 'at the
start of the following year, the consuls [or] when the consuls
. . . '.
e.g. (30.27.1) *principio insequentis anni M. Seruilius et Ti.
Claudius senatu in Capitolium uocato de prouinciis rettulerunt*,
'at the start of the following year, Marcus Servilius and Tiberius
Claudius convened the senate on the Capitol and raised the
question of the provinces.'

(b) *principio anni quo x et y consules fuerunt*, 'at the start of the
year in which *x* and *y* were consuls'.
e.g. (34.43.1) *principio anni, quo P. Scipio Africanus iterum et
Ti. Sempronius Longus consules fuerunt, legati Nabidis tyranni
Romam uenerunt*, 'At the start of the year in which Publius
Scipio for the second time and Tiberius Sempronius Longus
were consuls, ambassadors of the tyrant Nabis came to Rome.'

4. *x, y consulibus*, 'While *x* and *y* were consuls'.
(a) (27.7.7) *Q. Fabio Maximo quintum Q. Fulvio Flacco quartum
consulibus, idibus Martiis, quo die magistratum inierunt, Italia
ambobus prouincia decreta*, 'While Quintus Fabius Maximus

(for the fifth time) and Quintus Fulvius Flaccus (for the fourth time) were consuls, on the Ides of March, the day on which they entered office, Italy was assigned to the pair as their sphere of responsibility.'

(b) (32.28.1) *C. Cornelio et Q. Minucio consulibus omnium primum de prouinciis consulum praetorumque actum*, 'While Gaius Cornelius and Quintus Minucius were consuls, the first of all questions to be settled was about the provinces of the consuls and praetors.'

In general, there is no qualitative difference between the ablative absolute construction and the other forms of expression used by Livy to introduce the year. He uses all these formulae to focus the narrative on the first events of the year—the entry of the magistrates into office, the convening of the senate, the designation and distribution of provinces, and so forth. In several instances, in fact, Livy's employment of one formula or another would appear to be a matter of stylistic preference or the desire for variation.[7]

The ablative absolute construction alone, however, merely provides a date for the year; it gives no indication of when the events immediately following occurred within the year. To specify the latter, Livy has to provide further details, as he does in number 4a above, by the addition of the words *idibus Martiis*, 'on the Ides of March'. The essential difference between the two historians' use of the ablative formula is that Livy usually qualifies the ablative construction to provide a specific temporal setting, namely the inception of the consular year,[8] while Tacitus does not.[9] The opening of the Tacitean

---

[7] Compare e.g. 28.38.12 with 28.10.8 and 29.13.1; 42.1.1 with 32.28.1; 34.43.1, 34.55.1 and 42.10.9 with 44.19.1; 30.1.1 with 45.16.1.

[8] Livy occasionally uses the ablative formula to make a general comment on the year before turning to its first events. For example: *P. Licinio C. Cassio consulibus non urbs tantum Roma nec terra Italia sed omnes reges ciuitatesque ... conuerterant animos in curam Macedonici ac Romani belli*, 'During the consulship of Publius Licinius and Gaius Cassius not just the city of Rome, nor the Italian peninsula, but every king and city ... had become preoccupied with the war between the Macedonians and the Romans' (42.29.1); the narrative of the year proper begins at 42.30.8 (*consules, quo die magistratum inierunt* 'the consuls, on the day on which they entered office'). Cf. 31.5.1, 37.48.1.

[9] Tacitus provides an explicit date for the first narrated event only in the opening of the year 17: *C. Caelio L. Pomponio consulibus Germanicus Caesar a. d. VII. Kal. Iunias triumphauit de Cheruscis C<h>attisque et Angriuariis quaeque alias nationes usque ad Albim colunt*, 'With C. Caelius and L. Pomponius as consuls, on the seventh day

year 15, for example, tells us no more than that in this year a triumph was decreed to Germanicus: *Druso Caesare C. Norbano consulibus decernitur Germanico triumphus manente bello . . .*, 'With Drusus Caesar and C. Norbanus as consuls, a triumph was decreed to Germanicus—with the war still remaining . . .' (*A.* 1.55.1). Tacitus is simply not usually interested in the inauguration of the magistrates as a temporal event at the beginning of the narrative year, or, in fact, in consular activities. When he does deal with these topics, his purposes are quite different from Livy's. Let us look at the six instances in which Tacitus replaces the regular ablative construction by other introductory formulae:

> *A.* 2.53.1 (AD 18): *Sequens annus Tiberium tertium, Germanicum iterum consules habuit. sed eum honorem Germanicus iniit apud urbem Achaiae Nicopolim, quo uenerat per Illyricam oram uiso fratre Druso in Delmatia agente, Hadriatici ac mox Ionii maris aduersam nauigationem perpessus.*

The following year had as its consuls Tiberius for a third time and Germanicus for a second. But Germanicus entered upon his office at Nicopolis, a city in Achaea, to which he had journeyed down the Illyrian coast after visiting his brother Drusus, resident in Dalmatia, and having endured a troublesome voyage of the Adriatic and then of the Ionian sea.

> *A.* 3.31.1 (AD 21): *Sequitur Tiberi quartus, Drusi secundus consulatus, patris atque filii collegio insignis. nam biennio ante Germanici cum Tiberio idem honor neque patruo laetus neque natura tam conexus fuerat.*

There followed Tiberius' fourth and Drusus' second consulship, distinctive for the collegiality of father and son. (Three years earlier, Germanicus' same honour with Tiberius had been neither welcome to his uncle nor so connected in respect of birth).

> *A.*3.52.1 (AD 22): *C. Sulpicius D. Ha<te>rius consules sequuntur, inturbidus externis rebus annus, domi suspecta seueritate aduersum luxum, qui immensum proruperat ad cuncta, quis pecunia prodigitur.*

C. Sulpicius and D. Haterius were the following consuls—a year not undistinguished in foreign affairs and at home by the suspicion of strictness against luxuriousness, whose inordinate surge had reached everything on which money is squandered.

---

before the Kalends of June, Germanicus Caesar triumphed over the Cherusci, Chatti, Angrivarii, and the other nations who live as far as the Albis' (*A.* 2.41.2).

A.6.1 (AD 32): *Cn. Domitius et Camillus Scribonianus consulatum inierant, cum Caesar tramisso quod Capreas et Surrentum interluit freto
Campaniam praelegebat, ambiguus an urbem intraret, seu, quia contra
destinauerat, speciem uenturi simulans.*

Cn. Domitius and Camillus Scribonianus had embarked on the consulship when Caesar, having crossed the strait which washes between
Capri and Surrentum, was skirting Campania, in two minds whether
to go into the city—or because he had already decided otherwise,
simulating a scene of impending arrival.

A.6.40 (AD 36): *Quintus Plautius Sex. Papinius consules sequuntur.
eo anno neque quod L. Aruseius ... morte adfecti forent, adsuetudine
malorum ut atrox aduertebatur. sed exterruit quod ...*

Quintus Plautius and Sextus Papinius were the following consuls. In
that year neither the fact that L. Aruseius ... they had death inflicted on
them attracted notice as anything frightful, given the normality of evil;
but what did cause terror. . . .

A.6.45.3 (AD 37): *neque enim multo post supremi Tiberio consules, Cn.
Acerronius C. Pontius, magistratum occepere, nimia iam potentia
Macronis ...*

For not long afterwards Tiberius' final consuls, Cn. Acerronius and C.
Pontius, commenced their magistracy, with power already being exer-
cised successively by Macro ...

In two of the above cases, the years 22 and 36, there is no apparent
reason why Tacitus uses the main clause formula (*x, y consules
sequuntur*, '*x* and *y* were the following consuls') rather than the
regular ablative construction. Koestermann's explanation, that this
formula, in the simple style of the old annalistic, is a device for
denoting an event at the beginning of the year more emphatically,
is hardly convincing.[10] In other instances where Tacitus clearly
wishes to emphasize an event at the beginning of the year (e.g. years
24 and 28), he uses the regular opening formula. It might be argued
that the historian employs this main clause formula for the year 22
just because it provides a convenient introduction to a general comment on the year, but as the opening of the year 23 demonstrates, this
object could be achieved just as well under the regular rubric: *C. Asin<i>o
C. Antistio consulibus nonus Tiberio annus erat compositae rei
publicae, florentis domus ... cum repente turbare fortuna coepit,*

---

[10] Koestermann (1963: 516).

saeuire ipse aut saeuientibus uires praebere, 'With C. Asinius and C. Antistius as consuls, Tiberius was experiencing his ninth year with the state calm and his household flourishing ... when suddenly fortune started to turn disruptive and the man himself savage—or to present control to savages' (*A*. 4.1.1). Tacitus' use of this old annalistic formula had no other object than that of *uariatio*.[11]

The other variations on the opening formula are a different matter. Here Tacitus abandons the regular ablative absolute construction in favour of other traditional forms of expression precisely because it suits him to make the inauguration of the consuls a temporal event to which some other event, of interest to him, is to be linked in time. The year 18 opens with Germanicus taking up his consulship at Nicopolis in Achaea on the first leg of his fateful expedition to the east. It is not Germanicus' inauguration which interests Tacitus, however, but Germanicus' movements, for which the inauguration provides a temporal setting. The latter will occupy the historian's attention again in the opening of the year 20, where Germanicus' ashes make the homeward journey on the high seas, displacing the usual naming of the consuls at the beginning of the annual account. In the year 21 Tacitus follows the introductory formula (*sequitur Tiberi quartus, Drusi secundus consulatus*, 'There followed Tiberius' fourth and Drusus' second consulship', *A*. 3.31.1) with a remark on the joint consulship of Tiberius and Drusus (*patris atque filii collegio insignis*, 'distinctive for the collegiality of father and son'), comparing it to the earlier joint tenureship of the same emperor and Germanicus. The inauguration of father and son as consuls is connected with another event: though consul for the year with his son Drusus, Tiberius left Rome for Campania at the beginning of the year (*A*. 3.31.2). At the opening of the year 32 Tacitus uses the inauguration of the consuls in its temporal context to date another event. After the consuls entered office (*Cn. Domitius et Camillus Scribonianus consulatum inierant*, 'Cn. Domitius and Camillus Scribonianus had embarked on the consulship', *A*. 6.1.1), Tiberius left Capri to sail up the Campanian coast, apparently on course for Rome.[12] And in the year 37 the

---

[11] See Moore (1923: 7–8) for a discussion of the variations used by Tacitus even within the regular ablative formula.

[12] Rogers (1945: 43), on the basis of Suet. *Tib*. 65.2 (*uerum et oppressa coniuratione Seiani nihilo securior aut constantior per nouem proximos menses non egressus est uilla, quae uocatur Iouis*, 'Yet even after the conspiracy of Sejanus was crushed, he was by no means more self-assured or resolute, but for the next nine months he did not

entrance into office of the last consuls of Tiberius' principate dates, and thereby calls attention to, the emperor's failure to provide for the succession (*A.* 6.46.1–3).

Tacitus has little interest in retailing the official functions which began each year, notably the inauguration of the consuls. Even when he does diverge from the ablative absolute as an opening formula to treat the inauguration of the consuls as an event, Tacitus does so with ulterior purposes—to place another event in a temporal context. In these cases, it is that event, and not the inauguration itself, which has special significance for the historian.

THE TEMPORAL SETTING

The historian's opening formula allows him great freedom in selecting and arranging his material at the beginning of the annual narrative. How did Tacitus make use of this freedom? Let us begin by asking where the Tacitean year begins. If Tacitus shows little interest in the annual events which began the consular year and which Livy faithfully records, does he also disregard the traditional chronological framework for the beginning of the year's narrative?

The first events recorded by Tacitus in fourteen of the twenty-one years under consideration here can be placed in a temporal context.[13] The evidence for their dating is given below:

leave the villa which is called Jupiter's'), argues that Tiberius' journey to the outskirts of Rome occurred sometime after mid-year even though Tacitus places it first in his account of the year 32. The evidence of Suetonius, however, is hardly sufficient to cast doubt on Tacitus' chronology here. Suetonius' other statement on the subject of Tiberius' travels after the year 26—that Tiberius was near the city only twice (*Tib.* 72.1)—is demonstrably false.

[13] Those which cannot be dated: Artabanus' attack on Armenia and the imprisonment of Vonones in Syria (16), trial of Cremutius Cordus (25), collapse of the amphitheatre at Fidenae (27), marriage of Germanicus' daughters, Julia and Drusilla (33), appearance of the *auis phoenix* in Egypt (34), suicide of Vibullius Agrippa (36). The first event of the narrative year 29, the death of Livia (*A.* 5.1), cannot be dated precisely but belongs in the first half of the year when the *consul ordinarius* C. Fufius was still in office (cf. *A.* 5.2.2). [For more on Livia's birth and death dates, see Barrett (1999), who considers that she may well have died in January.] A *tessera nummularia* dated 1 May names the *consules ordinarii*, while the suffects of the year, A. Plautius and L. Nonius Asprenas, are named in an inscription dated 7 July and on a *tessera*

Year 15 (Spring). The year begins, after the statement that in this year a triumph was decreed to Germanicus though the war was not finished, with Germanicus' campaign against the Chatti *initio ueris,* 'at the beginning of spring' (*A.* 1.55.1). Timpe has argued convincingly that both the triumphal decree (*A.* 1.55.1) and the award of triumphal insignia to Germanicus' legates (*A.* 1.72.1) occurred in the autumn at the conclusion of the summer campaign.[14]

Year 17 (May 26). Tacitus begins the year with a description of the triumph celebrated by Germanicus *a. d. VII. Kal. Iunias,* 'on the seventh day before the Kalends of June' (*A.* 2.41.2).

Year 18 (1 January). The first event of this year is Germanicus' assumption of the consulship (on January 1) at Nicopolis in Achaea: *sed eum honorem Germanicus iniit apud urbem Achaiae Nicopolim,* 'But Germanicus entered upon his office at Nicopolis, a city in Achaea' (*A.* 2.53.1).

Year 19 (January). Tacitus himself does not date the first event of this year, Germanicus' visit to Egypt. However, an *ostrakon* from Thebes, dated 26 January, records the receipt of a contribution which was imposed for the occasion of Germanicus' visit (*A.* 2.60.2).[15] If, as Wilcken observes, preparations for the maintenance of Germanicus in Thebes were already under way by 26 January, he must have been at Alexandria (*A.* 2.59.2) at the beginning of the year.[16]

---

nummularia of 15 July. The *suffecti* took office at least by 6 July. See Degrassi (1947: 1.262) for the sources.

[14] Timpe (1968: 43–58, esp. 43–6). Timpe shows that the triumphal decree cannot refer to Germanicus' spring campaign of the year since at its conclusion Germanicus received the *nomen imperatoris* (*A.* 1.58.5), a distinction below that of a triumph. At the conclusion of the summer campaign Germanicus' legates were awarded triumphal insignia (*A.* 1.72.1). Germanicus must have received at this time a proportional honour, i.e., the triumphal decree. Tacitus has deliberately placed the triumph notice at the beginning of the year's account in order to emphasize the paradoxical situation: a triumph was awarded to Germanicus at the end of the campaigns of the year 15 although the war had not been completed. Syme (1978: 53–61, esp. 59–61) argues (*contra* Timpe) that Germanicus was already qualified to celebrate a triumph at the beginning of AD 15 by virtue of his campaign and imperial salutation in AD 13. The fact that Germanicus was qualified to celebrate a triumph at the beginning of AD 15, however, does not prove that a triumph was actually decreed at that time.

[15] Ostrakon Louvre 9004 (Wilcken 1928: 413).

[16] Ibid. 51 n.1, 63–4). [For discussion of Germanicus' trip to Egypt, see Kelly (2010).]

Year 20 (beginning of the year). The year opens with Agrippina's voyage to Rome. It is a wintry sea, *hiberni maris* (A. 3.1.1), and we are presumably at the beginning of the year.[17] Tacitus confirms this a chapter later when he introduces, at the head of the welcoming party that met Agrippina at Tarracina, the consuls Valerius and Aurelius (*iam enim magistratum occeperant,* 'they had already commenced their magistracy' A. 3.2.3).

Year 21 (beginning of the year). After an opening remark on the joint consulship of Tiberius and Drusus, Tacitus begins the year's narrative with Tiberius' withdrawal to Campania and Drusus' activities as consul, *eius anni principio,* 'at the beginning of that year' (A. 3.31.2).

Year 22 (beginning of the year). This year opens with Tiberius' response to the aediles' proposal for sumptuary legislation (A. 3.52–4). Whether or not the aediles took up the matter immediately upon entering office, as Mommsen assumes,[18] the discussion of their proposal clearly occurred before other events—the prorogation of Blaesus' command in Africa and the questions of procedure raised in the sortition for the province of Asia (A. 3.58)—which normally took place early in the calendar year.[19]

Year 23 (beginning of the year). Tacitus opens this year and Book 4 with an introduction to the second half of his account of Tiberius' principate. The first events of the year (the assumption of the *toga uirilis,* 'toga of manhood', by Drusus, the son of Germanicus, Tiberius' speech in praise of his own son Drusus, etc.) are introduced in A. 4.4 with the words *interim anni principio,* 'meanwhile at the beginning of the year'.

Year 24 (3 January). At the beginning of this year's account the *pontifices* and other priests included the names of Germanicus' sons, Nero and Drusus, in the prayers offered for the health of the

---

[17] [Woodman and Martin (1996: 87–8) cite evidence from a suggested restoration of a lacuna in the *Tabula Siarensis* and are cautious about when in Tacitus' narrative the year 20 actually begins.]

[18] Mommsen (1909a: 258).

[19] Mommsen (1887–8: 1.255–6): the sortition of provinces probably took place at the beginning of the calendar year for which the province was assigned and in which the senatorial governor was to set out before a designated day. Under Tiberius, this day was 1 June (cf. Dio 57.14.5).

emperor. The *pro salute principis uota*, 'vows for the safety of the emperor', were offered each year on January 3.[20]

Year 26 (summer–autumn). The Thracian campaign of Poppaeus Sabinus (*A.* 4.46–51) begins the narrative of this year. Near the end of this account, Tacitus says that the *praematura montis Haemi et saeua hiemps*, 'Mount Haemus' early and savage winter' (*A.* 4.51.3), caused the rest of the population to surrender and thus be spared reduction by assault or blockade. This campaign, then, must have taken place in the summer or autumn.

Year 28 (1 January). *Iunio Silano et Silio Nerua consulibus foedum anni principium incessit tracto in carcerem inlustri equite Romano Titio Sabino ob amicitiam Germanici,* 'With Junius Silanus and with Silius Nerva as consuls, a foul beginning to the year was made with the dragging to prison of the illustrious Roman equestrian Titius Sabinus owing to his friendship with Germanicus' (*A.* 4.68.1). Tacitus emphasizes Tiberius' sacrilegious behaviour in turning the formal *uota pro salute rei publicae*, 'vows for the safety of the state', on 1 January into an attack on Sabinus (*A.* 4.70).[21]

Year 32 (beginning of the year). The historian begins the narrative of this year with a description of Tiberius' journey from Capri up the Campanian coast (*A.* 6.1), shortly after the consuls took office, and then turns to events at Rome at the beginning of the year (*at Romae principio anni*, 'But at Rome at the beginning of the year', *A.* 6.2): senatorial resolutions against Livilla and Sejanus.

---

[20] Cf. Gaius Dig. 50.16.233: *post Kal. Ian. die tertio pro salute principis uota suscipiuntur*, 'vows are undertaken for the safety of the emperor on the third day after the Kalends of January'; Suet. *Tib.* 54.1: *sed ut comperit ineunte anno pro eorum quoque salute publice uota suscepta, egit cum senatu, non debere talia praemia tribui nisi expertis et aetate prouectis*, 'But as soon as he learned that at the beginning of the year vows were being undertaken for their safety also, he referred the matter to the senate, saying that such honours ought to be conferred only on those of tried character and mature years.'

[21] *sed Caesar sollemnia incipientis anni kalendis Ianuariis epistula precatus, uertit in Sabinum, corruptos quosdam libertorum et petitum se arguens, ultionemque haud obscure poscebat*, 'As for Caesar, having offered solemn prayers for the starting year by letter on the Kalends of January, he rounded on Sabinus, charging that certain of his freedmen had been bribed and that he himself was the target; and there was no obscurity about his demand for vengeance'. Cf. also Suet. *Tib.* 61.2. [The start of the year AD 28 is discussed by L. Morgan (1998).] For the sources for the *uota pro salute rei publicae*, 'vows for the safety of the state', see Degrassi (1963: 389).

Year 35 (summer). Tacitus' account of this year begins with a secret embassy of Parthian nobles, seeking Tiberius' sanction for setting up Phraates on the Parthian throne as a rival to Artabanus (*A.* 6.31). At the end of this account of affairs in the east, the historian says: *quae duabus aestatibus gesta coniunxi, quo requiesceret animus a domesticis malis,* 'These achievements of two seasons I linked together to provide some mental respite from domestic afflictions' (*A.* 6.38.1). Thus the embassy and the events immediately following must belong to the first summer, that of the year 35.[22]

Year 37 (first part of the year). Tacitus opens the last year of Tiberius' reign with a discussion of the excessive power of Macro and Tiberius' failure to provide for the succession (*A.* 6.45.3–46). Of the events of the year introduced at 6.47.1 with *interim Romae*, 'meanwhile at Rome', one of these, the trial of Albucilla (*A.* 6.47.2), occurred shortly before the death of Tiberius on 16 March. L. Arruntius, one of Albucilla's alleged co-conspirators, refused to prolong his life, declaring that although he could survive a few days and see Tiberius into his grave, he could not be secure under the emperor's successor.[23] This temporal setting is confirmed by Dio (58.27.4–5) and Suetonius (*Tib.* 75), who indicate that others accused with Albucilla were saved even after their condemnation because the ten days' grace period had not expired when the emperor died.

The accounts of several years (ten out of our fourteen) open with an event or events at or near the beginning of the calendar year. Tacitus describes the first events of three of these as occurring *anni principio*, 'at the beginning of the year' (21, 23, and 32), a phrase the historian uses to refer literally to the beginning of the calendar year.[24] Four other years open with events which can be placed in the month of January either on the direct testimony of Tacitus himself (18 and 28) or from external evidence (19 and 24). The first part of the calendar

[22] *Contra* Magie (1950: 2.1364, n.39). Magie dates the first events of Tacitus' account to the year 34. For the chronology of these events, see Garzetti (1956: 223–4).

[23] *sane paucos ad suprema principis dies posse uitari: quem ad modum euasurum imminentis iuuentam?*, 'Of course avoidance was possible during the few days to the princeps's final moments; but how would he escape the youth of the one who loomed over them?' (*A.* 6.48.2).

[24] Tacitus uses the phrase *anni principium*, 'beginning of the year', at the beginning of 28 (*A.* 4.68.1) to date an event, the trial and incarceration of Titius Sabinus, which occurred on 1 January of that year. See above, n. 21.

year, though not necessarily its very inception, is the temporal setting for the years 20, 22, and 37.

The Tacitean year need not, however, open with the calendar year, as is evidenced by the four years whose first events fall relatively late in the year (15, 17, 26, and 35). Nor is Tacitus' choice of a late beginning for these years fortuitous. For in two of these years he has chosen to begin the annual narrative not only with late events but with ones taken out of their proper places in the actual temporal sequence of the year's events. The year 15 opens with Germanicus' spring and summer campaigns on the German frontier (*A.* 1.55–71). Following these and the award of triumphal insignia to Germanicus' legates (*A.* 1.72.1), Tacitus turns to events at Rome which can be dated to the beginning of the consular year. Among these is Tiberius' refusal to allow the senate to swear obedience to his *acta* (*A.* 1.72.1), an incident which must have taken place on 1 January, the day on which these oaths were customarily sworn.[25] Similarly, the historian begins the account of the year 35 with affairs in the East (*A.* 6.31–7), events which he tells us occurred in the summers of the years 35 and 36, but which he has combined into one continuous narrative: *quae duabus aestatibus gesta coniunxi, quo requiesceret animus a domesticis malis*, 'These achievements of two seasons I linked together to provide some mental respite from domestic afflictions' (*A.* 6.38.1).[26] A date for the first of the events which follow, the suicide of Fulcinius Trio (*A.* 6.38.2–3) is provided by Dio's account of the same year. Trio was charged shortly after the new consuls had taken office.[27] In both

---

[25] Cf. Dio 57.8.4, 58.17.2

[26] [See Ash (1999b) for Tacitus' presentation of events in the east here.]

[27] Dio 58.25.2: 'After this Gaius Gallus and Marcus Servilius became consuls, and Tiberius was at Antium celebrating the marriage of Gaius. For he would not enter Rome even for such a purpose because a certain Fulcinius Trio . . . had been accused and handed over for trial . . .'. Despite the fact that Tacitus places the marriage of Gaius in the year 33 (*A.* 6.20), the other details of the two accounts accord well: see Rogers (1945: 43). The distance between Rome and Antium fits Tacitus' description of the time it took for news of the trials of Trio and others to reach Tiberius: *haec Tiberius non mari, ut olim, diuisus neque per longinquos nuntios accipiebat, sed urbem iuxta, eodem ut die uel noctis interiectu litteris consulum rescriberet, quasi aspiciens undantem per domos sanguinem aut manus carnificum*, 'These matters Tiberius learned, not cut off by the sea (as formerly) nor through long-distance messengers, but close to the City, so that on the very same day or after only a night's intermission he could write back to the consuls' letters, almost observing the gushing blood in the houses or the handiwork of the executioners' (*A.* 6.39.2). [See Morello (2006) on Tiberius as a writer of letters in the first hexad.]

these cases Tacitus could have opened the annual account with events near the beginning of the calendar year. He chose not to do so.

Moreover, in the opening of the year 17 Tacitus departs from the traditional framework for the beginning of the annual narrative self-consciously and with irony. The opening of this year is striking and exceedingly clever: *C. Caelio L. Pomponio consulibus Germanicus Caesar a. d. VII. Kal. Iunias triumphauit de Cheruscis C<h>attisque et Angriuariis quaeque aliae nationes usque ad Albim colunt,* 'With C. Caelius and L. Pomponius as consuls, on the seventh day before the Kalends of June, Germanicus Caesar triumphed over the Cherusci, Chatti, Angrivarii, and the other nations who live as far as the Albis' (*A.* 2.41.2). Tacitus is writing like an old-fashioned annalistic historian. He is quoting, or pretending to quote, an entry in the official records or calendar of the state. It was from just such compilations that the early annalists drew their material.[28] Yet at the very moment that he is imitating the annalists, he is breaking one of their central canons. For Tacitus this year began not on 1 January, but 26 May.

But it is not in these four years alone—the late starters—that we can see Tacitus purposefully selecting material for the opening of the annual account. The historian's selection and arrangement at the opening of the years 18, 20, 21, and 32 would appear to be equally deliberate, and all these years begin with events early in the calendar year. In each of these years Tacitus links the entry of the consuls into office on 1 January with a contemporary or near-contemporary event. The four instances divide into two couplets. The year 18 opens with Germanicus taking up his consulship at Nicopolis in Achaea on his way to the east; two years later his ashes make the homeward journey on the high seas. In 21 Tiberius departs from Rome for Campania at the beginning of the year—a withdrawal which Tacitus suggests is something of a dress rehearsal for the final departure in 26; in 32 Tiberius leaves Capri and sails up the Campanian coast toward Rome. The question we must ask is: does Tacitus, even when he begins the year early (and this is in the majority of cases), behave as a traditional annalist might be expected to behave?

---

[28] For a general discussion of the documentary sources from which the early annalists drew their material, see Packard (1969: 6–18). [Rawson (1971), Bucher (1995), and Oakley (1997: 21–108, esp. 24–38) are also relevant to this issue.]

TREATMENT OF MATERIAL

Let us consider first the most favourable case: the opening of the year 24. Here Tacitus begins very early indeed, on 3 January, with the annual prayers for the emperor's safety (the *uota pro incolumitate principis*, 'vows for the safety of the emperor'), the kind of official notice which traditionally opens the annalistic year. Tacitus' treatment of this event, however, is not that of a traditional annalist. The ceremony of 3 January will never again engage the historian's attention. He is not interested in it for its own sake; in the year in question it takes on thematic significance. In that year the priests unwittingly fanned the flame of Tiberius' hatred for Germanicus by including the two sons of Germanicus in the prayers for the emperor's safety. The incident is relevant to what Walker aptly terms the succession theme: Tiberius' uneasy, and ultimately hostile, relationship with the Julian house.[29]

In fact a number of the years beginning with early events take up this theme by focusing on the central characters of the drama: Germanicus himself, his family and friends. The year 18 opens on 1 January with Germanicus' assumption of his consulship in Greece. In the winter of 19 we witness Germanicus setting out for Egypt, a course of action which the emperor viewed with some displeasure (*A.* 2.59.2). At the beginning of 20 it is Germanicus' ashes which make the homeward journey on the wintry seas. The first event recorded under the year 23 and *anni principio*, 'at the beginning of the year', is the assumption of the *toga uirilis*, 'toga of manhood', by Drusus Caesar, Germanicus' son. In 28 Tiberius pollutes the ceremonies of New Year's Day by attacking, *ob amicitiam Germanici*, 'because of friendship with Germanicus', Titius Sabinus and demanding his immediate trial. Tacitus, it seems, is perfectly willing to obey a convention of annalistic history in beginning the annual account with events early in the calendar year—as long as this chronological framework allows him to construct the opening of the year around themes and persons of consequence.

In the year 23, indeed, Tacitus uses this convention of annalistic history to great advantage. The earliest event recorded under the year is the assumption of the *toga uirilis*, 'toga of manhood', by Drusus, the younger son of Germanicus, and the passage of senatorial decrees in his honour, *anni principio*, 'at the beginning of the year'. This is in chapter 4.

[29] Walker (1960: 18–20).

By now, however, the Tacitean year is three chapters old. It began at *A.* 4.1, and the intervening chapters contain an extended portrait of Sejanus, his background, character, ambitions, and, finally, the evil designs he harboured against the emperor's son Drusus. Tacitus is using the opening chapters of the year, emphatically placed, to signal a new turn in the plot. Sejanus and his machinations will dominate the narrative of the decade after the death of Germanicus. Tacitus is more concerned to establish this at the opening of 23 than to begin at the beginning.[30]

While making the advancement of Drusus Caesar yield the centre of the stage to Sejanus, Tacitus has found for it a most effective new home. There is dramatic irony in the honouring of the younger Drusus, Germanicus' son, immediately after a chapter devoted to the schemes of Sejanus against the elder Drusus, Tiberius' son. The younger Drusus, together with his brother Nero, will be the next victims of Sejanus.[31] In advancing Germanicus' children, the senate was merely fattening fresh lambs for the slaughter. In short, the Drusus entry is more properly seen as a pendant of the excursus on Sejanus than as an independent entry in its own right.

The *interim anni principio*, 'meanwhile at the beginning of the year', of *A.* 4.4, like the formal notice of Germanicus' triumph at the beginning of the year 17, is one of those false trails that Tacitus lays so expertly, another reminder that Tacitus is fully conversant with and respectful of the conventions of annalistic history. In reality, as we have seen, the beginning of the calendar year, *principium anni*, is by no means sure of a place in the *Annals*. Here, as elsewhere, it has earned inclusion by satisfying the criterion of thematic relevance.

One of the drawbacks of the annalistic method, we are often told, is that it breaks up the natural flow of events and themes from one year to the next. The necessity of beginning again each year, however, gives Tacitus a splendid opportunity to drive home his message. If we

---

[30] Tacitus uses the opening of the year 37 in much the same way. Before taking up the events of the year proper at *A.* 6.47 (*interim Romae*, 'Meanwhile, at Rome') he begins with an excursus on the excessive power of Sejanus' successor, Macro, and on Tiberius' failure to provide for the succession (*A.* 6.45.3, 6.46). The excursus looks beyond the death of Tiberius to the following principate. Cf. e.g. *A.* 6.46.4, where Tiberius characterizes Gaius: *et C. Caesari forte orto sermone L. Sullam inridenti omnia Sullae uitia et nullam eiusdem uirtutem habiturum praedixit*, 'and when C. Caesar in a chance conversation was deriding L. Sulla, he predicted to him that he would have all of Sulla's vices and none of his virtues.'

[31] Cf. *A.* 4.12.2.

expand our inquiry to include also those years beginning with events of uncertain or late date, we notice that eleven out of our twenty-one years open with entries relevant to the succession theme. As long as Germanicus is alive, and for a time after his death, it is he who leads off the Tacitean year.[32] A triumph is awarded him (15), he triumphs (17), he assumes his consulship in Greece (18), he leaves Syria for Egypt (19), his ashes return to Rome (20). The only exception is the year 16, which is begun with the announcement of a war brewing in the east: *Sisenna Statilio Tauro L. Libone consulibus mota Orientis regna prouinciaeque Romanae, initio apud Parthos orto*, 'With Sisenna Statilius Taurus and L. Libo as consuls, there were tremors in the kingdoms and Roman provinces of the east, the starting-point having originated among the Parthians' (*A.* 2.1). But here, a survey of Augustan developments in the east (*A.* 4.1–4) merely provide the background for Tacitus' point. Returning to the present at *A.* 2.5, we find the following comment: *ceterum Tiberio haud ingratum accidit turbari res Orientis,ut ea specie Germanicum suetis legionibus abstraheret nouisque prouinciis impositum dolo simul et casibus obiectaret*, 'But Tiberius was quite pleased that the East was disturbed because this gave him the chance of taking Germanicus away from legions that had grown used to him and of entrusting him with unfamiliar provinces, where he might be susceptible to intrigue and hazards.'

And after Germanicus' death, it is the family and friends of Germanicus which occupy the historian at the year's inception. To Drusus Caesar's assumption of the *toga uirilis*, 'toga of manhood' (23), the inclusion of Germanicus' sons in the *uota pro incolumitate principis*, 'vows for the safety of the emperor' (24), and the attack on Titius Sabinus *ob amicitiam Germanici*, 'because of friendship with Germanicus' (28), we may add the opening of the years 29 and 33. An event decisive for the fortunes of the family of Germanicus begins the year 29: the death of Livia. It is from that moment that Tacitus dates the *urgens dominatio*, 'oppressive despotism' (*A.* 5.3.1), which is to characterize the remainder of Tiberius' reign. For while Livia was still alive, he says, she was a refuge for Germanicus' family. Neither Tiberius nor Sejanus had dared to oppose her authority. Immediately after her death, however, a letter from Tiberius attacking Agrippina and Nero Caesar was read in the

---

[32] For the role of Germanicus in the first three books, see Syme (1958a: 254). [Germanicus has attracted lively interest from scholars over recent decades: see the article by Pelling reprinted as Ch. 12 below, with updated bibliography.]

senate (*A.* 5.3.1). And the year 33—a year full of calamities, including the deaths of Drusus Caesar and Agrippina—opens with the marriages of Germanicus' daughters, Julia and Drusilla.[33] Their husbands were chosen by Tiberius after long deliberation.[34] Tiberius' arrangement of the marriages, Tacitus implies, was merely another, if less extreme, method of disposing of Germanicus' children.

Tiberius' relationship with the Julians, moreover, is not the only theme of *Annals* 1–6. Throughout the Tiberian books Tacitus is concerned to demonstrate that the senate's traditional sphere of activity under the Republic no longer obtained under the principate.[35] The historian takes up this theme also in his selection of material for the opening of the annual account. Several years begin with senatorial activities: a dispute in the senate between Domitius Corbulo and Lucius Sulla (21), a discussion of the aediles' proposal for sumptuary legislation (22), the trial of Cremutius Cordus (25), the prosecution and imprisonment of Titius Sabinus (28), senatorial resolutions against Livilla and Sejanus (32), the trial and subsequent suicide of Vibellius Agrippa (36), the trial of Albucilla and others for *maiestas*, 'treason' (37). These are isolated items which in themselves seem randomly selected, but which take on significance when linked with others presented, often just as casually, in later books. Taken together, the senatorial entries illustrate the inability of that body to act decisively and free of external influence. For the emperor himself or one of his representatives is involved in these events. The senate refers the question of sumptuary legislation to Tiberius in 22; the emperor is present at the trial of Cremutius Cordus in 25; he requests the prosecution of Sabinus in 28; and he is on the outskirts of the city when the senate passes resolutions against Livilla and Sejanus in 32. At the beginning of the year 21 it is Drusus who intervenes and settles the dispute in the senate between Domitius Corbulo and Lucius Sulla. *Clientes Seiani*, 'clients of Sejanus', are behind the charges against Cremutius Cordus and Titius Sabinus heard by the senate in 25 and 28, while Macro's known enmity for Arruntius is suspected as a motive for the charges against Albucilla and others in the year 37.

---

[33] [On the year 33 (*A.* 6.15–27), see Syme (1983) and Woodman (2006a).]

[34] *A.* 6.15.1.

[35] The way in which Tacitus develops this theme through his selection of material for the annual account is the subject of Ginsburg (1981: 80–95).

Finally, Tacitus uses the year's beginning to develop minor as well as major themes. The historian presents Tiberius' withdrawal to Capri in AD 26/27 as the realization of Sejanus' plan to remove the emperor from Rome and thereby strengthen his own position.[36] But Tacitus was not altogether satisfied with this explanation. Tiberius, after all, remained on the island for six years after Sejanus' death. Might not the explanation lie in Tiberius' character? His cruelty and lusts were conspicuous; seclusion might hide them (*A.* 4.57.1).[37] Tacitus anticipates the emperor's final departure in the opening of the year 21 when he records Tiberius' departure from Rome at the beginning of the year and suggests that this was the first step in the emperor's prolonged and continuous absence from Rome (*A.* 3.31.2). He returns to the subject again at the beginning of the year 32: Tiberius leaves Capri, sails up the Campanian coast toward Rome, but does not actually enter the city. Instead, Tacitus adds, Tiberius returned to Capri, ashamed of the lust and crimes which now dominated him completely (*A.* 6.1.1). The two incidents—one predating Sejanus' plan to remove the emperor from Rome, the other following Sejanus' death—underline the historian's own view of the reasons for Tiberius' withdrawal.

CONCLUSION

In his treatment of the beginning of the annual account, Tacitus has rejected the Livian style of annalistic history writing. For clearly the function of the first reported events within Tacitus' narrative of the year differs from that in his predecessor. Livy begins the annual account with the official events at Rome which opened the calendar

---

[36] Cf. *A.* 4.41.

[37] *causam abscessus quamquam secutus plurimos auctorum ad Seiani artes rettuli, quia tamen caede eius patrata sex postea annos pari secreto coniunxit, plerumque permoveor, num ad ipsum referri uerius sit, saeuitiam ac libidinem, cum factis promeret, locis occultantem,* 'As to the reason for his retirement, although I have followed the majority of authors and ascribed it to the practices of Sejanus, nevertheless, because he spent six continuous years in seclusion after bringing about the latter's slaughter, I am often moved to ask whether it is more realistically ascribed to the man himself, concealing his savagery and lust by his location, though he exhibited them in his deeds . . .'.

year: the inauguration of the magistrates, the assignation or sortition of consular and praetorian provinces, the disposition of troops, the expiation of prodigies, and so forth. All these initial items lead up to, and indeed form a necessary prelude to, the substance of the annual account, the year's campaigning,[38] for such matters had to be dealt with before the consuls could depart for their provinces.[39] Moreover, as Phillips and others have suggested, these official notices recorded in the dry, monotonous manner of official documents, served his ends well. By recapitulating them at the opening of each annual narrative Livy emphasizes the 'regular repetition of constitutional processes' at home and suggests that in their regularity lies the explanation for Roman success abroad.[40]

Tacitus does not need to provide such setting for his narrative since campaigns do not usually form the major subject-matter of the Tacitean year. Nor is the historian interested in calling attention to the magisterial and senatorial activities which officially inaugurated the Roman year. These were forms without substance when in truth all power was in the hands of one man alone: *neque alia re Rom<ana> quam si unus imperitet*, 'and there is no salvation for Roman affairs other than if one man is in command' (*A.* 4.33.2). Tacitus, instead, chooses for the opening of his year events which are relevant to the themes of *Annals* 1–6, and he treats these items as significant in themselves.

There is little reason to believe, moreover, that Tacitus found his chosen medium restrictive. The historian has no compunction about departing from the traditional chronological framework for the opening of the annual account when it suits his purposes to do so. And Tacitus can use the annalistic method to advantage. We sympathize

---

[38] There are exceptions to this format. Livy occasionally begins years with *res externae*, 'external affairs' (after giving the consuls for the year): e.g 191 BC (36.1–36.45), 185 BC (39.23.5–39.32 with no clear indication of the beginning of the consular year), 184 BC (39.33–39.45.1). *Res internae*, 'internal affairs', can play a leading role in the annual narrative: e.g. 186 BC (39.8–39.23.4). For discussion, see Luce (1977: 80–81, 106–7, 260–61).

[39] Cf. the year 210 BC (26.26.5–27.7.6), where only after the exchange of provinces by the consuls, the hearing of embassies, and the completion of the levy do the consuls set out for their provinces: *paratisque omnibus ad bellum consules in prouincias profecti sunt*, 'When all the preparations for war were completed, the consuls left for their provinces' (26.36 12). See, however, 196 BC (33.25.4–33.42), where Livy breaks into the normal sequence to narrate Flamininus' proclamation at the Isthmian games (33.27.5) before recounting the departure of the consuls for their provinces (33.36.4).

[40] Phillips (1974: 265, 272–3); Hoch (1951: 55).

with him for having to break up his narrative. But Tacitus can make a virtue of this apparently grim necessity. The need to drop everything and begin again each year allows the historian to elucidate his point, not once, but again and again.

[POSTSCRIPT

Comparison with the inscription preserving the senatorial decree about the trial of Cn. Calpurnius Piso, charged with Germanicus' murder, is now crucial for any analysis of Tacitus' account of the year 20 (*A.* 3.1-30).[41] No doubt Ginsburg would have offered perceptive discussion of this evidence, had she been writing today, but her overview of Tacitus' narrative techniques remains invaluable.]

---

[41] [For bibliography, see the introduction to this volume, n. 94].

12

Tacitus and Germanicus

Christopher Pelling

THE PROBLEM

What exactly is the problem about the Tacitean Germanicus? There are at least four ways of putting the question. First, for Goodyear it is very much a question of consistency. He stresses the difficulties of reconciling the apparently inept Germanicus of much of Book 1 of the *Annals* with the generally heroic tone in which he is described, and indeed with the much more satisfactory figure presented in parts of Book 2; but Goodyear feels that this is adequately explained if we assume that Tacitus simply makes Germanicus what he needs to be for each episode, glorious when he is required as a foil for the blackened Tiberius, 'egregiously undignified and inept' when that is what the drama requires.[1]

But, second, others have found it more difficult to gauge how Germanicus is supposed to come out of particular scenes. This is an especially acute problem in Book 1, where, famously, there are several passages where any reasonable reading of the text seems to show Germanicus as strangely incompetent, despite the romantic aura that surrounds him. But it recurs with the death scenes at *Annals* 2.69–73: are we there supposed to be carried away by the hysteria and applaud

My thanks for full and rich comments on the original draft to Barbara Levick, Miriam Griffin, Simon Hornblower, Christiane Sourvinou-Inwood, Michael Comber, Alison Sylvester, and (especially) the editors of the volume in which it was published, T. J. Luce and A. J. Woodman. I am also most grateful to the editor of the present collection for her advice in the mild updating.

[1] Goodyear (1972, 1981: esp. 1.32–34, 239–41; and 2.65–68, 198–99, 253, 372–76, 415–17); the quotation is from 1.241. Notice also Goodyear (1976). Others too speak in similar terms, notably Krohn (1934: 481) and Edelmaier (1964: 167 n.42).

the legacy of hatred that his final speech bequeaths? Should we share the popular grief that Tacitus describes, and approve the comparison of this glorious figure to Alexander? So this is the second problem, and the one that has come to attract most critical attention: what impression does the text convey, and how well should Germanicus come out of a curiously indecisive narrative?

It is odd that this should be a problem. At least in *Annals* 1–6, Tacitus does not typically leave us in much doubt as to his general verdict on the principals—even if those verdicts are more nuanced than critics sometimes admit. But with Germanicus we seem to have a more irregular technique, one in which (to quote Goodyear again) 'Tacitus favours Germanicus by refraining from comment where comment was called for'.[2] That formulation may be a little misleading, because elsewhere Tacitus does not always proceed by direct comment or appraisal: sometimes he does, sometimes he does not (for instance with Seneca). But direct comment is anyway only the crudest way in which a skilled orator can suggest an appraisal, and it is quite true that Tacitus insistently thrusts his view of Tiberius (for instance) or Sejanus upon us by one technique or another. Yet if Germanicus is inept in handling a mutiny or managing a campaign, we seem to be left to a surprising extent to work that out for ourselves. So this is our third question: why, in the case of Germanicus, is Tacitus' characterizing technique so morally inexplicit?

There is an obvious answer to that. Perhaps Tacitus refrains from straightforward moral comment because straightforward moral comment is not his central interest or would not be adequate; perhaps this Germanicus serves a more sophisticated purpose in the general narrative strategy. That, surely, is the right approach. But that raises the fourth problem: what precisely is this role of Germanicus in the narrative? Far too often we rest content to say things like (to quote Goodyear yet again), 'In *A*. 1–2 T. sets off Germanicus against Tiberius. One way in which he does so is by depicting Germanicus as endowed with precisely those desirable qualities which Tiberius lacks, or which, if they sometimes appear to be manifested in Tiberius' conduct, he will, if he can, depreciate or explain away.'[3] In other

---

[2] Goodyear (1972, 1981: 2.66); cf. ibid. 1.240, 266, 298; Koestermann (1963–8: 1.157).

[3] Goodyear (1972, 1981: 1.252, commenting on 1.33.2); cf. e.g. Goodyear (1970b: 32; 1972, 1981: 1.33, 240); Koestermann (1963–8: 1.150).

words, Germanicus is Tiberius' foil; and this is often as far as criticism goes, sometimes in extraordinarily black-and-white terms.[4] Is this really the best we can do?

Indeed, the level of some of this is surely disappointing. So much of the discussion tends to treat characterization as a self-contained topic; so much centres on the simple question whether Tacitus approved of Germanicus or not. It is a little reminiscent of the British mock-history book *1066 and All That*, which divided historical events into good things and bad things: which sort was Germanicus? Yet, if we were talking about epic or tragedy, we would not dream of asking such crude questions as 'Was Antigone a good thing? Or Achilles? Or Aeneas?' Even characters like these *who invite our appraisal*, as Germanicus surely invites our appraisal, can seldom be analysed in such simple good-or-bad terms, or without more careful analysis of the role they play within their respective works.

CONSISTENCY

Take that first question, that of consistency. In fact, is Goodyear really talking of 'consistency' at all? It is easy to see that the leading characteristics of Germanicus are very consistent indeed: his *comitas* ('affability'), his *ciuilis animus* ('mentality appropriate to a citizen', which suggests polite 'civility' to others as well as a reluctance to give himself imperial airs), his impetuosity and theatricality; his readiness to allow his troops to take the lead; his swiftness to leap to conclusions or to sink into despair, whether at the prospect of a mutiny, the prematurely assumed loss of his comrades, or the precipitate inference that Piso is plotting his death.[5] If there is a problem, it is not in

---

[4] Thus Daitz (1960), 48 found Germanicus 'pure white' and Tiberius 'jet black'; so, effectively, did Drexler (1939: 175), Christ (1956: 67), Michel (1966: 121–30), and others. Koestermann's view (e.g. 1963–8: 1.89) is not too different. The 'foil' approach is most interestingly developed by Krohn (1934); cf., in less black-and-white terms, Martin (1981: 107, 116–17). Syme (1958a: 254) knew that there was more to it.

[5] For *comitas* cf. esp. 1.33.2, 1.71.3, 2.13.1, 2.72.2; for the *ciuile ingenium* cf. 2.82.2 and such instances as 2.53.2, 2.59.1; the *clementia* of 2.57.2 is a related form of courteous restraint (though it does not last long). For the theatricality, see my comments in the text along with n.11; cf. Koestermann (1963–8: 1.276), 'die etwas theatralische Wesenart des Germanicus', of the Henry-V-at-Agincourt tour of the troops at 2.12–13, and now Fulkerson (2006); Pomeroy (2006) traces the range of

the tracing of those characteristics; it is rather in the fact that they sometimes produce creditable results and sometimes are ludicrous and disastrous. It may be an excess of *comitas* or *ciuilitas* or theatricality that leads him to give so weak a lead in the mutiny of Book 1, but the same traits produce the popularity among the troops that conduces so helpfully to the German successes in Book 2. If there is a problem of consistency, it is not in the characterization itself, but rather in the favourable or unfavourable impression it seems to encourage (so our first question swiftly leads into our second). But there is nothing unusual in this at all. It simply reflects a common ancient insight, whereby a hero's faults and strengths are closely related and are often even facets of the same basic traits. That is familiar with an Oedipus, an Ajax, or an Antony, or even with the Persia of Herodotus or the Athens of Thucydides.

True, we should not operate with a transcultural notion of 'consistency'. Ancient assumptions were different from ours, and in particular ancient writers tend to posit a greater degree of coherence among an individual's traits. Each characteristic predicts the next, in a way or at least to a degree that we find alien.[6] Ancient traits come in clusters—which is not to say that they are necessarily stereotypes, only that the different characteristics of Antigone, Aeneas, even Odysseus hunt more naturally together than those of Prince André or Hamlet or Hedda Gabler. But Germanicus' traits cluster without discomfort. *Comitas* goes with the *ciuilis animus*, and the lack of pretence or restraint, that distinctive openness of Germanicus, is a natural extension of the same characteristics; that in turn goes well with the effusive theatricality, and that then with the impetuosity and swiftness to reach conclusions.

'theatrical' behaviour in the *Histories*. For Germanicus' readiness to let troops take the lead, cf. 1.44, 1.48.1–49.2, and 1.49.4 (see subsequent discussion and n.11); and even so small a touch as 1.43.1, where Germanicus assumes that, had he died, the troops would have picked a replacement leader (*legissetis ducem*; cf. Koestermann (1963–8: 1.172) and Goodyear (1972, 1981: 1.295). Germanicus here speaks very differently from the model Scipio Africanus at Livy 28.28.13–14 (see the section on Germanicus and the past, with works cited in n. 40; the Livy intertext is also relevant for Dillius Vocula's speech at *H*. 4.58, and Ash (2010b) illuminatingly brings the three passages together). For the rapidity of his despair cf. 1.35.4, 36 (mutiny: see the next section); 2.24.2 (friends scarcely restrain him from suicide after the storm); 2.69.3 (poison: see n.13).

[6] I have said more about this in Pelling (1988b) and (1990: esp. 235–44) = (2002: 283–300 and 301–38, esp. 315–21).

Similarly, if we were expecting to find Goodyear's consistency of *impression* in ancient authors, it swiftly becomes clear that we will not usually find it. Ancient qualities often belie a consistent or unqualified response. What are we to make of Antigone or Achilles, and are we always to think that they demand straightforward approval or disapproval? Evidently not. It is much easier to *describe* such characters, or Oedipus at Colonus, or Turnus, or Hannibal, or Cleopatra, than to be sure quite how to react, or quite whether we should react in the same way at different times. The moralism a characterization subserves—not just the portrayal of an individual as an *exemplum* for imitation or avoidance, but the moralism of the whole work, a moralism that typically traces a pattern of human behaviour or experience[7]—is usually too complex to allow a wholly even response. That is not inconsistency; it is simply ethical subtlety.

IMPRESSION

How uncertain, though, are we how to react to Germanicus? That is the second question; and it is in Book 1, with his handling of the mutinies, that this problem is acute. There are at least four instances where Germanicus seems peculiarly inept. There is his extravagant speech in chapter 35, where he ends by trying to kill himself, rather than play along with the mutiny, and is then rather discomfited when a certain Calusidius offers him a sword: not the best way to handle a hostile crowd.[8] There is the forged letter from Tiberius in the

---

[7] Both sorts of moralism are of course to be found in Tacitus. *Agr.* 46.3 and (rather differently) *A.* 3.65.1 suggest a concern with *exempla*, and his Agricola or his M. Lepidus provide genuine models for imitation; and models for avoidance are not hard to find. But *A.* 4.32–3 suggests a wider concern with exploring the imperial system and its character, in ways that might still provide political lessons for Tacitus' audience. Such lessons may be given by straightforward moral *exempla*, but are unlikely to be limited to them.

[8] True, such extravagant language was used by other generals, and was sometimes successful. Even here, as Tony Woodman stresses to me, Germanicus at least secures a lull, and good use could potentially be made of it: cf. also Williams (1997: 53–4) and Pigoń (2008: 294 and n. 22). But the distinctive style of Germanicus still emerges if we compare the similar story of Pompey at Plut. *Pomp.* 13. (The comparison is briefly noted by Borzsák 1982: 53.) Pompey's troops, like these, are indignant not with him, but because of a wider grievance; they too try to deploy their popular general against his superior (there Pompey against Sulla, here Germanicus against Tiberius). Pompey

following chapter, carried through with startling incompetence. A letter is produced, purportedly (it seems) written some time earlier, in which the emperor's offers happen to coincide with the demands the mutineers have made a moment ago: no wonder they see through it immediately. Then, in chapter 44, the soldiers are allowed to sit in judgement not merely on the ringleaders but even on their own centurions. That is indeed an odd experiment in military democracy, especially when there is a show of restoring discipline after the disruption: Tacitus several times criticizes similar things in the *Histories*.[9] And there are the vague instructions to the camp of Caecina in chapter 48, a camp where, Tacitus stresses, most of the soldiers are already loyal. Germanicus menacingly urges them to see to matters themselves: *uenire se ualida manu ac, ni supplicium in malos praesumant, usurum promisca caede*, A. 1.48.1 ('he was coming with a strong force, and unless they acted first to punish the wrongdoers, he would kill without discrimination'). No wonder they are so terrified, and the *caedes* they inflict upon themselves turns out to be so *promisca* that Germanicus himself, with a characteristic gesture, bursts into tears. But it is hard to acquit him of a fair measure of the responsibility.[10]

All that seems to come naturally out of the text. Nor do we have to strain to draw such conclusions, for Tacitus expands his detail at precisely the points where Germanicus is at his most undignified and

like Germanicus tries to calm them, then is physically buffeted as he tries to leave the tribunal. The difference is that Pompey's display of emotion (he was in tears, *Pomp.* 13.3) retains a dignity that Germanicus lacks as he makes his horrified leap from the platform; and that 'a good part of the day' was taken up with mutual pleas before Pompey finally threatened suicide, whereas Germanicus' gesture is spontaneous and immediate. It matters little whether Plutarch's story is literally true; it still shows what behaviour could figure naturally in a presentation of a popular but firm and dignified leader. Antonius Primus at *H.* 3.10 is another suggestive comparison, where similar points could be made; so is Agathocles at Diod. 20.33–4 (adduced by Edelmaier 1964: 154 n.16 and Borzsák 1982: 53). Blaesus at 1.18.3–19 and Drusus at 1.25–6, 29–30 are nearer contrasts, and doubtless intended as such; but they confront lesser threats than Germanicus. Cf. the section on character and theme below.

[9] Cf. *H.* 1.46.1, quoted by Koestermann (1963–8: 1.175) and alluded to by Goodyear (1972, 1981: 1.298), 'omnia deinde arbitrio militum acta'; also *H.* 2.79, 3.49.2.

[10] Pigoń (2008) has now perceptively pointed out that Tacitus uses a remarkable number of passive verbs when describing these events, and he explains this, at least partly, in terms of 'exculpating' Germanicus. But might one not equally interpret those passives as suggesting a lack of authority? At a time of crisis, a good general does not let things happen: he drives.

inept: the theatrical speech and suicide gesture, then the discomfiture with Calusidius (notice that this common soldier is even named, and Tacitus does not name people lightly); the *turpe agmen*, 'disgraceful column', as the victorious mutineers carry off the treasure chests; the humiliating departure of Agrippina and her train; the bloody punishment of the ringleaders (or those whom their fellows claim to be ringleaders) and the review of the centurions; the indiscriminate bloodshed at the second camp, and Germanicus' lack of strong leadership. The parallel tradition, slight as it is, confirms that Tacitus has dwelt on these passages more than he need; and the distinctively Tacitean material focuses on exactly the traits most central to his portrait, the spontaneity, the effusiveness, the theatricality, the reluctance to give a firm lead.[11] And he underlines the point with such suggestive juxtapositions: not merely with Drusus in Pannonia, who showed more aplomb in handling an admittedly lesser threat, but with M'. Ennius, inserted at chapter 38 just after Germanicus' most decisive failure: Ennius, who after a nervous start quelled a mutiny among the Chauci with the decisiveness that Germanicus lacked, grabbing a standard[12] and threatening to regard as a deserter anyone who disobeyed. Ennius' brand of theatricality worked; Germanicus' did not.

Yet all this has its problematic aspect too. For one thing, there is the highly enthusiastic tone in which Germanicus is introduced (*A.* 1.33.1–34.1):

---

[11] Thus at *A.* 1.35.4–5 he makes Germanicus' gesture and reaction less thoughtful than Dio 57.5.2; Koestermann (1963–8: 1.156) talks of Tacitus enhancing 'die Theatralik der Szene'. (On the story cf. also Plass 1988: 87.) Then at *A.* 1.41 Tacitus makes both army and Germanicus react more emotionally and spontaneously than Dio 57.5.5–6, and again we have more of a 'Theatercoup' (Koestermann (1963–8: 1.168). At *A.* 1.44 Tacitus puts more emphasis than Dio 57.5.7 on Germanicus' responsibility, both in suggesting that the troops take matters into their own hands ('cetera ipsi exsequerentur') and in not restraining them ('nec Caesar arcebat'). At *A.* 1.49.4 Tacitus' Germanicus follows the soldiers' lead ('sequitur ardorem militum'); Dio 57.6.1 gives the initiative to Germanicus himself (cf. Timpe 1968: 10, 24–30), arguing not quite decisively that Dio is closer to the version of the shared source; Goodyear (1972, 1981: 1.313–41). Koestermann (1963–8: 1.168), commenting on *A.* 1.41, suggests that the consistency of Tacitus' version with his earlier portrayal of Germanicus is a pointer to his greater reliability; one should rather find it suspicious that Tacitus' additional detail relates so closely to his own favoured emphases.

[12] Edelmaier (1964: 157–8) observes that the contrast is heightened by the undignified fate of Germanicus' own *uexillum* at *A.* 1.39.3. A standard is an especially suggestive symbol when military discipline is in point. Cf. also Borzsák (1970: 284).

*Interea Germanico per Gallias, ut diximus, census accipienti excessisse
Augustum adfertur. neptem eius Agrippinam in matrimonio pluresque ex
ea liberos habebat, ipse Druso fratre Tiberii genitus, Augustae nepos, sed
anxius occultis in se patrui auiaeque odiis, quorum causae acriores quia
iniquae. quippe Drusi magna apud populum Romanum memoria, credebaturque, si rerum poti<t>us foret, libertatem redditurus; unde in Germanicum fauor et spes eadem. nam iuueni ciuile ingenium, mira comitas
et diuersa a Tiberii sermone uultu, adrogantibus et obscuris. accedebant
muliebres offensiones nouercalibus Liuiae in Agrippinam stimulis, atque
ipsa Agrippina paulo commotior, nisi quod castitate et mariti amore
quamuis indomitum animum in bonum uertebat. Sed Germanicus
quanto summae spei propior, tanto impensius pro Tiberio niti.*

Meanwhile Germanicus was (as we have said) conducting a census in
Gaul when he received news of the death of Augustus. He was married
to Agrippina, Augustus' granddaughter, who had borne him several
children; he himself was son of Tiberius' brother [Nero] Drusus, and
grandson of Livia. But he was nervous of the unspoken hatred felt both
by his uncle and his grandmother, a hatred whose causes were the more
acute for being unjust. And indeed Drusus was clearly and fondly
remembered by the Roman people, and it was believed that, had he
become emperor, he would have brought back the free state; now they
had transferred the same enthusiasm to Germanicus, and the same
hopes as well. For the young man had an affable nature and a remarkable capacity for getting on with people; it was very different from the
haughty impenetrability of Tiberius' expression and style of speaking.
Besides, there were feminine antagonisms, sharpened by Livia's step-
motherly dislike for Agrippina. And Agrippina herself was rather too
easily provoked; but she was a faithful and loving wife, and those
qualities turned even that indomitable temperament into an asset. But
the nearer Germanicus was to the highest hopes, the more vigorously he
supported Tiberius.

Germanicus clearly has good reasons for apprehension, but his conduct ('the more vigorously he supported Tiberius') is shown to be as
immaculate as his character and qualities. True, nothing there says
that he is going to be marvellous at handling mutinies; Suetonius
(*Gaius* 1.1) might speak of his 'resoluteness' (*constantia*), but Tacitus
does not. Still, it is an odd and jarring way to introduce him if
criticism and derision are expected to be our principal verdict on
the next few chapters. Then again, there is that absence of explicit
criticism of the man's behaviour, the point especially stressed by
Goodyear. Tacitus does show that others criticized Germanicus

(*A.* 1.40.1, 1.46.1), and at *A.* 1.78.2 he even makes it clear that he shared those feelings himself: there he refers to the most significant of Germanicus' concessions as *male consulta*, 'mistakes', even if that phrasing has a euphemistic air (and Germanicus is not named). But he oddly separates that clear statement of his own view from the account of the events themselves.

So, by his own deployment of detail, Tacitus encourages the reader to dwell on the most questionable actions, and in that sense Germanicus clearly does invite appraisal. Yet Tacitus' own appraisal seems oddly positive, or at least strangely indirect in its negative elements. And the problem is not limited to Book 1, for the same sort of oddity recurs in the description of Germanicus' death. There again Tacitus elaborates the scene dramatically, with sinister and macabre colouring; he is also careful to distance himself from Germanicus' own conviction that he was being poisoned,[13] and at one point gives a strong hint that this conclusion was unjust and premature.[14] That would seem to make his dying speech a hysterical overreaction; yet that cannot be the first or principal conclusion we should draw, given that so much of the context is strongly coloured in Germanicus' favour, and the disquieting hints are so muted.

It is not easy to see what we are to make of this moral indecisiveness. One approach is that once outlined by Walker:[15] perhaps Tacitus is trying to allow Germanicus to come out as gloriously as possible, but the texture of the events is too intractable and, *try though he will*, the truer picture comes to the surface. But it is hard to be satisfied with this. If Tacitus had really wished to launder Germanicus, he would not have told the tale like this. He did not have to tell of

---

[13] Esp. at *A.* 2.73.4 and 3.19.2; contrast Dio 57.18, and cf. Koestermann (1957: 356, 358; 1963–8: 1.384).

[14] *A.* 2.69.3, 'saeuam uim morbi augebat persuasio ueneni a Pisone accepti': cf. *A.* 3.14.2 and Goodyear (1972, 1981: 2.409).

[15] Walker (1952: 9) on the mutinies, 'Tacitus' political hero Germanicus (who does not, when one reads carefully, acquit himself particularly well; but certainly the facts were against Tacitus here, and he did what he could for Germanicus, with difficult material)': an instance of the 'discrepancy between fact and impression' (1952: 8). Cf. then her ch. 6 on 'the divergence in some contexts of factual and non-factual material', esp. 110–31 on Germanicus. Koestermann is close to this view, e.g. (1957: 340 n. 24) and (1963–8: 1.39, 164, 175, 182). In discussion at the 1990 Princeton conference where this paper was first delivered, Miss Walker was kind enough to say that she would no longer present the matter in these terms; I was most grateful for her extremely helpful remarks, and for forgiving my continuing to take it as a stalking-horse.

the mutinies at such length at all: many have wondered whether their historical importance was such as to demand such extensive treatment.[16] And, once he had decided to tell of them, he did not have to expand his detail at those points, nor to emphasize those suggestive juxtapositions. If Tacitus was trying to do his best for Germanicus, he would have done a lot better than this.

So perhaps one ought to be tempted by the alternative approach, as argued most forcefully by Edelmaier and Ross. This suggests that Tacitus intends Germanicus to come out badly, to emerge as 'a figure of failure and futility'; and, if the people are carried away by enthusiasm, more fool them. They may think Germanicus is a different kettle of fish from Tiberius, but they are sadly deluded, and eventually these imperial fellows are not so very different. So far Edelmaier and Ross.[17] But it is hard to feel satisfied with this either. For one thing, these imperial fellows *are* very different: the contrast of manner between Tiberius and Germanicus is evident and irreducible, and there is surely no suggestion that Germanicus would have ended as the same sort of emperor as his uncle. There may be something in the view that we are supposed to contrast popular perceptions of Germanicus with the more dismal reality—just as often the converse is true with Tiberius, that malicious *rumores* are not a crude form of innuendo against the *princeps*, but rather invite the reader to consider the gulf between the malicious comment and the reality. With Tiberius we often sense unjustified unpopularity;[18] here we would have a

---

[16] Dio puts more weight than Tacitus on the political importance of the mutinies: for him they constituted a principal reason for Tiberius' hesitation in the accession debate. (Not that any historical weight should be attached to this, for Dio's freedom in reconstructing motives is too clear from elsewhere.) But the mutinies are still dismissed in one chapter apiece for Drusus (57.4) and Germanicus (57.5), even though it seems that his source material was closely similar to that of Tacitus.

[17] Edelmaier (1964: 148–73) and Ross (1973); the quotation is from Ross (1973: 227). The two analyses are sufficiently similar to be discussed together, though Edelmaier is more content to admit some positive elements, especially in Book 2 (1964: 167 n.42). Cf. also Shotter (1968), Rutland (1987); Borzsák (1970) has something in common with this view.

[18] *A.* 4.38.5 is perhaps the most suggestive example, where we are surely meant to sense the malicious and unfair quality of the remarks of Tiberius' critics: so, rightly, Martin and Woodman (1989: 186–7, 191–3); cf. also Syme (1958a: 315 n.6). In context the remarks may still point to an underlying disingenuousness in the emperor's speech, but they do so in a most unstraightforward way. Cf. also *A.* 3.44.2–4, where the popular criticism of Tiberius is clearly overreaction, and pointed as such by the subsequent narrative: cf. Tiberius' own remarks at *A.* 3.47.1–2. There too the issues are not wholly clear-cut: the people might have overreacted less had Tiberius explained himself earlier;

form of unjustified popularity. But it is hard to think that this is all there is to it, that we simply notice that the people get it wrong. This perception does not lead to much, not least because Germanicus comes out so much better in Book 2: if the people got it wrong, then they evidently did not get it *that* wrong. At least we need a clearer explanation of why such a misreading should fit into Tacitus' general narrative strategy. And Ross and Edelmaier leave it unclear why the characterizing method is so oblique, why Tacitus casts this negative verdict in so indirect and unexpressed a form, so that most readers end with something closer to the opposite impression.

CHARACTER AND THEME: GERMANICUS AND THE PRINCIPATE

So our second question has in its turn led into our third, which will occupy the rest of this paper: why it should be that Tacitus' appraisal of Germanicus should be so hard to pin down. This will prove impossible to separate from the fourth, the general function of Germanicus in the narrative. It may be that we should simply assume that this is one of the unresolved tensions in Tacitus' account. Perhaps Tacitus simply sets Germanicus the bumbler against Germanicus the hero, and it is untrue to his manner to try to resolve this into a more coherent generalized picture; perhaps this is yet another of the creative tensions his narrative presents to the reader.[19] But it is worth suggesting that there is a coherent implication here, but one that is

but the popular criticism is still clearly ill-conceived. The same partly goes for 1.46–7, where Tiberius' counter is largely vindicated by the narrative; but some of the popular points are there better aimed. These techniques are very complex, and I return to them in Pelling (2010), with particular reference to A. 4.37–8.

[19] Cf. Luce (1986: esp. 149). O'Gorman (2000: 46–77) now provides a sophisticated version of this approach, representing the difficulty of 'reading' Germanicus as one in counterpoint with the difficulties of observers in the text in knowing what to make of it all, and particularly their sense of a tension between the ways in which Germanicus recalls the past and those which portend the imperial future: 'his portrayal of Germanicus here demonstrates that the process of reading the past ultimately hinges on an image whose significance is continually reinvented by the present and whose absolute value is elusive' (69). Kelly (2010) similarly stresses Germanicus 'Janus-like' nature, looking both backwards and forwards.

complex, and is intimately connected with Tacitus' complex view of the Principate as a whole.

My main argument is simple.[20] It is not incorrect, but it is inadequate, to think of Germanicus as a foil for Tiberius; we should rather think of the whole world in which Germanicus moves, his style of fighting, leadership, and politics, as a contrast to the world and atmosphere of the Principate, so devious and complex, so subtle and unsavoury. Germanicus and his style serve as a sort of alternative, which helps to highlight what is distinctive about the Principate itself. No one would now suggest that Tacitus' view of the Principate was that of a simple denigrator. Of course he sees and emphasizes its unpleasant aspects, and of course he is nostalgic for those Republican days of brilliant and simple glory; but he also knows that the Republic was out of date, and that the Principate was a necessity, even if a necessary evil. Simple and straightforward denigration or praise would be inadequate for the Principate: should we be surprised if they are inadequate for Germanicus too, and the alternative atmosphere and world that he comes to embody? We are certainly encouraged to dwell particularly on the points where Germanicus' lack of sureness is plain, just as we are encouraged to notice the factors that make the Principate as a whole so inevitable. But simple derision or exculpation is unlikely to be the most important response, any more than it was with Antigone, Aeneas, or Achilles.

If this is right, then unqualified approval or disapproval is inadequate; but we should also consider ways in which simple ethical appraisal is not so much inadequate as irrelevant. Consider the mutinies again. If Germanicus fails to match up to the danger, then that may be less a commentary on him than on the seriousness of the threat. The Pannonian and German mutinies indeed follow a tellingly similar narrative pattern, as Ross emphasized,[21] and by various techniques Tacitus encourages us to compare them; but the point of the comparison may be one about the armies rather than the individuals. That is certainly the stress when the comparison becomes explicit; Velleius may compare the behaviour of Drusus and Germanicus, but

---

[20] It has something in common with that briefly presented by Borzsák (1970), but largely ignored since then (though cf. Rutland 1987: 153–4).

[21] Ross (1973: 211–20): so too Shotter (1968: 198) and cf. Everts (1926: 41, 48). Goodyear (1972; 1981: esp. 1.254–5) is too sceptical. On the parallels within the two sequences see now Williams (1997: 57–61) and esp. Woodman (2006b: 304–8).

Tacitus compares the two threats.[22] This is a greater danger than Blaesus (*A.* 1.19) or Drusus (*A.* 1.25–6, 29–30) had to confront in Pannonia: the point may be partly that *even* a Germanicus, with all his natural rapport with the troops, can do no better than this. Not that individuals can be left out of it completely. One thing that makes the German situation so much more menacing is that the Germans have a contender for the purple who needs to be taken seriously, Germanicus himself. These are troops, it is stressed, who might carry Germanicus to power—were he only willing.[23] In the part played by the mutinies within the *Annals* as a whole, that point is substantial—and of course the mutinies are 'historically unimportant' only in the crudest sense, for they introduce so many important themes to illuminate the crucial role an army can play in making or breaking a *princeps*. These themes are the more striking here for their stark juxtaposition with the polite nonsense of the accession debate,[24] and they would clearly have recurred ring-fashion in the closing books, where the power of the legions will at last be shatteringly unleashed.[25] An important notion in the *Annals* is this idea of the Roman world waking up to political reality, so that the initial hypocrisies can be abandoned: the legions are the central element of that reality. But, as far as this simple point is concerned, praise or blame of Germanicus is not very important. It is the legions, rather than Germanicus himself, who here absorb our interest.

---

[22] Thus *A.* 1.31.1, 'Isdem ferme diebus isdem causis Germanicae legiones turbatae, quanto plures tanto uiolentius'; *A.* 1.31.5, 'non unus haec, ut Pannonicas inter legiones Percennius, nec apud trepidas militum aures, alios ualidiores exercitus respicientium, sed multa seditionis ora uocesque'; cf. also Tiberius' arguments at *A.* 1.47.1, 'ualidior per Germaniam exercitus, propior apud Pannoniam; ille Galliarum opibus subnixus, hic Italiae imminens'. Contrast Vell. 2.125.4, 'quo quidem tempore ut pleraque ignouit Germanicus, ita Drusus . . . prisca antiquaque seueritate usus ancipitia sibi <sus>tinere <maluit> quam exemplo perniciosa' (Woodman's text).

[23] *A.* 1.31.1: 'et magna spe fore ut Germanicus Caesar imperium alterius pati nequiret daretque se legionibus ui sua cuncta tracturis'. Also perhaps the implications of *A.* 1.33.2 (see the section on consistency), 'quippe Drusi magna apud populum Romanum memoria, credebaturque, *si rerum poti<t>us foret,* libertatem redditurus; unde in Germanicum fauor et spes eadem . . . [34.1] Sed Germanicum *quanto summae spei* **propior**, tanto impensius pro Tiberio niti'. More clearly at *A.* 1.35.3, and already in Tiberius' fears at *A.* 1.7.6.

[24] The point becomes explicit in the popular grumbles at *A.* 1.46.1, 'trepida ciuitas incusare Tiberium quod, dum patres et plebem, inualida et inermia, cunctatione ficta ludificetur, dissideat interim miles neque duorum adulescentium nondum adulta auctoritate comprimi queat'.

[25] So Syme (1958a: 375).

Again, it is doubtless significant that Germanicus learns from his mistakes; just as he learns his lesson from the difficulties of the campaign of AD 15 (*A.* 1.55–71), and sensibly builds a fleet for the next campaign (*A.* 2.5–6).[26] Germanicus, in a crude sense, has the capacity to get better: that is one reason why unmasked derision would be an inapposite response to his initial uncertainties. Almost all Tacitus' other principals get worse. The explicit exception is Vespasian in the *Histories*, the first emperor to have shown any improvement;[27] and parallel points could be made about Vespasian's treatment when he first appears in the *Histories*, where the portrayal has to be similarly unstrident for similar reasons. His depiction is more morally explicit, but is again more positive than we might have expected, and his role in the more disquieting events is often blurred. Once again, crude dismissiveness would not be appropriate, not for a character with many good qualities already, and with the possibility of improvement.

There are more fundamental points. First, one could observe how Tacitus develops the theme of Germanicus' rapport with the troops, and here again we notice the contrast with Drusus, more austere and restrained, less warm and open. 'Promptum ad asperiora ingenium Druso erat,' says Tacitus when Drusus acts so effectively in eliminating the ringleaders, 'Drusus naturally inclined to the harsher option' (*A.* 1.29.4).[28] That is some way from Germanicus' *comitas* and *ciuile ingenium*. Suggestively, Drusus' harshness produces less bloodshed than Germanicus' openness; the warmer style does not always work. But Tacitus certainly introduces two ways of treating armies, the dignity of Drusus and the more intimate theatricality of Germanicus.

---

[26] Notice too the new surge of impetus when he turns to the campaigning, and a reversion to active rather than passive verbs: cf. n.10 and Pigoń (2008: 301–2).

[27] *H.* 1.50.4, 'et ambigua de Vespasiano fama, solusque omnium ante se principum in melius mutatus est': cf. Damon (2006). For his early characterization, cf. also esp. *H.* 2.5, 80, 82, 84; Mucianus, Antonius, Arrius Varus, even Titus and Domitian occupy the narrative focus to a notable degree, and (with the exception of Titus) they are also the ones who absorb any moral stigma.

[28] The point holds whether we take *promptum . . . erat* as a generalization about Drusus (thus e.g. Grant 1956: 49–50), 'Drusus had a natural preference for severe measures') or as relevant only to the immediate context, as Woodman (2004) prefers ('Drusus was instinctively ready for the more drastic of these alternatives'): when faced with the choice between a gentler and harsher course, Drusus was inclined to the *asperiora* of these two proposals. I agree with Woodman, but the choice still highlights the contrast between Drusus' 'natural' (notice *ingenium*) approach and that of Germanicus.

And Germanicus' way is the more sinister.[29] Certainly, his manner—and, importantly, Agrippina's too—inspires actions that strike fear into an imperial heart. Consider for instance the closing scene of the German campaign of 15. Agrippina ostentatiously greets the soldiers as they return from their near-destruction at the hands of Arminius, and 'acts the commander' in distributing clothes and medications, just as she did in forbidding the destruction of the Rhine bridge (*A.* 1.69). Then Germanicus uses his own money to help his men; and not merely does he fulfil the role of a good general and tour the wounded, he does so in his own distinctive style, with *comitas* (*A.* 1.71.3):

> *Vtque cladis memoriam etiam comitate leniret, circumire saucios, facta singulorum extollere; uulnera intuens alium spe, alium gloria, cunctos adloquio et cura sibique et proelio firmabat.*

> He softened the memory of their defeat by his personal warmth, going round the wounded and praising each man for what he had done; and inspecting their wounds he encouraged some with hope, others with pride, and all by his friendly greeting and care, strengthening them for battle and for himself.

No wonder Tiberius is incensed by their blithe actions—now, when he is convinced Agrippina's conduct is not straightforward (*A.* 1.69.3–5); later, when Germanicus cheerfully goes off to Egypt,[30] touristlike, then starts meddling with the corn supply (*A.* 2.59); or even earlier, at the suppression of the mutiny (*A.* 1.52.1):

> *Nuntiata ea Tiberium laetitia curaque adfecere; gaudebat oppressam seditionem, sed quod largiendis pecuniis et missione festinata fauorem militum quaesiuisset, bellica quoque Germanici gloria angebatur.*

> The news brought pleasure to Tiberius, but also concern. He was delighted that the mutiny had been suppressed, but he was distressed on the grounds that Germanicus had contrived to win[31] popularity with the soldiers by lavishing money upon them and allowing them early dismissal from the service; distressed too by his military glory.

---

[29] Cf. Borzsák (1970: 288), though he develops this idea rather differently.

[30] On this episode see now Kelly (2010).

[31] *Quaesiuisset* more likely suggests 'sought' than simply 'acquired' (*OLD* s.v. 'quaero' 7; Woodman [2004] has 'had won'), though my translation here keeps the ambiguity: cf. Goodyear (1972, 1981: 1.322). The unfriendly suggestions of *largiendis* should also be taken into account.

The perception may be a false one: notice the subjunctive rather than indicative *quaesiuisset*. This is the perception of Tiberius rather than of Tacitus. But one can understand it.

There is indeed a sense in which the natural successors of Germanicus are not only the later members of his own family (those on whom the mantle of his popularity descends), but people like Piso and Plancina, then Sejanus. Piso and Plancina foster the troops in the east, ironically in order to undermine Germanicus and Agrippina themselves; but when Piso removes the severe disciplinarians among the centurions and tribunes, or Plancina so disquietingly views the troops' exercises herself, even when Piso irregularly disobeys orders in trying to enter a debarred province, in each case they are tellingly mirroring the earlier actions of Germanicus and Agrippina themselves.[32] Germanicus had won popularity through his brand of informality; his review of the centurions had equally removed the severe and unpopular; Agrippina had been the one to greet the returning soldiers; Germanicus had not scrupled to enter Egypt against Tiberius' wishes. Now their own behaviour is being turned against themselves. Germanicus and Agrippina may themselves be presented as achingly innocent of any disloyalty, even perhaps of any malice against Tiberius, but they presage very sinister themes indeed.

And is it surprising that Tacitus fails to give explicit moral judgement? Straightforward approval or disapproval would again be hardly appropriate. The individuals may be innocent, their actions highly threatening. But it is natural that the instances are highlighted, because they are so suggestive of the future. To ask whether Tacitus

---

[32] 'Et postquam Syriam ac legiones attigit, largitione, ambitu, infimos manipularium iuuando, *cum ueteres centuriones, seueros tribunos demoueret* locaque eorum clientibus suis uel deterrimo cuique attribueret, desidiam in castris, licentiam in urbibus, uagum ac lasciuientem per agros militem sineret, eo usque corruptionis prouectus est, ut sermone uulgi parens legionum haberetur. nec Plancina se intra decora feminis tenebat, sed *exercitio equitum, decursibus cohortium interesse*, in Agrippinam, in Germanicum contumelias iacere, quibusdam etiam bonorum militum ad mala obsequia promptis, quod haud inuito imperatore ea fieri occultus rumor incedebat' (*A.* 2.55.5–6). Cf. Germanicus at *A.* 1.44 and Agrippina at *A.* 1.69; for the dangers of such feminine activity cf. *A.* 3.33.3, perhaps overstated, but an off-key version of something true: cf. Ginsburg (1993: 93–4). For Piso's attempt to return to Syria, cf. *A.* 2.69.1, 2.76–81, 3.12.2–3, etc.; for Germanicus' entry into Egypt, *A.* 2.59. Cf. also Sejanus, who equally tampers with the regular chain of command and appointments, and adopts a sinister *comitas* (*A.* 4.2.2); and later the younger Agrippina (*A.* 12.37.4, 13.18.2; cf. 14.7.2, 14.11.1), here as so often a darker counterpart of her mother: cf. now Ginsburg (2006: esp. 24, 26–7, 37–8 n.54, 42–4, 113–14, 129 n.94).

thinks Germanicus a good or bad thing is like asking whether Herodotus thinks Croesus or Cyrus, or whether Thucydides thinks Pericles, an unqualified good thing; and it is not coincidental that we
encounter similar critical problems in those cases too. In all these
cases we have brilliant figures, but ones that unleash or foster forces
that may eventually be destructive to the states they build, when those
forces recur with other, lesser figures.

GERMANICUS AND THE PAST

Yet there is a difference. Cyrus and Pericles are very shrewd. They
know the games they play, and the dangers. What of Germanicus?
That aching innocence is very suggestive: he is playing with forces far
more menacing than he seems to realize, and there is a lack of
sureness of touch in dealing with these central forces of the Principate—another quality that combines naturally with that *comitas* and
impetuosity and openness. The grimy and stifling realities of imperial
politics are not the stuff for the noble and brilliant Germanicus: even
when he senses something of their nature, when for instance he
recognizes Tiberius' envy (*inuidia*, A. 2.22.1, 2.26.5), we know he is
outmatched. He belongs in a simpler, older world.

Take for instance A. 2.43. Tacitus has just led back to the struggles
for the succession. He has prepared for them by a flashback to the
sordid realities *under Augustus* in chapter 42, when Archelaus of
Cappadocia so sadly misread the future by snubbing Tiberius at
Rhodes. It was not even the king's own fault: Augustus' closest friends
had advised him to favour the rising star of Gaius Caesar. The Roman
court had evidently been just as calculating then as we shall see them
now; and just as preoccupied with the succession, and just as astray.
Archelaus now eventually pays for it, lured to Rome by Livia's letters.
(Livia, so often underplayed by Tacitus, naturally recurs in such
contexts of intrigue.) Archelaus may well understand the deceit, but
has to come anyway; and he soon dies, rather mysteriously. Such are
the ways of the court.

Now we have the notice of Germanicus' and Piso's mission to the
east, with Livia again active, stirring Plancina to take on Agrippina.
The court was divided and at odds; sides were silently forming
for Drusus or Germanicus. Tiberius favoured Drusus, which itself

strengthened the support of others for Germanicus and Agrippina; the details of their descent allow some hints of earlier, much more destructive rivalries, for Germanicus' grandfather was Mark Antony and his great-uncle Augustus. But the brothers remained on splendidly good terms, unshaken by the rivalry and exertions of those closest to them: 'sed fratres egregie concordes et proximorum certaminibus inconcussi', 'Yet the brothers were exceptionally affectionate, and unshaken by the conflicts of their kin' (*A.* 2.43.6). The lack of contact, here between both brothers and the style of the whole court, is seldom clearer.[33] Neither Drusus[34] nor Germanicus fits naturally into the seething jealousies that surround them; and the flashback to Augustus reminds us that ruthless intrigue is no transient feature, but a familiar concomitant of the Principate and the court.

Other points in this part of Book 2 reinforce the impression. Germanicus continues to emerge, not merely as unworldly, but also as distinctively connected with the past.[35] That has really been true since his first mention at *A.* 1.3.5–6, where his war in Germany was immediately introduced as the great exception, the one decent war Rome was still fighting.[36] Then, in his formal introduction at *A.* 1.33

---

[33] Rhiannon Ash puts to me the comparison with Titus, who at *H.* 4.52 actually accosts Vespasian and intervenes on behalf of his brother (in his case, a most disreputable brother). Other themes too link Germanicus and Titus, e.g. Titus' taste for tourism and sightseeing (*H.* 2.2–4). As she suggests, the comparison between the complex foilings of Tiberius–Germanicus and of Titus–Domitian could also be taken further; possibly too the contrast of the two, very different brotherly relationships of Germanicus–Drusus and Titus–Domitian.

[34] Drusus duly continues some similar themes once Germanicus is dead. Thus his deluded faith in his marriage is strongly hinted at *A.* 3.34.6; it is not coincidence that Sejanus is introduced a few lines later (*A.* 3.35.2). Drusus' ill-judged openness is similarly stressed at *A.* 4.3.

[35] It is arguable that this impression is reinforced by literary allusion; in particular, echoes of Virgil cluster in the narrative of Germanicus' campaigns. But Goodyear in particular has emphasized the methodological problems in identifying Virgilian allusions. I believe he is too sceptical, but the issue is too complicated to pursue here. See now Pagán (1999: 305–6) and (2002: 52).

[36] 'at hercule Germanicum, Druso ortum, octo apud Rhenum legionibus imposuit adscirique per adoptionem a Tiberio iussit, quamquam esset in domo Tiberii filius iuuenis, sed quo pluribus munimentis insisteret. bellum ea tempestate nullum nisi aduersus Germanos supererat, abolendae magis infamiae ob amissum cum Quintilio Varo exercitum quam cupidine proferendi imperii aut dignum ob praemium' ['Yet by Hercules, he put Germanicus, Drusus' son, in charge of eight legions on the Rhine and ordered him to be taken up in adoption by Tiberius, although there was in Tiberius' household a son who was already a young man; but he did this in order to count on further safeguards. At that time, there was no war remaining except the one against

(quoted earlier), his popularity was influenced by people's memories of Nero Drusus, and the hopes that he might re-introduce the republic. Thus the association is not merely with the past *tout court*, but the political past in particular, and the flavour of the Republic (cf. *A.* 2.82.2, when the theme recurs after Germanicus' death). When Nero Drusus was mentioned again at *A.* 2.8.1, it was once more in a context that recalled the aggressive expansionist policy he, like Germanicus, had espoused.[37] Now, in the middle of Book 2, the hints of the past come thicker. There is his triumph, introducing (and presumably advanced in the year's chronology to introduce) the calendar year 17.[38] An old-fashioned style of notice for an old-fashioned thing. But as people watch they once more think back ominously to Nero Drusus, the Republican hero, and Marcellus: 'breues et infaustos populi Romani amores' (*A.* 2.41.2), 'the affections of the Roman people never lasted, their favourites never prospered'. Suitably enough, the next time they will compare father and son is when they hear of Germanicus' death (*A.* 2.82.2), then when they contrast the character of the two cortèges (*A.* 3.5).[39] But for the moment Germanicus reaches the east and begins to tour, 'eager to see these old and famous sites' (*A.* 2.54.1). He duly visits places like Actium, Athens, and Troy,

---

the Germans, and that was more to erase the disgrace of the army lost with Quintilius Varus than through any desire of extending the empire or for some worthy prize']: thus even this war is not as decent as all that. The initial 'at hercule' hardly evinces Tacitus' delighted satisfaction, as Koestermann (1963–68: 1.71) oddly suggests, but does emphasize the starkness of the contrast; note also *A.* 1.14.3, another mention of Germanicus, again in contrast ('*at* Germanico Caesari'). But such mentions of Germanicus, even as an exception or a contrast, are notably sparse in *A.* 1.1–15; cf. Koestermann (1963–8: 1.72, 89); Borzsák (1970: 280). Tacitus is at pains to exclude him from the distasteful savour of such meaningless politics.

[37] I owe this point to Miriam Griffin.

[38] 'C. Caelio L. Pomponio consulibus Germanicus Caesar a.d, VII Kal. Iunias triumphauit de Cheruscis C<h>attisque et Angriuariis quaeque aliae nationes usque ad Albim colunt', *A.* 2.41.2. On the chronology, cf. the commentators, and esp. Ginsburg (1981: 22, 36): she acutely observes that the evocation of the past is slightly off-key, as Tacitus suggests annalistic style at precisely the moment that he perverts it by his distortion of the year's internal sequence. The evocation of the past is reinforced by *A.* 2.41.1, with its suggestions of continuity both with Augustus (Bovillae: cf. Timpe 1968: 52–3) and with Julius (Fors Fortuna): there too Tacitus may have distorted precise chronology (Goodyear 1972, 1981: 2.312).

[39] Tony Woodman points out to me that the entire sequence of Germanicus' burial (*A.* 3.1–4) is strikingly reminiscent of the burial of Nero Drusus thirty years before; if the parallel is sensed, that underlines even more the importance of the family connection.

variously so rich in antique suggestions, and then, particularly, Egypt, 'for acquaintance with their antiquity' (*cognoscendae antiquitatis*, A. 2.59.1): an arch and mannered syntactic construction for an old-fashioned thing. Tacitus seizes the opportunity to discourse on the ancient origins of Canopus (*A.* 2.60), with talk of Menelaus and Hercules, Ramses and ancient hieroglyphs. And it is interesting that in Egypt Germanicus puts on his ostentatious show of civility 'in emulation of P. Scipio'. That too looks back to Book 1, making explicit what was there suggested allusively: for it was a speech of Scipio in Livy 28 that had been the model for Germanicus' speech at *A.* 1.42–3. How appropriate that Rome's most romantic general, as described in its most colourful and nostalgic historian, should serve as Germanicus' model.[40]

SYMPATHETIC AND UNSYMPATHETIC CHARACTERS

There is more to say about the processional arrival (*aduentus*) at Alexandria, where Germanicus again shows himself so *ciuilis*: for he is here repeating his performance at Athens a few chapters earlier (*A.* 2.53.3).

> *Hinc uentum Athenas, foederique sociae et uetustae urbis datum, ut uno lictore uteretur. excepere Graeci quaesitissimis honoribus, uetera suorum facta dictaque praeferentes, quo plus dignationis adulatio haberet.*

Next he arrived at Athens, and, as a mark of respect to the city's ancient traditions and her status as an ally, he entered with just one lictor. The Greeks greeted him with the choicest of honours, proclaiming the deeds and words of their ancestors to lend dignity to their flattery.

When Piso follows him to Athens, his entry is very different, part of the systematic contrast of the two figures that Tacitus is here developing (*A.* 2.55.1–2).

---

[40] The scepticism of Goodyear (1972, 1981: 1.288) is excessive; he is nearer the mark at (1972, 1981: 2.377). There is a good deal more to be said about the relation of Tacitus' narrative to Livy 28: see Woodman (2006b: 312–19, 321–2) and Ash (2010b).

At Cn. Piso, quo properantius destinata inciperet, ciuitatem Atheniensium turbido incessu exterritam oratione saeua increpat, oblique Germanicum perstringens, quod contra decus Romani nominis non Athenienses tot cladibus exstinctos, sed conluuiem illam nationum comitate nimia coluisset: hos enim esse Mithridatis aduersus Sullam, Antonii aduersus diuum Augustum socios. etiam uetera obiectabat, quae in Macedones improspere, uiolenter in suos fecissent, offensus urbi propria quoque ira, quia Theophilum quendam Areo iudicio falsi damnatum precibus suis non concederent.

But Piso, in a hurry to carry through his plans, burst violently into Athens, and delivered a fierce speech to reprimand the terrified city. He criticized Germanicus indirectly for being excessively affable and demeaning the dignity of Rome; these were not even Athenians, for that nation had been destroyed by its many disasters, these were just a mongrel mix of races; they were the people who had helped Mithridates against Sulla, then Antony against the divine Augustus. He even adduced ancient reproaches, their failures against the Macedonians, their violent crimes against their own people. And he also had his own reasons to be annoyed and angry with the city: he had interceded for a certain Theophilus, condemned by the Areopagus for forgery, and Athens had refused to yield to his request.

Yet this little instance also suggests that the 'sympathy' question is more complicated than we have yet seen. It is not difficult to see who wins in terms of attractiveness. Piso, like Tiberius so often, even has his own petty reasons for a grudge. Yet one cannot simply dismiss Piso's attack on the Athenians. That is partly because it has some style, particularly when aimed against Germanicus: two can play at the game of evoking the past, and Piso's historical allusions make some fair points. And, if one recalls Tacitus' own gibe at the end of *A.* 2.53.3—'proclaiming the deeds and words of their ancestors to lend dignity to their flattery'—it becomes clear that his own sympathies are not all on one side. That tone is closer to Piso than to Germanicus.[41] Piso may be unattractive, just as Tiberius is unattractive, but both of them often talk sense.

That reflection is supported by other features of this same part of Book 2. For one thing, there is the oddity of chapters 44–6, describing

[41] Thus, e.g., Hardinghaus (1932: 45–6) concluded that Tacitus' sympathies lean toward Piso, and that is why he has allowed him so sharp and pointed a view; cf. Syme (1958a: 513); Edelmaier (1964: 172 n.57). That too is an oversimplification.

the war of Inguiomerus and Maroboduus against Arminius. Tacitus' perspective notoriously tends to be limited to Rome, the city and its politics and its campaigns; yet here we have that rarity, a lengthy passage devoted to an internal foreign war. Why? Surely because this ties in with *A.* 2.26, the earlier account of Tiberius' reasons for recalling Germanicus from Germany. 'Now that enough had been done to win vengeance,' Tiberius had argued, 'the Cherusci too and the other rebel tribes could be left to their internal wranglings.' His motives are clearly suspect: 'Germanicus could see that his arguments were fictitious, and that he himself was being torn away through jealousy from the glory he had already won.' But still *what Tiberius says* is completely right, and Tacitus cares enough about bearing him out to vary his narrative technique, irregularly including those foreign wars. Tacitus is not doing his best for Germanicus with intransigent material, but going out of his way to ensure that the insight of Tiberius, along with some reservations about Germanicus, should be sensed.

Nor is this the first time, for Tacitus' treatment of the 'futile obsequies'[42] for Varus' legions had been very similar (*A.* 1.62.2).

Quod Tiberio haud probatum, seu cuncta Germanici in deterius trahenti, siue exercitum imagine caesorum insepultorumque tardatum ad proelia et formidolosiorem hostium credebat; neque imperatorem auguratu et uetustissimis caerimoniis praeditum adtrectare feralia debuisse.

Tiberius disapproved. Perhaps it was because he always took an un-favourable view of Germanicus' actions; perhaps he thought that the clear memory of the dead and unburied would make the army more reluctant to fight and more nervous of the enemy. He thought too that a general who was an augur, sanctified by the most ancient of rituals, should not have touched anything to do with the dead.

Once again, Tiberius comes out as unattractive: the possibility is raised that he would disapprove on principle of anything Germanicus did. Yet one of his substantial points is largely justified, for the Roman troops are indeed terrified by Arminius, and come within an ace of replaying the Varus disaster. However unpleasant, Tiberius is in touch with reality; and once again it is Tacitus' own narrative economy, and the

---

[42] The famous phrase of Furneaux (1896, 1907: 1.138). On the episode cf. esp. Woodman (1979; 1988a: 168–79) and now Pagán (1999; 2002).

extraordinarily dramatic style with which he goes on to describe the German attack, that ensure that the point goes home.

Not that in either case Tacitus' appraisal is unequivocal, and simple dismissiveness of Germanicus would be as inappropriate as simple enthusiasm for Tiberius. There is the questionable character of the emperor's motives, and at *A.* 2.26 the unattractive way he appeals to Germanicus' own best qualities, his unselfishness and fraternal affection. And the rights and wrongs of the issues are not straightforward. As far as *A.* 2.26 is concerned, if the future narrative justifies Tiberius, the immediately preceding narrative has done something to support Germanicus' view that only another year would be necessary to round off the campaign. The preceding chapter has stressed the amazement of the Germans that the Romans had recovered from the storm so quickly: they thought indeed that the Romans were invincible. Rather than right or wrong ways, we really just have two *different* ways of proceeding against enemies here, both of which have something to say for them: the way of Germanicus, old-fashioned, bloody, but glorious; and the way of Tiberius, diplomatic, modern, unglamorous, but highly effective.[43]

It should now be clear that either strident approval or strident disapproval would be inappropriate, either for Germanicus or for Tiberius; and that the whole question of Tacitus' treatment of Germanicus is a reflex of his approach to the Principate as a whole.[44] Just as Tacitus can regard the Principate as a regrettable necessity—'the Roman state could only survive with one-man rule', 'after the battle of Actium was fought and peace made it necessary for all power to be conferred on one man', 'there was no cure for the faction-ridden state except a single ruler'[45]—so he can regard Germanicus rather as he

---

[43] This also helps to explain the point stressed by Timpe (1968: esp. 8–23) that Tacitus strongly marks out the AD 14–16 campaigns as a separate war, whereas Velleius (2.120.2, 2.121.1, 2.122.2, 2.129.2), and possibly Aufidius Bassus, preferred to assume the continuity of this fighting with that begun in AD 10 by Tiberius himself. It is precisely the contrast of the two styles that engages Tacitus: a single *bellum Germanicum*, fought continuously and on a similar pattern by the two men, would not fit at all.

[44] This was briefly suggested by Ross (1973: 225–7); but he developed it rather differently, suggesting that Tacitus' view of the Republic was simply negative. Borzsák (1970: 291–2) is again more perceptive.

[45] 'neque alia re Rom<ana> [?] quam si unus imperitet' ['there is no way for the Roman state to function other than if one man is in charge'] (*A.* 4.33.2, though cf. Martin and Woodman 1989: 173–4 on the textual uncertainty); 'postquam bellatum

regards the past, particularly the Republican past: nostalgically attractive, brilliant, the sort of thing it is good to write about (*A*. 4.32–3); but out of keeping with the real needs of the modern world. Tiberius introduces many of the themes of the Principate, both the distaste and the sense of reality. In the same way, Germanicus helps us to grasp the alternative, with his style of politics and his style of war. Brilliant, yes, but brilliantly anachronistic.

A FOIL FOR TIBERIUS?

Let us return to Germanicus' death. So much of the emphasis falls on men's reactions as they hear the news, both in the east and in Rome and Italy, and reflect on the hero they have lost and the sad and sinister circumstances of his death. That should remind us of some reflections on another sinister death: *multus hinc ipso de Augusto sermo*, 'then there was much talk about Augustus himself', and the introductory reactions to *Augustus*' death at *A*. 1.9–10. When people thought of Germanicus, they thought of Alexander (*A*. 2.73). That is an extravagant comparison, of course, but it is suggestive again that the great romantic figure of the past should spring to their minds: the past, even if overlaid by unreality (as Alexander's memory was always overlaid by unreality).[46] When people thought of Augustus, they thought less of his merits than of the various features of the situation

---

apud Actium atque omnem potestatem ad unum conferri pacis interfuit' ['after the battle of Actium when the interests of peace were served by all power being conferred on one man'] *(H.* 1.1.1); 'non aliud discordantis patriae remedium quam <ut> ab uno regeretur' ['there had been no other remedy for his turbulent fatherland than for it to be ruled by one man'] *(A.* 1.9.4). This last passage is properly speaking not Tacitus' own judegment but that of Augustus' supporters; but, tellingly, it is one of the few points not countered in 1.10, nor qualified by Tacitus' own earlier narrative. Cf. Classen (1988) on Tacitus' acceptance of the Principate, and of the new unrepublican virtues that it made necessary. On this last aspect cf. also now Raaflaub (2008), who gives an incisive treatment of the 'regrettable' aspects but seems to me to underplay Tacitus' acknowledgement of the 'necessity'.

[46] Cf. esp. Borzsák (1969; 1970; 1982); Lehmann (1971). The Alexander comparison was implicit in earlier parts of the narrative (esp. at *A*. 1.61.1), when 'cupido Caesarem inuadit' rather as *pothos* often overcame Alexander; but as usual Tacitus adds a distinctive note, for he also hints that Germanicus shared the impulsive spontaneity of his troops (*A*. 1.49.3, 'cupido inuolat'). But on Germanicus' *cupido* and Alexander's *pothos* see now Kelly (2010), who is sceptical about any echo.

that made his rule so necessary, and the regrettable aspects which that rule still showed. The contrast with Germanicus is very clear. There are two views about Augustus and only one about Germanicus, but it trivializes the position to infer that this is because Tacitus is sympathetic to this favourable view.[47] Tacitus has done enough in the narrative itself to suggest the necessary qualifications, and there is no negative view because there was no similar strand of unpopularity at the time. People were keen on Germanicus, and that is itself an important historical fact; just as for Tacitus it is an important fact that people were cynical about Augustus.

This ring with Augustus' obituary is most suggestive. It reflects the unity of the first two books, and the poles of the comparison are here, not Germanicus and Tiberius, but Germanicus and Augustus. Or, better, the whole world of Germanicus and the world of the Principate: for so much of Tiberius is already there in Augustus, the murderousness, the hypocrisy, the bloody elimination of rivals, the *dissimulatio*, even the choice of a worse successor. These are qualities not just of individuals, but of the Principate as a whole, the patterns of behaviour the system recurrently imposes on each new *princeps*. The manner of Augustus might be different from that of Tiberius; Augustus has his own brand of *comitas* and civility, though a more calculating variety than that of Germanicus.[48] But the difference of style is a faint mask for the shared and deeper truth.

So we have by now two refinements of the view of Germanicus as a foil for Tiberius. First, insofar as he is a foil, the effect is anything but black and white. Even *1066 and All That* not merely divided kings into good things and bad things, but also introduced a subtler division, those who were right but repulsive and those who were wrong but romantic; and both aspects are here important, the rightness of Tiberius as well as his repulsiveness. Second, it is not just Germanicus

---

[47] Thus Goodyear (1972, 1981: 1.33 and n.1, and 2.416–17).

[48] Cf. *A.* 1.54.2, just before Tacitus reverts to Germanicus: notice 'ciuile *rebatur*'; then *A.* 1.76.4, again at the games, where the political benefit is plain. Even Tiberius can show *comitas* when it is politic (*A.* 3.81.1, 6.50.1), just as he can leave an impression of being *ciuilis* (*A.* 3.22.4, 4.21.2; cf. 2.34.3, 3.76.2; he can also fail, 1.72.2, 6.13.2). But this is the shrewd style of the accomplished autocrat (cf. Wallace-Hadrill 1982), not the natural manner of a Germanicus. Cf. also O'Gorman (2000: 48 n.5), who prefers to stress that with Augustus and Tiberius weight falls on what actions the emperors themselves thought *ciuile*; with Germanicus, the point is rather how contemporaries and the reader interpret his behaviour.

who is a foil, and not just Tiberius on the other side. It is also Augustus, and the whole pattern of the emperor's behaviour; and not just the emperor, but the whole shoddy business of politics at Rome, with senators who are as ruthless, as hypocritical, and as backbiting as their *princeps*. The whole court is split by their enthusiastic participation in the succession intrigues; Germanicus' so-called friends, the *amici accendendis offensionibus callidi* ('friends who know how to inflame mutual resentments', *A.* 2.57.2), have something to answer for in the east.[49] Emperor and courtiers deserve one another, and complement one another; and Germanicus and his world serve as a foil for the whole ambience, not just for Tiberius himself.

On Germanicus' side, one should also notice his adversary Arminius.[50] Germanicus and Arminius deserve each other too, and they have much in common. Both are often viewed in the context of their families: the first time we see Arminius we also see his pregnant wife (*A.* 1.57.4), a tableau as memorable as that of Agrippina at *A.* 1.40–41.[51] Both men are the popular figures who struggle against the forces of tyranny; both are associated with ideas of *libertas*. And we remember the way Arminius dies, *dolo propinquorum*, strangely and darkly 'tricked by his kinsmen'; we remember the struggles of Arminius with the jealous Inguiomerus, and such a perversion of the natural ordering of the family. Inguiomerus was uncle to Arminius; Tiberius was uncle to Germanicus.[52] There are also a number of more specific mirrorings of Tiberius in Inguiomerus' ally Maroboduus;[53] both were hypocritical, both sunk into a slothful old age, both were typified by jealousy and perfidy, both were deeply unloved by their subjects: the

---

[49] Like Agrippina's *proximi* later (*A.* 4.12.4, 4.54.1), and the friends of their children (*A.* 4.59.3). Some things do not change.

[50] On Arminius, cf. Edelmaier (1964); Timpe (1968: esp. 131–7). The mirroring is elaborate, but anything but mechanical: they can be contrasted too, e.g. in the juxtaposition of Arminius' emotion and ferocity and Germanicus' thoughtfulness at *A.* 2.10 and 2.11.1 (cf. *A.* 2.20.1). Then Arminius' misreadings of the Romans at *A.* 2.15 are proved false by the narrative, as surely as Germanicus' analysis of *A.* 2.14 is proved true. But Germanicus himself is not free of impetuosity and misreadings elsewhere.

[51] Cf. O'Gorman (2000: 72–3).

[52] Some of these points are noted by commentators (e.g. Koestermann 1963–8: 1.201, 414; Goodyear 1972, 1981: 2.447); Edelmaier (1964) brings them into a coherent scheme (followed by Borzsák 1970: 290–91).

[53] As Edelmaier (1964: 123 nn.105–7, 126 n.116) suggests. He also finds a parallel between Tiberius and Arminius' earlier antagonist Segestes (95–6 n.33): a little more far-fetched, perhaps.

strong, and totally perverted, praise that Tiberius gives to Maroboduus at *A.* 2.63 is strangely fitting to both. Arminius' sneer at this *satelles Caesaris*, 'Caesar's acolyte' (*A.* 2.45.3), is suggestively near the mark. Maroboduus, like Inguiomerus, is clearly less engaging than Arminius; yet the popular young hero, fighting wars in an old-fashioned way, is ultimately no match for the older, less attractive, but very shrewd modern manipulator. Neither Germanicus nor Arminius is at ease in the shoddy world of guile, and both are promptly removed from it. Book 2 is introduced, rather at the expense of chronology,[54] with a summary of the east, looking forward to the second half. It is closed, again at the expense of chronology, with the obituary of Arminius, which looks back to the beginning.[55] Germanicus and Arminius share the book, just as they share an anachronistic style. This sort of mirroring[56] may seem artificial to us; it would seem less so to a Roman audience that was acclimatized to ideas of *metus hostilis*, the notion that a worthy adversary is necessary to bring out the best in Roman military virtue. Arminius even brings out the best in Tiberius, inspiring him—of all people—to remark that deceit and concealment are not the Roman way (*A.* 2.88.1).[57] It will take adversaries of a different, more treacherous character to allow Tiberius to revert to his more natural style.[58] Sallust and Livy had presented pictures along the same lines, where antagonists of a particular

---

[54] Cf. Koestermann (1956: 478) and (1963–8: 1.264).

[55] Cf. Graf (1931: 20–21), and others since.

[56] It is very like the points of parallel that Tacitus elsewhere traces between campaigns and similar events in Rome; cf. esp. Keitel (1978; 1993).

[57] 'non fraude neque occultis, sed palam et armatum populum Romanum hostes suos ulcisci' ['the Roman people took vengeance on their enemies not by trickery or concealment, but openly and armed']: an expressive echo of Arminius' own proud claim at *A.* 1.59.3, 'non enim se proditione neque aduersus feminas grauidas, sed palam aduersus armatos bellum tractare' ['it was not his habit to conduct war by betrayal or against pregnant women, but openly against armed men']. Goodyear (1972, 1981: 2.446) notes the parallel but not its point; and e.g. Walker (1952: 124), Syme (1958a: 428), Edelmaier (1964: 101–2, 133–4, 140), Borzsák (1970: 290), and Straub (1980: 225–7) put it rather differently. Tony Woodman has also observed to me that the puzzling hints of Arminius' 'Romanness' continue at 2.88.2 with his description as 'proeliis ambiguus, bello non uictus' ['equivocal in battle, undefeated in war'], echoing a claim that Romans liked to make about themselves (cf. Goodyear ad loc.).

[58] *A.* 6.32.1, 'destinata retinens, consiliis et astu res externas moliri' ['maintaining his policy of handling foreign affairs by planning and stratagem']. Deception merits deception: *A.* 11.19.2, 'nec inritae aut degeneres insidiae fuere aduersus transfugam et uiolatorem fidei' ['nor was the ambush without result or improper, given that it was against a deserter and a violator of good faith'].

style elicit and foster similar virtues and vices: one need only think of how the new men Jugurtha and Marius share certain traits, or how the decline of the Jugurthine War into trickery elicits, in Sulla, the diplomatic trickster who can outsmart the African equivalents; or how the decline in impressiveness of Rome's eastern adversaries in the early second century allows and encourages Rome's armies to sink into the same moral excess.

Arminius is even treated with something like the same narrative rhythm as Germanicus. He is introduced as *turbator Germaniae* at *A.* 1.55.2, 'the disrupter of Germany', and there are other negative colours too: his impetuous audacity and his natural violence are both emphasized (*A.* 1.57.1, 59.1); his role in Varus' disaster is initially just 'treachery to the Romans' (*A.* 1.55.1). We immediately see the conflict between him and his father-in-law, Segestes, who had always advocated cooperation with Rome. The old way, Arminius' proud opposition, and the new way of collaboration are both explored; the issues are as ever not wholly simple, but for the moment Segestes is given many of the better tunes. Arminius is more clearly the emotional winner in his exchanges with Flavus at *A.* 2.9–10, and by the end of the book he is given a peculiarly warm farewell—even though, paradoxically, he falls victim to 'his countrymen's sense of freedom', precisely the *libertas popularium* that it had been his assiduous role to stimulate and exploit. *Libertas* is no less problematic and elusive in Germany than at Rome. But still it is hardly worthless, and in the final verdict Arminius is no longer *turbator Germaniae*, but *liberator haud dubie Germaniae*, 'beyond doubt Germany's liberator':[59] that is the keynote now.

We also again have the feeling that his natural affinities lay some way in the past.[60] 'He was not like those other kings and generals who attacked the Roman people in its infancy, but he challenged an empire at the height of its power'; that is why the Romans ignore him, with their penchant for ancient history and their neglect of the present (*A.* 2.88.2–3). So that is where Arminius' peers belong, in the romantic past—just as the emperor's proud response, deprecating

---

[59] This reshading of Arminius is again well traced by Edelmaier (1964: 89–93, 117–28; cf. also 144). Cf. also Koestermann (1963–8: 1.202) on the Flavus exchange.

[60] With Arminius, as with Germanicus, it is arguable that this impression is reinforced by an unusual clustering of Virgilian echoes, as Edelmaier (1964: 134–9) suggested: but here again (cf. n.31) this cannot be pursued.

deceit and treachery, explicitly belongs in the same distant world, for such were the words of Rome's commanders in the war with Pyrrhus (*A.* 2.88.1).[61] And we have passed from initial reservations about Arminius to final acclaim, just as at this point of the narrative the sense of loss for Germanicus is so insistent. Both receive a balanced treatment, with a sense of unreality as well as of heroic romance. But in each case the balance is not evenly spread, and the warmest tones are reserved for the end.

THE SEQUEL: GERMANICUS AND PISO

That, too, is not surprising, for it prepares for what is to come. It is rather the same technique as Cassius Dio uses, when he gives Augustus a more enthusiastic envoi than his own narrative had encouraged us to expect (56.43–5): that is surely guided by the growing desire of Dio to contrast Augustus and the even more hypocritical Tiberius, and there is a sense in which even the retrospect looks forward more than back.[62] In the case of Arminius, the first successor is Tacfarinas, a sort of moral heir but a shabby one. He too learned his warfare when serving with Rome, he too organizes his troops on a Roman pattern, he too has trouble on the home front, he too is able to tap his countrymen's taste for *libertas*. But he does so much less impressively, and it is not surprising that the war turns out to be a shabby one too, fought in a half-hearted way and compromised bitterly by the shadier aspects of imperial politics.[63] Tacfarinas too is ultimately repaid in his own coin, but this time the coin is inglorious, a response to his own deception and trickery.[64] Men like Arminius are indeed missed, for

---

[61] Ash (1999b: 129–30) also suggests that Tacitus' language in both 1.59.3 and 2.88.1 (n. 57) may evoke Livy 42.47.5, where some indignant senators object to the disingenuous tactics of Marcius Philippus during the war with Perseus.

[62] Manuwald (1979: 131–67) prefers to think that Dio follows different sources in the Tiberian narrative and in retrospect: cf. Pelling (1983) for the view presented here.

[63] Cf. esp. *A.* 2.52.1–2 (Roman experience, cf. Arminius at *A.* 2.10.3, and Roman organization, cf. *A.* 2.45.2); *A.* 2.52.3, 3.21.4, 3.74.3, 4.25.2 (various mistakes and bungles on both sides); *A.* 4.24.1 (*libertas*, cf. Arminius at *A.* 1.59.6, 2.44.2, 2.45.3, 2.46.3); *A.* 3.73.1–2 (Tacfarinas' empty bluster); *A.* 2.52.5, 4.23, 4.26 (Roman domestic jealousies complicating and compromising the conduct of the war).

[64] *A.* 3.73.3–74.1, 'mox aduersum artes Tacfarinatis hau<d> dissimili modo belligeratum. nam quia ille robore exercitus impar, furandi melior, pluris per globos

the degeneration that follows traces the increasing bleakness of the Principate. It is appropriate to bid them farewell with a nostalgic note, for nostalgia is what will dominate as we look back to them. That is even truer of Germanicus. He wins immense popularity, both for himself and his family; yet it will be the later, extremely bleak members of his own family—Caligula, Claudius, the younger Agrippina, Nero—who will especially evoke memories of that popularity; then we will know how sour it has turned.[65] No wonder that Germanicus' family is so highlighted from early on, with those memories of Nero Drusus, the children surrounding him at his triumph (*A.* 2.41.3), and earlier the pregnant Agrippina with their small son (*A.* 1.40.2–4). That son is of course Caligula, who has a named and important role in the German mutiny (*A.* 1.41.2; cf. 1.69.4); so, just as suggestively, does his future assassin, Cassius Chaerea, with an explicit mention of his role at *A.* 1.32.2, 'mox caede C. Caesaris memoriam apud posteros adeptus' ('soon to win his place in history by killing C. Caesar').[66] Brother Claudius is also brought in just as we leave the story of Germanicus and Piso, with pointed reflection on history's ironies (*A.* 3.18.3–4). But there are more immediate successors too, in different senses Drusus, Sejanus, and Piso; and finally it is worth turning to Piso and seeing how similar strands persist in the treatment of his trial.[67]

---

incursaret eluderetque et insidias simul temptaret' ['subsequently, war was waged against the techniques of Tacfarinas by very similar means. For since he was no match for the strength of the army but was better at stealth, by means of several groups, he made raids and slipped away, and at the same time he tried his luck at ambushes']. In fact, the subsequent narrative (*A.* 3.74) does not suggest much treachery or deceit, despite the connotations of *artes, furandi, eluderet,* and *insidias;* it is simply the Roman division of forces that mirrors Tacfarinas' tactics (cf. *pluris per globos).* But Tacitus' choice of language has by then already insinuated its effect.

[65] Cf. Walker (1952: 127–8) on Germanicus in the background of the Neronian narrative (esp. at *A.* 11.12.1, 12.2.3, 13.14.3, and 14.7.4); at the height of his criminality Nero can even affect a specious *comitas* (*A.* 14.4.4). I am less convinced than Walker that 'Tacitus did not pollute that name [Germanicus] by invoking it where Caligula was concerned'; the early mentions of Caligula and Chaerea look as if they are already establishing thematic links between Germanicus' campaigns and Gaius' Principate and death, and these would probably have been reinforced in the lost books. He is *Germanici filius,* pointedly, at the moment he is chosen to succeed Tiberius (*A.* 6.46.1). Cf. Ross (1973: 224), though he interprets it all rather differently.

[66] Tony Woodman writes: 'And is it significant that it is *memoriam* (not, e.g., *gloriam*) that he acquires among posterity? Nostalgia again, of a kind?'.

[67] My remarks on Piso are indebted to Alison Sylvester.

Of course, there are many narrative links between Germanicus and Piso, from the way they contend for the troops' affection onward; but, subtly, those mirrorings eventually mark not only points of contrast (as we had with the troop exercises, or the entry into Athens, or the two contrasting returns to Rome, or the loyalty or faithlessness of their wives and friends)[68] but also points of parallel. Piso's last letter (*A.* 3.16.3–4) shares various themes with Germanicus' dying speech (*A.* 2.71)[69]—the claim he is surrounded and outwitted by his enemies, the pleas for his children. Perhaps we infer only that he is perverting or abusing such language, but there seems more to it than this. Both react in similar ways to similar threats, and indeed Piso reads the forces marshalled against him with more unequivocal correctness than Germanicus does. In part, it is just that they are by now both 'Victims' (in Walker's terms).[70] Different though they may be, they are each unequal to the forces of hideous reality. But even these two have never been as different as all that. Piso had been introduced as the man with a distinctive brand of *independence* (*A.* 2.43.2–3). Tiberius had removed Creticus Silanus from Syria,

> *praefeceratque Cn. Pisonem, ingenio uiolentum et obsequii ignarum, insita ferocia a patre Pisone, qui ciuili bello resurgentes in Africa partes acerrimo ministerio aduersus Caesarem iuuit, mox Brutum et Cassium secutus concesso reditu petitione honorum abstinuit, donec ultro ambiretur delatum ab Augusto consulatum accipere. sed praeter paternos spiritus uxoris quoque Plancinae nobilitate et opibus accendebatur; uix Tiberio concedere, liberos eius ut multum infra despectare.*

and he had appointed Cn. Piso, a man of violent temperament and with no feelings of deference. He owed his natural truculence to his father Piso, who in the Civil War had served vigorously in the revival of the Republican cause in Africa, then had followed Brutus and Cassius; afterwards he was allowed to return but did not stand for office, until he was actually begged to accept the consulship that Augustus was offering. And, besides his father's spirit, our Piso was further inflamed by the nobility and wealth of his wife, Plancina. He was reluctant to give

---

[68] For the troop exercises, *A.* 2.55.6 versus 1.69.1–2, and the entries into Athens, *A.* 2.55.12 versus 2.53.3 (quoted earlier in the text); for the returns to Rome, cf. *A.*3.1 and 3.9.2–3; for the loyal or faithless wife and friends, *A.* 2.79, 3.1.2–4, 3.10.1 versus 3.11.2, 3.12.6, 3.15.1; cf. Seager (1977: 41–2).

[69] As Koestermann noted (1957: 372; 1963–8: 1.446).

[70] Walker (1952: 96, 218–20); cf. Krohn (1934: 66).

way even to the emperor himself, and despised Tiberius' children as far
beneath him.

So Piso has impeccably Republican antecedents, just as Germanicus
so often recalls the past; Tiberius appoints him as the man most likely
to embarrass Germanicus because of his violence, pride, and truculence—characteristics Piso shared with *his* Republican father, who
had similarly come to win the emperor's respect; and Piso too finds
his leading traits reinforced by the character of his wife. Violence,
pride, and truculence are hardly Germanicus' characteristics, though
(interestingly) they are Agrippina's; yet there is still a particular brand
of *openness* that typifies Piso just as it typifies Germanicus, and the
combination of these two opennesses is what lends the exchanges
their peculiar embarrassing character. Their disagreements were so
public: 'discesseruntque apertis odiis' ('they parted in open hatred',
A. 2.57.3); when they shared a tribunal, Piso's dissent was evident
(ibid.); and after Germanicus' death the disagreements progressed to
open war. Whatever Piso is, he is not particularly subtle or devious,
any more than Germanicus is subtle or devious, and he too seems out
of his time. He 'had behaved as if [the Republic] really existed and had
paid the inevitable penalty'.[71] When Piso is himself put on trial, it is
that same openness that now seems likely to embarrass Tiberius too,
as (if the story were true) he threatens to reveal those mysterious
occulta mandata (*A.* 3.16.1; cf. *A.* 2.43.4). Embarrassing Germanicus
is one thing, embarrassing Tiberius quite another, and this time Piso
is hopelessly outmatched. People who behave without concealment
are increasingly eliminated.[72] The next great imperial assistant will be
Sejanus: the times suit him, not the likes of Piso.[73]

So it is not surprising that Tacitus' attitude to Germanicus is so
hard to pin down, just as it is so difficult to pin down exactly what

[71] Seager (1972: 118); cf. Shotter (1974: 237; Goodyear (1972, 1981: 2.362–3, 426–7).
He duly has more than a breath of *libertas* about him: cf. *A.* 1.74.5 and the more acid
A. 2.35.2.

[72] Similar points could be made about *H.* 3–4. Antonius is powerful, unscrupu-
lous, and successful in his own style and area; but he lacks the accomplished
deviousness of a Mucianus, and is eclipsed by him, just as Mucianus will presumably
be eclipsed by Vespasian. Cf. esp. *H.* 3.49, 3.52–3, 3.78, 4.11, 4.39, 4.68, 4.80.

[73] Thus it is suggestive that Sejanus is already involved, obscurely, in the Piso trial:
A. 3.16.1. Sejanus' lurkings in Books 1–3 are seldom randomly placed, and this
juxtaposition is as eloquent as those with Drusus (*A.* 1.24.2; cf. 3.35 and n.30),
Agrippina (*A.* 1.69.5), and Sallustius Crispus and Maecenas (*A.* 3.29.4–30).

Thucydides thought about Pericles and Periclean Athens; and in each case we have an elaborate characterizing technique, but one that is not in the author's usual manner. For both historians the figure is vital, and the duality of the treatment is important: the brilliance, certainly, but also the vulnerability and fragility of what each figure stands for.[74] If Germanicus is a foil to Tiberius, it is far subtler than simple blackening; if Germanicus helps to highlight the emperor's unpleasant aspects, he also helps to bring out how his own style of generalship and politics is out of date. It is most expressive that his death comes just after that sequence of diplomatic initiatives and settlements, those of Drusus in Germany, Tiberius in Thrace, Germanicus himself in the east, grouped together here at the expense of yet another notorious chronological problem (*A.* 2.56–68).[75] It is a world where more delight is won by establishing peace through shrewdness than through winning a war (*A.* 2.64.1; cf. *A.* 6.32.1). Germanicus can play his own part in such diplomacy, though not in the most devious variety, and play it well; but it is not the style of heroism that we associate with him. It is Tiberius' way that now dominates.

Tacitus' characterization of Germanicus is thus complex and qualified, just as his attitude to the Empire and Republic is complex and qualified; and that comparison is not a casual one.

---

[74] In Pericles' case, not merely the personal vulnerability, which temporarily casts him from office (Thuc. 2.65.2–3), but the fragility of the ideals of the funeral speech, and the strong likelihood that Athens will not maintain the cautious, defensive policy so alien to its active and enterprising nature.

[75] For the problem cf. e.g. Goodyear (1972, 1981: 2.393–6); Syme (1982: 79) = (1979–91: 4.247–8).

13

Nero's Alien Capital: Tacitus as Paradoxographer (*Annals* 15.36–7)

A. J. Woodman

THE CONTEXT

According to Tacitus' narrative of AD 64, the centrepiece of which will be the Great Fire of Rome (15.38–41), Nero began the year with a keen desire to go on a concert tour of Greece (15.33.2).[1] Feeling that he needed some preliminary experience, however, the emperor decided to give a practice performance in Naples, because of its resemblance to a genuinely Greek city. The Neapolitan theatre was packed (15.33.3), and Suetonius tells us that Nero was captivated by the rhythmic applause of some visitors from Alexandria, whose techniques were subsequently taught to *equites* and others on the emperor's insistence (*Nero* 20.3).

When Nero had completed his performance (of which Tacitus pointedly omits all mention), and the crowds had dispersed, the theatre promptly fell to the ground (15.34.1). Most people interpreted the

An oral version of this paper was delivered at Case Western Reserve University, Cornell, Hunter College (where I had the honour of giving the Josephine Earle Memorial Lecture for 1990), Madison, Toronto, the University of California at Berkeley, Los Angeles, and Santa Barbara, the University of Pennsylvania, and Yale. I am extremely grateful for these invitations to speak and for the comments I received at each place; I am also glad to acknowledge help of various kinds from D. M. Bain, I. M. Le M. Du Quesnay, D. C. Feeney, J. R. Harris, T. J. Luce, R. H. Martin, and B. D. Shaw. All references to Tacitus are to the *Annals* unless stated otherwise.

[1] It cannot be taken for granted that Tacitus' narrative in the *Annals* reflects the historical order of events: see Ginsburg (1981: 18–30).

collapse as a sinister omen (*triste*), but the emperor himself looked on the bright side and interpreted his escape as providential (*prouidum*). Then, having duly composed his own *Te Deum* in thanksgiving, he proceeded on his way to Beneventum for the gladiatorial games of one Vatinius, during which a distinguished ex-consul, Silanus Torquatus, was forced to commit suicide for being a descendant of Augustus like Nero himself (15.35.1). A charge had been trumped up that he was set on revolution (15.35.2); and although Nero maintained that the man was indeed guilty, he also said that he as emperor would have shown *clementia* if Silanus had given him the chance (15.35.3). On this cynical note Tacitus then passes on to the episode which leads up to the Fire and which is the subject of this discussion (15.36–7).

THE TEXT

Nec multo post omissa in praesens Achaia (causae in incerto fuere) urbem reuisit, prouincias Orientis, maxime Aegyptum, secretis imaginationibus agitans. dehinc edicto testificatus non longam sui absentiam et cuncta in re publica perinde immota ac prospera fore, super ea profectione adiit Capitolium. illic ueneratus deos, cum Vestae quoque templum inisset, repente cunctos per artus tremens (seu numine exterrente seu facinorum recordatione numquam timore uacuus) deseruit inceptum, cunctas sibi curas amore patriae leuiores dictitans: uidisse maestos ciuium uultus, audire secretas querimonias, quod tantum itineris aditurus esset, cuius ne modicos quidem egressus tolerarent, sueti aduersum fortuita aspectu principis refoueri: ergo, ut in priuatis necessitudinibus proxima pignora praeualerent, ita populum Romanum uim plurimam habere parendumque retinenti.

Haec atque talia plebi uolentia fuere, uoluptatum cupidine et (quae praecipua cura est) rei frumentariae angustias, si abesset, metuenti. senatus et primores in incerto erant procul an coram atrocior haberetur.—dehinc (quae natura magnis timoribus) deterius credebant quod euenerat.—ipse, quo fidem adquireret nihil usquam perinde laetum sibi, publicis locis struere conuiuia totaque urbe quasi domo uti; et celeberrimae luxu famaque epulae fuere quas a Tigellino paratas ut exemplum referam, ne saepius eadem prodigentia narranda sit.

Igitur in stagno Agrippae fabricatus est ratem, cui superpositum conuiuium nauium aliarum tractu moueretur. naues auro et ebore distinctae, remigesque exoleti per aetates et scientiam libidinum componebantur.

uolucris et feras diuersis e terris et animalia maris Oceano abusque petiuerat. crepidinibus stagni lupanaria adstabant inlustribus feminis completa, et contra scorta uisebantur nudis corporibus. iam gestus motusque obsceni; et, postquam tenebrae incedebant, quantum iuxta nemoris et circumiecta tecta consonare cantu et luminibus clarescere. ipse per licita atque inlicita foedatus nihil flagitii reliquerat quo corruptior ageret, nisi paucos post dies uni ex illo contaminatorum grege (nomen Pythagorae fuit) in modum sollemnium coniugiorum denupsisset: inditum imperatori flammeum, <ad>missi[2] auspices, dos et genialis torus et faces nuptiales. cuncta denique spectata quae etiam in femina nox operit.

Not long afterwards, neglecting Greece for the present (his reasons were unclear), he revisited the City, with the provinces of the East, particularly Egypt, stirring in his private fantasizings. Subsequently, having testified by edict that his would be no long absence and that everything in the state would be as stable as it was prosperous, he approached the Capitol to consult about his departing thither. There he venerated the gods; but, after he had entered the temple of Vesta too, suddenly trembling in all his limbs (whether with the godhead terrifying him or, through the recollection of his actions, being never free from fear), he abandoned the project, insisting that his collective concerns were less weighty than his love for his country: he had seen the sad looks of his citizens, he could hear their private complaints that he was to approach so great a journey, given that they found even his limited excursions intolerable, accustomed as they were to being kept warm by the sight of the *princeps* as an antidote to accidents: therefore, just as in personal relationships one's closest connections counted most, so it was the Roman people who had the most control and, as they held him back, he must comply.

Words such as these were welcome to the plebs, with their desire for entertainments and dreading straitened corn-supplies (which are their primary concern) if he were absent. The senate and leaders were unclear whether to consider him more hideous at a distance or in their midst.— Subsequently (such is the nature of great terrors) they came to believe that what had happened was worse.—As for the man himself, to obtain additional credit that nothing anywhere was as delightful for him, he set up parties in public places and used the whole city as if it were his own

---

[2] The paradosis reads *misit*, which is conventionally emended to *missi*; yet the simple verb usually suggests 'send away', which would be mistaken here (cf. 11.27, quoted on p. 334), and exceptions are rare and apparently unambiguous (e.g. followed by *in* + accus., as Cic. *Planc.* 47, *Rab. Post.* 4; cf. *TLL* 8.2.1174.55–72). <in>missi would be a simpler correction, but this verb usually (and especially in Tacitus) has a hostile connotation. Another possibility is perhaps *iussi*; Rhenanus' *uisi* is adopted in *TLL* 2.1541.47–9.

house; and especially celebrated for its luxury and notoriety was the banquet organized by Tigellinus, which I shall recount as an example, to avoid too frequent a narrative of the same prodigality.

It was on Agrippa's lake, then, that he constructed a pontoon, on which a party was mounted and moved along by traction from other ships. The ships were picked out in gold and ivory, and their rowers, pathics, were arranged by age and expertise in sexual pleasures. He had tracked down birds and wild beasts from foreign lands, and marine animals all the way from the Ocean. On the embankments of the lake stood love-lairs filled with female luminaries, and, opposite, whores were visible, their bodies naked. Already obscene gestures and movements were in evidence, and, after darkness came on, every adjacent grove and the surrounding housing echoed to a symphony of song and shone with lights. As for the man himself, defiled by acts both permitted and proscribed, there was no outrage which he had forsaken in his search for increasingly deviant behaviour—except that after a few days he took one of that herd of perverts (his name was Pythagoras) in a mock-solemn wedding to be his husband: there was placed on the Commander a bridal veil, the officials were admitted, there was a dowry, marriage-bed, and nuptial torches. Everything, finally, was witnessed which even in the case of a woman is covered by night.

In the first paragraph Tacitus describes how Nero postponed his tour of Greece and decided instead on a visit to the east; but, after the shock he receives in the temple of Vesta, the emperor changes his mind about that too.[3] In the following paragraph Tacitus presents three reactions to Nero's change of plan, arranged in descending order of satisfaction.[4] The people were extremely satisfied, since all they wanted was the bread and circuses which Nero's presence guaranteed (15.36.4).[5] Leading politicians did not know whether to be satisfied or not,[6] although after the Fire, which is foreshadowed,[7] they realized that Nero's presence was a good deal more dangerous

---

[3] Nero's public explanation of his change of mind, in which he refers to 'personal relationships' (15.36.3), is of course ironical in view of his elimination of Silanus Torquatus, a distant relative, just previously (15.35.1). See also below, n. 7.

[4] The point is obscured by the conventional paragraphing of the passage.

[5] *uoluptatum cupidine* ('with their desire for entertainments') is Sallustian (*J.* 95.3, of Sulla).

[6] This sentence too is Sallustian (*J.* 46.8): see further Syme (1958a: 732).

[7] I assume that *quod euenerat* ('what had happened', 15.36.4) refers to the Fire, which has already been foreshadowed ironically at 15.36.3 also (*sueti aduersum fortuita aspectu principis refoueri*, 'accustomed as they were to being kept warm by the sight of the *princeps* as an antidote to accidents').

than his absence. Finally the emperor himself (15.37.1 *ipse*) was extremely dissatisfied, although his dissatisfaction has to be inferred from his efforts to convince people of the opposite: *laetum* ('delightful').

Nero's feigned *laetitia* ('delight') takes the form of organizing public parties and treating the whole city as if it were his own house, behaviour which Tacitus illustrates with an extended description of Tigellinus' *epulae* ('banquet'): *quas ... ut exemplum referam*, 'which I shall recount as an example' (15.37.1). This statement, with its combination of the noun *exemplum* and a first-person verb, is unique in the *Annals* and signals that the following description is digressive. The start of the digression is marked by *Igitur* ('therefore', 15.37.2), which picks up *ut exemplum referam*, and its closure is marked by *denique* ('finally', 15.37.4). But since so extended a description of revelling is itself unusual for Tacitus, he defends his practice on the grounds that he will thereby avoid the necessity of repeating similar material in the future (15.37.1 *ne saepius eadem prodigentia narranda sit*, 'to avoid too frequent a narrative of the same prodigality'). The claim to be seeking variety is of course standard, but Tacitus' authorial statements should rarely be taken simply at face value,[8] and here the almost tautologous expression *celeberrimae ... fama*,[9] 'celebrated for its notoriety', suggests that the present paragraph is motivated at least as much by the intrinsic unusualness of the material as by the desire to avoid monotony. Tacitus' implicit position at this point is in fact not unlike that adopted by Herodotus: 'I propose to lengthen my account when speaking about Egypt because it contains more remarkable features than any other country ... That is why more will be said about it' (2.35.1).[10]

The *stagnum* ('lake') on which Tigellinus' banquet takes place (15.37.2), is assumed to be a man-made reservoir serving the Thermae Agrippae. Whether it too, like the baths, was actually dignified with the name of its founder (as Tacitus implies) seems unknown,[11]

---

[8] See Martin and Woodman (1989: 95–6, 123–5, 223).

[9] There are parallels for this kind of expression (e.g. Ov. *Met.* 3.339 *fama celeberrimus*; Virg. *Aen.* 2.21–2 *notissima fama | insula*; cf. also Tac. *H.* 1.52.3 *ipsum celebri ubique fama* and Heubner ad loc.; Cic. *Arch.* 5 *hac tanta celebritate famae ... notus*), but Tacitus' phrase has been variously interpreted: see Koestermann ad loc., where the explanation of Nipperdey seems preferable.

[10] See Hartog (1988: 234, 344).

[11] See Platner and Ashby (1929: 496); Coarelli (1977: 816ff., esp. 826–30). Cf. Ov. *Ex P.* 1.8.37–8, Strabo 13.1.19.

but Tacitus no doubt relished pointing the contrast between the engineering of Agrippa, Nero's own great-grandfather, and that of Tigellinus, Nero's henchman: the one was intended for use and regular enjoyment, the other exclusively for irregular pleasures. Now pleasure-boats or *cumbae* had already been mentioned by Cicero and Seneca in connection with the infamous resort of Baiae;[12] but *cumbae* are small, lightweight craft, and those of Baiae in particular are mentioned by Juvenal precisely because of their fragility.[13] Tigellinus' construction, by contrast, was evidently massive; and whereas one might expect the construction of gigantic pontoons to meet a military emergency, as Livy describes (21.27.5 *ratesque fabricatae in quibus equi uirique et alia onera traicerentur*, 'pontoons were constructed on which horses and men and other burdens could be ferried across'), no such justification was provided by the large-scale *conuiuium* ('party') which Tacitus goes out of his way to report, emphasizing by his language the paradoxical nature of Tigellinus' feat: *superponere* ('to mount upon'), when used of building, would more normally suggest dry land.[14]

There are two aspects to Tigellinus' construction. By holding on water a party which more naturally would be held on land, he reveals that he and his emperor are victims of the same syndrome as those rich Romans of the late Republic and early Empire whose passion for building houses over the sea was attacked by moralizing authors as tyrannical, hubristic, and an affront to nature. 'In their sickness they need unnatural fakes of sea or land out of their proper places to delight them,' says a speaker whose words are reported by the elder Seneca.[15] Such men are the Roman counterparts of the Persian kings, who in Herodotus' narrative build bridges over rivers or over the sea and eventually pay the penalty for their hubris by an untimely

---

[12] Cic. *Cael.* 35 *nauigia*; Sen. *Ep.* 51.4 *comisationes nauigantium*, 12 *praenauigantes adulteras . . . et tot genera cumbarum*.

[13] Juv. 12.80 *interiora petit, Baianae peruia cumbae*; see further Tarrant (1985) on Sen. *Thy.* 592.

[14] As Suet. *Galba* 4.1 *uilla colli superposita*; contrast 12.57.2 *conuiuium effluuio lacus appositum*. Tigellinus' craft resembles Gaius' pleasure-ships, which Suetonius describes *(Gai.* 37.2) and the like of which were discovered at the bottom of Lake Nemi (see Barrett 1989: 201–2, 304 nn. 38–9); but Suetonius associates paradox rather with Gaius' subsequent activities (2–3 *nihil tam efficere concupiscebat quam quod posse effici negaretur. et iactae itaque moles . . . mari* etc.): see further below, n. 16.

[15] Sen. *Contr.* 2.1.13; for the topos see further Nisbet and Hubbard (1978) on Hor. *C.* 2.18.21.

death.[16] Yet not every case of building over water is a symptom of hubris in Herodotus' narrative: he tells his readers about the Paeonians, who lived in the area of Thrace and Macedonia and 'actually (καί) dwelt on the lake [of Prasias] as follows: platforms are supported on tall piles and stand right in the middle of the lake' (5.16.1). Such behaviour naturally has remarkable consequences ('to prevent their babies from tumbling out, they tie a string to their feet'), and Herodotus mentions the Paeonians' customs because they are the reverse of normal behaviour and hence typical of foreign peoples. So too the Egyptians are remarkable because 'they have reversed all the customs and habits of other men' (2.35.2), and the Scythians 'are completely opposed to adopting the customs of other peoples, but especially those of the Greeks' (4.76.1).[17] Hence Tacitus' account of Tigellinus' water-borne *conuiuium* ('party') not only suggests that such behaviour is morally defective but also that it is unnatural and foreign. And indeed, since the effect of the pontoon is to produce an island in the middle of Agrippa's lake, we should remember that islands attracted the particular attention of writers like Herodotus;[18] and, since Tigellinus' construction was also capable of floating along (*moueretur*, 'moved along'), it is tempting to recall in particular the floating island about which Herodotus was told in Egypt (2.156.2–6) and which was later ridiculed by Lucian in his parody *True History* (1.40).[19]

Tacitus tells us nothing about the aesthetic appeal of the pontoon, which we are obliged to infer from his description of the other boats as *auro et ebore distinctae*, 'picked out in gold and ivory'. If mere tugs, whose function was utilitarian, were decorated with ivory, 'a conventional symbol of regal magnificence' and 'often combined with gold',[20] then the *ratis* ('pontoon') itself must surely have been even more exotic.[21] The ships' crews are also paradoxical: they are male pathics (*exoleti*)[22] as

---

[16] See Hartog (1988: 331). Again cf. Suet. *Gai.* 19.1–3, where the parallel with Xerxes is made explicitly.

[17] Hartog (1988: 62–3 and *passim*); Wiedemann (1986: 189–92).

[18] See Wiedemann (1986: 191); Gabba (1981: 55–60).

[19] For this work and its genre see Morgan (1985). Floating islands are mentioned frequently in scientific, pseudo-scientific, and paradoxographical contexts: see e.g. Hecataeus, *FGrH* 1 F 305, Plin. *NH* 2.209 with Beaujeu ad loc.; Fensterbusch (1960). I owe this information to Prof. H. M. Hine.

[20] Nisbet and Hubbard (1978) on Hor. *C.* 2.18.1.

[21] Dio refers to purple rugs and soft cushions (62.15.3).

[22] It is maintained by Boswell (1980: 79) that '*catamiti* were passive, *exoleti* active', adding (n. 87): 'On the function *of exoleti*, see Lampridius 13.4, 26.4, 31.6; cf. Martial

much as rowers (*remiges*); they are evidently chosen for their *scientia libidinum* ('expertise at lust') rather than their *scientia naualis* ('naval expertise'); and the plural *per aetates* suggests that the criterion for inclusion was age at least as much as it was fitness.[23]

When Virgil in the *Aeneid* wished to emphasize that the Trojans have at last reached home, he contrasted the wild animals (*ferae, monstra*) of Circe's promontory, which Aeneas and his men successfully avoid (7.10–24), with the birds which enjoy their natural habitat at the mouth of the Tiber (7.32–3): *uariae circumque supraque | adsuetae ripis uolucres et fluminis alueo,* 'birds of various kinds around and above, accustomed to the river-banks and the channel'. Tacitus, on the other hand, here adopts an opposite technique in order to emphasize that the world created by Tigellinus in Rome was alien and unnatural (15.37.2). There was an abundance of birds and wild animals from a variety of other lands (*diuersis e terris*); and, since *stagnum* usually implies fresh water,[24] even the aquatic creatures are out of place, since they come all the way from the salt sea: *Oceano abusque,* 'all the way from Ocean'. This last is a most unusual phrase. The distance from which the creatures have been brought is underlined by the uncommon preposition *abusque* ('all the way from'), which itself is further emphasized by being placed after its noun.[25] And when Tacitus elsewhere refers to *Oceanus* in his own person (as opposed to in reported speech), he means a specific sea such as the English Channel or the North Sea;[26] only here does he use *Oceanus* without qualification, evidently referring to the sea or great river which,

---

12.91 etc.; Suetonius, *Galba* 21.' But there are objections. (*a*) By 'Lampridius' Boswell means *Historia Augusta* 17 (*Vita Heliog.*), to which only the third of his references is fully correct: the first contains no mention of *exoleti* at all, while the second should be 26.4–5. The reference to Suetonius should be *Galba* 22. (*b*) None of Boswell's references clearly supports his statement. (*c*) Boswell seems to contradict himself by saying '"*catamitus*" is supposedly derived from "Γανυμήδης"', the name of the Greek youth raped by Zeus', since Ganymede was himself described as *exoletus* (cf. *TLL* 5.2.1543.30–31).

[23] Tacitus' passage looks like a parody of a normal slave household, in which one would find 'beautiful slaves of varied ages', who 'may be subdivided into various specialist activities' (Horsfall 1989 on Nepos, *Att.* 13. 3, with further bibliography).

[24] As Catullus 31. 2–3 *in liquentibus stagnis | marique uasto;* see further *OLD* 1 and (of the sea) 2a.

[25] 'The effect is to make the "sea-beasts" very rare and exotic indeed' (Miller 1973: 87). For *abusque* see *OLD* 1 (in this sense only at Virg. *Aen.* 7.289 before Tacitus); for anastrophe of prepositions in Tacitus see Martin and Woodman (1989) on 4.5.1.

[26] See Gerber and Greef (1962: 1009).

according to ancient legend, encircled the world but about which even Herodotus expressed some scepticism on several occasions.[27] Facing each other on the banks of Agrippa's lake were upper-class women and low-class prostitutes (15.37.3). Normally the former would be parading themselves, behaviour to which *inlustribus* ('illustrious') perhaps partly alludes; but *scorta uisebantur* ('whores could be seen') suggests that the *feminae* ('ladies') are indoors, as the reference to their housing implies (*lupanaria adstabant . . . completa*, 'stood love-lairs . . . filled'). Conversely, the nakedness of the *scorta* ('whores') would normally mean that they were out of sight; yet it is they who are on display (*uisebantur*). These paradoxes and reversals lead to another. Since the *scorta* are naked (*nudis corporibus*), the suggestion is that the *feminae* are clothed;[28] and, since the *feminae* are also *inlustres*, there is a contrast between their presumed *haute couture* and their incongruous surroundings (*lupanaria*, 'love-lairs').[29] Indeed Tacitus' choice of the term *lupanaria*, rather than (say) *fornices* ('brothels') or Suetonius' *deuersoriae tabernae* ('lodging-houses', *Nero* 27.3), is itself revealing: it suggests that the aristocratic women were playing the role of *lupae* ('prostitutes'),[30] which, being a slang word, is therefore indicative of low-class behaviour[31] rather than the sophisticated dalliance associated with the more socially acceptable *meretrices* ('courtesans'). As the original meaning of *lupa* is of course 'she-wolf', there is a further implication of the adoption of animal behaviour. In particular, lycanthropy (if that is the right term) is 'the ultimate symbol' of barbarian as opposed to civilized man, and Suetonius makes a similar point about Nero himself, when, 'covered in the skin of a wild animal, he was released from a cave and attacked the sexual organs of men and women who had been bound to stakes' (*Nero* 29).[32]

---

[27] Hdt. 2.23, 4.8.2, 4.36.2; Hartog (1988: 295–6).

[28] Nakedness 'indicates the lowest class of whore' (Courtney 1980 on Juv. 6.121–5); for clothed prostitutes see Hor. *Epist.* 1.18.3–4 (by implication), Sen. *Contr.* 1.2.7, Juv. 3.135.

[29] There is a similar contrast earlier at 15.32: *feminarum inlustrium senatorumque plures per arenam foedati sunt.*

[30] For the sequence *scorta . . . exoletos . . . lupas* see Cic. *Mil.* 55.

[31] See *TLL* 7.2.1859. 23–4 (*uox*) *ad mulieres abiectissimas pertinere uidetur.*

[32] See Wiedemann (1986: 192) for lycanthropy and 190–91 for caves. The term 'lycanthropy' is not being used in its technical sense, which is evidently reserved for those who really imagine themselves to be wolves (Buxton 1987: 67–8).

If the women are seen in terms of animals, it is only natural that they should be surrounded by groves (*quantum iuxta nemoris*, 'every adjacent copse'), which more normally would be associated with life outside the boundaries of a city.[33] And whereas Suetonius says conventionally that Nero's banquets lasted from midday till midnight (*Nero* 27.2), Tacitus says that, when darkness fell, the area echoed with song and blazed with lights, as if the revellers turned night into day. The reversal of day and night is a well-known symptom of decadent and luxurious living:[34] it was a characteristic of the hedonist author Petronius (16.18.1 *illi dies per somnum, nox officiis et oblectamentis uitae transigebatur*, 'On his part, the day was spent in sleep, the night on duties and the delectations of life') and a point of pride with the later emperor Elagabalus (*Historia Augusta* 17.28.6 *transegit et dierum actus noctibus et nocturnos diebus, aestimans hoc inter instrumenta luxuriae*, 'he carried out the activities of the day at night and the activities of the night during the day, regarding this as one of the hallmarks of luxury'). A whole letter was devoted to the subject by the younger Seneca, who regarded the habit as an inversion of nature: the phrase *contra naturam* ('against nature') runs as a refrain through significant portions of his letter (122.5–9). And since such behaviour was unnatural, it was therefore also suitable for attribution to foreign peoples, for whom luxury was itself regarded as a defining characteristic.[35] Herodotus tells the story of King Mycerinus, who, by turning night into day, hoped to turn six years into twelve in order to frustrate an oracle: 'He had many lamps made, and would light them in the evening and drink and make merry; by day or night he never ceased from revelling, roaming in the marsh country and the groves and wherever he had heard of the likeliest places of pleasure' (2.133.4).[36] Phylarchus, a historian of the third century BC, alleged that the reversal of day and night was practised by some of the people of Colophon in Asia,[37] and as a motif it is perhaps

---

[33] Hartog (1988: 65). For groves in the city see further 15.42.1–2, where their unnaturalness is made explicit.

[34] See Mayor (1872–8) on Juv. 8.11. Night is again turned into day, but for different purposes, at 15.44.4 below.

[35] See e.g. Hall (1989: 80–83, 127–9, 209–10).

[36] The king is associated with other reversals in Herodotus' text: he was said to have committed incest with his daughter, for example, while his sister had been forced by their father Cheops to work in a brothel (2.131.1 and 126.1 respectively).

[37] *FGrH* 81 F 66 (= Athen. 12.526A–C).

taken to its paradoxical extreme once again by Lucian, who describes a land which enjoys neither day nor night but a kind of continuous twilight (*True History* 2.12).[38]

As the climax of his description, as of the preceding paragraph (above, p.319), Tacitus introduces the emperor 'himself' (15.37.4 *ipse*), using a polar expression (*per licita atque inlicita foedatus*, 'defiled by acts both permitted and proscribed') to embrace every possible vice except that which is described in the final episode of all (*nisi . . .* 'except').[39] This *nisi*-clause is a calculated exercise in paradox and suspense. *uni* ('one') is separated from its governing verb by three word-groups: *ex illo contaminatorum grege* ('of that herd of perverts'), where *grege* ('herd') keeps alive the animalism of *lupanaria* ('love-lairs') above and this time associates it with men;[40] *nomen Pythagorae fuit* ('his name was Pythagoras'), which is perhaps intended to be ironical in view of the famous philosopher's recommendation that one should abstain from sexual intercourse altogether;[41] and *in modum sollemnium coniugiorum* ('in a mock-solemn wedding'), which looks forward to the details of the following sentence. Up to this point there is no indication that Tacitus is not about to complete the sentence with an expression such as *puellam conciliasset* ('married a girl'), perhaps describing an episode like the bizarre under-age marriage portrayed in an early scene of Petronius' novel (25–6). Tacitus' actual verb *denupsisset* ('took as his husband') therefore comes as a shock: unlike his 'marriage' on another occasion, when Nero adopted the male role and his boyfriend Sporus the female,[42] on the present occasion the emperor is playing the role of the woman—a role which is worked out in all its paradoxical detail in Tacitus' penultimate sentence.

In keeping with his desire for a military reputation, Nero had accumulated nine salutations as *imperator* ('commander') by AD 64, and it is by this title that he is described here; but since 'the most

---

[38] Cf. also Hom. *Od.* 10.86. For some different examples of temporal inversion see Hartog (1988: 213 n. 4).

[39] For polar expressions in Tacitus see Voss (1963: 124–6).

[40] For *grex* of wild animals see e.g. Tac. *H.* 5.3.2 *grex asinorum agrestium*; Curt. 9.4.18 *immanium beluarum gregibus*; *OLD* 1a. Cf. also e.g. Sen. *Contr.* 10.4.17 *castratorum greges*.

[41] Cf. Diog. Laer. 8.9. Pythagoras himself was of unblemished sexual reputation (ibid. 8.19).

[42] See Suet. *Nero* 28.1–2; Dio 62.28.3.

tangible indication of the way the Emperor and his subjects regarded his role was his dress',[43] Tacitus' juxtaposition of the title with the 'bridal veil' (*flammeum*) could scarcely be more pointed or paradoxical. Any such reversal of roles was regarded as an affront to nature, as Seneca makes clear (*Ep.* 122.7 *non uidentur tibi contra naturam uiuere qui commutant cum feminis uestem?*, 'Doesn't it seem to you that men who exchange their clothing for women's garb are living in an unnatural manner?'), and a precisely analogous point to Tacitus' is made by Juvenal when describing the homosexual marriage of one Gracchus, who as a priest once carried the sacred shields of Mars but who now wears the bridal veil (2.124–6).[44] Gracchus too, like Nero, bestows a dowry (2.117–18); and Juvenal makes much of his inability to bear children (2.137–8), something to which, in the case of Nero, Tacitus makes only a brief, though telling, allusion (*genialis torus*, 'marriage-bed').[45]

These and other details of Tacitus' penultimate sentence are all in keeping with a Roman bride and hence with Nero's unnatural adoption of that role; but Roman brides were not expected to have sexual intercourse in public, something which Ovid associates with animals (*Ars Amatoria* 2.615–16). This final atrocity (*denique*) was, however, nevertheless accomplished by Nero, who therefore went even beyond the exchange of male and female roles (hence *etiam in femina*, 'even in the case of a woman') and practised sex in a manner more normally associated with foreigners and barbarians.[46] Herodotus tells us that in the Caucasus men and women have intercourse openly 'like animals' (1.203.2), and the same practice is attributed to the Mossynoeci on the shores of the Black Sea by both Xenophon and Apollonius, and to the Irish by Strabo (who adds incest for good measure).[47] Predictably the motif recurs in Lucian's parody (*True History* 2.19), and it is combined with its animal aspect by Herodotus when he says that in a certain part of Egypt a woman was seen mating with a goat 'openly'

[43] Griffin (1984: 222, and 231–2 for imperial salutations). We might also remember that the name 'Nero' denoted *fortis ac strenuus* in Sabine: see Suet. *Tib.* 1.2; Maltby (1991: 409).

[44] For the polarity in Greek thought between war and wedlock see Hartog (1988: 216–17). See also Mart. 12.42, and below, pp.331–2.

[45] 'The *genius* (a word derived from the root indicating procreation) is concerned with propagation of the family and therefore with the marriage-bed' (Courtney 1980 on Juv. 6.21).

[46] See also Hartog (1988: 221, 226).

[47] Xen. *Anab.* 5.4.33; Ap. Rhod. 2.1023–5 (1015–22 are also full of reversals); Strabo 4.5.4.

(2.46.4). Hence Nero's behaviour, as described by Tacitus, is not only foreign but also serves to keep alive the suggestions of animalism in *lupanaria* ('love-lairs') and *grege* ('herd') earlier.

THE SUB-TEXT: AUTHOR AND AUDIENCE

Although Tigellinus' revels are described also by Dio (62.15.1–6), he concentrates on the construction of the pontoon and on the hetero-sexual couplings which took place by the lakeside. Only Tacitus de-scribes the revels in terms of a series of reversals, the sheer number of which suggests that he intends to describe Rome as if it were an alien place. Reversals, as we have seen, are the standard method by which ancient authors described foreign countries and peoples. And, since Tacitus also presents the revels as the sequel to the incident in the temple of Vesta, his precise suggestion would seem to be that Nero himself turned Rome into a foreign city to compensate for the eastern tour which he had been obliged to call off. But can we go further, and identify any particular foreign city at which Tacitus may be hinting?

Later in his narrative of AD 64 Tacitus sarcastically implies that Nero's new house, under construction after the Great Fire, was almost co-extensive with the city of Rome itself: Tacitus refers to 'the parts of the city which were superfluous to the house' (15.43.1 *urbis quae domui supererant*).[48] Now this statement is a fruitful source of irony. Nero in a speech at the start of his reign had promised that he would keep his *domus* separate from the *res publica* (13.4.2 *discretam domum et rem publicam*, 'house and state were separate'), and had implied that he would follow in Augustus' footsteps (13.4.1), an implication which, in Suetonius' version, is made explicit: 'He de-clared that he would rule according to the principles of Augustus' (*Nero* 10.1). Yet Nero's house after the Fire, so far from being separate from the *res publica*, not only takes over practically the whole city but also represents a reversal of Augustus' behaviour, who had opened up

---

[48] This point was made much of at the time: see Suet. *Nero* 39.2; Griffin (1984: 138); cf. also, for the motif, Sall. *C.* 12.3 'domos atque uillas... in urbium modum exaedificatas'; Ov. *F.* 6.641 'urbis opus domus una fuit'. For recent studies of the Roman *domus,* and its significance for public and private life, see Saller (1984); Wiseman (1987); Wallace-Hadrill (1988).

his own property to the public (Velleius Paterculus 2.81.3 *publicis se usibus destinare professus est*, 'announced that he was designating [certain houses] for public use'). Yet these ironies become directly relevant only after the Fire: what is curious, therefore, is that Tacitus should make a very similar point here at 15.37.1 *before* the Fire: *totaque urbe quasi domo uti*, 'used the whole city as his own house'.

It is however interesting to recall that, according to the geographer Strabo (17.1.8), successive Ptolemies had so extended the royal residence at Alexandria that it came to occupy a large area of the city, which was actually called 'the Palaces' (τὰ βασίλεια). This area was connected to the headland of Lochias by 'the Inner Palaces', in which, says Strabo, there were 'groves and numerous lodges of various types' (17.1.9).[49] According to the *Memoirs* of Ptolemy Euergetes, this same area also contained a zoo, established by Ptolemy Philadelphus, which exhibited exotic birds and animals.[50] Alexandria had an artificial harbour called Cibotus, which, though placed by Strabo in the west of the city, is located in the eastern Palaces area by a papyrus of 13 BC.[51] And though I can find no evidence that parties were held actually in this harbour, we are told by Callixenus, a historian of the second century BC, that Ptolemy Philopator constructed a massive royal barge, with an assortment of cabins, the largest of which could hold twenty couches and was decorated with gold and ivory, and saloons for holding dinner parties.[52] This accumulation of details suggests that, if Tacitus is not describing Alexandria here, he is at least describing a city very like it.

At this point in the argument it is necessary to recall the observation (which has often been made) that Tacitus' description of Nero's entourage as *illo contaminatorum grege* ('that herd of perverts', 15.37.4) is an allusion to Horace, *Odes* 1.37.6–10:

> Capitolio
> regina dementis ruinas
> funus et imperio parabat
> *contaminato* cum *grege* turpium,[53]
> morbo uirorum.

---

[49] For the topography of Alexandria see Fraser (1972: i.14–15, 22–3).
[50] *FGrH* 234 F 2 (= Athen. 14.654C).
[51] *BGU* 1151, verso, ii.40; Strabo 17.1.10. See Fraser (1972: i.26, 144; ii.78–9).
[52] *FGrH* 627 F 1 (= Athen. 5.204F, 205 BC). See Rice (1983: 144–8).
[53] D. R. Shackleton Bailey's punctuation, now enshrined in his Teubner text (1985): see Brink (1971: 17).

the queen, together with her perverted herd of decadents, men only in vice, was preparing mad ruin for the Capitol and death for the Empire.

Horace was referring to the eunuchs who were conventionally associated with Egypt in the ancient world;[54] and in his ode their leader, being a woman (*regina*, 'queen'), is an appropriate analogue to Nero, who in his wedding to Pythagoras adopts the female role. Yet Cleopatra was not only a woman but queen of, precisely, Alexandria. Similarly Tacitus' account of Nero's wedding ends with the words *nox operit* ('night covered'), which are borrowed from the fourth book of Virgil's *Aeneid*.[55] There Aeneas says that, 'as often as night covers the earth' (4.351–2 *quotiens . . . | nox operit terras*), he dreams he must seek a foreign kingdom (4.350 *et nos fas extera quaerere regna*, 'it is right for me too to seek a foreign kingdom'). Aeneas' words may well seem significant enough in themselves, but we must also remember that this is his last speech to Dido—another queen 'reigning on the African continent' and regarded by many scholars as an allegory of Cleopatra.[56] And it was Cleopatra, we recall, who famously used a Ptolemaic barge for her meeting with Mark Antony. According to Plutarch's account (*Antony* 26.1–2, 4), it had a gilded poop and purple sails; Cleopatra herself reclined beneath a canopy spangled with gold; and, when Antony arrived on board for dinner, what most astonished him was 'the multitude of lights, . . . [which] were let down and displayed on all sides at once'. And though the meeting between the two took place at Tarsus in Cilicia, it seems safe to assume that the barge itself had voyaged there from its base at Alexandria.[57]

Tacitus' allusions to Virgil and especially Horace strongly support the suggestion that the author is providing a 'metonymical' description of Alexandria;[58] and that we as his audience are intended to recognize the description seems confirmed by what we are told at the very beginning of the episode. At 15.36.1 Tacitus said that, of all the eastern provinces which Nero had proposed to visit, it was

---

[54] Balsdon (1979: 277–8).

[55] The words also recur at e.g. Stat. *Theb.* 1.455.

[56] See Pease (1935) on *Aen.* 4, pp. 24–8 for discussion (quotation from p. 24).

[57] See Pelling (1988a: 188).

[58] For metonymy of this type elsewhere in Tacitus see Woodman (1988a: 188) and Martin and Woodman (1989: 242–4). Note that Augustus and his successors seem actually to have used Alexandria as a model for Rome when redeveloping their capital city: Castagnoli (1981: 414–23).

'particularly Egypt' (*maxime Aegyptum*) which he had in mind. Now we know from other authors that Alexandria was rumoured to be Nero's planned destination during the final days of his life;[59] but Suetonius also tells us that it was Alexandria which the emperor proposed to visit in the present year, AD 64, until he was deterred by the frightening incident in the temple of Vesta (*Nero* 19.1, cf. 35.5). Clearly it is this Alexandrian trip to which Tacitus refers with his mention of Egypt; but what is interesting is the way he presents the proposal as part of Nero's '<u>private</u> fantasizings' (<u>*secretis*</u> *imaginationibus*). If it was a private fantasy of the emperor's, there was no onus upon Tacitus to refer to it;[60] but, by doing so, he has activated the coded sub-text which the audience is meant to elicit from the description which follows at 15.37.2–4.

Such a procedure is very much in Tacitus' manner.[61] Earlier in this same book he has encouraged his readers to see the foreign campaigns of AD 62–3 in terms of the famous disaster which the Romans suffered at the hands of the Samnites several centuries previously at the Caudine Forks and which had been described in Book 9 of Livy. Tacitus records a rumour that, as a result of the leadership of the commander (Paetus), *sub iugum missas legiones* ('the legions had been sent beneath the yoke', 15.15.2), just as had famously happened in 321 BC, when, according to Livy, *primi consules . . . sub iugum missi . . . tum deinceps singulae legiones* ('first the consuls were sent beneath the yoke, then in turn the individual legions', 9.6.1). Tacitus says that when the troops of the commander-in-chief (Corbulo) met those of Paetus, *uix prae fletu usurpata consalutatio* ('scarcely were greetings exchanged through weeping', 15.16.4), which recalls the Capuans' report to their senate about the Romans after the Caudine disaster: in Livy's words *non reddere salutem salutantibus . . . prae metu potuisse* ('through fear they had not been able to respond to those greeting them', 9.6.12). And when Tacitus makes the Parthian envoys boast to Nero that their possession of Armenia was gained *non sine ignominia Romana* ('not without Roman ignominy', 15.24.1), that recalls Livy's authorial description of the Caudine

[59] Plut. *Galba* 2.1; Dio 63.27.2; cf. Suet. *Nero* 47.2; Griffin (1984: 229).

[60] I am not here concerned with the question of why Tacitus has chosen to represent as private something which in Suetonius is public, but with the fact that Tacitus so represents it.

[61] See Woodman and Martin (1996) on *A.* 3.33.4.

episode as one of *Romanae ignominiae* ('Roman ignominy', 9.15.10).
All these allusions to Livy and his account of the Caudine tragedy
have been activated earlier at 15.13.2, where Tacitus had depicted
Paetus' troops as actually calling to mind that very same event
(*Caudinae*, 'Caudine')—a depiction which itself constitutes an allusion to Livy (35.11.3 *Caudinaeque cladis memoria non animis modo
sed prope oculis obuersabatur*, 'the memory of the Caudine disaster
hovered not only in their minds, but also almost before their eyes').[62]

If Tacitus here at 15.36–7 has used similar techniques to prompt
his audience to believe that Nero transformed Rome into Alexandria,
the transformation is not simply a literary *jeu d'esprit* but plays a
significant part in the author's presentation of the emperor. Alexandria was an essentially ambiguous city, half Greek and half Egyptian.[63] Its Greekness not only provided a potential target for the
prejudice of Tacitus' audience but also meant that the city could be
represented as the object of Nero's personal enthusiasm and devotion,
since his love of all things Greek was notorious.[64] On the other hand,
the city's Egyptian character meant that it was at the same time
genuinely alien in a sense that Greece itself was not. In this respect
too it was target for popular prejudice, since 'Egyptians generally were
regarded by the Romans with hatred and contempt'.[65] Indeed Tacitus' allusion to Horace's Cleopatra ode may be intended to awaken
thoughts of the propaganda of the late Republic, in which it was
alleged that Mark Antony proposed to stay with Cleopatra in Alexandria and transfer the capital thither from Rome.[66] This propaganda
in its turn continued the taunts directed against Antony in 44 BC by
Cicero, who in his second *Philippic*, for example, had accused him of a
homosexual marriage in very similar terms to those used by Tacitus
about Nero (44):[67]

[62] I owe this reference to Dr Jane Chaplin.

[63] Balsdon (1979: 68).

[64] For Nero's philhellenism see Griffin (1984: 208ff.); Juvenal is perhaps an indication of contemporary attitudes to Greeks (Rudd 1986: 184–92); for Tacitus' own
attitude see Syme (1958a: 515–17).

[65] Balsdon (1979: 68). Cf. e.g. Juv. 6.82ff.

[66] See Dio 50.4.1. Gaius, Nero's uncle, was thought to have harboured similar
ambitions (Suet. *Gai.* 49.2), and Germanicus, his grandfather, had paid a famous visit
to Egypt and Alexandria in AD 19 (cf. 2.59–61). 'Alexandrianism' evidently ran in the
family.

[67] Cf. Opelt (1965: 155).

sumpsisti uirilem, quam statim muliebrem togam reddidisti. primo uul-
gare scortum, certa flagitii merces (nec ea parua); sed cito Curio inter-
uenit, qui te . . . , tamquam stolam dedisset, in matrimonio stabili et certo
collocauit.

'You assumed a man's toga, which you immediately exchanged for a
woman's one. At first you were a common prostitute, with a fixed
charge for your services (and that was not a small one); but Curio
quickly intervened, and as if he had given you a matron's dress, he set
you up in a stable and fixed marriage.'

It was of course the Battle of Actium in 31 BC between Antony and the
future Augustus which ensured that Alexandria, where Antony committed suicide a year later, would not become the capital of the
empire. There is thus considerable irony in the notion that Nero,
descended equally from both men, should proclaim himself a follower
of Augustus (above, p.327) but at the same time, having killed his
relative Torquatus for enjoying Augustan ancestry too (p.316), should
be depicted at the end of the Julian dynasty as adopting an overtly
'Antonian' lifestyle and as transforming Rome into Antony's hated
Egyptian city.

Yet the popular Roman hatred for Alexandria does not mean that
Nero himself did not share the same attitude to its Egyptian character.
One of the features which distinguishes Tacitus' portrayal of the
emperor is a complex of metaphors by which he is presented as an
aggressor attacking his own city.[68] These metaphors start right at the
beginning of Tacitus' narrative of the reign (13.25.1–2) but are particularly prominent in Book 15. For example, after hinting strongly
that the Fire at Rome was started by Nero himself (15.38.7),[69] Tacitus
says that he 'laid Italy waste' and 'looted the temples in the City'
(15.45.1 *peruastata Italia . . . spoliatis in urbe templis*). From the
standpoint of a Roman audience these metaphors identify Nero as a
foreign aggressor, as is made clear by a passage of indirect speech in
which Calpurnius Piso says that Nero 'built his house from the spoils

---

[68] Keitel (1984: 307–9). It is relevant to note that Egypt was an imperial province of a
special kind, which 'emperors treated as a sort of personal domain' (Brunt (1983: 61)).
See also Tacitus' remarks at 2.59.3, where Goodyear observes that Philo called Egypt the
greatest of the emperor's possessions (*Flacc.* 158).

[69] Unlike Rome before the Great Fire (cf. 15.43.1–5), Alexandria had been supposed to be *incendio fere tuta* ([Caes.] *Bell. Alex.* 1.3); yet it too suffered severe fire
damage in 48 BC (Fraser (1972: i.334–5, ii.493–4).

of the citizens' (15.52.1 *spoliis ciuium exstructa domo*); but the metaphors inevitably carry the further implication that Nero himself viewed Rome as a foreign city, which nothing prevented him from sacking. In terms of the analogy which I have been pursuing, Alexandria was the only foreign city in the whole Empire which had this dual capacity of attracting Nero's favouritism and hatred in equal measure, a city to be decorated or destroyed according to his changing whim. Thus, when Tacitus depicts Nero as transforming Rome into Alexandria, he is not merely illustrating the emperor's exorbitant compensation for his frustrated wanderlust[70] but is also underlining still further the schizophrenic element in the emperor's personality which we observed at the end of the preceding paragraph.

Since Rome's transformation into an alien capital has depended upon numerous reversals of situation and behaviour, as we have seen, it is at least arguable that Tacitus' authorial role has also changed: from that of historian in chapter 36 to that of paradoxographer in chapter 37.[71] Earlier in the *Annals,* for example, Tacitus had gone out of his way to scorn the technicalities of engineering as unworthy of inclusion in historiography proper (13.31.1); but feats of construction form a staple ingredient of paradoxographical narratives such as that of Herodotus, and Tacitus here provides an account, albeit brief, of the construction of Tigellinus' remarkable party pontoon. The exceptional nature of the account is reflected in Tacitus' use of language, for in this single sentence we meet *superponere* ('mounted upon'), which he does not employ elsewhere, *tractus*, which he does not employ elsewhere in the sense of 'traction' or 'towing', and *moueri* ('moved'), which in its simple form and primary sense he again seems not to employ elsewhere.[72] Yet at the same time none of these words is unusual in itself. Tacitus has evidently adopted one of the main

---

[70] As Nero had wanted to visit Greece as well as Egypt (cf. 15.33.2, 15.36.1), his transformation of Rome into the ambiguous city of Alexandria is peculiarly apposite.

[71] I am here using 'paradoxographer' in a broad sense, which might also include e.g. Herodotus, rather than in its technical sense, which would refer to an author such as Phlegon of Tralles (*FGrH* 257 F 35ff.), a contemporary of the emperor Hadrian: see *OCD* s.v. 'paradoxographer', Gabba (1981: 53–5), Rutherford (1989: 182), and below, p. 336 and n.84. For the notion that Tacitus manipulates his authorial role elsewhere too, see my discussions in Woodman (1988a: 180–90) and in Luce and Woodman (1993: 104–28).

[72] Gerber and Greef (1962: 1657a and 870); though Tacitus of course likes using simple for compound verbs, their statement in the latter place that *moueo* here = *amoueo* seems mistaken: if so, it is also mistaken to say that *moueo* is never literal in Tacitus.

techniques of producing an impression of 'otherness', which is 'to describe practices which are abominable (to us) in an altogether neutral fashion, even using technical vocabulary, as if they were the simplest and most common practices in the world'.[73]

Another example resides in the parenthetical reference to Pythagoras' name. The primary function of the reference is to guarantee the genuineness of an incident which otherwise seems beyond belief; but this in its turn implies the privileged stance of the paradoxographer, who has specialized knowledge and for whom naming is an activity which characterizes his role.[74] This explains why ancient historians, including Tacitus, tend to mention names in ethnographical or foreign contexts.[75] Yet it is the actual wedding of Pythagoras to Nero which provides the most notable example of all.

Earlier in the *Annals* (11.27) Tacitus had described a solemn wedding ceremony (termed *nuptiarum sollemnia*, 'solemnities of a wedding'; 11.26.3) involving Messalina, wife of the emperor Claudius, and C. Silius, consul designate:

Haud sum ignarus fabulosum uisum iri tantum ullis mortalium securitatis fuisse in ciuitate omnium gnara et nihil reticente, nedum consulem designatum cum uxore principis praedicta die, adhibitis qui obsignarent, uelut suscipiendorum liberorum causa conuenisse, atque illam audisse auspicum uerba, subisse <flammeum>, sacrificasse apud deos; discubitum inter conuiuas, oscula, complexus; noctem denique actam licentia coniugali. sed nihil compositum miraculi causa, uerum audita scriptaque senioribus trado.

I am not unaware it will seem mythical that, in a community aware of everything and silent about nothing, there were any members of humanity at all who felt such unconcern, still less that a consul designate and the wife of a *princeps*, on a pre-announced day and with signatories summoned, came together for the purpose of begetting children; that she for her part listened to the officials' words, put on the <bridal veil>, and sacrificed in front of the gods; that they reclined amongst guests, with kisses and embraces; and, finally, that their night was spent in wedded licence. Yet none of this has been composed for the purpose of producing a marvel; in reality I am recounting what was heard and written by an older generation.

---

[73] Hartog (1988: 256).

[74] Ibid. 247–8.

[75] e.g. Sall. *J.* 18.1 *quae mapalia illi uocant*; Liv. 23.24.7 *Litanam Galli uocabant*, 33.17.2 *ad Heraeum, quod uocant*; Vell. 102.3 *Limyra nominant*; Martin and Woodman (1989) on 4.73–4.

This wedding is conventional in the sense that it was heterosexual but unconventional in the sense that the woman was already married—and to the emperor at that. Inasmuch as it has a conventional aspect, the wedding falls squarely within the boundaries of *historia* ('history'), which was defined by the ancients as the narrative of an event which occurred.[76] But, in order to highlight just how extraordinary it was for someone to marry the emperor's wife, Tacitus in his role as historical author invites his audience to indulge in the momentary speculation that the wedding was actually the product of *fabula* ('myth'), which was defined by the ancients as the narrative which 'contains things neither true nor plausible'.[77] In fact, however, *fabula* was normally restricted to the narrative of things which were physically impossible or contrary to nature, such as the metamorphoses of mythology or the marvels of paradoxography proper (*miracula, τὰ θαυμαστά*);[78] and, since Messalina's wedding clearly did not fall into such a category, there was no real question that the event should *actually* be classified as *fabulosum* ('mythical').[79] Hence Tacitus, while affirming that the event belongs to *historia* (since *nihil compositum miraculi causa*, 'none of this has been composed for the purpose of producing a marvel'), is nevertheless able to make literary capital out of the explicit suggestion that it belongs to *fabula*.[80]

If readers of the account of Nero's wedding to Pythagoras remember the earlier marriage of Messalina to Silius (as they are surely intended to do, from the similarity of detail provided by Tacitus in each case), they will perhaps conclude that such a genuinely unnatural marriage does indeed belong to *fabula*; and, since many of the other descriptions in 15.37.2–4 are also contrary to nature, as we have seen, the audience may draw the further conclusion that the author is now writing *fabula* of the paradoxographical variety rather than *historia*. On this occasion Tacitus does not of course make any explicit reference to *fabula*, and he certainly makes no attempt to define his narrative in 'fabulous' terms. For otherwise he might have

---

[76] *Rhet. Herenn.* 1.13, Cic. *Inv.* 1.27.

[77] Ibid.

[78] See Walbank (1960: 226) = (1985: 234).

[79] 'The event was implausible but demonstrably true—a paradox with which the historians of the ancient world were ill-equipped to deal' (Wiseman (1981: 390) = (1987: 259)). Cf. esp. *Rhet. Herenn.* 1.16, Quint. 4.2.34, 56.

[80] Cf. how at 4.10–11, but for a different purpose, Tacitus makes similar capital out of his alternative account of Drusus' murder (Martin and Woodman 1989: 130–31).

invited the fate of Herodotus, from whose work, and especially the Egyptian narrative, so many of my paradoxographical illustrations have been taken. As Cicero said, 'in *historia* most things have their basis in *ueritas*, . . . although in Herodotus, the father of *historia*, . . . there are countless *fabulae*';[81] and it was for this reason that Herodotus became famous as 'the liar' quite as much as 'the father of history'.[82] Yet, from the accumulation of evidence in chapter 37,[83] it seems undeniable that Tacitus has produced the *implication* of *fabula*, without which he could not fully impress upon his audience that Nero's behaviour, though true, was beyond belief, and hence beyond the normal boundaries of *historia* also. These are the most telling paradoxes of all.[84]

[POSTSCRIPT

Takács (1995) offers a useful overview of shifting perceptions of Alexandria under the empire, and the collected essays in Hirst and Silk (2004) explore

---

[81] *Leg.* 1.5. On this passage see Woodman (1988a: 98–100 and 114–15 n. 141).

[82] Murray (1972: 205); Hartog (1988: 297–309).

[83] Miller (1973) on 37.1 remarks that *prodigentia* is 'a vigorous and allusive word ("monstrous behaviour")', evidently thinking that it is connected with *prodigium*. Unfortunately, though her instincts were clearly correct, there seems to be no evidence that this was or is the case. (I am not of course suggesting that the mythical and foreign are not attributed to Nero elsewhere in Tacitus or by other authors: cf. e.g. 11.11.3 *fabulosa et externis miracula adsimilata*, 16.6.2 *non . . . , ut Romanus mos*; Suet. *Nero* 6.4. It is merely the accumulation at 15.37.1–4 which I wish to emphasize)

[84] i.e. Tacitus not only resorts to the devices of *fabula*, which is the conventional antithesis of *historia*, but comes to adopt a position which is the mirror-image of that adopted by paradoxographers proper (above, n. 71), namely that their subject-matter, though beyond belief, is true. See e.g. Gabba (1981: 53–4): '[Paradoxography's] unifying characteristic was its acceptance without question of any available information; the problem of truth or credibility of the phenomena or facts, which were presented, was simply not raised, since the question of truth was not present in the minds of readers . . . Its concern was not to distinguish the true from the false . . . but to provide lively and highly-coloured pictures of milieus and situations, whose historicity was already accepted. Pseudo-historical or paradoxographical narrative was enriched with learned trivia, intended to ensure greater verisimilitude and hence win greater acceptance' (cf. the 'strange, therefore true' topos in the English novel: McKeon 1987: 528). Since the *ueritas* claimed by *fabula* in general and by paradoxography in particular is not that claimed by historiography, it is clear that Tacitus is here, as elsewhere (see n. 71), merely pretending to adopt a certain authorial role. If the role is not appreciated, its full effect in the narrative is lost; if the pretence is not recognized, mistaken conclusions might be drawn.

the tensions between Alexandria 'real' and 'imagined'. For the notion that, like 15.36–7, other episodes in the *Annals* are themed by a single dominant mode or metaphor see Woodman (2006a), (2006b), and (1993) on, respectively, 6.15–27 (food), 1.16–49 (madness), and 15.48–74 (theatre)].

14

Tacitus' Conception of Historical Change: the Problem of Discovering the Historian's Opinions

T. J. Luce

Reinhard Häussler's book, *Tacitus und das historische Bewußtsein*,[1] is centrally concerned with Tacitus' conception of historical change and might at first seem to leave little scope for further discussion of the topic: it is a long work of over 450 pages. Though it begins with Sartre and moves backward in time in fits and starts until it reaches Homer—and beyond—the latter 250 pages of the whole are devoted to Tacitus himself. The treatment of Häussler, though comprehensive, has not however proved exhaustive. Goodyear has made significant additional contributions to the discussion of an important relevant passage: namely, Tacitus' report at *Annals* 3.55 of a debate in the senate on luxury, together with the historian's thoughts on the cycle of development through which conspicuous consumption had passed from the days of Augustus to those of Vespasian and himself.[2]

Initially my own intention was to make some further additions and corrections to what Häussler had written. But doubts began to intrude as to the wisdom of some of my conclusions. The chief stumbling-block that developed, bluntly put, was an increasing uncertainty on my part as to how to come to know what Tacitus thought, not merely about historical change, but about a great many other topics as well. For the more I examined the text and compared passages within it,

---

[1] Häussler (1965).
[2] Goodyear (1970a). See further Woodman and Martin (1996: 376–413, esp. 407 on cyclical history).

the more uncertain I became as to what could properly be deduced, and whether any deductions I might make could be fitted together to form a tolerably consistent pattern of thinking.[3]

Why is it difficult to know Tacitean opinions? Professor Goodyear cites four chief reasons.[4] First, rhetoric. A man thoroughly imbued with rhetorical precepts, as Tacitus was, could and did argue on all sides of a question both in his own person and in the persons who populate the pages of his histories. Second, the desire to write a literary work that would delight, surprise, and enthral his readers. To that end he was prepared sometimes to sacrifice carefully weighed judgements, consistency, and verisimilitude.[5] Third, he himself was sometimes filled with doubt about certain questions, and expressed this doubt frankly in his writings: for example, on the role of the gods in human affairs, or whether moral behaviour goes through cycles of change as do the seasons of the year. Finally, his sources. They sometimes conflicted on matters of fact and of interpretation; these discrepancies may appear in Tacitus as he follows one or another.[6]

Professor Goodyear selected the portraits of Seneca and Germanicus for discussion. His aim was to demonstrate that these portraits are in fact inconsistent. My own purpose in the first part of this paper, the product of the above-mentioned scepticism about what can properly be deduced from the text of Tacitus about his opinions, is to explore some general problems connected with the business of extracting Tacitean opinions from ideas embedded in speeches, reported statements, and the like, and

---

[3] Goodyear seems to have had a similar experience: see his article (1976) entitled '*De inconstantia Cornelii Taciti*' and his change of opinion from the first to the second volume of his commentary on *Annals* 1–6 concerning Tacitus' narration of treason trials under Tiberius: Goodyear (1981: 150).

[4] Goodyear (1976: 198–9).

[5] A nice example of inconsistent treatment involves Tacitus' two different versions of the Nero–Otho–Poppaea love triangle (*H.* 1.13 and *A.* 13.45–6): the discrepancies between these two narratives have often been taken as Tacitus' inability to handle his sources, although they can arguably be seen to reflect the different narrative concerns at play within the *Histories* and the *Annals*. Similarly, we have the case of Antonius Primus in the *Histories*, whose apparently diverging presentation over the course of Bks 2 and 3 has been explained as a result of Tacitus changing in a clunking way from one anti-Primus source (consulted for *Histories* 2) and one pro-Primus source (consulted for *Histories* 3). Ash (1999a: 147–65) challenges such assumptions.

[6] I am doubtful that in most cases the nature and bias of Tacitus' several sources can be reconstructed from supposed discrepancies in his text. The assumption that the texts of ancient authors are 'transparent overlays' through which their sources can be seen is wrongheaded, especially in an author as idiosyncratic and complex as Tacitus. See my remarks on Livy's use of his sources: Luce (1977: xxii and 139ff.).

in so doing to suggest another reason for Tacitus' inconsistency. Having dealt with this prior problem, I want, in the second part, to turn to the much-discussed question of Tacitus' depiction of change in the reign of Tiberius, especially as it touches on the character of the emperor.

I

The problem of how one can extract Tacitean opinions from speeches, rumours, and views attributed to others is vexing and difficult. Some say it is impossible and should not be attempted. The *Dialogus* was the initial cause of the disquiet that recently came over me, since it is a central document for anyone interested in the problem of historical change in Tacitus.[7] The chief question the interlocutors raise concerns the decline of oratory. Much of the argumentation turns upon the question of how such a change is to be interpreted. There is a long dispute on what can be styled, or deserves to be styled, *antiquus* ('old-fashioned', *D.* 15–27). Even though some of the points brought up in the course of this discussion seem strained or specious, the question at bottom is not frivolous: namely, the relative way time can be viewed from the perspective of the present, and to what extent the mere passing of time can account for the differences between then and now. In the disagreement between Aper and Messalla over the relative merits of the ancients and the moderns, Aper argues for a change for the better: a refining of artistic taste from the backward days of yester-year. Messalla sees a regression over time: a decline in the standards of education (*D.* 27–35). The work climaxes with Maternus' speech, in which he pronounces in favour of neither view, substituting instead the notion that the social and political climates of the two periods are the decisive factors in explaining the difference (*D.* 36–41).

There was a time when I believed that Maternus' speech was the vehicle for expressing Tacitus' beliefs on historical change. After all, it comes last. And Maternus is presented as somewhat of a father figure—a man of courage and authority. And his chief argument—that works of oratorical genius require suitable historical circumstance in which to appear—seems reasonable. Which is to say, it answers to my own

---

[7] Luce (1993) explores these issues further.

prejudices. The argument also seems so right for our budding historian to have held. How remarkable to assert that the potential for greatness exists in every age and that the conditions for realizing that greatness constitute the crucial, indispensable factor! How remarkable not to be attracted into that attitude so beloved by all cultures, but never more than by the Roman, that the past is better because the men who lived then were better!

But fairly early on I realized that Maternus is not Tacitus, if only because of the obvious fact that he is not, and also because of Tacitus' obligation to present Maternus with at least some of the trappings of the man's milieu and temperament. I then began to concede that, of Maternus' arguments both before his last speech and in it, some are less than impressive, while others are at variance with Tacitus' beliefs expressed elsewhere. One example is Maternus' commendation of retirement from public life to the 'groves and glades' of poesy,[8] which is at odds with Tacitus' praise for men such as Agricola and Marcus Lepidus for serving the state actively and well even in the most parlous of times.[9] Further, while Agricola and Lepidus refrained from needlessly provoking their superiors, Maternus seems—lately, at least—to be making something of a career of it: writing a tragedy entitled *Cato* that has offended those in power, and currently engaged on a *Thyestes* that will make plain whatever he has failed to say in the *Cato* (*D.* 3.2–3, 10.5–8). Yet, seemingly at odds with these activities and with the lament Maternus makes concerning the erosion of free speech in the Empire is his attitude towards the imperial dispensation expressed in the last speech: he praises the security and happiness of the age, the near-unanimity of senatorial opinion, the wise rule by a single man, *sapientissimus et unus* ('a single supremely wise man', *D.* 41.4), the fact that there is little point in taking the initiative to prosecute because there is little wrongdoing, and little need of making impassioned defences when one may fall back upon the clemency of the emperor, which is what I take to be the meaning of *clementia cognoscentis*, 'the clemency of the one hearing the case' at *D.* 41.4. None of this fits well with the statements that Tacitus makes in his own person elsewhere in his writings, and some of it contradicts them.[10]

---

[8] *in nemora et lucos* (*D.* 9.6), echoed at *D.* 12.1 and by Pliny *Ep.* 9.10.2.

[9] *Agr.* 42.3–4, *A.* 4.20.

[10] Martin (1981: 63–5) and Williams (1978: 26–51, esp. 33–4) present the evidence against equating the views of Maternus with those of Tacitus.

Thus, both Tacitus' obligation to characterize the historical Maternus and the fact that some of Maternus' opinions clash among themselves or with those of the author militate against the simple identification of the interlocutor as Tacitus' spokesman. A third reason is the nature of the argumentation. Maternus, despite his championing the glories of poetry over the powers of rhetoric, uses all the devices of the rhetorical arsenal to buttress his case. Simple exaggeration is one: his argument necessitates giving a dim picture of the last years of the Republic and a favourable one of his own day; that he would heighten the contrast to make a stronger case is to be expected. One should be reluctant to maintain that Maternus' view of the Republic and Empire mirrors Tacitus' belief. Finally, the suggestion by some scholars that Maternus' decision to abandon forensic life for literary pursuits parallels Tacitus' shift from oratory to the writing of history is not to my mind persuasive. Tacitus did not abandon public life after he began to write history, nor do the affinities between poetry and history that some ancient and modern writers cite go very deep.[11]

How may Tacitean opinions be derived from the statements attributed to his historical characters? One approach is to say that, while single persons should not be viewed as Tacitus' spokesmen, his opinions may be embedded here and there in the speeches of various individuals, even at times of those in the same work who oppose one another in the argument.[12] Even if we grant that this may be so, how can we know which elements are Tacitean and which are not? Häussler believes that by excluding sarcasm and irony and by seeking out parallel sentiments expressed directly by Tacitus elsewhere, we can discover his true opinions.[13]

Certainly, cataloguing the sentiments Tacitus pronounces *in sua persona* would seem promising. I confess to some misgivings, however,

---

[11] e.g. Quint. *Inst.* 10.1.31; cf. Martin (1981: 65); Syme (1958a: 110, 362–3). There has been some recent interest in further exploring the relationship between poetry and history: see the collection of articles edited by Levene and Nelis (2002).

[12] So Häussler (1965: 235): 'Tacitus ist der Historiker Maternus (nicht der verträumte Utopist), Tacitus ist der Moralist Messalla (nicht der ewiggestrige Reaktionär), und Tacitus ist der Ästhetiker Aper (nicht der oberflächliche Utilitarist).'

[13] Ibid. 248 n. 36: 'Was sich nicht als Sarkasmus oder Ironie erweisen lässt und andererseits durch Parallelen wie *omnem potentiam ad unum conferri pacis interfuit* gestützt wird, kann inmitten aller Geschichtsdeutung als taciteische Überzeugung angesprochen werden.'

if only because of Sir Ronald Syme's misgivings, expressed at the start of his chapter entitled 'Tacitean Opinions': 'What are the true sentiments behind the narrative, the eloquence, and the drama? The first step is to mark down his own declarations. It will not take one very far.'[14] Despite this bleak outlook, collecting and comparing Tacitean opinions—at least on certain subjects—seems to me among the very few ways on the basis of which one can argue that views not expressed in his own person are indeed ones to which he subscribed. Something will be gained if this is successful, but I admit that the gain will not be particularly great—and especially for a reason that I will mention in a moment. Even this possibility of limited success, of course, is predicated on the hope that one will be able to take account of Tacitean inconstancy, caused by factors such as change in opinion, change in mood, striving for rhetorical point or literary effect, adoption for the moment of a particular *persona* (senator, moralist, annalist, advocate, prosecutor, and so forth).[15]

On the other hand, sarcasm and irony are not easily removed; they colour the text as dye permeates a piece of cloth.[16] Galba's speech in adopting young Piso at *Histories* 1.15–16 is an example.[17] However one judges the emperor's constitutional sentiments, he is culpably blind to his past conduct and present predicament, and has made a calamitous choice in Piso. He is the wrong man in the wrong position at the wrong moment: irony necessarily pervades the whole of what he says. Many scholars cite Nerva's recent adoption of Trajan as an important reason for Tacitus' composing Galba's speech. A parallel certainly exists. But what are we to make of it? That Galba's constitutional sentiments are laudable but his translation of them into fact deplorable? If so, what does this say about Nerva? No, whatever its

---

[14] Syme (1958a: 520).

[15] For more on the devices used by Tacitus for rhetorical point and literary effect, see Sinclair (1995) and Kirchner (2001).

[16] On such topics, see further Köhnken (1973), Plass (1988), and O'Gorman (2000) (reviewed by Luce 2002).

[17] Of *H*. 1.16.1, Häussler (1965: 248) says: 'Dieser Satz enthält das politische Credo des Tacitus.' In n.36, on p. 248 he criticizes the belief of Heubner (1963: 48ff.) that Galba's speech is meant to express the particular situation in which the emperor finds himself, rather than Tacitus' political credo: 'Doch um den Illusionismus Galbas zu enthüllen, bedurfte es nicht solch grossangelegter und programmatischer Rede.' The implication seems to be that Tacitus does not write long speeches unless they are vehicles for expressing his personal views. For further discussion of Galba's speech, see Keitel (1991: 2775–6); Keitel (2006: 219–23); Damon (2003: 136–41).

connection with the contemporary scene, Galba's speech is demolitionary.[18] The sentiments cannot be separated from the man who utters them or the situation in which he finds himself to form a residuum of pure Tacitean 'thought'.

The difficulty in attempting such distillations is well illustrated by the speech given to the *delator* Eprius Marcellus at *Histories* 4.8, which he delivered in the senate to defend himself from an attack by Helvidius Priscus. Häussler says of Marcellus that he ought not to represent Tacitean belief if only because he is basically 'on the opposite side'.[19] And yet, Häussler continues, the truth can sometimes be expressed by those 'on the other side'. What Marcellus says is identifiable with Tacitean belief if we 'remove it from its wrapping'—the wrapping being 'that of an abased man who leers longingly when those in power come his way'.[20] At the same time, Häussler criticizes Boissier for saying that so effective are Marcellus' words that we stand, at least for the moment, on his side: 'Boissier overlooks the fact that the ability *in utramque partem disserendi* [. . .] was a useful device for indirect characterization in Tacitus no less than in Thucydides. Bad and good arguments serve equally to characterize the respective speakers and are not a sign of the laxity, but of the objectivity, of the historian.'[21]

Well said. But the argument plunges us at once into difficulties. First, is it always so clear what the right and wrong sides are? Second, are the wrapping and its contents so separable, so easily disengaged? Third, how can we know how much wrapping to remove? That is, where does the historical character leave off and Tacitean conviction begin? Perhaps Häussler is right to begin by simply laying down the premise that Helvidius is on the right side and Marcellus the wrong. Certainly Tacitus praises Helvidius' devotion to Stoicism 'not in order to conceal a life of inaction under an imposing credo, as many do, but to undertake an active public career steeled against the vagaries of fortune'.[22] Moreover, Marcellus' role as a *delator* cannot have appealed to Tacitus, given his remarks at *Annals* 1.74 on that class of

---

[18] The description is that of Syme (1958a: 207). Note his summation (208): 'The quality of rulers matters more than any theory or programme.'

[19] Häussler (1965: 249): 'ein Mann, den man in toto von der taciteischen Meinung abziehen darf, nur weil er grundsätzlich auf der "Gegenseite" steht.'

[20] Ibid.

[21] Ibid. n. 39.

[22] *H.* 4.5.1. Cf. my discussion: Luce (1981: 1007–9).

men. And while in the *Dialogus* Aper holds up Marcellus as an example of the successful speaker (*D.* 5.7, 8.1–3), Maternus will have none of it: Marcellus' abasement before those in power is such that he seems neither servile enough to his masters nor free enough to Maternus and his coterie (*D.* 13.4). Yet in the context of the clash recorded in *Histories* 4.4–9, Helvidius does not escape censure. Certain unnamed critics said he was too eager for glory, that when danger threatened his resolve deserted him (*H.* 4.6.1–2). In his eagerness to embarrass Marcellus, he wants to alter the rules of the senate, which that body refuses to countenance. Moreover, when Helvidius proposes that the senate restore the ruined Capitol on its own initiative— without consulting the emperor—'senators of moderation let the motion pass in silence'.[23] This last observation illustrates well the double-edged sword Tacitus often presents to us. Is Helvidius to be admired for urging the senate to take an independent course, or criticized because the action would be a calculated slight to the emperor?

A nice question. It is one of many nice questions that Tacitus poses. Germanicus the bumbler versus Germanicus the hero. Seneca the time-serving minister versus the persecuted martyr in his last days. Tiberius sitting at one end of the praetor's tribunal to check the improper influence of great men, thereby improving justice but ruining freedom. A long list could be compiled.

Is there some way out of the dilemma of how to ascertain what Tacitus thought? As of this moment I am unsure, but am beginning to wonder whether the questions we are asking are not the wrong ones— or rather are not the ones to pose initially and not the most important ones. In our effort to understand Tacitus, we extrapolate ideas from the concrete events of which a history based on *res gestae* ('achievements') must chiefly consist and from speeches, rumours, and opinions of the *dramatis personae*. When we come upon remarks that Tacitus makes in his own person, we take them out of context, compare them, and apply the results to other events, speeches, or personal remarks in order to elucidate problems there. All these efforts involve basically the same procedure: divorcing ideas from their contexts, extrapolating with a view to forming a self-contained stockpile of Tacitean opinions from which we can draw for multiple use throughout the text. I want to suggest that this procedure may do

---

[23] *H.* 4.9.2.

more harm than good if it is carried to extremes or is our only procedure, because it runs counter to what Tacitus is trying to do and trying to make us see. After all, if it is so often difficult to know what Tacitus thought—to separate the package from the wrapping— perhaps he doesn't mean us to do so, at least not initially. It may even be that the very difficulty of making such a separation is precisely what he wishes us most to see. He is not trying to present us with a Chinese box-puzzle or a masked costume-party in which we must strip away the deceptive or superfluous in order to find the author underneath. Nor, in philosophic mode, should the accidents be separated out from the essences of individual things in order to ascertain the unchanging common denominator that obtains among groups of things. Quite the reverse. Many of the ideas, opinions, and beliefs we find in Tacitus do indeed form a stockpile, but they are not peculiar to him, being instead the common property of his contemporaries who were trained in ancient rhetoric, which is to say nearly the entire educated class. From their early schooling through their official careers and private pursuits to the ends of their lives they were immersed in the technique *in utramque partem disserendi*: the *loci communes* ('commonplaces'), the division of argumentation into the *honestum* ('honourable') and the *utile* ('practical')—each with their many subdivisions—the various *colores* to be applied, the different possibilities open to one thoroughly conversant with *inuentio* ('devising of arguments') and *dispositio* ('arrangement'). In the hands of a man of talent, almost any argument, idea, or attitude might be taken over successfully: the protean uses to which they lend themselves are nearly limitless. So Aper several times in the *Dialogus* is said not to believe what he says; his fondness for speaking on the opposite side gives him away, his opponents say.[24] Compare the passage at *Annals* 2.35, where Cn. Piso and Asinius Gallus disagree in the senate on whether there should be an adjourn- ment of business in the absence of the emperor. Piso argues that the organs of government should carry out their functions as usual,

[24] *D.* 15.2 (Messalla), 16.3 and 24.2 (Maternus). Williams (1978: 43) persuasively argues that these passages are not meant to excuse Aper from his views: they are indeed his own. But his argument that they are meant to undercut these views in the eyes of the reader is unconvincing. Messalla and Maternus are using a familiar rhetorical weapon: putting one's opponent on the defensive by claiming that the motives of the speaker belie his professions. Cicero's treatment of the young Atratinus in the *pro Caelio* is analogous (1-2). The credibility of Aper's views should not be decided or influenced by these allegations of Messalla and Maternus.

Gallus that all business should be conducted under the eyes of the emperor. Gallus took up this position, says Tacitus, only because Piso had got in ahead of him and had taken over the argument based on a specious display of freedom; so Piso adopted the opposite stance by default: *quia speciem libertatis Piso praeceperat*, 'because Piso had seized the initiative with a display of free speech' (*A.* 2.35.2).

Thus words and actions considered apart and divorced from their contexts are not what our attention should be chiefly directed to. What is crucial in Tacitus is how they are embodied in the situations of actual history: that is, who it is who speaks or acts, what sort of a person he is, what kind of circumstances he finds himself in, what motives he has in speaking or acting as he does. For Tacitus, I would argue, it is the particularity of each event that is more important than any universals that might be abstracted from it. Perhaps this is the reason why we find it so difficult to extract Tacitean opinions from the text: we are not meant to.

Tacitus is suspicious and impatient of generalizations and abstractions.[25] Put crudely, talk is cheap. Ideas are common. When they appear in real life, clothed in flesh or embodied in actions, there is the rub, there is where the trouble begins. Doubts assail us almost at once—or they should—for it is seldom that men and what they do are not compromised by a host of complicated, often conflicting circumstances. To discourse about the principles of political power, to cite extenuating circumstances, to derive rules of upright conduct—all such activities are easy, really. In life, as in the study of history, we want the packages to be tidy, we want clear answers. These Tacitus refuses to give because as he looks at history they are not there to give. The opposite is usually the case, and Tacitus takes pains to emphasize anomaly, inconcinnity, and complexity. This applies also, I think, to the stages, moments, and separate events in the life of a single man. The reason is simply that we human beings are, alas, frequently inconsistent. Even in the cases of such consistent heroes as Agricola or Marcus Lepidus, he is at pains to emphasize the necessity for them to walk a precarious tightrope between too much subservience and an excessive display of independence.

---

[25] So too are his protagonists, as when Petilius Cerialis observes: *eadem semper causa Germanis transcendendi in Gallias, libido atque auaritia et mutandae sedis amor, ut relictis paludibus et solitudinibus suis fecundissimum hoc solum uosque ipsos possiderent: ceterum libertas et speciosa nomina praetexuntur; nec quisquam alienum seruitium et dominationem sibi concupiuit, ut non eadem ista uocabula usurparet* (*H.* 4.73.2).

Note that the question is not *whether* one will comply with the wishes of those in power; one must, one must make compromises, one must flatter a bit. The question is one of degree, not of absolutes: how much to comply, who is complying to whom, and what the circumstances are that affect one's choices on a particular occasion. This is one reason why Tacitus' brand of history is so well suited to an annalistic format: each item needs to be taken up *seriatim* and dwelt upon separately. Through discrete episodes the milieu peculiar to a particular time is recreated; we can thereby appreciate the complexity of the individual moment, the interplay among events as precedents are established, one man responds to another, experiments of test and challenge are tried.

Throughout his works Tacitus expects us to judge the merits of the individuals who pass before us, however difficult the judging may be. In fact, it is often the difficulty that Tacitus wants us most to realize. In a reflective digression in the fourth book of the *Annals* he explains what benefit his readers will derive from his history: *sic conuerso statu neque alia <salute> rerum quam si unus imperitet, haec conquiri tradique in rem fuerit, quia pauci prudentia honesta ab deterioribus, utilia ab noxiis discernunt, plures aliorum euentis docentur,* 'Now that the nature of the Roman state has been changed and there is no salvation but the rule of a single man, it will be useful to record these events, because few men have the good sense to distinguish what is honourable from what is not, or what is useful from what is harmful, while most people learn from what happens to others' (*A.* 4.33.2). This passage is usually given perfunctory attention by scholars because the claim is a commonplace in Greco-Roman historiography: it seems tame and unexceptional. But when one considers how difficult it sometimes is to make clear distinctions in Tacitus between honourable and dishonourable, useful and harmful, the commonplace takes on an uncommon pertinence, if not irony. A small example concerns parsimony. It was a time-honoured virtue among the Romans, for which Tacitus can and does give praise. Yet it really depends upon persons and circumstance. For Galba it was disastrous: not to bribe the soldiers even a little bit was culpably blind.[26] Acting according to a rigid, outdated, or unseasonable principle, however laudable it is in the abstract, can be downright folly. Galba is judged accordingly.

---

[26] *H.* 1.18.3: *nocuit antiquus rigor et nimia seueritas, cui iam pares non sumus.* Sinclair (1995: 53–62) considers Tacitus' first person plurals, the 'associative we' marking collective connivance in the flawed imperial system.

II

I want to turn now to consider a much discussed, some might say too much discussed, topic: Tacitus' appraisal of change in Tiberius' reign. It illustrates well the problem of the protean nature of Tacitean judgements. I want to argue, however, that Tacitus' view is not as various and contradictory in at least some of its parts as has been claimed. Much of the change during the reign, of course, seems tied to the changes in Tiberius' character, or what appear to be changes in that character. For three emperors we know that Tacitus traced a course of character development that had significant repercussions: Tiberius and Nero, who changed for the worse, and Vespasian, who changed for the better. Claudius seems not to alter in the portion of the *Annals* that survives to us, although it is possible that in the missing part some sort of progression or turning-point was fixed upon.

Both Tiberius and Nero are depicted similarly in that their true characters—which is to say the things they really wish to do—emerge gradually over time, until they are able to give vent to desires that hitherto had been concealed. The reason for the concealment is the inhibiting presence of other people, which prevents them from acting as they secretly desire: shame and fear before these people are the commonest motives. Consequently, divesting themselves of these annoyances marks the stages in the revelation of the autocrat's true character. As the inhibiting people are eliminated, they are replaced by those who are willing to countenance, encourage, or participate in the activities in which the autocrat wishes to indulge. The end of the reign is marked by increasing frightfulness and by violence.

Having said this, even if we agree with it, we find ourselves facing in the case of Tiberius numerous problems: certain statements and episodes concerning him do not seem to fit well or at all among themselves. Let us begin with the famous obituary at the end, in which five stages are marked out. I give Professor Martin's translation, together with his annotation of the stages:[27]

---

[27] Martin (1981: 105). See too Martin (2001: 191–6) for detailed discussion of A. 6.51. Woodman (1989) (= Woodman (1998: 155–67)) offers rather a different interpretation of this passage from my own. I am unconvinced. See my review in *CP* (2000), 502–3.

His character too passed through different phases: (i) excellent both in achievement and reputation, as long as he was a private citizen or held commands under Augustus; (ii) given to concealment and an artful simulator of virtue (*occultum ac subdolum fingendis uirtutibus*), as long as Germanicus and Drusus survived; (iii) a similar mixture of good and evil during his mother's lifetime; (iv) then a period of loathsome cruelty, but concealed lusts, as long as he had Sejanus to love or fear; (v) then, finally, he threw himself into crimes and vices alike, casting aside all sense of shame and fear, following no inclination but his own. (*A.* 6.51.3)

Most readers of Tacitus find this appraisal somewhat puzzling. One reason is that the stages as described here have not received particularly strong stress in what precedes. The first under Augustus falls outside the period of our text. The second, whose end is marked by the deaths of Germanicus and Drusus, is a peculiar conflation: three years and a whole book intervene between these two events. In the narrative itself Tacitus does not single out the death of Germanicus as a turning-point, but only the death of Drusus: 'All of which Tiberius kept up—not in a gracious way, but irritating and alarming, until overturned by the death of Drusus. For as long as he was alive, they were in force, because Sejanus was only at the start of his power and wanted to be credited as a man of good counsel' (*A.* 4.7.1). The words *quae cuncta* ('all of which') that begin this sentence evidently refer to all the favourable aspects of the first half of Tiberius' reign enumerated in the previous chapter: the relative freedom of the senate, independence of the magistrates, integrity of Tiberius' appointments, fair treatment of the provinces, Tiberius' moderate style of living, and so on.

It is also somewhat puzzling to note that the third stage, which ends with Livia's death, is marked by no real change in Tiberius' character;[28] concealment and artful simulation of virtue remained the same: *idem inter bona malaque mixtus*, 'a similar mixture of good and evil' (*A.* 6.51.3). Note the seeming disagreement with what I just quoted in reference to the death of Drusus. The obituary says, in effect, that Tiberius was essentially the same under Germanicus, Drusus, *and* Livia: that is, from the start of the *Annals* to the beginning of the fifth book.

Yet the greatest cause of puzzlement concerning the obituary is the opening of the fourth book of the *Annals*, where a single great

[28] Barrett (1999: 632) argues that Livia died right at the start of the year AD 29 (or before 30 January at any rate).

turning-point is marked out: at the moment when Drusus dies and Sejanus emerges to full power—which is to say, six years and a book earlier than Livia's death and near the end of the obituary's second stage. On the other hand, Livia's death at the start of the fifth book ushers in a period in which Tiberius' behaviour changes markedly for the worse: *ceterum ex eo praerupta iam et urgens dominatio*, 'thenceforward, it was sheer, oppressive despotism' (*A.* 5.3.1). Tacitus notes that Tiberius' habitual obedience to his mother, as well as Sejanus' reluctance to risk combating her as long as she was alive, were the factors that ensured her hold over her son.

The role that Sejanus plays in the fourth stage of the obituary is also odd. Although in this stage Tiberius' savagery had free play, his sexual appetites were concealed as long as he loved or feared his minister. This is the only place in the obituary in which Sejanus appears, and he is depicted as much a force for good as for evil: his presence somehow prevented Tiberius' loathsome character from its full emergence, which happened only in the last phase, after Sejanus had gone.

How can the obituary be reconciled with the great division in Tiberius' Principate announced at the start of Book 4? One might well suppose, as some have done, that these seemingly conflicting schemata derived from different sources that Tacitus took over either without realizing it or, realizing it, but not caring to attempt a reconciliation among them.[29] Another is to suppose that in the course of writing Tacitus changed his mind about what made Tiberius tick—arriving in the end at a position that conflicts with what went before. I myself do not believe that this is correct. The chief supports for the theory are two passages sixteen chapters apart in the fourth book of the *Annals* (4.41 and 57). In the first, Sejanus urges the ageing emperor to retire from Rome. In the second, Tacitus informs us that he took over the first interpretation from his sources, but he now wonders whether the retirement was not more likely to have been the result of Tiberius' own wishes and temperament, seeing that he continued to live on Capri for the six remaining years of his life after Sejanus' death. Tacitus notes in passing (*A.* 4.57.2) the parallel of Tiberius' earlier retirement to Rhodes under Augustus, where he was able to avoid the common throng and give vent to his suppressed

---

[29] It is possible that they derive from different sources, but I doubt that Tacitus was unaware of their implications or that, if aware, he was indifferent to reconciling their supposed contradictions.

sexual urges. The realization of the import of the Rhodian parallel is taken by some scholars to be what prompted Tacitus to reconsider his statement sixteen chapters earlier; another reference to the retirement to Rhodes at the start of Book 1 (*A.* 1.4.4) is postulated as an insertion made in the light of this later awareness.[30]

This is possible, but I myself see no strong reason to suppose that these are later insertions into a completed text. Note that Tacitus did not venture to change or reconcile these two passages, which are close together and in the same book. To me, this means that he intended that we should read the passages as they stand. Note, too, that the two explanations do not exclude one another, but are, in a way, complementary (although I admit that Tacitus does not present them as such). Moreover, self-correction is a familiar rhetorical device—one that has parallels in other historians.[31] I am therefore not convinced that Tacitus' remark at *A.* 4.57 is necessarily proof of a new insight that came to him only then. Even if it is, Tacitus wanted both passages to stand as we see them. They should not be viewed as an inadvertent slip in which we can catch out the historian making rather a mess of things. I believe myself they are as they are because for Tacitus both motives were operative: Sejanus' prompting and Tiberius' inclination. It suited Tacitus to restrict the first passage to Sejanus' alarmed urging, coming as it does after the ominous and peculiar letter from Tiberius rejecting Sejanus' proposed marriage to Livia, Drusus' widow (*A.* 4.40). The second passage marks Tiberius' actual departure from Rome, in which a number of personal motives are canvassed: not only Tiberius' own inclination, but his desire to retire from public view because of his repulsive physical appearance, as well as to get clear of his domineering mother.

The obituary is based upon the premise that Tiberius' character, his *ingenium*, did not change: that seems inescapable. He was all along an evil man whose motives and passions were perverse and perverted. This view seems to me not to be something realized late or tacked on

---

[30] Sir Ronald Syme is the chief proponent of this hypothesis: Syme (1958a: 286, 425 n.5, 695–6).

[31] I know of two instances in Livy: 29.33.10 and 38.56–7. See Luce (1977: 92ff. and 199 n.19). The device is analogous to the rhetorical ploy of *reprehensio* or self-correction. In the orators correction usually comes quickly, as in Cicero's notorious confusion between Clodia's *uir* and *frater* in *pro Caelio* 32: *nisi intercederent mihi inimicitiae cum istius mulieris uiro—fratrem uolui dicere—semper hic erro.* The historians' use of the device is on a larger scale, but it is no less deliberate.

awkwardly at the end, but to inform Tacitus' portrait of Tiberius throughout. The most obvious sign of this is Tiberius' hypocrisy; during all the stages but the last he had to conceal wholly or in part what he really thought or desired.[32] This trait is present at the outset of the *Annals* and continues to be emphasized throughout. It is especially evident in the first three books, where Tiberius' motives in Tacitus' eyes are at such variance with the actions he feels constrained to perform, given the triply inhibiting presence of Livia, Germanicus, and Drusus for most of the period.

Compare, however, the unchanging nature of Tiberius' evil character with the pronouncement of Tiberius' friend, L. Arruntius, reported at *A.* 6.48, three chapters before the obituary. Tiberius, said Arruntius, despite his great experience, had been wholly perverted by holding supreme power: *Tiberius post tantam rerum experientiam ui dominationis conuulsus et mutatus sit*, 'Tiberius after so much experience of affairs had become unhinged and changed under the influence of being master' (*A.* 6.48.2). Many scholars see this as contradicting the obituary and hence as not what Tacitus thought; it is an example of inconstancy, where clashing alternatives are stated but not resolved—the mutability versus the immutability of character.[33] I think this view is unnecessary and mistaken: that is, I believe we do not have here a situation in which either Arruntius or the obituary is right. First, it will not do to say, as has been frequently said, that Tacitus *only* conceived of human character as unchanging and constant. One could argue that the majority of persons in his pages are mixed characters, in whom good and bad qualities intermingle and sometimes fluctuate. Moreover, Tacitus endorses the idea of change in a man. Vespasian is the best example; the same language, *mutatus* ('changed'), is applied to Vespasian as to Tiberius and describes a change that the Principate wrought upon its holder.[34] I therefore reject the argument that Tacitus must have believed in Tiberius' unchanging character because he believed that about all men.

---

[32] Yet even at the end he did not wholly abandon his practice of concealment. The anecdote of his response to the doctor Charicles' attempt to take his pulse surreptitiously is a marvellous and characteristic touch (*A.* 6.50.2–3).

[33] Cf. Goodyear (1976: 198).

[34] *H.* 1.50.4: *solus omnium ante se principum in melius mutatus est*. *A.* 6.48.2: *Tiberius post tantam rerum experientiam ui dominationis conuulsus et mutatus sit*.

The case of Tiberius should therefore be taken on its own terms. I do not doubt, let me reaffirm, that he viewed the emperor's *ingenium* as perverse and unchanging. But I want to propose that we shift our focus on the question, because it has been bedevilled by almost exclusive concentration on the constancy of character. Of at least equal importance are the *changes* that Tacitus delineates in the obituary. Now, what is changing here, if we agree that it is not character? Clearly, behaviour. And is it not what men do that is of special concern to the historian? This applies with particular force to an annalist such as Tacitus who writes of *res gestae* ('achievements'). What interests him are the circumstances in which men speak and act: the environment, the milieu, the circumstantial web in which they find themselves. For these are what test a man, what contribute to the reasons why he acts and reacts as he does, as much and possibly more than any inborn, genetic inheritance. Certainly, this is true for most of Tiberius' life as outlined in the obituary.

In short, the situation is similar to that concerning Tacitean ideas: our attention has been too much fixed on extracting the unchanging—whether ideas or character traits—from the temporal events that Tacitus is chiefly at pains to narrate. Thus, when Arruntius says *Tiberius . . . ui dominationis conuulsus et mutatus sit*, 'Tiberius . . . had become unhinged and changed under the influence of being master', I do not see that it contradicts the obituary. On the contrary, it can be taken to support and supplement it, which is how I understand it, for I take it to refer to what Tiberius did in his life, to how he behaved. I believe that, for Tacitus, Tiberius' behaviour did change, and for the worse. And when one says of someone that he 'changed', whether in English or in Latin, one can be referring to behaviour as much as to inborn character. Tacitus is admittedly not using precise language; on the other hand, I would not expect him to.

Collingwood maintained that Tiberius' unchanging character was central for Tacitus: 'Power does not alter a man's character; it only shows what kind of man he already was.'[35] Perhaps to a philosopher a man is corrupt if he has the potential to do evil, yet does not have the opportunity actually to commit evil acts. For the historian the chief emphasis must be on the actual, not the potential. If the historian is perceptive and curious, it is natural that, now and then, he will, like

---

[35] Collingwood (1946: 44).

Tacitus, be fascinated by 'might-have-been history'. The question of *capax imperii* ('capable of holding power'), for example: who would have made a good emperor, or a bad one, who would, if given the chance, have grasped for power and who would not. If Tiberius had died before Livia, would we have known the full extent of the evil in his character? Probably not. And think of poor Galba. If only he hadn't become emperor, everyone would have thought he would have made a good one. In short, circumstances may serve as the means or vehicle by which inborn character gradually becomes known; on the other hand, circumstances are what in large part determine behaviour.

I want to end by stressing once again the emphasis I see in Tacitus on the particularity of events: how necessary it is to appreciate the many circumstances that affect and control individual acts and words. As noble, as clear, as convincing as certain ideas, themes, and values may be when considered abstractly, their appearance in real life is all too often compromised by the sad state of the human condition: the *ludibria rerum mortalium cunctis in negotiis*, 'the mockeries made of mortal affairs in every activity' (*A.* 3.18.4). A remark of Dodds in the introduction to his edition of Euripides' *Bacchae* is pertinent: 'It is a mistake to ask what he is trying to "prove": his concern in this as in all his major plays is not to prove anything but to enlarge our sensibility.'[36] This is an illuminating observation which applies with equal force to Tacitus.

---

[36] Dodds (1960), xlvii.

15

Development of Language and Style in the *Annals* of Tacitus

F. R. D. Goodyear

THE PRESENT STATE OF THE QUESTION

The most fascinating aspect of the language and style of Tacitus is that they may be seen in evolution. If we set aside the *Dialogus* as a special case because of its subject-matter, for which a Ciceronian style was virtually obligatory, we may follow Tacitus' style through a continuous process of development from the two monographs to the *Histories* and then to its culmination in his most mature work, the *Annals*—though to use this word 'culmination' may be to prejudge the issue. Of course stylistic change and development may be found in the works of many writers, Cicero and Propertius for instance, but in few writers if any is the development so clear, yet also so complicated, as in Tacitus.

Wölfflin, who began the systematic investigation of Tacitus' language and style,[1] maintained that there is in Tacitus' writings a persistent and continuous movement away from normal, hackneyed and colourless expressions towards novelty, colour, and dignity,

[The editor has only supplied translations selectively, since the philological nature of this paper means that its primary focus is for a readership with a high level of Latin.]

* I am most grateful to Professor C. O. Brink for reading an earlier draft of this paper and making various helpful comments, to Mr R. H. Martin and Mr J. N. Adams for certain corrections, and to my wife for checking some of the figures in the statistical appendix. The paper has also benefited from discussion after it was read to the Oxford Philological Society.

[1] Wölfflin (1867; 1868; 1869).

towards what the Greeks called *semnotes* ('solemnity')—or, as some have chosen to put the matter, Tacitus in diverging more and more from the 'normal' became progressively more 'Tacitean'. The substance of Wölfflin's view, that there is a stylistic evolution in Tacitus, is today generally accepted. But, as a result of the work of Nutting, Löfstedt, and Eriksson,[2] one important modification of the picture Wölfflin presented has also gained acceptance, notably from Syme.[3] These scholars maintained that, while the movement away from the 'normal' is indeed continuous up to and including books 1–6 of the *Annals*, in books 13–16 of the *Annals* the tendency is reversed and there is a definite return in these books towards a more normal and more Ciceronian style.[4]

THE PURPOSE OF THIS PAPER

The main purpose of this paper is to examine the alleged change of development in books 13–16 of the *Annals*. While everyone would admit that Nutting, Löfstedt, Eriksson, and Syme have produced statistical evidence which indicates certain changes in vocabulary after Book 12, nevertheless in books 13–16 we still seem to be reading much the same kind of Latin as in books 1–6, the same unique and idiosyncratic creation, as Löfstedt at least is prepared to admit. I want to ask how radical is the change after book 12, to ask whether we may legitimately talk, as Syme does, of a 'great change of style towards the end', or whether the importance of a change which had to wait for statistical analysis before it was ever noticed may not have been more than a little exaggerated. I also hope to suggest certain new ways of approach to the problem as a whole, to raise various difficulties inherent in any investigation of this kind, but often overlooked, to consider which criteria are likely to be useful in gauging stylistic development, and to mention several matters which may deserve further exploration. Many of the

---

[2] Nutting (1923), Löfstedt (1933: 276–90), and Eriksson (1934).

[3] Syme (1958a: 711–45). It is appropriate to record here how much I am indebted to Syme's treatment of the subject, both for the information supplied and for the ideas suggested.

[4] It is possible to represent this development by a graph, showing the chronological sequence of Tacitus' writings and movement from 'normality' to *semnotes*. But, as my argument will imply, any such presentation would be far too schematic and over-simplified to be of serious use.

ideas I put forward are tentative and may be wrong; I put them forward in the hope of provoking further discussion and research. The whole problem needs much fuller examination than it has yet received, and it would be unfortunate if the views of Löfstedt and others, which are certainly in part disputable, should continue to be accepted (as they largely have been) without a hesitant word of dissent.[5]

THE DIFFICULTIES OF THE INQUIRY

Any inquiry into the development of Tacitus' language and style is subject to grave difficulties:

(1) The loss of so much of the *Histories* and *Annals* may well make the stylistic change from the *Histories* to the *Annals*, and similarly from the earlier to the later books of the *Annals*, seem more abrupt than it in fact was. If we had the whole of the two works the stylistic evolution both within them and from one to the other might be seen to be more gradual than it now appears to be—or it might not. We simply do not know.

(2) The loss of so much of Sallust and Livy and (with the exception of Velleius Paterculus and Curtius Rufus) the total loss of the historical prose of the first century AD largely deprive us of the standard of comparison we most need. Because of these losses it is hard to tell how original Tacitus is in his vocabulary, phraseology, and syntax. But we may reasonably guess that he is considerably less original than at first sight appears. In particular, many words which are first attested in Tacitus probably existed earlier, some as early as Sallust, and it is likely that the way had already been prepared for what seem to be Tacitean innovations in the use of words and in syntax, with no surviving antecedent in earlier writers. Occasional corroboration for this view is to be found in the poets of the first century AD, who sometimes wholly or partially anticipate 'Tacitean' usage. There were almost certainly other such anticipations in prose writers, particularly historians, contemporary with these poets.

(3) The question of Tacitus' originality leads on to a related difficulty. When we say that Tacitus diverges from the 'normal' or

---

[5] Martin has raised one or two pertinent objections to the views propounded by Löfstedt and Eriksson. See nn. 7 and 9 below.

returns to the 'normal', we clearly suppose the existence of a norm, yet what this norm is no one has so far defined and it is singularly hard to do so. Most scholars seem to assume that this norm is Ciceronian, an assumption which cannot be justified. In (say) AD 115 'normal' Latin of educated Romans, written or spoken, certainly owed much to Cicero, but it was very far from being Ciceronian; it also owed much to all the developments of the language in the first century AD and to the writers of that period, notably Seneca, even though Seneca had gone out of fashion quickly enough. And, further, one may justly question the relevance of any such general norm to the highly artificial language of historical writing in the Sallustian tradition. If any norm is strictly relevant to Tacitus it is either Sallust himself, the prototype of the genre of historical writing which Tacitus follows, or the latest development of historical prose in his immediate predecessors, the lost historians of the first century AD. Since, however, because of incompleteness or total lack of evidence, we cannot use this norm, we may accept as a convenient, though imperfect, substitute comparison with the language of Cicero. But we must remember that this standard of comparison, though convenient, is nevertheless unreal, since there was scarcely any possibility of Tacitus writing the kind of history he wrote in a Ciceronian style or even one approximating to the Ciceronian. As Löfstedt maintained, we may indeed find in *Annals* 13–16 more Ciceronian elements in Tacitus' language, but this language still remains worlds apart from that of Cicero. Whatever has happened in books 13–16, it is at most a readjustment of stylistic technique within a pre-existing genre, not a radical transformation.

(4) And this leads on to another difficulty, which is the immense complication of Tacitus' language and style. There is no one easily detectable pattern of development. For instance, the process is not simply one of accumulation, the adding of more new and colourful features of vocabulary and phraseology. The converse is equally important: the discarding of words and phrases which seem to Tacitus no longer acceptable; we find a continual reshaping and experiment, sometimes bringing in bold and unusual features, sometimes discarding them. No style can develop simply by accumulation. Some linguistic experiments will establish themselves permanently, some will not. And the taste of an author may change, producing either a greater refinement of his style or the opposite. In Tacitus there is, I believe, a continual refinement in general: the words and phrases

which seem over-rhetorical, over-poetical, and over-colourful tend increasingly to be discarded. But in detail there is no simple formula. For instance, it is mistaken to find an increasing preference for mildly poetical words. Of course Tacitus' language as a whole is deeply influenced by the poets, particularly Virgil, but all the time, while some poeticisms are making their first appearance, others are being discarded, and if anything there is a slight movement away from the poetical in Tacitus' later writings.[6] Many diverse tendencies intertwine in Tacitus' development, and it is not easy to find a wholly predominant movement in any one direction.

THE EVIDENCE FOR A CHANGE AFTER BOOK 12

The existence of a change in vocabulary after book 12 was first established by Nutting (1923), in an investigation of the relative frequency of *forem*/*essem*, etc. His figures for this group of words show a striking change of preference:

	Agr.	Germ.	Hist.	Ann. 1–6, 11–12	Ann. 13–16
essem	8	2	17	31	29
forem	4	–	51	62	1

This is an extreme example of the discarding of a word previously in favour, the more so because books 11–12, where we find seven examples of *essem* etc., and thirteen of *forem* etc., do not occupy an intermediate position, but show the same preference as books 1–6. But it is worth noting that there is a decline in the predilection for *forem* etc., after the *Histories*. As confirmation for the change found

---

[6] This too is far too simplified a picture to be wholly acceptable. There is not an even spread of poeticisms in Tacitus; rather he accumulates them in particular passages (e.g. A. 1.65) for special effect. Much the same applies to Livy, as Ogilvie (1965) has suggested in various notes on Livy 1–5. Nevertheless, granted that poeticisms tend to accumulate in particular passages, it may still be possible to find a general change in their use. The analogy of developments in Livy deserves further attention. There, too, no simple formula seems likely to present the truth.

in the use of *essem/forem* etc., Nutting noted that *ni* as a replacement for *nisi* virtually disappears in 13–16. The figures are:

Agr.	*Germ.*	*Hist.*	*Ann.* 1–6, 11–12	*Ann.* 13–16
4	–	30	36	1

Since it is the choicer and less commonplace alternatives which go out of favour, these figures indicate a movement towards a more ordinary vocabulary. And Löfstedt produced further evidence, such as the sharp drop in 13–16 in the use of *quis* as a replacement for *quibus:*[7]

Agr.	*Germ.*	*Hist.*	*Ann.* 1–6, 11–12	*Ann.* 13–16
1	–	23	54	7

Löfstedt also found confirmation of another kind, in the appearance or reappearance in books 13–16 of words excluded from the earlier books of the *Annals*, such as *grandis*, a word somewhat colloquial in tone. Then Eriksson, in the fullest investigation of the subject yet attempted, examined in particular the use of certain synonyms, variant forms, etc., and found evidence for an increase in the frequency of more commonplace words in 13–16. The examples I have given in the Statistical Appendix (hereafter App.) 2(g) show the kind of material on which Eriksson based much of his argument. They also suggest one of the main objections to Eriksson's conclusions: that they are based on words too infrequent in occurrence for their distribution to be significant statistically. Such evidence might be more weighty if it all pointed clearly in one direction. But it does not, as Eriksson himself admits. Nevertheless, though much of the evidence Eriksson produces is tenuous and disputable, it may serve as partial confirmation for a widespread, though not general, movement towards greater normality in vocabulary in *Annals* 13–16, since it is sometimes reinforced by investigation of certain linguistic features which do occur in large number, notably by a decline in the use of anastrophe of prepositions, always a feature of an artificial style (the figures for this are set out in

---

[7] For a fuller examination of the distribution of *quis* and *quibus*, see Martin (1968). He shows that the evidence is not so straightforward as has been supposed.

App. 2(d) and show a quite sharp drop in *Annals* 13–16), by a similar decline in the use of *e* rather than *ex* before consonants (this is set out in App. 2(e)), by the less striking, but perceptible, decline in the use of simple verbs for compound (as indicated by App. 2(c)), and, conversely, by an increase of Ciceronian elements in Tacitus' language (as indicated by App. 2(i) and perhaps 2(a)).

Such, in brief, is a selection of the evidence for a change after *Annals* 12. It is enough to indicate some movement towards an easier and less affected vocabulary. But if we are to see this change in true perspective, we must also consider: (1) its limitations; (2) what evidence there is to set against it, evidence for continuity rather than change; (3) whether the change is unique in Tacitus' writings or whether similar changes are to be found at earlier stages of his development.

THE LIMITATIONS OF THE CHANGE
AFTER BOOK 12

The change which Löfstedt and Eriksson detect after *Annals* 12 is limited in several ways: (1) it seems largely restricted to vocabulary, or rather to part of Tacitus' vocabulary, for many features remain unchanged. Little evidence has been found for any corresponding and widespread change in syntax, phraseology and sentence-structure.[8] (2) The number of words in the use of which the change is really abrupt is extremely small. Eriksson's diligent investigations hardly revealed anything else as startling as the changes in the use of *essem/forem*, *ni*, and *quis*. (3) Most of the changes Eriksson did find are matters of minor readjustment in the choice of words. For instance, he gives a good many examples of change in the relative frequency of two synonyms, but not many examples of one word being replaced entirely by another. (4) The change after book 12 is more by discarding than accretion. There seems to be no large-scale addition of new words, certainly not much more so than in earlier sections of Tacitus' writings.

---

[8] A very little perhaps. See Lindholm (1931: 196ff.).

EVIDENCE FOR LINGUISTIC AND STYLISTIC
CONTINUITY IN *ANNALS* 13–16

There is considerable evidence for continuity to set against the evidence for change. I give a selection of it.

Martin, in a valuable examination of that most characteristic feature of Tacitus' style, the use of *uariatio*,[9] shows that there is no diminution or substantial change in its use in *Annals* 13–16. It is indeed true that certain types of *uariatio* are most common in books 1–6, but equally true that certain other types are most common or occur only in books 13–16. In aggregate, as Martin suggests, *uariatio* is about equally common in *Annals* 1–6 and 13–16. Here then is one very important aspect of Tacitus' style in which, with some fluctuations in detail, his practice remains constant throughout his works. Another important feature in which there is continuity is in the use of metaphors. Tacitus is of all the great Latin prose writers remarkable for the frequency, boldness, and vividness of his metaphors; they contribute much to the unique coloration of his style.[10] If there were a general movement away from colourful forms of expression in books 13–16, we would expect a decrease in the frequency of the metaphors in favour before. But we hardly find it. If, for instance, we consider the favourite metaphor of fire, conveyed by such words as *ardesco, exardesco, ardeo,* and *flagro,* we find at least fifteen examples in books 1–6, six in books 11–12, and eleven in books 13–16, thus no diminution proportionately in the last books. As far as I can see, *Annals* 13–16 present language no less metaphorically coloured than *Annals* 1–6. Further evidence for this view is set out in App. 2(h). Again, in books 13–16 Tacitus is still prepared to experiment and innovate. It might have seemed that he had already strained the Latin language to its utmost in books 1–6, yet it is in books 13–16 that we find the most remarkable of all his syntactical innovations, the use of the genitive of the gerund with a sense like that of the infinitive. Further confirmation of continuity may be found in the occurrence for the first time in books 13–16 of various highly rare and colourful words, such as *praeumbro* ('I cast a shadow before') at *A.* 14.47.1. Their occurrence counterbalances the appearance

---

[9] Martin (1953).
[10] [For a stimulating recent study of the power of Tacitus' metaphors, see Woodman (2006b).]

or reappearance of flat and colourless words to which Löfstedt drew attention. Again no one has established any marked diminution in the influence of Sallust on Tacitus in *Annals* 13–16.[11] Finally, one other matter in which, if there were a general movement towards normality after book 12, we would expect a change: Tacitus' use of the endings *-erunt/-ere*. On the basis of the view propounded by Löfstedt and Eriksson, we would expect an increase in examples of *-erunt* in 13–16 and a decrease in examples of *-ere*, the choicer of the two forms. But we find no such change. As Martin has shown,[12] while there is considerable variation between individual books, on the whole there is no difference in proportion of examples between books 1–6 and 13–16. Book 4, for instance, has more occurrences of *-ere* than any of books 13–16, but, on the other hand, book 13 has more occurrences than book 1 or 3 or 6.

THE PROCESS OF DISCARDING

Löfstedt and Eriksson, when they drew attention to the change in vocabulary after *Annals* 12, failed to set this change in the right perspective. They failed to do so because they did not make it clear that the dropping of words and phrases previously in use is not something which happens only after book 12, but part of a process of discarding which goes on continuously throughout the writings of Tacitus. We can see this process on a limited scale after the minor works, we can see it very clearly on a larger scale after the *Histories*, and, in spite of the loss of *Annals* 7–10, an examination of *Annals* 11–12 gives us some reason to suspect that the same thing has happened after book 6. I will now mention some of the evidence for this process of discarding.

The figures given in App. 2(b) i show that there is some decline in liking for *nomina agentis* in *Annals* 13–16. They are most frequent in Books 1–6 and 11–12. But it is interesting to observe (App. 2(b) ii)

---

[11] Syme maintains that, though much Sallustian influence may still be detected in *Annals* 13–16, its extent has diminished. But he produces no wholly cogent evidence for such diminution. For instance, as to one matter he mentions, while it is true that there are character sketches in 13–16 not wholly in the manner of Sallust, so there are elsewhere in Tacitus' writings. On the other hand, nothing could be more Sallustian than the characterization of Poppaea at *A.* 13.45.2–4.

[12] Martin (1946: 17–19).

that the rarest and most colourful of them are fairly evenly spread. Of course many such *nomina agentis* are words which by their nature tend to be used only occasionally, for special effect. To show clearly the process of discarding we need to consider words of more common occurrence, such as the adjectives ending in *-osus*. These adjectives are not much in favour with Tacitus, who avoids a whole series of them altogether, including such common words as *calamitosus, furiosus, odiosus, pretiosus,* and *religiosus*. The most probable reason for Tacitus' dislike of these *-osus* adjectives is that many of them are too commonplace, too Ciceronian. He will tend to prefer a synonym, if one is available (thus, for instance, using *suspicax* instead of *suspiciosus*). If it were true that there is a general return to a more normal vocabulary in *Annals* 13–16, we would expect a marked increase in the frequency of *-osus* adjectives in this section. But, as App. 2(f) shows, we do not find it. What we find is a continual process of discarding after the *Histories*; there is no reversal of this tendency in *Annals* 13–16. But more substantial evidence for the discarding process is available, in the large number of words of all kinds which are dropped after the *Histories*. If the words dropped at this time were all commonplace and Ciceronian, this would be excellent evidence for a straightforward movement towards greater novelty and colour. While there are numerous common words amongst the discards, there are also many which are colourful and poetical, for instance, to mention but a few: *contemptim, crudesco, euilesco, grandaeuus, indigus, pauperies, temno*.[13] It seems that it is precisely because such words are too affected, too colourful that Tacitus rejects them after the *Histories*. If he strives increasingly after *semnotes*, he does so more by refining his vocabulary than by over-enriching it. It seems to me that this rejection of a large number of words after the *Histories* is essentially similar to what happens after book 12.

Syme rightly says that 'the *Annals* exhibit a strong movement away from rhetoric'. Indeed one may extend his observation. The crudest rhetoric in Tacitus is in the earliest works, notably the *Germania*, partly indeed because the subject-matter seemed to require embellishment, but also because the author's technique was as yet immature. A good indication of the progressive movement away from rhetoric may, I believe, be found in the decline in the frequency of epigrams or

---

[13] Many more examples of various kinds may be found in Syme (1958a: appendixes 45 and 46).

sententiae and indeed of pointed expression in general.[14] Tacitus' epigrams are sharpest and most frequent in the early books of the *Histories*; from then on there is a gradual decline. And not only are epigrams less frequent in the *Annals*; they are also on the whole milder. Of course this is a very subjective question, hard to judge, and the change may be determined by the subject-matter. The subject-matter of what has survived of the *Histories*, namely the momentous events of AD 69–70, provided ample opportunity for epigram. The subject-matter of the *Annals* is less tightly packed. But there is also, I should maintain, a change in technique. The *sententia* stands out too much from its context and is, if anything, too effective; the whole is obscured by the brilliance of a part. As the style of Tacitus matured, *sententiae* began to give way to more subtle devices.

Such then are a few indications of the existence of a process of discarding. And I must emphasize again that this movement towards greater simplicity, yet at the same time greater subtlety, is not found only after book 12.

THE POSITION OF *ANNALS* 11–12

The best confirmation of all that there is a continuous process of change, rather than an abrupt and isolated one after book 12, is provided by an analysis of *Annals* 11–12. Though their extent is insufficient to give us reliable evidence on all points, certain safe conclusions may be drawn from consideration of very common words and usages. As Eriksson perceived, *Annals* 11–12 are in many respects intermediate linguistically between books 1–6 and 13–16. He did not clearly perceive that, if the change of which he makes so much is already going on in books 11–12, it is not quite such a remarkable change as he would have us believe. I will now mention certain evidence relating to *Annals* 11–12.

In many respects *Annals* 11–12 maintain or even increase the preferences or tendencies shown in books 1–6, for instance in the decline in frequency of *cum* compounds, as indicated in App. 2(a). In other matters, books 11–12 are clearly intermediate. The use of *e/ex*

---

[14] [On Tacitus' use of epigrams and *sententiae*, see Sinclair (1995), Kirchner (2001), and Stegner (2004).]

before consonants set out in App. 2(e) is a particularly good example, because of the large number of cases involved. It is clear from the figures given that the use of *e* before a consonant begins to decline in frequency after books 1–6, since in 1–6 there are substantially more examples than we would expect on even distribution of the total, in 11–12 just about the number we would expect, and in 13–16 substantially less. Thus we find here a decline in preference beginning in books 11–12 and continuing in 13–16. Similarly App. 2(c) indicates a diminution in occurrences of simple for compound in books 11–12 which is continued in 13–16. In certain ways, however, books 11–12 share the characteristics of 13–16: in other words, the change from the language of books 1–6 is already in 11–12 as pronounced as it is in 13–16 or even more pronounced. The relative frequency of *nec/neque* is a very curious and interesting example of this, because, as App. 2(j) shows, in books 11–12 Tacitus reverses the strong preference for *neque* which he had shown in 1–6, and indeed seems to show a greater distaste for *neque* in books 11–12 than at any time later. The change from a proportion for *nec/neque* in books 1–6 of about 1/2.5 to one of about 1/0.5 in books 11–12 is a change almost as striking statistically as the discarding of *forem* etc. in books 13–16.[15] Those who believe (as I do not) that such figures are enough to prove a 'great change of style' may be compelled to accept that there is such a great change in books 11–12 as well as in 13–16.

EXPLANATION OF TACITUS' STYLISTIC EVOLUTION

Should we ask for an explanation of Tacitus' stylistic evolution? Or is it enough to note that his style does evolve? I think it may be enough, for it is doubtful whether any writer's style has ever remained absolutely constant, and it seems part of the nature of Tacitus' way of

---

[15] It seemed unnecessary to take account of the influence of the position in which the examples occur, i.e. whether before a vowel or a consonant, because, since so many examples are involved, any such influence is likely to even out. I have noticed a slight tendency for examples of *nec* and *neque* to cluster (probably through no other reason than subconscious harking back to a word used shortly before—the phenomenon is, of course, known elsewhere), but these clusters cancel one another out and do not affect the validity of figures taken from very numerous examples.

writing that it changes continuously—a similar and equally complicated pattern of development may be found in the sentence structure of Cicero's speeches, to name but a single parallel. One conventional mode of describing Tacitus' development seems to me quite unsound, indeed absurd in principle, namely the notion that Tacitus becomes more and more 'Tacitean'. It is absurd *inter alia* because it implies that, when Tacitus reached the point of being completely 'Tacitean', his style would become fixed, never to change again. What is essentially and invariably Tacitean is not the style of Tacitus at any one stage of its development, whether *Annals* 1–6 or the *Histories* or *Annals* 13–16, but the endless experiment with his medium, the discontent with and reshaping of what had been achieved before, the obsessive restlessness of a stylist never satisfied that he had reached perfection.

Though no special explanation is clearly necessary, since stylistic change is part of Tacitus' nature, certain factors may be relevant as at least contributory. One is obvious: lapse of time between the composition of the various sections of Tacitus' works. The lapse of a few years might bring self-criticism and change of taste. There is some evidence (not indeed very strong) for such a lapse of time between the composition of the *Histories* and the *Annals*. The same thing may have happened after *Annals* 12 and even perhaps after *Annals* 6.[16]

Other possible contributory factors are less plausible. It has, for instance, been maintained that books 13–16 show signs of lack of revision. Those who believe books 13–16 may be unrevised have remarked on one or two inconsistencies, some imprecision in the introduction of new characters and certain factual errors. Much of this alleged evidence is disputable, but some of it may be valid: *adhuc sub iudice lis est*. But, as far as the language is concerned, possible lack of revision explains little or nothing. It might indeed explain looseness and awkwardness in expression (if such is to be found in *Annals* 13–16), but it can hardly explain any general change in language, least of all a change which affects some of the most common words. As an

---

[16] To what extent change of source may have contributed to change of style is hard to assess. Certainly Tacitus' historical sources could sometimes serve as stylistic models—at least Tacitus seems prepared to borrow from them an epigram or turn of phrase. But I doubt whether a change of source could possibly affect the basic material of his language. And, though a partial change of source is likely after book 12, we know nothing of possible stylistic differences between Tacitus' sources.

explanation of such a change it may be dismissed by *reductio ad absurdum*: it could only be right if we are prepared to believe that in his first draft Tacitus was accustomed to write *essem, esset*, etc., then, when he came to revise, to substitute haphazardly *forem, foret*, etc. It is not impossible that this was the way he composed, but it is in a high degree improbable.

But may there be any external contributory factors? One possibility occurs to me, which I suggest very tentatively. Though it was in the nature of Tacitus' whole development to move towards greater simplicity, this process may have been accelerated by external influence. The influence I have in mind is the rise of the archaizing movement in Latin prose. The cult of archaism came into full fashion in the principate of Hadrian, but was certainly beginning many years earlier.[17] In so fastidious a stylist as Tacitus it may well have excited a strong reaction. As other writers moved towards greater affectation and unreality, he moved the more quickly towards greater simplicity. This is, of course, the merest speculation, but on such matters all we can hope to do is to speculate. Since the change after *Annals* 12, though consistent with Tacitus' evolution in general, is somewhat more pronounced than earlier changes (and this much I am prepared to concede), external influence may be the explanation—and reaction against the absurdities of the archaizers is the only remotely possible external explanation I can think of.

CONCLUSION

The main points I have tried to make are:

(1) That Tacitus' stylistic development is extremely complicated and hardly to be explained by any simple formula.

(2) That, while a definite change of vocabulary is found in *Annals* 13–16, its importance has been much exaggerated, because it affects only part of Tacitus' vocabulary, because there is substantial evidence for continuity of style in these same books, because an examination of *Annals* 11–12 shows the change already beginning earlier, and, above all, because the change,

---

[17] Sherwin-White (1966: 123).

which consists essentially in the discarding of various words in favour before, or a diminution in their use, is in no way different from other changes which had occurred previously in Tacitus' writings.

(3) That, this being so, it is mistaken to talk of a reversal of earlier tendencies in *Annals* 13–16: the same process continues, a process of discarding and replacement.

(4) That, if there is any one most characteristic tendency, it is a tendency towards greater refinement and subtlety, a movement away from the odd and affected. And this tendency continues right through from beginning to end—the linguistic change in *Annals* 13–16 is part of it. In the sense that this tendency does so continue, Wölfflin's picture of an unbroken development (however much it may need to be reinterpreted) seems to me nearer the truth than Löfstedt's picture of a change of direction after *Annals* 12.[18]

STATISTICAL APPENDIX

INTRODUCTORY NOTE

I make no claim to absolute accuracy in the information provided, but I believe the margin of error is not very great. A subjective element was inevitably involved in the selection of some of the evidence. Section 1 is simply for information, to show the basis on which certain calculations are made in section 2. In most of the subsections of 2, I have given first the actual number of occurrences in each part of Tacitus' writings or each part of the *Annals*, then another, hypothetical number produced by distributing the total number of occurrences evenly according to the size of each part. By comparing these two numbers we can see to some extent how Tacitus' use of particular words, types of word, etc., changes from one portion of his writings to another.

---

[18] Much still remains to be investigated before any really firm conclusion can be obtained. Amongst matters which might reward further exploration and supply further means to gauge stylistic change are Tacitus' use of brevity and ellipse, of asyndeton, and of the ablative absolute.

1. SIZE OF THE WORKS OF TACITUS

(a) On the basis of Koestermann's latest Teubner edition:

total pages	731	100%
Agr.	32	4% approx.
Germ.	26	4% approx.
Dial.	42	6% approx.
Hist.	237	32% approx.
Ann.	394	54% approx.
Ann. 1–6	202	28% approx.
Ann. 11–12	58	8% approx.
Ann. 13–16	134	18% approx.

Distribution within the *Annals*:

total pages	394	100%
Ann. 1–6	202	51% approx.
Ann. 11–12	58	15% approx.
Ann. 13–16	134	34% approx.

(b) Distribution within the *Annals* on the basis of Fuchs' edition:

total pages	359	100%
Ann. 1–6	194	54% approx.
Ann. 11–12	50	14% approx.
Ann. 13–16	115	32% approx.

2. DISTRIBUTIONS

(a) Distribution of *cum* compounds:

A.	G.	D.	H.	A. 1–6	A. 11–12	A. 13–16	
18	25	46	183	136	34	109	total 551

expect on even distribution:

22	22	33	176	154	44	99

so decrease in *A.* 1–6 and 11–12, increase in *A.* 13–16.

(b) *i.* Distribution of *nomina agentis* in *-tor*, excluding those of common occurrence.[19]

A.	G.	D.	H.	A. 1–6	A. 11–12	A. 13–16	
2	10	12	56	71	22	36	total 209

[19] I have excluded words which occur 10 times or more in Tacitus and a few which, though they occur fewer than 10 times in Tacitus, are particularly common elsewhere.

expect:

8   8   13   67   59   17   38

so these nouns are on the whole more in favour in *A.* 1–6 and *A.* 11–12 than elsewhere.

ii. Distribution of *nomina agentis* in *-tor* which occur only once in the works of Tacitus:

A.	*G.*	*D.*	*H.*	*A. 1–6*	*A. 11–12.*	*A. 13–16*	
–	3	1	11	11	4	9	total 39

so a fairly even spread proportionately.

(c) Distribution of a representative selection of examples of simple verbs used for compounds in the *Annals*:

A. 1–6	*A. 11–12*	*A. 13–16*	
68	13	30	total 111

expect:

60   16   35

so a decline in frequency both in *A.* 11–12 and *A.*13–16, but not a striking one.

(d) Distribution of prepositions in anastrophe in the *Annals:*

A. 1–6	*A. 11–12*	*A. 13–16*	
238	65	100	total 403

expect:

218   56   129

so a quite sharp drop in 13–16.

(e) Distribution of the use of *e/ex* before consonants in the *Annals*:

	A. 1–6	*A. 11–12*	*A. 13–16*	
e	67	14	21	total 102
ex	82	19	61	total 162

expect:

e	52	15	35
ex	83	24	55

so a clear decline in the frequency of *e* in *A.* 13–16, with an increase in the frequency of *ex*.

(f) Distribution of -*osus* adjectives in Tacitus:

A.	G.	D.	H.	A. 1-6	A. 11-12	A. 13-16	
12	12	14	75	49	5	28	total 195

expect:

8	8	12	62	55	16	35

so a general decline in frequency in the *Annals,* particularly in 11-12.

(g) Distribution of certain synonyms in the *Annals*:

	A. 1-6	A. 11-12	A. 13-16
impero	5	1	5
imperito	8	8	4
apiscor	8	–	4
adipiscor	18	8	8
firmo	9	2	–
adfirmo	–	1	1
confirmo	–	–	1
uerto	3	–	–
euerto	–	–	3

so no very clear indication of a change in A. 13-16.

(h) Distribution of twenty-two randomly selected metaphorical expressions in the *Annals*:

A. 1-6	A. 11-12	A. 13-16	
89	33	51	total 173

expect:

93	24	55

so no decrease in A. 13-16 and more than expected in A. 11-12.

(i) Estimate of the non-Ciceronian element in a sample of new words[20] in A. 1-6 and A. 13-16:

A. 1-6	A. 13-16
59/155	28/110

so no general drop in the number of new words[21] (155/110 gives about an even distribution proportionately), but a sharp drop in the non-

---

[20] The sample is of all 'new' words beginning with the letters *a, b, c, d, e,* and *s.* I have excluded all 'new' words which are highly specialized, i.e. by their nature likely to occur only very rarely. 'New' means 'not attested in any earlier part of the writings of Tacitus'.

[21] One might expect a progressive diminution in the number of 'new' words and, insofar as we do not find this in A. 13-16, see evidence here for a substantial change of vocabulary in A. 13-16. But most of the very common and basic words have

Ciceronian element in *A.* 13–16 (where one would expect 42 on even distribution).

(j) Relative frequency of *nec/neque* in the books of the *Annals*:

	nec	*neque*	
Ann. 1	21	55	1/2.6 approx.
Ann. 2	30	34	1/1.1 approx.
Ann. 3	24	66	1/2.7 approx.
Ann. 4	14	49	1/3.5
Ann. 5–6	16	36	1/2.2 approx.
Ann. 11	19	8	1/0.4 approx.
Ann. 12	25	13	1/0.5 approx.
Ann. 13	24	18	1/0.75
Ann. 14	27	15	1/0.6 approx.
Ann. 15	26	21	1/0.8 approx.
Ann. 16	10	8	1/0.8

neque is least frequent in *A.* 11–12.

[POSTSCRIPT

Goodyear's discussion of the difficulties of pinning down Tacitean divergences from 'normal' Latin could also be considered from the point of view of regional diversification, on which see the crucial study of Adams (2007). On the poetic register of the Latin language, see the volume edited by Adams and Mayer (1999), while Lyne (1989: 1–19) remains informative.]

appeared already in the *Histories* and earlier. My figures relate not to them, but to words which are not indispensable and therefore tend to be occasional in occurrence.

16

Tacitus' Excursus on the Jews through the Ages: An Overview of its Reception History

René Bloch

Auguror (nec me fallit augurium) historias tuas immortalis futuras. (Pliny, *Ep.* 7.33.1)

The complete works of the Roman historian Publius Cornelius Tacitus have, in recent decades, been repeatedly examined for the process of their reception at particular times and places, and Stefan Borzsák's 'research call' on this topic, issued a good thirty years ago, is probably now somewhat behind the times.[1] So far, however, no examination has been forthcoming of the reception of the Jewish Excursus.[2] These twelve chapters have had enormous influence ever since the late classical period, are constantly referred to, and have even had something of a collateral effect on the reception of the entire Tacitean

[The editor comments: I am extremely grateful to David Ash for translating this extract from Bloch's book. Some of the longer quotations in French, German, and Italian have been cut from Bloch's original footnotes, but where quotations have been retained, they have generally been translated into English.]

[1] Borzsák (1968: 509): 'The need to investigate the survival record of Tacitus—as well as of Virgil, Horace, etc.—should rank high on the list of *desiderata*.' Among the more important recent studies may be mentioned Schellhase (1976); Volpilhac-Auger (1985); Chevallier and Poignault (1992); Volpilhac-Auger (1993); Luce and Woodman (1993); Mellor (1995). On the reception of the *Germania*, see Lund (1995) and Krebs (2011).

[2] Schmitthenner (1981: 27) has already drawn attention to this *desideratum*: 'The profound effect produced by this portrayal of the Jews by Tacitus in particular and by other classical authors since the revival of classical antiquity has not to my knowledge been studied in any cohesive fashion.'

oeuvre. The entire palette of reception possibilities has been deployed in the process: sober commentaries alongside militant pamphlets, protests about the Tacitean portrayal of the Jews, attempted rebuttal or even enthusiastic appropriation of its sometimes invidious propositions. In the following study, these kinds of reactions and (where possible) their background in intellectual history will be traced in broadly chronological order. As with all studies of the reception of ancient authors, completeness can never be the aim.

PAGAN RECEPTION AND TERTULLIAN'S CRITIQUE

A pagan reception of Tacitus' works is discernible only with difficulty.[3] Certainly, the work of the Senator Tacitus must have found an interested readership in senatorial circles, and his correspondence with his younger contemporary and friend Pliny the Younger indicates that Tacitus' work indeed faced reception during his lifetime.[4] But his difficult Latin acted even in ancient times as a barrier to wider reception, and for that reason Tacitus 'in no way [took] the place to which he might have laid claim'.[5] In the few and sometimes heavily disputed Greek and Roman responses to Tacitus, no trace of the Jewish Excursus can be detected. Ammianus Marcellinus seems to have allowed himself to be inspired stylistically and intellectually by Tacitus, but in the four passages of his historical work in which he deals with Judaea and the Jews, no Tacitean influence can be established.[6] So all that may be said about this first phase of Tacitus'

---

[3] For Tacitus' reception in ancient times, cf. the early studies by Cornelius (1888), Fabia (1895), and Haverfield (1916).

[4] Fabia (1895: 2). Cf. Pliny *Ep.* 1.6; 6.16.20; 7.20.

[5] Schanz and Hosius (1935: 639). Fabia (1895: 10): 'If we maintain that the fashion for Tacitus was considerable, we acknowledge that it was brief . . .'.

[6] Amm. 14.8.11f.; 22.5.4f.; 23.1.2f.; 24.4.1f. Conspicuously absent from Ammianus' description of Judaea (14.8.11f.) are lists of the distinguishing features of Judaic geography such as balsam, the Dead Sea, etc. Nor is Ammianus referring back to Tacitus when he describes in polemical tones Marcus Aurelius' alleged aversion to the Jews, cf. 22.5.5: *Ille* [sc. *Marcus Aurelius*] *enim cum Palaestinam transiret Aegyptum petens, Iudaeorum faetentium et tumultuantium saepe taedio percitus*, 'For Marcus Aurelius, as he was passing through Palestine heading for Egypt, often being disgusted with the foul-smelling and troublesome Jews . . .'.

reception, among pagan authors, is that few traces can be found, none of which involves the Jewish Excursus.

The oldest and most significant reference to Tacitus' Jewish Excursus is that by Tertullian in his *Apologeticus* (197 CE). Tertullian alludes to Tacitus' description of the Exodus, especially the episode of the wild asses which were said to have led Moses to abundant sources of water (Tac. *H.* 5.3.2), and the corresponding worship by the Jews of the image of an ass (*H.* 5.4.2). Tertullian reckons that with this story Tacitus opened up the Christians, through their relationship to the Jews (*Iudaicae religionis propinquos*, 'associates of the Jewish religion' *Apol.* 16.3), to the suspicion that they would worship an ass's head. Tertullian argues, moreover, that Tacitus directly contradicts himself on this point, because in the same historical work (*H.* 5.9.1) he reports that Pompey on entering the temple found *no* images of gods.[7] On the strength of this contradiction, Tertullian derides Tacitus as *sane ille mendaciorum loquacissimus* ('to be sure, that most eloquent of liars', *Apol.* 16.3).[8]

The (indirect) reception of Tacitus's Jewish Excursus has been strongly influenced by this critique of Tertullian's. His derisive comment has echoed down the centuries. His critique is above all a Christian one: besides the contradictory information about the Jews' form of worship, Tacitus' work could have offered up many another contradiction for criticism. On just the same topic—religious ceremony without images—Tacitus reports in the *Germania* that the Germanic tribes did not model their gods on the human form (*G.* 9.2). This

---

[7] Tert. *Apol.* 16.1–3 (cf. also the parallel passage Tert. *Nat.* 1.11.2; the two passages are completely identical in content and virtually so in their language). Surprisingly, Tertullian shows no interest at all in the passage where Tacitus, in his discussion of Jewish monotheism, states that there were no images of gods in Jewish temples (*H.* 5.5.4). This passage would have bolstered Tertullian's argument by making the contradiction even more apparent.

[8] Tertullian does not quote Tacitus accurately; in particular he misses the fact that Tacitus does not speak of an ass's *head*, but refers less specifically to an *image* of an ass (*H.* 5.4.2: *effigiem animalis, quo monstrante errorem sitimque depulerant, penetrali sacrauere*, 'In the innermost part of the temple, they dedicated an image of the animal who had guided them and ended their wandering and thirst'). Such imprecision is found in many later recipients, directly or indirectly linked to Tertullian. There are two probable reasons for Tertullian's lack of precision: first he is thinking predominantly of reproaches made against the *Christians* of worshipping the *head* of an ass (cf. Tert. *Nat.* 1.14f; Min. Fel. 9.3 (Caecilius' criticism of Christianity)). Secondly, there does exist a reproach of *Jewish* worship of an ass's head: Flavius Josephus mentions an assertion by Apion that the Jews had worshipped an ass's head at the time of Antiochus Epiphanes (Jos. *Ap.* 2.80). Tertullian may have known this passage from Josephus (*Apol.* 19.6 quotes Josephus' *Contra Apionem*).

statement stands in contradiction to the description of the Nerthus festival, involving the washing of this goddess (*G*. 40). It is clear from this just how decisive it was for the early reception of this chapter that Tacitus had expressed himself on the Jews and thus—in the eyes of Christian authors such as Tertullian—on the Christians also. The Christian reception, as will become even clearer in what follows, played a large role in determining the effect made by the Jewish Excursus.[9]

Tertullian's comments are significant in another respect. Beatus Rhenanus noticed that Tertullian referred to the fifth book of the *Histories*, whereas the numbering at that time listed the Jewish Excursus as the twenty-first book of Tacitus' work. It also occurred to Rhenanus that there was a gap between Books 16 and 17. From this, Justus Lipsius drew the conclusion that the text must constitute two different works: sixteen books of *Annals* and five books of *Histories*.[10] So this allocation of the books arose from an observation of Tertullian's comment about the relevant passage in the Jewish Excursus. Also important in this regard is a passage in St Jerome's commentary on Zachariah, which refers to Tacitus' account of the fall of Jerusalem and gives the size of Tacitus' complete historical work (*Annals* and *Histories*) as thirty books.[11] Here too it is apparent that the reception of the Jewish Excursus played an important role in the manuscript tradition of Tacitus' collected output.

SULPICIUS SEVERUS, OROSIUS, AND HEGESIPPUS

Tacitus' account of the Jewish–Roman War was accorded its first more or less detailed reception by the Christian historiographers

---

[9] Tertullian makes use of the Jewish Excursus in other places also. In his discussion of the Roman god Saturn (*Nat*. 2.12), he refers to Tacitus' mention of this god at *H*. 5.4.4 in the context of his remarks about the sabbath. Elsewhere Tertullian describes the burnt region of Sodom and Gomorrah in terms which recall those of Tacitus: compare Tert. *Apol*. 40.7 with Tac. *H*. 5.7.1. It is noteworthy that Tertullian, in his *Aduersus Iudaeos*, does not appear to refer to the aggressive language of Tacitus' Jewish Excursus.

[10] Etter (1966: 29–30).

[11] Hieronymus *Comm. in Zach*. 3.14: *Cornelius quoque Tacitus, qui post Augustum usque ad mortem Domitiani Vitas Caesarum triginta uoluminibus exarauit*, 'Cornelius Tacitus, who set down in thirty books the Lives of the Caesars after Augustus all the way to Domitian's death'. Whether Hieronymus actually read Tacitus is questionable: cf. Barnes (1985: 200).

Hegesippus, Sulpicius Severus and Orosius, for whom Tacitus was a welcome source for their literary retelling of the war. Severus and Orosius have already featured more fully above in connection with the reconstruction of the lost narrative of Tacitus.[12] It is highly important for the reception of Tacitus in general and the Jewish Excursus in particular that Orosius was so commonly read in the Middle Ages, at a time when Tacitus' reception seems to have been largely at a standstill. Thus the Jewish Excursus remained known even in the 'dark' years of Tacitus' reception.

(Pseudo-)Hegesippus (*c.*370 CE), a Jew converted to Christianity, produced a Latin description of the Jewish War in five books. Even if it is not an actual translation of the *Bellum Judaicum* of Flavius Josephus, Hegesippus quite clearly followed the Flavian historian. Josephus was not his only source, however: he also used pagan Roman authors, including Tacitus. In particular he draws on the geographical chapters of the Jewish Excursus (Tac. *H.* 5.6-7).[13] The passages which depend on Tacitus are not always paraphrased consistently: Hegesippus' description of the burnt-out region of Sodom and Gomorrah owes much to Tacitus, but in contrast to Tacitus, who gives a rational interpretation of the region's destruction, Hegesippus adopts the biblical explanation.[14] Like Sulpicius Severus, and Orosius (and also St Jerome[15]), Hegesippus supplements the information he takes from Josephus with material from the *Histories* of Tacitus.[16] Hegesippus distances himself from Josephus in that—showing himself here as a convert—he interprets the destruction of the Temple of Jerusalem, in an anti-Jewish reversal of Josephus' critical Jewish insider's account, as a punishment for the perfidy of the Jews and the killing of Jesus.[17] It is worth noting that this undisguised anti-Jewish sentiment is not fuelled by any Tacitean arguments or expressions.

---

[12] See Bloch (2002: 116-19).

[13] Tac. *H.* 5.6.1: *septemtrionem e latere Syriae longe prospectant*; Heg. 3.6: *septentrionalia eius a dextero latere Tyrus claudit.*

[14] Hegesippus 4.18 (on Sodom and Gomorrah): *haec propter impiorum supplicia de Sodomitano territorio conperta silentio obducere non oportuit*, 'just because of the punishments inflicted on the wicked, one should not conceal in silence these things which have been discovered about the territory of Sodom.' Cf. Tac. *H.* 5.7.2.

[15] Cf. note 11 above.

[16] Cornelius (1888: 26): 'Besides, in several places Hegesippus adds various words drawn from the books of Tacitus to the words of Josephus.' This is especially clear at Hegesippus 4.18, where he combines Josephus *BJ* 4.476 with Tac. *H.* 5.6.2.

[17] Cf. Sorscher (1973) on this point.

Striking and explicit evidence of the early reception of Tacitus is provided by a *scholion* on Juvenal (*c.* 400 CE?).[18] It relates to an extended section of Juvenal *Satire* 14.96–106, which mentions amongst other things Jewish law said to have been handed down by Moses in some kind of secret book.[19] At the word 'Moses' the scholiast has noted that this may be a priest or king of the Jews, or—and here he relies on Tacitus' Jewish Excursus—the 'founder of their religion' (*inuentor religionis*).[20] So here the Jewish Excursus is used as an aid to understanding (who was Moses?).[21]

Summing up, one can say that the early Christian reception of Tacitus is in a large part a reception of the Jewish Excursus. The perspective of this reception is a distinctly Christian one: for Tertullian, the contradiction which he detected in Tacitus' presentation of Jewish monotheism is a convenient example of the false ideas spread by the heathens about the Christians. Similarly, Orosius refers repeatedly to Tacitus in order to illustrate, on the basis of his handling of Israelite history, the arbitrariness with which pagan historians presented biblical history. Sulpicius Severus, on the other hand, uses Tacitus in accordance with his purpose of convincing 'unbelievers' of Christianity also by taking pagan sources into account.[22] For St Jerome, finally, Tacitus' description of the capture of Jerusalem is an illustration of the veracity of Zachariah's prophesy. These authors name or use Tacitus 'on the coat-tails', so to speak, of Josephus: Tacitus is used as an ancillary (and occasionally contradictory) source for what in the first instance is reported by Josephus. In none of the authors covered can any recourse be demonstrated to the sometimes invidious language of the Jewish Excursus (*H.* 5.4f.). Tacitus' anti-Jewish

---

[18] Wessner (1931: 215) on Juvenal *Sat.* 14.102: [*Volumine*] *Moyses: sacerdos uel rex eius gentis. aut ipsius quidem religionis inuentor, cuius Cornelius etiam Tacitus* (*H.* 5.3) *meminit*, '[In a book] Moses: priest or king of that people; or indeed the founder of that religion itself, as Cornelius Tacitus also says.'

[19] Juvenal *Sat.* 14.102.

[20] The scholiast therefore can be connected with Tac. *H.* 5.4.1: *Moyses quo sibi in posterum gentem firmaret, nouos ritus contrariosque ceteris mortalibus indidit,* 'In order to strengthen the bond with his people in the future, Moses prescribed for them novel religious rites which were quite different from those practised by other mortals.'

[21] It has been mooted that the Juvenal scholiast knew Tacitus only indirectly, via Orosius; see Townend (1972). The Juvenal scholia then cannot have been written before 400 CE. Militating against any earlier dating are, among other things, the many obvious factual errors which no contemporary of Juvenal would have made; cf. Wessner (1931: xxxviii) and Mommsen (1909b).

[22] Cf. Bloch (2002: 116–17).

formulations in these passages are neither adopted nor criticized by their recipients. Tertullian's harsh critique is concerned with Tacitus' inconsistency and the reproach made (by others) against the *Christians* of worshipping an ass's head.

For the wider reception history of the Jewish Excursus it is significant that, through the use made of it by Christian authors, parts of it became accessible even to readers who did not read Tacitus, especially in the Middle Ages.

BUDÉ'S REPROACH AND THE FIRST
COMMENTARIES ON THE *HISTORIES*

During the Middle Ages, the reception of Tacitus' writings can be brought to light only with very great difficulty.[23] Tacitus seems to have fallen almost entirely into obscurity, so that from the seventh to the fourteenth centuries only isolated traces of his reception can be shown. Of course, parts of the Jewish Excursus did remain known, thanks to the rejoinders of Tertullian and above all Orosius. Alongside the actual reception of Tacitus, there emerged quite early on an indirect one which, given the strong resonance of the works of these two Christian authors, is not to be underestimated.[24]

The fifteenth and sixteenth centuries finally saw the rediscovery of Tacitus, and gradually even a veritable Tacitus renaissance.[25] In completely different contexts, the Jewish Excursus was now being referred to once more.[26] However, this renaissance was soon to be

---

[23] See on this point Haverfield (1916) and Tenney (1931).

[24] So in the 9th century, the chronicler Freculph, bishop of Lisieux, is seemingly able to quote Tacitus' version of the Exodus in his own description. In fact, he is citing Orosius *Hist.* 1.10.3!

[25] Cf. here Etter (1966) and Schellhase (1976).

[26] The Florentine Leon Battista Alberti in his work *On the Art of Building* (1452) refers at one point to Tacitus' description of the strong and impregnable walls of Jerusalem (Tac. *H.* 5.11): *ceterum, quod alibi diximus, omnium erit capacissima urbs, quae sit rotunda; tutissima, quae sinuosis amfractibus murorum obualletur, qualem fuisse Hierosolimam scribit Tacitus*, 'yet as I have said elsewhere, the most capacious city will be one which is round, but the safest will be one which is fortified with curving sinuous walls, just like the city of Jerusalem about which Tacitus writes' (L. B. Battista, *De Re Aedificatoria* 4.3, ed. G. Orlandi (Milan, 1966)). In the *Liber Chronicarum* of Hartmann Schedel (1493) the etymology of Jerusalem, probably following Tacitus, is clarified in the following way: 'The Solymi were people living

faced with a new derogatory judgement of Tacitus. The French humanist Guillaume Budé reproached Tacitus with having taken up Nero's scapegoating of the Christians for the fire of Rome in order to please his patron Domitian. Budé called Tacitus in this regard a 'nefarious man', his stylus 'smeared with the poison of falsehood'.[27] This attack by Budé had devastating consequences and was 'more than a mere repetition of Tertullian's harsh judgement of Tacitus'.[28] Budé's critique would rumble on in the same far-reaching way as Tertullian's.

Yet in Jean Bodin, Michel de Montaigne, and Marc-Antoine Muret, Tacitus found eloquent defenders against the reproaches of Tertullian and Budé.[29] In a letter written in 1572 Muret, newly installed as professor of rhetoric, reacted against reservations which the Church had raised concerning a proposed lecture on Tacitus. It was put to Muret that Tacitus had somewhere said bad things about the Christians and the Jews.[30] The French humanist did not allow himself to be deterred from his lecture plans, but he did feel himself obliged to justify his liking for Tacitus.[31] This polemic indicates what a heavy burden Tacitus' chapters about the Jews and the Christians were now charged with.

in the land of Lycia in the mountains, who named Hierosolima after themselves' (*Die Schedelsche Weltchronik von 1483* (Dortmund, 1988), 4th edn, fo. XVII); cf. Tac. *H.* 5.2.3, *clara alii Iudaeorum initia, Solymos, carminibus Homeri celebratam gentem, conditae urbi Hierosolyma nomen e suo fecisse*, 'Others posit a famous ancestry for the Jews in the Solymi, a tribe celebrated by Homer in his poems: these people allegedly founded Jerusalem and named it after themselves.'

[27] G. Budé, *De Asse et Partibus Eius* (Basel, 1556 [Paris, 1514]), 192–3.

[28] Von Stackelberg (1960: 160).

[29] Reacting to Budé's judgement, Bodin attempts to place Tacitus' remarks on the Jews in a historical context. See J. Bodin, *Methodus ad facilem historiarum cognitionem* (Paris, 1572), 96. In this piece, Bodin recognizes Tacitus' accomplishments as historian, politician, and stylist. For the reactions to Bodin, cf. Momigliano (1947: 91 n. 8). See M. de Montaigne, *Essais*, bk 3, ch. 8 in R. Barral (ed.), *Œuvres complètes* (Paris, 1967 [1586]), 380: 'He [sc. Tacitus] needs no excuse for agreeing with the religion of his own times, in accordance with the laws which governed him, and for being ignorant of the true religion. This is his misfortune, not his failing.' On the reception of Tacitus by Montaigne, cf. von Stackelberg (1960: 164–86), Etter (1966: 65–9), and Malissard (1992). On Muret, cf. the following notes.

[30] See M.-A. Muret, *Lettres inédites* (P. de Nolhac (ed.), *Mélanges Ch. Graux* (Paris, 1884), 389), cited by von Stackelberg (1960: 107). Muret also defends Tacitus against the then widespread reproach that he was a poor stylist. For Muret and Tacitus in detail see von Stackelberg (1960: 106–18).

[31] He did this in a somewhat sarcastic tone: 'If we think that at this time nothing should be read except that which agrees with the Christian religion, of course we should lay aside all those ancient Greek and Latin writers. Or is any one of us so weak as to be in danger of starting to waver in the Christian faith if he recognizes that Tacitus was not a Christian?' (M.-A. Muret, *Orationes, epistulae, hymnique sacri, editio nova* (Leipzig, 1629 [1st edn: Ingolstadt, 1604], 2.14).

A key reason for Tacitus' advancing at this time to become one of the most widely read ancient authors was that his work could serve as a substitute for one placed on the Index of prohibited books: Machiavelli's *The Prince*. In this intensive phase of his reception ('Tacitism', *c.*1580–1680), Tacitus was called into evidence by both supporters and opponents of absolutism.[32] 'Tacitism' also meant that the old critiques of the Jewish Excursus and the chapter on the Christians could now also be deployed against Machiavelli. Religious criticism was sometimes just a cover for political criticism.[33]

After the *editio princeps* of 1470 (Vindolino de Spira, Venice), Tacitus' work over the next two centuries saw a regular flurry of new editions and commentaries.[34] While the first commentators, self-evidently great admirers of the rediscovered Tacitus, did express their astonishment at the malicious tone and false allegations in the Jewish Excursus, they nonetheless strove visibly and sometimes touchingly to comment on these chapters of the *Histories* in a sober manner. Even so, Andrea Alciato (1517) is put off by Tacitus' *impietas* in questioning divine power.[35] Marcus Vertranius Maurus (1565) believes that despite the audaciousness with which Tacitus speaks of the Jews, one cannot help laughing; Tacitus has clearly carried his inaccuracies across from his sources.[36] Justus Lipsius (1585) rallies to Tacitus' defence and repudiates in relatively strong terms the Tertullianic polemic against Tacitus' assertion that Jews

---

[32] Von Stackelberg (1960: 63–93); Etter (1966: 15–26); Burke (1969); Volpilhac-Auger (1985: 23–6).

[33] Cf. Etter (1966: 62).

[34] Between 1580 and 1700 there appeared more than 100 commentaries on Tacitus (Burke 1969: 150). It would of course have been impossible for me to consult all the commentaries on the *Histories*. However, those summarized in the following pages must be representative. The extraordinarily large collection of commentaries on Tacitus in Basel University Library was very useful to me. J. Gronovius' publication *C. Cornelii Taciti Opera quae exstant* (Utrecht, 1721) includes, alongside his own commentary, notes on many earlier commentaries (by among others B. Rhenanus, M.-A. Muret, and H. Grotius. In the following discussion, for the sake of simplicity, quotations will be taken from this publication of Gronovius. An overview of editions, commentaries, and translations of the 15th–17th centuries is given by Etter (1966: 213–15).

[35] Alciato, in Gronovius, *Taciti Opera*, 355 on Tac. *H.* 5.5.5. On Alciato, cf. Etter (1966: 27–8).

[36] M. Vertranius Maurus, in Gronovius, *Taciti Opera*, 349 on Tac. *H.* 5.2.1. On Vetranius, cf. Etter (1966: 32–3).

worshipped an ass's head; he points to even more absurd passages in other pagan authors.[37] Tacitus' unpolemical handling of Jewish monotheism is accordingly noted with relief by Lipsius.[38] In similar vein to Lipsius, the Frenchman Julianus Pichon (1686) a hundred years later attempts to relativize Tacitus' errors. For him there is no question in the Excursus of onolatry by the Jews; they may, as Tacitus declared, have consecrated an image of an ass, but they did not worship it.[39]

Generally Tacitus received only restrained criticism from the early historical commentators for his apparent errors, and his standing as a historian was not called into question. It was pointed out that Tacitus was after all only a heathen (*ethnicus*), and as such could not understand Judaism and hence Christianity.[40] The outcry raised by Tertullian and Budé had not in the end stood in the way of sober-minded commentaries.

In none of the recognized commentaries can there be seen any anti-Jewish attitude such as might seek to endorse or 'contemporize' reproaches of Tacitus, though this would scarcely have been surprising against the background of the heavy burden of Tertullian and Budé with which the commentators had to contend. But even the openly anti-Jewish polemics in sixteenth- and seventeenth-century literature seem not to have resorted to Tacitus' diatribes against the Jews.[41] Also after the rediscovery of Tacitus, the Jewish Excursus did not serve as a source for anti-Semitic observations.

Not all of the commentators were so lenient with Tacitus' errors as the aforementioned sixteenth- and seventeenth-century interpreters. The two earliest essays (probably) to deal extensively with the Jewish

---

[37] J. Lipsius, *C. Cornelii Taciti Opera quae exstant* (Antwerp, 1585), on Tac. *H.* 5.4.2.

[38] Ibid. on Tac. *H.* 5.5.4.

[39] J. Pichon, *C. Cornelii Taciti Opera* (Paris, 1682–7; *Histories*: 1686) on Tac. *H.* 5.4.2.

[40] The chapter on the Christians (*A.* 15.44) receives similar comments. Cf. e.g. Beatus Rhenanus in Gronovius, *Taciti Opera*, 662 on Tac. *A.* 15.44: 'He calls Christian piety a "deadly superstition", but he speaks as a heathen, and one ignorant of the mysteries of our religion.'

[41] Melamed (1984) examined anti-Jewish polemics of the 16th and 17th centuries for echoes of Tacitus, and reaches the conclusion that Tacitus is not referred to anywhere (147: 'In all the anti-Jewish literature consulted, Tacitus is not mentioned'). Melamed suggests that this is because Tacitus expressly describes the Christians as stemming from the Jews (Tac. *A.* 15.44: Judaea as *origo eius mali*, 'the source of that wickedness'), so that using Tacitus as 'raw material for anti-Jewish literature' could also be interpreted as anti-Christian (149).

Excursus in isolation from the *Histories*, by Georg Caspar Kirchmaier (1676 and 1679) and Christian Worm (1694), were distinctly harder on Tacitus.[42] Worm was not concerned exclusively with Tacitus, but also with erroneous reporting on the Jews by other ancient authors. Kirchmaier's commentary, on the other hand, is probably the oldest specialized essay on the Jewish Excursus. Both authors assail Tacitus' observations with other pagan authors' statements about the Jews and with relevant passages from the Bible and the Talmud. Their commentaries thus become miniature treatises on ancient Judaism. For Worm, it is ultimately inexplicable that Tacitus can report on the origin of the Jews in the way he does. Rather than such self-contradiction, he would have done better to remain silent.[43] Kirchmaier, for his part, believes Tacitus' Jewish Excursus has scarcely anything to do with historiography, Tacitus did not know what he intended, his opinions jump first this way then that.[44]

The difference could not have been greater between these commentaries drawn up on more firmly theological lines and the first philological-historical (not to say political) commentaries. Worm and Kirchmaier are not afraid to pillory Tacitus for his errors. For them, what

---

[42] G. C. Kirchmaier, *Exercitatio academica ad C.C. Taciti Histor. Lib. V Capita aliquot priora de rebus moribusque Judaeorum* (Wittenberg, 1676); C. Worm, *De corruptis antiquitatum Hebraearum apud Tacitum et Martialem vestigiis libri duo* (Copenhagen, 1694). Both in Blasius Ugolinus, *Thesaurus Antiquitatum Sacrarum complectens selectissima clarissimorum virorum opuscula, in quibus veterum Hebraeorum mores, leges, instituta, ritus sacri et civiles illustrantur*, vol. 2 (Venice, 1744), 1–300 (Worm), 301–28 (Kirchmaier). Kirchmaier also wrote a separate commentary on the historical section (Tac. *H.* 5.1, 8–13): *De obsidione Hierosolymitana, ex V. Hist. C.C. Taciti* (Wittenberg, 1679).

[43] See Worm, *De corruptis antiquitatum Hebraearum* 21. Worm attempts in somewhat sophistical fashion to explain Tacitus' statements through false conclusions from Jewish sources—as though Tacitus had consulted these himself. On the first account of the *origo*, that the Jews came from Crete, Worm remarks that he rates this theory as completely unfounded (*tanta & vesana hallucinatio*, 'an enormous and mad delusion'), but that it may have arisen through confusion with the Philistines, whose homeland is described in the Old Testament (*Jer.* 47, 4; 1 *Sam.* 30, 14) as 'the south of Crete' (30–31.).

[44] In the short introduction to his commentary, *Exercitatio*, 301, Kirchmaier writes, 'There is more ignorance and malice apparent here than historical truth.' On Tac. *H.* 5.2.1 (Cretan origin of the Jews; Jews driven out at same time as Saturn; the *Ida-Judaei* etymology): 'Tacitus begins from traditions which are false and derive from fables', 'These matters should be ascribed to the mythology of poets, not to a chronological account', 'a most wretched proof, sought from name-play' (ibid. 301–3). On Tac. *H.* 5.2.3 (Assyrian origin of the Jews): 'Tacitus hurtles this way and that, uncertain about his thoughts' (p. 305).

stands pre-eminent is the biblical truth which they consider to have been disparaged by Tacitus' misconstructions. Thus both commentaries turn into Christian *apologiae* against Tacitus' portrayals. Concerning the prodigies described at Tacitus *H.* 5.13, Kirchmaier remarks that neither Roman nor Jew had recognized the true prodigy, Jesus Christ.[45]

JEWISH REACTIONS IN THE SEVENTEENTH CENTURY

What reactions were there from the Jewish side to Tacitus' ethnography? Here there are three significant Jewish authors of the seventeenth century to be noted, who either received or made use of Tacitus' Jewish Excursus: the Venetian rabbi Simone Luzzatto, the Spanish Marrano[46] emigré to Italy Isaac Cardoso, and the Dutch philosopher Baruch (Benedictus) de Spinoza. Prior to Luzzatto, Tacitus' Jewish Excursus was addressed only very marginally in Jewish writings.[47]

---

[45] Kirchmaier, *De obsidione*, 24: 'But indeed neither Jews nor Romans were willing or had the power to discern the prophecy (*Book of Micah*, ch. 5) about the leader of Israel and heavenly king of the Jews, Jesus of Nazareth.' Julianus Pichon, *C. Cornelii Taciti Opera* (Paris, 1682–7, *Histories*: 1686), in his note on *H.* 5.5.3 (*hinc generandi amor*), relates the 'passion for propagation' to the expectation of Christ: 'There was some more forceful explanation, without doubt because they were expecting Christ.'

[46] A Marrano was an Iberian 'crypto-Jew' legally obliged to convert, but doing so only nominally.

[47] Azariah de Rossi, in his Hebrew work *Light of the Eyes* (2nd edn, Berlin 1794, Mantua, 1573–5), refers repeatedly to Greek and Roman authors, among them Tacitus. In ch. 26, drawing specifically on Tacitus, he points out that until Pompey no Roman had harmed the Jews. Rossi here relies on the analogous statement in the Jewish Excursus: *Romanorum primus Cn. Pompeius Iudaeos domuit*, 'Gnaeus Pompey was the first of the Romans to conquer the Jews' (Tac. *H.* 5.9.1; Rossi's Hebrew translation of this passage also evokes a biblical verse: cf. *Lamentations* 4.6). Rossi does not cite Tacitus directly but—as he himself states—via J. L. Vives' commentary on Augustine (Basel, 1543). Thus Rossi, whose work combines Jewish tradition and Italian Renaissance culture (Yerushalmi 1982: 69), uses Tacitus as a historical source; on this; cf. also the introduction to the English translation by Weinberg (2001: xli–xlii). A first (albeit very brief) Jewish rebuttal of Tacitus' depiction of Judaism appears in Menasseh (Manasseh) ben Israel. In his *Conciliador* (Amsterdam, 1632, *non vidi*), in the course of a discussion of imageless worship, he examines how this topic is dealt with in Tacitus: 'We . . . clearly see the falsehood recorded by Tacitus to vilify the Jews, stating that they worshipped the head of an ass, originating, as he says, in their following the steps of a wild ass in the wilderness, when they were in want of water, until they came to a fountain at which he drank; which tale not only shows his

Simone Luzzatto

Simone Luzzatto's annotations on the Jewish Excursus of Tacitus, the 'famoso Historico Romano' as he called him, form the longest chapter of his *Discorso circa il stato degl'Hebrei et in particolàr dimoranti nell'inclita Città di Venetia*.[48] Among a number of reasons for these being of interest is the fact that, in contrast to many other commentators, Luzzatto's focus is expressly not on the six different accounts of Jewish origins offered by Tacitus, but on those points which relate to Jewish everyday life.[49] Just how far he links Tacitus' polemic, between the lines, to his own milieu in Venice is not easy to judge. It has certainly been demonstrated that Luzzatto's essay is not exclusively apologetic in character. Luzzatto shows himself, rather, to be a Tacitist and Machiavellist.[50]

Luzzatto takes seven anti-Jewish 'slanders' (*diffamationi*) which he explains in turn and refutes with quotations from the Bible. The slanders comprise: the worship of an ass's head, immorality, misanthropy, contrast between the Jewish god and the Roman Bacchus, renunciation of pork, prodigies of Jerusalem, and the Sabbath. The fact that here, too, the first item on the list is the worship of asses is no coincidence. Luzzatto was aware of the numerous reactions regarding this issue.[51] Just like the Christian commentators of Tacitus, Luzzatto

---

ignorance of Holy Writ, but also his hatred and evil disposition' (from the English translation by E. H. Lindo, *The Conciliator of R. Manesseh ben Israel* (New York, 1972 [1842]), 157). On the reception of Tacitus by Rossi and Manesseh ben Israel, cf. Melamed (1984: 151–2).

[48] Simone Luzzatto, *Discorso circa il stato degl'Hebrei et in particolàr dimoranti nell'inclita Città di Venetia* (Venice, 1638), 58–73 on Tacitus. The following citations refer to this publication, though its pagination is not always consistent. On Luzzatto and Tacitus, see at length Melamed (1984). At the start of his treatise Luzzatto pays tribute to Tacitus the historian thus: 'The famous Roman historian Cornelius Tacitus, through his learning and experience of political affairs deservedly numbered amongst the leading masters of civil government' (*Discorso*, 58).

[49] See ibid.

[50] Melamed (1984: 157): 'Luzzatto does not use Tacitus only in order to attack Christian anti-Semitism. He uses him also since he accepted him, like many other contemporary thinkers, as a supreme authority on political thought. . . . In the Jewish context he uses him as a secure means of assailing Christian anti-Semitism. Likewise, in the political context he uses him as a secure means of presenting the Machiavellian position. Christian anti-Semitism, on the one hand, and Machiavellism, on the other, thus appear in Tacitean disguise.' Melamed demonstrates (161–4) that Luzzatto in part uses the language of Machiavelli.

[51] *Discorso*, 60: 'A lie which has already been refuted by many learned men, and in particular by Tertullian.'

also finds himself torn between, on the one hand, his intellectual affinity with Tacitus and, on the other, the polemical Excursus on the Jews. Luzzatto tries to show that Judaism too is based on meaningful *political* principles. Judaism and Rome are not two different worlds. Rather, the banning of pork, for example, should be understood as a political matter—precisely in the Tacitean sense. Such laws serve to bind the faithful to their authorities.[52] Likewise, Luzzatto defends the Sabbath with political and social arguments and makes connections with parallel Roman institutions. However, whereas the Jewish day of rest served to bring spiritual relaxation and greater dedication to commercial matters on the remaining days of the week, Roman rest days were mainly to do with licentiousness.[53] Luzzatto goes on to explain the political background to the sabbatical year: it benefits efficient farming, makes enough food available for everyone after seven years, and gives the land workers the chance, every seventh year, to devote themselves to military training. The sabbatical year makes it possible to have a civilian army without economic hardship.[54]

Isaac Cardoso

Isaac Cardoso is the author of the important Spanish apologia *Excelencias* (1679), a work shaped by Cardoso's recollections of anti-Semitism in Spain.[55] Cardoso has quite frequent recourse to Tacitus' Jewish Excursus, and he seems to assume that the educated of his time were familiar with Tacitus' *Histories* and therefore also the Jewish Excursus.[56] Cardoso defends Judaism against anti-Semitic slanders, among others that Jews are misanthropic. As his prime evidence for this reproach he names Tacitus' Jewish Excursus, and refutes it with numerous biblical references—and also with Tacitus' own statement that the Jews did not kill posthumously born babies (*H.* 5.5.3: *nam et necare quemquam ex agnatis nefas,* 'for it is a sin to

---

[52] See *Discorso,* 66.
[53] See ibid. 71.
[54] See ibid. 73. Cf. Melamed (1984: 167–70).
[55] Isaac Cardoso, *Las excelencias de los Hebreos* (Amsterdam, 1679, *non vidi*). I cite from the Hebrew translation by Joseph Kaplan (Jerusalem, 1971). For a discussion of Cardoso's work at length, see Yerushalmi (1971: 417–22).
[56] Ibid. 418.

kill any surplus children'), which in Cardoso's view is proof of humanity.[57]

Like many a Christian recipient of Tacitus (Worm for instance), Cardoso is surprised that such a critical and truthful historian as Tacitus should have uncritically adopted such far-fetched tales as that of Moses leading the way to water with the help of a herd of asses; and that he relied on Apion rather than on either Josephus, the Septuagint, or direct information from Roman Jews.[58] Cardoso's respect for Tacitus is reflected in his resolution of Tacitus' contradictory portrayals of the Jewish concept of God (worship of asses (*H.* 5.4.2) vs. aniconic worship (*H.* 5.5.4)): his explanation is that Tacitus corrected his original view at a later stage, having either acquired better information or, perhaps through pure impulse, realized that the Jews had an imageless God.[59] Cardoso uses a Tacitean reference to counter the anti-Semitic stereotype that Jews smell bad, arguing that if even an author such as Tacitus says of the Jews that they have healthy and resilient bodies (*H.* 5.6.1: *corpora hominum salubria et ferentia laborum*, 'the bodies of these people are healthy and tolerant of hard work'), then this reproach must be absurd, for how can a healthy body smell bad?[60]

Baruch de Spinoza

Baruch de Spinoza quotes Tacitus with some frequency.[61] When, for example, in chapter 17 of his *Tractatus Theologico-Politicus*, which deals with the Jewish state, he introduces the topic of a government endangered by its own citizens, he refers his readers to Tacitus' description of civil war turmoil during the Year of the

---

[57] *Excelencias* (trans. Kaplan), 109–11.

[58] Ibid. 41. Cf. Yerushalmi (1971: 419).

[59] *Excelencias* (trans. Kaplan), 44. In connection with his defence against the reproach of onolatry, Cardoso argues that this belief may have had a real basis insofar as it might be related to Samson's heroic deeds—Samson slew 1,000 Philistines with the jawbone of an ass (*Jud.* 15, 14–20) (*Excelencias*, trans. Kaplan, 48). Luzzatto had earlier argued in similar fashion: objects associated with biblical miracles—manna vase, Aaron's rod, etc.—were kept in holy places (*Discorso*, 60).

[60] *Excelencias* (trans. Kaplan), 55.

[61] Baruch de Spinoza, *Tractatus Theologico-Politicus* (Amsterdam, 1670), abbreviated in subsequent notes as *TThP*; my citations are from the edition by C. Gebhardt, *Spinoza Opera*, vol. 3 (2nd edn, Heidelberg, 1925, repr. 1972). On Spinoza and Tacitus, cf. Wirszubski (1955).

Four Emperors.[62] In his historical contextualization of the Jewish theocracy—proposing that after the exodus from Egypt the Jews handed their natural right to self-government over to God—Spinoza poses the question of how far this kind of constitution was capable of keeping both governors and governed in check. Fundamental to this, he suggests, had been a patriotic love of country expressing itself on the one hand as religious piety and on the other—and here Spinoza begins to echo the Tacitus of the Jewish Excursus—as hatred of other nations.[63] Nonetheless Spinoza makes no explicit reference here to the Jewish Excursus. When giving an example of the strength of this double-sided Jewish 'policy' (strengthening inwardly, exclusion outwardly) and the associated difficulties for others in prevailing over the Jews, Spinoza does then explicitly reference Tacitus, who in the second book of the *Histories* (Spinoza does not explicitly refer to the fifth!) alludes to the difficulties anticipated by the Flavians in conquering Jerusalem.[64] Finally, in the same chapter Spinoza asks why it is that the Jews have so often fallen away from the law. He considers the fault to lie not with the Jews but with their laws and customs. These, Spinoza declares with astonishment, were given by God not as laws but as a punishment for their disobedience. At this, Spinoza feels compelled, as he himself states, to repeat Tacitus' words: '*quae mutatio* (that as a punishment for worshipping the golden calf, the firstborn should be cast aside and the Levites chosen in their stead) *quo eam magis ac magis considero, in uerba Taciti me cogit erumpere, illo tempore non fuisse Deo curae securitatem illorum, fuisse ultionem*, 'the more and more I ponder that exchange, I feel compelled to blurt out

---

[62] *TThP*, 204: 'Concerning this matter, see Tacitus at the start of *Histories* 4, where he depicts the utterly wretched appearance of the city.'

[63] *TThP*, 215, where Spinoza's use of *odium*, *separati*, and *contrarius* recalls Tacitus' Latin: *hostile odium* (*H.* 5.5.1), *separati epulis* (*H.* 5.5.2), and *nouos ritus contrariosque* (*H.* 5.4.1).

[64] *TThP*, 215, as Tacitus himself attests in the following words from *Histories* 2: *profligauerat bellum Iudaicum Vespasianus, oppugnatione Hierosolymorum reliqua, duro magis et arduo opere ob ingenium gentis et peruicaciam superstitionis, quam quo satis uirium obsessis ad tolerandas necessitates superesset*' ('Vespasian had already given the decisive turn to the Jewish war, although the siege of Jerusalem still remained. This was a difficult and uphill task, more because of the peculiar characteristics of the people and the bigotry of its inhabitants than because the besieged had enough strength left to endure a desperate struggle'). It appears from this quotation from Tacitus (*H.* 2.4.3) that Spinoza used the edition of Lipsius. Lipsius has *ob ingenium gentis*, whereas the *Codex Mediceus* has *ob ingenium montis*, as noted by Wirszubski (1955: 180).

the words of Tacitus, that at that time God cared not for our peace of mind, but only for vengeance'.[65] The gods, wrote Tacitus in his general description of the period to be covered in the *Histories*, were concerned with punishment, not with a carefree existence.[66] This remarkable transfer of a statement coined by Tacitus about Rome and its relationship with its gods to the relationship of the Jews with theirs serves, therefore, as an illustration of God as punitive authority.

In the third chapter of his *Tractatus*, which deals with the vocation of the Hebrews and their gift of prophesy, Spinoza relies on Tacitean formulations from the Jewish Excursus. He attributes the phenomenon of Jewish continuity to the peculiarity of Jewish customs and the consequent hatred among other nations which holds the Jews together.[67] Here again, however, Spinoza dispenses with a specific reference to Tacitus' Jewish Excursus. Finally, an almost literal echo of Tacitus is to be found in the *Praefatio* of the *Tractatus*. Spinoza is discussing in general terms—not specifically applying to the Jews— the phenomenon of superstition to which people in their fear and insecurity constantly cling. Once again without expressly quoting Tacitus, he makes his borrowing from the Jewish Excursus quite apparent: *Si quid porro insolitum magna cum admiratione uident, id prodigium esse credunt, quod Deorum aut summi Numinis iram indicat, quodque adeo hostiis, et uotis non piare, nefas habent homines superstitioni obnoxii, et religioni aduersi,* 'If moreover they see with great astonishment anything unusual, they believe that this is a prodigy indicating the anger of the Gods or of the highest power, and men steeped in superstition and hostile to proper religious practice regard it as wrong not to atone for it by sacrifices and vows.'[68]

---

[65] *TThP*, 218.

[66] Tac. *H.* 1.3.2, *nec enim umquam atrocioribus populi Romani cladibus magisue iustis indiciis adprobatum est non esse curae deis securitatem nostram, esse ultionem,* 'For it has never been verified by more terrible disasters for the Roman people or by fuller portents that the gods care not for our peace of mind, but only for vengeance.'

[67] *TThP*, 56. Spinoza's use of *separauerunt*/*odium*/*ritibus caeterarum nationum*/*contrariis*/*circumcisionis* recalls Tacitus' *ritus contrariosque ceteris* (*H.* 5.4.1), *odium* (*H.* 5.5.1), *separati epulis* (*H.* 5.5.2), *circumcidere* (*H.* 5.5.2). Cf. Wirszubski (1955: 183–4), who points out that Spinoza here speaks only of *ritus*, whereas elsewhere he uses *caerimonia* or *cultus*.

[68] *TThP*, 5 (*Praefatio*). Cf. Tac. *H.* 5.13.1: *euenerant prodigia, quae neque hostiis neque uotis piare fas habet gens superstitioni obnoxia, religionibus aduersa,* 'Various prodigies had occurred, but a nation steeped in superstition and hostile to proper religious practices considered it unlawful to atone for them by offering victims or solemn vows.' Cf. Wirszubski (1955: 181–2). Admittedly Tacitus is saying the exact

Although Spinoza frequently credits Tacitus as a source (five times altogether in chapter 17 of the *Tractatus Theologico-Politicus*), in his allusions to the Jewish Excursus he expressly chose not to refer to it. Despite his high regard for Tacitus as a historian, Spinoza evidently baulks at declaring him as the source—in not just words but content—for his account of Jewish concepts of law: it may be that Tacitus' strongly anti-Jewish propositions ruled out any reference to these chapters. Yet there, among Tacitus' observations on Jewish separatism, Spinoza found some very acceptable formulations for his critique of Jewish law.[69] It is striking that Spinoza, in setting out his philosophy of religion, makes use of the partially hostile Jewish Excursus, and in the preface to his *Tractatus* even employs a phrase from Tacitus that is clearly directed against the Jews as a general critique of religion, and broadens it into a general anthropological observation.

It does, however, appear that in the end, Spinoza distances himself from Tacitus' polemic. In this same chapter 17 of the *Tractatus Theologico-Politicus*, Spinoza criticizes those who view the end of the Jewish state as a consequence of the closed-mindedness of the Jews (*gentis contumacia*, 'the stubbornness of the people'). For Spinoza it is Jewish laws, not the Jews themselves, that are narrow-minded. Nature creates only individuals, not nations.[70] It seems possible that Spinoza is including Tacitus in this criticism. For Tacitus' ethnographical account of the Jews culminates in precisely the Jewish obsessiveness which Spinoza repudiates: *obstinatio uiris feminisque par; ac si transferre sedis cogerentur, maior uitae metus quam mortis* (Tac. *H*. 5.13.3), 'The women were no less determined than the men, and the thought that they might be forced to leave their homes made them fear life more than death.' If Spinoza's criticism is indeed directed against Tacitus, or at least includes him, it is worth noting that Spinoza does not name him.

---

opposite of what Spinoza here expresses: according to Tacitus, *superstitio* caused the Jews (in contrast to the Romans) to refrain from expiating the omens with vows and sacrifice, whereas for Spinoza, who already saw belief in omens as in itself a superstition, vows and sacrifice were marks of *superstitio*.

[69]   Also in his description of the Israelites' rebellion against Moses, Spinoza echoes a Tacitean formulation, without explicitly citing Tacitus; cf. *TThP*, 219, *quare tunc temporis seditio magis desierat quam concordia coeperat* ('Accordingly, it was more that the revolt of that time had stopped rather than that a state of harmony had begun') with Tac. *H*. 4.1.1: *interfecto Vitellio bellum magis desierat quam pax coeperat*, 'After the murder of Vitellius, it was more that the war had stopped than that peace had begun.'

[70]   See *TThP*, 203.

Spinoza's handling of Tacitus' Jewish Excursus is the reception-history equivalent of shadow-boxing.

Reviewing these three examples of the first Jewish reception, it can be seen that Luzzatto and Cardoso pursued mainly apologetic goals, with the former author's *apologia* for Tacitus involving Tacitist ideas. Spinoza, on the other hand, uses Tacitus for a quite different purpose: Tacitus' statements are for him convenient arguments in bringing out his own concepts of tolerance as he weans his critical writing away from his own Jewish tradition. Detectable in all three authors is a certain uneasiness with the great Roman historian's anti-Jewish polemic. Luzzatto and Cardoso, like the Christian recipients before them, struggle to find explanations for Tacitus' errors. As to whether Spinoza also shared this uneasiness, circumstances appear to suggest that in his several linguistic allusions to Tacitus' Jewish Excursus—in contrast to other passages in Tacitus—he never explicitly names the source and at one point, moreover, even seems to repudiate it. Ultimately, however, it is apparent what an important author Tacitus was for the political discourse of the seventeenth century.

THE EIGHTEENTH CENTURY AND THE AGE OF ENLIGHTENMENT

Following in the tradition of Spinoza are the French philosophers of the Enlightenment.[71] For many of them, Tacitus was an *esprit critique* and thus, even if not unconditionally, one of their own.[72] It is important for the reception of the Jewish Excursus that during the Enlightenment Judaism was often the target of freethinking and anti-clerical polemics,[73] and that Tacitus' Jewish Excursus was turned to in the process. In Voltaire, 'Jewish misanthropy', very much as Tacitus described it, is a negative example of his own concept of tolerance.[74] In another context Voltaire refers to the myth of the Jews worshipping an

---

[71] Hertzberg (1968: 39–45).
[72] For readings of Tacitus in the 18th century, cf. the works of Volpilhac-Auger (1985; 1992; 1993: 215–29): 'L'esprit critique de Tacite.'
[73] Cf. Hoffmann (1990: 23–4).
[74] Cf. Hertzberg (1968: 304–5).

ass's head, and attempts to place this 'error' in a historical context and make it understandable. In the article 'Idole, idolâtre, idolâtrie' from his *Dictionnaire philosophique*, Voltaire writes that Judaism was full of images representing God, and that his messengers, the cherubim, also had physical form, with human bodies and animal heads. No wonder, then, that ancient authors such as Tacitus had mistakenly reproached the Jews for worshipping an ass's head.[75] Like other authors of his time,[76] Voltaire endeavoured to see meaning behind Tacitus' errors with the aid of (dubious) attempts at reconstructing historical reality.

Linked to Voltaire through his Enlightenment views, Edward Gibbon, a great admirer of Tacitus, makes conspicuous use of phrases from the Jewish Excursus in his *Decline and Fall of the Roman Empire*.[77] When Gibbon describes the successful expansion of Christianity as something which would have been alien to the misanthropic Jews, he too makes use of the corresponding Tacitean charge of misanthropy.[78] Ultimately however the Jewish Excursus serves Gibbon more as an indirect argument against Christianity, which he saw as retrograde, than as a polemic against Judaism.[79]

---

[75] See Voltaire, *Dictionnaire philosophique*, in U. Kölving (ed.), *Les Œuvres Complètes de Voltaire* (Oxford 1994 [1764]), s.v. 'Idole, Idolâtre, Idolâtrie', 219.

[76] For Voltaire and other examples, cf. Volpilhac-Auger (1993: 210–14).

[77] E. Gibbon, *The History of the Decline and Fall of the Roman Empire* (1776), with an introduction by C. Dawson (London, 1910), 1,430–41 (ch. 15).

[78] Ibid. 1,432: 'who boldly professed, or who faintly disguised, their implacable hatred to the rest of humankind', cf. Tac. *H.* 5.5.1, *sed aduersus omnes alios hostile odium*, 'but against all others a hatred reserved for enemies' (though Gibbon may have in mind the *odium humani generis*, 'hatred of the human race' from Tac. *A.* 15.44, referring to the Christians). Other apparent allusions to the Jewish Excursus are: ibid., 1,431, 'The Jews, who under the Assyrian and Persian monarchies, had languished for many ages as the most despised portion of their slaves . . . ', cf. Tac. *H.* 5.8.2, *dum Assyrios penes Medosque et Persas Oriens fuit, despectissima pars seruientium*, 'While the Assyrian, Median and Persian empires dominated the East, the Jews were considered to be the lowliest element of those enslaved'; ibid., 1,433, 'The mad attempt of Caligula to place his own statue in the temple of Jerusalem was defeated by the unanimous resolution of a people who dreaded death much less than such an idolatrous profanation', cf. Tac. *H.* 5.9.2, *dein iussi a C. Caesare effigiem eius in templo locare arma potius sumpsere, quem motum Caesaris mors diremit*, 'Then, after being ordered to put up a statue of Gaius Caesar in the Temple, the Jews chose to fight instead, although the rebellion came to nothing since the emperor was assassinated.'

[79] However, Gibbon's antipathy towards the Jews was genuine (cf. ch. 23 on Julian, in his *History*), and he followed Tacitus' account of Jewish history out of conviction. He defended his close adherence to Tacitus' arguments in 'A Vindication of Some Passages in the Fifteenth and Sixteenth Chapters of the History of the Decline and Fall of the Roman Empire' (London, 1779), in P. B. Craddock (ed.), *The English Essays of Edward Gibbon* (Oxford, 1972), 229–313 (240–48 on Tacitus). Cf. Hoffman (1988: 16).

The reproaches of Tertullian and Budé, albeit less widespread, continued to have their effect in the eighteenth century. Of particular interest here are the two editions of Tacitus by Gabriel Brotier (1771) and Jean Henri Dotteville (1772).[80] Both commentators attempt to do justice to two irreconcilable claims. They want to bolster Tacitus' credibility without making any concessions to their own religious stances (Brotier was a Jesuit and a priest, Dotteville an Oratarian).[81] Brotier does his level best to defend Tacitus. In the introduction to his lengthy commentary on the Jewish Excursus, he strives to find explanations for Tacitus' gaffes: his lack of interest in religion (his own as well as that of foreigners), the already unsavoury reputation of the Jews in Graeco-Roman literature, and the exacerbation of this in the wake of the Judaeo-Roman War, are enlisted to explain Tacitus' curious portrait of the Jews. Nonetheless Tacitus did get many things right; it is possible to extract truth from error—Brotier's cue for a very detailed commentary.[82] Brotier does in fact criticize Tacitus' charge of misanthropy, for example,[83] but commends the sections on proselytes and monotheism.[84] Even Tacitus' closing swipes against Judaism (Jewish ritual is *absurdus sordidusque*, 'discordant and degrading', whereas Bacchus instituted *festos laetosque ritus*, 'festive and joyous rites') are not completely unfounded in Brotier's view.[85] And finally Brotier aligns himself with those commentators who see the fall of Jerusalem as God's punishment for the Jews' non-recognition of Jesus Christ.[86] Thus Brotier

---

[80] *C. Cornelii Taciti Opera. Recognouit, emendauit, supplementis expleuit, notis, dissertationibus, tabulis geographicis illustrauit G. Brotier*, vol. 3 (Paris, 1771). To his already extensive footnotes on the Jewish Excursus, Brotier adds further detailed notes at the end of the volume (537–80). See too J. H. Dotteville, *Tacite, Œuvres complètes en latin et en français* (Paris, 1780). On Brotier and Dotteville, cf. Volpilhac-Auger (1993: 210–14).

[81] Ibid. 213.

[82] See Brotier, *Taciti Opera*, vol. 3, 537. As with Kirchmaier's commentary, Tacitus' Jewish Excursus also triggers in Brotier a detailed discussion of biblical and early Jewish history.

[83] See Brotier, *Taciti Opera*, vol. 3, on Tac. *H.* 5.5.1.

[84] Ibid. on Tac. *H.* 5.5.2 (proselytes): 'most carefully spoken' and 'still true'; on *H.* 5.5.4 (monotheism): 'truly and excellently spoken'.

[85] See Ibid. on Tac. *H.* 5.5.5.

[86] Both Jews and Flavians misinterpreted the prodigies; ibid. on Tac. *H.* 5.13.1: 'Yet it is utterly certain and clear to anyone thinking back over the course of eras and events that the kingdom of Jesus Christ was foretold by this oracle and by several other ones'.

interprets the section on prodigies in the same way as Kirchmaier a hundred years earlier.

The balancing act between admiration for Tacitus and his own religious beliefs also causes Dotteville some strains in his line of argument. On the one hand, like Bodin, Montaigne, and Lipsius before him, he adopts the position that Tacitus should not be held responsible for the evident errors in the Jewish Excursus as he is basically not interested in Judaism (he refers to the phrase *hi ritus quoquo modo inducti*, 'these observances, whatever their origin', *H.* 5.5.1), and has merely echoed the judgements on the Jews which were circulating at that time.[87] On the other hand Dotteville wishes to detect Tacitus' own handwriting in his description of the Jews' imageless and monotheistic form of worship.[88] These examples show very clearly the tensions under which Dotteville was writing his commentary. Dotteville's purpose, to portray Tacitus as a credible historian, does sometimes involve anti-Semitic stereotypes,[89] and draws the line at Tacitus' interpretation of the Jerusalem prodigies (*H.* 5.13). In Dotteville's view, too, these are not portents of Vespasian's successful campaign in the east, but of the emergence of Christianity which occurred in the same period.[90]

---

[87] Dotteville, *Tacite*, on Tac. *H.* 5.5.1: 'It is clear from these words that Tacitus relates these explanations without adopting them.' In contrast to those commentaries which assiduously refute Tacitus' errors, Dotteville prefers to dispense with proof of the individual statements: 'Tacitus relates these explanations without adopting them, so I will not waste time refuting them,' he writes in introducing his notes on the Jewish Excursus.

[88] Ibid. on Tac. *H.* 5.4.4: 'Tacitus speaks here of the Jews based on his own experiences and not on the evidence of other authors. Must he not have been struck by the sublimity of an idea which he expresses with so much justness and accuracy?'

[89] Already, in the introduction to his notes on the Jewish Excursus, Dotteville (ibid.) observes: '[The Jews] rendered themselves too contemptible for Tacitus to be willing to take the trouble to examine the facts.' At one point he calls the Jews a 'coarse and carnal people' (on Tac. *H.* 5.4.4). On Tacitus' polemical comparison of Jewish and Roman festivals (Tac. *H.* 5.5.5), Dotteville remarks: '*dies festus* amongst the Romans signified a day dedicated to enjoyment, spectacles, banquets. There is none of that in a Jewish holiday. Even the sacrifice of the paschal lamb, their greatest ritual, had something depressing about it: doors daubed with blood, a modest meal eaten in haste, the apparel of a traveller ready to depart.' Cf. similar arguments in Brotier, *Taciti Opera*, vol. 3.

[90] See Dotteville, *Tacite*, on Tac. *H.* 5.13.1.

THE NINETEENTH CENTURY

During the nineteenth century, when the role of Jews in society became a subject for heated debate, a whole series of scholarly works on the ancient Jews began to emerge.[91] In 1843 there appeared the first scholarly treatise on the Jewish Excursus in the German language. Its author, the theologian J. G. Müller, confined himself to the six different accounts of Jewish origins provided by Tacitus.[92] Müller's introductory remarks are typical of a whole range of authors of his time, who, though they might denounce Tacitus' falsehoods, nonetheless share his view that the Jewish religion is depraved. Müller writes:

> while he [sc. Tacitus] and other contemporaries sometimes unjustly ascribed to them [sc. the Jews] many strange characteristics, and sometimes mistook defective outgrowths for the whole, can anybody really take him to task for the overall impression given, the scant affection shown; anybody, that is, who knows from purer sources not accessible to Tacitus with what ossified conformity this prejudiced people so disdainfully thrust off the Salvation of the World which the German people would soon so fervently espouse and cherish? However, with the knowledge we now possess we can scarcely avoid some sense of how the great man was able to pass down such strange views concerning the origins and characteristics of the Jews.[93]

Behind this attitude, where Germanophilia goes hand in hand with hatred of the Jews, lies the widely held nineteenth-century view that the first century CE marked the beginning of so-called 'Late Judaism'. This concept holds that with the fall of the temple the historical role of Judaism is lost: Judaism, now frozen in the legalistic orthodoxies of 'Late Judaism', is supplanted by Christianity.

A few years after Müller, another essayist on Tacitus' Jewish Excursus, F. X. Leonhard, argued along very similar lines: 'Circumstances decreed that the greatest historian of Rome, at a time when that city's approaching doom too was making itself strongly felt, should set forth the origins and character of another nation which

---

[91] Cf. the bibliographical data in Labhardt (1881).
[92] Müller (1843).
[93] Ibid. 895–6. Müller elsewhere tries to come to Tacitus' defence (899): 'For him to have achieved the path of critical truth would have been an almost superhuman step beyond that stage of human development.'

had fulfilled its world-historical significance, and in which all that had refused to follow spiritually the principle newly arisen in its midst was now about to lose the visible symbol of its outmoded way of life'.[94] A similar line can already be observed in the early work of the historian H. Leo, particularly in his Berlin lecture 'On the History of the Jewish State', delivered from 1828 onwards.[95] Despite his assurances to the contrary,[96] his arguments are steeped in anti-Semitic polemic and wholly focused on the break-up of the Jewish state.[97] For Leo this was a direct consequence of the Jewish revolt against the Romans. The severity with which the Romans suppressed the Jews was a reaction to their religious and political fanaticism. In this connection Leo, invoking Tacitus, writes: 'It is understandable, therefore, that the Romans regarded the Jews as the most degraded race on earth, as Tacitus said of them: *profana illic omnia quae apud nos sacra, rursum concessa apud illos quae nobis incesta*—and even more understandable that he could add *apud ipsos fides obstinata, misericordia in promptu, sed aduersus omnis alios hostile odium*.'[98] Leo, who was later to distance himself from some of his rhetoric,[99] is here quite simply projecting Tacitus' words onto Roman opinion in general, and using the Jewish Excursus for his

---

[94] Leonhard (1852: 4). Leonhard's work (apart from the generalized introduction) also deals mainly with the alternative theories of Jewish origin. Leonhard (1852: 6) also sees the Jews of the 1st century CE as a kind of 'discontinued model', and thus can just as readily accept Tacitus' theory of depravation (*H.* 5.4f.) as denounce 'his blatant misjudgment' concerning individual Jewish customs.

[95] H. Leo, *Vorlesungen über die Geschichte des Jüdischen Staates: gehalten an der Universität zu Berlin* (Reutlingen, 1829). On Leo's treatment of Judaism, see at length Hoffmann (1988) 42–73. According to Hoffmann (1988: 43 n.8) Leo first delivered this lecture in 1828.

[96] In his preface (*Vorlesungen*, v), Leo asserts that he is writing 'impersonally and dispassionately'.

[97] Leo's portrayal of Judaism has clear anti-Semitic undertones from the very first lecture (ibid., first lecture, 8): 'As far as the characteristics of the Jewish people are concerned, what distinguishes them from all other peoples in the world is that they possess a truly corrosive and destructive mind.'

[98] Ibid., 24th lecture, 250, quotes from Tac. *H.* 5.4.1 ('Among the Jews everything that we hold sacred is regarded as sacrilegious; on the other hand, they allow things which we consider immoral') and 5.5.1 ('amongst themselves there is stubborn loyalty and a ready benevolence, but they confront all others with a hatred reserved for enemies'). Ibid., 24th lecture, 250, then refers to the passage in the *Annals* which tells of the expulsion of the Jews to Sardinia (*A.* 2.85): '[It then becomes understandable], how, in another passage, he [*sc.* Tacitus] was able to cast them away in a manner which barely allows them to appear human [this is followed by the quotation from *A.* 2.85].'

[99] Hoffmann (1988: 63–7).

own anti-Semitic interpretation of the Judaeo-Roman War. Leo follows Tacitus in depicting a Judaea which is not only fanatical in its religion but obdurate in its politics. 'The once proud and self-contained Israelites', writes Leo, 'had been turned by the fate which had befallen them into a misanthropic nation which snuggled up to superior powers yet took revenge on its enemies with deceit and dagger, and had cast aside all morality.'[100] To the eighteenth-century Enlightenment's religious criticisms is now added a political dimension.[101]

In 1885 the fifth volume of Theodor Mommsen's *Roman History* appeared, with a long chapter tackling the subject of 'Judaea and the Jews'. In it, Mommsen distinguishes between two radically different philosophies of Judaism. The dividing line is once again the destruction of the temple of Jerusalem: the earlier cosmopolitan, proselytizing Judaism and, set against it, the frozen, misanthropic Judaism of the 'rabbi state' which succeeded this event. To illustrate the two periods, Mommsen makes reference to Horace and Tacitus:

> The Jews had always been foreign, and wished to be so; but the feeling of estrangement mounted in horrifying fashion, both among them and towards them, and its hateful and pernicious consequences were extended starkly in both directions. From the disparaging satire of Horace against the importunate Jew from the Roman ghetto, it is quite a step to the solemn resentment which Tacitus harbours towards this scum of the earth for whom everything clean is unclean and everything unclean is clean; in between are those uprisings of the despised nation, the need to defeat it and perpetually expend money and people on keeping it down.[102]

Thus for Mommsen the aggressive tone of Tacitus' Jewish Excursus is a reaction to the Jewish revolts and their consequences. The dichotomy yet again expressed here between 'cosmopolitan' and 'frozen' Judaism is distinguished from that evoked by the theologian J. G. Müller forty years earlier only by the fact that for the latter, the counterpoint to 'rabbi state' was not assimilation but Christianity.[103]

---

[100] Leo, *Vorlesungen*, end of the 24th lecture, 250.

[101] According to Hoffmann (1988: 73).

[102] Th. Mommsen, *Römische Geschichte*, vol. 5 (2nd edn, Berlin 1885), 551. On Mommsen's relations with the Jews, cf. the commentary of Täubler (1936), also Hoffmann (1988: 87–132; 1995: 195–201) and Malitz (1996).

[103] Applicable here is Hoffmann (1988: 114): 'Mommsen's account could be seen as a secularised form of the traditional Christian interpretation.'

Mommsen's argument, which incidentally resembles Gibbon's in reflecting a more general anti-clerical polemic, is a typical nineteenth-century political judgement of Judaism, which in the age of the nation-state was viewed as the prototype of particularism and unwillingness to integrate—'the importunate Jew from the Roman ghetto'.[104]

When the so-called 'anti-Semitic dispute' was raging in Berlin in 1879–80, Tacitus was brought into the ring. In an article in the *Preußische Jahrbücher* the historian H. von Treitschke denounces the alleged particularism of the Jews and mentions Tacitus' reproach against them for their *odium generis humani*, 'hatred of humankind' (*A.* 15.44.4): 'A gulf between western and Semitic natures has existed through the ages, since Tacitus complained of the *odium generis humani*; there will always be Jews who are nothing but German-speaking Orientals....'.[105] In polemical tones, von Treitschke calls for the total assimilation of the Jews. Whereupon, in reply to this article, the Jewish historian H. Graetz points out that the Tacitus quotation in question comes from the chapter in the *Annals* concerning the Christians: 'In support of your anti-Jewish position you quote Tacitus' phrase against the Jews' *odium generis humani*: you should be aware, however, that this one-sided aristocratic Roman historian uses this phrase only about the Christians, when describing their persecution by Nero: *correpti (Christiani) qui fatebantur, deinde indicio eorum multitudo ingens haud proinde in crimine incendii quam odio humani generis conuicti sunt.*'[106] This exchange of blows was followed

---

[104] Elsewhere, in connection with the role of the Jewish diaspora at the time of Caesar, Mommsen sees Jewish 'cosmopolitanism' as an important aid (or 'ferment') for the 'national decomposition' that was an important part of Caesar's politics. Mommsen ascribes an important political role to the Jews in this development. His assessments of diasporic Judaism are ambivalent, but viewed overall are scarcely anti-Semitic; the fact that the phrase 'ferment of cosmopolitanism and national decomposition' soon became an anti-Semitic slogan and would later be exploited by the National Socialists (including Goebbels and Hitler) is not Mommsen's fault. When the 'Berlin anti-Semitic dispute' broke out at the end of the 1870s, Mommsen opposed the anti-Semites in plain terms: see Th. Mommsen, *Auch ein Wort über unser Judenthum* (Berlin, 1880). Cf. Hoffmann (1988: 92–103).

[105] H. von Treitschke, 'Unsere Aussichten', *Preußische Jahrbücher* (Nov. 1879), quoted in Boehlich (1965: 14).

[106] H. Graetz, 'Erwiderung an Herrn von Treitschke', *Schlesische Presse* (7 Dec. 1879), quoted in Boehlich (1965: 28). Cf. Tac. *A.* 15.44.4: *igitur primum correpti qui fatebantur, deinde indicio eorum multitudo ingens haud proinde in crimine incendii quam odio humani generis conuicti sunt*, 'The first then to be seized were those who confessed, then, on their information, a mighty number was convicted, not so much on the charge of the conflagration as for their hatred of the human race.'

by another, with von Treitschke arguing that Tacitus made no distinction between Christians and Jews, and Graetz remaining unimpressed by these 'interpretive arts'.[107] What is striking about this dispute between the two historians is that it involves only the *Annals* and not the Jewish Excursus in the *Histories*. When replying to Graetz's correction, von Treischke does not even mention Tacitus' formulation from the Jewish Excursus *aduersus omnes alios hostile odium*, 'against all others a hatred reserved for enemies' (*H.* 5.5.1).[108]

As has been seen, in the view of many nineteenth-century authors Tacitus, with his distinction between Jewish customs that are sanctioned by their age (*antiquitas*) and those that are perverted (*prauitas*), brings handy evidence of Jewish depravation.[109] In nineteenth-century commentary editions of the *Histories*, however, attempts at this kind of interpretation do not feature. During this period there is a

---

[107] H. von Treitschke, 'Herr Graetz und sein Judenthum', *Preußische Jahrbücher* (Dec. 1879), quoted in Boehlich (1965: 38–9): 'In the course of this I mentioned Tacitus' well-known phrase *odium generis humani*. Then along comes Herr Graetz and cites the phrase, which refers to the Christians, and of course in the eyes of unscholarly readers he is right. But every historian knows—and Herr Graetz better than anyone—that the Christians were regarded as a Jewish sect until the time of Trajan. In the days of Nero about which Tacitus is speaking, the Christians were still frequently called *Judaei*, and the charge of "hatred for humanity" was levelled equally against the Old Jews and the New Jews, the Christians . . . That passage of Tacitus has never been understood otherwise, and cannot be understood otherwise, than as bearing witness both to the citizens' repugnance for the new religion and to the hatred of the Jews that prevailed in the Eastern lands. Almost all the authors of the late Classical period agreed about this hatred: Pliny, Quintilian, Tacitus, Juvenal and many others.' To which H. Graetz replied, in 'Mein letztes Wort an Professor von Treitschke', *Schlesische Presse* (28 Dec. 1879), quoted by Boehlich (1965: 49): 'No amount of interpretive art will extricate you from your blunder over *odium generis humani*. Tacitus is speaking only of the Christians and not the Jews. Only the Christians were accused by Nero of starting the fire and brutally tortured by him, not the Jews.'

[108] The phrase *odium humani generis* from the chapter on the Christians (Tac. *A.* 15.44) had already been applied to the Jews by Hegel. According to Hegel, the Jews' hate-filled relationship with those around them is a direct result of their self-segregation: the 'soul of Jewish nationality' is '*odium generis humani*'. Cf. G. W. F. Hegel, *Frühe Schriften* vol. 1 (Frankfurt am Main, 1971), 293. Cf. Hoffmann (1988: 17–18).

[109] This one-sided depiction of the ancient Jews was redressed by various Jewish authors (such as M. Güdemann, E. Täubler, I. Heinemann, and E. Bickermann). On this, cf. the observations and references in Hoffmann (1988: 287 and *passim*). Finally, as indicated (Bloch 2002: 42–54), Posidonius lies behind Tacitus' account of the depravation of Jewish customs. Heinemann (1919: 121) remarks very aptly and perhaps not without irony that Posidonius, with his theory of a gradual ritualization of Judaism, 'has become in a certain sense the precursor of the concept of the development of the Israelite religion which today is usually attributed to Wellhausen'.

discrepancy between commentaries and essays on the Jewish Excursus. The commentaries of Th. Kiessling (1840) and I. G. Orellius (1848) describe the Jewish Excursus with restraint, and tend to criticize the more invidious sections.[110] The same can be said of the commentaries of W. Heraeus (1884), and later those of E. Wolff and G. Andresen (1886).[111]

An indication meanwhile of the momentum acquired by the reception history of the Jewish Excursus is provided by a remark by Friedrich Nietzsche. Nietzsche, in *Beyond Good and Evil*, evokes Tacitus in connection with his religious criticism, which here again is aimed mostly at Christianity: 'The Jews—"a people born to slavery" as Tacitus and the whole world say, "the chosen people out of all people" as they themselves say and believe.'[112] Nietzsche is of course wrong to attribute this quotation to Tacitus; it comes in fact from a speech by Cicero.[113]

---

[110] Th. Kiessling, *C. Cornelii Taciti Historiarum libri quinque* (Leipzig, 1840); I. G. Orellius, *C. Cornelii Taciti Opera quae supersunt*, vol. 2 (Zürich, 1848). Orellius provides a special appendix on the Jewish Excursus (323–9). On the reproach of misanthropy on the part of the Jews (Tacitus *H.* 5.5.1), Kiessling notes: 'By law there was no hostile hatred.... The same charge of hatred is cast at Christians jumbled together with Jews.' In their *Breviaria* on Book 5 of the *Histories*, Kiessling and Orellius reject Tacitus' representation of Judaism as 'spiteful opinions of the ignorant'. To redress this, Orellius repeatedly points to passages in the Bible. On the other hand, just as Lipsius before him, he explicitly praises Tacitus' description of Jewish monotheism as distinct from the less accurate one by Diodorus. Orellius, *Taciti Opera*, 327–8. [on *H.* 5.5.4]: 'Tacitus has examined much more subtly and truthfully than Diodorus (40 p.543) the innermost power and special source of the Jewish religion.'

[111] W. Heraeus, *Cornelii Taciti Historiarum libri qui supersunt* (4th edn, Leipzig and Berlin, 1899, 1st edn, 1884); E. Wolff and G. Andresen (2nd edn, Berlin 1926, 1st edn, 1886; 2nd edn by G. Andresen). Heraeus comments unequivocally on Tacitus' malicious observations, speaking of 'absurdity', 'the wrong end of the stick', 'prejudice and libel'. On *H.* 5.13.1 (*gens superstitioni obnoxia, religionibus aduersa*, 'a nation steeped in superstition and hostile to proper religious practices'), Heraeus notes: 'Viewed from an unbiased position, one would expect the opposite judgment.' Wolff and Andresen have a similar comment, speaking of 'Tacitus' narrative, riddled with mistakes' and 'distorted by elements of fable'. In questioning the reproach of misanthropy (*H.* 5.5.1), Wolff and Andresen respond that 'the law was different' and cite Exodus 22.20.

[112] F. Nietzsche, *Jenseits von Gut und Böse* (Leipzig, 1886), no. 195. Cf. Schmitthenner (1981: 127).

[113] Cic. *Prov.* 5.10: *iam uero publicanos miseros . . . tradidit in seruitutem Iudaeis et Syris, nationibus natis seruituti*, 'Then too he has handed over the wretched revenue farmers to servitude under the Jews and Syrians, peoples born to slavery.'

THE NATIONAL SOCIALIST PERIOD

Tacitus certainly offered the anti-Jewish rhetoric of some recipients a convenient peg for anti-Semitic polemics. This is particularly so in the period of National Socialism (1933–45). At this time an extensive literature on the ancient Jews appeared in Germany. This is for the most part vehemently anti-Jewish in tone.[114] Here just one representative work will be considered, by the 'race researcher' E. Fischer and the New Testament scholar G. Kittel; its tendentious title, *World Jewry in Antiquity*, already hints at the use (or misuse and distortion) of ancient records to bolster National Socialist conspiracy theories concerning the Jews. This will be clear from the following extract, in which the two authors seek backing from Tacitus:

> As far back as Tacitus the emergence of the Jewish community is closely analogous to modern Zionism: international World Jewry artificially creates and sustains a central point which does nothing to impede World Jewry but serves to maintain and strengthen its role as a destructive element throughout the world. At the same time this increased concentration quite obviously facilitates proselytism: the proselyte is completely freed from his traditional ties to become a factor in the power ranking of World Jewry: 'Also they stick firmly together, and among themselves display ungrudging generosity, while hating the rest of mankind as enemies' (Tacitus).[115]

Here Tacitus is patently misused in the service of National Socialist racial theory. Neither the literary nor the historical context is taken into account. The authors wish to demonstrate that 'always, at all times, whether in the first or the twentieth century... World Jewry dreams of absolute world domination at either end of history'.[116] But even such a plainly anti-Semitic book as that of Fischer and Kittel may still find itself surprised by Tacitus' somewhat abstruse passages. In the chapter 'Ancient Antagonism Towards the Jews', which again was intended to appear fully researched, they write: 'This antagonism

---

[114] On the 'Image of Judaism in German scholarship of antiquity under the Nazis', cf. Hoffmann (1988: 246–79).

[115] E. Fischer and G. Kittel, *Das antike Weltjudentum: Forschungen zur Judenfrage*, vol. 7 (Hamburg, 1943), 79ff. (cf. Tac. *H.* 5.5.1, *et quia apud ipsos fides obstinata, misericordia in promptu, sed aduersus omnes alios hostile odium*). On Kittel, cf. Hoffmann (1988: 254–9). The book of Fischer and Kittel is part of an 8-vol. series, 'Forschungen zur Judenfrage'.

[116] Fischer and Kittel, *Das antike Weltjudentum*, 11.

towards the Jews sometimes took the form of fanciful stories; [for instance that of] the ass's head they were said to worship as a god, which was taken up by Tacitus.'[117]

CONCLUSION

How is it that Tacitus' ethnographical study of the Jews can have had such a strong effect? Various moments appear to have been decisive in securing the Jewish Excursus its intensive reception.

1. The sparse early reception of Tacitus' collected works cannot be explained by the anti-Jewish and anti-Christian propositions in the *Histories* and the *Annals*. On the contrary, it would appear that Tacitus' reception was boosted by the chapters on the Christians and the Jews, as these passages were of particular interest to Christian authors and commentators. Right from the start, ever since Tertullian's polemic, the Jewish Excursus has held a special place in the reception of Tacitus. Tertullian's critique gained further impetus in the sixteenth century through Budé. Thereafter the religious components of the reception became somewhat secondary, but still found a place in the work of commentators.

2. Tacitus presents the Jewish religion as being in complete antithesis to the Romans'. Jewish customs are part of a negative and perverted world. Hence Tacitus became the emblem of an antithetical mindset which runs like a red thread through subsequent periods of anti-Jewish rhetoric. Tacitus' richly detailed polemic provided numerous opportunities for this.[118]

3. In addition to this antithetical mindset there was another moment of considerable importance for the reception: the chronological dividing line Tacitus draws between 'customs that were sanctioned by

---

[117] Fischer and Kittel, *Das anlike Weltjudentum*, 90.

[118] Cf. Hoffmann (1988: 285f.; 1990). Hoffmann sets out a list of various dualities for gauging the anti-Jewish polemics of ancient historians of the 19th and 20th centuries: 'universal spirit religion' vs. 'particular law religion', 'enlightened free scientific culture' vs. 'clerical dogmatism', 'secular national state' vs. 'theocracy/church', 'popular national consciousness' vs. 'homeland-lacking cosmopolitanism'. Judaism at that time represented the negative, and Tacitus could be called into evidence for all of this.

their age [*antiquitas*]' and those that 'owed their value to their perverted nature [*prauitas*]'. In this way Tacitus gave the antithetical position a chronological cloak which was particularly to the taste of nineteenth-century authors.

This survey of the reception history has made it clear how large was the effect of Tacitus' little chapters. On the other hand the potential significance of the Excursus for hatred and anti-Semitism has by and large been kept within bounds. With the exception of the anti-Jewish polemics of nineteenth-century authors mentioned above, and those of National Socialist literature, Tacitus' description of the Jews has very seldom been used to launch or justify anti-Jewish rhetoric. This may be related to the complexity and difficulty of the Excursus, but also to the fact that Tacitus' criticism of Christianity was a complicating factor for Christian authors contemplating the adoption of his arguments.

Moreover, the 'reputation' of the great Roman historian has scarcely been dented by the old criticisms of Tertullian, Budé, and a few later commentators. Certainly a great many authors, both Christian and Jewish, found themselves struggling to preserve their high regard for Tacitus over questions of *ira et studium* in the Jewish Excursus. But usually the historiographical brilliance of Tacitus caused critics to exercise restraint. Occasionally there are signs of wishing to separate the character of anti-Jewish polemicist from that of far-sighted historian. A final example may help to make this clear: the *Josephus* trilogy by the German-Jewish novelist Lion Feuchtwanger, written between 1932 and 1940.[119] The first part of the trilogy features a Roman captain who will later attack the temple of Jerusalem with fire. Feuchtwanger gives this character lines of anti-Jewish dialogue which are almost literally (somewhat beefed up) drawn from Tacitus' Jewish Excursus:

Vol. 1, p. 376: 'You hate and despise all others. You circumcise yourself only as a mark of difference.' (cf. Tac. *H.* 5.5.1: *sed aduersus omnis alios*

---

[119] L. Feuchtwanger, *Josephus Trilogie*, vol. 1, *Der jüdische Krieg* (1932, English translation published as *Josephus*); vol. 2, *Die Söhne* (1935, English translation published as *The Jews of Rome*); vol. 3, *Der Tag wird kommen*, also published as *Das gelobte Land* (1942, English translation published as *The Day Will Come* or *Josephus and the Emperor*). I cite from the edition of the *Aufbau Taschenbuch* press (Berlin, 1994).

hostile odium. 5.5.2: *circumcidere genitalia instituerunt ut diversitate noscantur*)

Vol. 1, p. 376: 'These stupid people believe that the souls of those who keep their squalid commandments will be preserved for eternity by their God.' (cf. Tac. *H.* 5.5.3: *animosque proelio aut suppliciis peremptorum aeternos putant*)

Vol 1, p. 377: 'and some even say they worshipped an ass in their holy of holies.' (cf. Tac. *H.* 5.4.2: *effigiem animalis . . . penetrali sacrauere*)

Vol. 1, p. 377: 'But that's not right, these lunatics and criminals believe in a god you can't see or taste, a god as shameless as themselves existing only in their minds.' (cf. Tac. *H.* 5.4.4: *Iudaei mente sola unumque numen intellegunt*)

Feuchtwanger is obviously drawing on Tacitus here, but does not name his source. Later in the book Feuchtwanger actually brings Tacitus the historian into the action. Feuchtwanger presents him— doubtless autobiographically—as an intelligent and eloquent man standing up for freedom under the tyrant Domitian (somewhat Hitleresque in Feuchtwanger's portrayal), but who sees himself for the time being condemned to silence. Feuchtwanger depicts Tacitus as a cool-headed champion of freedom who reads people and politics with the utmost care.[120] The anti-Jewish statements quoted above— derived from Tacitus' Jewish Excursus!—are placed by Feuchtwanger in the mouth of a fierce Roman captain. However, Feuchtwanger allows other authors such as Quintilian to express explicit anti-Jewish views.[121]

---

[120] For Feuchtwanger's depiction of the historian Tacitus, cf. e.g. *Josephus Trilogie*, vol. 3, 61: 'I [sc. Tacitus] am here to write down what happens under the tyrants. If I didn't constantly tell myself that, then I wouldn't know how I could bear this life either'; 201: 'And Cornelius could no longer restrain himself, and in his dark, grave, threatening voice he added, "Freedom is no prejudice, my dear Regin, freedom is something very definite and palpable. If I have to reflect whether I'm allowed to say what I have to say, then my life becomes narrower, I become poorer, I can no longer think without constraint, I oblige myself against my will to think only the 'permissible', I deteriorate, I hem myself in with a thousand paltry reflections and hesitations, instead of looking out to the wide horizons my brain grows fat. In servitude one merely breathes: only in freedom can one live"'; 377: 'In dark and mighty sentences which piled up like boulders he set out the crimes and terrors of the Palatine, and found words as wide and as bright as an early summer's day for the heroism of his friends.'

[121] Feuchtwanger (ibid. vol. 2), 208: 'Quintilian was never fond of the Jews, and the influence of the "Jewish Venus" [meaning Berenice] on Roman politics always made him uneasy.' Cf. Quint. 3.7.21, *et parentes malorum odimus et est conditoribus urbium*

Feuchtwanger's disparate handling of the polemical sections of the Jewish Excursus on the one hand and the serious-minded figure of Tacitus on the other does not square with the fact that Tacitus is the author of this polemic, and is in the end a further example of the unease felt by many recipients that the great historian Tacitus should have written so negatively about the Jews.

infame contraxisse aliquam perniciosam ceteris gentem qualis est primus Iudaicae superstitionis auctor, 'We tend to hate the parents of evil children, and founders of cities have a bad reputation for having brought together a people destructive to others, such as the man who was the founder of the Jewish superstition.'

17

Tacitus and the Tacitist Tradition

Arnaldo Momigliano

I

For about three centuries, from the Reformation to the French Revolution, Tacitus inspired or troubled politicians, moralists, and even theologians, not to speak of the subjects he provided for poetry and painting. He operated in two different camps. First, he helped the Germans to reassert their nationality and consequently to attack the foreign rule of the Roman Church. Second, he disclosed the secrets of political behaviour both to those who governed and to those who were governed. He taught the former more than one sleight-of-hand and warned the latter that such tricks were cruel and inevitable: everyone had to know his place. Aphorisms and political discourses on Tacitean themes multiplied. There was of course also a great deal of imitation of Tacitus in historical prose. But only the German antiquarians found in Tacitus—and more specifically in the *Germania*—a precise model for their historical work. The events of modern Europe at large could not be satisfactorily narrated within a Tacitean framework. Tacitus had never dealt with geographical discoveries, colonization, wars of religion, and trade competition. Though he had perceived the future importance of Germans and Christians, he had been spared the fulfilment of his forebodings. It is therefore more appropriate to speak of 'Tacitism' in relation to the political thought of the age of absolutism, though few historians of that age remained insensitive to his art of discovering substance under appearances. On the eve of the French Revolution, Gibbon gave the supreme example of Tacitean style adapted to a different type of historiography. Even so, Gibbon's subject was not modern history. Whatever Tacitus' lesson for the age of absolutism, its roots were in his own choice of subjects and in his own ambiguities. Tacitism was not an arbitrary interpolation into Tacitus. To understand Tacitism, we must first consider Tacitus.

II

We must resist any attempt at presenting Tacitus as a researcher on original evidence in the sense in which a historian of the twentieth century is a researcher. We know that ancient historians normally did research only in connection with contemporary events which they were the first to describe: Pliny the Younger, a friend of Tacitus, confirms this. Tacitus, no doubt, read with care the *acta senatus* and the *acta diurna*—the records of the senate meetings and the city journal—for the period of Domitian, in which he broke new ground. But we cannot assume without very good reasons that he did the same thing systematically for the period from Tiberius to Titus, for which he could use literary sources. The *Histories* offer the best opportunity for examining Tacitus' methods of work. We can compare Tacitus with Suetonius, Plutarch, and Dio on the events of the year AD 69. Tacitus' account is very similar to that of the other authorities, and clearly derives from a common source. In the *Annals*, the similarities with the parallel sources are not so close—a fact that admits of more than one explanation. But even in the *Annals*, Tacitus claims in only one place to have gone back to the *acta senatus* ('records of the senate', A. 15.74), whereas he implies at least twice that he did not trouble to consult them on controversial issues. At A. 2.88.1, Tacitus states: *reperio apud scriptores senatoresque eorundem temporum Adgandestrii principis Chattorum lectas in senatu litteras, quibus mortem Arminii promittebat, si patrandae neci uenenum mitteretur,* 'I find from contemporary authors who were members of the Senate that a letter was read in the Curia from the Chattan chief Adgandestrius promising the death of Arminius, if poison were sent to do the work.' Here Tacitus says that he got his information from senatorial historians: he does not mention the *acta senatus*, though the letter from the German chieftain was read in the Senate. Mommsen tried to avoid the inevitable inference by suggesting that in a question of political murder the *acta senatus* would remain silent.[1] But if Tacitus had been in the habit of checking the historians against the *acta senatus*, he would have told us that the *acta senatus* did not confirm the story of the senatorial historians. In another passage, *A.* 1.81, Tacitus admits his inability to form a clear picture of the procedure of the consular elections of AD 15, though he had consulted the historians and Tiberius' speeches. Here again he excludes the *acta senatus* by implication. Incidentally we must not take the reference to Tiberius' speeches as a reference to the *acta senatus*: Tiberius' speeches had been collected and could be read without going to the *acta senatus*. If a confirmation of these deductions was needed, it was provided by the discovery of the *Tabula Hebana*. The inscription contains some at least of the details about the elections which Tacitus had been unable to discover for himself. As the *Tabula Hebana* is substantially, if not formally, a deliberation of the senate, it must have been reported in the *acta senatus*. Tacitus' ignorance of its contents can be explained only if he did not consult the relevant protocols of the senate meetings.

Sir Ronald Syme is prepared to believe that Tacitus used the *acta senatus* to make a special study of the speeches of the Emperor Claudius. Tacitus' antiquarian excursuses would derive, not from an antiquarian handbook, as Friedrich Leo suggested, but from Claudius' antiquarian speeches in the senate.[2] This is an amusing thought; and there is certainly an element of truth in it. Tacitus read with great care Claudius' speech about the admission of the Gauls to the senate because he remembered it in a different context for his excursus on Mons Caelius (*A.* 4.65). We can easily believe that he took a whimsical pleasure in other pieces of Claudian pedantry. He devoted an excursus in *Annals* 11.14 to the history of the alphabet, for instance: we know that problems connected with the alphabet were a favourite subject with the emperor Claudius. But there is nothing to suggest that Tacitus' acquaintance with Claudius' speeches was wide. The further suggestion that Tacitus knew Claudius' speeches from direct consultation of the *acta senatus* is even less probable. One example will make my point clear. Tacitus states that Augustus preceded Claudius in enlarging the *pomerium*, that is, the sacred boundary of Rome (*A.* 12.23.2). This statement Sir Ronald Syme takes to come from a speech by Claudius in the Senate on the proposed extension of

---

[1] Mommsen (1909a: 253).   [2] Syme (1958a: 295).

the sacred boundary.[3] Overwhelming evidence shows that Augustus never extended the *pomerium*. Augustus himself never mentions such a performance in his *Res Gestae*; and the *Lex de imperio Vespasiani* does not cite Augustus as a predecessor of Claudius in extending the *pomerium*. Furthermore, the respectable antiquarian who is behind Seneca in the discussion on the *pomerium* in the *de Breuitate uitae* (13.8) does not know of an extension of the *pomerium* by Augustus. *De Breuitate uitae* itself was written within a few months of the extension of the *pomerium* by Claudius when the subject was topical. The only explanation for this silence is that Augustus did not in fact extend the *pomerium*. But if he did not, then Claudius is unlikely to have lied to the senators in an official speech. He was too good an antiquarian to discredit himself by inventing facts. We do not know who first made the mistake of attributing the extension of the *pomerium* to Augustus, but we can at least say that it was not Claudius. Somebody between Claudius and Tacitus must have thought fit to attribute a widening of the sacred border of Rome to the first emperor. Tacitus here depends not on the *acta senatus*, but on a literary tradition later accepted by Dio Cassius and also by the *Historia Augusta*. The extent of Tacitus' original research is bound to be a matter of doubt and controversy because only in a few cases do we have enough evidence to assess it. For instance, we cannot say where Tacitus found his information about the debate between Helvidius Priscus and Eprius Marcellus which now figures so conspicuously at *Histories* 4.6–8. He may have read about it in the *acta senatus*, but more probably in the biography of Helvidius Priscus which had been written by Herennius Senecio. Indeed Tacitus may simply have based his account on another historian who had already used the biography of Helvidius written by Herennius Senecio. What we can say is that our present evidence offers nothing to support the anachronistic image of a Tacitus passing his mornings in the archives of the Roman Senate.

If Tacitus was not a researcher in the modern sense, he was, however, a writer whose reliability cannot be seriously questioned. When we question Tacitus' account of Tiberius or doubt his information about the Parthian campaigns of Nero, we are really discussing details. To put it more sharply, if you do not believe Livy on Romulus, this means that you cannot know anything about Romulus, but if you

---

[3] Syme (1958), 378.

do not believe Tacitus on Tiberius, this means only that you have to think again about certain details of Tiberius' reign. Suetonius, Dio, Plutarch—not to speak of the inscriptions—support Tacitus in all his main facts and reduce the controversy about his truthfulness to narrow margins. While the discovery of the *Tabula Hebana* has shown that Tacitus overlooked certain aspects of the consular elections under Tiberius, we must not forget that Tacitus had admitted his inability to get sufficient information about them. I know of only one case in which Tacitus may be suspected with some justification of having consciously altered the truth for the sake of rhetorical effect. He makes Cremutius Cordus recite a speech in the senate during his trial (*A.* 4.34). Yet we know from Seneca that Cremutius Cordus committed suicide before he was tried in the senate (*Cons. Marc.* 22.6). It is hard to avoid the conclusion that Tacitus made Cremutius go before the senate because he had thought of a good speech to put into his mouth. But it is fair to add that this idea may already have occurred to a predecessor of Tacitus. In that case, Tacitus would have been at fault in trusting a predecessor instead of going to read the *acta senatus* for himself.

Tacitus never claimed to be a historian with a method of his own, as Thucydides or Polybius did. The claims he makes for himself—to write *sine ira et studio* ('without anger and partiality') and to disdain trivial details—belong to the conventions of Graeco-Roman historiography. He accepts the pattern of Roman annalistic writing; he makes it plain that he studied his Sallust, Caesar, and Livy. He does not want to appear as an innovator. Neither the subjects he chooses nor the materials he uses were new or particularly difficult to handle.

Yet in another sense Tacitus is one of the most experimental historians of antiquity. Only Xenophon, among the historians who have come down to us, can be compared with him in this respect. Xenophon tried biography, historical novel, military history with an autobiographical element, mere historical narrative, and finally a collection of philosophical sayings. Superficially Tacitus is not so many-sided. He tried only biography, ethnography, historical discussion of the decline of eloquence, and finally plain annalistic narrative. But almost all his experiments are complex. Each big experiment includes other experiments. The *Agricola* is biography with an ethnographic-historical background: the combination cannot have been common. The *Germania* is ethnography with a political message. I may be permitted to take the dialogue *De Oratoribus* as Tacitus' work without further discussion. It combines an attempt to describe the subjective reactions of various persons to the political regime under which they live with an attempt to clarify the causes of the decline of eloquence. Even in his most mature historical writing Tacitus experimented. What we have of the *Histories* is a picture of a civil war in which the leaders are no more and perhaps less important than the crowds—soldiers, provincials, Roman mob. In the *Annals* the perspective is changed. The personalities of the emperors and of their women, of a few generals and philosophers, dominate the scene. We take the change to be natural because Tacitus makes it appear natural, but other solutions were possible. We may suspect that the complexities of that dark emperor-maker, Antonius Primus, as described in the *Histories,* would have been more interesting to Tacitus ten years later when he wrote the *Annals*; while the open-air scenes of the fire of Rome as told in the *Annals* would have been better described ten years earlier, when he wrote the *Histories.*

Some of the experiments were never developed in full. The lesser works after all are lesser works just because they do no more than hint at the most serious historical problems. The *Agricola* might have developed into a study of the impact of Romanization on the natives of Britain. The *Germania* is potentially an enquiry into the relations between the free Germans and the Roman Empire; the *Dialogus* outlines research on the interrelations between political liberty and intellectual activities. None of these themes is taken up in earnest and turned into a full-scale history. Tacitus would have become a very different type of historian if he had done so. He would have become a critic of the structure of the Roman Empire. He would have told us explicitly whether or not he believed that there was a reasonable alternative to the present regime of Rome. The very fact that Tacitus wrote the *Agricola* and the *Germania* in AD 98, before the *Histories* and the *Annals,* shows that at the beginning of his career as a historian he wanted to ask some fundamental questions about Roman provincial government. But he did not pursue these themes fully; nor did he develop the theme of the decline of eloquence outside the *Dialogus.* Any development of this kind would have implied a complete break with the political and historiographical tradition of Rome. Politically, Tacitus would have had to give up the society of the senatorial class for which he had probably been the first member of his family to qualify. Historiographically he would have had to repudiate the traditions of Roman annalistic writing, confined as it was to political and religious events in the narrow sense. We can only speculate on the form Tacitus' historical work would have taken had he chosen to describe the slow transformations of intellectual life in Rome and of tribal life in the provinces.

Breaks of such far-reaching proportions were not unheard of in the world in which Tacitus lived. Christians and Cynics were prepared to leave behind them the forms and substance of Roman political life. The Christians had even invented new historiographical forms—the Gospels and the Acts of the Apostles—to express their new outlook. But Tacitus was neither a Christian nor a Cynic; and to be fair to him, neither the Christians nor the Cynics came near to asking the sort of questions we see implied in the *Germania* and in the dialogue *De Oratoribus*.

In short, Tacitus did not pursue his most daring experiments, but devoted his major historical works to a subject which was less revolutionary without being conventional. He began to work in an analytical way on the most undesirable features of tyrannical government. The surviving part of the *Histories* is largely about civil war under tyrants, with its interconnected features of mob irresponsibility and upper-class greed for power. The *Annals* defy simple definition. Each emperor is analysed at his worst, his collaborators share his fate, and only a few individuals—mainly senators with a philosophical faith— escape condemnation because they face martyrdom.

A sober evaluation of the originality of such a historiographical enterprise is almost impossible. The evidence is missing. The works of Tacitus' predecessors are all lost. He may have learned something from Hellenistic historians who wrote chronicles of tyrants. The Athenian Demochares, who in the first part of the third century BC gave a passionately hostile account of the government of Demetrius Poliorcetes in Athens, certainly qualified as a model for anti-tyrannical historians. But tyranny in Greece was something provisional, something violently and uneasily superimposed on a democratic structure. It seems highly unlikely that any Greek historian could really be of great use to a historian like Tacitus, who was describing the consequences of the permanent suppression of liberty. Tacitus was bound to learn much more from his immediate predecessors, who were also his immediate sources. Yet we must make a distinction between borrowing facts and borrowing interpretations. I should be very embarrassed to assess the originality of Tacitus as an interpreter of history on the present evidence. The comparison of Tacitus with Dio,

Plutarch, and Suetonius is conclusive about the existence of a common source for the facts, but quite inconclusive about the existence of a common source for the interpretation of the facts. Yet where the comparison is easier, in the *Histories*, the differences of interpretation between Tacitus and the other surviving historians are conspicuous. Only Tacitus interprets the crisis of 69 as the collapse of the discipline of the Roman army made possible by the demoralization of the Roman aristocracy. Neither Plutarch nor Dio interprets the events of 69 as the crisis of a society. When we read Tacitus, we immediately feel that he gives us something different from the other historians. His analysis of human behaviour is deeper, his attention to the social traditions, to the precise circumstances, is far more vigorous. He conveys his interpretation by a subtle and accurate choice of details which are expressed in an entirely personal language. The picture which sticks in our mind is his own. To admit that Tacitus had real predecessors is to admit that there was a Tacitean style before Tacitus. This is enough for our purpose, because ultimately our purpose is to show how his picture of despotism became classic.

Tacitus' theoretical remarks on the beginning of the decline of Rome, on the relative merits of fate and providence, and on the developments of political institutions are notoriously vague and even self-contradictory. He consistently cared for the honour of Rome, for the victory of its armies, for the extension of the borders of the Roman state, even when he was clearly not certain about the merits of the Roman case. One of his accusations against Tiberius is that he was not interested in extending the Roman Empire (*A*. 4.32.2). His accounts of wars are founded upon the presupposition that once a war was started the victory of Rome was automatically desirable. He took for granted the right of the Roman state to conquer and win— though he questioned the consequences. He liked fairness towards the provincials, but never doubted the right to repress any rebellion of the provincials. He extended his prejudice to include a great number of Roman upperclass likes and dislikes. Greeks, Jews, and Christians are looked down on, and there is the conventional contempt for *liberti* and more in general for mere plebeians. This means that the area in which he was prepared effectively to question the Roman imperial structure was limited. He had no ideas of his own about foreign policy, and in the matter of provincial policy he shared the widely felt opinion that the Latin west was more promising than the Greek east. The emperors of the first century AD very nearly practised what

Tacitus preached about the rights of Rome, the policy of conquest, the dangers of aliens and mobs. On these points Tacitus' disagreement was marginal. His notoriously ambiguous account of the persecution of the Christians under Nero, though critical of the emperor, does not question his ultimate right to persecute.

Tacitus' real aim was to unmask the imperial rule, insofar as it was government by debasement, hypocrisy, and cruelty. He did not exclude any class from the consequences of such a regime, but concentrated on the imperial court itself and on the senators. Individual exceptions he allowed. They were either the martyrs, like Thrasea Paetus, or the wise men, like Agricola, but it is characteristic of his more mature judgement that in the *Annals*, the martyrs figure much more prominently than the wise men. To see the prostitution of the Roman aristocracy, to have to recognize that there was often more dignity in a German or British chieftain than in a Roman senator—that was the last bitterness of tyranny. The whole history of the years 68–70 is the consequence of the shameful weakness of the Roman senate in changing masters five times. Nothing said against Tiberius equals the indictment of his Senate: *pauor internus occupauerat animos, cui remedium adulatione quaerebatur*, 'domestic panic had preoccupied their minds, for which the remedy was sought in sycophancy' (*A.* 4.74.1). *Adulatio* is the recurring word. Domitian's mind was corrupted by adulation: adulation is promised by Galba to Piso. On the other hand protests against the tyrant, if ever uttered, are not invariably praiseworthy: they run the risk of being useless and frivolous, *inane*. One of the aspects of tyranny is to impose a difficult choice between adulation and empty protest or, to put it in Tacitean words, *inter abruptam contumaciam et deforme obsequium*, 'between sheer truculence and grotesque compliance' (*A.* 4.20.3).

Such a situation, in which even the free word is only seldom appropriate, is the indication that something is radically wrong with human nature. Tyranny ceases to be an isolated phenomenon and becomes a symptom of a basic evil. Men are ready to forsake freedom for adulation—or to make fools of themselves by empty words of freedom. The more Tacitus pursues this point, from the *Histories* to the *Annals*, the more pessimistic he becomes. The deeper he looks, the more evident the contrast becomes between reality and appearances, between deeds and words in human behaviour. Yet, we must insist, Tacitus is no nihilist. His pessimism is perhaps more superficial than we are inclined to admit. Almost every story he tells us has a bad end, and he may give the impression that man cannot avoid going wrong. But there is much he does not tell us. What remains untold is safe enough. Family, property, rank, education on the whole do not seem to be in danger. Certainly Tacitus does not worry about them. Thucydides and Polybius registered much greater upheavals and were less querulous about them. Even power as such is not distrusted by Tacitus. He only dislikes tyrannical power.

Perhaps there is an insoluble conflict in Tacitus' approach to the Roman Empire. There is much that he approves of—so much, indeed, that he cannot criticize the institution as a whole. But he dislikes intensely the despotism which goes with it. Just because he cannot criticize the Empire as a whole, he comes to accept it as unmodifiable. And because he accepts it as unmodifiable, he cannot really see how it is possible to have an Empire without tyranny. He may have had hopes in that direction when he began to write the *Histories*, but those hopes had vanished long before he started the *Annals*. Thus he was led to admit an unchangeable element of evil in the Roman Empire. The psychology of the tyrant turned out to be only a prominent manifestation of the permanent greed, lust, and vanity of man as such. Paradoxically it is his conservatism which forces Tacitus to be a pessimist. He is a pessimist because he cannot even conceive of an alternative to the Roman Empire.

It is part of the insoluble conflict in Tacitus' mind that he never forgets that human nature is capable of true courage, true frankness, true liberty. Where so much adulation and hypocrisy prevail, he can give examples of freedom of speech. Furthermore, he envisages distant worlds where virtue could reign unimpaired: primitive Rome, or perhaps untouched barbarian lands. Admittedly these fairy lands are of limited practical importance. Tacitus makes it clear that any idea of a Roman Republic in the old sense is by now obsolete and, with tragic irony, emphasizes the danger that freedom-loving barbarians represent for the Roman state. But the individuals who at their own peril managed to keep alive the old freedom are of immense importance to Tacitus. He does not include himself among them. He never judges from the security of a morally superior position. One of his very rare personal notes is to confess that he had accepted Domitian's tyranny without offering resistance.

Tacitus had no intention of competing with the philosophers. He would have been very annoyed to be taken for one. Towards the greatest philosopher of the previous generation, Seneca, he maintained a guarded attitude. Modern scholars have been given plenty of scope to discuss whether Tacitus liked Seneca. His very admission of relative cowardice in the time of Domitian also serves the purpose of preventing any confusion between himself and the philosophers. He speaks from the middle of the Roman state and does not claim any exemption from its evils. Yet both the methods and the results of his historical writing recall the contemporary philosophers. He transferred to history the subtlety of analysis which philosophers had developed through the centuries of Hellenistic and Roman rule. He confirmed the opinion of those philosophers who thought that *uirtus* was the rare achievement of individual effort, more often to be obtained by standing up against the government of the day than by governing others.

III

Tacitus' teaching about despotism was ambivalent. It was never meant to encourage revolutions, but would obviously open the eyes of anyone who cared to see the effects of despotism. Other people, however, could take it as an object lesson in the art of government, a lesson of realism.

In antiquity few people were prepared to ponder such a complex message. A Tacitus could mature only in solitude. Even his contemporary Pliny the Younger, with all his admiration for Tacitus, was unable to grasp his friend's thought. Later Tacitus seems to have found a public among the last Romans of the fourth and fifth centuries. Ammianus Marcellinus sharpened his wits on Tacitus' pages. But nostalgia rather than ruthless objectivity was the keynote of the age: while Ammianus recaptured some of the spaciousness, nobility, and bitterness of the *Histories*, he no longer questioned human nature in the agonizing way which is characteristic of Tacitus. Like El Greco many centuries later, Ammianus came to be interested in the world (visually) because it appeared ill-proportioned and quaint. Other aristocrats with learned tastes, especially in Gaul, enjoyed their Tacitus without further probing into his teaching. There was a friend of Sidonius Apollinaris who even claimed descent from Tacitus (*Ep.* 4.14); Sulpicius Severus and Orosius used him extensively. People went on quoting him in the sixth century. But he must by then have been a very dim figure if Cassiodorus, who used his *Germania*, could refer to him as a 'certain Cornelius', *Cornelio quodam* (*Variae* V, 2.).

During the Middle Ages only a few read Tacitus, and almost all of them were in Benedictine monasteries either in Germany (such as Fulda) or connected with Germany (such as Montecassino). Our most important manuscript of the later part of the *Annals* and of the *Histories* (the *Mediceus secundus* in the Laurentian Library) was apparently stolen from Montecassino in the fourteenth century. The story that Boccaccio was the thief has unfortunately proved to be unreliable. The minor works were brought from Germany to Italy in the fifteenth century: here again the details are notoriously uncertain, but the minor works were in Rome by about 1455. For the rest of the century there was no further increase in the knowledge of Tacitus' text; but what people had was enough to make minds work. Florence was the first intellectual and political centre to react to Tacitus' message, just as it was the first to appreciate Polybius. Characteristically, Leonardo Bruni used Polybius to supplement Livy for the story of Roman wars and extracted from Tacitus the notion that great intellects vanish when all power is concentrated in one man. Bruni's quotation of Tacitus in his *Laudatio Florentinae Vrbis* (of about 1403)—*Nam posteaquam res publica in unius potestatem deducta est, preclara illa ingenia* (*ut inquit Cornelius*) *abiere*, 'For after the state was restricted to the control of one man, those preeminent and talented writers disappeared (so Tacitus says)'—is the first evidence for the appearance of Tacitus in modern political thought.[4] About thirty years later Poggio Bracciolini turned to Tacitus again to support, against Guarino Guarini, the superiority of republican Scipio over monarchic Caesar. This, however, was a use of Tacitus which derived its significance from the special position of Florence in its struggle against Milan ruled by the Visconti, and lost importance with the general decline of republican ideals in Florence itself and in the rest of Italy. Furthermore, the Florentine interpretation of what was known of Tacitus did not provide a clue to the understanding of the only conspicuous exception in this decline—the republic of Venice.

---

[4] [This is a paraphrase of Tacitus *H.* 1.1.1: *postquam bellatum apud Actium atque omnem potentiam ad unum conferri pacis interfuit, magna illa ingenia cessere*, 'After the battle of Actium had been fought and the interests of peace demanded that power should be concentrated in one man's hands, this great line of historians came to an end'.]

As far as I know (though I am not a specialist in the political literature of the Quattrocento), Tacitus was put aside in Italy about 1440 for a good sixty years. These are the years in which the Germans were learning to read the *Germania*. Enea Silvio Piccolomini first brought it to the attention of the Germans in 1458. By 1500 it had become a mirror in which the Germans liked to look at themselves. Conrad Celtis was apparently the first to lecture on Tacitus in a German university, in about 1492. He started the tradition of investigation into German antiquities which his pupil Johannes Aventinus, together with Beatus Rhenanus, Sebastian Münster, and many others, was to continue. The learned enquiry both implied and fostered a claim of independence and perhaps of superiority in relation to the imperial Rome of the past and the papal Rome of the present. Tacitus was beginning to repay the hospitality he had received in German monasteries during the Middle Ages.

At this point the manuscript of Books 1–6 of the *Annals,* according to contemporary evidence, was stolen from Corvey and brought to Rome about 1509. There seems to be no serious reason to doubt this story. Philippus Beroaldus published the *editio princeps* of the first books of the *Annals* in 1515. Tiberius' ghost was returning at the right time. Machiavelli had written *Il principe* (*The Prince*) two years before. He was working at the same time on those *Discorsi sulla Prima Deca di Tito Livio* ('Discourses on the first ten books of Livy') which destroyed any illusion the Florentines might ever have had about the similarity of their government with that of republican Rome.

Tiberius was accompanied by another no less timely ghost, that of Arminius, *liberator haud dubie Germaniae* ('without doubt the liberator of Germany', *A.* 2.88.2). Almost on the heels of Beroaldus' edition Ulrich von Hutten wrote the *Arminius dialogus* (*c.*1520), a momentous event in the history of German nationalism. Tacitus is called in as witness by Arminius and is asked to recite *elogium illud meum quod in historiis tuis est* ('that epitaph for me which is in your histories'). In the *Ragguagli del Parnaso* ('Advertisements from Parnassus') by Traiano Boccalini, the reactionary god Apollo puts together Luther and the manuscript of Tacitus as the two worst things which had ever come out of Germany. Tacitus found himself at the confluence of the two great movements of the sixteenth century, religious reform and monarchic absolutism. In the later *Discorsi,* Machiavelli himself quoted little of Tacitus and almost nothing of the newly discovered section on Tiberius. His few quotations, however, showed something of more general importance than his obvious sympathy for Tacitus. They showed that Tacitus' books made sense only if used to explain why even republican Rome—for all her ability to turn political struggles into sources of political strength—fell under the control of monarchs. Tacitus was the complement to Livy—the historian who more than Tacitus had been the guide of earlier humanistic historians. Francesco Guicciardini, with his talent for the right word, produced the formula for the new movement of ideas: 'Tacitus teaches the tyrants how to be tyrants and their subjects how to behave under tyrants.'[5] The ambivalence of Tacitus is here recognized—perhaps for the first time. It is this ambivalence that explains why he might alternatively serve the purposes of the friends and of the enemies of absolutism. Cosimo I Medici and Pope Paul III Farnese were among the most diligent readers of Tacitus. It has even been suggested that the Medici and the Farnese as family groups became special devotees of Tacitus.

There were resistances to be overcome before Tacitus could be accepted as a major teacher of political wisdom. The truest classicists stuck to Cicero and Livy. The pious remembered that Tacitus had been attacked by Tertullian (*Ad Nat.* 1.11) for his pages on the Christians. Budé could not forgive Tacitus on grounds of religion: *hominem nefarium Tacitum* ('that nefarious man Tacitus'). The circumstance that another dubious character, Jean Bodin, took up the case of Tacitus against Budé was perhaps not a recommendation. Only when the split between Catholic and Protestant Europe became an accepted fact—and theological disputes lost something of their urgency—did Tacitus gain full authority. We may put the turning point around 1580, when Marc-Antoine Muret started to give lectures on Tacitus' *Annals* at the University of Rome—the very centre of the Counter-Reformation. Tacitus was both the exegete and the critic of political absolutism: the ambiguity pleased almost everyone. He helped the new search into the obscurities of the human soul. Montaigne studied and admired him, and all the later French moralists from Charron to La Rochefoucauld owed something to him, especially in the study of hypocrisy. Modern Dutch literature was almost brought to life by the contact of Dutch intellectuals with Tacitus. Two other factors contributed. The condemnation of Machiavelli's works by the

---

[5] Spongano (1948: ch. 18).

Catholic Church (1559) had left an empty space which Tacitus could easily fill. What could not be said in the name of Catholic Machiavelli could be said in the name of pagan Tacitus. If somebody objected to Tacitus, one could always reply that a pagan was not supposed to know the whole truth. Second, Ciceronianism was undergoing a crisis. The popularity of Seneca both as a stylist and as a philosopher was mounting; Neo-Stoicism became the faith of those who had lost patience with theology, if they had not lost faith altogether. The fortunes of Seneca and Tacitus became indissolubly connected towards the end of the sixteenth century. In the controversy between the Italians and the French about the superiority of their respective languages, the ability to translate Tacitus became a test case. As is well known, Davanzati's translation of Tacitus was the answer to some derogatory remarks by Henricus Stephanus. Davanzati tried to prove that one could write as concisely in Italian as Tacitus had done in Latin. Davanzati was successful in writing short sentences, but Italian remained a language of interminable sentences.

One man represented the new synthesis of Seneca and Tacitus: Muret's disciple, Justus Lipsius. If his mind was more with Seneca, his heart, his personal experience, were for Tacitus. Justus Lipsius loved Tacitus so much, interpreted him so learnedly, pressed his case so authoritatively, and combined his teaching with that of Seneca so ingeniously that it was impossible not to listen to him. Because Justus Lipsius, who was born a Catholic and ended a Catholic, spent part of his learned life in the Protestant camp, he made propaganda for Tacitus on both sides of the fence. His contemporaries regarded Lipsius as the real discoverer of Tacitus, and they were substantially right. But I was able to show many years ago[6] that another current of thought contributed to the same result. The study of Tacitus as a political thinker was introduced in Paris by an Italian émigré, who like Lipsius wavered between Protestantism and Catholicism, Carolus Paschalius, or Carlo Pasquale. Both Paschalius and Lipsius published a commentary on Tacitus in 1581. But whereas Lipsius was chiefly interested in illustrating the historical allusions in Tacitus and in interpreting his words, Paschalius treated Tacitus as a collection of political *exampla*. Lipsius availed himself of Tacitus as a political thinker only in 1589, when he published his *Politicorum libri VI*

---

[6] Momigliano (1947).

('Six books on politics'), but not even then did he use Tacitus so extensively, indeed exclusively, as Paschalius had done in his commentary of 1581. Though all the later Tacitisti, as they were called, were encouraged by the authority of Justus Lipsius, they depended more directly on Carolus Paschalius for the type of their enquiry and for the form of presentation. The rapid progress of Tacitus' reputation as a political thinker in those years can be shown by this significant chronological sequence. The Jesuit Giovanni Botero did not yet know of Tacitus as an important political thinker when he wrote his *De Regia Sapientia* ('On royal wisdom') in 1582. In 1589, when he published his *Ragion di Stato* ('Reason of state'), after a stay in Paris, he put together Machiavelli and Tacitus as the leading writers on politics.

The commentaries and dissertations on Tacitus of the next hundred years are innumerable; Machiavellian Italy led the Tacitist movement, and Spain, France, and Germany followed—I venture to believe—in this order. England contributed comparatively little, and Holland too was not conspicuous in this type of production. England and Holland were the countries which were to give Europe her modern political thought with Hobbes, Grotius, Spinoza, and Locke. The defeat of the Armada saved England, among other things, from being invaded by Tacitus, or by the Tacitisti. But if Ben Jonson got into trouble for his *Sejanus* in 1603, some connection with the mounting wave of the Tacitism of those years must be admitted. Ben Jonson himself had greeted Sir Henry Savile's translation and supplementation of the *Histories* in 1591 by an epigram (no. 95) which is an interesting characterization of Tacitus from the Tacitist point of view:

> We need a man, can speake of the intents,
> The councells, actions, orders and events
> Of state, and censure them: we need his pen
> Can write the things, the causes, and the men.

Books of foreign Tacitists were translated into English—Boccalini, Virgilio Malvezzi. Others were read in the original or in Latin translations. What is perhaps true is that in England there was a tendency to emphasize the anti-tyrannical aspects of Tacitus. Bacon took him for an enemy of absolute monarchy. The Dutch Dr Isaac Dorislaus, who became the first holder of a lectureship in History at Cambridge in 1627, had soon to leave his chair because he interpreted Tacitus in an obviously anti-monarchical spirit. Ultimately, however, in England the most serious thinkers worried about the divine rights of kings, not about the psychology of tyranny. As the dispute between Salmasius and Milton shows in an exemplary way, biblical texts counted for more than Tacitus. The Tacitist literature of the Continent can be divided into four groups:

(1) Excerpts from Tacitus in the form of political aphorisms. For instance, Abraham Golnitz in his *Princeps* ('Prince') of 1636 describes what a prince must do in peace and war by means of excerpts from Tacitus.

(2) Excerpts from Tacitus accompanied by a detailed political commentary: Virgilio Malvezzi's *Discorsi* are a good sample. They belong to what Bacon would have called *historiae ruminatae* ('Ponderings on historical writings').

(3) General theories on politics vaguely founded on Tacitus, such as the *Quaestiones ac Discursus in duos primos libros Annalium* ('Questions and discourses on the first two books of the *Annals*') by Petrus Andreas Canonherius (Canoniero).

(4) Political commentaries on Tacitus, which wavered somewhat ambiguously between an analysis of Tacitus' opinions and an analysis of the facts related by Tacitus. The commentaries by Annibale Scoto and by Traiano Boccalini are of this type.

Tacitus became fashionable. He was even put into Italian verse by Alessandro Adimari.[7] Like every other fashion 'Tacitismo' became tiresome after a time and found itself in conflict with more modern trends. As I have already implied, doubts on Tacitus had always been maintained in certain Catholic circles. The Spanish Jesuit Pedro Ribadeneira put together in one bunch Tiberius, 'a very vicious and abominable emperor', Tacitus, 'a pagan historian and enemy of Christianity', Machiavelli, 'the impious counsellor', and Bodin, who 'was neither learned in theology nor accustomed to piety'.[8] The other Jesuit authority on Machiavelli, Antonio Possevino, complained that too many of his contemporaries seemed to forget that one syllable of the Gospel is preferable to the whole of Tacitus. And in 1617 Famiano Strada, better known to the English for his influence on Richard Crashaw's poetry, published a determined attack on Tacitus. He

---

[7] Adimari (1628).   [8] Ribadeneira (1603).

renewed the accusation of atheism and also tried to revive, against Tacitus, the declining cult for Livy. The fact that Spinoza liked Tacitus for his anti-Jewish and anti-Christian bias did not improve the pagan author's popularity in pious circles.

About a century later, dislike for Tacitus was expressed both on the right and on the left, by Catholics and by rationalists. While he was too much of a pagan for the Catholics, the libertines and rationalists disliked him for being too cynical and anyway too clearly connected with the Counter-Reformation. The decline of Spanish supremacy in Europe, the ascendancy of England and the Netherlands, the rise of Cartesian rationalism and of Jansenism in France, were destroying the presuppositions upon which Tacitus had gained his authority. For once Fenelon and Bayle found themselves in agreement on the point that Tacitus defeated his own purposes by too much subtlety: 'il a trop d'esprit, il rapine trop' ('He has too much wit, he plunders too much'). Saint-Evremond complained that Tacitus turned everything into politics: Voltaire himself had no use for Tacitus, who, according to the *Traite sur la Tolerance* ('Treatise on tolerance'), preferred slander to truth. In a letter to Madame du Deffand (no. 14202), Voltaire explained that Tacitus did not comply with the new standards of a History of Civilisation: 'I [Voltaire] should like to know the rights of the senate, the forces of the empire, the number of the citizens, the form of government, the customs, the habits. I do not find anything of the sort in Tacitus. *Il m'amuse, et Tile-Live m'instruit.*' People interested in the new idea of parliamentary government spreading from England found Tacitus less instructive than the historians of the Roman Republic, such as Polybius and Livy. On the other hand the supporters of continental enlightened despotism discovered that Tacitus was an embarrassment to their cause: his emperors were only too clearly unenlightened despots.

This might well have been the end of the Tacitist period in modern political thought if Tacitus had not found new allies in unexpected circles. To begin with, Giambattista Vico recognized in Tacitus one of his four guides to the discovery of the laws of history. He was interested in Tacitus as the student of primitive, violent impulses—a complement to Plato. Following a suggestion by Francis Bacon (*De augmentis scientiarum*, 'On the advancement of learning' 7.2), Vico regarded Tacitus as the portrayer of man as he is, while Plato contemplates man as he should be. Vico revalued Tacitus and Machiavelli, as it were, from a higher point of view. The same was done—independently and more crudely, but with greater consequences—by the French Encyclopedists. Machiavelli was rescued by the French Encyclopedists partly because his works had been put on the Index, partly because they adopted the old extreme Baconian interpretation that he was secretly hitting at despotism. Rousseau produced the new formula in the *contrat social*: 'The Prince of Machiavelli is the book of the Republicans.'[9] What was good for Machiavelli was even better for Tacitus. D'Alembert, who wrote the article on Machiavellianism in the *Encyclopédie,* also published an anthology of Tacitus. Rousseau, too, translated some Tacitus. They turned Tacitus into an enlightened enemy of obscurantist princes. This is the Tacitus, wise and mild, who prevailed in Europe immediately before the French Revolution. We recognize him in Gibbon's definition of Tacitus as 'the first of historians who applied the science of philosophy to the study of facts'.[10] Gibbon learned more than one stylistic trick from Tacitus. With due acknowledgement to d'Alembert and Gibbon, John Hill treated him in a similar way in a really important paper published in the *Transactions* of the Royal Academy of Edinburgh in 1788. But in England the interpretation inspired by the French Encyclopedists had been somewhat anticipated in 1728 by Walpole's friend Thomas Gordon, the 'snoring Silenus' of the second *Dunciad.* Gordon was an 'unsparing critic of the priesthood'. He compared Tacitus with St Jerome to the advantage of the former: 'in Tacitus you have the good sense and breeding of a Gentleman; in the Saint the rage and dreams of a Monk.'[11] I suspect that when in 1752 the Reverend Thomas Hunter published his *Observations on Tacitus. In which his character as a writer and an historian, is impartially considered, and compared with that of Livy,* he was hitting at Gordon as much as at Tacitus. It is no wonder that Gordon found a French publisher during the Revolution.

Meanwhile the enlightened Tacitus of d'Alembert and Gibbon had advanced further and had turned into a revolutionary republican: 'Et son nom prononcé fait pâlir les tyrans' ('The utterance of his name makes tyrants turn pale').[12] He was a republican to be used against

---

[9] J.-J. Rousseau, *Du contrat social* (Amsterdam, 1762), 3.6.
[10] E. Gibbon, *The History of the Decline and Fall of the Roman Empire* (1776), ed. J. B. Bury (New York, 1906), 230.
[11] T. Gordon, *The Works of Tacitus,With political discourses upon that author, by Thomas Gordon, Esq; in five volumes* (London, 1728), discourse 2, I.i.
[12] M.-J. Chénier, *Épître à Voltaire* (Paris, 1806).

tyrannies of every kind. Camille Desmoulins quoted Tacitus—or rather, Gordon's Tacitus—against Robespierre in the pages of his *Vieux Cordelier*.[13] Vittorio Alfieri fed on Tacitus' works, and in Foscolo's juvenile novel the hero, Jacopo Ortis, equally hostile to monarchic and to democratic terror, commits suicide after having translated 'the whole second book of the *Annals* and the greater part of the second of the *Histories*'. The mere name of Tacitus made Napoleon I angry. We could tell a long story about the part played by Tacitus in the struggle against the Caesarism of both Napoleons. French intellectuals were divided between those who admired Caesar and those who admired Tacitus. The Bonapartist *Revue contemporaine* ('Contemporary journal') was definitely against Tacitus. The *Revue des deux mondes* ('Review of the Two Worlds') can approximately be described as pro-Tacitus. Gaston Boissier, who wrote the best book on Tacitus of the nineteenth century, was a contributor to the *Revue des deux mondes*.

The battle over French Caesarism—the word 'Caesarism' was invented by Auguste Romieu in 1850—was the last episode of modern political life in which Tacitus played a direct, unsophisticated role. This is not to deny that in even more recent times—for instance, during Fascism or the Vichy regime—books on Tacitus were inspired by modern political passions. Concetto Marchesi's well-known book on Tacitus, for instance, was written in hatred of Fascism (1924). But in the course of the nineteenth century it became increasingly difficult to talk about modern problems as if they were Roman ones. The French battle about Caesarism closed an epoch which had started at the beginning of the sixteenth century.

For three centuries Tacitus taught modern readers what tyranny is. No doubt there were philosophers and moralists, from Plato to Epictetus, who had something very important to convey on the same subject. But philosophers talk in abstract terms. Tacitus portrayed individuals. He was so lucid, so memorable, that no philosopher could compete with him. It was Tacitus who transmitted the ancient experience of tyranny to modern readers. Other historians and biographers—such as Diodorus, Suetonius, and Plutarch—were far less authoritative: they had been unable to produce a convincing,

---

[13] [The *Cordeliers* were members of a populist club during the French Revolution; and the *Vieux Cordelier* was the name of a short-lived journal published between 1793–4 and edited by Desmoulins. See Boissier (1903: 156–9).]

life-size picture of a despot. Thucydides, Xenophon, Polybius, Livy, Sallust competed with each other for the attention of the modern reader in the matter of republican government. Tacitus on despotism was left without rival. True, at least in the sixteenth and seventeenth centuries the image of the Tacitean despot was reproduced for the benefit of the modern reader in works of political theory rather than in books of history. I have already explained why this is perhaps not surprising. It was the essence of Tacitism to furnish indirectly that analysis of the political contemporary situation which it would have been technically difficult—and perhaps also more politically dangerous—to formulate in plain historical works.

But this is perhaps the moment to add that the historiography of these two centuries is insufficiently explored, and studies on the imitation of ancient models are needed especially. Mariana, John Hayward, William Camden, Grotius, Davila, and later Johannes Müller are names that immediately come to mind as historians who admired and imitated Tacitus. How much do we know about the exact forms of this imitation? Similarly, I do not know of an adequate study of A.-N. Amelot de La Houssaye, the greatest Tacitist of France and the translator of Baltasar Gracián, who was also the writer of the *Histoire du gouvernement de Venise* (1676), a classic in the interpretation of the Venetian constitution. Even in the early nineteenth century there are still historians who stylistically and psychologically imitate Tacitus in a way requiring some explanation. Such are the three most important Italian historians of that time, Carlo Botta, Pietro Colletta, and Carlo Troya. Indeed it is impossible to describe Italian historiography of the early nineteenth century without reference to Tacitus. The influence of Tacitus as a historian was inherent in his authority as a source for the history of the Roman Empire. Every educated man read Tacitus, accepted his picture of Tiberius and Nero, and learned from it how to understand the psychology of tyranny.

It is not difficult to see why such a situation should change in the nineteenth century, and why the change first became apparent in Germany. The Romantic revolution gave preference to those historians who expressed conflicts of ideas rather than conflicts of personalities. To be called a pragmatic historian became a term of abuse in certain circles. At the very beginning of the nineteenth century, Schelling declared that Herodotus and Thucydides were to be preferred to Polybius and Tacitus. At least as far as Thucydides was concerned, his judgement was generally accepted. Later, under the guidance of Mommsen, the studies on the Roman Empire were increasingly directed towards the provinces, the army, the administration—all subjects to which Tacitus could contribute less than the *Corpus Inscriptionum Latinarum*. Tacitus was declared to be the least military of the historians and was accused of being badly informed about Roman provincial administration. It was also shown that he followed his sources very closely— which seemed to cast a shadow on his competence as a historian. All the basic criticisms were made or at least confirmed by Mommsen. In a famous memoir of 1870, he opened a new phase in the analysis of the sources of Tacitus. He himself refrained from any derogatory remark and always respected Tacitus' judgement of life under the emperors. The definition of Tacitus as a monarchist from despair comes from him. Mommsen himself was a pessimistic supporter of the German Empire. But scholars who followed Mommsen too narrowly were bound to dislike or to underrate Tacitus.

Admirers of Tacitus had to try various lines of defence. Some did their best to cover him by pointing out that he was not a pragmatic historian, but an artist. This was a valid defence against Schelling's criticism because Schelling put art—*Kunst*—above everything else. In this sense J. W. Süvern wrote his famous paper 'Ueber den Kunstcharakter des Tacitus', published by the Berlin Academy in 1823. Other students of historiography suggested that Polybius and Tacitus were nearer than Herodotus and Thucydides to Christian truth and were therefore to be preferred. But the definition of Tacitus as an artist could easily turn into an admission that he was not a historian. At the end of the century Friedrich Leo, who owed so much to Mommsen, proclaimed Tacitus a poet, one of the few great poets Rome had ever had, only to damn him as a historian. Few or none of those people who defended Tacitus in Germany were so bold or so naive as to say that Tacitus was true, as French scholars still did. Finally, the negative appreciation of Tacitus prevailed everywhere, even in France, where he had found his steadiest admirers, as the works by Fabia and Courbaud showed.

Today we can see the point of these nineteenth-century discussions about the merits of Tacitus without having to agree. The dispute about Tacitus has definitely passed to another stage. Tacitus has his own obvious limits. Within these limits there can be no doubt on our part that he saw something essential: the demoralization that goes together with despotism. Mussolini and Hitler and Stalin have done something for his reputation. Furthermore, we cannot now judge an ancient writer without asking ourselves what he represented in the history of medieval and modern humanism. The transition from the Roman Republic to the Roman Principate remains to the present day a problem of immediate relevance to us. This would never have happened without Tacitus. He is our master in the study of despotism. His methods can be applied, and have been applied, to other periods. His analysis of human motives has been discussed, and often accepted, by the leading moralists of the last centuries. But there is perhaps something even simpler and more immediate to be said about Tacitus. He was interested in individual men and women. He went beyond appearances and made an effort to interpret their minds. He wrote as a man who was inside the process of tyrannical corruption which he was describing. He makes us realize that we, too, are inside.

[POSTSCRIPT

I have supplemented some of the skeletal bibliographical detail in Momigliano's original version of this paper and moved it into footnotes, but apart from supplying English glosses of the titles of some works, my editorial interventions in this piece have been sparing. For some additional items of bibliography on points raised, see Griffin (1982) on Tacitus' version of Claudius' speech on the possible admission of Gauls to the senate; Moles (1998) on the speech of Cremutius Cordus; Ash (1999a: 147–65) on the rogue general Antonius Primus; Riedl (2002) and Kelly (2008) on the relationship between Tacitus and Ammianus Marcellinus; and Krebs (2005) on the *Germania* and Enea Silvio Piccolomini and Conrad Celtis.]

18

Tacitus Now

Lionel Trilling

The histories of Tacitus have been put to strange uses. The princelings of Renaissance Italy consulted the *Annals* on how to behave with the duplicity of Tiberius. The German racists overlooked all the disagreeable things which Tacitus observed of their ancestors, took note only of his praise of the ancient chastity and independence, and thus made of the *Germania* their anthropological primer. But these are the aberrations; the influence of Tacitus in Europe has been mainly in the service of liberty, as he intended it to be. Perhaps this influence has been most fully felt in France, where, under the dictatorships both of the Jacobins and of Napoleon, Tacitus was regarded as a dangerously subversive writer. In America, however, he has never meant a great deal. James Fenimore Cooper is an impressive exception to our general indifference, but Cooper was temperamentally attracted by the very one of all the qualities of Tacitus which is likely to alienate most American liberals, the aristocratic colour of his libertarian ideas. Another reason for our coolness to Tacitus is that, until recently, our political experience gave us no ground to understand what he is talking about. Dictatorship and repression, spies and political informers, blood purges and treacherous dissension have not been part of our political tradition as they have been of Europe's. But Europe has now come very close to us, and our political education of the last decades fits us to understand the historian of imperial Rome.

It is the mark of a great history that sooner or later we become as much aware of the historian as of the events he relates. In reading Tacitus we are aware of him from the first page: we are aware of him as one of the few great writers who are utterly without hope. He is always conscious of his own despair; it is nearly a fault in him; the attitude sometimes verges on attitudinizing. Yet the great fact about

Tacitus is that he never imposes or wishes to impose his despair upon the reader. He must, he says, be always telling of *saeua iussa, continuas accusationes, fallaces amicitias, perniciem innocentium et easdem exitii causas*, 'savage orders, constant accusations, deceitful friendships, the ruin of innocents and always the same reasons for their extermination' (*A.* 4.33.3), and he complains that his subject-matter has *minimum oblectationis*, 'very little enjoyment' (*A.* 4.33.3). But the reader never feels the monotony; despite the statements which seem to imply the contrary, Tacitus never becomes the victim of what he writes about—he had too much power of mind for that.

His power of mind is not like that of Thucydides; it is not really political and certainly not military. It is, on a grand scale, psychological. We are irresistibly reminded of Proust when Tacitus sets about creating the wonderful figure of Tiberius and, using a hundred uncertainties and contradictions, tries to solve this great enigma of a man, yet always avoids the solution because the enigma is the character. In writing of political events his real interest is not in their political meaning but rather in what we would now call their cultural meaning, in what they tell us of the morale and morals of the nation; it is an interest that may profitably be compared with Flaubert's in *L'Éducation sentimentale*, and perhaps it has been remarked that that novel, and *Salammbô* as well, have elements of style and emotion which reinforce our sense of Flaubert as a Tacitean personality.

Tacitus's conception of history was avowedly personal and moral: *quod praecipuum munus annalium reor, ne uirtutes sileantur utque prauis dictis factisque ex posteritate et infamia metus sit*, 'which I deem to be a principal responsibility of annals, to prevent virtues from being silenced and so that crooked words and deeds should be attended by the dread of posterity and infamy' (*A.* 3.65.1). This moral preoccupation finds expression in a moral sensibility which is not ours and which in many respects we find it hard to understand. It has often been pointed out that slaves, Christians, Jews, and barbarians are outside the circle of his sympathies; he rather despised the Stoic humanitarianism of Seneca. Yet, as he says, half his historical interest is in the discovery of good deeds, and perhaps nothing in literature has a greater impact of astonishment, a more sudden sense of illumination, than the occurrence of a good deed in the pages of his histories. He represents the fabric of society as so loosened that we can scarcely credit the account of any simple human relationship, let alone a noble action. Yet the simple human relationships exist—a soldier weeps at having killed his father in the civil war (*H.* 3.25), the aristocrats open their houses to the injured thousands when the great amphitheatre falls down (*A.* 4.63.2); and the noble actions take place—the freed-woman Epicharis, when Piso's enormous conspiracy against Nero was discovered, endured the torture and died, implicating no one, *alienos ac prope ignotos protegendo*, 'defending others whom she scarcely knew' (*A.*15.57.2). But the human relationship and the noble deed exist in the midst of depravity and disloyalty so great that we are always surprised by the goodness before we are relieved by it; what makes the fortitude of Epicharis so remarkable and so puzzling is that the former slave screened strangers and those whom she hardly knew: *cum ingenui et uiri et equites Romani senatoresque intacti tormentis carissima suorum quisque pignorum proderent*, 'when the freeborn—men and Roman equestrians and senators, all untouched by torture—were each betraying the dearest of those to whom they were bound' (*A.* 15.57.2). From these pages we learn really to understand those well-worn lines of Portia's about the beam of the candle, for we discover what Portia meant by a naughty world, literally a world of naught, a moral vacancy so great and black that in it the beam of a candle seems a flash of lightning (*Merchant of Venice*, v. ii).

The moral and psychological interests of Tacitus are developed at the cost of what nowadays is believed to be the true historical insight. The French scholar Boissier remarks that it is impossible to read the *Histories* and the *Annals* without wondering how the Roman Empire could possibly have held together through the eighty years of mutiny, infamy, intrigue, riot, expenditure, and irresponsibility which the two books tell us of.[1] At any moment, we think, the political structure must collapse under this unnatural weight. Yet almost any modern account of the post-Augustan Empire suggests that we are wrong to make this supposition and seems to imply a radical criticism of Tacitus' methods. Breasted, for example, includes the period from Tiberius to Vespasian in a chapter which he calls 'The First of Two Centuries of Peace'.[2] And Rostovtzeff in his authoritative work gives us to understand that Rome, despite the usual minor troubles, was a healthy, developing society.[3] Yet Tacitus finds it worthy of comment

---

[1] Boissier (1903).   [2] Breasted (1927).   [3] Rostovtzeff (1926).

that at this time a certain man died a natural death—*rarum in tanta claritudine*, 'a rarity in the case of such brilliance' (*A.* 6.10.3), he says.

It is not, as I gather, that Tacitus lacks veracity. What he lacks is what in the 1930s used to be called 'the long view' of history. But to minds of a certain sensitivity 'the long view' is the falsest historical view of all, and indeed the insistence on the length of perspective is intended precisely to overcome sensitivity—seen from sufficient distance, it says, the corpse and the hacked limbs are not so very terrible, and eventually they even begin to compose themselves into a 'meaningful pattern'. Tacitus had no notions of historical development to comfort him; nor did he feel it his duty to look at present danger and pain with the remote, objective eyes of posterity. The knowledge, if he had it, that trade with the east was growing or that a more efficient bureaucracy was evolving by which well-trained freedmen might smoothly administer affairs at home and in the provinces could not have consoled him for what he saw as the degradation of his class and nation. He wrote out of his feelings of the present and did not conceive the consolations of history and the future.

What for many modern scholars is the vice of history was for Tacitus its virtue—he thought that history should be literature and that it should move the minds of men through their feelings. And so he contrived his narrative with the most elaborate attention to its dramatic effects. Yet something more than a scrupulous concern for literary form makes Tacitus so impressive in a literary way; some essential poise of his mind allowed him to see events with both passion and objectivity, and one cannot help wondering if the bitter division which his mind had to endure did not reinforce this quality. For Tacitus hated the Rome of the emperors, all his feelings being for the vanished Republic; yet for the return of the Republic he had no hope whatever. He served the ideal of the Republic in his character of historian; the actuality of the Empire he served as praetor, consul, and proconsul, and complied with the wishes of the hated Domitian. The more he saw of the actuality, the more he despaired of his ideal—and the more he loved it. And perhaps this secret tension of love and despair accounts for the poise and energy of his intellect.

We can see this poise and energy in almost all his judgements. For example, he despised the Jews, but he would not repress his wry appreciation of their stubborn courage and his intense admiration for their conception of God. The one phrase of his that everyone knows, *ubi solitudinem faciunt pacem appellant*, 'They make a desert and call it peace' (*Agr.* 30.4), he put into the mouth of a British barbarian, the leader of a revolt against Roman rule; it will always be the hostile characterization of imperialist domination, yet Tacitus himself measured Roman virtue by imperialist success. He makes no less than four successive judgements of Otho: scorns him as Nero's courtier and cuckold (*H.* 1.13), admires him as a provincial governor (*H.* 1.13), despises him as emperor (*H.* 2.50.1), and praises him for choosing to die and end the civil war (*H.* 2.50.1). Much as he loved the Republican character, he knew that its day was past, and he ascribes Galba's fall to his old-fashioned inflexibility in Republican virtue (*H.* 1.18.3).

The poise and energy of Tacitus's mind manifests itself in his language, and Professor Hadas in his admirable introduction to the useful Modern Library edition tells us how much we must lose in translation.[4] Yet even a reader of the translation cannot help being aware of the power of the writing. When Tacitus remarks that Tiberius was an emperor *qui libertatem metuebat, adulationem oderat*, 'who feared freedom while he hated sycophancy' (*A.* 2.87), or that the name of Lucius Volusius was made glorious by his ninety-three years, his honourable wealth, and his *inoffensa tot imperatorum amicitia*, 'uninterrupted friendship of so many emperors' (*A.* 13.30.2), or that *an satias capit aut illos, cum omnia tribuerunt, aut hos, cum iam nihil reliquum est quod cupiant*, 'or else satiety afflicts either one party, when they have bestowed everything they can, or the other, when there no longer remains anything they desire' (*A.* 3.30.4), we catch a glimpse of the force of the original because the thought itself is so inherently dramatic. Sometimes we wonder, no doubt foolishly, if we really need the original, so striking is the effect in translation, as when Sabinus is being led to his death through the streets and the people flee from his glance, fearing that it will implicate them: *quo intendisset oculos, quo uerba acciderent, fuga uastitas*, 'Wherever he turned, wherever his eyes fell, there was flight and solitude' (*A.* 4.70.2); or when the soldiers undertake to 'absolve' themselves of a mutiny by the ferocity with which they slaughter their leaders (*A.* 1.48–9); or when, in that greatest of street scenes, the debauchees look out of their brothel doors to observe with casual interest the armies fighting for the possession of Rome (*H.* 3.83.2).

---

[4] Hadas (2003: xxv).

Tacitus is not a tragic writer as, in some strict use of the word, Thucydides is often said to be. It has been conjectured of Thucydides that he conceived his *Peloponnesian War* on the model of actual tragic drama, Athens being his hero; and certainly the downfall of Athens, which Thucydides himself witnessed, makes a fable with the typical significance of tragedy. But Tacitus had no such matter for his histories. The Republic had died before his grandfather was born and he looked back at it through a haze of idealization—the tragedy had ended long ago; what he observed was the aftermath which had no end, which exactly lacked the coherence of tragedy. His subject is not Rome at all, not Rome the political entity, but rather the grotesque career of the human spirit in a society which, if we may summarize the whole tendency of his thought, appeared to him to endure for no other purpose than to maintain the long and lively existence of anarchy. From this it is easy, and all too easy, to discover his relevance to us now, but the relevance does not account for the strange invigoration of his pages, which is rather to be explained by his power of mind and his stubborn love of virtue maintained in desperate circumstances.

[POSTSCRIPT

My editorial interventions in this piece have been minimal. I have added footnotes with details of the modern discussions to which Trilling refers, and since the original piece included quotations from Tacitus in English without any indication of their provenance, I have incorporated the Latin text and added precise references.]

References

ABBREVIATED JOURNAL TITLES

AHB	*Ancient History Bulletin*
AJAH	*American Journal of Ancient History*
AJP	*American Journal of Philology*
ANRW II	*Aufstieg und Niedergang der römischen Welt*
AU	*Der altsprachliche Unterricht*
BICS	*Bulletin of the Institute of Classical Studies*
CA	*Classical Antiquity*
CAH XI [2]	*Cambridge Ancient History*
CISA	*Contributi dell'Istituto di storia antica*
CJ	*Classical Journal*
CP	*Classical Philology*
CQ	*Classical Quarterly*
CR	*Classical Review*
CW	*Classical World*
G&R	*Greece and Rome*
HSCP	*Harvard Studies in Classical Philology*
ICS	*Illinois Classical Studies*
IJCT	*International Journal of the Classical Tradition*
JRS	*Journal of Roman Studies*
MD	*Materiali e discussioni per l'analisi dei testi classici*
MEFRA	*Mélanges de l'École française de Rome*
MGWJ	*Monatszeitschrift für Geschichte und Wissenschaft des Judentums*
MH	*Museum Helveticum*
PBSR	*Papers of the British School at Rome*
PCPS	*Proceedings of the Cambridge Philological Society*
PLLS	*Papers of the Leeds International Latin Seminar*
RFIC	*Rivista di filologia e di istruzione classica*
RhM	*Rheinisches Museum für Philologie*
SCI	*Scripta Classica Israelica*
SO	*Symbolae Osloenses*
TAPA	*Transactions of the American Philological Association*
WJA	*Würzburger Jahrbücher fur Altertumswissenschaft*
WS	*Wiener Studien*
YCS	*Yale Classical Studies*

OTHER

AE	*L'Année épigraphique*
BGU	*Berliner griechische Urkunden* (Berlin 1895-)
LSJ	H. G. Liddell, R. Scott, and H. Stuart Jones, *A Greek-English Lexicon* (Oxford, 1996, 9th edition)
OLD	*Oxford Latin Dictionary*
PIR	E. Klebs, H. Dessau, and P. Rhoden, *Prosopographia Imperii Romani*, 3 vols (Berlin 1897-98)
*PIR*²	E. Groag, A. Stein, and L. Petersen, *Prosopographia Imperii Romani*, 2nd edition, vol 1- (Berlin 1933-)
RE	*Paulys real-Encyclopädie der classischen Altertumswissenschaft*
TLL	*Thesaurus Linguae Latinae*

ADAMS, J. N. (1972), 'The Language of the Later Books of Tacitus' *Annals*', *CQ* 22, 350–73.

——(1973), 'The Vocabulary of the Speeches in Tacitus' Historical Works', *BICS* 20, 124–44.

——(2007), *The Regional Diversification of Latin, 200BC–AD600* (Cambridge).

——and MAYER, R. G. (eds) (1999), *Aspects of the Language of Latin Poetry* (Oxford).

ADIMARI, A. (1628), *La Polinnia, ovvero cinquanta sonetti d'Alessandro Adimari fondati sopra sentenze di G. Cornelio Tacito* (Florence).

ADLER, E. (2008), 'Boudica's Speeches in Tacitus and Dio', *CW* 101, 173–95.

ALFÖLDY, G. (1995), 'Bricht der Schweigsame sein Schweigen?', *Mitteilung des deutschen archaeologischen Instituts: Römische Abteilung* 102, 251–68.

ALLISON, J. (1999), 'Tacitus' *Dialogus* and Plato's *Symposium*', *Hermes* 127, 479–92.

AMIOTTI, G. (1987), 'Cerne: "*ultima terra*"', *CISA* 13, 43–9.

ANDERSON, J. G. C. (ed.) (1938), *Cornelii Taciti de origine et situ Germanorum* (Oxford).

ANDRÉ, J.-M. (1991), 'Tacite et la philosophie', *ANRW* II 33.4, 3101–54.

ARNALDI, F. (1945), *Due capitoli su Tacito* (Naples).

ASH, R. (1997), 'Warped Intertextualities: Naevius and Sallust at Tacitus *Histories* 2.12.1', *Histos* 1, http://www.dur.ac.uk/Classics/histos/1997/ash.html

——(1998), 'Waving the White Flag: Surrender Scenes at Livy 9.5–6 and Tacitus *Histories* 3.31 and 4.62', *G&R* 45, 27–44.

——(1999a), *Ordering Anarchy: Armies and Leaders in Tacitus' Histories* (London and Ann Arbor, Mich.).

——(1999b), 'An Exemplary Conflict: Tacitus' Parthian Battle Narrative (*Annals* 6.34–35)', *Phoenix* 53, 114–35.

——(2002), 'Epic Encounters? Ancient Historical Battle Narratives and the Epic Tradition', in D. S. Levene and D. P. Nelis (eds), *Clio and the Poets: Augustan Poetry and the Traditions of Ancient Historiography* (Leiden), 253–73.

——(2003), '*Aliud est enim epistulam, aliud . . . historiam scribere* (*Epistles* 6.16.22): Pliny the Historian?', *Arethusa* 36, 211–25.

——(2006a), 'Following in the Footsteps of Lucullus? Tacitus' Characterisation of Corbulo', *Arethusa* 39, 355–75.

——(2006b), *Tacitus* (London).

——(2007a), *Tacitus Histories II* (Cambridge).

——(2007b), 'The Battle of Mons Graupius: An Historiographical Route Map?', in J. Marincola (ed.), *Blackwell Companion to Ancient Historiography* (Oxford), 434–40.

——(2010a), 'Rhoxolani Blues (Tacitus *Histories* 1.79): Virgil's Scythian Ethnography Revisited', in Woodman and Miller (2010).

——(2010b), 'Fighting Talk: Dillius Vocula's Last Stand (Tacitus *Histories* 4.58)', in D. Pausch (ed.), *Stimmen der Geschichte: Funktionen von Reden in der antiken Historiographie* (Berlin).

——(2010c), 'The Great Escape: Tacitus on the Mutiny of the Usipi (*Agricola* 28)', in C. S. Kraus, J. Marincola, and C. Pelling (eds), *Ancient Historiography and its Contexts: Studies in Honour of A. J. Woodman* (Oxford), 275–93.

——and MALAMUD, M. (eds) (2006), *Ingens Eloquentiae Materia: Rhetoric and Empire in Tacitus*, *Arethusa* Special Issue 39 (Baltimore, Md.).

AUERBACH, E. (1957), *Mimesis: the Representation of Reality in Western Literature* (Garden City, NY).

BABCOCK, C. L. (2000), '*Principe interfecto*: Tacitus' Sense of Aftermath in the *Histories*', in S. K. Dickison and J. P. Hallett (eds), *Rome and her Monuments: Essays on the City and Literature of Rome in Honor of Katherine A. Geffcken* (Wauconda, Ill.), 563–86.

BABLITZ, L. (2007), *Actors and Audience in the Roman Courtroom* (London and New York).

BAILEY, C. (1947), *Titi Lucreti Cari 'De Rerum Natura' Libri Sex*, 3 vols (Oxford).

BALSDON, J. P. V. D. (1946), review of Pippidi (1944), *JRS* 36, 168–73.

——(1959), review of Syme (1958a), *CR* 9, 258–61.

——(1979), *Romans and Aliens* (London).

BANNON, C. J. (1997), *The Brothers of Romulus: Fraternal Pietas in Roman Literature, Law, and Society* (Princeton, NJ).

BARDON, H. (1940), *Les Empereurs et les lettres latines d'Auguste à Hadrien* (Paris).

——(1953), 'Tacite et le "Dialogus des orateurs"', *Latomus* 12, 166–87.

——(1956), *La Littérature latine inconnue* , vol. 2 (Paris).

444 *References*

BARNES, J. (1989), 'Antiochus of Ascalon', 51–96 in Griffin and Barnes (1989: 51–96).

BARNES, T. D. (1981), 'Curiatius Maternus', *Hermes* 109, 382–4.

——(1985), *Tertullian: A Historical and Literary Study* (Oxford).

——(1986), 'The Significance of Tacitus' *Dialogus de Oratoribus'*, *HSCP* 90, 225–44.

BARRETT, A. A. (1989), *Caligula: The Corruption of Power* (London).

——(1999), 'The Year of Livia's Birth', *CQ* 49, 630–32.

BARTSCH, S. (1994), *Actors in the Audience: Theatricality and Doublespeak from Nero to Hadrian* (Cambridge, Mass.) [pp. 101–25 reprinted as Chapter 4 in this volume].

BARWICK, K. (1954), 'Der *Dialogus de Oratoribus* des Tacitus: Motive und Zeit seiner Entstehung', *Sitzungsberichte der Sächsische Akademie der Wissenschaften*, Philologisch-Historische Klasse 101 (Leipzig).

BATOMSKY, S. J. (1985), 'The Not-So-Perfect-Man: Some Ambiguities in Tacitus' Picture of Agricola', *Latomus* 44, 388–93.

BAXTER, R. T. S. (1971), 'Virgil's Influence on Tacitus *Histories* 3', *CP* 66, 93–107.

——(1972), 'Virgil's Influence on Tacitus in *Annals* 1 and 2', *CP* 67, 246–69.

BECK, M. (2001), 'Das dramatische Datum des *Dialogus de Oratoribus'*, *RhM* 144, 159–71.

BENARIO, H. (1964–5), 'Recent Work on Tacitus: 1954–63', *CW* 58, 69–83.

——(1969–70), 'Recent Work on Tacitus: 1964–68', *CW* 63, 253–67.

——(1977–8), 'Recent Work on Tacitus: 1969–73', *CW* 71, 1–32.

——(1986–7), 'Recent Work on Tacitus: 1974–83', *CW* 80, 73–147.

——(1990), 'Tacitus' *Germania* and Modern Germany', *ICS* 15, 163–75.

——(1993), *Thusnelda: A German Princess in Ancient Rome* (New York).

——(1995–6), 'Recent Work on Tacitus: 1984–93', *CW* 89, 91–162.

——(2005), 'Recent Work on Tacitus: 1994–2003', *CW* 98, 251–336.

BENVENISTE, E. (1971), *Problems in General Linguistics* (Coral Gables, Fla.).

BEWS, J. (1987), 'Language and Style in Tacitus' *Agricola'*, *G&R* 34, 201–11.

BIRLEY, A. R. (2000), 'The Life and Death of Cornelius Tacitus', *Historia* 49, 230–47.

BLOCH, R. S. (2002), *Antike Vorstellungen vom Judentum. Historia Einzelschriften* 160 (Stuttgart) [pp. 187–216 reprinted in translation as Chapter 16 of this volume].

BLOOM, A. (1986), *Prodigal Sons: The New York Intellectuals and Their World* (Oxford).

BO, D. (1993), *Le principali problematiche del Dialogus de Oratoribus* (Zurich).

BOEHLICH, W. (ed.) (1965), *Der Berliner Antisemitismusstreit* (Frankfurt).

BOISSIER, G. (1903), *Tacite* (Paris).

BOOTH, J., and VERITY, A. C. F. (1978), 'Critical Appreciations IV: Ovid *Amores* 2.10', *G&R* 25, 125–40.

BORNECQUE, H. (1902), *Les Déclamations et les déclamateurs d'après Sénèque le Père* (Lille).

BORZSÁK, I. (1968), 'P. Cornelius Tacitus', *RE* supplement 11, 375–512 (Stuttgart and Munich).

——(1969), 'Das Germanicusbild des Tacitus', *Latomus* 28, 588–600.

——(1970), 'Zum Verständnis der Darstellungskunst des Tacitus', *Acta Antiqua* 18, 279–92.

——(1973), '*Spectaculum*: ein Motiv der "tragischen Geschichtsschreibung" bei Livius und Tacitus', *Acta Classica Vniversitatis Scientarum Debreceniensis* 9, 57–67.

——(1982), 'Alexander der Grosse als Muster taciteischer Heldendarstellung', *Gymnasium* 89, 37–56.

BOSWELL, J. (1980), *Christianity, Social Tolerance, and Homosexuality* (Chicago and London).

BÖTTICHER, W. (1830), *Lexicon Taciteum, siue de Stilo C. Cornelii Taciti* (Berlin).

BRAMBLE, J. C. (1973), 'Critical Appreciations I: Propertius 3.10', *G&R* 20, 155–61.

BRAUND, D. (1996a), *Ruling Roman Britain: Kings, Queens, Governors and Emperors from Julius Caesar to Agricola* (London).

——(1996b), 'River Frontiers in the Environmental Psychology of the Roman World', in D. Kennedy (ed.), *The Roman Army in the East, JRA* Supplementary Series 18 (Ann Arbor, Mich.), 43–8.

BRAUND, S., and GILL, C. (1997), *The Passions in Roman Thought and Literature* (Cambridge).

BREASTED, J. H. (1927), *A Brief History of Ancient Times* (London).

BRIESSMANN, A. (1955), *Tacitus und das flavische Geschichtbild*, Hermes Einzelschriften 10 (Wiesbaden).

BRINGMANN, K. (1970), 'Aufbau und Absicht des taciteischen *Dialogus de Oratoribus*', *Museum Helveticum* 27, 164–78.

BRINK, C. (1989), 'Quintilian's *De Causis Corruptae Eloquentiae* and Tacitus' *Dialogus de Oratoribus*', *CQ* 39, 472–503.

——(1993), 'History in the *Dialogus de Oratoribus* and Tacitus the Historian', *Hermes* 121, 335–49.

——(1994), 'Can Tacitus' *Dialogus* be Dated? Evidence and Historical Conclusions', *HSCP* 96, 251–80.

BRINK, C. O. (1952), 'Justus Lispius and the Text of Tacitus', *JRS* 42, 32–51.

——(1971), 'Horatian Notes II: Despised Readings in the Manuscripts of the *Odes* Book II', *PCPS* 17, 17–29.

BROCK, R. (1995), 'Versions, Inversions, and Evasions: Classical Historiography and the "Published" Speech', *PLLS* 8, 209–24.

BRUÈRE, R.T. (1954), 'Tacitus and Pliny's *Panegyricus*', *CP* 49, 161–79.

BRUNT, P. A. (1982), 'The Legal Issue in Cicero, *pro Balbo*', *CQ* 32, 136–47.

——(1983), '*Princeps* and *Equites*', *JRS* 73, 42–75.

BUCHER, G. S. (1995), 'The *Annales Maximi* in the Light of Roman Methods of Keeping Records', *AJAH* 12, 2–61.

BÜCHNER, K. (1955), *Tacitus: die Historischen Versuche, Agricola, Germania, Dialogus* (Stuttgart).

——(1956), 'Das Proemium zum *Agricola* des Tacitus', *WS* 69, 321–41.

BURKE, P. (1969), 'Tacitism', in Dorey (1969b: 149–71).

BURN, A. R. (1949), '*Mare pigrum et graue*', *CR* 63, 94.

——(1969), 'Tacitus on Britain', in Dorey (1969b: 35–61).

BUXTON, R. (1987), 'Wolves and Werewolves in Greek Thought', in J. Bremmer (ed.), *Interpretations of Greek Mythology* (London), 60–79.

BYRE, C. S. (1994), 'The Rhetoric of Description in *Odyssey* 9.116–41, Odysseus and Goat Island', *CJ* 89, 357–67.

CALVINO, I. (1997), *Invisible Cities* (London).

CAMERON, A. D. E. (1967), 'Tacitus and the Date of Curiatius Maternus' Death', *CR* 17, 258–61.

CANCIK, H., LICHTENBERGER, H., and SCHÄFER, P. (eds) (1996), *Geschichte-Tradition-Reflexion: Festschrift M. Hengel* (Tübingen).

CAPLAN, H. (1944), 'The Decay of Eloquence at Rome in the First Century', in *Studies in Speech and Drama in Honor of Alexander M. Drummond* (Ithaca, NY), 295–325.

——(1970), *Of Eloquence* (Ithaca, NY).

CARMODY, W. M. (1926), *Tacitus' Use of the Subjunctive* (Chicago, Ill.).

CASTAGNOLI, F. (1981), 'Influenze alessandrine nell' urbanistica della Roma Augustea', *RFIC* 109, 414–23.

CHAMPION, C. (1994), '*Dialogus* 5.3–10.8, A Reconsideration of the Character of Marcus Aper', *Phoenix* 48, 152–63.

CHAPLIN, J. D., and KRAUS, C. S. (eds) (2009), *Livy*, Oxford Readings in Classical Studies (Oxford).

CHARLESWORTH, M. P. (1923), 'Tiberius and the Death of Augustus', *AJP* 44, 145–57.

——(1927), 'Livia and Tanaquil', *CR* 41, 55–7.

CHEVALLIER, R., and POIGNAULT, R. (eds) (1992), *Actes du Colloque Présence de Tacite* (Tours).

CHILVER, G. E. F. (1979), *A Historical Commentary on Tacitus Histories I and II* (Oxford).

CHRIST, K. (1956), *Drusus und Germanicus* (Paderborn).

CIZEK, E. (1983), *L'Époque de Trajan: circonstances politiques et problems idéologiques*, trans. C. Frantescu (Paris and Bucharest).

CLARKE, K. (1999), *Between Geography and History: Hellenistic Constructions of the Roman World* (Oxford).

——(2001), 'An Island Nation: Re-Reading Tacitus' *Agricola*', *JRS* 91, 94–112 [reprinted as Chapter 1 in this volume].

CLASSEN, C. J. (1988), 'Tacitus: Historian Between Republic and Principate', *Mnemosyne* 41, 93–116.

COARELLI, F. (1977), 'Il Campo Marzio occidentale: storia e topografia', *MEFRA* 89, 816–46.

COLLINGWOOD, R. G. (1946), *The Idea of History* (Oxford).

COMBER, M. (1991), review of Martin and Woodman (1989), *JRS* 81, 209–10.

CONSTANTAKOPOULOU, C. (2007), *The Dance of the Islands: Insularity, Networks, the Athenian Empire and the Aegean World* (Oxford).

CORBEILL, A. (2004), *Nature Embodied: Gesture in Ancient Rome* (Princeton, NJ).

CORDANO, F. (1992), *La geografia degli antichi* (Rome).

CORNELIUS, E. (1888), *Quomodo Tacitus, Historiarum Scriptor, in Hominum Memoria Versatus Sit ad Renascentes Litteras Saeculis XIV et XV* (Wetzlar).

COSTA, C. D. N. (1969), 'The Dialogus', in Dorey (1969b: 35–61).

COURBAUD, E. (1918), *Les Procédés d'art de Tacite dans les Histoires* (Paris).

COURTNEY, E. (1980), *A Commentary on the Satires of Juvenal* (London).

CRANE, N. (1999), *Two Degrees West: A Walk Along England's Meridian* (London).

CROOK, J. A. (1995), *Legal Advocacy in the Roman World* (Ithaca, NY).

DAITZ, S. G. (1960), 'Tacitus' Technique of Character Portrayal', *AJP* 81, 30–52.

DAMMER, R. (2005), 'Wenn das Temperament mit einem Durchgeht . . . Marcus Aper im *Dialogus de oratoribus*', *RhM* 148, 329–48.

DAMON, C. (2003), *Tacitus Histories Book I* (Cambridge).

——(2006), '*Potior utroque Vespasianus*: Vespasian and his Predecessors in Tacitus's *Histories*', *Arethusa* 39, 245–79.

——and TAKÁCS, S. A. (eds) (1999), *The Senatus Consultum de Cn. Pisone Patre*. American Journal of Philology Special Issue 120 (Baltimore, Md.).

DAVIDSON, J. (1991), 'The Gaze in Polybius' *Histories*', *JRS* 81, 10–24.

DAVIES, J. P. (2004), *Rome's Religious History: Livy, Tacitus, Ammianus and their Gods* (Cambridge).

DEGEL, F. (1907), *Archaistische Bestandteile der Sprache des Tacitus* (Nuremberg).

DEGRASSI, A. (1946), 'Osservazioni su alcuni consoli suffecti dell'età di Augusto e Tiberio', *Epigraphica* 8, 34–52.

——(ed.) (1947, 1963), *Inscriptiones Italiae*, 2 vols (Rome).

——(1952), *Fasti Consolari dell'Impero dal 30 avanti Cristo al 613 dopo Cristo* (Rome).

DENCH, E. (2009), 'Tacitus' Syme: The Roman Historians and Twentieth-Century Approaches to Roman History', in Feldherr (2009).

DEUSE, W. (1975), 'Zur *Advocatus-Diaboli*-Funktion Apers im *Dialogus* und zur Methode ihrer Deutung', *Grazer Beiträge* 3, 51–68.

DEVILLERS, O. (2003), *Tacite et les sources des Annales: enquêtes sur la méthode historique* (Louvain, Paris, and Dudley, Mass.).

DICKINSON, B., and HARTLEY, B. (1995), 'Roman Military Activity in First-Century Britain: The Evidence of Tacitus and Archaeology', in R. Brock and A. J. Woodman (eds), *Papers of the Leeds International Latin Seminar* 8, 241–55.

DION, R. (1977), *Aspectes politiques de la géographie ancienne* (Paris).

DODDS, E. R. (1960), *Euripides' Bacchae*, 2nd edn (Oxford).

DOMINIK, W. (2007), 'Tacitus and Pliny on Oratory', in W. Dominik and J. Hall (eds), *A Companion to Roman Rhetoric* (Oxford), 323–38.

DOREY, T. A. (1969a), '*Agricola* and *Germania*', in Dorey (1969b: 1–18).

——(ed.) (1969b), *Tacitus* (London).

DOVER, K. J. (1974), *Greek Popular Morality in the Time of Plato and Aristotle* (Oxford).

DRAEGER, A. A. (1868), *Über Syntax und Stil des Tacitus* (Leipzig). 2nd edn 1874; 3rd edn 1882.

DREXLER, H. (1939), *Tacitus: Grundzüg einer politischen Pathologie* (Frankfurt am Main).

DUDLEY, D. R. (1968), *The World of Tacitus* (London).

DURET, L. (1986), 'Dans l'ombre des plus grands: poètes et prosateurs mal connus de la latinité d'argent', *ANRW* II 32.5, 3152–3346.

EARL, D. C. (1961), *The Political Thought of Sallust* (Cambridge).

——(1967), *The Moral and Political Tradition of Rome* (London).

ECK, W., CABALLOS, A., and FERNÁNDEZ, F. (1996), *Das Senatus Consultum de Cn. Pisone Patre*, Vestigia 48 (Munich).

EDELMAIER, W. (1964), 'Tacitus und die Gegner Roms' (dissertation, Heidelberg).

EDWARDS, C. (1993), *The Politics of Immorality in Ancient Rome* (Cambridge).

EDWARDS, R. (2008), 'Hunting for Boars with Tacitus and Pliny', *CA* 27, 35–58.

EGERMANN, F. (1935), 'Der *Dialogus* des Tacitus und Platons *Gorgias*', *Hermes* 70, 424–30.

ERIKSSON, N. (1934), *Studien zu den Annalen des Tacitus* (Lund).

ETTER, E.-L. (1966), *Tacitus in der Geistesgeschichte des 16. und 17. Jahrhunderts. Basler Beiträge zur Geschichtswissenschaft* 103 (Basel and Stuttgart).

EVERTS, P. S. (1926), *De Tacitea historiae conscribendae ratione* (Kerkrade).

FABIA, Ph. (1893), *Les Sources de Tacite dans les Histoires et les Annales* (Paris).

——(1895), 'Les ouvrages de Tacite: réussirent-ils auprès des contemporains?', *Revue de philologie de literature et d'histoire anciennes* 19, 1–10.

FANTHAM, E. (2004), *The Roman World of Cicero's de Oratore* (Oxford).

FEAR, A. T. (2009), 'Greater than Caesar? Rivalry with Caesar in Tacitus' *Agricola*', in J. Pigoń (ed.), *The Children of Herodotus: Greek and Roman Historiography and Related Genres* (Newcastle upon Tyne), 304–16.

FELDHERR, A. (1998), *Spectacle and Society in Livy's History* (Berkeley, Calif.).

——(ed.) (2009), *The Cambridge Companion to Roman Historians* (Cambridge).

FENSTERBUSCH, C. (1960), 'Schwimmende Ziegel, schwimmende Inseln', *RhM* 103, 373–7.

FLACH, D. (1973), *Tacitus in der Tradition der antiken Geschichtsschreibung*, Hypomnemata 39 (Göttingen).

FLETCHER, G. B. A. (1964), *Annotations on Tacitus*, Collection Latomus 71 (Brussels).

FLORES, E. (1999), 'Francesco Arnaldi e Tacito', *Vichiana* 4a: 3–5.

FLOWER, H. (1996), *Ancestor Masks and Aristocratic Power in Roman Culture* (Oxford).

——(2006), *The Art of Forgetting: Disgrace and Oblivion in Roman Political Culture* (Chapel Hill, NC, and London).

FORNARA, C. W. (1983), *The Nature of History in Ancient Greece and Rome* (Berkeley, Calif.).

FORNI, G. (ed.) (1962), *De Vita Iulii Agricolae* (Rome).

FORTENBAUGH, W. W. (1975), *Aristotle on Emotion* (London).

FOUCHER, A. (2000), *Historia Proxima Poetis: l'influence de la poésie épique sur le style des historiens latins de Salluste à Ammien Marcellin*, Collection Latomus 255 (Brussels).

FRANK, T. (1937), 'Curiatius Maternus and his Tragedies', *AJP* 58, 225–9.

FRASER, P. M. (1972), *Ptolemaic Alexandria*, 3 vols (Oxford).

FREEMAN, P. (2001), *Ireland and the Classical World* (Austin, Tex.).

FRIER, B. (1985), *The Rise of the Roman Jurists* (Princeton, NJ).

FUCHS, H. (1938), *Der geistige Widerstand gegen Rom in der antiken Welt* (Berlin).

FUHRMANN, M. (1960), 'Das Vierkaiserjahr bei Tacitus', *Philologus* 104, 250–78.

FULKERSON, L. (2006), 'Staging a Mutiny: Competitive Role-Playing on the Rhine (*Annals* 1.31–51)', *Ramus* 35, 169–92.

FURNEAUX, H., rev. J. G. C. Anderson (1922), *Cornelii Taciti de Vita Agricolae* (Oxford).

——(1883; 1907), *The Annals of Tacitus*, 2 vols (Oxford). First volume 1883, rev. edn 1896; second volume 1907.

GABBA, E. (1981), 'True History and False History in Classical Antiquity', *JRS* 71, 50–62.

GABRIELLI, C. (2007), 'Insularità e impero nell'*Agricola*', in M. A. Giua (ed.), *Ripensando Tacito (e Ronald Syme): storia e storiografia: Atti del Convegno Internazionale (Firenze, 30 novembre–1 dicembre 2006)*, Memorie e atti di convegni 41 (Pisa).

GALLIA, A. (2009), '*Potentes* and *Potentia* in Tacitus' *Dialogus de Oratoribus*', *TAPA* 139, 169–206.

GALTIER, F. (2001), 'La Mort de Junius Blaesus ou l'illusion tragique (Tacite, *Histoires* III, 38–39)', *Latomus* 60, 637–46.

GARZETTI, A. (1956), 'La data dell'incontro all' Eufrate di Artabano III e L. Vitellio', in *Studi in onore di A. Calderini e R. Paribeni* (Milan), 211–29.

——(1960), *L'impero da Tiberio agli Antonini* (Bologna).

References

GERBER, A., and GREEF, A. (1962), *Lexicon Taciteum* (Hildesheim).

GIBSON, B. J. (1998), 'Rumours as Causes of Events in Tacitus', *MD* 40, 111–29.

GILL, C. (1983), 'The Question of Character-Development: Plutarch and Tacitus', *CQ* 33, 469–87.

——(1984), 'The *Ethos/Pathos* Distinction in Rhetorical and Literary Criticism', *CQ* 34, 149–66.

——(1986), 'The Question of Character and Personality in Greek Tragedy', *Poetics Today* 7, 251–73.

——(1990), 'The Character–Personality Distinction', in C. B. R. Pelling (ed.), *Characterization and Individuality in Greek Literature* (Oxford), 1–30.

GILL, C. (1996), *Personality in Greek Epic, Tragedy, and Philosophy: The Self in Dialogue* (Oxford).

——(2006), *The Structured Self in Hellenistic and Roman Thought* (Oxford).

GILLIVER, C. M. (1996), '*Mons Graupius* and the Role of Auxiliaries in Battle', *G&R* 43, 54–67.

GILMARTIN, K. (1975), 'A Rhetorical Figure in Latin Historical Style: The Imaginary Second Person Singular', *TAPA* 105, 99–121.

GILMORE, G. D. (1970), 'Tacitus, *Germania* 36.1', *CQ* 20, 371.

GINSBURG, J. (1981), *Tradition and Theme in the Annals of Tacitus* (New York) [pp. 10–30 reprinted as Chapter 11 in this volume].

——(1993), '*In Maiores Certamina*: Past and Present in the *Annals*', in Luce and Woodman (1993: 86–103).

——(2006), *Representing Agrippina: Constructions of Female Power in the Early Roman Empire* (New York and Oxford).

GIUA, M. A. (1991), 'Paesaggio, natura, ambiente come elementi strutturali nella storiografia di Tacito', *ANRW* II 33.4, 2879–2902.

GOLDBERG, S. (1999), 'Appreciating Aper: The Defence of Modernity in Tacitus' *Dialogus de Oratoribus*', *CQ* 49, 224–37 [reprinted as Chapter 5 in this volume].

——(2009), 'The Faces of Eloquence: the *Dialogus de oratoribus*', in A. J. Woodman (ed.), *The Cambridge Companion to Tacitus* (Cambridge), 73–84.

GOODYEAR, F. R. D. (1968), 'Development of Language and Style in the *Annals* of Tacitus', *JRS* 58, 22–31 [reprinted as Chapter 15 in this volume].

——(1970a), 'Cyclic Development in History: A Note on Tacitus *Annals* 3.55.5', *BICS* 17, 101–6.

——(1970b), *Tacitus* (London).

——(1972), *The Annals of Tacitus Volume 1, Annals 1.1–54* (Cambridge).

——(1976), '*De Inconstantia Cornelii Taciti*', in *Acta omnium gentium ac nationum conuentus Latinis litteris linguaeque fouendis* (Malta), 198–204.

——(1981), *The Annals of Tacitus Volume 2, Annals 1.55–81 and Annals 2* (Cambridge).

GOTTSCHALK, H. B. (1987), 'Aristotelian Philosophy in the Roman World', *ANRW* II 36.2, 1079–1174.

GOWERS, E. (1993), *The Loaded Table: Representations of Food in Roman Literature* (Oxford).

GOWING, A. (2005), *Empire and Memory: The Representation of the Roman Republic in Imperial Culture* (Cambridge).

GRAF, F. (1931), *Untersuchungen über die Komposition der Annalen des Tacitus* (Thun).

GRANT, M. (trans.) (1956), *Tacitus: The Annals of Imperial Rome* (Harmondsworth).

GREENWOOD, E. (2006), *Thucydides and the Shaping of History* (London)

GRIFFIN, J., and HAMMOND, M. (1982), 'Critical Appreciations VI: Homer *Iliad* 1.1–52', *G&R* 29, 126–42.

GRIFFIN, M. T. (1982), 'The Lyons Tablet and Tacitean Hindsight', *CQ* 32, 404–18.

——(1984), *Nero: The End of a Dynasty* (London).

——(1999), 'Pliny and Tacitus', *SCI* 18, 139–58.

——and BARNES, J. (eds) (1989), *Philosophia Togata: Essays on Philosophy and Roman Society* (Oxford).

GRUEN, E. S. (1968), *Roman Politics and the Criminal Courts, 149–78* B.C. (Cambridge, Mass.).

——(1984), *The Hellenistic World and the Coming of Rome* (Berkeley, Calif.).

——(1992), *Culture and National Identity in Republican Rome* (Ithaca, NY).

GUDEMAN, A. (1894), *P. Cornelii Taciti Dialogus de Oratoribus* (Boston, Mass.).

——(1914), *P. Cornelii Taciti Dialogus de Oratoribus: mit Prolegomena, Text, und Adnotatio Critica, exegetischem und kritischem Kommentar, Bibliographie, und Index nominum et rerum* (Leipzig and Berlin).

——(1928), *De Vita Iulii Agricolae and De Germania* (Boston).

GUGEL, H. (1964), *Zu Stil und Aufbau von Tacitus, Dialogus de Oratoribus* (dissertation, Graz).

GÜNGERICH, R. (1951), 'Der *Dialogus* des Tacitus und Quintilians *Institutio Oratoria*', *CP* 46, 159–64.

——(1955), review of Barwick (1954), *Gnomon* 27, 439–43.

——(1956), 'Tacitus' *Dialogus* und der *Panegyricus* des Plinius', in H. Erbse (ed.), *Festschrift für Bruno Snell zum 60. Geburtstag* (Munich), 145–52.

——(1980), *Kommentar zum Dialogus des Tacitus*, ed. H. Heubner (Göttingen).

HABINEK, T. (2000), 'Seneca's Renown: *Gloria*, *Claritudo*, and the Replication of the Roman Elite', *Classical Antiquity* 19, 264–309.

HADAS, M. (ed.) (2003), *Tacitus: The Annals and the Histories*, trans. A. Church and W. Brodribb (New York) (originally published 1942).

HALL, E. (1989), *Inventing the Barbarian* (Oxford).

HALL, J. (1994), 'Persuasive Design in Cicero's *de Oratore*', *Phoenix* 48, 210–25.

——(2004), 'Cicero and Quintilian on the Oratorical Use of Hand Gestures', *CQ* 54, 143–60.

HALLIWELL, S. (1986), *Aristotle's Poetics* (London).

HAMMOND, M. (1963), 'Res Olim Dissociabiles: Principatus ac Libertas', *HSCP* 67, 93–113.

HANSEN, O. (1989), 'Did Poseidonios Give Germania Her Name?', *Latomus* 48, 878–9.

HANSON, W. S. (1991a), 'Tacitus' *Agricola*: An Archaeological and Historical Study', *ANRW* II 33.3, 1741–84.

——(1991b), *Agricola and the Conquest of the North*, 2nd edn (London).

HARDINGHAUS, B. (1932), 'Tacitus und die Griechentum' (dissertation, Münster).

——(1991), *Agricola and the Conquest of the North*, 2nd edn (London).

HARDWICK, L. (2003), *Reception Studies, Greece and Rome* New Surveys in the Classics 33 (Oxford).

HARTMAN, J. J. (1916), 'De Domitiano Imperatore et de Poeta Statio', *Mnemosyne* 44, 338–73.

HARTOG, F. (1988), *The Mirror of Herodotus*, trans. J. Lloyd (Berkeley, Calif., and London).

HASS-VON REITZENSTEIN, U. (1970), *Beiträge zur gattungsgeschichlichen Interpretation des Dialogus de Oratoribus* (Cologne).

HAUPT, H. (1885), 'Cassius Dio: Jahresbericht', *Philologus* 44, 132–63.

HÄUSSLER, R. (1965), *Tacitus und das historische Bewußtsein* (Heidelberg).

——(1969), 'Zum Umfang und Aufbau des *Dialogus de Oratoribus*', *Philologus* 113, 24–67.

——(1996), 'Thukydides und Tacitus', in E. G. Schmidt (ed.), *Griechenland und Rom: vergleichende Untersuchungen zu Entwicklungstendenzen und höhepunkten der antike Geschichte, Kunst, und Literatur* (Tbilisi and Erlangen), 433–52.

HAVERFIELD, F. (1916), 'Tacitus during the Late Roman Period and the Middle Ages', *JRS* 6, 196–201.

HAYNES, H. (2003), *The History of Make-Believe: Tacitus on Imperial Rome* (Berkeley, Calif., and London).

——(2004), 'Tacitus's Dangerous Word', *Classical Antiquity* 23, 33–61.

——(2006), 'Survival and Memory in the *Agricola*', *Arethusa* 39, 149–70.

HEINEMANN, I. (1919), 'Poseidonios über die Entwicklung der jüdischen Religion', *MGWJ* 63, 113–21.

HEINZ, W.-R. (1975), *Die Furcht als politisches Phänomenon bei Tacitus* (Amsterdam).

HELDMANN, K. (1982), *Antike Theorien über Entwicklung und Verfall der Redekunst* (Munich).

HENDERSON, J. (1992), 'Tacitus: the World in Pieces', *Ramus* 18 (1992), 162–98; revised version in Henderson (1998: 257–300).

——(1998), *Fighting for Rome: Poets and Caesars, History and Civil War* (Cambridge).

HERRMANN, L. (1939), 'La Mort de Curiatius Montanus', *Latomus* 3, 58–60.

HERTZBERG, A. (1968), *The French Enlightenment and the Jews* (New York).

HEUBNER, H. (1963), P. *Cornelius Tacitus. Die Historien*, vol. 1 (Heidelberg).

HILTBRUNNER, O. (1979), '*Prisce, iubes . . .* ', *Zeitschrift der Savigny-Stiftung für Rechtsgeschichte* 96, 31–42.

HIRST, A., and SILK, M. (2004), *Alexandria, Real and Imagined* (Aldershot and Burlington, Vt.).

HOCH, H. (1951), *Die Darstellung der politischen Sendung Roms bei Livius* (Frankfurt am Main).

HOCHART, P. (1890), *De l'authenticité des Annales et des Histoires de Tacite* (Paris).

——(1894), *Nouvelles considerations au sujet des Annales et des Histoires de Tacite* (Paris).

HOFFMANN, B. (2004), 'Tacitus' *Agricola* and the Role of Literature in the Archaeology of the First Century AD', in E. Sauer (ed.), *Archaeology and Ancient History: Breaking Down the Boundaries* (London), 151–66.

HOFFMANN, C. (1988), *Juden und Judentum im Werk deutscher Althistoriker des 19. und 20. Jahrhunderts*, Studies in Judaism in Modern Times 9 (Leiden).

——(1990), 'Das Judentum als Antithese. Zur Tradition eines kulturellen Wertungsmusters', in W. Bergmann and R. Erb (eds), *Antisemitismus in der politischen Kultur nach 1945* (Opladen), 20–38.

——(1995), 'Ancient Jewry—Modern Questions: German Historians of Antiquity on the Jewish Diaspora', *Illinois Classical Studies* 20, 191–206.

HORSFALL, N. (1989), *Cornelius Nepos: A Selection, including the Lives of Cato and Atticus* (Oxford).

HÜBNER, E. (1866), 'Zu Tacitus *Agricola*', *Hermes* 1, 438–48.

JACOB, C. (1991), *Géographie et ethnographie en Grèce ancienne* (Paris).

JANSON, T. (1964), *Latin Prose Prefaces*, Studies in Literary Conventions (Stockholm).

JUMONVILLE, N. (2007), *The New York Intellectuals Reader* (London).

KAHN, V. (1985), *Rhetoric, Prudence and Skepticism in the Renaissance* (Ithaca, NY).

KAPPELMACHER, A. (1932), 'Zur Abfassungszeit von Tacitus' *Dialogus de Oratoribus*', *WS* 50, 121–9.

KASTER, R. (ed.) (1995), *Suetonius, de Grammaticis et Rhetoribus* (Oxford)

——(2007), *Emotion, Restraint, and Community in Ancient Rome* (Oxford).

KEITEL, E. (1978), 'The Role of Parthia and Armenia in Tacitus' *Annals* 11 and 12', *AJP* 99, 462–73.

——(1984), 'Principate and Civil War in the *Annals* of Tacitus', *AJP* 105, 314–26.

——(1987), 'Otho's Exhortations in Tacitus' *Histories*', *G&R* 34, 73–82.

——(1991), 'The Structure and Function of Speeches in Tacitus *Histories* I–III', *ANRW* II 33.4, 2772–94.

KEITEL, E. (1992), '*Foedum Spectaculum* and Related Motifs in Tacitus *Histories* II–III', *RhMus* 135, 342–51.

——(1993), 'Speech and Narrative in Tacitus *Histories* 4', in Luce and Woodman (1993: 39–48).

——(1995), 'Plutarch's Tragedy Tyrants: Galba and Otho', *PLLS* 8, 275–88.

——(2006), '*Sententia* and Structure in Tacitus *Histories* 1.12–49', *Arethusa* 39, 219–44.

KEITEL, E. (2007), 'Feast Your Eyes on This: Vitellius as a Stock Tyrant (Tac. *Hist*. 3.36–39)', in J. Marincola (ed.), *A Companion to Greek and Roman Historiography* (Malden, Mass.), 441–6.

——(2008), 'The Virgilian Reminiscences at Tacitus *Histories* 3.84.4', *CQ* 58, 705–8.

KELLY, B. (2010), 'Tacitus, Germanicus, and the Kings of Egypt', *CQ* 60, 221–37.

KELLY, G. (2008), *Ammianus Marcellinus: The Allusive Historian* (Cambridge).

KENNEDY, D. F. (1992), *The Arts of Love* (Cambridge).

KENNEDY, G. (1972), *The Art of Rhetoric in the Roman World* (Princeton, NJ).

KEYSSNER, K. (1936), 'Betrachtungen zum *Dialogus* als Kunstwerk und Bekenntnis', in *Studien zu Tacitus: Carl Hosius zum siebzigsten Geburtstag am 21. März 1936*, Würzburger Studien 9 (Stuttgart), 94–115.

KIMMAGE, M. (2009), *The Conservative Turn: Lionel Trilling, Whittaker Chambers, and the Lessons of Anti-Communism* (Cambridge, Mass.).

KIRCHNER, R. (2001), *Sentenzen im Werk des Tacitus* (Stuttgart).

KLINGNER, F. (1932), 'Tacitus', *Die Antike* 8, 151–69.

KOESTERMANN, E. (1930), 'Der taciteische *Dialogus* und Ciceros Schrift *de Re Publica*', *Hermes* 65, 396–421.

——(1952), *P. Cornelii Taciti Libri qui Supersunt* (Leipzig).

——(1956), 'Der Feldzüge des Germanicus 14–16 n. Chr.', *Historia* 6, 429–79.

——(1957), 'Die Mission des Germanicus im Orient', *Historia* 7, 331–75.

——(1963–8), *Cornelius Tacitus: Annalen*, vols 1–4 (Heidelberg) (vol. 1, 1963; vol. 2, 1965; vol. 3, 1967; vol. 4, 1968).

KÖHNKEN, A. (1973), 'Das problem des Ironie bei Tacitus', *Museum Helveticum* 30, 32–50.

KONSTAN, D. (2001), *Pity Transformed* (London).

KRAGELUND, P. (1987), 'Vatinius, Nero, and Curiatius Maternus', *CQ* 37, 197–202.

KREBS, C. (2005), Negotiatio Germaniae: *Tacitus' Germania und Enea Silvio Piccolomini, Giannantonio Campano, Conrad Celtis und Heinrich Bebel* (Göttingen).

——(2006), 'Imaginary Geography in Caesar's *Bellum Gallicum*', *AJP* 127, 111–36.

——(2011), *A Most Dangerous Book: Tacitus' Germania from the Roman Empire to the Third Reich* (New York).

KROHN, F. (1934), 'Personendarstellung bei Tacitus' (dissertation, Leipzig).

KÜHNER, R., and STEGMANN, C. (1955), *Ausführliche Grammatik der lateinischen Sprache: Satzlehre*, 2 vols, 3rd edn, rev. A. Thierfelder (Leverkusen).

LABHARDT, Th. (1881), *Quae de Iudaeorum Origine Iudicauerint Veteres* (Augsburg).

LADA, I. (1993), 'Empathetic Understanding: Emotion and Cognition in Classical Dramatic Audience-Reponse', *PCPS* 39, 94–140.

LAIRD, A. (ed.) (2006), *Oxford Readings in Ancient Literary Criticism* (Oxford).

LAULETTA, N. (1998), *L'intreccio degli stili di Tacito: intertestualità prosa-poesie nella letteratura storiografica* (Naples).

LAURENCE, R. (1994), 'Rumour and Communication in Roman Politics', *G&R* 41, 62–74.

LAVAN, M. (2011), 'Slavishness in Britain in Rome in Tacitus' *Agricola*', *CQ* 61, 294–305.

LEAR, J. (1988), 'Katharsis', *Phronesis* 33, 297–326; repr. in A. O. Rorty (ed.), *Essays on Aristotle's Poetics* (Princeton, NJ, 1992), 315–40.

LEEMAN, A. D. (1975), 'The Structure of Cicero's *de Oratore* 1', in A. Michel and R. Verdière (eds), *Ciceroniana: hommages à Kazimierz Kumaniecki* (Leiden).

——and PINKSTER, H. (1985), *De Oratore Libri III* (Heidelberg).

LEHMANN, G. A. (1971), 'Tacitus und die *Imitatio Alexandri* des Germanicus', in G. Radke (ed.), *Politik und literarische Kunst im Werk des Tacitus* (Stuttgart), 23–36.

LEIGH, M. (2004), 'Quintilian on the Emotions (*Institutio Oratoria* 6 Preface and 1–2)', *JRS* 94, 122–40.

LENDON, J. E. (2009), 'Historians Without History: Against Roman Historiography', in Feldherr (2009).

LEO, F. (1896), 'Die staatsrechtlichen Excurse in Tacitus' *Annalen*', *Göttingische gelehrte Nachrichten*, 191–208; repr. in Leo (1960: 299–317).

——(1898), review of Gudeman (1894), *Göttingische gelehrte Anzeigen* 92, 169–88; repr. in Leo (1960: 277–98).

——(1901), *Die griechisch-römische Biographie nach ihrer literarischen Form* (Leipzig).

——(1960), *Ausgewählte kleine Schriften* 2 (Rome).

LEONHARD, F. X. (1852), *Über den Bericht des Tacitus über die Juden, Hist. 5.2–6* (Ellwangen).

LÉTOUBLON, F. (ed.) (1996), *Impressions d'îles* (Toulouse).

LEVENE, D. S. (1993), *Religion in Livy* (Leiden).

——(1997), 'Pity, Fear and the Historical Audience: Tacitus on the Fall of Vitellius', in S. Braund and C. Gill (eds), *The Passions in Roman Thought and Literature* (Cambridge), 128–49 [reprinted as Chapter 8 in this volume].

LEVENE, D. S. (1999), 'Tacitus' *Histories* and the Theory of Deliberative Oratory', in C. S. Kraus (ed.), *The Limits of Historiography: Genre and Narrative in Ancient Historical Texts* (Leiden), 197–216.

—— (2004), 'Tacitus' *Dialogus* as Literary History', *TAPA* 134, 157–200.

—— (2006), 'History, Metahistory, and Audience Response in Livy 45', *CA* 25, 73–108.

—— (2009), 'Warfare in the Annals', in A. J. Woodman (ed.), *The Cambridge Companion to Tacitus* (Cambridge), 225–38.

LEVENE, D. S., and NELIS, D. P. (eds) (2002), *Clio and the Poets: Augustan Poetry and the Traditions of Ancient Historiography* (Leiden).

LEVI, M. A. (1959), review of Syme (1958a), *Historia* 8, 251–6.

LEVICK, B. (1999), *Vespasian* (London).

LIEBESCHUETZ, W. (1966), 'The Theme of Liberty in the *Agricola* of Tacitus', *CQ* 16, 126–39 [reprinted as Chapter 2 in this volume].

LIER, H. (1996), 'Rede und Redekunst im Diskurs. Tactus' *Dialogus de oratoribus* als Schullekture', *AU* 39, 52–64.

LINDHOLM, E. (1931), *Stilistische Studien: zur Erweiterung der Satzglieder im Lateinischen* (Lund).

LÖFSTEDT, E. (1933), *Syntactica: Studien und Beiträge zur historischen Syntax des Latein* (Lund).

LOVEJOY, A. O., and BOAS, G. (1973), *Primitivism and Related Ideas in Antiquity* (New York).

LUCAS, D. W. (1968), *Aristotle: Poetics* (Oxford).

LUCE, T. J. (1977), *Livy: The Composition of his History* (Princeton, NJ).

—— (1981), 'Tacitus', in *Ancient Writers: Greece and Rome*, 2 vols (New York), 1003–33.

—— (1986), 'Tacitus' Conception of Historical Change: The Problem of Discovering the Historian's Opinions', in I. S. Moxon, J. D. Smart, and A. J. Woodman (eds), *Past Perspectives: Studies in Greek and Roman Historical Writing* (Cambridge), 143–57 [reprinted as Chapter 14 in this volume].

—— (1991), 'Tacitus on "History's Highest Function": *praecipuum munus annalium* (*Ann.* 3.65)', *ANRW* II 33.4, 2904–27.

—— (1993), 'Reading and Response in the *Dialogus*', in Luce and Woodman (1993); repr. in Laird (2006: 380–413).

—— (2002) review of O'Gorman (2000), *Phoenix* 56, 374–6.

—— and WOODMAN, A. J. (1993), *Tacitus and the Tacitean Tradition* (Princeton, NJ).

LUND, A. A. (1995), *Germanenideologie im Nationalsocialismus: zur Rezeption des 'Germania' des Tacitus im 'Dritten Reich'* (Heidelberg).

LYNE, R. O. A. M. (1989), *Words and the Poet: Characteristic Techniques of Style in Vergil's Aeneid* (Oxford).

——and MORWOOD, J. H. W. (1973), 'Critical Appreciations I: Propertius 3.10', *G&R* 20, 38–48.

MAGIE, D. (1950), *Roman Rule in Asia Minor* (Princeton, NJ).

MALISSARD, A. (1992), 'Montaigne lecteur de Tacite', in Chevallier and Poignault (1992: 157–64).

MALITZ, J. (1985), 'Helvidius Priscus und Vespasian: zur Geschichte der "stoischen" Senatsopposition', *Hermes* 113, 231–46.

——(1996), 'Mommsen, Caesar und die Juden', in Cancik, Lichtenberger, and Schäfer (1996: 371–87).

MALTBY, R. (1991), *A Lexicon of Latin Etymologies* (Leeds).

MANOLARAKI, E. (2005), 'A Picture Worth A Thousand Words: Revisiting Bedriacum (Tacitus *Histories* 2.70)', *CP* 100, 243–67.

MANUWALD, B. (1979), *Cassius Dio und Augustus*, Palingenesia 14 (Wiesbaden).

MARCHESI, C. (1924), *Tacito* (Messina).

MARINCOLA, J. (1999), 'Genre, Convention, and Innovation in Greco-Roman Historiography', in C. S. Kraus (ed.), *The Limits of Historiography: Genre and Narrative in Ancient Historical Texts* (Leiden, Boston, and Cologne), 281–324

——(2003), 'Beyond Pity and Fear: The Emotions of History', *Ancient Society* 33, 285–315.

MARTIN, R. H. (1946), '*-ere* and *-erunt* in Tacitus', *CR* 60, 17–19.

——(1953), '*Variatio* and the Development of Tacitus' Style', *Eranos* 51, 89–96.

——(1955), 'Tacitus and the Death of Augustus', *CQ* 5 (1955), 123–8 [reprinted as Chapter 9 in this volume].

——(1964), 'The Leyden Manuscript of Tacitus', *CQ* 14,109–19.

——(1968), '*quibus* and *quis* in Tacitus', *CR* 18, 144–6.

——(1981), *Tacitus* (London and Berkeley, Calif.).

——(1994), *Tacitus*, 2nd edn (London and Berkeley, Calif.).

——(2001), *Tacitus Annals V and VI* (Warminster).

——and WOODMAN, A. J. (1989), *Tacitus Annals Book IV* (Cambridge) (rev. repr. 1994, 1997).

MATTHIESSEN, K. (1970), 'Der Dialogus des Tacitus und Cassius Dio 67.12', *L'Antiquité classique* 39, 168–77.

MATTINGLY, H. (1948), *Tacitus on Britain and Germany: A Translation of the Agricola and the Germania* (Harmondsworth).

MAYER, R. (2001), *Tacitus Dialogus de Oratoribus* (Cambridge).

——(2003), 'A Lost Allusion Recovered: Tacitus *Histories* 3.37.1 and Homer *Iliad* 19.301–2', *CQ* 53, 313–15.

MAYOR, J. E. B. (1872–8), *Thirteen Satires of Juvenal with a Commentary* (London).

McGING, B. C. (1982), 'Synkrisis in Tacitus' *Agricola*', *Hermathena* 132, 15–25.

McKEON, M. (1987), *The Origins of the English Novel 1600–1740* (London).

MELAMED, A. (1984), 'Simone Luzzatto on Tacitus: *Apologetica* and *Ragione di Stato*', in I. Twersky (ed.), *Studies in Medieval Jewish History* (Cambridge, Mass., and London), 143–70.

MELLOR, R. (1993), *Tacitus* (New York).

——(1995), *Tacitus: The Classical Heritage* (New York).

MENDELL, C. W. (1957), *Tacitus: The Man and His Work* (Oxford).

——(1959), review of Syme (1958a), *AJP* 80, 321–4.

MEYER, G. (ed.) (1933), *Eduard Wölfflin: Ausgewählte Schriften* (Leipzig).

MICHEL, A. (1962), *Le Dialogue des orateurs de Tacite et la philosophie de Cicéron* (Paris).

MICHEL, A. (1966), *Tacite et le destin de l'Empire* (Paris).

MILLER, N. P. (1966), review of Koestermann (1965), *CR* 16, 345–7.

——(1968), 'Tiberius Speaks', *AJP* 89, 1–19.

——(1973), *Cornelii Taciti Annalium Libri XV* (London).

——(1986), 'Virgil and Tacitus Again', *PVS* 18, 87–106.

——and JONES, P. V. (1978), 'Critical Appreciations III: Tacitus *Histories* 3.38–9', *G&R* 20, 70–80 [reprinted as Chapter 7 in this volume].

MITSIS, P. (1988), *Epicurus' Ethical Theory: The Pleasures of Invulnerability* (Ithaca, NY).

MOLES, J. (1998), 'Cry Freedom: Tacitus *Annals* 4.32–5', *Histos* 2, http://www.dur.ac.uk/Classics/histos/1998/moles.html

MOMIGLIANO, A. (1932), 'Osservazioni sulle fonti per la storia di Caligola, Claudio, Nerone', *Rendiconti della Reale Accademia Nazionale dei Lincei* 8 (Rome), 293–336.

——(1947), 'The First Political Commentary on Tacitus', *JRS* 37, 91–101; repr. in Momigliano (1955: 37–59).

——(1955), *Contributo all storia degli studi classici* (Rome).

——(1990), *The Classical Foundations of Modern Historiography* (Berkeley, Calif., and Oxford) [pp. 109–31 reprinted as Chapter 17 in this volume].

MOMMSEN, TH. (1870), 'Tacitus und Cluvius Rufus', *Hermes* 4, 295–325; repr. 1909 in *Gesammelte Schriften* 7 (Berlin), 224–52.

——(1887–8), *Römisches Staatsrecht*, 3 vols, 3rd edn (Leipzig).

——(1909a), 'Das Verhältniss des Tacitus zu den Acten des Senats'; repr. in *Gesammelte Schriften* 7 (Berlin), 253–63.

——(1909b), 'Zeitalter des Scholiasten Juvenals'; repr. in *Gesammelte Schriften* 7 (Berlin), 509–11.

MOORE, F. G. (1923), 'Annalistic Method as Related to Book Divisions in Tacitus', *TAPA* 54, 5–20.

MORELLO, R. (2002), 'Livy's Alexander Digression (9.17–19): Counterfactuals and Apologetics', *JRS* 92, 62–85.

——(2006), 'A Correspondence Course in Tyranny: The *Cruentae Litterae* of Tiberius', *Arethusa* 39, 331–54.

MORFORD, M. P. O. (1993), 'Tacitean *Prudentia* and the Doctrines of Justus Lipsius', in Luce and Woodman (1993: 129–51).

MORGAN, J. R. (1985), 'Lucian's *True Histories* and the *Wonders Beyond Thule* of Antonius Diogenes', *CQ* 35, 475–90.

MORGAN, L. (1998), 'Tacitus *Annals* 4.70: An Unappreciated Pun', *CQ* 48, 585–7.

MORGAN, M. G. (1991), 'An Heir of Tragedy: Tacitus *Histories* 2.59.3', *CP* 86, 138–43.

——(1992a), 'Dispositions for Disaster: Tacitus *Histories* 1.31', *Eranos* 90, 55–62.

——(1992b), 'The Smell of Victory: Vitellius at Bedriacum (Tacitus *Histories* 2.70)', *CP* 87, 14–29.

——(1992c), 'Tacitus and the Battle of Tarracina (*Histories* 3.76–7)', *MH* 49, 124–30.

——(1993a), '*Commissura* in Tacitus *Histories* 1', *CQ* 43, 274–91.

——(1993b), 'Tacitus *Histories* 1.58.2', *Hermes* 121, 371–4

——(1993c), 'Two Omens in Tacitus' *Histories* (2.50.2 and 1.62.2–3)', *RhM* 136, 321–9.

——(1993d), 'The Unity of Tacitus, *Histories* 1.12–20', *Athenaeum* 81, 567–86.

——(1994a), 'The Long Way Round: Tacitus *Histories* 1.27', *Eranos* 92, 93–101.

——(1994b), 'A Lugubrious Prospect: Tacitus *Histories* 1.40', *CQ* 44, 236–44.

——(1994c), 'Rogues' March: Caecina and Valens in Tacitus *Histories* 1.61–70', *MH* 51, 103–25.

——(1994d), 'Tacitus *Histories* 2.83–4, Content and Positioning', *CP* 89, 166–75.

——(1994e), 'Vespasian's Fears of Assassination: Tacitus *Histories* 2.74–5', *Philologus* 138, 118–28.

——(1995a), 'Tacitus *Histories* 2.7.1', *Hermes* 123, 335–40.

——(1995b), 'Tacitus *Histories* 2.68.1', *Mnemosyne* 48, 576–9.

——(1996a), 'Recriminations after Ad Castores: Tacitus *Histories* 2.30', *CP* 91, 359–64.

——(1996b), 'Vespasian and the Omens in Tacitus *Histories* 2.78', *Phoenix* 50, 41–55.

——(1996c), 'Cremona in AD69, Two Notes on Tacitus' Narrative Techniques', *Athenaeum* 84, 381–403.

——(1997), 'Caecina's Assault on Placentia: Tacitus *Histories* 2.20.2–22.3', *Philologus* 141, 338–61.

——(2000), 'Clodius Macer and Calvia Crispinilla', *Historia* 49, 467–87.

——(2002), 'Greed for Power? Tacitus *Histories* 1.52.2', *Philologus* 146, 339–49.

——(2003a), 'The Shackles of Misfortune: Tacitus *Histories* 3.18.1', *Hermes* 131, 350–57.

——(2003b), 'Galba, the Massacre of the Marines and the Formation of the *Legio I Adiutrix*', *Athenaeum* 91, 489–515.

MORGAN, M. G. (2003c), '*Disserere* and *Edisserere* in Tacitus', *Latomus* 62, 642–7.

——(2004), 'Tacitus *Histories* 2.4.4 and Mucianus' Legion in AD69', *MH* 61, 129–38.

——(2005a), 'Martius Macer's Raid and its Consequences: Tacitus *Histories* 2.23', *CQ* 55, 572–81.

——(2005b), 'The Opening Stages in the Battle for Cremona, or the Devil in the Details (Tacitus *Histories* 3.15–18)', *Historia* 54, 189–209.

——(2006), *69 AD: The Year of the Four Emperors* (Oxford).

MACMULLEN, R. (1993), *Enemies of the Roman Order* (Cambridge, Mass.).

MÜLLER, C. (ed.) (1855), *Geographi Graeci Minores I* (Paris).

MÜLLER, J. G. (1843), 'Kritische Untersuchung der taciteischen Berichte über den Ursprung der Juden, *Hist.* 5.2ff', *Theologische Studien und Kritiken* 16, 893–958.

MURGIA, C. E. (1980), 'The Date of Tacitus' *Dialogus*', *HSCP* 84, 99–125.

——(1985), 'Pliny's *Letters* and the *Dialogus*', *HSCP* 89, 171–206.

MURPHY, T. (2004), *Pliny the Elder's Natural History: The Empire in the Encyclopedia* (Oxford).

MURRAY, O. (1972), 'Herodotus and Hellenistic Culture', *CQ* 22, 200–213.

——(ed.) (forthcoming), *Peace and Liberty in the Ancient World: The Cambridge Lectures by Arnaldo Momigliano* (Cambridge).

NEHEMAS, A. (1992), 'Pity and Fear in the *Rhetoric* and the *Poetics*', in A. O. Rorty (ed.), *Essays on Aristotle's Poetics* (Princeton, NJ), 291–314.

NICOLET, C. (1991), *Space, Geography and Politics in the Early Roman Empire* (Ann Arbor, Mich.).

NISBET, R. G. M., and HUBBARD, M. (1978), *A Commentary on Horace, Odes Book II* (Oxford).

NISSEN, H. (1863), *Kritische Untersuchungen über die Quellen der vierten und fünften Dekade des Livius* (Berlin).

NORDEN, E. (1898), *Die antike Kunstprosa* (Berlin).

NUSSBAUM, M. (1986), *The Fragility of Goodness: Luck and Ethics in Greek Tragedy and Philosophy* (Cambridge).

——(1992), 'Tragedy and Self-Sufficiency: Plato and Aristotle on Fear and Pity', *Oxford Studies in Ancient Philosophy* 10, 107–59.

NUTTING, H. C. (1923), 'The Use of *Forem* in Tacitus', *University of California Publications in Classical Philology* 7, 209–19.

OAKLEY, S. P. (1997), *A Commentary on Livy Books VI–X*, vol. 1 (Oxford).

OGILVIE, R. M. (1965), *A Commentary on Livy Books 1–5* (Oxford).

——(1991), 'An Interim Report on Tacitus' "Agricola"', *ANRW* II 33.3, 1686–1713.

——and RICHMOND, I. (1967), *Cornelii Taciti De Vita Agricolae* (Oxford).

O'GORMAN, EDMUNDO (1972), *The Invention of America: An Inquiry into the Historical Nature of the New World and the Meaning of its History* (Westport, Conn.).

O'GORMAN, ELLEN (1993), 'No Place like Rome: Identity and Difference in the *Germania* of Tacitus', *Ramus* 22, 135–54 [reprinted as Chapter 3 in this volume].

——(2000), *Irony and Misreading in the Annals of Tacitus* (Cambridge).

OLIVER, J. H. (1947), 'The Descendants of Asinius Pollio', *AJP* 68, 147–60.

OPELT, I. (1965), *Die lateinischen Schimpfworter* (Freiburg).

PACKARD, J. (1969), 'Official Notices in Livy's Fourth Decade: Style and Treatment' (dissertation, University of North Carolina).

PAGÁN, V. (1999), 'Beyond Teutoburg: Transgression and Transformation in Tacitus *Annales* 1.61–2', *CP* 94, 302–20.

——(2002), 'Actium and Teutoburg: Augustan Victory and Defeat in Vergil and Tacitus', in D. Levene and D. Nelis (eds), *Clio and the Poets: Augustan Poetry and the Traditions of Ancient Historiography* (Leiden), 45–59.

——(2004a), *Conspiracy Narratives in Roman History* (Austin, Tex.).

——(2004b), 'Speaking before Superiors: Orpheus in Vergil and Ovid', in I. Sluiter and R. M. Rosen (eds), *Free Speech in Classical Antiquity*, *Mnemosyne* Supplement 254 (Leiden), 369–89.

PANTZERHIELM-THOMAS, S. (1936), 'The Prologues of Sallust', *Symbolae Osloenses* 15–16, 140–62.

PARATORE, E. (1951), *Tacito* (Rome); 2nd edn 1962 [pp. 182–90 reprinted in translation as Chapter 6 in this volume].

PAUSCH, D. (2010), *Stimmen der Geschichte: Funktionen von Reden in der antiken Historiographie* (Berlin and New York).

PEARS, D. F. (1978), 'Aristotle's Analysis of Courage', *Midwest Studies in Philosophy* 3, 273–85.

PEASE, A. S. (1935), *Publi Vergili Maronis Aeneidos Liber Quartus* (Darmstadt).

PELLING, C. B. R. (1983), review of B. Manuwald, *Cassius Dio und Augustus* in *Gnomon* 55, 221–6.

——(1988a), *Plutarch: Life of Antony* (Cambridge).

——(1988b), 'Aspects of Plutarch's Characterisation', *ICS* 13, 257–74.

——(1990), 'Childhood and Personality in Greek Biography', in C. B. R. Pelling (ed.), *Characterization and Individuality in Greek Literature* (Oxford), 213–44.

——(1993), 'Tacitus and Germanicus', in Luce and Woodman (1993: 59–85) [reprinted as Chapter 12 in this volume].

——(2002), *Plutarch and History* (Swansea).

——(2010), 'The Spur of Fame: Tacitus, *Annals* 4.37–8', in C. S. Kraus, J. Marincola, and C. Pelling (eds), *Ancient Historiography and Its Contexts* (Oxford), 364–84.

PENWILL, J. (2003), 'What's Hecuba to Him . . . ? Reflections on Poetry and Politics in Tacitus' *Dialogue on Orators*', *Ramus* 32, 122–47.

PERCIVAL, J. (1980), 'Tacitus and the Principate', *G&R* 27, 119–33.

Peretti, A. (1979), *Il periplo di Scilace: studio sul primo portolano del Mediterraneo* (Pisa).

Phillips, J. E. (1974), 'Form and Language in Livy's Triumph Notices', *CP* 69, 265–73.

Pigoń, J. (1992), 'Helvidius Priscus, Eprius Marcellus and the *Iudicium Senatus*: Observations on Tacitus *Histories* 4.7–8', *CQ* 42, 235–46.

——(2008), 'The Passive Voice of the Hero: Some Peculiarities of Tacitus' Portrayal of Germanicus in *Annals* 1.31–49', in J. Pigoń (ed.), *The Children of Herodotus* (Newcastle upon Tyne), 287–303.

Pippidi, D. M. (1944), *Autour de Tibère* (Bucharest).

Plass, P. (1988), *Wit and the Writing of History: The Rhetoric of Historiography in Imperial Rome* (Madison, Wis.).

Platner, S. B., and Ashby, T. (1929), *A Topographical Dictionary of Ancient Rome* (London).

Pomeroy, A. (1991), *The Appropriate Comment: Death Notices in the Ancient Historians* (Meisenheim am Glan).

——(2006), 'Theatricality in Tacitus' *Histories*', *Arethusa* 39, 171–91.

Putnam, M. C. J. (1989), 'Virgil and Tacitus *Annals* 1.10', *CQ* 39, 563–4.

Questa, C. (1960), *Studi sulle fonti degli Annales di Tacito* (Rome).

Raaflaub, K. (2008), 'The Truth about Tyranny: Tacitus and the Historian's Responsibility in Early Imperial Rome', in J. Pigoń (ed.), *The Children of Herodotus* (Newcastle upon Tyne), 253–70.

Rademacher, U. (1975), *Die Bildkunst des Tacitus*, Spudasmata 29 (Hildesheim).

Ramin, J. (1976), *Le Periple d'Hannon/The Periplus of Hanno* (Oxford).

Ramsay, G. G. (1904, 1909), *The Annals of Tacitus: An English Translation with Introduction, Notes, and Maps*, 2 vols (London).

Rawson, E. (1971), 'Prodigy Lists and the Use of the *Annales Maximi*', *CQ* 21, 158–69.

——(1985), *Intellectual Life in the Late Roman Republic* (Baltimore, Md.).

Reinhardt, T., and Winterbottom, M. (eds) (2006), *Quintilian, Book 2* (Oxford).

Reitzenstein, R. (1915), 'Bemerkungen zu den kleinen Schriften des Tacitus', *Nachrichten von der Königlichen Gesellschaft der Wissenschaften zu Göttingen* 22, 173–276; repr. in Reitzenstein (1967: 17–120).

——(1967), *Aufsätze zu Tacitus* (Darmstadt).

Renz, W. (1905), *Alliterationem bei Tacitus* (Aschaffenburg).

Reynolds, L. D. (1983), *Scribes and Scholars* (Oxford).

Ribadeneira, P. (1603), *Princeps Christianus adversus Nicolaum Machiavellum, ceterosque huius temporis politicos* (Cologne).

Rice, E. E. (1983), *The Grand Procession of Ptolemy Philadelphus* (Oxford).

Rich, J. (1996), 'Structuring Roman History: The Consular Year and the Roman Historical Tradition', *Histos* 1, http://www.dur.ac.uk/Classics/histos/1997/rich1.html

RICHMOND, I. (1944), 'Gnaeus Iulius Agricola', *JRS* 34, 34–45.

RIEDL, P. (2002), *Faktoren des historischen Prozesses. Eine vergleichende Untersuchung zu Tacitus und Ammianus Marcellinus* (Tübingen).

RIVES, J. B. (1999), *Tacitus: Germania* (Oxford).

——(2002), 'Structure and History in the *Germania* of Tacitus', in J. F. Miller, C. Damon, and K. S. Myers (eds), *Vertis in Vsum: Studies in Honour of Edward Courtney* (Leipzig), 164–73.

ROBBERT, L. (1917), *De Tacito Lucani Imitatore* (Göttingen).

ROBERTS, M. (1988), 'The Revolt of Boudicca (Tacitus *Annals* 14.29–39) and the Assertion of *Libertas* in Neronian Rome', *AJP* 109, 118–32.

ROBIN, P. (1973), *L'Ironie chez Tacite* (Lille).

ROBINSON, R. P. (1935), *The Germania of Tacitus: A Critical Edition* (Middletown, Conn.).

ROGERS, R. S. (1935), *Criminal Trials and Criminal Legislation under Tiberius* (Middletown, Conn.).

——(1945), 'Tiberius' Travels, AD26–37', *CW* 39, 42–4.

——(1960), review of Syme (1958a), *CP* 55, 40–43.

ROLLER, D. W. (2006), *Through the Pillars of Herakles: Greco-Roman Exploration of the Atlantic* (New York and London).

ROMM, J. S. (1992), *The Edges of the World in Ancient Thought* (Princeton, NJ).

ROOD, T. (1998), *Thucydides: Narrative and Explanation* (Oxford).

ROSE, M. (1979), *Parody/Metafiction* (London).

ROSENSTEIN, N. (1990), *Imperatores Victi: Military Defeat and Aristocratic Competition in the Middle and Late Republic* (Berkeley and Los Angeles, Calif.).

ROSS, D. O., Jr. (1973), 'The Tacitean Germanicus', *YCS* 23, 209–27.

ROSS, J. W. (1878), *Tacitus and Bracciolini: The Annals Forged in the Fifteenth Century* (London).

ROSTOVTZEFF, M. I. (1926), *The Social and Economic History of the Roman Empire* (Oxford).

RUDD, N. (1986), *Themes in Roman Satire* (London).

RUDICH, V. (1985), 'Accommodation to Corrupt Reality: Tacitus' *Dialogus de Oratoribus*', *Ancient World* 11, 95–100.

RUSSELL, D., and WINTERBOTTOM, M. (1972), *Ancient Literary Criticism* (Oxford).

RUTHERFORD, R. (1989), *The 'Meditations' of Marcus Aurelius: A Study* (Oxford).

RUTLAND, L. W. (1987), 'The Tacitean Germanicus: Suggestions for a Reevaluation', *RhM* 130, 153–64.

RUTLEDGE, S. H. (1999), '*Delatores* and the Tradition of Violence in Roman Oratory', *AJP* 120, 555–73.

——(2000), 'Tacitus in Tartan: Textual Colonisation and Expansionist Discourse in the *Agricola*', *Helios* 27, 75–95.

RUTLEDGE, S. H. (2001), *Imperial Inquisitions. Prosecutors and Informants from Tiberius to Domitian* (London).

SAGE, M. M. (1991), 'The Treatment in Tacitus of Roman Republican History and Antiquarian Matters', *ANRW* II 33.5, 3385–3419.

SAID, E. (1985), *Orientalism* (Harmondsworth).

SAILOR, D. (2004), 'Becoming Tacitus: Significance and Inconsequentiality in the Prologue of *Agricola*', *Classical Antiquity* 23, 139–77.

——(2008), *Writing and Empire in Tacitus* (Cambridge).

SALLER, R. P. (1984), '*Familia, Domus*, and the Roman Conception of the Family', *Phoenix* 38, 336–55.

SALLMAN, K. (1987), 'Reserved for Eternal Punishment: The Elder Pliny's View of Free Germania', *AJP* 108, 108–28.

SALWAY, B. (2004), 'Sea and River Travel in the Roman Itinerary Literature', in R. Talbert and K. Broderson (eds), *Space in the Roman World: Its Perception and Presentation* (Münster), 43–96.

SANDBACH, F. H. (1975), *The Stoics* (London).

SANTORO L'HOIR, F. (2006), *Tragedy, Rhetoric, and the Historiography of Tacitus' Annales* (Ann Arbor, Mich.).

SCHAMA, S. (1995), *Landscape and Memory* (New York).

SCHANZ, M., and HOSIUS, C. (1935), *Geschichte der römischen Literatur bis zum Gesetzgebungswerk des Kaisers Justinian, Handbuch der Altertumswissenschaft* 8.2 (Munich).

SCHELLHASE, K. C. (1976), *Tacitus in Renaissance Political Thought* (Chicago).

SCHMAUS, H. (1887), *Tacitus ein Nachahmer Vergils* (Bamberg).

SCHMITTHENNER, W. (1981), 'Kennt die hellenistich-römische Antike eine "Judenfrage"?', in B. Martin and E. Schulin (eds), *Die Juden als Minderheit in der Geschichte* (Munich), 9–29.

SCHUNCK, P. (1964), 'Studien zur Darstellung des Endes von Galba, Otho, und Vitellius in den *Historien* des Tacitus', *SO* 39, 38–82.

SCHWINDT, J. P. (2000), *Prolegomena zu einer Phänomenologie der römischen Literaturgeschichtsschreibung von den Anfängen bis Quintilian* (Göttingen).

SCHWINGE, E. R. (1963), '*Festinata Mors*', *RhM* 116, 363–78.

SEAGER, R. (1972), *Tiberius* (London).

——(1977), '*Amicitia* in Tacitus and Juvenal', *AJAH* 2, 40–50.

SEVERINI, P. (2004), *Cornelio Tacito, Agricola. Introduzione, testo critico, traduzione e commento* (Alessandria).

SHATZMAN, I. (1974), 'Tacitean Rumours', *Latomus* 33, 549–78.

SHAW, B. (2000), 'Rebels and Outsiders', in A. Bowman, P. Garnsey, and D. Rathbone (eds), *CAH XI: The High Empire, A.D. 70–192* (Cambridge), 361–403.

SHERWIN-WHITE, A. N. (1959), review of Syme (1958a), *JRS* 49, 140–46.

——(1966), *The Letters of Pliny: A Historical and Social Commentary* (Oxford).

SHOTTER, D. C. A. (1968), 'Tacitus, Tiberius, and Germanicus', *Historia* 17, 194–214.

——(1974), 'Cn. Calpurnius Piso, Legate of Syria', *Historia* 23, 229–45.

——(2004), *Romans and Britons in North-West England*, 3rd edn (Lancaster).

SHUMATE, N. (1997), 'Compulsory Pretence and the "Theatricalization of Experience" in Tacitus', in C. Deroux (ed.), *Studies in Latin Literature and Roman History* 8 (Brussels), 364–403.

SINCLAIR, P. (1995), *Tacitus the Sententious Historian: A Sociology of Rhetoric in Annales 1–6* (University Park, Penn.).

SOLL, J. (2000), 'Amelot de la Houssaye (1634–1706) Annotates Tacitus', *Journal of the History of Ideas* 61, 167–87.

SOLMSEN, F. (1941), 'The Aristotelian Tradition in Ancient Rhetoric', *AJP* 62, 32–50, 169–90.

SÖRBOM, G. (1935), *Variatio Sermonis Tacitei Aliaque apud Eundem Quaestiones Selectae* (Uppsala).

SORSCHER, E. (1973), *A Comparison of Three Texts: The Wars, the Hegesippus, and the Yosippon* (New York).

SPONGANO, R. (ed.) (1948), *Per l'edizione critica dei 'Ricordi' del Guicciardini* (Florence).

STEGNER, K. (2004), *Die Verwendung der Sentenzen in den Historien des Tacitus* (Stuttgart).

STERNBERG, R. H. (ed.) (2005), *Pity and Power in Ancient Athens* (Cambridge).

STEWART, J. J. (2003), 'Some Connections Between the Speech of Calgacus and the *Laus Caesaris*', *AHB* 17, 1–4.

STORONI MAZZOLANI, L. (1972), *The Idea of the City in Roman Thought* (Bloomington, Ind.).

STRAUB, J. (1980), '*Liberator haud dubie Germaniae*', *WJA* 6a: 223–31.

STRAY, C. (1998), *Classics Transformed: Schools, Universities, and Society in England, 1830–1960* (Oxford).

STROUX, J. (1931), 'Vier Zeugnisse zur römischen Literaturgeschischte der Kaiserzeit', *Philologus* 86, 338–68.

STUART, D. R. (1928), *Epochs of Greek and Roman Biography* (Berkeley, Calif.).

SYME, R. (1955), 'Marcus Lepidus: *Capax Imperii*', *JRS* 45, 22–33.

——(1956), 'Some Pisones in Tacitus', *JRS* 46, 17–21.

——(1958a), *Tacitus* (Oxford).

——(1958b), 'Obituaries in Tacitus', *AJP* 79, 18–31; repr. in Syme (1970: 79–90) [reprinted as Chapter 10 in this volume].

——(1970), *Ten Studies in Tacitus* (Oxford).

——(1978), *History in Ovid* (Oxford).

——(1979–91), *Roman Papers*, vols 1–7 (Oxford).

SYME, R. (1982), 'Tacitus: Some Sources of his Information', *JRS* 72, 68–82.

——(1983), 'The Year 33 in Tacitus and Dio', *Athenaeum* 61, 3–23.

——(1991), *Roman Papers*, vol. 7, ed. A. R. Birley (Oxford).

SYSON, A. (2009), 'Born to Speak: *Ingenium* and *Natura* in Tacitus's *Dialogus de Oratoribus*', *Arethusa* 42, 45–75.

TAKÁCS, S. A. (1995), 'Alexandria in Rome', *HSCP* 97, 263–76.

TARRANT, R. J. (1985), *Seneca's Thyestes* (Atlanta, Ga.).

TENNEY, M. F. (1931), 'Tacitus in the Middle Ages and in England to about 1650' (dissertation, Cornell University).

THIEL, J. H. (1959), review of Syme (1958a), *Mnemosyne* 12, 369–75.

THOMAS, R. F. (1982), *Lands and Peoples in Roman Poetry: The Ethnographic Tradition* (Cambridge).

THOMPSON, J. O. (1948), *History of Ancient Geography* (Cambridge).

TIMPE, D. (1968), *Der Triumph des Germanicus: Untersuchungen zu den Feldzügen der Jahre 14–16 n. Chr. in Germanien*, Antiquitas 1.16 (Bonn).

TOWNEND, G. (1964), review of Paratore (1962), *CR* 14, 53–5.

——(1972), 'The Earliest Scholiast on Juvenal', *CQ* 22, 376–87.

——(1973), 'The Literary Substrata to Juvenal's Satires', *JRS* 63: 148–60.

TRAUB, H. W. (1953), 'Tacitus' Use of *ferocia*', *TAPA* 84, 250–61.

TRILLING, L. (1976), *The Liberal Imagination: Essays on Literature and Society* (New York) [pp. 198–204 reprinted as Chapter 18 in this volume].

VILLE, G. (1981), *La Gladiature en occident des origins à la mort de Domitian* (Rome).

URMSON, J. O. (1988), *Aristotle's Ethics* (Oxford).

VIANEY, J. (1896), *Quomodo Dici Possit Tacitum Fuisse Summum Pingendi Artificem* (Paris).

VOLPILHAC-AUGER, C. (1985), *Tacitus et Montesquieu*, Studies on Voltaire and the Eighteenth Century (Oxford).

——(1992), 'Tacite du XVIIIe au XIXe siècle: les causes d'une révolution', in Chevallier and Poignault (1992: 281–9).

——(1993), *Tacite en France de Montesquieu à Chateaubriand*, Studies on Voltaire and the Eighteenth Century (Oxford).

VON STACKELBERG, J. (1960), *Tacitus in der Romania: Studien zur literarischen Rezeption des Tacitus in Italien und Frankreich* (Tübingen).

VOSS, B.-R. (1963), *Der pointierte Stil des Tacitus* (Aschendorff).

WALBANK, F. W. (1938), 'Φίλιππος τραγωγούμενος: A Polybian Experiment', *JHS* 58, 55–68.

——(1960), 'History and Tragedy', *Historia* 9, 216–34; repr. in *Selected Papers* (Cambridge, 1985).

——(1972), *Polybius* (Berkeley, Calif.).

WALKER, A. D. (1993), '*Enargeia* and the Spectator in Greek Historiography', *TAPA* 123, 353–77.

WALKER, B. (1952), *The Annals of Tacitus* (Manchester).

—— (1960), *The Annals of Tacitus*, 2nd edn (Manchester).

WALLACE-HADRILL, A. (1982), '*Ciuilis Princeps*: Between Citizen and King', *JRS* 72, 32–48.

—— (1988), 'The Social Structure of the Roman House', *PBSR* 56, 43–97.

WALSER, G. (1951), *Rom, das Reich und die fremden Völker in der Geschichtsshreibung der frühen Kaiserzeit. Studien zur Glaubwürdikeit des Tacitus* (Baden-Baden).

WALSH, P. (1958), 'Livy and Stoicism', *AJP* 79, 355–75.

—— (1961), *Livy: His Historical Aims and Methods* (Cambridge).

WARD, A. M. (1987), *The New York Intellectuals: The Rise and Decline of the Anti-Stalinist Left from the 1930s to the 1980s* (Chapel Hill, NC, and London).

WARDLE, D. (1996), 'Vespasian, Helvidius Priscus, and the Restoration of the Capitol', *Historia* 45, 208–22.

WEINBERG, J. (2001), *Azariah de' Rossi, The Light of the Eyes. Translated from the Hebrew with an Introduction and Annotation*, Yale Judaica Series 31 (New Haven, Conn.).

WELLESLEY, K. (1965), review of Fletcher (1964), *CR* 15, 124.

—— (1969), 'Tacitus as a Military Historian', in Dorey (1969b: 63–97).

—— (1970), 'Tacitus, *Germania* 36.1', *CQ* 20, 371.

—— (1972), *Cornelius Tacitus: The Histories Book III* (Sydney).

—— (2000), *The Year of the Four Emperors*, 3rd edn (London and New York).

WESSNER, P. (1931), *Scholia in Iuuenalem Vetustiora, Collegit Recensuit Illustrauit P. Wessner* (Leipzig).

WEST, S. (1996–7), 'Tacitean Sidelights on *The Master and Margarita*', *IJCT* 3, 473–84.

WHITAKER, G. (2007), '*Breuique adnotatione critica . . .* A Preliminary History of the Oxford Classical Texts', in C. Stray (ed.), *Classical Books: Scholarship and Publishing in Britain since 1900* (London), 113–34.

WHITE, P. (1993), *Promised Verse: Poets in the Society of Augustan Rome* (Cambridge, Mass.).

WHITMARSH, T. (2006), '"This in-between book": Language, Politics, and Genre in the *Agricola*', in B. McGing and J. Mossman (eds), *The Limits of Ancient Biography* (Swansea), 305–33.

WHITTAKER, C. R. (1983), 'Trade and Frontiers of the Roman Empire', in P. Garnsey and C. R. Whittaker (eds), *Trade and Famine in Classical Antiquity* (Cambridge).

WHITTON, C. (2007), 'The Rhetoric of Accession: Tacitus' Early Historical Works as Trajanic Legitimation' (dissertation, Cambridge).

WIEDEMANN, T. E. J. (1986), 'Between Men and Beasts: Barbarians in Ammianus Marcellinus', in I. S. Moxon, J. D. Smart, and A. J. Woodman (eds), *Past Perspectives: Studies in Greek and Roman Historical Writing* (Cambridge), 189–202.

——(1992), *Emperors and Gladiators* (London).

——(1993), 'Sallust's *Jugurtha*: Concord, Discord, and the Digressions', *G&R* 40, 48–57.

WIENER, L. (1920), *Contributions toward a History of Arabico-Gothic Culture*, vol. 3: *Tacitus' Germania and Other Forgeries* (New York).

WILCKEN, U. (1928), 'Zum Germanicus-Papyrus', *Hermes* 63, 48–65.

WILFORD, H. (1995), *The New York Intellectuals: From Vanguard to Institution* (Manchester).

WILKES, J. (1972), 'Julio-Claudian Historians', *CW* 65, 177–92, 197–203.

WILLIAMS, G. W. (1978), *Change and Decline: Roman Literature in the Early Empire*, Sather Classical Lectures 45 (Berkeley, Calif.).

WILLIAMS, M. F. (1997), 'Four Mutinies: Tacitus, *Annals* 1.16–30; 1.31–49 and Ammianus Marcellinus, *Res Gestae* 20.4.9–20.5.7; 24.3.1–8', *Phoenix* 51, 44–74.

WILLIAMS, R. D., and CARTER, C. J. (1974), 'Critical Appreciations II: Virgil *Aeneid* 12.843–86', *G&R* 21, 165–77.

——and KELSALL, M. (1980), 'Critical Appreciations V: Joseph Addison *Pax Gulielmi Auspiciis Europae Reddita, 1697*, lines 96–132 and 167–end', *G&R* 27, 48–59.

WINTERBOTTOM, M. (1964), 'Quintilian and the *Vir Bonus*', *JRS* 54, 90–97.

——(1999), 'Tacitus, *Dialogus* 13.4', *CQ* 49, 338.

——(2001), 'Returning to Tacitus' *Dialogus*', in C.W. Wooten (ed.), *The Orator in Action and Theory in Greece and Rome* (Leiden), 137–55.

WIRSZUBSKI, C. (1950), *Libertas as a Political Idea at Rome during the Late Republic and Early Principate* (Cambridge).

——(1955), 'Spinoza's Debt to Tacitus', *Scripta Hierosolymitana* 2, 176–86.

WISEMAN, T. P. (1979), *Clio's Cosmetics: Three Studies in Greco-Roman Literature* (Leicester).

——(1981), 'Practice and Theory in Roman Historiography', *Historia* 66, 375–93; repr. in *Roman Studies: Literary and Historical* (Liverpool, 1987), 244–62.

——(1986), 'Monuments and the Roman Annalists', in I. S. Moxon, J. D. Smart, and A. J. Woodman (eds), *Past Perspectives: Studies in Greek and Roman Historical Writing* (Cambridge), 86–100.

——(1987), '*Conspicui postes tectaque digna deo*: The Public Image of Aristocratic and Imperial Houses in the Late Republic and Early Empire', in *L'Urbs: espace urbain et histoire* (Rome), 393–413.

——(1988), review of Woodman (1988a), *CR* 38, 262–4.

——(1994), *Historiography and Imagination* (Exeter).

—— (1998), *Roman Drama and Roman History* (Exeter).

WÖLFFLIN, E. (1867), 'Jahresberichte über Tacitus 1', *Philologus* 25, 92–134.

—— (1868), 'Jahresberichte über Tacitus 2', *Philologus* 26, 92–166.

—— (1869), 'Jahresberichte über Tacitus 3', *Philologus* 27, 113–49.

WOMERSLEY, D. (1991), 'Sir Henry Savile's Translation of Tacitus and Political Interpretation of Elizabethan Texts', *Review of English Studies* 42, 313–42.

WOODMAN, A. J. (1972), 'Remarks on the Structure and Content of Tacitus *Annals* 4.57–67', *CQ* 22, 150–58.

—— (1979), 'Self-Imitation and the Substance of History', in D. West and T. Woodman (eds), *Creative Imitation and Latin Literature* (Cambridge), 143–55; repr. in Woodman (1998: 70–85).

—— (1988a), *Rhetoric in Classical Historiography* (London, Sydney, and Portland, Or.).

—— (1988b), review of N. P. Miller, *Tacitus Annals 14: A Companion to the Penguin Translation with Introduction and Commentary* (Bristol, 1987), *CR* 38, 417–18.

—— (1989), 'Tacitus' Obituary of Tiberius', *CQ* 39, 197–205.

—— (1992), 'Nero's Alien Capital: Tacitus as Paradoxographer', in J. Powell and A. J. Woodman (eds), *Author and Audience in Latin Literature* (Cambridge), 173–88 [reprinted as Chapter 13 in this volume].

—— (1993), 'Amateur Dramatics at the Court of Nero: *Annals* 15.48–74', in Luce and Woodman (1993: 104–28).

—— (1998), *Tacitus Reviewed* (Oxford).

—— (2004), *Tacitus: the Annals*, translated, with introduction and notes (Indianapolis and Cambridge).

—— (2006a), 'Tiberius and the Taste of Power: The Year 33 in Tacitus', *CQ* 56, 175–89.

—— (2006b), 'Mutiny and Madness: Tacitus *Annals* 1.16–49', *Arethusa* 39, 303–29.

—— (2007), 'Readers and Reception: A Text Case', in J. Marincola (ed.), *A Companion to Greek and Roman Historiography* (Oxford), 133–44.

—— and MARTIN, R. H. (1996), *The Annals of Tacitus Book 3* (Cambridge).

—— and MILLER, J. F. (2010), *Latin Historiography and Poetry in the Early Empire: Generic Interactions* (Leiden).

YERUSHALMI, Y. H. (1971), *From Spanish Court to Italian Ghetto. Isaac Cardoso: A Study in Seventeenth-Century Marranism and Jewish Apologetics* (New York and London).

—— (1982), *Jewish History and Jewish Memory* (Seattle, Wa., and London).

ZANGARA, A. (2007). *Voir l'histoire: théories anciennes du récit historique. IIe siècle avant J.-C.–IIe siècle après J.-C.* (Paris).

ZERNIAL, U. (1864), *Selecta Quaedam Capita ex Genetiui Vsu Tacitus* (Göttingen).

Index